CITIES AND URBAN LIFE

FOURTH EDITION

CITIES AND URBAN LIFE

JOHN J. MACIONIS
KENYON COLLEGE

VINCENT N. PARRILLO
WILLIAM PATERSON UNIVERSITY

PEARSON

Prentice
Hall

Upper Saddle River, New Jersey 07458

Library of Congress Cataloging-in-Publication Data

Macionis, John J.
  Cities and urban life / John J. Macionis, Vincent N. Parrillo.—4th ed.
    p. cm.
  Includes bibliographical references and index.
  ISBN 0-13-226040-9
  1. Cities and towns. 2. Cities and towns—History. 3. Sociology, Urban. 4. City and
town life. I. Parrillo, Vincent N. II. Title.
  HT151.M335 2006
  307.76—dc22   2006002780

Editorial Director: Leah Jewell
Editorial Assistant/Supervisor: Christina Walker
Publisher: Nancy Roberts
Production Liaison: Joanne Hakim
Director of Marketing: Brandy Dawson
Senior Marketing Manager: Marissa Feliberty
Manufacturing Buyer: Brian Mackey
Cover Art Director: Jayne Conte
Cover Design: Bruce Kenselaar
Cover Image: "Sunday Afternoon" by Ralph
  Fasanella. A stickball game on a New York
  City street bustles with life while demonstrat-
  ing the "daily necessity of the streets."

Director, Image Resource Center: Melinda Reo
Manager, Rights and Permissions: Zina Arabia
Manager, Visual Research: Beth Brenzel
Manager, Cover Visual Research &
  Permissions: Karen Sanatar
Photo Coordinator: Debbie Hewitson
Photo Researcher: Sheila Norman
Cartographer: International Mapping Associates
Line Art Coordinator: Scott Garrison
Full-Service Project Management: Jessica
  Balch/Pine Tree Composition, Inc.
Composition: Laserwords Private Limited
Printer/Binder: RR Donnelley & Sons Company

Credits and acknowledgments borrowed from other sources and reproduced, with permission, in this textbook appear on appropriate page within text. Photo credits appear on p. 455.

Pearson Education LTD., London
Pearson Education Singapore, Pte. Ltd
Pearson Education, Canada, Ltd
Pearson Education—Japan
Pearson Education Australia PTY, Limited

Pearson Education North Asia Ltd
Pearson Educación de Mexico, S.A. de C.V.
Pearson Education Malaysia, Pte. Ltd
Pearson Education, Upper Saddle River, New Jersey

10 9 8 7 6 5 4 3 2 1
ISBN 0-13-226040-9

To the memory of E. Digby Baltzell
mentor, friend,
and maverick sociologist
—John J. Macionis

To Donald L. Halsted
mentor, friend,
and inspiration
—Vincent N. Parrillo

CONTENTS

SPECIAL FEATURES

CITYSCAPE

CRITICAL THINKING

PREFACE

We are now several years into a new century—indeed, a new millennium—and the world stands on the brink of a historic landmark: In a few years, a majority of the planet's people will live in cities. Urban living is rapidly becoming the *norm* for members of our species. Surely, there is no more compelling reason to undertake the study of cities and urban life.

THE BASIC APPROACH

The approach of this text is multidisciplinary but fundamentally sociological. Readers will find here the enduring contributions of the classical European social thinkers, including Max Weber, Karl Marx, Ferdinand Tönnies, Georg Simmel, and Emile Durkheim, as well as those of early pioneers in North America, including Robert Park and Louis Wirth. Of course, many men and women have stood on the shoulders of these giants and extended our understanding. Thus, this text also considers the ideas of a host of contemporary urbanists, including Henri Lefebvre, Jane Jacobs, Manuel Castells, John Logan, Harvey Molotch, Kevin Lynch, Lyn Lofland, Carol Stack, Herbert Gans, Michael Sorkin, and Michael Dear.

Yet, as this string of well-known names suggests, urban studies rests on research and theory developed within many disciplines. *Cities and Urban Life,* therefore, is truly a multidisciplinary text that draws together the work of historians (Chapter 2: "The Origins and Development of the World's Cities," and Chapter 3: "The Development of North American Cities"); sociologists (Chapter 4: "Cities

and Suburbs of the Twenty-First Century," Chapter 5: "Urban Sociology: Classic and Modern Statements," Chapter 10: "Stratification and Social Class: Urban and Suburban Lifestyles," Chapter 11: "Race, Ethnicity, and Gender: Urban Diversity," and Chapter 12: "Housing, Education, Crime: Confronting Urban Problems"); social psychologists (Chapter 6: "Social Psychology: The Urban Experience"); geographers and urban ecologists (Chapter 7: "Geography and Spatial Perspectives: Making Sense of Space"); political economists working within various disciplines (Chapter 9: "The New Urban Sociology: The City and Capitalism"); anthropologists (Chapter 8: "Comparative Urbanism: The City and Culture," and Chapter 13: "Cities in the Developing World"); and architects as well as city planners (Chapter 14: "Planning the Urban Environment").

THE ORGANIZATION OF THIS TEXT

Part I of the text, "Understanding the City," introduces the main questions and themes that resonate throughout the book (Chapter 1). Part II, "History of Cities and New Trends," surveys the historical development of cities, noting how urban life has often differed in striking ways from contemporary patterns we take for granted (Chapters 2 and 3), and the current trends of sprawl, edge cities, and gated communities that are shaping the cities and suburbs of the new century (Chapter 4). Part III, "Disciplinary Perspectives," highlights the various disciplinary orientations that, together, have so advanced our understanding of cities (Chapters 5 through 9). Part IV, "The Structure of the City," focuses on the social organization of today's cities in North America, highlighting how urban living reflects the importance of stratification and social class (Chapter 10), race, ethnicity, and gender (Chapter 11), as well as forcing us to confront vexing problems such as housing, education, and crime (Chapter 12). Part V, "Global Urbanization," offers a look at the history and current urbanization in four major world regions: Latin America, Africa, the Middle East, and Asia (Chapter 13). It is in these areas of the world that urbanization is now most rapid, with cities reaching unprecedented size. Finally, Part VI, "The Planning and Evaluation of Cities," examines the architectural, social, and political dimensions of urban planning, and points out the problems that prevent cities from living up to their promise of improving everyone's lives (Chapter 14).

FOUR KEY THEMES

This attempt to tell the urban story will lead us to consider a wide range of issues and to confront countless questions. Yet four main themes guide this exploration, and it is useful to make these explicit. To put it another way, whatever else a student entering the field of urban studies might learn, he or she must pay attention to these themes:

1. *Cities and urban life vary according to time and place.* Since the idea of the city came to our ancestors some 10,000 years ago, the urban scene has been re-created time and again, all around the world, in countless ways. The authors—informed by their own travels to some 60 of the world's nations—have labored to portray this remarkable diversity throughout this text.
2. *Cities reflect and intensify society and culture.* Although cities vary in striking ways, everywhere they stand as physical symbols of human civilization. For example, nowhere do we perceive the inward-looking world of the Middle Ages better than in the walled medieval cities of that era. Similarly, modern

U.S. cities are powerful statements about the contemporary forces of industrial capitalism.
3. *Cities reveal the best and the worst about the human condition.* Another way to "read" cities is as testimony to the achievements and failings of a way of life. Thus, while New York boasts some spectacular architecture, exciting public parks, vital art galleries, and vibrant concert halls, it also forces us to confront chronic prejudice, wrenching poverty, and sometimes explosive violence.
4. *Cities offer the promise—but not always the reality— of a better life.* At least since the time of the ancient Greeks, people have recognized that the city holds the promise of living "the good life." Yet all urban places fall short of this ideal in some ways, and in a number of today's cities, people are struggling valiantly simply to survive. The great promise of urban living, coupled with the daunting problems of actual cities, provokes us to ask how (or, indeed, if) we can intentionally and thoughtfully make urban places better. Although we are realistic about the problems, we remain optimistic about the possibilities.

SPECIAL FEATURES OF THE TEXT

Two special features warrant the attention of readers.

Boxes   Each chapter contains several boxed inserts. These boxes are of three kinds. *Critical Thinking* boxes ask readers to grapple with a particular problem or question, assess some evidence, and reach a reasoned conclusion. *Urban Living* boxes provide a picture of the city "at street level"—that is, a close-up look at how people really live. Finally, *Cityscape* boxes present an extended literary account or scholarly analysis of some significant dimension of urban life.

Case Studies   The text includes eight case studies that offer a broad sociohistorical look at major cities in various regions of the world as they illustrate a chapter's key points. The cities profiled in these case studies are London (Chapter 2), New York (Chapter 3),

Portland, Oregon (Chapter 4), Ming Peking (Chapter 8), Hellenic Athens (Chapter 8), Communist Beijing (Chapter 8), Chicago (Chapter 11), and Toronto (Chapter 14).

WHAT'S NEW IN THE FOURTH EDITION

This new edition reflects a number of changes. First, and most important, is the continuance of our policy to provide a thorough updating of all data and information, and the inclusion of the most recent and relevant studies not only in sociology but in many other related fields as well.

Second, the devastation of New Orleans from Hurricane Katrina prompted the addition of two new sections. In the discussion in Chapter 7 ("Geography and Spatial Perspectives") about water as a prime factor in most cities' location, a new Cityscape box examines the good and bad that such a location has meant for New Orleans. A new Critical Thinking box in Chapter 14, on urban planning, explores what approach should be taken to rebuild the city.

Third, the information on the evolution of suburbs formerly in Chapter 10 has been incorporated into Chapters 3 and 4, on the development on North American cities and suburbs, while the theoretical views of Wirth and Gans are now contained within Chapter 5, on sociological perspectives.

Fourth, Chapter 8, on the city and culture, contains a new section on the importance of civic culture in building a sense of community and molding urban public behavior.

Fifth, the discussion in Chapter 9, on the global economy, has been significantly expanded to provide greater insight into how deindustrialization and economic restructuring impact on cities.

Sixth, Chapter 10 has been completely rewritten to include a thorough discussion of stratification and inequality in North America generally, and in its cities specifically. In addition, there is a detailed discussion of social class differences in both cities and

suburbs—together with numerous examples— to show the diversity that exists in both.

Seventh, discussions on race, ethnicity, and gender have been expanded throughout the book, particularly in Chapter 11.

Eighth, a new section in Chapter 12 on urban problems examines the impact of the No Child Left Behind Act on urban schools.

In addition, a new photo program and supplemental materials further enhance the fourth edition, both for readers and instructors.

ACKNOWLEDGMENTS

The authors wish to thank the editorial team at Prentice Hall for their efforts in making this text a reality. Particular thanks go to Nancy Roberts, publisher–sociology, for originally signing the project and helping to get the work under way, and to Chris De-John, former managing editor for sociology, for handling the reviews and consulting on the revision. Joanne Hakim of Prentice Hall and Jessica Balch of Pine Tree Composition did a masterful job in guiding the book through technical production and an on-time delivery date. We are grateful to Pat Daly for copyediting and to Diane Burke for preparing the index. Finally, we wish to thank Sheila Norman for selecting the striking photographs that appear in the book.

The authors also wish to acknowledge the role played by James L. Spates, of Hobart and William Smith Colleges, in an earlier version of this book, titled *The Sociology of Cities,* coauthored by Spates and Macionis. Although Vince Parrillo and John Macionis have significantly revised that effort at many levels, elements of Jim's ideas and his enthusiasm for cities still remain.

For their efforts reviewing part or all of the manuscript and generously sharing their ideas with us, we gratefully acknowledge the reviewers for this edition: Daniel J. Monti Jr., Boston University; Stephanie Moller, University of North Carolina at Charlotte; and Robert J.S. Ross, Clark University. For the third edition: Mark Abrahamson, University of Connecticut; Robert L. Boyd, Mississippi State University; and Jerome Krase, Brooklyn College. For the second edition: Leo Pinard, California Polytechnic State University–San Luis Obispo; David Prok, Baldwin Wallace

College; and James D. Tasa, Eric Community College–North. For the first edition: Ronald S. Edari, University of Wisconsin; and Daniel J. Monti, Boston University.

John J. Macionis
Kenyon College
Gambier, Ohio 43022
E-mail: macionis@kenyon.edu
http://www.TheSociologyPage.com

Vincent N. Parrillo
William Paterson University
Wayne, New Jersey 07470
E-mail: parrillov@wpunj.edu
http://www.wpunj.edu/cohss/sociology/parrillo

CITIES AND URBAN LIFE

CHAPTER 1

EXPLORING THE CITY

❖ ━━━━━━━━━━ ❖ ━━━━━━━━━━ ❖

"This music crept by me upon the waters"
And along the Strand, up Queen Victoria Street.
O City city, I can sometimes hear
Beside a public bar in Lower Thames Street,
The pleasant whining of a mandolin
And a clatter and a chatter from within
Where fishmen lounge at noon: where the walls
Of Magnus Martyr hold
Inexplicable splendour of Ionian white and
   gold.

                T. S. Eliot, "The Waste Land"

Let us go then, you and I,
When the evening is spread out against the sky
Like a patient etherised upon a table;
Let us go, through certain half-deserted streets,
The muttering retreats
Of restless nights in one-night cheap hotels

And sawdust restaurants with oyster-shells:
Streets that follow like a tedious argument
Of insidious intent
To lead you to an overwhelming question . . .
Oh, do not ask, "What is it?"
Let us go and make our visit.

    T. S. Eliot, "The Love Song of J. Alfred Prufrock"

WHY STUDY THE CITY?

Cities! Most of us share poet T. S. Eliot's fascination with urban places—settings of intense
excitement, great mystery, and striking human
diversity. With the poet, most of us probably
agree that cities (London was the object of
Eliot's interest) are places we would love to
visit—but, of course, we wouldn't want to live
there! On the one hand, little compares with
the excitement of visiting a major city such as
New York, Toronto, Chicago, or San Francisco. Arriving at the airport (there may be
several), we make our way through crowds of
people in search of the baggage claim area
(checking the monitor to see which carousel is
the correct one), then grab a cab for downtown and watch for the skyline coming up. We
pull up in front of a downtown hotel and
check in, staying just long enough to drop off
our bags. Then, out on the streets, we find
block after block of shops selling all kinds of
things we never find at home, and pass by
every imaginable sort of person—the old and
the young, the rich and the poor, the up and
coming as well as the down and out. People
say that virtually anything can and does happen in big cities—and it doesn't take long to
realize that they're right!

Across North America, more than three
out of four of us live in urban places, and
even more of us build our lives around cities.
We are born in cities (or near them), grow up
in or near one (probably in a suburb), go to a
college in or near a city (maybe one some
distance away from our hometowns), and
eventually settle down in or near a city that becomes "home." Across the continent, much of
our favorite entertainment—including sports

contests, films, and musical events—is city
based. We might as well admit it: We are a nation of city slickers, and the urban way of life,
or urbanism, has become the norm in both
Canada and the United States. To study the
city, therefore, is to study ourselves.

Yet the city is more than what our personal
experiences reveal. It is a dynamic entity unto
itself, the most powerful drawing card in
human history. In 1900, cities were home to
just 9 percent of the world's population. In
1950, cities were home to 30 percent and
then to 47 percent in 2000. If present trends
continue, by 2025 cities will be home to 58
percent of humanity (Brockerhoff 2000:7).

The city is thus the setting for all aspects of
the human drama: the highest learning colliding with the grossest ignorance, unimagin-
able wealth juxtaposed with the most abject
poverty. Historically, most people drawn to the
city have been able to realize their hopes of a
higher standard of living—but will this continue to be true in the new megacities such as
Mexico City, Rio de Janeiro, Cairo, New Delhi,
and Tokyo? (See the world map preceding this
chapter to locate these and other prominent
cities.) Such places are adding millions of new
residents so rapidly that they cannot provide
basic services (water, housing, electricity) to
many of their people. If such growth is not
checked soon, poverty and suffering for billions may be inescapable, not to mention
ecological disasters unparalleled in history.
To study the city, therefore, is also to study a
uniquely powerful form of human settlement:
a physical and social environment with the
potential for both satisfying and frustrating
the entire spectrum of human needs.

An important theme of this book is the fact
that cities do not exist entirely by themselves.
They are inextricably bound up with the
larger societies of which they are a part. For
centuries, the city has been the heart, the
lifeblood, of various civilizations—the center
of economic, political, and artistic events. In
cities we find both the triumphs and the
tragedies of the human story. For example, we
associate Hellenic Athens, Renaissance Florence, and Elizabethan London with great

achievements of the human spirit, while we link classical Rome and Nazi Berlin with savage human degradation. In each case, a cultural setting helped shape the city's character: During the fourth century B.C.E.,[1] the Greeks raised Athens to a pinnacle of human accomplishment, while the rise of Nazism in Germany in the post–World War I era led to Berlin's infamous decadence.

The connection between the city and a broader culture is no less evident today. In its cities exists much of what is great about the United States: intellectual excellence, political freedom, and artistic vitality. Of course, these same cities exhibit this country's greatest failings, including grinding poverty and sometimes-savage racial prejudice. To study the city, then, is also to examine the society in which it exists.

Understanding the city, therefore, is crucial in order to comprehend modern existence. But how we choose to study the city is also important. The city is a complex reality that yields few easy answers. Our approach here is to study the city much as we would a poem. In encountering a new poem, most people wonder, "What does it mean?" We may ask, "What is the poem's topic?" "What meter does it use?" "What is its place in the poet's works?" For example, someone might ask what T. S. Eliot means by "the walls of Magnus Martyr" in the lines that opened this chapter—a reference to a particularly beautiful London church, Saint Magnus Martyr, built by Sir Christopher Wren in the seventeenth century. Or we might examine the phrase "inexplicable splendour of Ionian white and gold"—a reference to the startling white and gold interior of Magnus Martyr, which reminded Eliot of the glories of the Ionian period of classical Greece.

Central as these "what" questions are, U.S. poet John Ciardi (1990, chap. 1) believed that we also need to consider the mood the poem creates in us, its readers, as well as the deeper subtleties conveyed in how the poem's words play together. Our concern, wrote Ciardi, should not be "to arrive at a definition and close the book, but to arrive at an experience." In other words, Ciardi maintains, only by asking *how* a poem transmits its meaning—by experiencing how all its complex elements fit together—will we fully comprehend the poem. The same is true of cities.

If we look only at the facts of urban life, we will surely miss its dynamic soul. The city will appear dull and lifeless, a collection only of concrete buildings, bureaucracies, unemployment rates. But if we also ask the "how" questions, which link these factual elements to human lives, the city springs to life as a set of vital, dynamic forces.

In studying the city, then, we must not ask merely "What is it?" We must, as Eliot suggests in his poem, "go and make our visit." We must probe beyond the descriptions and the statistics to the broader and deeper reality of urban life. This book will help you do just that, and the remainder of this chapter offers an overview of the steps we will follow.

THE COMPLEXITY OF THE CITY: VARIOUS PERSPECTIVES

The city may well be the most complex of all human creations. As a result, it cannot be understood using any single point of view. While this book is fundamentally sociological in its orientation, it draws together insights, theories, and statistics from a wide variety of related disciplines, among them history, archaeology, psychology, geography, economics, and political science. As we now explain, all these perspectives are vital for grasping the living entity that is the contemporary city.

The City in History

Today, cities are so much a part of our lives that they seem both natural and inevitable. You may be surprised to learn, then, that in the larger picture of human history, cities are a very new idea, indeed. Although the human

---

[1]The designation B.C.E. ("before the common era") is used in place of B.C. ("before Christ") in recognition of the religious pluralism of North American society. Similarly, we use C.E. ("common era") in place of A.D. (*Anno Domini,* "in the year of our lord").

species has existed on the earth for at least 100,000 years, cities began to appear a scant 10,000 years ago. Moreover, it wasn't until the last 3,000 years that cities became relatively numerous and inhabited by significant numbers of people. And only today are we reaching the point at which most of the world's people will be urbanites.

Then, too, urban life itself has changed dramatically over time. As an example, consider the massive changes undergone by San Francisco. Today San Francisco is a thoroughly modern U.S. city, famed for its hills, cable cars, fog, and natural beauty. It also has a particularly easygoing lifestyle, about which Geoffrey Moorhouse once wrote:

> No one who visits San Francisco for the first time can fail to be aware of the pleasantly relaxed atmosphere. You are not perpetually admonished by well-wishers about the dangers of getting mugged, as visitors usually are in New York. It seems true that shop assistants here are more amiable than elsewhere, less bent on treating their customers as components of the cash register; when they say "Have a nice day," they sound as though they mean it and not as if it were a ritual phrase learned to help trade. Watch people move about the streets if you want to appreciate what San Francisco has done to them. Except at rush hour, they tend to stroll. There is nothing comparable here to downtown New York or the heart of London, where the word "perambulation" may now be considered redundant except at weekends, having long since been banished by the general push and shove. (1979:24)

But such was not always the case. Changes to San Francisco through its brief century and a half of existence have been profound, as historic documents attest. One such document is Richard Henry Dana's *Two Years Before the Mast* (2001, originally published in 1862), one of the greatest of nineteenth-century seagoing journals, a part of which you can read in the Cityscape box on page 5.[2]

What happened to San Francisco between Dana's two visits was gold, discovered in 1849.

Almost overnight the sleepy little village of Yerba Buena, the nearest port for outfitting the Sierra Nevada mines, was transformed into a feverish city. Not for another 70 years would Moorhouse's sophisticated, "laid-back" San Francisco begin to appear. Thus, we can see the importance of studying the city historically. Without benefit of hindsight, we might easily fool ourselves into thinking that cities, although perhaps smaller in the past, were always more or less like those we know today.

Luckily, our understanding of past cities doesn't rely only on historical documents such as Dana's account of early San Francisco. In recent years urban archaeologists have made major strides in the study of urban settings about which little or no written material is available.

Abandoned cities, or cities rebuilt on earlier foundations, still contain traces of their earlier existence, providing clues for archaeologists trained in the careful excavation and analysis of artifacts. From such clues, they can piece together a picture of how a city's people lived: how they built their houses and organized their families, what they thought important enough to portray in paintings, what level of technology they employed, what they commonly drank or ate. By unearthing many such clues, archaeologists allow long-dead cities to spring back to life.

One of the most important finds in recent years was the 1965 discovery of the pre-Incan site of Gran Pajatén, a legendary lost city of Peru, located 360 miles north of Lima, the capital. Imagine trekking through the high jungles of South America and finding the ruins of a vast system of

> walls and terraces, buildings and tombs and statuary, all perched on the steep, cloud-shrouded eastern slope of the Andes [Mountains] overlooking a nameless river, [ruins] of an early, resourceful and mysterious people whose civilization flourished long before the glory days of the Incas. (Wilford 1985:A1)

Lost for centuries, Gran Pajatén appears to be only one of the region's lost urban sites (another was found nearby in 1997). Archaeologists regard the Gran Pajatén site as one of the

---

[2]Various kinds of boxes are included in each chapter to illustrate key points and themes. When you encounter a reference to a particular box, take a minute or two to read it before going on with the chapter.

CITYSCAPE

San Francisco's Massive Changes

Shipping from New York, Richard Henry Dana first visited San Francisco, then called Yerba Buena ("good herbs"), in 1835. Here is what he saw:

[Near the] mouth of the bay . . . is a high point on which the [Presidio Mexican military outpost] is built. Behind this point is the little harbor, or bight, called Yerba Buena, in which trading vessels anchor, and, near it, the Mission of Delores. There was no other habitation on this side of the Bay, except a shanty of rough boards put up by a man named Richardson, who was doing a little trading between the vessels and the Indians. . . . We came to anchor near the mouth of the bay, under a high and beautifully sloping hill, upon which herds of hundreds and hundreds of red deer, and the stag, with his high branching of antlers, were bounding about, looking at us for a moment, and then starting off, affrighted at the noises we made at seeing the variety of their beautiful attitudes and motion.

That was hardly the San Francisco of Geoffrey Moorhouse; nor does it much resemble this description of Dana's, written in 1859 after a second visit:

We bore round the point toward the old anchoring ground of hide ships, and there, covering the sand hills and the valleys, stretching from the water's edge to the base of the great hills, and from the old Presidio to the Mission, flickering all over with lamps of its streets and houses, lay a city of one hundred thousand inhabitants. . . . The dock into which we drew, and the streets about it, were densely crowded with express wagons and hand-carts to take luggage, coaches and cabs for passengers, and with men. . . . Through this crowd I made my way, along the well-built and well-lighted streets, as alive as by day, where boys in high keyed voices were already crying the latest New York papers; and between one and two o'clock in the morning found myself comfortably abed in a commodious room, in the Oriental Hotel, which stood, as well as I could learn, on the filled-up cove, and not far from the spot where we used to beach our boats from the Alert.

When I awoke in the morning, and looked from my windows over the city of San Francisco, with its townhouses, towers, and steeples; its courthouses, theaters, and hospitals; its daily journals; its well-filled learned professions; its fortresses and light houses; its wharves and harbor, with their thousand-ton clipper ships, more in number than London or Liverpool sheltered that day . . .; when I looked across the bay to the eastward, and beheld a beautiful town on the fertile wooded Shores of the Contra Costa [the area of today's Oakland and Berkeley] and steamers, large and small, the ferryboats of the Contra Costa, and capacious freighters and passenger- carriers to all parts of the great bay and its horizon—when I saw all these things, and reflected on what I once was and saw here, and what now surrounded me, I could scarcely keep my hold on reality at all, or the genuineness of anything, and seemed to myself like one who had moved in "worlds not realized."

Source: Richard Henry Dana, *Two Years Before the Mast* (New York: Heritage, 2001), pp. 196, 203, 320–22.

most important pre-Columbian ruins discovered since the 1911 finding of Machu Picchu, also in Peru, hundreds of miles to the south. The citadel of Gran Pajatén dates back to 2000 B.C.E., and was occupied until the Incas conquered it in the early sixteenth century. What astonishes the scholars is how the city, clearly part of a highly developed civilization, thrived in such an inhospitable environment—within a dense jungle, surrounded by almost perpetual clouds and rain, some 8,600 feet above sea level. Only five authorized expeditions have gone to study the city thus far, although 21 others went to loot (Salzar 1997).

Built by the Incas in the mid-fifteenth century, Machu Picchu remained hidden until 1911. Now a tourist attraction receiving 400,000 visitors annually, it is one of the world's most impressive archeological sites. It is a masterpiece in urban planning, civil engineering, architecture, and stonemasonry; its many buildings still intact except for their thatch and reed roofs.

Archaeology also plays a role in contemporary cities. Most cities exist on the rubble of their own past. Take London, for example. Over the course of its 2,000-year history, this city has risen some 30 feet, building on its own refuse. In 1997, ten excavation sites in and around London Bridge unearthing Roman London—established in the first century C.E.—brought new discoveries. Archaeologists found two different types of Roman building, one type made with timber frames and clay walls and floors, and later, more substantial masonry buildings, some with mortar floors and plaster walls, both of which served as the homes of artisans, with shops or workshops in front and living quarters behind. Also uncovered were many artifacts of everyday life, including oil lamps for lighting homes and vessels used for cooking and drinking (Jubilee 1997).

Closer to home, archaeologists completed an excavation on New York's Wall Street in 1979–1980, uncovering artifacts from the original Dutch settlement of 1625. In 1991, excavation for a new federal building between Broadway and Duane Street in Lower Manhattan unearthed an eighteenth-century African burial ground.

Two chapters of this text survey cities in human history. Chapter 2 reviews major urban developments from the beginnings of cities some ten millennia ago right up to the urban events of this century. We will see that the urban story is one of continuous and striking change. Chapter 3 highlights how cities have developed in the United States and Canada. Here, too, we will find astonishing changes—changes hinted at in Dana's account of San Francisco. We will see the alterations of North American urban life as cities grew from the small, isolated colonial centers of the seventeenth century to sprawling environments with populations often reaching into multimillions. Next, in Chapter 4, we examine recent urban trends that will shape urban and suburban lifestyles for at least part of the twenty-first century: sprawl, edge cities, gated communities, and common-interest developments (CIDs).

The Emergence of Urban Sociology

One key goal of this text is to understand how sociologists study the city. Although historians have been looking at cities for centuries, sociologists are more recent arrivals on the scene. As Chapter 5 explains, early sociologists in the late nineteenth century lived during a period of dramatic urban upheaval and, naturally, they turned their attention to cities. They tried to understand just how the Industrial Revolution transformed the small villages of both Europe and North America into huge, chaotic metropolises.

Many early sociologists shared a pessimistic vision of the city. Their works portray the city as a dangerous place where the traditional values of social life—a sense of community, a caring for other people—were systematically torn apart. However, recent sociological research shows that many of these concerns about the destructiveness of urban living were based on faulty evidence. In the light of contemporary research, the city emerges as a more neutral phenomenon. Neither good nor bad in and of themselves, cities have been pushed in one direction or the other by the cultural forces at work in a particular time and place. Thus, the horrors of nineteenth-century London appear to be primarily a product of the massive industrialization that took place within a capitalist society, and not a result of something inherently urban.

Social Psychology: The Urban Experience

With more than three-fourths of North Americans living in cities, any student of cities needs to explore the urban experience. How and why do cities stimulate us so much? Do cities change people in one way or another?

We know that the city trips our emotions—a point clearly illustrated in the Cityscape box on pages 8–9, as one sociologist recalls his visit to "the Big Apple": New York. Although these reactions are certainly personal, they are also *social* in two senses. First,

it is the social environment of the city itself that generates them. Second, they are social in that they are common; they resonate with most of us as well.

These social dimensions of the urban experience also figure in our analysis. **Urbanism**—a concept referring to those social–psychological aspects of life, personality patterns, and behavioral adaptations influenced by the city—is the focal point of Chapter 6.

Urban Geography and Ecology

Why did people cluster together to form cities in the first place? In the fourth century B.C.E., the Greek philosopher Aristotle provided a timeless answer: People come together in cities for security; they remain there in order to live the good life. For the ancient Greeks, cities satisfied a need for security. In an age of few laws and fewer treaties, groups frequently preyed on one another. For protection, people came together in a single location, often a natural fortification such as the Acropolis in Aristotle's Athens. Where natural defenses were not available, people built walls. But a site could become a city only with other geographical assets: water, access to transportation routes, and the ability to produce or import enough goods to meet the population's needs.

But once cities began, people made a remarkable discovery. Mixing together in large numbers not only afforded protection; it generated more profitable trade and stimulated intellectual life as well. People began to hail the city as offering the potential for what Aristotle termed "the good life."

The importance of a city's physical location, and of how people come to arrange themselves within the urban area, has led urbanists to develop two related areas of study: (1) **urban geography,** which focuses on the significance of the city's location and natural resources; and (2) **urban ecology,** which analyzes how people spread out within an urban area. Let us illustrate each of these areas of study.

A city's geographical location has a great deal to do with how life in that city is lived. Take the two largest U.S. cities, New York and Los Angeles. Centered on Manhattan Island,

CITYSCAPE

New York, New York!

As a child, I lived in a suburb of Springfield, Massachusetts. I must've been about eleven years old the first time I ever went to New York City. I remember I was so excited that I could hardly sleep for a week before.

New York? It seemed absolutely incomprehensible. To my mind, Springfield and Boston weren't even cities compared to New York. They were outposts, back country. New York was in a class by itself—gargantuan, mysterious, the city of cities, the place where everything important (other than the Red Sox) happened. I had read about it; I had seen it in the movies; I knew about people who lived there. I was going.

We took the train from Springfield. Four hours! Imagine being eleven years old and waiting four hours on a train to get to New York! I counted the cities (hardly looked at them, couldn't care less) as we went by—Hartford, New Haven, Stamford, whatever. Finally: the outskirts!

Our approach was through the Bronx and Harlem, tenement areas. I had never seen so many buildings. They went on for miles and all seemed huge and alike. I saw the back alleys, the clothes strung from windows, and pigeon cages on the roofs. I knew tremendously exciting things were happening here. This was where the boxer Rocky Graziano grew up (I had read his autobiography, *Somebody Up There Likes Me,* a dozen

times), where *West Side Story* gang wars took place, where the people who worked *On the Waterfront* lived. (In retrospect, it seems crass, even cruel, this attitude about the poor. I had no comprehension of the suffering, the degradation that more often than not accompanied such existences. I was a suburban kid, hyped up by all the media I had been exposed to.)

After what seemed an eternity, during which the train repeatedly slowed, stopped, and went slowly forward again, we finally stopped for good. All the people on the train except my mother and myself (bumpkins both!) got up, put their coats on, grabbed their briefcases, and started out. We piled onto the platform; I pulled myself, our three suitcases, and my mother after the crowd. Inside the main lobby of Grand Central, I was awestruck. I knew it was going to be big, this was *cavernous! I mean, you could hardly see the roof!* And there were the haze, the incredible echoes, the indecipherable voices of the train announcers, and no fewer than five hundred thousand people going every which way. We were in New York!

Somehow we got to the street—I have no recollection how—and once again I was stupefied, this time by the traffic, the hurrying people, the huge buildings. My mother suggested we take a cab to the hotel. Although excited by this prospect, I argued against it: "Let's not," I said, "It's only 14 blocks to our hotel. It's just around the corner. Nobody can get lost in New York. Everything's numbered, the streets

surrounded by rivers, New York City has a land base of bedrock physically able to support tall buildings. By contrast, Los Angeles stretches out across a semiarid basin that, geologically speaking, makes the building of skyscrapers a shaky business indeed. These

different settings translate into very different daily routines, as Joseph Giovannini, a part-time resident of both cities, noted:

New York and Los Angeles have fundamentally different spatial premises. Space in New York go one way, the avenues another (I wasn't sure which). Let's walk." A bit skeptical, my mother agreed. Carrying our not inconsiderable baggage, we headed over to Fifth Avenue.

What do I remember? The lions on the steps of the New York Public Library. They were larger than any statues I had ever seen. The library itself was huge: The library in Springfield was about a third the size, and the library in my suburb wasn't even as large as one of the lions. People: in suits, in dresses, in uniforms and clothing that I hardly imagined existed. Orthodox Jews in their traditional raiment; Blacks and Asians; young kids in motorcycle jackets with their hair slicked back (delinquents); bums lying in the street or panhandling.

And, I remember the street—the newsstands, with more papers and magazines than I could believe. I took mental notes on one block: a department store, a book store, a record store, a fashion shop, a Florsheim shoe store. Then another: a department store, a Kelly Girls office, a restaurant . . . , and another Florsheim shoe store! Springfield had three shoe stores within its entire city limits, all different companies. Two Florsheim shoe stores in two blocks? I could hardly believe it. How could they stay in business?

The next thing I remember is my mother grabbing my shoulder and yelling at me to be careful. I was three steps into the street on a "Don't Walk" signal. Yellow cabs and Cadillacs were coming at me, honking like crazy. They weren't about to stop. In my daze I had just kept walking, looking at everything and astonished by a third Florsheim

shoe store across the street. As I leaped back onto the curb, the horns were honking and the cabbies were glaring and shaking their fists.

At this point, my mother said we were taking a cab the rest of the way to the hotel, no matter how close it was. I didn't argue. I was exhausted. I hailed a cab like a native (I'd seen them do it in hundreds of movies). We got in. The cabbie looked around and said, "Where to, Mack?" A bit ruffled by his demeanor, I said in a confident, firm voice: "The Hotel——" (I've forgotten the name). The cabbie looked at me, frowned, looked impatient, and then asked gruffly, "Where's that, Mack?"

What? In every story I'd ever read, in every film I'd ever seen about New York, you just got into the cab, said the name of the hotel, and the cab took off. Cabbies knew all the hotels in New York. I suddenly realized New York was so big they didn't know all the hotels. And this cabbie couldn't care less. I fumbled about for the address, my suave facade completely blown. My mother finally found it. The cabbie grabbed it, snorted, and turned around. We roared off.

I smashed back into the seat, sliding through a piece of fresh gum thoughtfully left by a prior passenger. All I remember about the ride is that we almost got in twelve accidents, that the cabbie yelled at other drivers a lot, that the meter went up awfully fast, and that we passed eight more Florsheim shoe stores on the way.

Source: James L. Spates, Hobart and William Smith Colleges.

collects people; in Los Angeles it separates them. New Yorkers occupy a community; Angelenos occupy their own privacy. New York is an environment of people; Los Angeles is an environment of vehicular movement. New York is a vertical city, and Los Angeles, despite its hills and mountains, is horizontally organized. . . .

The urban patterns that shape attitudes in the two cities are as simple as the daily commute. In Los Angeles, I coasted downhill in my '59 Studebaker Lark, accompanied by **FM** music. If I timed the freeways correctly to avoid bottlenecks, the drive to work from my office in Venice was a rumination. . . .

In New York, the half-hour commute is a very different half hour. It starts in the elevator, where I might encounter another tenant: We chat. Then, a brief conversation with the door-man; perhaps a passing greeting to a neighbor on the street, and then another chat at the cor-ner newsstand. [After my subway ride, when] I arrive at Times Square, I sometimes head for my morning coffee and pastry at the Lucky Star Delicatessen, where I talk to Mervat, an Egypt-ian waitress; then, on the elevator in The Times building, I meet more people before sitting down at my desk. (1983:147)

Geography is only one cause of the differ-ing social dynamics that distinguish cities. Various categories of people stake out partic-ular areas within the city, particular activities come to dominate certain districts—and both of these change over time. Such shifts interest urban ecologists, who seek to understand how people choose to locate and rearrange them-selves in urban space. One well-documented ecological process is **invasion-succession,** by which whole sections of a city change. A new "high-tech" area in an adjacent suburb may rather suddenly upstage an old industrial dis-trict. Almost overnight, the older district starts to look tawdry. Secondhand stores, "gentlemen's clubs," and pornographic book-stores replace the older, more respectable businesses. Before long, income levels in the area drop and the few remaining original businesses close their doors. Where once ex-ecutives and working people trod the city sidewalks, now one finds only prostitutes, drug dealers, and petty criminals. With this succession, the process of change is complete.

The same process of invasion and succession may occur in residential areas as new categories of people enter an established neighborhood. An example is contained in the Cityscape box on page 11, in which novelist Paul Theroux de-scribes the reaction of Mr. Gawber, a traditional British civil servant and long-term London resi-dent, to ethnic changes in his neighborhood. The very presence of these new people offends Mr. Gawber, who refuses to see any good in his new neighbors—a hard attitude not likely to foster good relations.

Mr. Gawber has seen a lot of change in Lon-don; understanding some of these changes offers some insight into this man's rancor. Gaw-ber is a member of London's old middle class. His father, impoverished, had come to the city early in the twentieth century to work for the huge civil service that had evolved to control London's growth. Over the years, the Gawbers, proud of their accomplishments, enjoyed solid, well-ordered lives in a "good" neighborhood.

After World War II, however, London changed radically. The soldiers came home, fol-lowed closely by thousands upon thousands of the British Empire's far-flung subjects: Africans; Asians; people from the islands of the West In-dies such as Jamaica, Trinidad, and Tobago; and immigrants from India. Postwar conditions prompted the immigration, for the war had devastated many colonies' economies. To make matters more complicated, many colonies were in the midst of political turmoil. In such a cli-mate, many of the empire's colonial subjects decided to seek a better life in England. Many who arrived in London had little money and few skills to support themselves.

Some settled in Gawber's neighborhood partly because the massive wartime bombing of London had decreased property values in that area. Speculating real-estate agents bought up the available housing and rented it to the newcomers at affordable prices. The poverty and colonial lifestyles of the newcomers of-fended and threatened traditionalists, many of whom packed up and left. Gawber was among the few who remained to fume at the newcomers, who symbolized the demise of his "orderly and decent life."

Such study of ecological changes over time helps our understanding of the social dynam-ics of city life, just as geography provides in-sight into the physical arrangements. These interrelated elements provide the subject matter of Chapter 7.

Comparative Urbanism: The City and Culture

As we have already suggested, the city does not exist in a vacuum. It is "powered" by its

CITYSCAPE

Mr. Gawber's London—A Neighborhood in Transition

Once, this road had the preserved well-tended look of . . . [houses with] painted trim, owned by families for their cozy size and kept in repair. But the houses on Volta—with servants' bells in every room and names like The Sycamores—had fallen into the hands of speculators and building firms and enterprising landlords, who partitioned them with thin walls, sealing off serving hatches and doors, building kitchens in back bedrooms, installing toilets in broom cupboards, bolting a sink or a cooker on a landing so the stacked dishes were in full view of the street. . . .

Mr. Gawber had been born in number twelve and he had grown up in it. . . . He had attended the boys' school, Saint Dunstan's, at the top of the road and the Anglican church at the bottom. Now the church was Baptist and mostly black. . . . He stayed away. He had seen the street's residents grow old and die or retire to the country, and after the war the houses had moved into a phase of decline that was, even now, unchecked. The new occupants were numerous, they were every human color, and the street was made nearly impassable by their parked cars. . . . The window boxes were empty, the hedges torn out, the gardens paved for cars and motorbikes. . . . It was not a bad road—there were many worse—but it would never improve. Eventually it would be . . . pulled down and tan apartment blocks built on it. That was the pattern. . . .

Mr. Gawber thought: I am a relic from that other age. Lately, he had studied the new families. They were . . . Negroes and Irishmen who wore bicycle clips; dog-faced boys in mangy fur coats and surly mothers with red babies and children with broken teeth and very old men who inched down the sidewalk tapping canes. . . .

In the warm weather . . . the life in those houses spilled into Volta Road—babies were wheeled out for approval, youths met and tinkered with motorbikes and taunted girls; arguments turned into fights, shameless courtships into loud weddings. . . . This evening they were out: Wangoosa mending his bicycle, Churchill dandling his baby, the Indian tuning his Land Rover, each one claiming his portion of the road. He wished these families away.

Mr. Gawber destroyed it with his eyes. He policed the ruins and found the idlers guilty of causing a nuisance and a breach of the peace, of unlawful assembly, uttering menaces, outraging the public modesty, and tax evasion. He blew a shrill whistle and had them carted off, then leveled the road, reducing the houses to a field of broken bricks and lumbers, and he let the grass reassert itself and cover the rubble with its green hair. It would serve them right.

Source: Paul Theroux, *The Family Arsenal,* reprint ed. (New York: Penguin, 1996), pp. 34–37.

people, who represent a particular way of life, or culture. By the term **culture,** we mean the basic beliefs, values, and technology that characterize a city in a particular historical era. Any society's culture is reproduced and intensified in the city.

Technology provides a good example. If we were to visit the London of a century and a half ago, we likely would be shocked to see how different it was from the cities of today. Yes, we would find a bustling business district and lots of people—but there the similarity

The congested, bustling activity captured in this woodcut drawing of London in the 1870s helps us visualize the sights and sounds, the grandeur and squalor, that attracted millions of people to live, work, play, or visit within its boundaries.

would end. Rather than a sprawling metropolitan area with extensive suburbs and shopping centers, crisscrossed by superhighways and adorned with skyscrapers, we would find a relatively compact city, with all its hustle going on in narrow, winding streets of astonishing filth. Charles Dickens, who lived there, provides us with an illustration:

> LONDON. . . . Implaccable November weather. As much mud in the streets as if the waters had but newly retreated from the face of the earth. . . . Smoke lowering down from chimney pots, making a soft black drizzle, with flakes of soot in it as big as full-grown snow-flakes—gone into mourning, one might imagine, for the death of the sun. Dogs, undistinguishable in mire. Horses, scarcely better; splashed to their very blinkers. Foot passengers, jostling one another's umbrellas, in a general infection of ill-temper, and losing their foothold at street-corners, where tens of thousands of other foot passengers have been slipping and sliding since the day broke (if this day ever broke), adding new deposits to the crust upon crust of mud . . . and accumulating at compound interest. (*Bleak House* 1853, p. 1)

Inevitable as they may seem, clean, paved streets, clean air, the skyscraper, the superhighway, and the large, sprawling suburb are very recent urban phenomena, all products of a certain level of technological development. The skyscraper only became feasible in the latter part of the nineteenth century, when steel-frame buildings and electrically powered elevators were developed. Similarly, sprawling suburbs are unthinkable without superhighways or mass public transportation linking cities and suburbs; these, in turn, are dependent on technological innovations such as steel, railroads, electricity, and the private automobile. Finally, paved streets became common in cities only in the twentieth century, and it wasn't until the 1950s and 1960s that clean air acts were passed in the United States to curtail exhaust excesses like those Dickens described. A given level of technology, then, has much to do with the urban experience.

In the same way, cultural beliefs play a major role in shaping city life. Americans, for instance, live out distinctly American beliefs and values in an urban setting. Consider that well-known urban institution, the cabdriver, who earns a living performing essentially a public service: transporting people from one location to another. Because of differing cultural orientations, an examination of London cabbies would turn up rather striking differences from, say, New York cabbies.

First, the relationship between drivers and fleet owners is less adversarial in London. Although there are some "gypsy cabs"—taxis privately owned or leased by their drivers—large companies control most of the cabs in New York and other U.S. cities (Moreno 1997; Vidich 1976). The central U.S. value of maximizing private profit no doubt plays a role in fleet owners trying to pay drivers the smallest portion of the fare possible and drivers either cheating the fleet owner (and sometimes the public) or learning to skillfully maximize tips. In London, however, little conflict exists between drivers and fleet owners, mainly because more than 40 percent of London's drivers (compared with a mere handful in New York) own their own cabs and are beholden to no one. Because of the threat that any driver may "go independent," fleet owners in London must be more solicitous of drivers and more competitive in terms of benefits offered (Buckland 1968).

Second, the British maintain far more government control of the cab industry than is the case in the United States, and there are stringent requirements concerning the character and ability of drivers and strict enforcement of the regulations on the upkeep of cabs (Buckland 1968; Georgano 1973). This control reinforces a traditional value that competes with profit making in the minds of London's drivers and owners: pride. With cabs in good repair and personnel "up to a certain mark," London's taxi people have the *esprit de corps* of an elite group. Although restricted from cutting corners to maximize profit, most British drivers and fleet owners would not do so even if they could. Similarly, although many of London's cabbies struggle to make ends meet, they find it undignified to manipulate passengers for tips, as often happens in U.S. cities (Buckland 1968, chap. 7).

In comparison, government control is anathema to many Americans. New York fleet owners have lobbied long, hard, and successfully to keep government regulation to a minimum. With fewer restrictions and a powerful profit motive, they have been able to hire less-experienced drivers and let cabs deteriorate tremendously (Vidich 1976, chaps. 6–7). The result is more profit but also a lower quality of service and noticeably less pride.

It would be impossible to understand the differences between English and American cabdrivers without a careful study of the role that cultural beliefs play in the urban setting. So central is this issue to the study of cities that we devote all of Chapter 8 to it.

The New Urban Sociology: The City and Capitalism

Just as important as a city's geographical setting and its cultural framework is its ability to generate trade—to be economically prosperous. Aristotle said that initially people came to cities for security. True enough, particularly at the time he was writing. But throughout history, people have flocked to the city for many reasons, chief among them the belief that, in the city, they would significantly improve their material standard of living. An excellent case in point is Hsiang Tzu, a Chinese peasant who went to Peking, China's capital city, in the 1930s:

> When he saw the bustle of people and horses, heard the ear-piercing racket, smelled the dry stink of the road, and trod the powdery, churned-up gray dirt, Hsiang Tzu wanted to kiss it, kiss that gray stinking dirt, adorable dirt, dirt that grew silver dollars! He had no father or mother, brother or sister, and no relatives. The only friend he had was this ancient city. This city gave him everything. Even starving here was better than starving in the country. There were things to look at, sounds to listen to, color and voices everywhere. All you needed was to be willing to sell your strength. There was so much money it couldn't be counted. There were ten thousand kinds of grand things here

> that would never be eaten up or worn out. Here, if you begged for food, you could even get things like meat and vegetable soup. All they had in the village was cornmeal cakes. (Lao 1979:31)

Although Hsiang Tzu's experience occurred half a world away from North America, it might have taken place anywhere. His hope that life in the city would fulfill his dreams is the same as the hopes of the millions upon millions of immigrants who came to Canada and the United States from rural and poor backgrounds around the turn of the last century. These people, including many of our grandparents and great-grandparents, settled in cities across both nations in an attempt to make their fortunes.

Comparisons of medieval and contemporary cities reveal the growing importance of the economic function of cities over the centuries. In the Middle Ages, although cities were already important centers of trade, other areas of life also were thriving. All one has to do is look at the physical layout of cities built in the Middle Ages—with their central cathedral as the tallest building—to see the importance of religion in the lives of the people. With the coming of the Industrial Revolution, however, all that began to change. Cities became ever more important as centers of wealth. Skyscrapers, large factories, and office buildings sprang up to meet the economic demands of millions. The churches that had previously dominated the skyline were dwarfed by the new "central business district."

Study of the economics of land use was, until the 1960s, dependent on an ecological model (see Chapter 7). Since then, many social scientists from a variety of disciplines have embraced a new perspective called **urban political economy.** Looking at the decline of manufacturing in cities, the migration to the suburbs and the Sunbelt, mushrooming cities in poor nations, and a growing world economy, the new breed of urban researchers concluded that natural processes could not explain these changes and their economic impact on cities.

The Church of Our Lady before Tyn, with its magnificent Gothic steeples, dominates the cityscape of Prague in the Czech Republic. The Old Town retains many medieval qualities: visual domination by the cathedral, no central business district, narrow streets, buildings with commercial enterprises at street level and residences on the floors above.

Instead, they argue, decision making within political and economic institutions, often thousands of miles away, affects a city economically, politically, socially, and even physically. Some, but not all, advocates of this perspective are neo-Marxists. Regardless of their philosophical orientation, their theoretical emphasis focuses on investment decisions and economic trends that determine a city's fortunes. We will look at the structural imperatives of urban political economy, and their ramifications on urban poverty, in Chapter 9.

THE ANATOMY OF MODERN NORTH AMERICAN CITIES

Chapters 2 through 9 provide the basic framework for a detailed analysis of the cities of the contemporary world. Then our attention returns to North America for a detailed analysis of the cities most of us know best. Even though urban population growth has slowed in Canada and the United States, this by no means suggests that the situation of our cities today is stagnant and unchanging. Far from it. Recent decades have been a period of enormous change for North American cities.

In the United States, the much-publicized movement to Sunbelt (southern and western) cities is one such change. As Table 1–1 indicates, with a few exceptions, Sunbelt cities have gained markedly in population in the last decade, while midwestern and northeastern cities have generally declined. Growing significantly were the cities of Austin, Phoenix, San Jose, Charlotte, and San Antonio, all in the South and West. Declining substantially were Detroit, Milwaukee, Washington, D.C., Baltimore, and Philadelphia, all in the Midwest or Northeast. Moving against the trend were New York City, which increased in population, and New Orleans and Birmingham, which lost people.

Unlike the medieval Old Town section of Prague with its central cathedral and lower surrounding buildings, North American cities typically include a central business district with few residences, expressways, wider streets for cars, and a skyline dominated by tall commercial buildings, as illustrated in this view of Atlanta, Georgia.

A second recent development is a nation-wide trend toward living in smaller cities or in areas farther away from the central cities. For instance, the census shows that the areas surrounding the suburbs are growing most rapidly. Thus, just as people moved from central cities to suburbs a generation ago, now they are moving still farther from the urban core.

What accounts for these marked changes? Demographers suggest that, although many older Americans prefer to remain in the community where they spent most of their adult lives ("aging in place"), retirement magnet areas attract many affluent seniors. A retirement home in Dade County, Florida (Miami's home county), Austin, Texas, or Sun City, Arizona (near Phoenix) has become an attraction that millions have no desire to resist. Second, the last several decades have seen an increasing exodus of business and industry from center cities, occasioned by a desire to escape high taxation, congestion, outmoded

plants, high union wages, and excessive heating costs (the latter two factors primarily in the North). In many cases, firms have moved south or west. In other instances, they have moved to areas on the periphery of the center city. In either case, they have pulled their employees with them. The employees' choice to live in smaller cities, towns, and rural areas results partly from their desire to be near relocated businesses or industries and partly from the long-standing desire to be free of congestion and to have "living space" in affordable housing. Earlier suburbs, built primarily in the 1950s and 1960s, were the first manifestation of this cultural value. The decentralization indicated by recent census data confirms that this trend is continuing.

Whatever the final explanations for these demographic changes, their effects are profound. Those cities with declining population lose federal funding and political representation. As a result, such cities must cut budgets,

TABLE 1–1   Populations of the Thirty Largest U.S. Cities, 2000

2000 Ranking	City	2000 Population	1990 Population	1990 Ranking	Percent Change
1	New York	8,008,000	7,323,000	1	+10.7
2	Los Angeles	3,695,000	3,486,000	2	+6.0
3	Chicago	2,896,000	2,783,000	3	+4.0
4	Houston	1,954,000	1,698,000	4	+15.1
5	Philadelphia	1,518,000	1,586,000	5	−4.3
6	Phoenix	1,321,000	989,000	10	+33.6
7	San Diego	1,223,000	1,111,000	6	+10.1
8	Dallas	1,189,000	1,007,000	8	+18.1
9	San Antonio	1,145,000	997,000	9	+26.9
10	Detroit	951,000	1,028,000	7	−7.5
11	San Jose, CA	895,000	783,000	11	+14.2
12	Indianapolis	782,000	732,000	13	+6.9
13	San Francisco	777,000	724,000	14	+7.3
14	Jacksonville, FL	737,000	635,000	16	+15.8
15	Columbus, OH	711,000	636,000	15	+11.8
16	Austin	657,000	494,000	25	+32.8
17	Baltimore	651,000	736,000	12	−11.5
18	Memphis	650,000	619,000	18	+5.0
19	Milwaukee	597,000	628,000	17	−6.0
20	Boston	589,000	574,000	20	+2.6
21	Washington, DC	572,000	607,000	19	−5.7
22	El Paso	564,000	516,000	22	+9.3
23	Seattle	563,000	516,000	21	+9.1
24	Denver	555,000	468,000	28	+18.6
25	Nashville-Davidson	546,000	488,000	20	+11.7
26	Charlotte, NC	541,000	427,000	33	+26.7
27	Fort Worth	535,000	448,000	29	+20.2
28	Portland, OR	529,000	486,000	27	+8.9
29	Oklahoma City	506,000	445,000	30	+13.8
30	Tucson	487,000	417,000	34	+16.7

Source: U.S. Bureau of the Census.

services, and aid to the poor and elderly, decreasing further their attractiveness as places to live. Because of lost revenues, inner suburbs also begin to deteriorate as people move away. On the other hand, the small cities and towns gaining population are likely to "get rich quick." This growth is a mixed blessing, however—many long-time residents of outlying areas, accustomed to traditional rural lifestyles, now find themselves assailed by an invasion of "city slickers."

What is life like in these cities of ours? Who lives in them? Why do they live there? What are the problems these cities face? Such questions will be answered in three chapters (Chapters 10, 11, and 12) that look at North American urban social structure. By **social structure,** we mean the recurrent patterns of city life that are shaped significantly by the unequal distribution of important urban resources, including wealth, power, and prestige.

One aspect of social structure concerns the wide variety of lifestyles within our cities. Often, these lifestyles coincide with different geographical districts of the city. In downtown areas, for example, we are likely to see well-dressed businesspeople—many of whom live in apartments. Older residential neighborhoods may provide the sights, sounds, and even smells of exotic cultural diversity. Still other neighborhoods contain the city's poor, who struggle every day to survive. In many suburban areas, single-family homes dominate—replete with children and the ever-present automobile.

Lifestyles are, of course, much more than matters of individual choice. They reflect dimensions of social difference, often taking the form of social inequality—the focus of Chapters 10 and 11. Like virtually all other societies, the United States and Canada contain marked **social stratification,** the hierarchical ranking of people in terms of valued resources. Wealth is certainly one important dimension of social stratification; U.S. cities, especially, provide striking contrasts between well-heeled urbanites who live lives of material comfort and others who must persevere just to survive.

Very often, this difference is closely related to other dimensions of social difference: race, ethnicity, and gender. Once ignored in the urban public sphere, women are now more likely to hold public office, at least in cities with populations of 25,000 or more (MacManus and Bullock 1995:162). From both historical and contemporary viewpoints, however, women's lives and city experiences have reflected the realities of gender, interwoven with those of social class, race, and ethnicity. In a still-continuing historic pattern, North American cities attract immigrants of different races and ethnic origin; on arrival many find themselves at or near the bottom of the urban hierarchy. With time, many improve their situation, but others continue to suffer from a wide range of problems associated with poverty and/or prejudice.

Social power—the ability to achieve one's ends and to shape events—is yet another important dimension of inequality. For those

As this scene of New Year's revelers in Times Square shows, a city is a dynamic, living entity, but not just on such special occasions. A city's night life—with its excitement, bright neon lights, variety of activities, crowds of people, and sense of adventure—lures people of all ages and backgrounds to come and be part of one of its many simultaneous happenings.

with considerable wealth, urban living is often the experience of shaping their own lives (and, indeed, the lives of others); by contrast, for poorer urbanites, many of whom are members of racial and ethnic minorities, life in the city is a grim matter of trying to cope with forces that seem overwhelming.

Of course, none of these structural patterns exists exclusively in cities. Social stratification is as important in small towns in New Hampshire as it is in Concord, the capital; people perceive racial distinctions as keenly in rural Ohio as they do in Columbus; and "power politics" is the name of the game in rural Wyoming, just as it is in Cheyenne. Nevertheless, because these structural patterns have shaped our cities so strongly, we can hardly ignore them.

On another level, however, because cities concentrate everything human in a small space, they intensify the effects of class, race, ethnicity, gender, and power. If we care to look, we can be buffeted by visions of wealth and poverty, of power and powerlessness of such extremity as to be nearly incomprehensible. A walk through the poor neighborhoods of almost any major North American city will reveal numerous examples of numbing poverty. Indeed, poverty for millions continues as only one of the significant problems that beset the urban environment. Three other closely related, significant urban issues are problems related to housing, education, and crime. An analysis of these problems and their implications is the focus of Chapter 12.

THE CITY IN WORLD PERSPECTIVE

If any one thing should astound us, it is how popular cities have become the world over. As a human invention, cities are scarcely 10,000 years old; but, as the centuries have passed, they have become both much larger and far more numerous. To put it slightly differently, once people become aware of the advantages of cities—protection, increased material standard of living, a more stimulating mental and social life—they don't want to live anywhere else. The process of **urbanization**—the concentration of people in cities and other densely populated areas—continues as strongly today as ever before. Demographers measure this process by the growing proportion of a population living in urban locales.

For example, in 1800 only one city, Beijing, had 1 million residents; now the world contains 130 cities where a million or more people reside. Table 1–2 makes the point even more powerfully. Reporting the percentage of urban people living in the world's seven major geographical areas between the years 1920 and 2000, the table shows that urbanization is an unmistakable trend everywhere. In fact, the world's cities are growing by 1 million people each week. This dramatic pattern means that by 2025, as mentioned earlier, almost three-fifths of the planet's people will be urban dwellers.

But there are distinct regional patterns in urban growth. If we examine the table for the percentages of growth between 1960 and 2000, we see that all regions gained urban population. Yet in the more industrialized areas of the world—North America

TABLE 1–2 Percentage of Urban Population in Major Areas of the World, in Millions

Area	1920	1960	2000	2030 (projected)
Europe	32	41	73	80
North America	38	57	79	87
Latin America (Central and South America)	14	32	77	85
Africa	5	13	39	54
Asia	7	17	39	55
Oceania	34	50	73	75
The World	14	25	47	61

Source: "Growth of the World's Urban and Rural Population: 1920–2000," *International Social Development Review* 1 (1969), p. 52; People & the Planet at *http://www.peopleandplanet.net*, accessed January 20, 2006.

and Europe—urban growth has slowed considerably in recent years. For instance, the urban population of the United States in 1960 was 69.9 percent; by 2000 it had inched upward to just 77 percent.

The area of greatest urban growth is now in the developing world—in Latin America, Africa, the Middle East, and Asia (see Figure 1–1). In fact, when we consult the figures on urban growth rates by country, we find that the ten countries with the highest urban growth rates are all in these four regions; those with the lowest rates, with one exception (Uruguay, in South America), are all in Europe, North America, and Japan. Moreover, when we scan a list of all the world's nations ranked in order of their urban growth rates, we must look down through 150 countries before we encounter an industrial nation—Canada (UN 2003).

Why should this concern us? Aren't growing cities generally a good thing? After all, cities produce jobs, generate better health care, and stimulate improvements in technology and the arts. The answer to this question is double edged: Sometimes they do these things, but not always; and often, when they do them, they do them for only some of the city's people.

In fact, throughout most of the developing world, the urban situation is desperate and, in some places, is even getting worse. Recent decades have witnessed hundreds of millions of people, enticed by the promise of a better life, moving into the cities of Latin America, Africa, the Middle East, and Asia. Most of these cities cannot keep up with the incoming tide. The results are poverty, malnutrition, and disease for many people. The Urban Living box on page 22 provides a poignant example of this in the Dominican Republic and elsewhere. Fortunately, the kind of disaster that prompted this story does not happen often, but the conditions reported still exist in many shantytowns throughout the world.

The grave situation in these countries is common throughout the world's poor nations. Chapter 13 examines the cities of Latin America, Africa, the Middle East, and Asia,

and offers analysis highlighting their urban problems and successes.

URBAN SOCIOLOGY AND THE QUALITY OF CITY LIFE

The city is a living, dynamic entity. Its capacity to concentrate human efforts means that urban places contain the greatest potential for improving the quality of human life.

From its beginnings millennia ago, people have come to the city with hopes and dreams of living "the good life." But when all is said and done, has the city lived up to its billing? True, many cities boast material living standards that are higher than they ever have been in history; but this is not the case for everyone. Further, in many cities of the developing world, material living standards are appallingly low—destitution in many cities is not the exception but the rule. Then, too, focusing on material standards alone may be a mistake. What about security, which was Aristotle's first concern? Despite a steadily declining urban crime rate in recent years, many areas in U.S. cities are so dangerous that people cannot go out alone, especially at night, without fear of being mugged, raped, or murdered. What about strong, community-oriented neighborhoods? Once a primary element of U.S. cities, these, too, have weakened in recent decades—and, in some areas, have disappeared altogether.

We need to understand the whole range of conditions that contribute to a more stimulating, fulfilling urban life. In bits and pieces throughout this book, evidence regarding the positive and negative elements of the city will emerge. We will comment on some of this evidence as we proceed and, in the final chapter, we will pull together these ideas as we examine urban planning and offer some thoughtful speculation about the future of cities.

Because of the ever-increasing importance of the city to the future of human civilization, sizing up the potential of urban places for meeting human needs is clearly essential. Are we necessarily heirs to the city of rage, racial prejudice, and exploitation that Mr. Gawber,

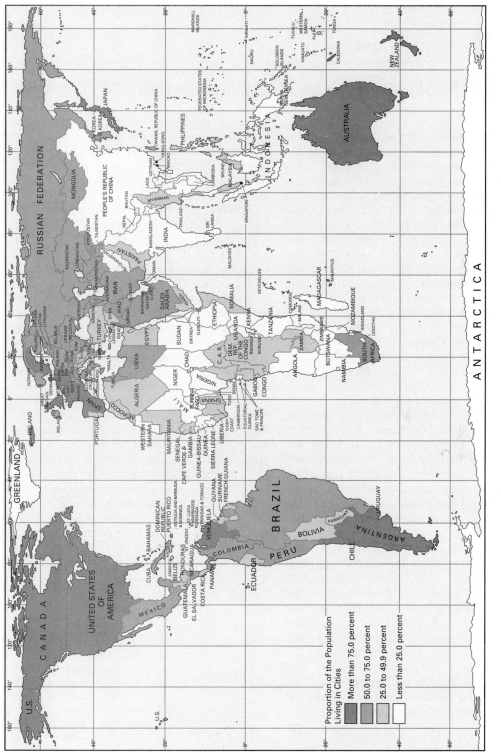

FIGURE 1–1 Urbanization in Global Perspective [*Source: Peters Atlas of the World* (1990).]

Proportion of the Population
Living in Cities

More than 75.0 percent

50.0 to 75.0 percent

25.0 to 49.9 percent

Less than 25.0 percent

URBAN LIVING

The Shantytowns of the Developing World

Communities of squatters, so poor that they cannot pay any amount of rent, can be found on the outskirts of major cities throughout Africa, Asia, the Caribbean, and Latin America. Millions of people throughout the developing world live in comparably unhealthy and dangerously situated shantytowns, most of them without indoor plumbing or electricity. Built from castoff scraps of lumber and tin by people who often have not even heard of building codes, they sprawl across river flood plains and low-lying coastal strips where tidal flooding is common, or else on hillsides where deadly mudslides take their toll.

In September 1998, San Juan de la Maguana, a banana-producing region of the Dominican Republic to the west of the capital city, Santo Domingo, fell victim to Hurricane Georges, with heavy rains and winds up to 130 miles an hour that lashed this area for 16 hours. The storm entombed five entire shantytowns there, including a basin area called Mesopotamia, in several feet of mud and rock, burying about 200 people.

In December 1999, mudslides and floodwaters destroyed thousands of flimsy homes in mountainside shantytowns above Caracas, Venezuela, along a 60-mile swath on the northern Caribbean coast. An estimated 30,000 people were killed. Today, on one of the hills overlooking the eastern edge of the city lies Petare, a shantytown of about 1,500 residents. The house-sized scars along the steep, unpaved road are grim reminders of that mudslide.

In July 2005, the city of Mumbai (Bombay), India, was deluged during a monsoon with 37 inches of rain in a 24-hour period. In Saki Naka, a shantytown in the city's northern area, a water-soaked hill collapsed and buried over 150 people.

In each of these areas and in many others, relief agencies attempted to provide food, provisions, and emergency shelter. Governments, working in tandem with these agencies, built new housing and pledged not to allow residents to again live in dwellings on such unstable ground. However, this relief effort has not been enough for the displaced, ever-growing population people who abandon the countryside in search of better jobs and are unable to find affordable housing. Instead, they continue to occupy these shantytowns throughout the developing world. Until the economic problems in these countries are solved, better housing will not be the answer, because people still won't be able to pay even a minimal amount for housing. So the shantytowns exist again, the squatters living in houses stacked so close to one another that the edges often overlap, hoping they will be spared when the next heavy rains come.

encountered? Or can the city become the ideal suggested by historian Lewis Mumford in the following passage?

The mission of the city is to further [the human being's] conscious participation in the cosmic and historic process. Through its own complex and enduring structure, the city vastly augments [human beings'] ability to interpret these processes and take an active, formative part in them, so that every phase of the drama it stages shall have, to the highest degree possible, the illumination of consciousness, the stamp of purpose, the color of love. That magnification of all the dimensions of life, through emotional communion, rational communication, technological mastery, and above all, dramatic representation, has been the supreme office of the city in history. And it remains the chief reason for the city's continued existence. (1961:576)

To answer, we must "go and make our visit."

❖ ━━━━━━━━ ❖ ━━━━━━━━ ❖

KEY TERMS

Culture
Invasion-succession
Social power
Social stratification
Social structure
Urban ecology
Urban geography
Urbanism
Urbanization

CHAPTER 2

THE ORIGINS AND DEVELOPMENT OF THE WORLD'S CITIES

Can you imagine the United States without great cities such as New York, Chicago, or San Francisco? It would be like thinking about Egypt without Cairo, Japan without Tokyo, France without Paris, or England without London. Why are entire countries so closely bound up with cities? The answer, as this chapter will explain, is that much of the story of human history is centered in cities. In fact, the words *city* and *civilization* are both derived from a single Latin root—*civitas.* Indeed, to be civilized is to live in or near a city.

This was not always the case, however. Most knowledgeable people today recognize the importance of cities because we live in an era in which the city is the dominant form of human association and is becoming more so every day. In the larger picture of human history, however, the city is a "wide-eyed infant"— a very recent arrival on the human scene.

URBAN ORIGINS

When and where did the first cities develop? What were they like? How did they change over time? Here we shall offer brief answers to these crucial questions. Before we can do so, however, we must look far back in time to see just how recently we human beings began making history on this earth.

To get a better perspective on where we are in relation to human history, let us utilize astronomer Carl Sagan's concept of a **cosmic calendar.** Sagan (1977) suggested that we imagine the entire history of our planet compressed into a single calendar year. What does such a vision suggest? To begin with, for almost the entire history of the universe (beginning with the "Big Bang"—corresponding to January 1), the human species did not exist. In fact, our species, *Homo sapiens,* appeared on earth roughly 100,000 years ago (December 31 in Sagan's year). Another 90,000 years passed before permanent settlements—even in the form of small villages—existed. The emergence of the first cities, then, and with them of the way of life we commonly call "civilization," occurred only about 10,000 years ago (8000 B.C.E.)—in the last minute of Sagan's

year! It would be several thousand years more, around 3000 B.C.E., before cities became common. Even then they contained only a small proportion of the world's population.

It is only in the last several centuries (the last second in Sagan's year) that the world has acquired a sizable urban population. As recently as 1940 the proportion of the world's population living in cities was only 19 percent. In 2000, this figure had grown to 47 percent. The existence of the city and of the urban way of life that we so readily take for granted, in other words, is a very recent and momentous change in the history of the world.

Archaeology: Digging the Early City

Learning about the first cities has been a gradual process filled with difficulties. Urban scholars have relied heavily on the work of archaeologists to gain an understanding of early settlements. Through excavation and techniques for determining the age of artifacts, we have learned much about the social life of people who left little formal record of their existence. Often, however, simply finding the sites of early cities—frequently buried beneath the surface, hidden by dense plant growth, or even covered by a current metropolis—is a matter of hard work and a bit of luck. Once an ancient city is found, excavation must proceed carefully to avoid damaging the remains. Finally, even when a city has been excavated successfully, archaeologists do not always offer the same interpretations of findings at a given site.

Moreover, our understanding of early urban settlements is subject to continuous revision. Ongoing investigations at old sites, and the discovery of new locations (such as the recent excavation of the Gran Pajatén Complex in Peru), provide a steady stream of new data. In addition, techniques of analysis continually improve, often leading to a reformulation of beliefs that urbanists held with certainty only a few years before.

We still have much to learn; nevertheless, there is much that we do know about early cities, and this chapter summarizes a great deal of that knowledge. First, we examine cities as they took form in the ancient world, and then we consider how, as the centuries passed, cities reflected the changing character of human civilization.

The First Permanent Settlements

Human beings like us first appeared on the earth about 100,000 years ago. For the next 90,000 years, our ancestors lived as hunters and gatherers—hunting game and gathering vegetation over large areas. Most followed the animals and moved with the seasons, without permanent settlements, in small groups ranging in size from 25 to 50 individuals. Frequently these family bands would camp in a place for a few weeks because the hunting was good or the vegetation was plentiful. When the game left the area or the vegetation went out of season, the people moved on.

Then, around 10,000 years ago, near the end of the last Ice Age, a change occurred. It happened slowly and without any evident drama. Nonetheless, it was to be one of the most momentous changes in human history: People began to settle down in one place and to evolve more complex social structures. Civilization as we know it was beginning. Why did it happen?

As time passed, the number of hunter-gatherer tribes grew. Gradually, they began to deplete the natural resources that had formed the mainstay of their existence for millennia. Game became scarce and vegetation was depleted. How could these nomads solve the food shortage problem? They could wander over larger areas, but that was difficult and threatened to place them in direct competition with other groups. They could carry extra food from areas of abundance, but this would be burdensome without the use of animals—which had not yet been domesticated. A better possibility was to settle in the most fertile areas and raise their own food. This option was the one that won out. Many experts view the domestication of plants, sometimes called the agricultural revolution, as the single most

important event in human history (Mumford 1961:55). For the first time, people could stay in one place and—once a food surplus could be produced—could allow some members of the group to pursue interests other than seeking food, such as crafts and science.

Over a period of some 5,000 years, villages began and multiplied. Humans created permanent settlements where they raised crops and learned to domesticate animals for use in the fields or as a food supply. Permanent settlements also transformed patterns of social structure. Most important, these settlements were all characterized by a more **complex division of labor.** For the first time people began doing many different, specialized tasks to "earn a living." This was a radical shift from the social structure that prevailed in hunter-gatherer tribes. In nomadic groups everyone knew a bit about everything. No one was a full-time doctor, lawyer, priest, or trader. Only permanent settlements afforded people the opportunity to specialize, not just in food production, but also in religion, military affairs, trade, and a host of other occupations.

Specialization benefited everyone: The farmer gained the protection of the military and the value of the priest's greater insight into matters religious, while the priest and the soldier received the fruits of the farmer's labors. In short, these early settlements provided the possibility of living a life based more on choice than on tradition. As Dora Jane Hamblin (1973:9) suggested, "No longer was every man forced to be a hunter or a farmer, every woman a mother and a housekeeper." Such a tantalizing variety, "offering the possibility of following a personal bent rather than a parent's footsteps, must have been as powerful a lure in 8000 B.C.E. as in the twentieth century."

Linked to the more complex division of labor was a second major element in the social structure of these early settlements: a **hierarchical power structure.** Hunting and gathering societies tend to be egalitarian. That is, while people perform a few different tasks in daily life, all work is deemed equally important to the welfare of the group. For example, hunting (typically done by men) is no more important than gathering food or caring for children (usually women's tasks). Furthermore, with the limited productive technology possessed by hunter-gatherers, there are few resources beyond those needed for daily life; no one is able to amass much more wealth than anyone else.

Given a more complex division of labor and the development of a hierarchical power structure, a third element was necessary for cities to emerge: the development of a **productive surplus.** Earlier we noted that many archaeologists believe that the rise of agriculture was the main reason people traded hunting and gathering for permanent settlements. A similar process was at work in the gradual transition from village to town to city. Specifically, a growing population could not be supported without an increasing surplus of food. This notion of "agricultural primacy"—food surplus supporting permanent settlements—has been reinforced by the discovery of the remains of domesticated plants and animals at early urban sites around the world.

To sum up, around 8000 B.C.E., hunting and gathering societies began to increase in size. As a response to population increase, people began to settle down and take up agriculture as a way of life. These permanent settlements were characterized by increasingly complex social structures organized around a division of labor and a hierarchical power structure. Such settlements depended on a productive surplus. As these elements coalesced, they fed on each other: The division of labor led to more efficient use of human and natural resources, which in turn led to a greater division of labor and a more intricate power structure, and so on. As this happened, villages turned into towns, and then towns became the first cities.

The City Emerges

What do we know of these earliest cities? We begin with what is thought to be the first city: Jericho. The modern city of Jericho and its ancient ruins lie just to the north of the Dead Sea, in present-day Israel (see Figure 2–1 on pages 28–29).

Jericho. For generations, archaeologists thought that the first cities arose in the Fertile Crescent region of Mesopotamia (present-day Iraq) about 3500 B.C.E. However, with the excavation of Jericho over the past several decades, the history of cities has been largely rewritten. There archaeologists found evidence of the oldest city yet to be discovered anywhere in the world. We now know that Jericho was an emerging city as early as ten millennia ago. Put differently, it was already an ancient city when the pyramids were built.

Research at Jericho, however, sparked a debate: At what point can we speak of a permanent settlement as being a "city"? Some archaeologists argue that, given total population statistics in that period, a population of about 600 people and substantial buildings allow Jericho to be considered a city about 8000 B.C.E. Others disagree, citing Jericho's small size by today's standards. Size, however, is not the only important factor. Density and the complexity of social life—involving a broad range of activities and a hierarchy of power relations—add to Jericho's claim to city status.

What made Jericho different from other settlements of its time was the presence of houses made of sun-dried brick, a surrounding wall, a tower, and a large trench, all suggesting an advanced division of labor and a hierarchical social order that could oversee large-scale public works. The wall further points to a recognition of the need for defense and for protection from the elements. Even after 10,000 years of erosion, its ruins are some 12 feet high and 6 feet thick at the base. The trench, cut into solid rock, is about 27 feet across and 9 feet deep. Although archaeologists are not sure what it was used for (to hold water?), certainly a complex, cooperative effort was necessary to create it.

A short account of the later history of Jericho holds an interesting lesson in the history of urban settlements. It would seem that the original settlers of Jericho did not remain after about 7000 B.C.E., when a second group

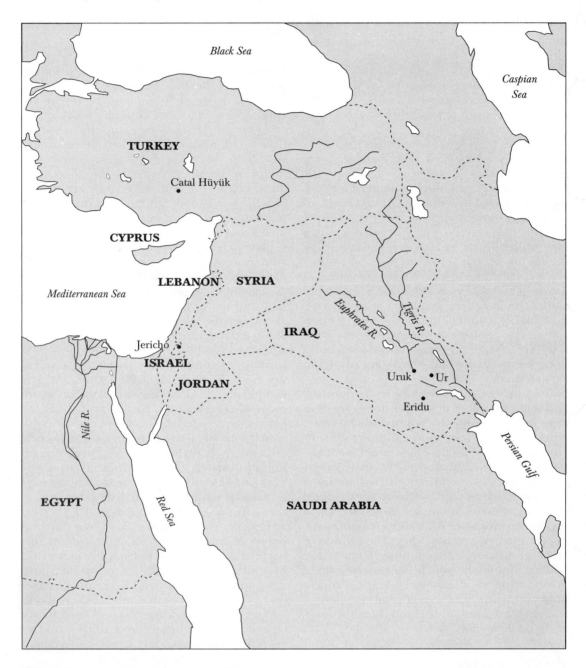

FIGURE 2–1   Asia Minor: The Earliest Cities

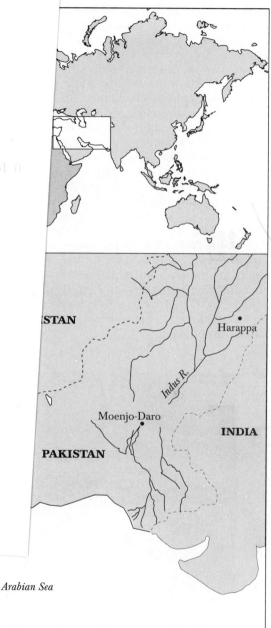

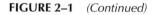

FIGURE 2–1   *(Continued)*

took up residence. This second group was more technologically advanced than the original settlers, constructing rectangular houses of bricks and mortar with plaster walls and floors. Around this time, trade with outsiders appears to have developed, adding to Jericho's cosmopolitan character. Then, about 1,000 years later—close to 6000 B.C.E.—the site was inexplicably abandoned, and remained so for a millennium.

Resettlement began about 5000 B.C.E., providing yet another twist to Jericho's story. The later settlers were markedly less advanced in their technology, digging only primitive shelters, and no public works are traceable to this period. Then, with the coming of the Bronze Age about 3000 B.C.E., a far more advanced culture prevailed. Artwork is evident, possibly linked to the civilization in Mesopotamia to the east or Egypt to the southwest. By the time settlement of ancient Jericho came to an end about 1500 B.C.E., many other groups had lived within the city.

The story of Jericho teaches us that the history of cities must not be oversimplified. Cities do not always grow in population and gain technical capacity. Discontinuity and unexpected events change developmental patterns again and again, as we shall see in the remainder of this chapter.

Catal Hüyük. Evidence produced by excavation at Jericho places the beginning of city life between 8000 and 7000 B.C.E. By 6000 B.C.E., other sites, such as Catal Hüyük (pronounced Sha-tal Hoo-yook) in present-day Turkey, had become well developed. Originally settled on a 32-acre site (three times larger than Jericho), Catal Hüyük eventually supported a population of some 6,000. This strange, streetless city was composed of mud-brick dwellings clustered together like the cells of a beehive with windowless walls facing outward. Small windows built high in the inner walls provided light, and the only entrances were on the roofs, reachable by ladders. This construction

The partial excavation of the Neolithic city of Catal Hüyük has already provided archaeologists with many clues about the social life of its inhabitants. Discovered in the late 1950s, the site rapidly became internationally famous due to the large size and dense occupation of the settlement, as well as the spectacular wall paintings and other art uncovered inside the houses.

CITYSCAPE

Daily Life in Catal Hüyük, 6000 B.C.E.

When the first light of dawn struck . . . on a spring morning in the year 6000 B.C.E., it brushed lightly across the flat roofs of tightly built mud-brick houses. . . . The houses turned blank, doorless walls to the world. The household entrance was by way of the roof through either a wooden doorway or a thatch opening onto a ladder. Doors at ground level could have let in anything from floodwaters to wild animals: the roof holes and ladders provided security. . . .

Inside one of the houses the father stirred. . . . From his leather pouch he grasped a lump of yellowish, crystalline sulfur collected on his last trip to the hills, and a flint tool that he had fashioned to his needs. . . . With this prehistoric Boy Scout knife the man could make wood shavings, strike a spark, feed the spark with sulfur and produce a fire within minutes. . . . The man made a fire on the hearth while his wife went through a small doorless opening in the mud-brick wall to the family food-storage niche. In it was a bin about a yard high, made of clay and very clean. She drew some grain from a small hole at the bin's bottom: it was always filled from the top and emptied from the bottom so that the oldest grain, or that most exposed to damp, would be used first. The wife moved slowly. She was heavy with another child, and she was getting old: almost 28.

On that mythical morning the family ate a gruel of grain and milk, supplemented by bits of meat left over from a previous meal. The mother nursed the baby while she fed the next-oldest with a spoon made from a cow's rib bone. . . .

Then there was work to do. . . .

The man and the woman might have tended fields or flocks, but not many towns-folk could have been farmers—no compact community of 6,000 people could have grown enough food to support itself while doing all the other things that Catal Hüyük residents did. The city must have traded goods and services for supplies from the surrounding region. The woman of the house might conceivably have made baskets for such trade. Or the man might have spent his days as a craftsman, for although no specialized tools were found in his home, there is ample evidence in the city of skillfully woven textiles, good pottery and beautiful art work.

Source: Dora Jane Hamblin, *The First Cities* (New York: Time–Life, 1973), pp. 43–46, excerpts.

design was so secure that no trace has been found of any plunder or massacre during the city's nearly 1,000 years of existence. The Cityscape box above offers a portrait of life in this early city.

THE FIRST URBAN REVOLUTION: CITY-STATES AND URBAN EMPIRES

Although scattered cities such as Jericho and Catal Hüyük thrived in the period between 7000 and 4000 B.C.E., it was not until about 3500 B.C.E. that urban development accelerated to a point where large numbers of cities flourished.

The earliest cities, like Jericho, clearly demonstrated their ability to generate security and wealth for fairly large numbers of people. Thus, more and more people came to the city to share in these benefits. The *idea* of the city was taking hold. No longer were many people content to live the relatively backward life of the tribe, the village, or the town. They wanted the benefits of the city: more choice, unprecedented material wealth, and ongoing excitement.

So cities grew in number and in population. But growth also brought problems: A rising population demanded more and more goods and services. And the needs of the city's inhabitants had to be managed in some way. Some cities responded to this challenge by making their social structure even more complex: They created the state.

The central feature of the state is its ability to wield power over many people—essentially to dictate everyone's rights and responsibilities: who has to live where, who has to serve in the military, and so on. With such power the city's leaders can do pretty much what they like in order to solve (or create) the city's problems—they can reorganize production, determine who will be educated, and, perhaps most important, make alliances and wage war to capture land, population, and resources.

With the emergence of the state as a form of social organization came the first city-states—cities that controlled surrounding regions, including a number of other towns, villages, and rural lands. As time passed, some of these city-states conquered or made alliances with others to form the world's first urban empires—much larger regions, usually dominated by a single central city. These early urban empires emerged around the world—in Mesopotamia, Egypt, the Indus River Valley, China, Central America, and South America—and they "pushed" the city as a form of human settlement to ever-greater complexity and population size.

This, then, was the period of the **first urban revolution** (Childe 1950). From approximately 4000 B.C.E. to 500 C.E., urban sites multiplied and their populations grew to sizes previously unknown in human history (Rome at its apex, for example, surpassed a million people). In retrospect, the first urban revolution appears to have been something of a mixed blessing. The city's greatest positive attributes are its ability to improve people's standard of living, provide choice in the conduct of life, and stimulate the human imagination. On the other hand, these first cities also had rigid social class divisions that extended the city's benefits to only a small minority of the urban population. With the emergence of city-states and urban empires, human warfare and bloodshed rose to unparalleled levels.

With all this in mind, then, we now turn to brief descriptions of some of the first urban empires.

The Near East: Mesopotamia and Egypt

The first urban empire was in the Fertile Crescent region of the Tigris and Euphrates Rivers in the southern portion of present-day Iraq. This region, known in ancient times as Mesopotamia or Sumer, began evolving significant cities as early as 4000 B.C.E. Cities such as Uruk, Eridu, and Ur (see Figure 2–1) represent a significant extension of world urbanization not only because they were larger than their earlier counterparts but also because of their more complex social structures. Wheat and barley were important domesticated crops, and city dwellers enjoyed the advantages of major technological advances such as oxen-pulled plows and the wheel (Sjoberg 1965; Stavrianos 1998).

Rise of Mesopotamian Cities.   The cities of the region reached their greatest development about 2800 B.C.E. Uruk, it is estimated, covered an area of about 1,100 acres (Adams 1966:69) and supported a population as high as 50,000 (Hamblin 1973:89). All the Mesopotamian (Sumerian) cities were theocracies, ruled by a priest-king. A ruling elite that controlled and protected the area around the city, including its agricultural land, exacted a portion of the agricultural surplus as tribute and stored it in the major temple (Sjoberg 1965).

Uruk and other Mesopotamian cities had highly complex social structures, including a power hierarchy and a pronounced division of labor. Excavations have established the existence of monumental public buildings, including ziggurats (religious shrines); extensive trade arrangements; a system of writing (cuneiform); mathematics; and a code of law. Sumerian texts noting the concerns of everyday life still survive. In these accounts, sheep, goats, and cattle are tabulated, taxed, and exchanged; children are shepherded to school— as today, often against their will—by concerned parents; a council of elders meets to consider grievances against the inhabitants of an adjoining city-state; and a politician attempts to win the favor of the populace with tax reductions (Wenke 2005). Clearly these cities had advanced to a point at which parallels may easily be drawn with cities of our own experience.

Early Mesopotamian urban life was centered, however, on the temple and on religious beliefs. The populace recognized thousands of gods, and the temples, like the palaces, were large and opulently decorated. People of less favorable social position lived in irregularly organized houses along the narrow, unpaved, winding streets (Sjoberg 1965). The complex social structure also resulted in a strong military elite and made possible an increasing capacity to wage war. Frequently under attack, Mesopotamian cities were walled defensively (Hamblin 1973).

After about 3500 B.C.E., the cities began to be organized as politically distinct city-states, each exerting its influence over a broad region. Although these city-states were independent of one another and were often at war, they did represent a common civilization. They shared a common cultural heritage and, as far as the outside world was concerned, saw themselves as possessors of a unique, even superior, culture (Wenke 2005). By 700 B.C.E., the Assyrian Empire dominated the region and the Persian Empire followed around 500 B.C.E.

The importance of this continual trading of urban dominance was that it spurred the development of cities and their influence throughout the Near East. In an effort to maintain control of their empires, each set of rulers tried to develop their cities as much as their culture and technology would permit. The cities of the region were continually renewed with inventions, innovations, and new ideas supplied by trade and people of different backgrounds.

Although it would be too much to say that these cities contained all of the civilization that existed in their era, they were key centers. They were "containers" in a double sense: They literally encircled their population and their valued goods with walls, and, more figuratively, they served as the place where all the themes of Mesopotamian culture could be found.

Egyptian Cities.   The Great Pyramids of Giza are modern reminders of another empire that flourished shortly after the rise of cities in Mesopotamia. The archaeological record of Egyptian cities is less detailed than that of their Mesopotamian counterparts, but it appears that by 3100 B.C.E., Menes, the first pharaoh of a united Egypt, was in control of the cities of Memphis and Hierakonopolis.

There are a number of reasons why the record of the earliest Egyptian cities is less clear. First, their buildings were made of unbaked brick and other materials that have not stood the test of time. Second, the early Egyptians apparently built and abandoned their cities frequently. As a result, although the cities were crucial centers of Egyptian civilization, none maintained its dominance long enough to reach a very large size (Sjoberg 1965; Kemp 1992). The sites of many of these cities are mapped in Figure 2–2 on page 34.

Although the cities that emerged in Egypt went through what we now think is the normal process of early development—from village to town and, finally, to city—they were rather distinct from those in Mesopotamia. Egyptian civilization was focused on the ruling pharaoh, and each had his city—a religious and political center built to reflect his power, which, by 2500 B.C.E., was virtually absolute. More than a secular leader or priest, the pharaoh was believed to be a god, and his singular dominance of the Nile region created a relatively peaceful history.

Thus we find little evidence in early Egypt of city walls. Each capital city became a pharaoh's administrative center, and much of the activity of urban artisans was directed toward construction of a palace for his pleasure

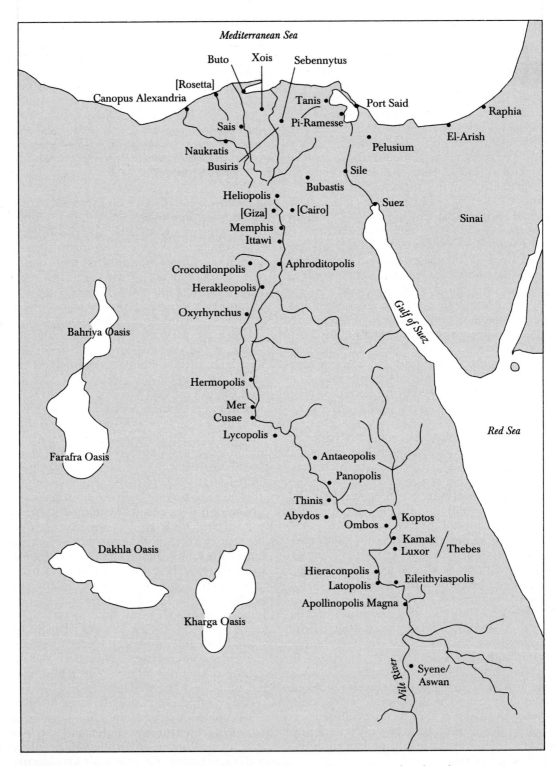

FIGURE 2–2 Egypt and the Nile: The Pharaonic Cities (modern cities are bracketed) [*Source:* Adapted from Jacquetta Hawkes, *The First Great Civilizations* (New York: Knopf, 1973), p. 287.]

in this life and an opulent tomb to provide for his needs in the life to come. Although not as large as those of Mesopotamia, these Egyptian cities were characterized by distinctive urban traits, including a clear power structure and division of labor, social inequality, and an administrative organization (utilizing hieroglyphic writing, papyrus paper, and ink) to oversee public needs and maintain the pharaoh's control.

But if the early Egyptian cities were peaceful, those that followed were not. Egypt's later history, like that of Mesopotamia, is riddled with conflict within the empire and with other empires. During the period known as the Old Kingdom (2700–2180 B.C.E.), the pharaohs made forays into neighboring territories to procure goods. Successful in many of these adventures, they used their plundered wealth and captured slaves to build cities and palaces. It was two pharaohs of this period—Cheops and his son, Cephren—who built the Great Pyramids of Giza between 2600 and 2500 B.C.E., still the most colossal monuments ever constructed. Cephren was also responsible for the Sphinx at Giza.

Then, around 2180 B.C.E., the Old Kingdom collapsed, famine spread, and rioting in the cities was rampant. For the next 600 years, Egypt went through several alternating periods of disarray and reunification. Urban greatness once again reappeared in the New Kingdom era (1500–1100 B.C.E.). This was the period of the minor pharaoh Tutankhamun—the only pharaoh whose gravesite in the Valley of the Kings was undisturbed by pillaging robbers—and of Ramses II, the pharaoh who conquered much of the Near East for Egypt and may have been Moses' adversary in his attempts to free the Jews from Egyptian servitude. Ramses rebuilt many of Egypt's cities; created a new capital, Pi-Ramesse, on the Mediterranean; and constructed self-glorifying yet magnificent temples at Karnak, Luxor, and Abu Simbel. The Asian territories were lost around 1100 B.C.E., and the next 300 years saw the last decline of pharaonic Egypt. From 800 to 671 B.C.E., the African rulers of Kush—a former Egyptian outpost to the south—controlled Egypt.

Near Eastern empires inflicted the final indignities. The Assyrians conquered Egypt in 671 B.C.E. and, though expelled less than 20 years later, were followed by the Persians in 525 B.C.E. The Persians more or less dominated the region until 332 B.C.E., the year Alexander the Great arrived, was accepted as pharaoh, and built his city, Alexandria, at the head of the Nile. From then on, Egypt was at the mercy of foreign overlords.

The development of cities in the Nile region raises an interesting question as to the possible diffusion of urban influence from Mesopotamia. History records frequent contact between the two regions. Were the Egyptian cities created independently, or was the city idea imported? Debate continues, but the currently dominant belief is that traders or nomads from early cities in Mesopotamia carried at least some urban influences toward both Egypt in the west and the Indus Valley in the east (Stavrianos 1998). In all three regions, however, city life emerged in its own special fashion and included clearly distinct and unique aspects that revealed the stamp of the local civilization (Sjoberg 1965:49).

The Indus Region

To the east of Mesopotamia, along the Indus River of present-day India and Pakistan, was a third ecologically favorable area where early cities emerged. Excavations have yielded the remains of two highly developed cities that were centers of a regional civilization beginning about 2500 B.C.E. Both were prominent in urban history until about 1500 B.C.E. Moenjo-Daro was situated on the Indus River about 175 miles from the Arabian Sea; Harappa was about 350 miles further north on one of the river's tributaries. Each had a population as high as 40,000 and represented an urban civilization distinct in many ways from those we have considered thus far.

Trade routes linked the Indus cities with Mesopotamian cities through other outposts such as Tepe Yahya, midway between the two areas (see Figure 2–1). It is also likely that

The excavated site of ancient Moenjo-Daro in the Indus River Valley reveals a surprisingly modern grid pattern of housing (left) and a sanitation system of brick-lined open sewers (trench, bottom and right). What the photo does not reveal is the uniformity of its north–south boulevard, 30 feet wide, and east–west cross streets about every 200 yards.

trading in such products as jade linked this area eastward with central Asia (Magee 2005).

Moenjo-Daro would have seemed familiar to a modern visitor. A thriving seaport, the city was constructed with the same gridiron pattern common to most Western cities today. Hamblin writes:

> As long ago as 2500 b.c., [Moenjo-Daro] and the half dozen cities of the Indus Valley had already put to use the crisscross gridiron system of street layout—an urban convention long thought to have been invented by the Greeks of a later era. Moenjo-Daro was planned with a broad boulevard 30 feet wide, running north and south, and crossed at right angles every 200 yards or so by somewhat smaller east-west streets. Along these impressive avenues were shops and food stands. The blocks between were served by narrow curving lanes five to ten feet wide. (1973:123)

Perhaps the most remarkable discovery about this city was the uncovering of a well-established city sanitation system. Along the streets were brick-lined open sewers that carried away house drainage. Bathrooms—including several sit-down toilets—have been discovered by archaeologists, indicating the presence in 2500 B.C.E. of an urban luxury not commonly found in European cities until the nineteenth century.

Within the city numerous craft specialists were in operation, including potters, weavers, brick makers, and copper and bronze metalworkers (Sjoberg 1965). A citadel, the city's administrative center, may have included a granary for storage of food surplus.

Unlike either Mesopotamia or Egypt, however, Moenjo-Daro does not show evidence of a single, all-powerful leader or a preoccupation with temples and god-monuments. Rather, Moenjo-Daro shows evidence of extensive "good living." Hamblin suggests that the city

must have been among the first places to provide its citizens with a broadly based, comparatively high standard of living. Most of its people seem to have lived in considerable comfort, in near identical mud-brick houses, along near identical streets that were served by near identical drainage systems. The ruins of residential areas struck one archaeologist as "miles of monotony." But that monotony suggests, in its uniformity, an even distribution of the population, and thus the well-being that goes with a large, prosperous middle class. (1973:144)

Until the mid-twentieth century, it was commonly thought that Mesopotamia, Egypt, and the Indus River Valley contained the cities from which all later cities took their pattern. Archaeological research since then makes this claim doubtful. Apparently, cities emerged in many places around the world independently of one another. Two other regions where this occurred were China and the Americas.

A Glance Eastward: China

Cities in China go back to at least 2000 B.C.E. Present knowledge suggests that the earliest was Po, the first capital of the Shang Dynasty. Very little is known about this city because excavations are incomplete.

Fortunately, the second and third Shang capitals have been studied in more detail. The second capital, Cheng-chou, was at its height about 1600 B.C.E. A rectangular wall 4.5 miles in length and over 30 feet high enclosed an area of about 1.5 square miles, which contained the city's administrative and ceremonial centers. In this fortified area the political and religious elite lived apart from the common people. Outside the enclosure lived artisans— bronze workers and craftspeople.

An-yang was the third Shang capital. Archaeological excavation has uncovered remnants of its larger pattern, by which the central city was linked to the surrounding area. As in Cheng-chou, the residences of artisans and craft workers were just outside a walled area. In the region immediately beyond, numerous villages formed a network of trade, supplying agricultural and other specialized products to the city (Chang 1977).

What existed in China, then, was a type of urban settlement somewhat more diffused

than in the areas already considered. Rather than concentrating all their political, religious, and craft activities in a single, center-city area, the Chinese set priests and rulers apart from the remainder of the urban population. At some distance from their protected, walled enclosure, residents of satellite villages participated in the life of the urban area as a whole.

A Glance Westward: The Americas

The last major region in which early cities developed was nearer home—in Mesoamerica, specifically the area of present-day central Mexico, the Yucatan Peninsula, and Guatemala; and in South America, particularly the western part of that continent. The history of these areas reveals, once again, several familiar patterns: A more productive agricultural technology and the formation of a complex social structure accompanied the rise of cities. But the case of Mesoamerica is also of interest because it represents several significant areas of contrast to urban development elsewhere.

The area was inhabited at least as early as 20,000 B.C.E. Cultivation of plants had been achieved by 7000 B.C.E., but in contrast to other areas of the world where cities arose, the area was not well suited to the production of large surpluses, partly because of its rocky, mountainous terrain and partly because the people lacked domestic animals and a solid source of agricultural protein. The traditional digging stick rather than the plow remained the primary tool of cultivation for millennia, and Mesoamerica never embraced farming in the sense that other regions did. Rather, its groups developed a mixed economy in which hunting and other undomesticated resources continued to play a very important part. Nevertheless, one cultivated crop, maize (corn), contributed to a sturdy and nutritious diet.

By 1500 B.C.E. early villages of mud-walled houses had been established. Because hunting continued to play a major role in the economy, these village sites moved with some frequency. In some villages, Olmec and Maya tribes built elaborate ceremonial centers that served large populations, employing many craftspeople in their design and construction. Serving as a place of permanent residence for only a small number of priests at the outset, these ceremonial centers slowly grew in size and complexity. Before the birth of Christ they had become full-fledged cities.

The same process occurred later on the western coast of South America in present-day Peru and Bolivia. Perhaps the most famous urban empire of this region was that of the Incas, with its capital in the city of Cuzco. Less well known, but as important, was the urban empire of Chimor on the north coast of Peru (Mosley 1975). Its capital, Chan Chan, began as a city around the same time that the Inca urban centers evolved—about 800 C.E. At its height (approximately 1450 C.E.), Chan Chan ruled over a large hinterland as a major challenger to the Inca empire.

Note that this was a **regal/ritual city**—an important urban center with a population of no more than 30,000. As the term suggests, a regal/ritual city is used primarily by the ruling class: Chan Chan's rulers lived there year round and used most of the city's buildings for their own pleasure and for the rituals of Chimor culture. Only a small group of artisans, servants, and peasants were allowed to share in that part of the urban environment. All the rest of the empire's people were forced to live in the surrounding towns or rural areas and do the ruling class's bidding, including paying taxes and laboring on city projects.

In 1470 Chan Chan's challenge provoked the Incas to conquer the Chimor empire and subjugate its inhabitants. However, even this dominance was not to last. By the end of the century, Columbus was to land in the New World. Not long after that, the Spanish, and later the Portuguese, would arrive in Mesoamerica and South America in force. Under the European onslaught these proud urban empires would fall like dominoes and a new type of city would arise—a process described in Chapter 13.

Despite conditions that were unique to the hemisphere, cities arose indigenously in the Americas as they had in other regions of the world. These cities, from a historical standpoint, were highly sophisticated and equal in complexity to those found elsewhere. For example, a thousand years before the Aztecs, Teotihuacan was the religious capital of Mexico. An urban center of massive structures that was at its peak around 600 C.E., it supported a population of perhaps 200,000 in a city physically larger than imperial Rome itself (Austin and Lujan 2001:109). Its 8 square miles were laid out in a specific grid plan, with its north–south avenues containing palaces and pyramid temples with impressive sculptures. The city's housing complexes were large and contained a number of rooms, all opening out onto patios. Some were built, like the pyramid temples, of a red volcanic rock that was mined locally. Towering over the city was the Pyramid of the Sun, rising at a sharp angle from its 720-by-760-foot base to a height of 216 feet. Probably constructed in the first century C.E., it would have taken thousands of laborers 50 years to build, according to expert estimates (Matos 1990).

Summary: Traits of Early Cities

Human beings first devised cities about 10,000 years ago. As shown graphically in Figure 2–3, they had become quite common in the Near East by 4000 B.C.E., in the Indus River Valley by 2500 B.C.E., and in China by 2000 B.C.E. Their appearance in the Americas came somewhat later, around 500 B.C.E.

All early cities were characterized by some combination of favorable ecological conditions, some sort of trade or food surplus, and a complex social structure (a fairly sophisticated division of labor and a power hierarchy). Beyond these important characteristics, some other similarities and a few differences may be mentioned.

First, early cities do not show any smooth progression of growth. On the one hand, the transition from the first permanent settlements to full-fledged cities took a long time—from about 8000 B.C.E. to 3000 B.C.E. On the other hand, city histories the world over are

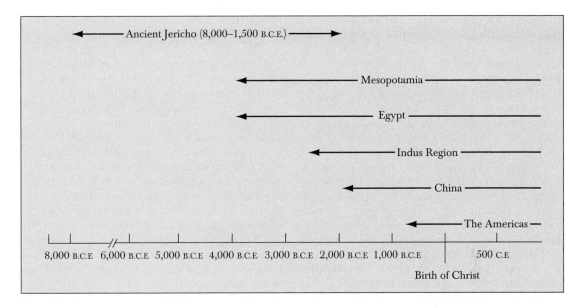

FIGURE 2–3   The Chronology of the First Cities

marked by discontinuity and change, rise and fall. Sometimes, as in Teotihuacan, one group occupied a city for its entire duration; sometimes, as in Jericho, many groups came and went.

Second, as population centers, early cities were small. Most were mere towns by today's standards. A population of about 10,000 was usual, and even the largest settlements never went much beyond the quarter-million mark.

Third, regarding the power structure, many early cities had a theocratic character—a fused religious and political elite in which kings were also priests and, not infrequently, "gods." This fusion allowed a type of double control over the city's population and its problems. Royalty could, in the name of heaven, impose taxes and even servitude. Of course, the character of this elite structure varied. It was sharply evident in Egypt, China, and Teotihuacan, while it was more subdued in the Indus city of Moenjo-Daro. But everywhere, the first cities were characterized by inequalities in power and benefits: Usually the few prospered and the many got by as best they could.

Finally, what of the quality of life in early cities? In comparison with modern Western cities, it was probably not very high—life was usually hard, relatively short, and subject to considerable uncertainty. Yet there is substantial variation here as well. Moenjo-Daro appears to have afforded a higher standard of living to more residents than was the case in more sharply class-divided cities elsewhere. Other factors, such as war and slavery, also must have had a powerful effect on the quality of life experienced by many early city dwellers.

The city, particularly after it reached the state and empire stage, was more often than not an instrument of death and destruction as one urban center tried to conquer another. To some extent this increase in bloodshed cannot be blamed on the city as such. Rather, the use of systematic warfare seems more coincident with primitive agriculture and the coming of the first permanent settlements around 8000 B.C.E. Apparently, agricultural techniques produced a productive surplus for the first time. This surplus, in turn, attracted people to settlements and induced some of them to conquer other groups in an effort to procure even more surplus. When urban areas became common around 4000 B.C.E., these human appetites were magnified to a level unknown before in history.

In short, the development of the city was a most decisive event in human history. The early city magnified human activity in all its dimensions. People knew more, did more, and found more possibilities open to them. Such has always been the city's promise: to provide a better life. As we turn to the development of Western cities in the next section, we shall find that cities in our own tradition also have held out the promise of "the good life." Certainly some progress has been made along that road. We shall also find, however, that these cities, like their earlier counterparts, have had a tragic capacity for harboring the human indignities of coercive inequality, militaristic expansion, and war.

Crete and Greece

Western cities—those of Europe and North America—are relative latecomers in the urban story. Cities had been in existence for many thousands of years before urbanization took hold in the northern Mediterranean region on the island of Crete.

About 1800 B.C.E., possibly traders or migrants from the urban settlements of Mesopotamia established settlements in Crete. Little is known of these early cities, yet by all accounts they were thriving centers. A series of ornamental tiles found in the Palace of Minos depict what appears to be a typical city. Writes Sir Arthur Evans, "The central features consisted of the towers and houses and a fortified town. . . . Also depicted were: trees and water, goats and oxen, marching warriors, spearmen and archers, arms and equipment, the prow apparently of a ship. . . ." (quoted in Mumford 1961:121). Then for some reason the record breaks off inconclusively about 1400 B.C.E. Like Teotihuacan two centuries later, the cities of Crete were simply abandoned. Was this the result of some catastrophic volcanic eruption? No one knows for sure. In any event, it was not until seven centuries later

that urban development appeared again in Europe, this time in Greece.

The early Greek polis, or city-state, did not follow the pattern of the cities of Mesopotamia and Egypt, which magnified the power of the elite at the expense of their other citizens. The fiercely independent Greek city-states—among them Athens, Corinth, and Sparta—experienced war, as well as peaceful rivalry symbolized by the Olympic games. Compared with earlier cities of the Near East, Greek cities were more egalitarian; in Lewis Mumford's phrase, they were cities "cut closer to the human measure . . . and delivered from the claims of quasi-divine monarchs" (1961:124).

Classes whose commercial influence reached outward from Sicily to northern Africa ruled these cities. The Greeks founded such cities as Messina in Sicily and Marseilles in France (Sjoberg 1965). Unfortunately, however, in the end the Greek city-states turned on each other in the destructive Peloponnesian Wars (431–404 B.C.E.), leaving behind a remarkable legacy that highlighted the positive possibilities of urban civilization, including outstanding painting, sculpture, and architecture, as well as a political system and body of philosophy that influence the world to this day.

Rome

As Greek culture slipped into decline, another great civilization was gathering strength to the west. It was centered, perhaps more than any cultural system before or since, on a single city; indeed, the city's name is synonymous with the culture itself. As Aelius Aristedes claimed in the second century B.C.E.: "Rome! Everything is found here. All the skills which exist or have existed, anything that can be made or grown. If something can't be found here, then it simply doesn't exist!"

Aristedes was right. By the final centuries of the pre-Christian era, Rome was the dominant power of the Western world. By the time of Christ, the city on which the Roman Empire was based was gargantuan by all previous urban standards, approaching a population of approximately 1 million.

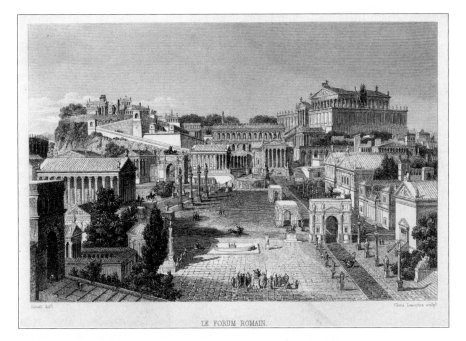

LE FORUM ROMAIN.

At its height Imperial Rome was the center of a vast militaristic empire. The city, a mixture of magnificent buildings and squalid slums, contained carefully planned broad thoroughfares and an impressive water supply and drainage system. Here the Roman Forum, the heart of the city's ceremonial life, was crowded with temples, arches, statues, and public buildings.

Rome displayed the same characteristics we have encountered in the earliest cities: a favorable ecological setting, the ability to produce an economic surplus, and a complex social structure. Also, like Greece, Rome was characterized by developed arts and sciences and by public monuments and buildings.

Yet Rome was an urban civilization almost exclusively based on the expression of militaristic power. For the several centuries during which the city thrived, Rome explored and revealed for all history the consequences of concentrating a city's resources almost entirely on the accumulation of power and wealth.

If the Greek conception of the good life was a city founded on the principles of moderation, balance, and human participation, the Roman conception was based on the celebration of sheer excess and unremitting domination. At its height the empire extended from Rome across the Mediterranean to northern Africa, from present-day Germany to the British Isles, from Egypt to the Near East; it included almost half the world's population (Gibbon 1932; Stavrianos 1998).

What can we say of the city that served as the center of this vast empire? In physical design Rome was similar to cities discussed earlier. At its center were a market, a forum, and a complex of monumental buildings. Radiating outward in orderly fashion across the breadth of the city—some 7 square miles overall—were major broad thoroughfares constructed according to a careful plan. Indeed, roads were one of Rome's greatest achievements. In all, over 50,000 miles of roads were constructed by the Roman work force. Extremely well built, they served as links between Rome and the empire's vast hinterland, from which the city drew tribute. Many of the major cities of Europe today—including London, York, Vienna, Bordeaux, Paris, and Cologne—were once provincial outposts of Rome.

Waterworks were another engineering achievement. The city had large public baths, fountains, hydrants along main streets, and a system of water drainage begun as early as the sixth century B.C.E. (Mumford 1961). Perhaps most striking was the city's aqueduct system, completed during the second century B.C.E. and copied in many provincial cities founded by the Romans throughout Europe. These spillways—some still in use today—brought fresh water, from as far away as 57 miles, to the city, just as today's aqueduct system brings water from as far away as 120 miles to New York City, or California's massive aqueduct system delivers water from many hundreds of miles away.

The motive for Rome's impressive engineering was ultimately to serve the interests of the ruling military and political elite. While the elite enjoyed incredible riches, Rome's poorer residents benefited little from the wealth that was brought continuously to the city, living in largely unplanned and squalid tenements. This underside of Roman life had a further dimension—one that could hardly find sharper contrast with the Greek ideal of human dignity:

> The main population of the city that boasted its world conquests lived in cramped, noisy, airless, foul smelling, infected quarters, paying extortionate rents to merciless landlords, undergoing daily indignities and terrors that coarsened and brutalized them, and in turn demanded compensatory outlets. These outlets carried the brutalization even further, in a continuous carnival of sadism and death. (Mumford 1961:221)

The enduring, if horrible, example of Rome's "carnival of sadism and death" was the Circus. In the Cityscape box on page 43, Mumford describes this ritual around which the later city revolved.

Taken as a whole, Rome was a parade of contrasts: engineering excellence and technical achievement juxtaposed with human debasement and militaristic cruelty. Eventually, its empire extended so far that it no longer could control its home base, and, rotting from within, Rome sank into decline. It fell in 476 C.E. under the onslaught of northern invasion, and by the sixth century it had become a mere town of 20,000.

Decline: The Middle Ages

As Rome collapsed, so did the empire that had sustained urban life throughout much of Europe. With this eclipse came a period of about 600 years during which European cities either fell into a pattern of minimal survival or ceased to exist entirely. The commercial trade that had been the source of life to the empire and its cities was drastically curtailed. The danger of pillaging by barbarians increased. Once-great cities, which had boasted populations in excess of 100,000, became virtually isolated hamlets. There evolved an almost singular concern for security. Surviving cities became fortified—surrounded by great walls—a revival of an older urban feature that had been rendered unnecessary by the establishment of Roman control of nearly the entire continent.

The pattern of settlement typical of the fifth through the eleventh centuries was a mosaic of local manors, villages, and small towns in many ways reminiscent of the earliest urban settlements we considered at the beginning of this chapter. The dominance over a large hinterland so characteristic of Greek and Roman cities all but vanished. This is, of course, the essence of the image conveyed by the phrase "Dark Ages."

During this period arose a feudal system, in which a local lord provided security in exchange for service on his lands. In most cases, however, manors were situated in the countryside, weakening urban influence even further. A few highly fortified small cities and manor towns survived, but a delicate balance was struck in these settlements. Given the state of medieval technology, protection could be provided for only a limited population. A small population made a low level of production inevitable, and this, in turn, caused the city to stagnate.

CITYSCAPE

Classical Rome: The Dance of Death

The existence of a parasitic economy and a predatory political system produced a typically Roman urban institution that embraced both aspects of its life and gave them a dramatic setting: the old practice of the religious blood sacrifice was given a new secular form in the arena.

Roman life, for all its claims of peace, centered more and more on the imposing rituals of extermination. In the pursuit of sensations sufficiently sharp to cover momentarily the emptiness and meaninglessness of their parasitic existence, the Romans took to staging chariot races, spectacular naval battles set in an artificial lake, theatrical pantomimes in which the strip tease and lewder sexual acts were performed in public. But sensations need constant whipping as people become inured to them: so the whole effort reached a pinnacle in the gladiatorial spectacles, where the agents of this regime applied a diabolic inventiveness to human torture and human extermination. . . . To make attendance at these spectacles even easier, as early as the reign of Claudius, 159 days were marked as public holidays, and as many as 93, a quarter of the whole year, were devoted to games at the public expense. Vast fortunes were spent on staging even a single one of these events. . . .

No body of citizens, not even the Athenians at the height of their empire, ever had such an abundance of idle time to fill with idiotic occupations. . . . after the hour of noon, in addition, the Roman workers, who had doubtless risen at daybreak, suffered no further demand on their time. The transformation of the active, useful life of the early Republican city into the passive and parasitic life that finally dominated it took centuries. But in the end, attendance at public spectacles, terrestrial and nautical, human and animal, became the principal occupation of their existence; and all other activities fed directly or indirectly into it. . . .

The gladiatorial games were first introduced into Rome in 264 B.C. by the consul Decimus Junius Brutus on the occasion of his father's funeral; but the Romans gave them a more utilitarian turn by employing the deadly contests as a popular means for the public punishment of criminals, at first presumably as much for an admonitory deterrent as an enjoyment. Too soon, unfortunately, the ordeal of the prisoner became the welcome amusement of the spectator; and even the emptying of the jails did not provide a sufficient number of victims to meet the popular demand. As with the religious sacrifices of the Aztecs, military expeditions were directed toward supplying a sufficient number of victims, human and animal. Here in the arena both degraded professionals, thoroughly trained for their occupation, and wholly innocent men and women were tortured with every imaginable body-maiming and fear-producing device for public delight.

Source: From *The City in History, Its Origins, Its Transformation and Its Prospects.* Copyright © 1961 and renewed 1989 by Lewis Mumford. Reprinted by permission of Harcourt, Inc.

Revival: Medieval and Renaissance Cities

The low point of urban life in Europe was reached in the ninth century (Holmes 2002). Then, around the eleventh century, a general "awakening" began to take place. The reasons for this change, which occurred gradually over several centuries, are numerous and complex, but a general development of urban trade and crafts was a key factor.

The Crusades (armed marches by Christian European groups against the possessors of "The Holy Land," where, more often than not, the Europeans found ultimate defeat) took place between 1096 and 1291; they contributed to a rebirth of trade routes linking Europe and the Near East. Pirenne (1980) contends that the reopening of trade began bringing new ideas and products to cities in Europe by the twelfth century. Mumford (1961) turns the argument around and suggests that trade rebounded as cities once again became effective "stepping stones" across Europe and Asia. In any event, the growth of local trade began stimulating the long-dormant urban division of labor.

The emergence of a complex and competitive commercial class at the center of this trade, dominated from the eleventh century onward by craft guilds, contributed to a newly vibrant city life. However, the merchants alone did not dominate these cities. Many groups—including the church, the landed gentry, and the feudal royalty—vied for position. Small and self-contained, medieval cities allowed no single focus to dominate urban life in the way the military and political elements had dominated Rome.

As for their populations, medieval cities were small—both in relation to Roman cities (many of which supported more than 100,000 people) and in comparison with the industrial cities that would follow them. Although a few cities such as Paris and Venice were much larger in area, the physical dimensions of most medieval cities also were modest. Cities typically occupied a few hundred acres, about the size of a small town of about 5,000 people today. Walls surrounding the cities often were supplemented by a moat, as shown in Figure 2–4. Major roads connected the city gates to the center of the city—generally the cathedral, the

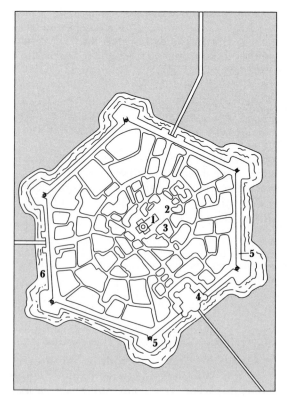

FIGURE 2–4 The medieval city, circa 1350, developed on a new site in response to the needs and patterns of the new trading system and for defense. The site was chosen at the intersection of rivers and roads, a natural route center that offered plentiful water, natural defenses, and an ample food supply from the surrounding agrarian area of the valley. The city was a trading and commercial center; craft industries produced goods for trade and for exchange with farmers of the surrounding area who supplied food, as well as many of the items involved in long-distance trade. Movement within the city was mainly pedestrian, so narrow streets with many angles were not constricting. Some wider, more open streets allowed passage of horse traffic involved in long-distance trade.

1. Cathedral
2. Market plaza
3. Guildhalls, craft and trade centers
4. Fortress of local lord
5. Defensive walls with turrets at intervals
6. Moat outside defensive walls

[*Source:* Janet Roebuck, *The Shaping of Urban Society,* pp. 48–49. Copyright © 1974 by Janet Roebuck.]

marketplace, or major buildings such as the guilds or town halls.

Mumford (1961) suggests that if any one center was of greatest importance, it was the cathedral, often towering over the rest of the city. Indeed, the importance of the church to the social life of medieval Europe is difficult to exaggerate. All members of mainstream medieval society—both urban and rural—were Roman Catholics. The Catholic Church was an unchallenged dominant force, and exclusion from it—whether through excommunication or as a member of a religious minority (particularly Jews)—relegated one a social outcast on the fringe of society.

The medieval city did not produce the sense of awe and massive scale that mark the modern Western city. Other than the cathedral and perhaps a palace, there were no tall buildings, and streets were narrow and winding rather than wide and straight as they are today. Paving of streets, done on a large scale in Rome during the empire, did not become common in medieval European cities until the twelfth and thirteenth centuries. Houses typically were built together—in rowhouse fashion—often with open space for cultivation in the rear. Despite the lack of such conveniences as indoor plumbing, the small population and relatively low density of these cities allowed life to proceed under conditions far more healthful than those of many postindustrial tenements today (Mumford 1961).

The city of Carcassonne in France remains an outstanding example of a medieval walled city. Compare this picture to Figure 2–4. The local lord's fortress is on the right and the cathedral is slightly to the left and above it. Such cities were characteristic of Europe for nearly 1,000 years after the fall of Rome (479 C.E.).

These European cities grew gradually—not only in population and area, but also with a renewed idea of the human possibilities of the city. The period from the twelfth century until about the sixteenth century was an age of general urban rebirth, or renaissance. First evident in Italian city-states such as Venice, Florence, Palermo, and Milan, this rebirth is easily linked to the humanistic conception of city life that flourished some 1,500 years earlier in Athens. During the Renaissance, the city gradually recaptured an interest in art, literature, and architecture.

Although once again the city generated the ideal of full human development, the real contradiction of the era was that it was an ideal that the great bulk of the city's citizens had little chance to realize. Wealth, for example, was highly concentrated. In Lyon, a French city, in 1545, over half the wealth belonged to a mere 10 percent of the population (Hohenberg and Lees 1996:147).

THE SECOND URBAN REVOLUTION: THE RISE OF MODERN CITIES

Within the walls of the Renaissance city, the seeds of another type of city altogether were being sown. The old feudal power structure was breaking down, giving people more freedom to live their lives where they chose; trade was becoming more important, increasing the available wealth. Cities were gaining rapidly in prominence.

Throughout Europe, commerce slowly began to replace agriculture as the dominant mode of making a living. A new middle class began to rise to power. This class—the **bourgeoisie** (the French word means, literally, "of the town")—was composed of shopkeepers, traders, bureaucrats, government officials, and people engaged in commercial ventures of all sorts. As wealth increased in the cities, they began to attract ever more people who hoped to share in the obvious material benefits of this process.

By the mid-seventeenth century, feudalism was all but dead, and with it went the last remnants of the rural-centered life of the Middle Ages. In its place stood capitalism, a mode of life fundamentally grounded in the trade possibilities offered by the city. By the eighteenth century, the Industrial Revolution had begun, a process that fueled even more strongly the dominance of the city-based market economy.

The change was striking: City populations everywhere exploded (see Table 2–1). If the first urban revolution took place when cities first appeared some 10,000 years before, the second urban revolution occurred from about 1650 on: Europe became a continent of cities.

The preindustrial era had been characterized by low-efficiency technology and primitive health care. Both birth and death rates were high. In other words, people typically had many children, but many did not live to maturity. Even for those who did, life expectancy was much lower than today (usually under 40 years). As a result, natural population growth (the difference between the birth and death rates) was slow and frequently checked by massive numbers of deaths occasioned by outbreaks of plague. From the 1340s to the early 1350s, for example, the Black Plague raced across Europe, killing one-third of the population, and up to 60 percent in the continent's cities (Kelly 2005).

TABLE 2–1   Population of Selected European Cities, 1700–2005, in Thousands

City	1700	1800	1900	2005
Amsterdam	172	201	510	742
Berlin	—	172	2,424	3,398
Hamburg	70	130	895	1,734
Lisbon	188	237	363	518
London	550	861	6,480	7,421
Madrid	110	169	539	3,103
Naples	207	430	563	981
Paris	530	547	3,330	2,118
Rome	149	153	487	2,644
Vienna	105	231	1,662	1,569

Source: Adapted from T. Chandler and G. Fox, *3000 Years of Urban History* (New York: Academic Press, 1974); *The World Gazetteer,* accessed online at *www.gazetteer.de* on May 29, 2005.

But plague did not wreak its vengeance forever. In time a larger portion of the urban population enjoyed more wealth, more efficient means of production, and better health and sanitation conditions. Death rates fell dramatically, while birth rates remained high: What population experts call a demographic transition was underway. A major population explosion began throughout Europe, primarily centered in the cities. Although migration caused much urban growth—that is, from people coming to the city from the countryside—natural population growth was also extremely high. Together, both forces began to produce cities with population sizes undreamed of in antiquity. Recall that Rome, at its peak, contained around a million people. London in 2005 (see Table 2–1) contained more than seven times that number.

In European and North American countries, the urban demographic transition continued well into the twentieth century. Recently, however, a rising standard of living—making more children for "productive purposes" unnecessary—and effective means of contraception have begun to halt the trend. In most industrial nations, population growth has slowed as both birth and death rates have continued to decline. The situation is not so hopeful in many other areas of the world, however. As will be made clear in later chapters, overpopulation produced by an even more powerful demographic transition continues to create incredible suffering and threatens to overwhelm many nations.

Part of that explosive population growth can be found in the evolution of **megacities**—metropolitan areas with populations of 10 million or more. By 2015, the number of megacities will be 22, with 16 of them in developing countries, including some of the poorest nations in the world (see Table 2–2). These huge urban areas are filled both with danger signs of overwhelming problems and with great promise in the now-visible stirrings of self-reliance. In the twenty-first century we will learn which potential dominates.

To conclude this chapter, we turn to a case study focusing on London, a city that many

TABLE 2–2   Population of the World's Megacities, in Millions

	2004	2015 (projected)
Shanghai	13.3	18.0
Mumbai (Bombay), India	12.6	26.2
Buenos Aires	11.9	13.0
Moscow	11.3	9.3
Karachi, Pakistan	10.9	19.4
Delhi, India	10.4	16.9
Manila	10.3	14.7
São Paolo, Brazil	10.3	20.3
Seoul	10.2	13.0
Istanbul	9.6	12.3
Jakarta, Indonesia	9.0	13.9
Mexico City	8.7	19.2
Lagos, Nigeria	8.7	24.6
Lima, Peru	8.4	9.4
Tokyo	8.3	28.9
New York City	8.1	17.6
Cairo, Egypt	7.6	14.4
London	7.6	7.6
Tehran, Iran	7.3	10.3
Beijing	7.2	15.6

Based on defined city borders.

Source: The World Gazetteer, accessed online at *www.gazetteer.de* on May 31, 2005.

consider, perhaps with Paris and Rome, the greatest of European urban centers. As we examine this city of kings, queens, Shakespeare, Dickens, and Churchill, we shall see reflected all the stages of urban development we have just discussed.

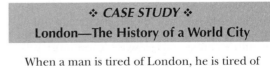

❖ CASE STUDY ❖
London—The History of a World City

When a man is tired of London, he is tired of life; for there is in London all that life can afford.

Dr. Samuel Johnson (1709–1784)

There are certain great cities, suggests British urban geographer Peter Hall (1988:1), in which a disproportionate part of the world's most important business is conducted. These are the "world cities," such as London.

For nearly a thousand years, London has been a focus of European urban life. It is one of the three or four most important economic centers of the world. Its metropolitan area has a population of about 18 million people, and over 8 million foreign tourists besiege it each year. Despite this vitality, the city has problems. Even though tourism annually brings in over $3 billion, the time-honored image of a relatively sedate city is changing rapidly. Some Londoners feel the quality of life is being destroyed as a fleeing middle class and growing racial/ethnic diversity changes the city's texture. They see "too many" foreign-born who come to stay without regard for traditions and customs, and who fill up hospital casualty wards, police stations, and magistrate's courts.

More seriously, the city lost over 1 million jobs in recent decades. Despite an improving economy, an occupational bipolarization continues, with high unemployment among the less skilled and less educated, and increased demand and good pay for business professionals. Most of London's middle class, however, has moved to the suburbs, leaving the city bereft of its traditional tax base and increasingly polarized into a home for the very rich and the poor. Tension between whites and minorities still exists, although not with the violent confrontations of the mid-1980s.

So London remains, as Dr. Johnson put it, a mix of "all that life can afford." Why? What forces are at work in making a city a world city? To answer this question, we need to look at London's history.

Beginnings: 55 B.C.E.–1066 C.E.

London's story begins with Rome and Julius Caesar. After his conquest of Gaul in the first century B.C.E., Caesar was told of a large island to the north that had important natural resources. His expedition to the island in 55 B.C.E. met with little success, however: He encountered fierce resistance from the local Celtic tribes, and so he retreated to Rome to enjoy his other victories. But he brought back with him knowledge of the island.

A hundred years later, in 43 C.E., the fifth Caesar, the emperor Claudius, conquered the island. Claudius set up his main encampment at the first point upstream on the River Thames (pronounced "tems") where a bridge could be built, thereby allowing access across the river by troops to the south. The place was called "Londinium" (meaning "wild" or "bold" place), after the Celtic name for the area. A deep-water port, London's site facilitated the shipment of goods into the heart of England. The Romans built major roads in all directions and enclosed the city within a wall for protection. By 60 C.E., London was thriving: The Roman historian Tacitus wrote that the city was "famed for commerce and crowded with traders."

The Romans remained for nearly 400 years. By the beginning of the fifth century, Roman rule was being challenged continually by the remnants of the Celtic tribes (who had long before been forced into the nether regions of the country: Cornwall, Wales, and Scotland) and by invading tribes from northern Europe. Eventually, the cost of maintaining the British Isles, combined with the necessity of protecting the parts of the empire closer to Rome itself, became too great, and the islands were abandoned in 410 C.E. Virtually all remnants of the Roman occupation, including the Roman remains in London, were destroyed with great relish by the reemergent tribes. Nevertheless, the Romans left two legacies crucial to London's later history: the established city and a superior road system that linked it with the hinterland.

From the time of the Roman retreat until the Norman Conquest in 1066, Britain came under a variety of political overlords. Different tribes—the original Celts, Danes, Angles, Saxons, and Vikings—vied for control of the island, gaining and losing it numerous times. To take but one example, in 1013 the Danes conquered the city, driving out the Saxon king, Ethelred. Ethelred formed an alliance with King Olaf of Norway and together they quickly reattacked the city. Knowing that London Bridge was the key to London's southern

Ancient Rome's domination of Europe had a profound influence on its urban development, both physically and culturally. In many European cities today we can find the remains of vast building projects, roads, bridges, enormous baths and aqueducts, temples and theaters. Situated near the Tower of London, for example, is this portion of a Roman wall built in 200 B.C.E.

supply route, they attached ropes to its huge pilings and sailed downstream, pulling the bridge in their wake (hence the origin of the eleventh-century song "London Bridge Is Falling Down"). Following the Saxon–Norwegian takeover, the Danes returned in 1016 and again they took the city. This seesaw pattern was typical.

Despite changing political fortunes, London thrived. Eager to maintain their success, its merchants usually threw in with whoever was in power, thus maintaining and strengthening London's importance as the economic center of England.

The Medieval City: 1066–1550

The year 1066 brought political stability. The Norman invader, William the Conqueror, defeated the Saxon king, Harold, in the Battle of Hastings and marched on London. Finding the city well fortified and recognizing the vital importance of the trade connections it maintained elsewhere, William attacked the community of Southwark (pronounced "sutherk") at the opposite end of London Bridge. Leaving

a standing army, he took the remainder of his forces to the smaller, less protected cities to the west and north. These he systematically destroyed (ravaged might be a better word), always sending back news of his conquests. The message to Londoners was all too clear: Surrender or face utter devastation. Londoners opened the gates of the city and welcomed William as their king. Without a shot fired, William had gained his prize. By not sacking the city, William not only gained access to virtually all its wealth but also ensured that the city would be able to produce more wealth in the future. Slaughtered merchants trade with no one.

Twenty-five years before William's conquest, the Saxon king, Edward the Confessor, a devout Christian, had decided to build a great abbey west of the original City of London, around a sharp bend in the Thames. (Technically, and still true today, the "City of London" is the original one-square-mile area encompassed by the Roman walls.) It was in this abbey, called Westminster (literally, "the church in the west"), where William chose to have himself crowned king of all England. He then took up residence in the nearby palace that had been constructed by Edward.

The site of William's coronation and residence was critical to the history of London for three reasons. First, an important political residence was established in the immediate vicinity of the financial capital, giving London the power of a "double magnet" as both a financial center and a political center. Second, the establishment of the City of Westminster to the west of the City of London meant that the land between would be filled with incoming people, thus "dragging" greater London in a westward sprawl out of the original Roman walled city. Third, the establishment of the royal residence in London inextricably tied London's local history to the nation's history. Henceforth, the history of London would be, to a large degree, part of the history of England.

For five and a half centuries, medieval London grew steadily. Nevertheless, it was an out-of-the-way place, an important, but not major, European city. This changed radically with the onset of world exploration. By 1550 London had become a world city.

The World City Emerges: 1550–1800

There are three reasons for the transformation of London. First, with the discovery of the Americas, London suddenly became a stop "on the way" for most northern European expeditions heading west to the Americas. It thus became a place where goods could be unloaded conveniently and transferred to the ships of other nations or processed in some manner for reshipment.

Second, because of its geographic isolation from the rest of Europe and the paucity of its natural resources, England became a seafaring nation, with the world's most efficient sailing fleet. Third, there was wool. Isolated from war-ravaged Europe for centuries, England was able to produce more of this precious material than any other country. With wool in ever-increasing demand, London quickly became the port where by far the largest proportion of the world's wool was traded, and London merchants established a virtual monopoly.

As a result of all these factors, London exploded in population, wealth, power, and influence. By the mid-1500s, the English Renaissance—comparable to those of Florence and Venice—had begun. Not only did commerce thrive; so did art, literature, music, and drama. It was the era of Henry VIII, Sir Thomas More, Elizabeth I, Roger Bacon, Sir Walter Raleigh, and, of course, Shakespeare.

Shakespeare, in fact, is a marvelous example of a city's nourishing effect on human creativity. In the late 1500s, Shakespeare arrived in London—the only place where serious dramatists could have their work produced. There he found patrons and competitors who pushed him to his peak. All his greatest work was written in London. As Oscar Wilde, the great nineteenth-century poet and playwright, put it, "Town life nourishes and perfects all the more civilized elements in man. . . . Shakespeare wrote nothing but doggerel lampoon before he came to London and never penned a line after he left."

It is important to see the link between a thriving city and the advance of cultural ideas. First, a dynamic city draws to it people from different backgrounds. As the population grows, the possibilities of permutations and combinations of ideas and lifestyles become legion. Second, a thriving city is usually a wealthy city, and there has been a very intimate historical link between wealth and the development of cultural ideas. Simply, wealth supports leisure. Creative artists with wealthy patrons or buyers for their work can literally afford to develop their art in ways that would be impossible if leisure time were not available. In addition, the rich demand drama, architecture, and music, thereby enhancing the creative arts in another way.

People came to Renaissance London in droves. In 1500 the city was home to 75,000 people. By 1600 that number had nearly tripled to 220,000; by 1650 it had doubled again to over 450,000. But London had no plan for accommodating these huge numbers of people. Housing became scarce and overcrowded, streets virtually impassable. The water became polluted, as—not surprisingly—did the streets themselves. As one historian notes:

> A whole network of officials, from the mayor down to the four [officials] attached to each ward, were continuously battling with the problems of street cleaning. People like William Ward, who caused great nuisance and discomfort to his neighbors by throwing out horrible filth onto the highway, the stench of which was so odious that none of his neighbors could remain in their shops, were prosecuted as public menaces. Many people defied regulations and simply emptied their slops into the street, or, like one ingenious fellow, piped them into the cellar of a neighbor. (Gray 1986:133–34)

Then, in a single year, the city was hit twice by catastrophe. The first was directly connected with the unsanitary conditions we have just described. The Black Plague had visited London before, but never with the virulence of the epidemic of 1665–1666. The population of the city was nearly halved; more than 100,000 people died in the space of eight months.

A major contributor to ending the bubonic plague by killing the rats who transmitted it was the Great Fire that began the evening of September 2, 1666. By the end of the fire four days later, some four-fifths of the City had been destroyed, approximately 13,200 houses, 87 churches, and 50 Livery Halls over an area of 436 acres. But, like the mythical phoenix, London rose from its own flames. Less than 40 years later, in 1700, the London area had a population of over half a million people and the city had been entirely, even spectacularly, rebuilt. It was more powerful than ever. By 1750 the population had grown to over 675,000; by 1800 it was nearly 900,000, almost twice the size of Paris.

Industrialization and Colonization: 1800–1900

The onset of the Industrial Revolution in the late 1700s spurred the growth of London as never before. London was already the center of British trade; what the city did not produce, it shipped; what it did not ship was simply not available for human consumption. To fuel its voracious industrial machine, England needed cheap raw materials in huge portions. Unable to supply all these materials itself, England, like many European nations of the period, colonized much of the globe as quickly as possible. Thus grew the British Empire, on which the sun never set and which, from its center in London, controlled the destinies of a quarter of the earth's population.

To accommodate the burgeoning empire and its industry, the city grew immensely. The docks expanded and provided huge numbers of jobs in the East End; the government civil service expanded to oversee the empire; growing industry provided still more jobs.

The Industrial Revolution brought a tide of urban migrants by the millions to cities such as London. Misery and despair, a life of squalor living in unbelievable slum conditions, were the lot of many, as poignantly shown in this picture of London's Harrow Alley, drawn by French artist Gustav Doré in the 1870s.

London became like a huge, expanding mouth, swallowing up people by the millions. By 1861, the population of London had risen to nearly 3 million. By 1901, the figure was almost 6.5 million, thus increasing by more than 3 million in just 40 years.

The city developed a level of poverty among millions of its residents that was unlike anything experienced before. Many—including Charles Dickens, Karl Marx, and Friedrich Engels—described the suffering of the poor in nineteenth-century London, but few captured it as well as the French illustrator Gustave Doré, whose drawing accompanies this discussion.

The Modern Era: 1900 to the Present

After 1900, life improved. World War I united the country against a common enemy, and, ironically, the Great Depression of the 1930s helped equalize the suffering, as it cut the economic bottom out from under the country's middle and upper-middle classes. Then, in 1940, Adolf Hitler's *Luftwaffe* destroyed much of the city once again through continuous bombings.

After the war, the city regenerated itself once more. Rebuilt offices in the devastated city boomed, tourists came by the millions; and yet, much was lost. London lost population, partly due to the policy of shifting people out of the slums and into new towns, and partly because of the decline in heavy industries. The docklands—an 8.5-square-mile area in the East End that housed the world's largest complex of enclosed docks and warehouses—went into rapid decline as the advent of container ships and other technological changes rendered the docks obsolete. As England's colonies became independent states, the empire disappeared, and with it the immense wealth that made the city grow.

Long-term unemployment was virtually unknown in London until the 1960s and 1970s, when massive commonwealth immigration brought racial–ethnic minorities (primarily Indians, Pakistanis, and Bangladeshis) into the city's inner-city districts. Roy Porter (1994) noted that Londoners viewed these areas as decaying and dangerous, filled with an emerging outcast group poorly integrated into the ties of workplace and neighborhood as unemployment remained two to three times above the city average. With an increase in crime and violence and a decrease in social services, many thought London's future lay between dismal and dire. Commerce no longer served as a unifying force, and poor areas were becoming urban ghettos. Race riots in the city's Brixton district in 1981 and 1985 demonstrated that its social fabric, as well, was unraveling. Londoners began to fear that the city had lost its ability to integrate diverse elements of society and survive social upheaval without shattering into fragments. Porter further observed:

> London's problems mirror those of many U.S. and other world cities, and its plight worries many Londoners: Homelessness, single-parent families, the isolation of the old, classroom violence, joblessness, rising crime, poverty, drug-dealing, neo-Nazi racial attacks—all these now-familiar troubles foretell alienation, anti-social behaviour and despair. Poverty and deprivation deepen, and fears rise of the emergence of a new, permanent underclass, resented by the rest, reinforcing polarisation. . . . As the able and the aspirant leave, quitting Greater London for cleaner, greener pastures elsewhere, the capital is being saddled with a disproportionate population of problem people—resource consumers rather than producers: the old, sick and disabled, broken and lone-parent families, the chronic unemployed, children in care, alcoholics, addicts, new immigrants (some illegal) and derelicts. (Porter 1994:30)

As the first city to develop an infrastructure able to sustain millions of people living and working in a relatively confined area, London can rightly be called the "mother of the modern megacity." That infrastructure—including water, gas and electricity supplies, sewage and waste disposal systems, an underground and suburban railway network—has since been copied by other large cities worldwide. However, although it was once a forerunner in creating a livable, modern metropolis, beset by a recession, high inflation, and burdensome costs in the 1980s, voters elected a conservative government that eliminated the Greater London Council, which was responsible for maintaining the infrastructure of the London metropolitan area (Girardet 1994:12). Now, the mayor of London works with a wide range of environmental groups to draw up strategies and implement them, while the 25-member London Assembly scrutinizes the mayor's approach and issues reports that comment on those strategies.

In analyzing occupational and housing improvements in London in the 1970s and 1980s, Peter Congdon (1995) offered a more optimistic view. While acknowledging the city's problems, he also found revitalization underway:

> The continuing growth of financial, business and information services in the central city, and their deregulation in the 1980s, increased demand for

. . . higher-income professional and managerial workers as a proportion of the London workforce. Despite the recent rise in regional unemployment [the city experienced] an improvement in average prosperity exceeding the national average. (Congdon 1995:523)

Today, mixed trends still are evident. *The Economist* reported in 2004 that office rentals were again on the upturn, with Canary Wharf leading the way as one of the busiest and most important areas of commerce. This thriving community is in the docklands area, at the famous "U" bend in the River Thames, with its blend of restored warehouses and historic buildings, contemporary housing complexes and office developments, many with award-winning glass and steel designs. In the past 15 years, this area has undergone a massive, landscape-changing development, with towering skyscrapers, including Britain's tallest building, the 50-story Canary Wharf Tower, and the uniquely designed, 41-story Swiss Re

London effectively blends its past and present, its modern buildings serving as a backdrop to the eleventh-century Tower of London and complex along the Thames River. The city continues successfully to modernize to remain competitive, but its rich traditions and charm of bygone years remain an important part of London and are major attractions for millions of visitors each year.

CITYSCAPE

The East End and West End of London

These two ends of central London appear to have little in common. The West End and its neighbours, Whitehall and Westminster, are linked together by centuries of state power and by the wealth of its royal, aristocratic, and (more recently) bourgeois residents. They contain most of the principal contemporary tourist sites, as well as monuments and buildings redolent of empire and pre-colonial, medieval elites. The East End, on the other hand, has long been a poor suburb of the City of London. During the nineteenth century it rapidly expanded into a vast working-class area containing substantial pockets of intense poverty. Its residents were excluded from the centers of political and social power until the early twentieth century. Here the struggle for survival operated over a terrain sharply divided by occupational, ethnic, racial, and gender distinctions.

While Soho shares many of the characteristics associated with the East End, it is nevertheless a small enclave contained within a generally prosperous area of central London. Soho became a central London locality where middle- and upper-class visitors could easily find "low life" entertainment. In the East End the scale of its social and economic problems, and its overwhelmingly working-class population, has deterred all but the most determined visitors from the West End and other more prosperous areas of London.

The terms "West End" and "East End," therefore, conjure up two sharply different images of London—images shaped by the realities of social and economic inequality. Yet the gap between these two ends of central London has recently narrowed as the dockland neighbourhoods have been redeveloped.

Source: John Eade, *Placing London: From Imperial Capital to Global City* (London: Berghahn Books, 2000), p. 123.

building, known to Londoners as the "Gherkin." Nearby is the popular promenade on the south bank of the Thames, with its new attraction, the London Eye, the world's largest observation wheel, standing at about 443 feet and attracting 15,000 visitors daily.

Meanwhile, the influx of immigrants has driven London rents and property prices higher, placed a serious strain on public services, and resulted in more children in the schools with a poor command of English. As Londoners flee the crime and congestion, and higher costs of living, the city has become more foreign and diverse than the rest of Britain. London has also become more economically polarized, its cost of living making it difficult for those struggling to find economic security and a home of their own.

Thus, even as London improves, not everyone is necessarily better off.

Perhaps Dr. Johnson was right after all. With several trends occurring simultaneously, there is no one portrait of this city. London in the modern era is still as it was in Johnson's day: a world city that inevitably contains "all that life can afford."

❖ ———————— ❖ ———————— ❖

SUMMARY

Cities have been with us for 10,000 years. They began after the last Ice Age in favorable ecological settings in many areas of the world. Slowly and tentatively they established themselves, fueled by a surplus of goods and materials, whether developed by agriculture, trade, or military dominance. As they grew, they evolved a complex social structure—most particularly, a specialized division of labor and a hierarchical power structure. All these elements allowed cities, in time, to increase their dominance in human affairs. Thus began the first urban revolution.

The earliest cities, such as Jericho and Catal Hüyük, were scattered, independent units, often linked by trade but not much more. Sometime after 4000 B.C.E., however, the first urban empires began to appear. In Mesopotamia and later in Egypt, China, the Indus River Valley, and the Americas, systems of cities emerged. These became not only centers of culture but centers of regional domination as well. This link between city and empire was a central factor in the development of civilization for nearly 5,000 years. Urban empires pulled into their sphere diverse peoples, ideas, and great wealth and power. This was as true of Teotihuacan in North America as it was of Egypt in the Middle East.

Early Western civilization also centered around its cities—first those of Greece and then those of the Roman Empire. When the latter finally crumbled in the late fifth century C.E., most of the other cities of Europe—outposts in the Roman chain—lost their reason for being. The next 500 years—roughly from 500 to 1000 C.E.—were a decidedly antiurban period. Many cities disappeared entirely. The few that managed to survive limped along, shadows of what they had been.

In the first few centuries of the second millennium C.E., a halting urban revival began. Slowly trade began to revive and the old feudal system began to break down as a new merchant class gained power. This revival reached its peak between 1400 and 1600 with the evolution of the Renaissance cities—most effectively symbolized by the Italian **city-states** of Florence, Venice, and Milan.

Then, around 1600, a turning point was reached. The old feudal social order was weakened beyond repair, and the merchant class, generating greater wealth through increasingly successful business ventures, began to control

urban life throughout Europe. Seeing new possibilities for a better life in material terms, people streamed into cities all over the continent. This influx, coupled with technological improvement and advances in health and sanitation services, created what is known as a demographic transition. Europe generally, but cities especially, exploded in population as death rates plummeted, birth rates stayed high, and migrants arrived by the millions. From 1650 on, cities—many huge in population and dominance—began sprouting all over Europe and in North America. This was the second urban revolution, spurred on primarily by the twin engines of capitalism and industrialization.

Today, cities exist in the farthest reaches of the globe. In many cases the growth of cities created immense problems and widespread suffering amid successes. Now, in areas of the world where the urban demographic transition first occurred (notably Europe and North America), urban growth has slowed dramatically. Unhappily, in other areas—as Chapter 13 explains—it has not.

Our case study of London illustrates, in the life of a single city, nearly all of these processes. London began as an outpost of the Roman Empire, achieved initial success, and then, with the Roman retreat in 410, fell into its own dark age—unheard of for centuries and the object of multiple invasions. It began to recover after the victory of William the Conqueror in 1066. For five centuries it built its prominence as the center of British life and, around 1600, blossomed into one of the greatest Renaissance cities in history. Its success was linked primarily to international trade. Through the next two centuries London grew and gained even greater control of world markets. Then, with the Industrial Revolution and intensive British colonization in the nineteenth and early twentieth centuries, the city exploded in population, undergoing a major demographic transition. Despite its incredible wealth-generating capacity, London has had massive problems that it has carried into this century. It now faces, as do many Western industrial cities, a future of changing demographics and a transformation of its economic activities.

CONCLUSION

The emergence of cities as a dominant force in human affairs is one of the crucial events of history. In many instances, cities have been the driving wheel behind the development of civilization. They have combined ideas in new ways, produced great wealth, wielded incredible power (often injudiciously and inhumanely), and become home to an increasing proportion of the world's population.

Yet, throughout history, cities have not always had the same character. As we suggested at the opening of this chapter, the city is largely synonymous with civilization itself. Each chapter in the story of human civilization has thus brought distinctive cities: cities of the early empires, the medieval city, the Renaissance city, and, most recently, the industrial-capitalist city.

Thus, there is both constancy and flux to city history. Together, these processes create urban living. We shall see both clearly evident again as we consider the development of North American cities in the next chapter.

KEY TERMS

Bourgeoisie
City-states
Complex division of labor
Cosmic calendar
Hierarchical power structure
Megacities
Productive surplus
Regal/ritual city

CHAPTER 3

THE DEVELOPMENT OF NORTH AMERICAN CITIES

❖ ━━━━━━━━━ ❖ ━━━━━━━━━ ❖

Come hither, and I will show you an admirable Spectacle! 'Tis a
Heavenly CITY. . . . A CITY to be inhabited by an Innumerable
Company of Angels, and by the Spirits of Just Men. . . .
Put on thy beautiful garments, O America, the Holy City!

Cotton Mather,
seventeenth-century preacher

American urban history began with the small town—five villages hacked out of the wilderness . . . each an "upstart" town with no past, an uncertain future, and a host of confounding and novel problems.

Alexander B. Callow, Jr. (1982)

To the visitor from London, the cities of North America may seem to lack the rich texture that accumulates over centuries of history. In no city of North America, for example, does a single building rival in age the Tower of London—whose foundations were erected in the eleventh century during the reign of William the Conqueror. Even the current Houses of Parliament and Buckingham Palace—relative newcomers on the London scene dating from the mid-nineteenth century—are older than all but a few urban structures in the United States and Canada. Indeed, throughout Europe and much of the non-Western world, one can find abundant examples of exquisite old architecture that suggests a vibrant, urban past that long predates the founding of Canada and the United States.

However, if the cities of North America are rather recent developments in the course of world urban history, they have a fascinating history of their own, spanning over 370 years. This chapter examines this urban history from the earliest settlements on the Atlantic coast, literally "hacked out of the wilderness," to the suburbs and massive metropolitan regions of the new century, which contain more than 250 million North Americans.

The first European settlements in North America were founded in the early seventeenth century at the time when the medieval city in Europe was being transformed by industrialization. Perhaps not surprisingly, the New World cities were founded specifically as trade- and wealth-generating centers to fuel the growth of cities across the Atlantic in Europe. The forces of postmedieval culture—commercial trade and, shortly thereafter, industrial production—were the primary shapers of urban settlement in the United States and Canada. These cities, like the new nations themselves, began with the greatest of

hopes. Cotton Mather was so enamored of the idea of the city that he saw its growth as the fulfillment of the biblical promise of a heavenly setting here on earth. Has that promise been realized? To find out, this chapter examines the development of urban North America in terms of four phases: the colonial, growth and expansion, metropolitan, and modern eras.

THE COLONIAL ERA: 1600–1800

The potential of a good river or sea port and a strategic location for trade were principal reasons for the founding of the early cities of Boston, Charles Town (Charleston), New Amsterdam (New York), Newport, Philadelphia, Quebec City, and Toronto. With the exception of Newport (eclipsed in prominence by Providence in the nineteenth century), all of these settlements became important North American cities. During their earliest stages, however, they were so different from the cities we know today that they would appear virtually unrecognizable were we to visit them.

Colonial City Characteristics

To begin with, colonial cities were exceptionally small, both in physical size and in population. New Amsterdam, for example, occupied only the southernmost tip of Manhattan Island, a far cry from the huge, five-borough City of New York that was incorporated in 1898. As for population, until the eighteenth century, neither New Amsterdam nor any of the other North American urban settlements had populations approaching even 10,000. Not until the Revolutionary War did any of these places begin to develop the population sizes we associate with a city today.

Second, the small size of these settlements and the common ethnic and religious background of most of their population resulted in a very personalized urban existence. The town's inhabitants experienced a social life that was, in a real sense, collective, continually interacting with one another throughout their lives. Community life remained cohesive, as adults had daily contact with neighbors and

BROADWAY. NEW-YORK.

North American preindustrial cities were bustling port cities of commerce. Their concentrations of people and multitude of activities impressed visitors then, but they contained only about 5 percent of the total population. Not until the nineteenth century did any reach today's minimum standard of 100,000 for large cities, as this 1830s view of New York's Broadway suggests.

other townsfolk during the week and expected to see one another each Sunday at church.

Third, the building patterns of early towns were unlike those common today. Boston was "one story structures, covered with thatch, and flung at random over the peninsula" (Bridenbaugh 1964:9). The lack of regular street patterns in early Boston and New York gave both settlements the look of medieval towns. Even today that original pattern can be observed: Both central Boston and Manhattan below 14th Street still retain their initial pattern of irregular streets. Furthermore, hard-surfaced streets were not commonly found in the United States until well into the eighteenth and nineteenth centuries. Only Philadelphia, settled half a century later than the others, was built from the beginning on the more familiar grid system now found in many North American cities (see Chapter 7, Figure 7–3).

Although many of these cities had a medieval feel to them, such qualities were deceptive. Beneath the surface they were part and parcel of the change that was sweeping European urban civilization: They were unabashed trading centers bent on profit and growth. New Amsterdam was probably the most clearly commercial, but Puritan Boston and Quaker Philadelphia were no slackers when it came to money making.

The underlying concept of all these cities was that they would serve as export centers for colonial raw materials going to the European home country. Boston, for example, supplied lumber for the ships of the British Royal Navy; for its part, Charles Town (Charleston) shipped rice and indigo back to the British Isles; New York and Montreal served as bases for the lucrative fur trade.

As time wore on, however, U.S. cities, distant from England geographically, prospered and became more and more independent.

Colonial merchants began to compete with the British and established separate trade agreements with the West Indies and even with Europe. Enterprising craftspeople produced goods for local consumption equal in quality to those imported from England. On the civic front, more and more city governments, technically responsible to their "home offices" in Europe, found reason to cave in to local demands for more freedom in trade.

Many newcomers to the United States moved inland as the eighteenth century progressed, and numerous new, secondary cities, such as New Haven and Baltimore, were established. Although only a small fraction of the population lived in towns, an urban society was emerging along the eastern shore of what soon would become a new nation. By the late 1760s, the 13 colonies had at least 12 major cities and a total population (city and hinterland) of 2 million English, half a million of other European backgrounds, and nearly 400,000 slaves, almost all of whom were in the South (Parrillo 2005:45–48). The major cities were rapidly losing their "backwater" status.

The City-Instigated Revolutionary War

Although the struggle for U.S. independence did not take place entirely in cities, it was in many ways a city-instigated war. The bulk of the economic trade of the colonies was carried out in its cities. American merchants and colonists wanted freedom to pursue their life's interests as they saw fit, and in most cases economic interests were uppermost in their minds. The growth and development of the northern seaport towns generated numerous changes that affected labor relations, the distribution of wealth, the restructuring of social groups, and the emergence of the laboring class into the political arena. As historian Gary B. Nash (1979:383) notes,

> This led, as the Revolution approached, to the rise of a radical consciousness among many and to an interplay between calls for internal reform and insurgency against external forces that adversely affected the lives of city people.

After the war, leadership of the new nation continued to be urban centered. New York became the first capital in 1789, and Philadelphia took over the title in 1790.

Despite this urban dominance, however, most of the population was not urban at this point. When the first census was completed in 1790, only 5 percent resided in urban places (places with 2,500 or more persons), and only 24 such places existed. Philadelphia was the largest settlement, with a population of only 42,000.

If the first phase of the urban history of the United States was marked by the establishment of a chain of important urban settlements on the East Coast, the next phase revealed a dramatic shifting of attention westward as the new nation began an expansion that, before the middle of the nineteenth century, would reach the Pacific Ocean.

GROWTH AND EXPANSION: 1800–1870

At the outbreak of the Revolutionary War, the western frontier of the northern colonies extended barely past the Hudson River, and the southern colonies reached outward only to the Appalachian Mountains. By the time the war was over, the territory of the United States extended roughly to the Mississippi River. The tremendous economic potential of this new region captured the interest of business leaders in established cities and, by the early decades of the nineteenth century, plans were under way to link the new territories with cities in the East.

The first of these links westward was established in 1818, when the National Road (now Interstate 40) pushed through the Appalachians from the city of Baltimore. This trade route, along with Baltimore's large shipbuilding industry, caused that city to grow in size and wealth. Philadelphia attempted to keep pace, opening both canal and turnpike routes west, although with more modest success. Not to be outdone, New York opened the Erie Canal in 1825. Although it was not fully recognized at the time, the canal was to be the key to New York's increasing dominance over East Coast urban trade in the mid-nineteenth century. By cutting across upstate New York from the Hudson, the canal opened a water route to the entire Great Lakes region and much of Canada. Undaunted, Baltimore began another round in this interurban rivalry by opening a railroad line to Ohio in 1828. Other cities followed suit. Soon many railroad lines stretched westward, linking coastal cities to the hinterland.

By 1830, New York, Philadelphia, and fast-growing Baltimore had emerged as the main coastal cities, largely due to their control of the lion's share of commerce with the Ohio Valley. The remarkable rate of growth of these cities in comparison with Charleston, an original East Coast city still focused on tobacco and cotton production, is suggested in Table 3–1. As westward expansion proceeded, many new cities were incorporated. A glance at Table 3–2 shows that fully 39 major urban areas appeared between 1816 and 1876, the height of the westward expansion movement.

Canadian cities also benefited from new transportation links, especially in the 1850s. Toronto experienced rapid development with the coming of the Grand Trunk and Great Western railways and the signing of a trade treaty with the United States. From 9,000 in the 1830s, its population ballooned to 45,000 by 1861. Similarly, Montreal's railroad linkage to Toronto and initiation of shipping service with Europe brought its population to 270,000

by the end of the nineteenth century. Quebec City and its surrounding region numbered about 1 million by 1850, due mostly to rapid natural growth. Thereafter, lack of additional fertile lands in a favorable climate for this mostly agrarian economy prompted many French Canadians to migrate to work in the new industries in the United States.

Economic gain was clearly the major objective of the urban growth of the early nineteenth century. As Europe had sought economic reward through colonization of the New World, so, in turn, did the cities of the East Coast seek to enrich themselves through expansion of trade networks with the West. Pittsburgh, Cincinnati, Louisville, Kansas City, Chicago, and other cities all attempted to gain their share of trade with their region and beyond.

The Beginnings of Industrialization

As the nineteenth century wore on, the North American Industrial Revolution took root. This process gave birth to new and important cities inland. Secretary of the Treasury Alexander Hamilton played a major role in the founding in 1792 of Paterson, New Jersey, at the site of the Passaic Falls, second only to Niagara Falls in its width and height. Pierre L'Enfant, the French-born engineer who would later plan Washington, D.C., designed a water raceway system to harness this water power for mills. As the first planned industrial

TABLE 3–1   Population Growth of Selected East Coast Cities, 1790–1870

	1790	1810	1830	1850	1870
New York	33,131	100,775	214,995	515,500	942,292
Philadelphia	44,096	87,303	161,271	340,000	674,022
Boston	18,320	38,746	61,392	136,881	250,526
Baltimore	13,503	46,555	80,620	169,054	267,354
Charleston	16,359	24,711	30,289	42,985	48,956
Total U.S. urban dwellers	202,000	525,000	1,127,000	3,543,700	9,902,000
Total percent urban	5.1	7.3	8.8	15.3	25.7

Source: Statistics derived from U.S. Censuses in 1850, 1860, and 1910 (Washington, DC: U.S. Government Printing Office).

TABLE 3–2   Incorporation Dates of the 50 Largest U.S. Cities by Historical Period

Pre-1776 (3)	1776–1820 (7)	1821–1860 (25)	1861–1880 (8)	1881–1910 (7)
New York (1685)	Nashville (1784)	Boston (1822)	Denver (1861)	Virginia Beach (1887)
Philadelphia (1701)	Baltimore (1797)	St. Louis (1822)	Tucson (1864)	Long Beach, CA (1888)
Charlotte (1774)	Dayton (1805)	Detroit (1824)	Minneapolis (1867)	Oklahoma City (1890)
	New Orleans (1805)	Memphis (1826)	Seattle (1869)	Miami (1896)
	San Antonio (1809)	Jacksonville (1832)	Phoenix (1871)	Tulsa (1898)
	Pittsburgh (1816)	Columbus (1834)	Fort Worth (1873)	Honolulu (1909)
	Cincinnati (1819)	Cleveland (1836)	Fresno (1874)	Las Vegas (1909)
		Chicago (1837)	Indianapolis (1874)	
		Houston (1837)		
		Toledo (1837)		
		Austin (1840)		
		Milwaukee (1846)		
		Atlanta (1847)		
		Albuquerque (1847)		
		Kansas City (1850)		
		Los Angeles (1850)		
		El Paso (1850)		
		Sacramento (1850)		
		San Diego (1850)		
		San Francisco (1850)		
		San Jose (1850)		
		Portland (1851)		
		Oakland (1854)		
		Dallas (1856)		
		Omaha (1857)		

Source: Based on data from *Statistical Abstract of the United States 2001* and from *Encyclopaedia Britannica,* 2002.

city, Paterson quickly emerged as *the* cotton town of the United States and then as a loco-motive-building center. Soon, New England emerged as the leader in textiles. By the 1830s around Boston, factory towns "were rising on every hand, in Eastern Massachusetts and New Hampshire—Lawrence, Lowell, Fitchberg, Manchester, Lynn. Every village with a water-fall set up a textile mill or a paper mill, a shoe factory or an iron foundry" (Brooks 1936:4). Slowly, industrialization supported by private investment began to transform the developing continent, particularly in the North. As it did so, new tensions began to mount.

Urban–Rural/North–South Tensions

U.S. culture has always contained a streak of anti-urbanism. As long as the early North American settlements remained small and kept their relatively homogeneous character, few tensions existed between urban and rural sections. Yet some of the founders of the United States worried greatly about how growing cities might transform the new na-tion. Thomas Jefferson, who was nurtured in the rural aristocratic tradition of Virginia, con-demned cities as "ulcers on the body politic" and saw their growth as an invitation to all the corruption and evil that had befallen the Old World across the Atlantic. Commenting on an outbreak of yellow fever, Jefferson wrote to Benjamin Rush in 1800:

When great evils happen I am in the habit of looking out for what good may arise from them as consolations to us, and Providence has in fact so established the order to things, as that most evils are the means of producing some good. The yellow fever will discourage the growth of great cities in our nation, and I view great cities as pestilential to the morals, the health and the liberties of man. (White and White 1977:28)

As if in defiance of Jefferson's wishes, America's cities grew in number and prominence. To escape their influence, some people moved westward. The cities followed and brought with them the more mechanized existence of the industrial age. By 1850, many rural Americans were deeply alarmed about these developments. Agrarian periodicals regularly touted the superiority of country life over the deceitful ways of city life.

The debate on the pros and cons of city life soon took on a new and powerful dimension on the regional level: hostility between the North and the South. This conflict resulted from the fact that the unparalleled growth of U.S. cities between 1820 and 1860 was largely centered in the North. Cities such as New York, Philadelphia, and Baltimore simply outdistanced the conservative, slowly growing cities like Charleston and Savannah. The northern cities had the canal routes and the bulk of the railroad lines to the West, which produced tremendous increases in wealth and population. Moreover, they were dominating ever-greater shares of regional and national markets, outstripping the South in overall production as industrialization spread.

The Civil War broke out in 1861. Although its causes were numerous, many historians believe that it was, in a very fundamental sense, a confrontation between urban and rural, industrial and agricultural values. The North's victory was a symbolic turning point. The world of Jefferson was dying. America's commitment to urban industrial expansion was now unchallenged. The stage was set for an urban explosion comparable to the one that had shaken Europe a century before.

THE ERA OF THE GREAT METROPOLIS: 1870–1950

The record number of small cities incorporated in the United States during the 50-year period that ended in 1870 had not yet acquired many of the urban characteristics most familiar to us: towering buildings, populations in the millions, and blazing lights downtown. Two historical events would provide the impetus for this transformation: (1) the technological advance of industrialization and (2) the migration of millions of people to urban North America.

Technological Advance

Industrialization involved much more than simply a proliferation of factories in and around the enlarging urban areas. Several inventions emerged that changed the face of the North American city. The construction of buildings with iron, and then steel, pushed the city skyward. In 1848, a five-story factory built with an iron frame had made news in New York; by 1884, a ten-story steel structure in Chicago had ushered in the era of urban skyscrapers. The success of these taller buildings was further ensured as another invention, the Otis elevator (devised in the 1850s), became widespread in the 1880s. By the end of the nineteenth century, some buildings reached 30 stories; by 1910, a few were as high as 50. By 1913, New York had 61 buildings taller than 20 stories, and the famous city skyline was beginning to take form (Still 1994:206–207).

As cities grew upward, they also pushed outward, aided by a new technology in street-level transportation. Prior to the Civil War, pedestrians had only horse-drawn vehicles to contend with. By the 1870s steam-powered trains were running on elevated tracks in New York. Soon after, "els" were built in other large cities. People's ability to move about certainly was enhanced, but the thunderous noise, billowing smoke, and cascading sparks and cinders of these trains surely did little to preserve the peace and quiet of local neighborhoods or the quality of the environment.

In the 1880s, the electric street trolley came into use. Still in operation today in Philadelphia, Boston, New Orleans (temporarily out of service after Hurricane Katrina in August 2005), and Vancouver, these devices also helped make mass transit a reality. Indeed, streetcars, and the subways that followed, were primarily responsible for making suburban life possible for millions.

Suburbs and the Gilded Age

In the mid-nineteenth century, railroads stretched outward from the central city and carried an increasing number of affluent and fashionable people to their new summer residences in outlying settlements. Of fashionable Philadelphians, E. Digby Baltzell wrote:

> The early suburbanites usually spent only the summer months in the country, the more wealthy in their country houses and their less affluent friends in various popular boarding houses. With the improvement of rail service in the last few decades of the nineteenth century, large suburban estates began to multiply, suburban developments were built, and many families remained the year round. (1989:197)

The trains and trolleys allowed fast and inexpensive transportation beyond the city limits. Quick to see the possibilities of such transportation, real-estate speculators built housing tracts by the dozens. For example, Sam Bass Warner studied the growth of the suburbs of Roxbury, Dorchester, and West Roxbury to the south of central Boston. From 1850 to 1900, these communities increased in population from 60,000 to about 227,000 (1978:35). For the burgeoning middle class, an escape from the city's dirt and din was at last possible:

> The . . . general satisfaction with suburbs came from their ability to answer some of the major needs of the day. . . . To middle class families [they] gave a safe, sanitary environment, new houses in styles somewhat in keeping with their conception of family life, and temporary neighborhoods of people with similar outlook. . . . In addition to benefiting [the middle class] the suburbs [also served that portion of the city's]

Although their numbers were fairly small, the movement of affluent urbanites in the late nineteenth century to suburban areas not too far from the city conferred a quality of prestige on suburban living that persists today. Here, a New Jersey family, wearing their Sunday best, plays croquet on the well-mowed lawn behind their house.

population which could not afford them. The apparent openness of the new residential quarters, their ethnic variety, their extensive growth, and their wide range of prices from fairly inexpensive rental suites to expensive single-family houses—these visible characteristics of the new suburbs gave aspiring low-income families the certainty that should they earn enough money they too could possess the comforts and symbols of success. (Warner 1978:157)

The key to this increase was the streetcar, which carried people beyond the bounds of the old "walking city" of Boston, making frequent stops at stations that soon became centers of suburban housing. Suburban living and streetcar service, Warner concluded, "moved together"—the more there was of one, the more there was of the other. Later, crosstown service filled in the area between the original suburbs and downtown. By 1900, the old "walking city" was surrounded by a mosaic of "streetcar suburbs," which contained about half of the population of greater Boston (Warner 1978:3).

The process repeated itself across North America. As urban subway and elevated systems pushed ever farther from the central city early in the twentieth century, suburbs appeared everywhere. Technology thus spawned the suburban dream, enabling the middle class to move out of the city, separating their place of work from their place of residence. Unlike the more mixed pattern of the earlier walking city, the new housing tracts created homogeneous economic and social communities that by and large excluded the poor. This pattern of social class segregation and the attempt of many to escape to the suburbs have remained two powerful aspects of urban history ever since.

Nothing did more to encourage people to move outward than the automobile. Before cars were common, suburbs were long corridors, stretching out along the streetcar tracks that led from the city core. Suburban settlement spread all around the city, however, as cars made every part of the region accessible to commuters. With the paving of more and more roads, the percentage of people living in suburbs moved ever upward. Even so, from 1900 to 1940, growth was moderate. "Suburban fever" would not seize the nation until the 1950s.

The Great Migration

Between 1870 and 1920, U.S. urban places (places with over 2,500 residents) increased their populations from just under 10 million to over 54 million. The country became, for the first time, a predominantly urban nation. (The United States passed the 50 percent urban population mark in 1913.) The rate of growth for many of the largest cities was nothing short of astonishing. By 1920, Chicago had over 12 times its 1870 population and was fast approaching the 3 million mark. New York, not yet a city of 1 million in 1870, was by 1920 approaching the 6 million mark.

Two demographic trends were primarily responsible for this striking increase in city dwellers: (1) depopulation of rural areas as people moved into cities and (2) immigration to the United States from abroad. The movement from the countryside to the city was brought about by automation—machinery was making old forms of hand-powered labor obsolete—and the possibility of greater wealth in the city. Between 1880 and 1890, nearly 40 percent of the nation's 25,746 townships actually lost population (Glaab 1963:176). Unable to survive in the country and lured by the cities, thousands abandoned their farms to seek their fortunes elsewhere. As might be expected, migration was most intense in the Northeast and Midwest, where the largest cities were.

The absolute number of foreign immigrants to the United States (20 million) was a bit smaller than the number of city-bound Americans who left rural areas during this period, but the changes wrought by immigrants from abroad were far greater. Representing dozens of different nationalities and ethnicities, they introduced staggering cultural diversity to the large cities of the United States. Glaab and Brown give some hint of the transformation:

The influx of immigrants to the cities, particularly during the decade of the 1880's when over five million arrived in the United States, produced some striking statistics for individual cities. In 1890, New York . . . contained more foreign born residents than any city in the world. The city had half as many Italians as Naples, as many Germans as Hamburg, twice as many Irish as Dublin, and two and a half times the number of Jews in Warsaw. In 1893, Chicago contained the third largest Bohemian community in the world; by the time of the First World War, Chicago ranked only behind Warsaw and Lodz as a city of Poles. (1967:138–39)

One important effect of all this migration was the clustering together of cultural groups in distinctive city districts. The tremendous variety of these groups gave cities of the late nineteenth century a degree of diversity and excitement that was quite new in the United States—and would affect the character of the city from that time on. To travel the breadth of Chicago, Cleveland, Pittsburgh, or New York was—and still is today—to experience a succession of differing worlds, each characterized by its own shops and products, its own sounds and smells, its own language. Hence, in addition to upward and outward expansion and raw population growth, cultural heterogeneity became a third major characteristic of the new American metropolis.

When immigration laws in 1921 and 1924 curtailed immigration, the industrial machine that had been developing since the late nineteenth century simply looked elsewhere for cheap labor and found African Americans in the South all too eager to find a better way of life. Between 1920 and 1929, more than 600,000 southern African Americans migrated to northern cities. By the end of the decade, Chicago's South Side and New York's Harlem had the largest concentrated black populations anywhere in the world. In Hartford, Baltimore, Washington, Philadelphia, Cincinnati, and Detroit, the black population grew enormously. Soon racial tensions developed in many northern cities, sometimes leading to riots.

Many cities also grew through annexation. The independent suburbs of Dorchester, Roxbury, and West Roxbury, for example, became part of Boston. In Canada, between 1883 and 1900, Toronto annexed adjacent villages and towns and doubled its area, again doubling its size through further annexation by 1920. In 1930, Toronto's metropolitan area included the central city, four towns (Leaside, Mimico, New Toronto, and Weston), three villages (Forest Hill, Long Branch, and Swansea), and five townships (Etobicoke, East York, North York, Scarborough, and York). Montreal also annexed several cities, towns, and villages on its outskirts, thereby significantly expanding its municipal boundary as well.

Politics and Problems

With the enormous changes that reshaped cities in this period came equally enormous problems. How were the incoming millions to be fed and provided with water, electricity, jobs, and protection against unscrupulous exploitation? Only the city government was empowered to cope with these issues; however, the pressures against fairly representing the public interest were great. All the utility companies required franchises to use the streets— water and gas companies to lay pipes, electric companies to erect poles, and transit companies to lay iron rails. Local or out-of-town entrepreneurs offered to pay large sums for these lucrative franchises, and their bribes sometimes corrupted city officials.

Certain dictatorial political figures—"the bosses"—began to take control of many city governments. They got the job done, but in the process they usually lined their pockets with graft and kickbacks. By the turn of the century many city officials were as corrupt as any organized crime figure.

Another problem of the times was that large-scale immigration sparked an increasingly bitter reaction against newcomers. It was not just their numbers. By 1900, immigrants were more often from southern and eastern Europe, more likely to be Roman Catholic or Jewish than Protestant, and more likely to have darker eyes, hair, and skin tone than whites of northern and western European descent. Moreover, these newcomers often had manners and dress that made them stand out as "different." These "less desirable" immigrants added significantly to anti-city sentiment because, even more than earlier arrivals, they were overwhelmingly urban settlers. By 1910, in fact, over one-third of the inhabitants of the eight largest U.S. cities had been born abroad; another one-third were second-generation Americans. In sharp contrast, fewer than one in ten rural Americans were foreign born at this time (Glaab 1963:176). Within the city, people from "good stock" tried valiantly to get away from the newcomers. As a result, the wealthier suburbs often had a decided antiethnic and racist tinge to them.

The Quality of Life in the New Metropolis

Some profited greatly in this age of great economic expansion. Tremendous fortunes were made and urban industrial empires became established. In 1892, the *New York Times* published a list of 4,047 U.S. millionaires; in 1901, J. P. Morgan founded U.S. Steel, the first billion-dollar corporation; and "by 1910 there were more millionaires in the United States Senate alone than there were in the whole nation before the Civil War" (Baltzell 1964:110).

But times were not equally good for all. As the enormous mansion-retreats of the "robber-baron" industrialists rose across the urban fringe, the blight of the inner-city tenements became more and more conspicuous. With a steady stream of people entering the large cities of the North, property owners responded to the rising demand for housing by making the most profitable use of building space. New York tenements, denounced as "hideous" by Charles Dickens in 1842, had become even worse by 1900, as designs cheapened and more and more people moved into them. The word *tenement* now symbolized an airless, congested slum dwelling. By the turn of the century, perhaps 35 percent of New York City's population lived in such quarters, but the situation in most other industrial cities was somewhat more favorable. Despite periodic attempts at reform through legislation, the urban housing problem remains a controversial issue to the present day (see Chapter 12).

Quality-of-life problems in the rapidly expanding industrial cities, unfortunately, were not limited to housing. Health hazards were great where high-density living was combined with inadequate sewerage and generally unsanitary conditions. Through the end of the nineteenth century, toilet facilities were grossly inadequate for immigrant tenement dwellers. Moreover, until the 1880s most Philadelphians drank water from the Delaware River, into which some 13 million gallons of sewage were being dumped weekly (Marshall 1969:150). The frequency of epidemics was high. The *Chicago Times* summed up the problem with appropriate bluntness:

> The river stinks. The air stinks. Peoples' clothing, permeated by the foul atmosphere, stinks. . . . No other word expresses it so well as stink. A stench means something finite. Stink reaches the infinite and becomes sublime in the magnitude of odiousness. (cited in Glaab and Brown 1967:165)

Of course, attempts were made to remove many of these problems. Urban activists attempted to help the situation of immigrants and improve living conditions. But for decades the battle was uphill. The cities were growing uncontrollably, a trend that ended with World War II (1941–1945) and the suburban housing boom afterward.

THE NORTH AMERICAN CITY TODAY: 1950 TO THE PRESENT

Today's U.S. cities are in the process of three major changes: (1) people and businesses still abandon the central cities, continuing a suburbanization trend that began nearly 100 years ago, a process aptly called **decentralization;** (2) major population growth is occurring in cities in the South and West, the so-called **Sunbelt expansion;** and (3) the work typically performed in the central city is more and more oriented to white-collar jobs, high technology, and services, as Canadian and U.S. cities adjust to the *postindustrial era of* **globalization.**

Decentralization

If the first three eras of North American urban history can be characterized as a time of **urban implosion,** of ever-greater numbers of people converging on the central city itself, then the period since 1950 has seen the beginnings of a major **urban explosion,** of people moving out from the core to the surrounding regions. One indication of this decentralization can be seen in the census data, shown in Table 3–3, for major northern cities between 1910 and 2000. Notice that all the cities in this table became large metropolises by 1910, and that each grew rapidly in the following few decades. However, by 1950, that growth was slowing. By 1970 there was an actual decline in central-city populations, and by the 1980s, it seemed a full-scale central-city retreat was under way. By 2000, though, a few cities had reversed this trend.

The people moving, however, are not leaving the metropolitan region. They are relocating in suburbs near the cities. Table 3–4 on page 69 makes this clear by examining metropolitan area populations for selected cities across the continent, including those examined in Table 3–3. With few exceptions, suburbs are growing everywhere and have been doing so for over 30 years. Why?

Economic Considerations. By about 1950, more and more businesses, particularly in industry and manufacturing, were moving away from the industrial districts of central cities. The costs of refurbishing older buildings were high and, given high rents, expansion wasn't always possible. Further, some new assembly-line procedures required large, low-level structures rather than the multistory buildings characteristic of an earlier era. Concerns over rising crime rates, taxes, and traffic congestion also played their part in a proliferation of new **industrial parks** in the outer urban areas. Workers often moved from the central city to be near their relocated jobs. The result was a growth in suburban population and a decline in central-city population.

Economics is the driving force that prompts some urban critics to suggest governance changes. One view is to utilize regional planning, even regional government, to reduce sprawl, ghettoization, and economic competition among municipalities—often at their own expense by giving tax breaks to companies (Orfield and Rusk 1998; Miller 2002). Another proposal is to allow older cities to be **elastic cities** through annexation of suburbs. In capturing suburban growth, elastic cities promote greater economic progress for the entire metropolitan community and reduce fragmented local government that typically fosters segregation and poverty concentrations (Rusk 1995:5–48).

TABLE 3–3   Population of Selected U.S. Northern Cities, 1910–2000 (in thousands)

	1910	1930	1950	1970	1990	2000
Baltimore	588	805	950	906	736	651
Boston	671	781	801	641	574	589
Chicago	2,185	3,376	3,621	3,367	2,784	2,896
Cleveland	561	900	915	751	506	496
Detroit	466	1,569	1,850	1,511	1,028	951
New York	4,767	6,930	7,892	7,895	7,323	8,008
Philadelphia	1,549	1,951	2,072	1,949	1,586	1,518

Source: U.S. Census Bureau.

TABLE 3–4   **Population of Selected Metropolitan Areas, 1990–2000**

	2000 Population (in thousands)	Change Since 1990 (in thousands)	Percent Change Since 1990
Northern Cities			
Baltimore	2,553	1171	17
Boston	3,407	1179	16
Chicago	8,283	1862	112
Cleveland–Lorain–Elvira	2,251	149	12
Detroit	4,442	1175	14
New York	9,314	1767	19
Philadelphia	6,101	1179	14
Southern Cities			
Atlanta	4,112	11,153	139
Birmingham	921	181	110
Dallas	3,519	1843	132
Houston	4,178	1856	126
Miami	2,253	1316	116
New Orleans	1,338	152	14
Orlando	1,645	1420	134
Tampa–St. Petersburg–Clearwater	2,396	1328	116
Western Cities			
Los Angeles–Long Beach	9,519	1656	17
Phoenix–Mesa	3,252	11,013	145
Portland–Vancouver	1,918	1403	127
Salt Lake City–Ogden	1,334	1262	124
San Francisco	1,731	1128	16
Seattle–Bellevue–Everett	2,415	1381	119

Source: U.S. Census Bureau.

Technology.   As noted earlier, technological changes in energy (steam power) and building techniques (steel-frame skyscrapers) were important in the creation of a centralized metropolis in the nineteenth century. Since then, the development of electric power, interstate highways, the telephone, and—most recently—computers and telecommunications have been equally important in the decentralization of the urban area.

As rail lines pushed out of the cities in earlier decades, the first suburbs clustered around the railroad stations. But motor vehicles made it possible to live in a far wider area while still having access to the urban area as a whole. As late as 1920, the average commute was still only about 1.5 miles (B. Duncan 1956). By 1960, however, this distance had grown to almost 5 miles (Hawley 1981), and it is not uncommon today to travel 20 miles or more to work.

Taken together, these technological changes have changed the meaning of urban space. Because we move more easily across space—in minutes by car or milliseconds by telecommunications—physical proximity is no longer as necessary to tie together all the activities within the urban area. In fact, most of us who live in cities routinely think in terms of time ("We live about 40 minutes from the airport") rather than distance; we may not even know how many miles away the airport is.

The Postwar Era: 1945–1970.   Once the Great Depression and World War II were in the past, North America's suburbs exploded. Millions of Americans returned from overseas to find their old neighborhoods in increasing disrepair (in the war effort many neighborhood maintenance projects had been shelved and the ability of private homeowners to maintain full upkeep was curtailed). In many instances, returning white soldiers also found minority groups, especially African Americans, living in or close to their former homes. (Many African Americans had migrated north during the war to operate the industrial machinery vacated by whites.) Finally, like almost all Americans, these men wanted their own place out of the congested city, a place with a little more room where they could raise their kids in clean air and send them to good schools, without fear of crime and other urban ills. This was, of course, the classic suburban dream.

What made its realization possible for millions was the federal government. The Federal Housing Authority (FHA) and the Veterans Administration (VA) made low-interest construction loans available to veterans or to anyone else who could supply some assurance of their ability to repay. Millions of veterans took the FHA and the VA up on their offer and elected to build or buy new homes that, because of federal funding policies, were mostly built outside the central city, in suburban tracts. All across North America, new housing developments appeared. None, however, illustrates "suburban fever" better than Levittown on New York's Long Island.

Some 30 miles east of Manhattan, Levittown rose from spinach and potato fields. Begun in 1947 by developer Abraham Levitt and his sons, it was originally planned as 2,000 rental units for veterans. However, the project escalated to 6,000 units within a year, and with construction of the last house in 1951, Levittown contained 17,447 homes. Each ranch house (almost all of which were sold, not rented) was small (32 feet by 25 feet) and strikingly uniform in appearance. It sold for $7,990, with a $90 deposit and $58 monthly payment, and came in five different models, differing only by exterior color, roofline, and the placement of windows. Built on a concrete slab with radiant heating coils, it had no garage and came with an expandable attic

(Matarrese 1997). Soon, similar housing developments were built elsewhere.

Retail businesses were quick to follow the flow of population into these bedroom communities, and local shopping malls increasingly became part of suburban living. Although a suburban shopping center broke ground as early as 1907 in Baltimore and another shortly afterward in the Country Club district of Kansas City, in 1946 only eight such centers existed in the entire United States (Jackson 1973). By 1960, the number soared to 3,800 and then tripled again to 13,000 "malls" by 1970 (King 1974:102; Tobin 1976). No wonder that, by 1970, there were as many people working in the suburbs as there were in the central cities (Rosenthal 1974).

As the white middle class moved out to the separately incorporated suburbs, the cities lost even more of the tax base that departing industry was already eroding. To add to the problem, the population that was left behind in the city core was increasingly composed of minorities and the poor. As industry abandoned the central city, many of these people were unable to find jobs and went on public relief. Thus the city was faced with an increasing demand for services and a shrinking ability to provide them. By the mid-1960s a true urban crisis—largely created by the decentralization phenomenon—was upon the country as a whole. Urban poverty was on the increase, minorities were justifiably angry over their standard of living, services were getting worse, and many cities were facing bankruptcy.

The Metropolitan Statistical Area. With decentralization well under way by 1910, U.S. cities were growing well beyond their traditional boundaries. In the North, for example, workers, unable to find adequate housing in the central city, spilled over into the surrounding towns and small cities. To take a single case, Boston's workers began to settle in Wakefield and Lynn to the north, in Wellesley and Natick to the west, and in Quincy and Braintree to the south. While technically these people were residents of their newly adopted local communities, on another level they were still clearly linked to Boston and under its sphere of influence.

Noticing this trend, the U.S. Bureau of the Census was faced with a problem: how to measure accurately the way cities were really growing. If it merely counted the residents of the central city—in this case, Boston—it would get a relatively small population count that would not reflect the fact that many of the people who lived in Braintree and Wakefield were really tied to Boston in a fundamental way. Consequently, the Census Bureau decided to count not only the central city population in its surveys, but the surrounding towns and cities that were obviously tied to that central city as well. Thus was born the idea of the metropolitan area.

Since 1910, a series of terms have been used to designate such sprawling urban regions. From 1959 until 1983, the term *standard metropolitan statistical area* (or SMSA) was employed. Then, in 1983, the Census Bureau introduced the concept **metropolitan statistical area** (or MSA). An MSA is currently defined as including at least one city with 50,000 or more inhabitants, the county or counties containing the city, and any surrounding counties that have a high population density and a large proportion of inhabitants commuting to and from the central city. As of 2000, the Census Bureau recognized 273 MSAs within the United States, containing roughly three-fourths of the total population.

The Toronto Metropolitan Area.   In 1953, Toronto created a federated form of government unique to North America to deal with the metropolitan phenomenon. Going beyond merely labeling a metropolitan area as such, this action created a consolidated governance system. The 13 municipalities of this metropolitan area formed a 25-member, elected Council of Metropolitan Toronto. Through united effort the Council succeeded in establishing a common property assessment and tax rate to deal with such regional problems as water supply, sewage disposal, mass transit, school building needs, housing for the elderly,

parks, and urban development. This metropolitan governance approach is found in many European countries but is virtually nonexistent in the United States. Subsequently, the Council was modified to include 33 members but from only six municipalities.

Megalopolis and the Consolidated Metropolitan Statistical Area.   French geographer Jean Gottmann was one of the first urbanists to look closely at the sprawling urban regions and to note the linkages between many independent urban municipalities. The first such area, which he called a **megalopolis,** was the unbroken urban region that emerged along the eastern seaboard of the United States, and he dubbed it the "BosWash corridor." In Cityscape on page 72, he describes this development.

The BosWash corridor was the first North American megalopolis, but not the last. Since the publication of Gottman's seminal book in 1961, other megalopolises have emerged—in Southern California ("SanSan") and across the northern Midwest from Chicago ("ChiGary") to Cleveland ("CleveAk"). Once again, such growth has not gone unnoticed by the Census Bureau, which coined the term **consolidated metropolitan statistical area** (or CMSA) to describe these areas. By 2000, 18 CMSAs were recognized as part of the urban landscape, including Dallas–Forth Worth, Denver–Boulder–Greeley, Detroit–Ann Arbor–Flint, Houston–Galveston–Brazoria, Miami–Fort Lauderdale, Milwaukee–Racine, and Seattle–Tacoma–Bremerton.

Nonmetropolitan Growth.   The decentralization of the U.S. population has dispersed people outward from central cities not just to nearby suburbs, but to the outlying rural hinterland as well. Small towns and rural areas had steadily lost population for the first 70 years of this century. In the 1960s rural America lost 2.8 million people, but during the 1970s, the trend reversed itself as rural areas gained 8.4 million people, up some 15.4 percent. Between 1990 and 2000, the nonmetropolitan population increased by 5.1 million, a 19.7 percent increase (U.S. Census Bureau 2002a).

CITYSCAPE

Megalopolis: The BosWash Corridor

The Northeastern seaboard of the United States is today the site of a remarkable development—an almost continuous stretch of urban and suburban areas from southern New Hampshire to northern Virginia and from the Atlantic shore to the Appalachian foothills. . . .

. . . As one follows the main highways or railroads between Boston and Washington, D.C., one hardly loses sight of built-up areas, tightly woven residential communities, or powerful concentrations of manufacturing plants. Flying this same route one discovers, on the other hand, that behind the ribbons of densely occupied land along the principal arteries of traffic, and in between the clusters of suburbs around the old urban centers, there still remain large areas covered with woods and brush alternating with some carefully cultivated patches of farmland. These green spaces, however, when inspected at closer range, appear stuffed with a loose but immense scattering of buildings, most of them residential but some of industrial character. That is, many of these sections that look rural actually function largely as suburbs in the orbit of some city's downtown. . . .

Thus the old distinctions between rural and urban do not apply here any more. Even a quick look at the vast area of Megalopolis reveals a revolution in land use. Most of the people living in the so-called rural areas, and still classified as "rural population" by recent censuses, have very little, if anything, to do with agriculture. In terms of their interests and work they are what used to be classified as "city folks," but their way of life and the landscapes around their residences do not fit the old meaning of urban.

In this area, then, we must abandon the idea of the city as a tightly settled and organized unit in which people, activities, and riches are crowded into a very small area clearly separated from its nonurban surroundings. Every city in this region spreads out far and wide around its original nucleus; it grows amidst an irregularly colloidal mixture of rural and suburban landscapes; it melts on broad fronts with other mixtures, of somewhat similar though different texture, belonging to the suburban neighborhoods of other cities. Such coalescence can be observed, for example, along the main lines of traffic that link New York City and Philadelphia. Here there are many communities that might be classified as belonging to more than one orbit. It is hard to say whether they are suburbs, or "satellites," of Philadelphia or New York, Newark, New Brunswick, or Trenton. The latter three cities themselves have been reduced to the role of suburbs of New York City in many respects, although Trenton belongs also to the orbit of Philadelphia. . . .

This region indeed reminds one of Aristotle's saying that cities such as Babylon had "the compass of a nation rather than a city. . . ."

Source: Jean Gottmann, *Megalopolis* (New York: Twentieth Century Fund, 1961), pp. 3, 5–7.

No doubt improved transportation and communications are an important foundation of this change. Yet Americans moving to small towns or rural areas also may be reacting to the problems of cities in the same way that those moving to the suburbs have done for decades: They are looking for a greater sense of security and reaffirming the value of simpler living. Still, the people moving to these areas are in no way traditionally rural. Most are well educated, have sophisticated tastes, and work in nearby cities. Local stores often spring up, supplying such items as gourmet wines and sophisticated books.

The Sunbelt Expansion

A glance back to Table 3–4 reveals the other main trend that is affecting contemporary U.S. cities. Although suburban population is growing everywhere, the table shows that it is growing fastest in the South and West. Figure 3–1 drives home the point even more effectively, showing that the population of virtually every state below the Mason-Dixon Line and west of the Rocky Mountains increased considerably between 1990 and 2000.

During most of U.S. history, the Northeast and Midwest regions and their cities dominated national affairs. No more. An immense power shift has occurred; the South has risen again and the West has also come into preeminence.

Table 3–5 on page 74 illustrates just how dramatic the change has been by comparing the raw population figures and national rankings for the ten largest U.S. cities in 2000. New York, Chicago, Philadelphia, and Detroit still remained in the top ten but the latter two have lost significant population since 1950. If present trends continue, only New York and Los Angeles may appear on the next list. In addition, seemingly from nowhere, Houston, Dallas, San Diego, San Antonio, and, especially, Phoenix have leaped onto the top ten list. Why has this change occurred?

Snowbelt Debits/Sunbelt Assets.   To begin with, the northern cities experienced the strains of age, and businesses found costs and taxes rising to the point where many were not willing to stay. Built around the cruder industrial machinery of the nineteenth century, these cities found their physical plants outmoded by newer, particularly "high-tech"

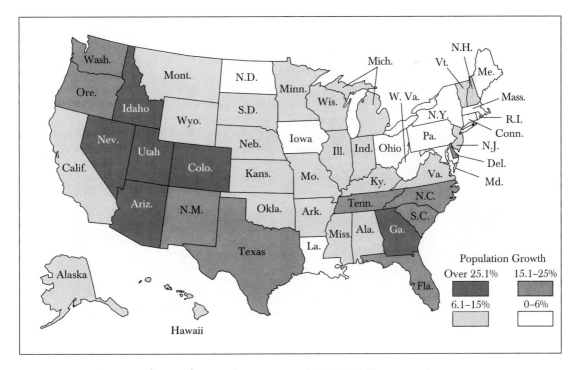

FIGURE 3–1   State Population Changes (in percentages), 1990–2000 [*Source:* U.S. Census Bureau.]

TABLE 3–5 **The Ten Largest U.S. Cities in 2000 Compared with Rank in 1950 (population in thousands)**

	2000		1950	
	Population	Rank	Population	Rank
New York	8,008	1	7,892	1
Los Angeles	3,695	2	1,970	4
Chicago	2,896	3	3,621	2
Houston	1,954	4	596	14
Philadelphia	1,518	5	2,072	3
Phoenix	1,321	6	107	96
San Diego	1,223	7	334	28
Dallas	1,189	8	434	21
San Antonio	1,145	9	408	24
Detroit	951	10	1,850	5

Note: Center city data only.

Source: U.S. Census Bureau.

industry. Renovation was exorbitantly costly. City streets were in disrepair. Services were declining. Because of the financial burden they labored under, these cities could not offer tax breaks to businesses as liberally as they once had. Energy costs were skyrocketing. Superhighways (so vital to modern commerce) typically did not terminate conveniently in the industrial area. Union pay scales made labor very expensive.

The Sunbelt had few of these problems. With many cities industrialized only recently, they were able to build modern, efficient plants linked easily to superhighways. With stronger economies than their northern counterparts due to booming population growth, they could offer substantial tax breaks to businesses. Energy costs were also much lower. A less unionized labor force was an added attraction to businesses. The result was that businesses by the thousands deserted the North and headed for the cities of the South and West.

Private citizens also enjoyed many benefits living in the South and West. Sunbelt cities are warmer, cheaper to live in, and offer more jobs. Home heating and electricity typically cost twice as much in the Snowbelt cities as in

Snowbelt cities such as Minneapolis–St. Paul, unlike Sunbelt cities, have high-density land use. The tight clustering of buildings—and therefore a closer proximity of shops, offices, and restaurants, not to mention apartment residences—places more activities within walking distance and results in more crowds, congestion, and reliance on mass transit.

the Sunbelt. Responding to such incentives, people head south or west.

The movement out of the North and Midwest has not only affected whites. From Virginia to Texas (the states of the Old Confederacy), the black population increased 19 percent between 1970 and 1980, as more than a million more African Americans moved into the South than moved out. This was the first major reversal of the northward black migration pattern since it began after the Civil War, and the trend has continued. Black migration to the South accelerated dramatically between 1990 and 2000; seven of the ten metropolitan areas that gained the most black residents in this period were in the South. By 2000, 62 percent of all African Americans lived in the Sunbelt. But there is a difference between the earlier migration northward and the present one southward. Previously, most African Americans moving north were unskilled workers looking for any type of employment that would pay them more than the bare subsistence income they had earned in southern rural areas or cities. Today, most African Americans migrating southward are of working age, and about one-fifth are college graduates, and thus they contribute to the growth of the black middle-class population in cities such as Atlanta, Charlotte, and Washington, D.C. Another 7 percent are aged 65 or older, moving south to retire (Frey 1998).

Finally, many Sunbelt cities have been permitted, by law, to annex new territory, as the northern cities once did before municipal boundaries became rigid. Because of this territorial flexibility, Sunbelt economic and political boundaries are more congruent, and so far these cities have been able to avoid the financial straits of northern cities, becoming urban regions unto themselves. In contrast, most northeastern cities have the same boundaries that they had half a century ago and are surrounded by legally independent suburbs that wish no part of the problems of the old central cities.

The Sunbelt cities are on a growth spurt that resembles the one that Canadian and northern U.S. metropolises underwent in the period between 1870 and 1950. They are reshaping the face of urban North America. The process is feeding on itself. Business follows people; people follow business.

California provides just one example. For decades, people moving to the so-called golden land at the western edge of the continent tended to settle in that state's coastal cities—San Diego, Los Angeles, Santa Barbara, San Francisco—or their suburbs. Many are still doing so. However, in recent years the growth of California's inland cities has been nothing short of astounding. Growing as though there is no tomorrow are cities like Stockton, Bakersfield, Fresno, San Bernardino, Modesto, and Sacramento. Once again, it is quality-of-life issues that seem behind the change. Housing costs in coastal cities are astronomical, jobs are scarce (especially those that pay well), and smog and congestion are omnipresent. Inland, these problems are less intense.

BosWash Assets.   Despite the Sunbelt expansion, the BosWash megalopolis remains a major part of U.S. urban life. It is a region where over 51 million people—almost one in five Americans—live. This 18 percent holds its share (19 percent) of the nation's wealth, compared with the 57 percent produced by the South and West, which contain 58 percent of the total population (Federal Reserve System 2000). Nearly one-half of all investment capital available nationwide in 2000 was concentrated in the Northeast, where bank assets of $2.1 trillion accounted for 33 percent of the nation's total bank assets (U.S. Federal Deposit Insurance Corporation 2002).

Why does this region still attract job-creating investments? With nearly one-fifth of the U.S. population on one-nineteenth of the land mass, it is the nation's most concentrated market region. Manufacturers in the BosWash corridor can reach over half the U.S. and Canadian industrial firms and retail sales outlets within 24 hours by truck. Also, the corridor states are, by air and sea, close to the 271 million people in the European Union (EU) countries. In addition, the 11-state region has the highest concentration of higher-education institutions, sending 2.8 million students annually to 875 colleges and universities. Proximity to top colleges has influenced the location choices of high-technology firms. Massachusetts's famous Route 128 (now called "America's Technology Highway") is near Massachusetts Institute of Technology (MIT) and Harvard. New Jersey—with only 3.3 percent of the nation's population—has laboratories along Route 1 near Princeton University that do 9 percent of the research and development work in the United States (Parrillo 2005b:107).

Sunbelt Debits. Just as all is not negative in the Snowbelt, all is not rosy in the Sunbelt. A 2004 FBI report indicated that reported violent crime in the Sunbelt region constituted 66 percent of the total (42 percent in the South and 24 percent in the West), compared with 19 percent in the Midwest and only 18 percent in the Northeast. Pollution is increasing, water is running short (particularly in the Southwest), and population growth is just too great to absorb in many areas. Many of the fast-growth cities have not yet developed adequate infrastructure systems (roads, bridges, water and sewage systems) and the cost of doing so is rising rapidly.

THE COMING OF THE POSTINDUSTRIAL CITY

In the 1960s, it looked as though our central cities were in an irreversible process of self-destruction. Dozens of cities experienced major riots, as thousands of poor minorities reacted in desperation to their poverty, lashing out at our white-dominated society. In 1968, the National Advisory Commission on Civil Disorders studied 75 of these violent outbreaks and warned that the United States was "moving toward two societies, one black, one white—separate and unequal." Part of this problem showed itself in changing demographics. The central city was literally falling apart, and whites and the affluent were leaving for the suburbs. Industry was close behind as old factories became obsolete. Left in the decay were those who had little choice—the trapped and the poor, many of them minorities, increasingly embittered as

the American Dream passed them by. It looked like the end of the city as we knew it, and many doubted that North American cities would ever rise again. In stark contrast, Canadian cities dealt with their problems more effectively, causing U.S. urbanist Jane Jacobs to refer to Toronto—by the 1960s a cosmopolitan city with a distinct racial/ethnic mix—as "a city that works."

Deterioration and Regeneration

Since the mid-nineteenth century, U.S. cities had been industrial machines. They were the location of factories and their associated support industries. By and large, the people who worked in those industries lived in the city. But all that changed. As cities became more congested, more affluent people moved to the suburbs, leaving declining neighborhoods in their wake. With time, factories too fell into disrepair. Equally important, in the last few decades transportation services improved, making it more efficient for industries to locate outside of the central city on interstate loops. Together, these processes produced a city apparently rotting at the core, populated less and less by the rich and more and more by minorities and the poor.

But, as Chapters 1 and 2 have shown, cities are remarkably resilient human creations with a built-in facility for regeneration because they are so vital to human life. Probably the city's most important trait, as we will discuss in detail in Chapter 7, is its ability to centralize and concentrate human affairs. Cities allow more efficient and intense activity in all areas of social existence: politics, religion, the arts and sciences, as well as the economy.

In the late 1960s, as central cities deteriorated or, worse, went up in smoke, scholars, politicians, and nearly everyone else wrung their hands and wondered what could be done. One voice suggested that we need do nothing: With time the city would save itself. That voice belonged to Edward C. Banfield, whose book *The Unheavenly City* (an obvious reference to Cotton Mather's wish for a "heavenly city" in the seventeenth century) created an enormous stir. The book, published in

1970, was controversial because of its basically conservative thesis that the city was too powerful an economic machine to remain down and out for long. Allow enough time and new businesses and people would see that they could get back into the central city and enjoy its great communicative advantages cheaply. They could buy up that land, renovate those deteriorated factories, houses, and apartment complexes, and thus avail themselves of the city's many benefits.

To some, Banfield's "do nothing" approach to urban destitution seemed callous and mean-spirited, and they roundly criticized him. And yet, well over three decades later, many of his predictions have come to pass. Cities across the nation are in the midst of a rejuvenation, and with little help from the federal government. The postindustrial city has arrived, and recent research suggests strongly that a general economic revitalization is under way (Teaford 1990).

In many cities today, the contrast with the earlier picture of older U.S. cities in disrepair is nothing short of amazing. All over the United States, new urban construction is in progress—from Pittsburgh to Seattle, from New York to Phoenix. Office towers are multiplying almost as fast as contractors can build them. Many residential areas of the city are being totally transformed as young urban professionals—the "yuppies"—move in, renovate old buildings, or settle into new apartment complexes. Although many older cities, particularly smaller ones, are still hurting, the urban economy is alive once more. In most areas of the country, a true urban renaissance is under way as U.S. cities complete a shift to a postindustrial economy.

The reasons for this turnaround are two: (1) the growth of white-collar businesses tied to new computer technology; and (2) a major shift in the way many industries do business. Regarding the first change, high-tech businesses

The night mosaic photographed from space illustrates the urban concentrations of people in North America more dramatically than could any artist or cartographer. The electric lights easily reveal where to find a megalopolis or metropolis and how much of the land is nonurban.

were more than happy to take over, renovate, or rebuild the structures left by departing heavy industry. They needed the central-city location to maximize their efficiency.

As to the second element in the turnaround, many corporations are in the midst of a radical transformation, changing their structure and operations. In the nineteenth century, major industries believed in a "beginning-to-end" process. That is, they oversaw and controlled their product from raw material to finished marketable item. This was true of most of the "giants," such as the Carnegie Corporation (steel) and the Ford Motor Company (which went so far as to raise sheep to produce wool for its cars' upholstery fabric!).

Now all that is changing. Big industries are divesting themselves of parts of their operations that are no longer profitable and are contracting out important products to other firms or to foreign companies. Thus, General Electric no longer makes microwave ovens or the icemakers that go into its refrigerators;

instead other firms in the United States, Korea, Japan, and elsewhere supply them. Taking a more flexible approach, firms decide which parts of the production process they can perform profitably themselves and which would be more efficiently done by others (Prokesch 1985).

But such changes, which are happening all over the country, have important implications for the city: On the one hand, U.S. companies no longer require as many blue-collar workers or as many buildings geared to heavy industrial production. On the other hand, these corporations, which play so large a role in our urban scene, have created more white-collar jobs—jobs that depend on regular contact with other corporations, whether in the United States or abroad.

Naturally, many of the people employed by these postindustrial, high-tech industries want to live near their work, and while some (particularly those with families) continue to commute from the suburbs, many have opted

One of the best examples of an urban renaissance occurring in many North American cities is New York City's Times Square. Once the locale of sleazy porn stores and theaters and other seedy enterprises, it has undergone a facelift that is more than cosmetic. New hotels, theaters, and family-oriented businesses now dominate the area.

to live in the central city. Illustrating this trend in the past several decades has been the process of gentrification, in which white-collar professionals have moved into and transformed older, decaying neighborhoods of many cities.

The Future

The postindustrial city will likely dominate North America's future, but what form will it take? One vitally important trend is globalization, a subject we will explore in Chapter 9. Two other trends are occurring simultaneously, and it is uncertain which will prevail in the twenty-first century. One trend is the appearance of edge cities, discussed more fully in Chapter 4. It is the evolution of edge cities on the fringe of older urban areas in the past two decades that helps explain the previously mentioned increases in population in nonmetropolitan areas. Joel Garreau (1991) suggested that North Americans have reinvented the city and that these new urban agglomerations are now the future. Numbering over 200 in Canada and the United States, these edge cities with their malls and office parks now dominate the nation's retail trade and office facilities.

The second trend is the revitalization of older cities, a significant process that shows no sign of stopping. More people, not fewer, are taking on the yuppie lifestyle. Since edge cities do not offer the residential ambience that young adults can find in a central city's brownstone houses, loft apartments, cozy restaurants, and shops, the upgrading of many older city neighborhoods continues. In addition, the office-building boom in many cities persists, to meet the needs of postindustrial corporations (Zipp and Cook 1999).

Cleveland is a good example. In the 1960s and 1970s, this Ohio premier city was a symbol of urban despair. Severe social problems exploded into race riots in 1966 and 1968. Pollution was thick in the air and, in 1969, the Cuyahoga River actually burned for days because of the pollutants it contained. Cleveland's heavy industry was dying, its middle class was fleeing to the suburbs, and, by 1979, the city was on the verge of financial collapse.

A public–private partnership, forged by city government and business leaders in the early 1980s, breathed new life into the city. Perhaps the linchpin of the revitalization was the restoration of Cleveland's famous but abandoned landmark—the Terminal Tower commercial complex—into a rail transit station, a multilevel shopping center with upscale national stores, an 11-screen movie theater, a Ritz-Carlton hotel, and several high-rise office buildings. The complex created over 3,000 permanent jobs and contributes more than $4 million in taxes to the city treasury (Greengard and Solomon 1994:65).

Tourist attractions include the six-story Rock and Roll Hall of Fame and Museum, two new stadiums, and nearby Cedar Point amusement park with its 11 roller coaster rides (Herbert 1996:72). Yuppies have turned abandoned warehouses into lofts and apartments. City residents can enjoy a lakefront park and trendy restaurants along the Cuyahoga River, where one can sit on the patios while barges and pleasure boats navigate the river. Although the city lost 5 percent of its population in the 1990s, that marked the smallest decline since the 1950s, and several hundred new homes sprout up each year, reinforcing the spirit of urban revival that many residents feel (Schmitt 2001:A1). To offset the city's loss of its former industrial base, Cleveland's leaders have rediscovered its waterfronts and made waterside development and amenities an important part of their economic strategy.

Strategy is exactly the right word. As the nation's central cities regenerate, many are engaging in a type of competition reminiscent of the interurban competition of the mid-1800s, when North American cities were growing by leaps and bounds. An increasing number of urban governments are hiring marketing professionals whose job it is to spiff up the city's image so that it can attract more businesses and tourists.

The Human Cost of Economic Restructuring

It is clear that the postindustrial process is not benefiting all of the city's residents, however.

As gentrification progresses, the poorer residents of many city neighborhoods are simply displaced. Unable to pay the rising rents, they have to find somewhere else to live. Similarly, the fact that a few areas of our cities have become havens for the affluent has done little to change the very poorest areas of those cities: New York still has its Harlem and South Bronx, Chicago its South Side, Los Angeles its Watts, and Cleveland its Hough. Even more worrisome, the postindustrial economy is exacerbating the plight of the city's poor and unskilled.

This occupational restructuring creates a "skills mismatch" as our cities' economy becomes ever more white collar. The cities' gradual shift away from manufacturing and goods processing eliminates many of the blue-collar jobs that were the first step up for millions of unskilled migrants and immigrants. The rising skill requirements of today's urban job market, demanding educated employees able to work with words and numbers in information-processing jobs, puts these new jobs out of reach for the urban poor. Thus, even as some urban neighborhoods improve, unemployment rates and welfare dependency among the unskilled remain high (Handel 2003; Bauder and Perle 1999). Gentrification is all well and good as far as it goes, but not everyone agrees that the changes benefit all.

In the 1980s several urban observers viewed postindustrial cities pessimistically (Berry 1985; Downs 1985; Bradbury, Downs, and Small 1982). They saw the postindustrial city as increasingly characterized by two labor markets that fostered two dramatically unequal lifestyles—that of the well-paid white-collar professional and that of the low-paid service worker. Seeing these lifestyle inequities worsening in the foreseeable future, they concluded that the decline of the U.S. city was all but irreversible. Postindustrialism and the windfall of the urban upper classes may be flashy and hopeful on the surface but in reality, the critics contended, these "improvements" did not penetrate far beyond a small, favored group. In contrast, Roger Waldinger (1999) speaks of the interdependence between the city's affluent and poor and of how the instability in the labor market and then the transformation of the ethnic division of labor is leading to positive developments in the case of the first postindustrial city, New York.

Historically, then, the North American city is engaged in a dynamic process that extends from its origins—those five communities "hacked out of the wilderness" in the seventeenth century—to the present configuration—much larger and still embroiled in rapid and significant change, as decentralization, the growth of the Sunbelt, and postindustrialization unfold. All these changes can be seen in the case study that closes this chapter, an analysis of North America's world city, New York.

❖ CASE STUDY ❖
New York—The "Big Apple"

Jim said everything was in New York. Jim said that he was happy, just standing in Grand Central Station, catching scraps of people's conversations. Jim said he would not mind standing all day on Sixth Avenue where they had the joke shops and the Orange Drinks, just watching the crowds go by. Jim said he would not mind standing all day in Radio City, where the French and British shops and the travel offices were, and the evergreens at Christmas and the tulips in the spring and where the fountains sprayed ceaselessly around Mr. Manship's golden boy and where exhibition fancy skaters salved their egos in the winter. If he grew tired of skaters, Jim said he would not mind standing and staring up and up, watching the mass of buildings cut into the sky.

John P. Marquand, *So Little Time* (1943)

Through almost all of the nation's history, New York has been the Great U.S. City. It symbolizes the United States to the world and, in many ways, reveals the rest of the world to the United States. New York not only represents the distinctive course of North American urban history, it is a timeless display of what urban life is all about. Here are just a few of the features that make it so outstanding.

First, New York is huge, an enormous concentration of population. Over 8 million people live within the city limits, and almost three times that many reside in the urban region that sprawls outward around the city. Second, it has the nation's greatest concentration of business and finance: By sales volume, New York City ranks first as the world's largest corporate headquarters, including five of the six largest banks, and more than 100 of the *Fortune* 500 largest industrial corporations have their home offices there. In addition, it is a major location for most international businesses located in North America. Third, it is the third largest U.S. port and has dominated American commerce since the early 1800s. Fourth, it is a mosaic of virtually every race and ethnic group in the world—over 50 different foreign-language newspapers are published in the city. Many of these groups have clustered together in such well-known districts as Chinatown, Harlem, Spanish Harlem, Little Italy,

and the Lower East Side. Fifth, other New York districts are world famous: Wall Street (finance), Madison Avenue (advertising), the garment district (center of the nation's clothing industry), Central Park (arguably the greatest urban park in the world), Fifth Avenue (for fashionable shopping and living), Greenwich Village (a longtime bohemian, student, and counterculture enclave), and Broadway (center of the most vibrant theater district in the world). Sixth, New York is also a key center of the arts, music, and publishing.

At street level New York abounds with crowds, traffic, musicians, and vendors—multiple sights and sounds that bombard the senses. Indeed, the first experience of New York City is one many carry with them all their lives. On another level the city is deceptive. Its very size tricks us into thinking things are other than they are—something that the Urban Living box below reveals about that grandest of illusion makers, Radio City Music Hall.

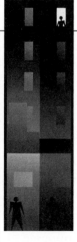

URBAN LIVING

All New York's a Stage

I'll tell you an old joke that will sum up Radio City Music Hall for you. It seems a man and his wife went to the Music Hall one Sunday afternoon, arriving toward the end of the film. When it ended, the house lights came up for a few minutes before the stage show and the man rose, murmuring to his wife: "I'm going to the men's room."

He located an exit on his floor—orchestra, loge, mezzanine, balcony or second balcony—but he couldn't find a men's room on it. He descended a staircase and looked on the next floor and couldn't find a men's room and descended another staircase. He walked along corridors and pushed open doors, he went along dark

passages and up and down steps, getting more and more lost and more and more frantic. Just as his need became intolerably urgent, he pushed open a heavy door and found himself on a small street lined with houses, trees and shrubs. There was no one in sight and the man relieved himself in the bushes.

All this had taken time, and it took him additional time to work his way back up to his own floor and locate his own aisle and section. By the time he finally reached his seat, the stage show had ended and the movie had begun again. The man slid into his seat whispering to his wife: "How was the stage show?" To which his wife replied: "You ought to know. You were in it."

Source: Helene Hanff, *Apple of My Eye* (New York: Doubleday, 1978), p. 129.

One cannot escape, however, the great contradictions, contrasts, and inconsistencies of New York life. The city is home to the richest and poorest of North Americans. Some of the worst social problems stand, literally, in the shadow of the proudest cultural achievements. Inevitably, perhaps, New York is the most loved and most hated city in the United States. Say outsiders, "A nice place to visit, but . . . I wouldn't want to live there." Some New Yorkers even boast about how awful it is—but most probably would never live anywhere else. In short, if something is to be found at all, it is to be found in New York. It is a world city par excellence. And, since September 11, Americans elsewhere have expressed a special bond with New York as the symbol of America united and defiant against terrorism.

New York, always at the center of U.S. life, has a varied history. Since its changes serve to illustrate the themes of North American urban history generally, we shall look briefly at its development during each of the four phases discussed in this chapter.

The Colonial Era

New York was the earliest of the five major colonial settlements. By 1624, a small Dutch settlement, based primarily on the fur trade, was permanently in place on the southern tip of Manhattan Island. New Amsterdam, the center of the Dutch New Netherlands, prospered in the decades that followed: Houses were built and farmland was cultivated. A row of logs was put in place for protection along the northern edge of the settlement, which later became known as Wall Street. In 1638, a ferry service to Breukelen (later Brooklyn) began and the first settlers reached Staten Island.

In 1653 a charter granted by Holland allowed the town to organize a local government featuring a mayor and a city council. When the first survey was completed in 1656, the "city" had about 1,000 people living in 120 houses on 17 irregularly placed streets. Within a few years, some of the streets were stone-covered and a greater measure of security was provided by a town-watch (the earliest direct ancestor of New York's police force). Outside of town to the north were farms the Dutch called "boweries." This area, the point at which the irregular streets end (at about Houston Street today), was long known as "The Bowery." A farming village called Haarlem was established much farther up the island in 1658, at the end of a long dirt road known as "Broadway."

The first Jews arrived in the 1650s, establishing a long tradition that was to influence the city's history, and the first Quakers settled in the city in 1657. An English fleet anchored in 1664 and gained control of the town, renaming the settlement New York in honor of Charles II's brother, James, the Duke of York. The English commander continued a policy of religious freedom for all groups, reaffirming the tradition of religious tolerance initiated by the Dutch. Millions in later years would be drawn to this city where it was possible to worship and to express oneself as one chose.

In 1680, New York City began its climb to economic preeminence when it gained a monopoly on the sifting of flour for export. Docks multiplied, trade prospered, and support businesses of all sorts became established. The population grew steadily; from 4,000 in 1703, New York grew to 7,000 in 1723, and passed the 10,000 mark in 1737. The first newspaper appeared in 1725; a stagecoach link to Philadelphia started in 1730; and the New York Public Library opened in 1731.

As this growth occurred, New York, like the other colonies, was beginning to resent ever more sharply the British impositions on trade. In 1765 the English government instituted the Stamp Act, placing a levy on all transactions. The colonists bitterly opposed it. Swayed, Parliament repealed the act in 1766, causing a New York group dubbed the "Sons of Liberty" to build a triumphant "Liberty Pole" in the city. The British took strong offense, an altercation followed, and some of the Sons of Liberty were killed. This was the first blood of the American Revolution.

When the revolution began, the British occupied New York for seven years. The war drove many New Yorkers temporarily out of the city, reducing its population by several thousand from a peak of 21,500. However, with the end of the war, the city leapt once more to life. George Washington was inaugurated as the first president of the United States in Federal Hall at the corner of Wall and Nassau Streets and, for a year thereafter (1790), New York served as the U.S. capital.

Growth and Expansion

By 1800 the city's population surpassed 60,000. The growth of New York during this second period continued to be spectacular. The population exceeded 96,000 by 1810 and 202,000 by 1830. Yet this was only a hint of things to come. Earlier, in 1792, a group of traders had met in the Wall Street area and planned what was to become the New York Stock Exchange. In 1807 the city approved its famous grid plan for street development. In 1825 the Erie Canal was completed, linking the Hudson with the Great Lakes and giving New York a long-sought trade advantage over its East Coast urban competitors. With direct access to the North American heartland, in the next few decades the city became the economic center of the United States.

In 1838 overseas steamship service began, establishing a connection with Europe that truly opened immigration. In 1840, for example, more than 50,000 people arrived in New York harbor from abroad, and most settled in the city. In 1846, the first telegraph line between New York and Philadelphia began operation. In 1848, a five-story factory (also a sign of things to come) opened its doors. Urban transportation improved with the introduction of the rail-mounted horsecar in 1850. This made "suburbanization" of the upper island more feasible by establishing a fare—a nickel—that was within financial reach of most New Yorkers. In 1853, New York hosted the nation's first "expo," symbolic of the grand optimism that by now was part of the city's character. In 1858, the plan for one of the greatest of urban landmarks—Central Park—was approved (though the park itself

was not substantially completed until after the Civil War). In 1860, although still officially consisting of only Manhattan Island, the city boasted a population of 814,000, with another 250,000 nearby in Brooklyn, Staten Island, and Jersey City.

The Great Metropolis Emerges

After the Civil War, which temporarily slowed its growth, New York matured as a great metropolis. An unprecedented surge in the city's population occurred between 1870 and 1930, dwarfing all previous gains. Table 3–6 shows that New York City as a whole quintupled its population in the six decades after 1870. However, until January 1898, the five boroughs remained legally separate municipalities.

The period between 1870 and 1920 was an era of extensive foreign immigration to the United States, and New York was the major port of disembarkation for the entire country. Some nationalities arrived in huge numbers. For example, Chinatown began to take form in 1884; Italian immigration intensified after 1885; and Jews began to make their way through the Ellis Island immigration facility to the Lower East Side in large numbers after 1890. Many of these new urbanites went directly to work in industries that produced items such as garments and shoes.

TABLE 3–6   Population of New York City, by Borough, 1870–2000 (in thousands)

	1870	1900	1930	1960	2000
New York City	1,476	3,437	6,929	7,782	8,008
Borough					
Manhattan	942	1,850	1,867	1,695	1,537
Bronx	37	201	1,265	1,425	1,333
Brooklyn	419	1,167	2,560	2,627	2,465
Queens	45	153	1,079	1,810	2,229
Staten Island	33	67	158	222	444

Note: The five boroughs were not officially incorporated as New York City until 1898.

Source: U. S. Census Bureau.

As amazing as it sounds, by 1890 four out of five people living in the New York area were either born abroad or had foreign-born parents (Glaab and Brown 1967). New York, like other American metropolises of the era, began to take on a characteristic "ethnic mosaic" pattern of settlement, as described by social reformer Jacob Riis in the Cityscape box below. Although citywide residential density in 1890 was about 60 people to an acre, in immigrant areas densities reached alarming levels—as much as seven times greater. The frightful concentration continued to increase to almost 750 persons per acre—about 12 times the city average—in 1898 (Glaab and Brown 1967). Today, the density of central Manhattan has fallen to about 100 persons per acre.

Sometimes, when immigrants mixed, the results were explosive. One area of midtown, from about West 15th Street to West 50th Street along Eighth, Ninth, and Tenth Avenues, was home to blacks and whites of different ethnic groups. During the work week trouble was minimal, but on weekends in the summer, when much drinking and carousing occurred, violent fighting often broke out between groups. So intense were the confrontations that police nicknamed the area "Hell's Kitchen."

Governing this incredible and growing mass of people was difficult, at best. City Hall became increasingly corrupt as interest groups vied with one another for contracts, favors, and patronage. The greatest symbol of corruption in New York's history was that of political boss William "Boss" Tweed. In 1870, by means of $1 million in bribes to the New York State legislature and other groups, Tweed and his gang were able to gain complete political control over the city. It is estimated that they stole nearly $200 million in

CITYSCAPE

The Crazy-Quilt Pattern of New York, 1890

A map of [New York], colored to designate nationalities, would show more stripes than the skin of a zebra, and more colors than any rainbow. . . . [G]reen for the Irish prevailing in the West Side tenement districts, and blue for the Germans on the East Side. . . . [I]ntermingled . . . would be an odd variety of tints that would give the whole the appearance of an extraordinary crazy-quilt. From down in the Sixth Ward . . . the red of the Italian would be seen forcing its way northward along the line of Mulberry Street to the quarter of the French purple on Bleecker Street and South Fifth Avenue. . . . On the West Side, the red would be seen overrunning the old Africa of Thompson Street pushing the black of the negro rapidly uptown.

. . . [T]he Russian and Polish Jew, having overrun the district between Rivington and Division Streets, east of the Bowery, to the point of suffocation, is filling the tenements of the old Seventh Ward to the river front. . . . Between the dull gray of the Jew, his favorite color, and the Italian red, would be seen squeezed in on the map a sharp streak of yellow, marking the narrow boundaries of Chinatown. . . . Dots and dashes of color here and there would show . . . the Finnish sailors . . . the Greek pedlars . . . and the Swiss. . . . And so on to the end of the long register, all toiling together in the galling fetters of the tenement.

Source: Jacob Riis, *How the Other Half Lives* (New York: Hill and Wang, 1957), pp. 18–20. Originally published in 1890.

Until suburban malls became dominant in the 1960s, cities were the shopping meccas for almost everyone. By car, bus, and train, shoppers from outlying towns came to the city to shop, for that was where the best and biggest stores, with the widest selections, were. In this 1950s photo, a crowd lines up to shop on the ground floor of Macy's New York City department store.

funds from the city treasury and garnered even more from kickbacks and payoffs. Finally exposed by the *New York Times* in 1871, Tweed was arrested and brought to trial. So confident was he that he would be acquitted that he haughtily said, in response to an allegation about his misappropriation of funds, "What are ya gonna do about it?" His confidence was misplaced. He went to jail in 1872. Nevertheless, extensive graft in city government continued to plague the city until well into this century.

Certain physical changes linked to technology contributed to the growth of the city during this period as well. In 1881, the Brooklyn Bridge opened, and remains, along with the Golden Gate Bridge in San Francisco, one of the world's most beautiful. It was followed in

1903 by the Williamsburg Bridge and in 1904 by the first tunnel under the Hudson River connecting the city to the New Jersey shore. In 1906, the Pennsylvania Railroad also tunneled under the Hudson, establishing major rail transport in the heart of Manhattan at Penn Station. Subways soon followed. People now could live far from midtown and still get there cheaply and quickly.

At the lower end of Manhattan, the dazzling New York skyline began to take shape. Today, it is difficult to imagine New York without a forest of skyscrapers. Yet, before 1890, Manhattan below Central Park was completely covered by structures of less than five stories. The first steel structure in New York appeared in 1889 and reached a "towering"

11 stories. From this point, New York grew upward as if the clouds had become great magnets. The number of buildings with 20 or more floors increased from 61 in 1913 to 188 in 1929. Indeed, half of all such buildings in the country were in New York (Armstrong 1972).

Before the Depression stalled construction of office buildings, New York witnessed the completion of three famous architectural innovations that survive to the present day. The Chrysler Building, opened in 1930, is a marvelous 77-story example of Art Deco architecture—topped with six stories of magnificent stainless-steel arches. The following year marked the opening of the Empire State Building, which, at 102 floors, has symbolized New York ever since. Rockefeller Center was begun in the same year. It was designed to include "everything" in one place, as urban critic Paul Goldberger observes:

> . . . skyscrapers, plazas, movement, detail, views, stores, cafes. It is all of a piece, yet it is able to appear possessed of infinite variety at the same time. . . . It was conceived as a place in which monumental architecture would spur both business and culture to new heights, and it has come remarkably close to fulfilling that somewhat naive goal. It is surely the parent of every large scale urban complex every American downtown has built since—from Atlanta's Peachtree Center to Hartford's Constitution Center to San Francisco's Embarcadero Center—and it is no insult to say that Rockefeller Center still remains far and away the finest such development ever built (1989:168–69).

New York Today

> New York? It'll be a great place if they ever finish it.
>
> Short-story writer O. Henry

By the 1950s New York had grown from being a metropolis to being the center of that vast urban region that Jean Gottmann called a megalopolis. The 2000 census places the city at the heart of a vast metropolitan statistical area covering some 4,000 square miles with more than 21 million people. To illustrate the point another way, nearly one American in fourteen lives in the New York MSA.

From another perspective, however, this incredible region is a product of the decentralization that has affected so many cities in contemporary America. Bridges, highways, tunnels, cars, costs, and congestion—all led to a rapid move away from the city itself between 1970 and 1980, as New York City lost over 860,000 people (a loss greater than the entire central city population of San Francisco!). However, between 1980 and 1990, New York gained 251,000 inhabitants, and by 2000, the city had grown by another 685,000, due primarily to an influx of immigrants.

Economic Problems

By the late 1990s the nation as a whole had recovered all the jobs lost in the recession of the late 1980s and early 1990s, but the New York region regained only about a third of the 770,000 jobs it lost. The numbers reflected deep structural problems in this metropolitan region, especially in the concentration of the company headquarters of 46 of the nation's top 500 corporations. Many large businesses continue to shrink as corporate America merges, downsizes, and lays off workers. The merger of Chase Manhattan and Chemical Bank, for example, eliminated about 12,000 jobs (Johnson and Lueck 1996).

Then the destruction of the World Trade Center and its immediate surroundings caused a severe blow both to the corporate and neighborhood economies of lower Manhattan. The loss of or severe damage to 20 million square feet of office space, as well as the loss of tens of thousands of jobs, also directly affected 14,000 small businesses because there was less foot traffic and there were far fewer customers (Ploeger 2002).

Beyond the Devastation

On that infamous day of September 11, 2001, New York City suffered the worst tragedy in its history. In addition to the heartbreaking loss of so many innocent lives were the severe economic losses. These losses included billions of dollars of damaged or destroyed private capital and public infrastructure; thousands of dislocated workers; millions of dollars of lost sales due to business interruption; and significant disruption to the financial services industry that makes New York the capital of the global securities and banking markets.

Sudden unemployment and business losses fell not just on the many small businesses dependent on customers who worked at or visited the World Trade Center, but also on those dependent on tourism—including hotels and restaurants, theaters, the taxi industry, airlines, and airport-related industries. A study by the Center for an Urban Future found that LaGuardia and Kennedy Airports suffered larger economic losses than most other major hub airports in the country. Those losses caused the elimination of 16.5 percent of all airport-related jobs—10,000 jobs. That was by far the largest percentage loss of any industry in the city, including the securities industry, which lost 9 percent of its jobs (Kennedy 2002).

Through federal and state government aid, New York City slowly rebounded. The rebuilding of Ground Zero is yet to be completed, but hopes are high. Once it is completely rebuilt, lower Manhattan will no doubt thrive again as well. In the near future that locale will combine commercial buildings with cultural, performing arts, and transportation centers all linked to a memorial park and pedestrian walkway. Its composition will, advocates say, "reassert New York's cosmopolitan identity" and "re-establish New York's skyline as the most thrilling in the world" (Muschamp 2002).

Major cities like New York are constantly changing. Just as immigration repeatedly remade the city throughout its history, so too have its economic fortunes rebounded despite the "gloom and doom" experts who sounded the city's death knell. New York and the other cities survived, and—despite recessions in the late 1980s, early 1990s, and early 2000s—they have worked their way back to financial solvency. Partially back, at least. And the city is back for many of the same reasons that Boston, Baltimore, and other cities are coming back: The postindustrial economy is remaking New York. New positions for highly trained professional workers, particularly in the information-processing and finance sectors, are available, along with lower-paying jobs in the service sectors of food, delivery, and tourism. Parts of the city, such as midtown, thrive as white-collar service centers where business professionals can remain in close contact with one another, have lunch, and socialize after work at a wide variety of places catering to their tastes. As in other cities, the proportion of people who work in postindustrial jobs is small—perhaps on the order of 10 percent. Many people are working in the service sector in restaurants, hotels, and retail stores, or as public employees (police, fire, transit, sanitation, social services). Although the city's manufacturing sector has declined somewhat, its 500,000 jobs represent 15 percent of the city's labor force, and the city in 2005 initiated a comprehensive industrial policy that involves designing new business zones and creating new incentives to encourage long-term investment in manufacturing, warehousing, and other industrial businesses throughout the five boroughs (Lyne 2005:180).

In 2004, tourism soared to a record-breaking 39.6 million, generating about $23 billion in business activity. Air passenger arrivals; hotel occupancy; attendance at Broadway shows; ticket sales at tourist attractions like the Empire State Building, Ellis Island, and the Statue of Liberty; and retail sales all improved, partly encouraged by the city's plummeting crime rate (City of New York 2005). Its 2004 total crime index for violent and property crimes put New York among the lowest for U.S. cities with 100,000 or more, and the safest city among those with 1 million or more inhabitants (Federal Bureau of Investigation 2005). Retail sales went up, helped in part by the opening of numerous bank branches and chain stores. In fact, in mid-2002 a strong demand for store space bolstered the city's economy (Holusha 2002). More feature films and television series are now shot in the city than at any time since the 1950s, and New York hosts the second largest concentration of motion picture activity.

Throughout the city one can find clubs, coffee bars, chic shops, and trendy restaurants springing up, and attendance at concerts, museums, theaters, sports contests, and special events has risen as well. Rental housing is scarce and expensive, especially in Manhattan, where a month's rent for a one-bedroom apartment averaged $2,210 in 2004 (Boss-Bicak 2004:24).

Upgrading the City

Construction is omnipresent. In the 1970s, the twin towers of the World Trade Center in lower Manhattan boosted both the image and the economy of the city. In the 1980s, it was the construction of Battery Park City, a $1.5 billion, 92-acre commercial and residential complex that is home to the New York Mercantile Exchange, the Commodity Exchange, and American Express. There are also 2,000 apartments in eight buildings, a Ritz-Carlton and an Embassy Suites hotel, four ferry slips, and a 15-screen multiplex theater (Dunlap 1999). The site also includes a museum, parks, plazas, playgrounds, public arts, and schools. In 2004, Time Warner moved into its new world headquarters, one of the largest projects ever built in New York City, the Time Warner Center at Columbus Circle. Besides its office space the complex, with its two towers, includes one of the largest malls in the city (four floors of retail space), a screening theater, five restaurants, and a café with a marvelous view of Central Park.

At 125th Street in Harlem, the neighborhood's first supermarket, the New Harlem USA shopping center and cinema multiplex, and the renovation of the Apollo Theater

As the first office tower of several to be rebuilt on the World Trade Center site, the Freedom Tower will soar to 1,776 feet in the sky and serve as an inspirational and enduring beacon in the New York City skyline. The tower's footprint, measuring 200 feet by 200 feet, is the same size as the footprints of the original Twin Towers that will be left intact in the adjoining memorial park.

improved the physical environment and quality of life (Pristin 1999). In lower Harlem, the completion of 3,500 new apartments in rehabilitated buildings revitalized commercial activity along 116th Street west of Malcolm X Boulevard. East New York, a once-devastated area in Brooklyn dubbed the "murder capital of New York City," was transformed into a livable area of new multifamily homes and rental housing, with plans for 2,300 more new homes around a new mall (Hevesi 2001).

Perhaps, though, the most dramatic symbol of New York's revival is construction in the South Bronx. Its image as a lawless, burned-out, drug-infested area whose rampant crime rate inspired the movie *Fort Apache, the Bronx* is no longer true, after what officials call the nation's largest urban rebuilding effort. With more than $1 billion in public dollars trained on the South Bronx since 1986, 19,000 apartments were refurbished and more than 4,500 new houses built for working-class home buyers. More than 50 abandoned buildings that once stood like rotten teeth along major arteries like the Cross Bronx and Major Deegan expressways were reclaimed as midrise apartment houses.

Other signs of an urban renaissance are found everywhere. They range in scale from massive residential enclaves like Queens West and Riverside South, both loosely modeled after Battery Park City, to the Starbucks-style cafes that have sprouted up all over. The transformation of 42nd Street, once the center of sex and sleaze, into a family entertainment center with Disney as the linchpin is simply amazing, and the renovation of Grand Central Terminal with upscale shopping malls is another positive sign.

Creation or restoration of parks offers another example of the improvement in the quality of life in New York. At Pier 25 in TriBeCa, for example, there is now a recreation area with miniature golf, volleyball, and a children's playground. Similar restorations at Pier 45 at Christopher Street and Pier 64 in Chelsea have made these areas available for recreation as well. Now these parks have been combined into Hudson River Park, 550 acres stretching from Battery Park City to 59th Street, with esplanades, waterfront activities, biking and rollerblading paths, dog runs, athletic facilities, gardens, and sculptures. The success of the 1992 transformation of Bryant Park—once an unsafe, sequestered area overrun by drug dealers—into one of New York's busiest public spaces, where thousands go day and night for lunch, concerts, outdoor movies, or simply to mingle surprised even city planners. Directly behind the New York Public Library, it has become a hot spot for young adults, serving—in an odd manifestation of a small-town tradition—as Manhattan's town square.

On another front, over 130 Business Improvement Districts, or BIDs, exist in virtually every section of the city, from Harlem to Brighton Beach. More than 1,200 have been created in cities across North America in the last two decades, but their greatest impact has been in New York (in Times Square, for instance), where their numbers, size, and financial clout dwarf those of BIDs elsewhere. BIDs are self-taxing districts set up to clean, patrol, and upgrade their neighborhoods, providing services that were once the sole responsibility of city government. Cities, faced with budget problems, have welcomed the privatizing of municipal services. Once a majority of owners in a designated area agree, they work out a plan for services, which must be approved by the City Council. The city then collects an annual assessment (above the property taxes) from all property owners and turns the money over to the district. The resulting services and improvements—new sidewalks, signs, street lights, planters, wastebaskets, flags and banners, street sweepers, and unarmed uniformed security patrols—have reduced crime, cleaned up streets, and restored a sense of pride among merchants and the public (Mitchell 2001).

Changing Population

Since the end of World War II, over 3 million whites have left the central-city area, replaced by minority migrants and immigrants. In 1950 the population of the five boroughs was 87 percent white, 9 percent black, and 3 percent Hispanic. By 2000 the city's profile had shifted to 34 percent non-Hispanic white, 28 percent black, 27 percent Hispanic, and 11 percent Asian (U.S. Census Bureau 2002b).

Although many minorities work in the information-processing and service sectors, unemployment and poverty are high within the city's African American and Hispanic American communities. The Community Service Society of New York reported that about 21 percent of New York City residents lived in poverty in 2003. Poverty was highest among Hispanic residents at 29 percent compared to 26 percents for blacks; 31 percent of New

York's children were poor (almost double the national rate), as were 19 percent of the city's elderly. All of these rates were above the national average (Community Service Society 2004).

In the midst of the difficulties, some continue to try to improve their lives, placing their faith in an improving neighborhood. Many new-style New York homeowners of lower-income status, tired of their urban lifestyle but not of the city—investing their life savings and adding faith, determination, and hard work—have helped revitalize parts of run-down neighborhoods that only a few years ago seemed hopelessly lost. Whether moving into new housing improved by others or employing "sweat equity" to upgrade a run-down dwelling, a surprising number of lower-income New Yorkers have been successful in these efforts. Their combined efforts are giving a much-needed facelift to some of the city's worst neighborhoods.

And so New York goes on, with its successes and failures, its ability to symbolize simultaneously all that is great and tragic about all cities. To many, New York is the quintessential city. If New York fails, in some sense cities everywhere fail, but if it succeeds, it offers hope for all.

❖ ▬▬▬▬▬ ❖ ▬▬▬▬▬ ❖

SUMMARY

The development of North American cities has been, in its own way, as dynamic and varied as that of European cities. Neither Canada nor the United States began as an urban nation; in fact, that idea would have been anathema to many of either country's founders. Nevertheless, in three and a half centuries, that is what both have become.

The process of urbanization began just as European feudalism was breathing its last. Begun as places of religious and political freedom, the new colonies rapidly established themselves as major trading centers. By 1700, coastal villages were becoming bustling towns. By the late eighteenth century, these small cities began to develop into major urban

areas. They traded up and down the coast and with Europe and became rich by establishing links with the vast and rich heartland of the country. Inland cities appeared. By the middle of the nineteenth century, industrialization was transforming the northern cities of the United States and, to some degree, their Canadian and newer midwestern counterparts, into manufacturing centers. The South, still operating on the "small city" pattern associated with agriculture, fell behind. With victory for the North, the Civil War effectively ended the small- versus large-city "debate" in the United States.

After 1870, North American cities, particularly in the North, the Midwest, and Lower Canada, exploded into metropolises of millions. Trade and industry were the driving wheels behind this development. More and more jobs generated more and more wealth. Drawn to this opportunity, millions came from abroad, resulting in the ethnic–racial–religious mosaic that characterizes so many North American cities. With this influx came great problems, particularly in the United States. Quality of life began to deteriorate, and poverty and exploitation became rampant. New technological advances enabled many to escape to streetcar suburbs. Consequently, cities began to spread over the countryside. Losing revenue because of this exodus, and greatly hampered by the Depression, cities began to depend on federal assistance.

After World War II, decentralization accelerated. People and businesses departed the central cities, leaving the innermost areas increasingly populated by the poor and minorities (unable to escape because of poverty or prejudice) and by service-oriented or professional businesses. Huge metropolitan regions became more the norm, replacing earlier central-city cores.

In the older Snowbelt cities of the United States, decentralization had particularly disastrous results. When the cities lost people and businesses, billions in tax and sales revenues and hundreds of thousands of jobs were lost as well. Many cities faced a continual threat of bankruptcy. The South and West, however, experienced an urban boom. Sunbelt cities were the direct beneficiaries of northern cities' problems such as their old industrial systems, poor inner-city transportation for products, and deteriorating services. The Sunbelt cities built new plants, surrounded by efficient superhighways; they provided good or brand-new service systems; and they offered lower costs—particularly for energy and labor. Some Sunbelt cities were able to expand their physical boundaries—for example, in Texas, one of the states with greatest urban expansion, suburbs were annexed almost as fast as they appeared, thus keeping the tax and business base within the city jurisdiction.

In a contemporary trend that may turn out to be the most important of all, North American cities are rapidly developing a postindustrial economy based on high technology, white-collar jobs, and services. As a result, in recent years cities have been rebuilding the deteriorating office and housing stock left from earlier decades and improving many other amenities that define the quality of urban life. Older cities once in the throes of economic disaster are rebounding, although problems clearly remain, particularly with the poorer residents. Serving as white-collar service centers, these cities have attracted young, relatively affluent professionals whose presence has had great impact. Another trend is the formation of edge cities on the fringes of established metropolitan areas.

The evidence suggests that all three trends—decentralization, the move to the Sunbelt, and the growth of a postindustrial economy—will continue in force in the new century. As a result, northern cities such as New York will continue to adapt to a changing economic structure and a new population. Meanwhile, the Sunbelt picture is not as rosy as it once was. The population boom, in many instances, has been too much to cope with, crime rates are high, and racial tensions are on the rise as Hispanics move up from Mexico and Latin America and African Americans move back to the South. Furthermore, even in cities where postindustrialization is in full sway, there is no indication that the new-found wealth of the few who are participating in this lifestyle will spread to the urban population as a whole. On the contrary, it appears that the gap between the urban rich and poor is widening, not narrowing.

CONCLUSION

It seems evident that in the three centuries since urbanization took hold in the New World, North Americans have not built Cotton Mather's hoped-for "Heavenly City." Nevertheless, there are signs that cities are being revitalized, if only partially, as we move further into the twenty-first century. Whether this rebuilding process will continue or whether the North American version of the urban experiment will come, as it did in the late 1960s and early 1970s, to resemble Edward Banfield's "Unheavenly City" more than likely will depend on the decisions made by the people living in these cities in the next several years. If we continue to see the city as something to "use," but not something to be collectively concerned about, the outlook probably is not very bright. If, on the other hand, we see the city as a human creation and thus subject to understanding and human control, then we might be justified in being more optimistic about the outcome.

Chapters 2 and 3 have provided an overview of the long path that cities have followed from their origins thousands of years ago until a few decades ago. The new patterns of urban and suburban development are significantly different and so widespread that they clearly will be important factors for the foreseeable future. In the next chapter we will examine these newest components of urban life.

KEY TERMS

Consolidated metropolitan statistical area (CMSA)
Decentralization
Elastic cities
Globalization
Industrial parks
Megalopolis
Metropolitan statistical area (MSA)
Sunbelt expansion
Urban explosion
Urban implosion

CHAPTER 4

CITIES AND SUBURBS OF THE TWENTY-FIRST CENTURY

❖ ──────── ❖ ──────── ❖

We can't always predict the future, but we do invent it. Today's decisions affect tomorrow's realities, just as we are living out the decisions made by preceding generations. For example, the change in public preference from urban to suburban living owes much to federal legislation in the late 1940s and 1950s that provided low-cost builder and buyer loans, as well as to a massive highway-building program that made it easier to live away from city jobs and activities. That growth in middle-class suburban housing, and the subsequent exodus of many businesses to suburban campuses or shopping malls, eroded the cities' economic vitality and tax base, which, in turn, worsened the quality of urban schools and the quality of life for many city dwellers who remained. The suburban lifestyles that most North Americans favor today, as well as the problems besetting many U.S. cities, are the result of social forces unleashed two generations ago. So too will the decisions of recent decades affect urban and suburban lifestyles for decades to come.

Four patterns in particular—sprawl, edge cities, gated communities, and common-interest developments—have grown so fast and had such a strong effect on urban areas that we can discuss both their current influence on the quality of life as well as their importance for the foreseeable future.

URBAN AND SUBURBAN SPRAWL

Stretching across North America—from the West Coast to the East Coast, from Toronto to Miami, from Vancouver to Tucson—are large metropolitan areas fused into a series of megalopolises. Gobbling up the land are strip malls and large suburban tracts of cookie-cutter housing of such striking similarity that they are creating an unvarying sameness everywhere, blurring traditional regional differences. Within this vast homogeneous panorama, one could be almost anywhere on the continent and find few visual clues as to locale.

What Is Sprawl?

Sprawl is the term used to describe spread-out or low-density development beyond the edge of services and employment. It separates where people live from where they work, shop, and pursue leisure or an education, thereby requiring them to use cars to move between these zones. This type of development results from decades of unplanned, rapid growth and poor land-use management. *Sprawl* thus identifies the cumulative effects of development that is automobile-dependent, inefficient, and wasteful of natural resources.

As people move farther from core cities and into outlying regions, so do all the trappings of urban life: stores, offices, factories, hospitals, crime, congestion, and pollution. Developments claim more and more open land as the population increases and disperses. One town looks like another, stores on the highways erect signs to shout out their wares to the fast-moving traffic going by, and every activity requires a separate trip by car (see the Critical Thinking box on page 94).

According to the Regional Plan Association—a nonprofit organization dedicated to improving the quality of life in the New York metropolitan region—if the office space needed for each 5 million increase in population were built only in suburban office parks it would cut a swath a half-mile wide and 54 miles long. However, in a large city with skyscrapers, 200 acres would fulfill the same need. The reason is that each million square feet of suburban office space requires, on average, 80 acres (25 of those acres for parking lots) as compared with 1 acre in a large city, half of which is for an office plaza. In smaller cities, the same 1 million square feet would take up about 6 acres, with the construction of 25-story buildings with landscaping and parking lots (Caldwell 1973:45–56).

Two striking examples of suburban sprawl-development patterns consuming far more land than urban development patterns are in Pennsylvania and Arizona. Since 1950, Pennsylvania has lost more than 4 million acres of farmland to sprawl—an area larger

CRITICAL THINKING

Something Is Wrong

Americans *sense that something is wrong* with the places where we live and work and go about our daily business. We hear this unhappiness expressed in phrases like "no sense of place" and "the loss of community." We drive up and down the gruesome, tragic suburban boulevards of commerce, and we're overwhelmed at the fantastic, awesome, stupefying ugliness of absolutely everything in sight—the fry pits, the big-box stores, the office units, the lube joints, the carpet warehouses, the parking lagoons, the jive plastic townhouse clusters, the uproar of signs, the highway itself clogged with cars— as though the whole thing had been designed by some diabolical force bent on making human beings miserable. And naturally, this experience can make us feel glum about the nature and future of our civilization.

When we drive around and look at all this cartoon architecture and other junk that we've smeared all over the landscape, we register it as ugliness. This ugliness is the surface expression of deeper problems—problems that relate to the issue of our national character. The highway strip is not just a sequence of eyesores. The pattern it represents is also economically catastrophic, an environmental calamity, socially devastating, and spiritually degrading.

. . . We reject the past and the future, and this repudiation is manifest in our graceless constructions. Our residential, commercial, and civic buildings are constructed with the fully conscious expectation that they will disintegrate in a few decades. This condition even has a name: "design life." Strip malls and elementary schools have short design lives. They are expected to fall apart in less than fifty years. Since these things are not expected to speak to any era but our own, we seem unwilling to put money or effort into their embellishment. Nor do we care about traditional solutions to the problems of weather and light, because we have technology to mitigate these problems— namely, central heating and electricity. Thus in many new office buildings the windows don't open. In especially bad buildings, like the average Wal-Mart, windows are dispensed with nearly altogether. This process of disconnection from the past and the future, and from the organic patterns of weather and light, done for the sake of expedience, ends up diminishing us spiritually, impoverishing us socially, and degrading the aggregate set of cultural patterns that we call civilization.

Source: James Howard Kunstler, "Home from Nowhere," *The Atlantic Monthly* 278 (September 1996), 43–66. Reprinted by permission of the author.

---

than Connecticut and Rhode Island combined. The city of Phoenix now covers some 600 square miles, an area larger than the state of Delaware. In the next 50 years, sprawl is expected to consume more than 3.5 million acres of California's Great Central Valley, the nation's prime greengrocer (Purdum 1999). Elsewhere, trends are similar. Between 1970 and 1990, metro New York's population grew

only 5 percent but consumed 61 percent more land, while metro Chicago's population grew by just 4 percent but consumed 46 percent more land.

Opponents cite figures for the loss of rural land that vary from about 400,000 to 1.4 million acres a year. Advocates counter that there is no shortage of empty land in the United States, that 95 percent of the land is undeveloped, and that the rate of land development is an infinitesimal .07 percent a year. Although that is a low figure, it does mean that during the lifetime of a child born today, the developed area of the nation would double. Which side's figures are accurate? Actually, they both are. The problem is that this development is concentrated in a relatively few areas, close to the big cities (Pedersen, Smith, and Adler 1999:24).

Why Do We Have Sprawl?

Sprawl is like that cartoon snowball rolling down the hill, growing in size and momentum, becoming practically unstoppable. In the past half-century, government policies on taxation, transportation, and housing—nurtured by society's embrace of *laissez faire* development—subsidized virtually unlimited low-density development. And the more this development occurred, the more people clamored for it.

A house in the suburbs became, for many, the personification of the ideal lifestyle. Massive road-building projects and community planning designed around the car encouraged people to abandon the cities for the greener pastures of suburbia. As these nonmetropolitan areas grew in population, a new phenomenon—the shopping center—came into existence, with large department stores from the city serving as anchors for the variety of retail enterprises along the indoor corridors. Office and industrial parks followed, either lured by tax incentives, induced by management preferences, or prompted by the relocation of competitors. Whatever the reason, the snowball effect generated more and more growth farther and farther away from cities into outlying regions. As a result, much of the natural landscape around the largest cities in Canada and the United States was transformed.

Where Does Sprawl Occur?

Sprawl occurs everywhere. It is most obvious and grows most spectacularly in the rapid growth areas of the South and West. For instance, on the periphery of Denver, farmland is yielding to sprawl at a rate of 90,000 acres per year. Significantly, though, land development is no longer proportional to population growth. Studies show that a 1 percent increase in population results in 10 to 20 percent growth in land consumption (Florian 1999:24). West Palm Beach, Florida, for example, experienced a 15 percent population increase between 1990 and 1996 but a 25 percent decrease in population density during the same period.

Yet sprawl doesn't occur only because of population growth. Cincinnati, which lost 15 percent of its population between 1970 and 1980, then another 10 percent between 1980 and 2000, nonetheless increased its land area from 335 square miles in 1970 to 573 square miles. Metro Cleveland's population declined by 11 percent between 1970 and 1990, but it still consumed 33 percent more land. Also, between 1990 and 1996, Akron, Ohio, experienced a 37 percent decrease in population but a 65 percent increase in developed land area use (Florian 1999:25).

An important study, *The Dark Side of the American Dream* (1998), conducted by the Sierra Club, an environmentalist group, identified the 30 most sprawl-threatened cities (see Table 4–1). Some cities—such as Phoenix, Spokane, Boise, and many California cities—are not in this group because they evolved as sprawled cities from the beginning and are thus not sprawl threatened. However, most of these qualify for a "dishonorable mention" because of their continuing patterns of sprawl.

The Problems of Sprawl

Most people don't realize all the negative aspects of sprawl. To them it is the means of owning a house on a large lot and enjoying the convenience of one-stop mega-mall shopping. Yet these suburbanites pay a price in air pollution, traffic congestion, and visual blight. Longer commutes take time away from families, increase gasoline consumption as well as wear and tear on cars, cause traffic congestion, and increase instances of road rage. For example, the typical worker in Atlanta drives 37 miles round trip to work, while

This aerial view of Las Vegas shows the spread-city phenomenon occurring in the U.S. Sunbelt area. Like other Sunbelt cities in which climate and work opportunities attract many, its rapid growth strains the existing infrastructure and water supply and gobbles up the land, as its sprawling development pattern increases dependence on the automobile.

those in Dallas drive 30 miles, and in Los Angeles the daily drive is 21 miles (Florian 1999:25). When people complain that it takes an hour and a half to go 30 miles, some suggest that the answer is more highways. But the building of more roads and the widening of others result in the cutting down of more trees, creating an ugly and desolate landscape devoid of vegetation and full of strip malls.

We pay a high social price for sprawl as well. By spreading residences, medical and commercial offices, and industries throughout a region on large tracts of land, we increase residents' dependence on automobile transportation. Everything and everyone is too spread out to make public transportation economically feasible. With insufficient coordination of work sites and highways, traffic congestion results. Nor can everyone get around by car: A lifestyle that requires a car discriminates against poor families, the elderly, the disabled, and the young. Suburban

teenagers, for instance, usually lack sufficient activities in their town but are unable to travel to locations where such diversions do exist. Suburban parents thus spend a large part of their time chauffeuring their children to stores, cinemas, juvenile activities, and other events.

Green space advocates, disparagingly called "tree-huggers" by developers and business interests, have long deplored the decades-old growth pattern that consumes large expanses of prime farmland and woodland. However, in recent years other individuals, groups, and organizations—realizing the costs and consequences of sprawl—have suggested that these costs may outweigh the benefits. Joining their ranks are low-income housing advocates, social service organizations, church leaders, and others concerned about urban decay and poverty (McMahon 1997). Those seeking to curb sprawl base their concerns around environmental damage, loss

TABLE 4–1   The Most Sprawl-Threatened U.S. Cities

Large Cities (Population: 1 million or more)		Medium Cities (Population: 500,000–1 million)
1. Atlanta, GA	11. Detroit, MI	1. Orlando, FL
2. St. Louis, MO	12. Baltimore, MD	2. Austin, TX
3. Washington, DC	13. Cleveland, OH	3. Las Vegas, NV
4. Cincinnati, OH	14. Tampa, FL	4. West Palm Beach, FL
5. Kansas City, MO	15. Dallas, TX	5. Akron, OH
6. Denver, CO	16. Hampton Roads, VA	
7. Seattle, WA	17. Pittsburgh, PA	
8. Minneapolis–St. Paul, MN	18. Miami, FL	
9. Fort Lauderdale, FL	19. San Antonio, TX	
10. Chicago, IL	20. Riverside–San Bernardino, CA	

Small Cities (Population: 200,000–500,000)	Dishonorable Mention
1. McAllen, TX	1. Los Angeles, CA
2. Raleigh, NC	2. San Diego, CA
3. Pensacola, FL	3. Phoenix, AZ
4. Daytona Beach, FL	
5. Little Rock, AR	

Source: From *The Dark Side of the American Dream,* © 1998 Sierra Club Books. Reprinted by permission.

of farmland and historic centers, financial costs, and transportation issues.

Environmental Damage.   As new structures arbitrarily emerge in scattered fashion across the countryside, they disrupt wildlife habitats and fragment rural regions once abounding in farmland, fields, forests, lakes, and ponds. An example of the latter is the runoff from streets, parking lots, lawns, and farms that empties pollutants and sediment into waterways, degrading water quality and smothering habitat. In *The Dark Side of the American Dream,* the Sierra Club gave two examples of this problem:

Around the Chesapeake Bay, sprawl is gobbling up open space and forest lands quickly. According to the Chesapeake Bay Foundation, more than 90,000 acres are consumed by sprawl each year in the bay states. Today, 4 to 5 times more land is used per person than 40 years ago. As a result, toxins and sediments are flowing into the bay in increasing amounts and upsetting the

delicate balance of the watershed's ecosystem. Sprawl is undermining progress in cleaning up the Chesapeake Bay and protecting habitat for fish and wildlife.

The Sonoran Desert is the largest desert in North America, covering about 120,000 square miles. Daily summer temperatures exceed 100 degrees Fahrenheit. Most parts of the desert receive less than 10 inches of rainfall a year. But, far from being a parched and barren wasteland, the Sonoran Desert is one of the most botanically diverse deserts in the world. More than 2,500 plant species and various desert animals call the Sonoran Desert home.

Today, more than 80 percent of Arizona's population lives in the Sonoran Desert, which includes the rapidly growing areas around Phoenix and Tucson. For the natural habitat of the Sonoran Desert, which evolved gradually over millennia, the rapid changes brought by man-made development, including fragmented habitats, new competition for food and water by imported non-native species, and changes in air and climate conditions, could pose a very serious threat. (Sierra Club 1998)

Sprawl has also had disastrous consequences involving the destruction of wetlands and building on flood plains. Wetlands act as natural sponges that soak up and store rain and runoff. When they are bulldozed over and asphalted under, water that would have been stopped or slowed is free to flood. With few exceptions, floods are most frequent, and loss of life and property are greatest, in counties that have lost the most wetlands—especially in the past 30 years.

According to the Federal Emergency Management Agency (FEMA)—the government entity responsible for disaster response and prevention—many of the floods, flood deaths, and property losses caused by flooding are preventable. Nationwide, floods have killed over 2,000 people since 1991 and cost the nation an average of $5.1 billion in damage each year. And FEMA believes that a principal cause of flooding is poor planning and unwise development that destroys the wetlands and open space that protect communities.

Worsening pollution is another negative effect of sprawl on the environment. In Seattle, for example, experts blame development around Puget Sound for the polluted water and habitat destruction that resulted in the proposed Endangered Species listing of chinook salmon. Another form of pollution is found in the suburbanized areas of Las Vegas, one of the fastest-growing cities in the United States. This midsized city, which increased its population by 84 percent between 1990 and 2000, gains a new resident every nine minutes. As a result, the city now has serious air- and water-quality problems.

Three environmental groups—the National Wildlife Federation, Smart Growth America, and NatureServe—projected that over the next 25 years, more than 22,000 acres of natural resources and habitat will be lost to development in 35 of the largest and most rapidly growing metropolitan areas. According to the groups, as many as 553 of the nearly 1,200 at-risk species are found only in those areas (Heilprin 2005).

Loss of Farmland. Sprawl threatens farmland all across the North American continent.

The American Farmland Trust (2005) reported that more than 75 percent of our fruits and vegetables are produced near urban areas, directly in the path of relentless development, and that every single year, we lose an area of productive farmland the size of Delaware. Texas lost more "high quality" farmland than any other state, followed by Ohio, Georgia, North Carolina, Illinois, Pennsylvania, Indiana, Tennessee, and Michigan. The study found that Americans' wasteful use of land rather than economic growth is causing the problem. From 1982 to 1997, for example, the U.S. population grew by 17 percent, while urbanized land grew by 47 percent. Over the past 20 years, the acreage per person for new housing almost doubled. Along the East Coast, writes the Sierra Club:

> Even places like Vermont, a state with a powerful rural legacy, are not immune to development pressures. The very name of the state, "Vermont," is practically synonymous with rural life in this country. Its rural personality is largely responsible for the area's economic health as millions of tourists visit Vermont each year and produce billions of dollars in revenue for state coffers.
>
> Yet, beginning in the 1980s, as more and more people moved to Vermont in search of a better quality of life, development (often in the form of malls and superstores) began to slice up this bucolic countryside. In just two years, the state lost 10 percent of its farmland. (Sierra Club 1999)

Antisprawl advocates argue that this contagious—so far unstoppable—march across fertile, high-quality farmland is quickly undermining the nation's agricultural productivity. Furthermore, the trend is a worldwide phenomenon, with cities growing outward and absorbing peripheral farmland in their inexorable drive to accommodate their burgeoning populations. As the world population expands from 6 billion to 9 billion in the twenty-first century, we may require more arable land for agriculture, not less.

In contrast, others argue that negative claims about sprawl and vanishing farmland are vastly overstated. People's freedom to choose low-density suburban living arrangements over high-density living arrangements, they contend, is a positive aspect of life. Moreover, as the late economist Julian L Simon noted in *Hoodwinking the Nation* (1999), much farmland is left idle to limit crop surpluses. James Legacy (2000) adds that the introduction of new crops in developing nations such as Nigeria has markedly increased local food crop production. However, he cautions, we should nonetheless carefully examine our land-use policies so that marginal agricultural lands get used for housing and roads, while our best farmlands are kept in agriculture.

Loss of Historic Treasures.   The centrifugal shift of businesses and residences into outlying areas takes people away from the older, established central cities, downtowns, and neighborhoods where so much of the heritage of both Canada and the United States is concentrated. These areas then lose their economic health, and the buildings and other historical reminders that define these once bustling places fall into disrepair. Sprawl thus robs cities of character, as abandoned factories, boarded-up homes, and decaying retail centers dominate the urban landscape. Smaller, older cities in the northeastern United States are especially vulnerable to this process. A good example is Greensboro, North Carolina, the anchor point to Guilford County, which a 2004 Sierra Club report identified as the national leader in sprawl. As its boundaries expanded far more than its population growth, its population density declined by more than half after 1950, even as it more than doubled outside the old city limits.

> Sprawl in Greensboro has also been associated with the movement of shopping and entertainment to the periphery and the decline of the city's once lively downtown. . . . [D]owntown Greensboro in the 1960s . . . was still a center for shopping, recreation, and many businesses. In subsequent decades, retailers, employers, and entertainment facilities followed residents to the periphery, leaving a downtown full of empty and underutilized buildings. Empty buildings pay little tax; instead they swallow large amounts of taxpayer money devoted to

downtown redevelopment plans. Recent years have seen a gradual upward trend in downtown activity, but the problems of empty buildings and storefronts are far from solved. (Doss and Markham 2004)

In contrast, historic Spokane, Washington, once called "The City Beautiful," is reeling under the pressures of growth, with 50,000 newcomers expected in the next 20 years. Many city residents—believing that sprawl and automobile dependency were taking over and crushing the city's charm—banded together to form the Spokane Horizons project to develop a comprehensive plan to address issues like parking, new roads, and infrastructure capacity while calling for a healthy downtown and surrounding neighborhoods. Adopted in 2001, the 20-year Comp Plan designates 21 mixed-use centers and corridors within and adjacent to the city limits, yet will maintain the downtown as the heart of the city and the region's cultural and economic center (City of Spokane Planning Services Department 2003).

Financial Costs.   Conventional wisdom says that development strengthens the municipal tax base. That may have been true in the 1980s, but by the 1990s local officials had discovered that increases in tax revenues were eaten up by costs to their communities for delivering new services (including water and sewer lines, schools, police and fire protection, and roads) to people who lived far away from the existing infrastructure. Here are some examples:

- Between 1970 and 1995, Maine spent over $338 million building new schools while the number of public school students declined by 27,000.
- Fresno, California, doubled in size since 1980, producing $56 million in yearly revenues, but the cost of services rose to $123 million (not including costs for roads and sewers).
- From 1970 to 1990, Minneapolis–St. Paul closed 162 physically adequate schools in urban and central suburban areas and opened 78 brand-new schools in the outer suburbs.

- Prince William County, a sprawling suburb of Washington, D.C., has the highest tax rates in the state of Virginia yet it still cannot keep pace with the expenditures needed to accommodate new growth (American Planning Association 2005).

In contrast, a master plan for the state of New Jersey evaluated the costs of conventional sprawl growth patterns against a mix of "infill" development, higher-density concentrated new development, and traditional sprawl. The projected differences are large. Infill and higher-density growth would result in a savings of $1.18 billion in roads, water, and sanitary sewer construction (or more than $12,000 per new home) and $400 million in direct annual savings to local governments. Over 15 years, it amounts to $7.8 billion. This does not take into account reductions in the cost of other public infrastructure that result from infill growth: decreased spending on storm drainage, less need for school busing (and parent taxi service), fewer fire stations, and less travel time for police, ambulance, garbage collection, and other services (Clean Water Action Council 2005).

A Maryland study predicted that, in the first two decades of the twenty-first century, sprawl will cost state residents about $10 billion more for new roads, schools, sewers, and water than would be necessary if growth were more concentrated. Similar studies in California, Florida, and elsewhere have demonstrated a direct relationship between sprawl and the spiraling costs of government (McMahon 1997:4). These additional costs don't occur only in the growing communities. As people flock to the outlying suburbs, cities—their tax base eroded—must raise taxes on the remaining taxpayers to pay for city services. Yet, in 2005, Maryland citizens found themselves fighting a $1 billion proposal to build a new Potomac River bridge and highway, despite a study showing little need for such a bridge except to encourage sprawl development (Solutions Not Sprawl 2005).

Traffic Problems.   Because sprawl, by definition, is low-density, automobile-dependent development on the edge of service and employment areas, it generates longer commutes and greater traffic congestion. Cars zipping along highways, or worse, cars stuck in traffic jams, spew millions of tons of carbon dioxide and other greenhouse gases into our atmosphere each year.

The 2005 Urban Mobility Report identified time wasted in traffic (beyond normal commuting time) in 2003 as part of its study of the effect of sprawl. The top five urban areas in time squandered because of traffic congestion were (1) Los Angeles–Long Beach–Santa Ana; (2) San Francisco–Oakland; (3) Washington, D.C.–Virginia–Maryland; (4) Atlanta; and (5) Houston. Other findings were as follows:

- Los Angeles drivers wasted 93 hours per person in traffic, highest in the country.
- Atlanta drivers spent 176 percent more time in traffic than in 1993.
- Baltimore drivers spent 167 percent more time in traffic than in 1993.
- Boston drivers spent 134 percent more time in traffic than in 1993.
- New York Metropolitan drivers wasted 49 hours per person caught in traffic, eighteenth in the country.

The problem is most acute in Southern California, where traffic congestion is growing by about 3 percent a year, as measured by the number of miles of clogged freeways. The congestion will get worse as this region of 18 million absorbs a projected 6 million new residents in the next 20 years—the equivalent of twice the population of Chicago. The Southern California Association of Governments (SCAG) predicts that if population trends and transportation demand continue at their current pace, the daily delay from congestion will probably double by 2030. The term *rush hour*, whether in Southern California or elsewhere, is in actuality no longer accurate. Where once the rush hour was exactly that—typically an hour between 7 and 8 A.M. and another between 4 and 5 P.M.—today the peak traffic periods last from 6 through 9 A.M. and from 3 until 7 P.M. (Southern California Association of Governments 2003:55).

Atlanta's afternoon rush-hour traffic snarls at what commuters refer to as "spaghetti junction"—the intersection of Interstates 85 and 285. Many of these drivers are heading from their jobs to homes in suburban Gwinnett County. In two decades, Gwinnett's population has more than tripled to exceed 465,000. Atlanta's phenomenal growth and lack of adequate mass transit are the main reasons why the area suffers from traffic congestion, air pollution, and urban sprawl.

Harm to Cities.   Sprawl may be primarily a suburban phenomenon, but it has a powerful urban counterpart. People are only beginning to realize that it wastes generations of investment in urban infrastructure—that abandoned buildings in the city, clogged highways, and the new mega-malls in farm fields have something in common: Although seemingly unrelated, they are all the direct results of sprawl. As Jeff McLaughlin (1999) observes:

> Sprawl is not just a 20-minute drive in a $40,000, 12-miles-per-gallon sport utility vehicle to buy a half-gallon of milk. Sprawl is also a 20-minute wait by a core-city resident for a dilapidated municipal bus that will lug its passenger over pot-holed streets to a "convenience store" for that half-gallon of milk.

Sprawl hurts cities in several ways:

1. It erodes the city's tax base as people flock to the suburbs, forcing cities to raise taxes on remaining taxpayers to pay for city services.

2. It destroys downtown commerce by pulling shoppers from once-thriving locally owned stores and restaurants to large regional malls.
3. It increases unemployment and concentrates poverty in urban centers.
4. It robs cities of character as abandoned factories, boarded-up homes, and decaying retail centers dominate the landscape (Sierra Club 1999).

Solutions to Sprawl

Sprawl by definition is a regional problem, and solving the problem requires convincing people that comprehensive, rational planning and strategies to combat it are in their self-interest. "Smart growth" public policies seek ways to stop the bulldozing of forests and farms and instead encourage reinvestment in cities and urbanized towns through sustainability, denser development, mass transit, and pedestrian-friendly areas. An increasing number of community leaders, concerned citizens, environmental groups, and government officials are exploring alternative growth and development approaches to sprawl, some of which are still on the drawing boards while others are gaining more widespread adoption.

Land Purchases.   In the 1960s, the federal government began setting aside a percentage of its royalties from offshore oil drilling to acquire or expand recreational land and open space. Now, through referendums and local or state government initiatives, efforts to protect open space and slow suburban sprawl are growing. In 1998, New Jersey voters approved a $1 billion referendum to raise the gasoline tax to set aside half the state's remaining 2 million acres of open space over the next 10 years. Earlier, voters in Monroe County in Pennsylvania approved a $25 million bond referendum to purchase undeveloped land over a ten-year period. Voters in Austin, Texas, approved an increase in water rates to protect thousands of acres of environmentally sensitive land around the city. Maryland's Smart Growth and Neighborhood Conservation Program includes $71 million to buy agricultural, forest, or natural areas that are in danger of development. Elsewhere, in Florida and Michigan, for example, communities are also purchasing land to prevent development.

Urban Growth Boundaries.   Oregon and Washington require all communities to designate official boundaries in order to separate urban areas from their surrounding greenbelt of open lands, including farms, watersheds, and parks. The intent is to funnel growth to areas with existing infrastructure while protecting the wide diversity of natural resources wrapped around these population centers. Portland, Oregon—featured in this chapter's case study—has had an urban growth boundary in place since 1975. Although Portland has grown almost 50 percent in population since then, it has consumed only 2 percent more land. Home prices are lower than in other major West Coast cities, and builders support the growth boundaries because there is less red tape and more flexible zoning within the designated growth areas. As

a result, Portland is one of the healthiest and most livable cities in the United States (McMahon 1997). Other cities that have been successful in this approach are Boulder, Colorado, and the California cities of San Jose, Morgan Hill, Napa, and Santa Rosa (Sierra Club 1999).

Revitalizing Existing Cities and Towns.   The rejuvenation of once-thriving cities and towns—where mass transit, existing infrastructure, and high-density living can support growth—will attract new residents and limit urban flight. Many communities are preserving their unique architecture through restoration and are utilizing good planning to restore a sense of community, improve livability, and enhance economic vitality. Through innovative public–private redevelopment strategies, they are creating vibrant urban environments that reconnect to their histories and cultural identities. Chattanooga, Tennessee, cleaned up its once seriously polluted river, the Tennessee, and created a riverfront park and a promenade that now attract both wildlife and people. Suisun, California, in the San Francisco Bay area, converted an area containing a polluted waterway, decaying warehouses, and a high-crime neighborhood of dilapidated houses into a charming place filled with shops, affordable homes, and a canal for boating. As part of its smart growth plan to encourage revitalization by drawing people to the inner city, Maryland gives at least $3,000 to people to buy a home in areas closer to their places of work.

Transit-Oriented Approaches.   Some proposed solutions for relieving traffic congestion focus on building more highway lanes, using "smart corridors" with synchronized traffic lights to move vehicles through congested areas, adding carpool or high-occupancy vehicle (HOV) lanes, or building more rail lines alongside the highways that connect cities and suburbs. While these proposals may alleviate traffic congestion somewhat, they do nothing to slow sprawl. Indeed, they may intensify it. Instead, planners seek to strengthen ridership on public transit by encouraging or

An excellent example of revitalizing an urban environment to reconnect to the city's history is the San Antonio River Walk, one of the world's great urban linear parks and a tourist's delight. Shops, restaurants, and hotels line the San Antonio River, as people take advantage of sightseeing boats or paddleboats, walkways, footbridges, or stairs to street level to tour historic sites.

requiring more compact mixed-use development around transit stops. Some companies, worried that congested roads and long commutes hurt their ability to hire and retain workers, have taken such steps. Bell South consolidated 75 scattered work sites (with 13,000 workers) into three near the Atlanta rapid transit system. Adobe Systems moved its headquarters to downtown San Jose and pays 300 workers $30 monthly subsidies to ride mass transit (Jones 1999).

In Vancouver, British Columbia, sprawl spread eastward and carpeted the Fraser River Valley with dozens of suburbs; as a result, rush-hour traffic headed out of the city over Lion's Gate Bridge was routinely backed up for three miles. Unable to stop the sprawl, planners sought to reduce the traffic congestion. Determined to avoid further "Los Angelization," regional leaders rejected the idea of building more highways as the backbone of their local transportation network. Instead, they set up an extensive transit system—utilizing trains

and ferries, but anchored by 1,000 buses (20 times the number in the Atlanta region). Significantly, as more suburbanites and commuters converged on the Vancouver metropolitan region, area planners opted to spread the population around by creating self-sustaining job centers in the suburbs to the east. They did so through SkyTrain, an automated light-rail train system along the Expo and Millennium lines that can, technically, move up to 30,000 people per hour in both directions. Its elevated electric cars zip along into the suburbs, taking passengers to and from their homes or work in far less time than on the clogged highways. Metrotown, once a suburban warehouse district on the wane, has become SkyTrain's busiest station, as office buildings, apartments, movie theaters, and a mall now ring the station (Wolinsky 2004).

These four approaches—land purchases, growth boundaries, revitalization, transit solutions—and other grass-roots efforts at comprehensive land-use planning to designate growth and nongrowth areas are essential to revitalizing our urban cores and protecting our open space, outdoor lifestyles, and farmland. If public policy invests money, effort, and vision into our communities rather than into sprawl and stops subsidizing new roads, utilities, and development at the expense of our urban centers, the public will have more options to make environmentally responsible lifestyle choices.

EXURBS

A. C. Spectorsky (1957) was the first to use the term **exurb** in describing the appearance of new residential areas developing on the metropolitan fringe. He based his account of such communities from his observations (none too systematic, it should be noted) of an exclusive residential area on the fringes of the New York City metropolitan area. He noted that the lifestyle of these exurbanites was an intriguing mix of high tech, high culture, and rustic charm. Although they lived in a rural locale, they (1) commuted to jobs in the central business district; (2) combined their love for old things with attraction to new electronic gadgets; and (3) maintained a strong interest in books, theater, and art.

The small trend that Spectorsky noted in *The Exurbanites* has morphed into a stampede. Indeed, the term *exurb* often appears in newspaper articles about urban sprawl. Then the exurbanites settled heavily in counties such as Fairfield (Connecticut), Rockland and Westchester (New York), and Bucks (Pennsylvania). Today, there are exurban counties surrounding every major city, from Marin near San Francisco to Dacula near Atlanta. Nowadays, new exurbanites are more likely to be moving from a suburb, not from a central city, and are less likely to work in a central city (Eiesland 2000).

As Jon Teaford (1997) noted, within the past 20 years the development of shopping malls, office towers, and sit-down restaurants has expanded metropolitan areas far beyond central business districts and traditional suburbia. A diverse mixture of inner suburbs, large suburban edge cities, office parks, retail centers, "captured" small towns, and even low-density rural territory now comprise the metropolitan fringe.

> Businesses were drawn to the less crowded metropolitan periphery where—developers promised—their operations would be free from traffic congestion and would gain access to an underutilized rural population. Whether they were termed "edge cities," "techno-burbs," "outer cities," or "transformed suburbs," these relatively recent formations changed the patterns of metropolitan life as well as of small towns and rural areas now within the metropolitan orbit. (Eiesland 2000:5)

Once viewed by their residents as physically and socially distant from the city, small towns now often merge into the sprawling metropolitan region, as outsiders view them as historic "subdivisions" adjacent and economically linked to the newly developing cities with their high-density housing, offices, shopping, and service centers (Eiesland 2000:6). As the exurbanization process unfolds and small towns are absorbed within metropolises, there is a cost. The small-town traditions and values that first attracted the newcomers morph into more cosmopolitan ones, resulting in social tensions between old and new residents (Fischer 1991, Dobriner 1963; Vidich and Bensman 1958). In addition, these once rural areas and small towns become more expensive places to live as land values, taxes, and the overall cost of living increase.

Small towns thus become new suburbs to new cities, dramatically altering the region. As Nancy Eiesland notes, "The resulting changes in demographics, organization patterns, and lifestyle in these once small towns signal a broad pattern of urban/rural spatial and social restructuring in the United States" (2000:6). We will now examine this social phenomenon of the new cities that so impact on small towns.

THE NEW CITIES

Not since the expansion of small cities into huge metropolises a century ago have we seen as profound a change in our urban world as the emergence of what are commonly called edge cities. An **edge city** is a new, sprawling, middle-class, automobile-dependent center typically located at the fringe of an older urban area, at the intersection of major highways, where little except villages or farmland existed three decades earlier.

We should note that the term *edge city* is most likely a temporary one. Since it denotes a new creation, as such entities continue their evolution, there will cease to exist any rationale for calling them "edge cities," for they will not be on the edge of anything, but simply be newer cities interlinked with older ones. Yet,

CITYSCAPE

Atlanta's Edge Cities

He looked away from the buildings and out over the ocean of trees. Since Atlanta was not a port city and was, in fact, far inland, the trees stretched on in every direction. They were Atlanta's greatest natural resource, those trees were. People loved to live beneath them. Fewer than 400,000 people lived within the Atlanta city limits, and almost three quarters of them were black; if anything, over the past decade Atlanta's population had declined slightly. But for the past thirty years all sorts of people, most of them white, had been moving in beneath those trees, into all those delightful, leafy, rolling rural communities that surrounded the city proper. By the hundreds of thousands they had come, from all over Georgia, all over the South, all over America, all over the world, into those subdivided hills and downs and glens and glades beneath the trees, until the population of Greater Atlanta was now more than 3.5 million, and they were still pouring in. How fabulous the building booms had been!! As the G-5 banked, Charlie looked down. . . . There was Spaghetti Junction, as it was known, where Highways 85 and 285 came together in a tangle of fourteen gigantic curving concrete-and-asphalt ramps and twelve overpasses. . . . And now he could see Perimeter Center, where Georgia 400 crossed 285. Mack Taylor and Harvey Mathis had built an office park called Perimeter Center out among all those trees, which had been considered a very risky venture at the time, because it was so far from Downtown; and now Perimeter Center was the nucleus around which an entire edge city, known by that very name, Perimeter Center, had grown. . . .

Edge city . . . Charlie closed his eyes and wished he'd never heard of the damn term. He wasn't much of a reader, but back in 1991 Lucky Putney, another developer, had given him a copy of a book called *Edge City* by somebody named Joel Garreau. He had opened it and glanced at it—and couldn't put it down, even though it was 500 pages long. He had experienced the *Aha!* phenomenon. The book put into words something he and other developers had felt, instinctively, for quite a while: namely, that from now on, the growth of American cities was going to take place not in the heart of the metropolis, not in the old Downtown or Midtown, but out on the edges, in vast commercial clusters served by highways.

Source: Excerpt from "Atlanta's Edge Cities," from *A Man in Full* by Tom Wolfe. Copyright © 1998 by Tom Wolfe. Reprinted by permission of Farrar, Straus & Giroux LLC.

as this is still the fashionable term, we will use it in this edition to discuss them more fully.

In the second half of the twentieth century, North Americans went through three waves of centrifugal movement away from the older cities. First came the suburbanization of North America, most notably after World War II, as people moved into new homes beyond city boundaries. Next came the malling of North America, particularly in the 1960s and 1970s, when we moved our stores out to where we lived. And now, says Joel Garreau (1991), we have moved our means of creating wealth, the essence of urbanism—our jobs—out to where most of us have lived and shopped for two generations. This has led to the rise of edge cities, resulting in profound changes in the ways we live, work, and play.

It is the evolution of edge cities in the past quarter-century that helps explain the increases in population in nonmetropolitan areas, as discussed in the previous chapter. Garreau suggests that North Americans have reinvented the city in recent decades and that these new urban agglomerations are the future. Numbering over 200 in the United States, these edge cities with their malls and office parks now dominate the nation's retail trade and office facilities.

Edge cities have appeared in Canada as well as in the United States, but apparently for different reasons. Unlike the United States, the Canadian government does not provide suburb-enhancing tax deductions for home mortgages, and it has greater control over planning and development. In Canada also, there is a greater emphasis on mass transit; a relative lack of freeways; vibrant, bustling urban centers; and a relative lack of racial problems. Nevertheless, edge cities are flourishing. Toronto, for example, has only 46 percent of the area's market. The rest is found in the nine edge cities growing up around it. These are Midtown–Yorkville and North York–North Yonge to the north; Mississauga, the Downsview Airport area, and the Etobicoke–427 area to the west; and the Don Valley Parkway–401 area, Markham–404 area, Eglington–Don Mills area, and Scarborough to the east.

Characteristics and Commonalities

The new cities possess many of the same characteristics of older cities: extensive office and retail space, a large-scale influx of workers each weekday morning, and a recognized mixed use of work, shopping, and entertainment (Garreau 1991:425). What one rarely finds, however, is a clearly defined territorial boundary, for edge cities do not have the same look (the compactness of closely adjacent buildings and high pedestrian traffic), political organization (elected officials or civic codes), or even visual clues of older cities (signs, edges) to mark their perimeters. As Garreau explains:

> The reason these places are tricky to define is that they rarely have a mayor or a city council, and just about never match boundaries on a map. We're still in the process of giving each Edge City its name—a project, incidentally, that could use more flair. In New Jersey, for example, there is one with only the laconic designation "287 and 78." The reason there are no "Welcome to" signs at Edge City is that it is a judgment call where it begins and ends. (1991:6)

A common feature of edge cities is that they have sprouted far from the old downtowns, in locales where, 30 years ago little existed save villages and farmland. They typically evolve adjacent to two or more major highways, usually with shopping malls serving as anchor points. Figure 4–1 on pages 108–109 shows two of the more densely concentrated Edge City regions—the Los Angeles and New York areas.

Types of Edge Cities

Edge cities fall into one of three major categories: (1) **uptowns,** built on top of preautomobile settlements, such as Pasadena, California, or Arlington, Virginia; (2) **boomers,** the typical edge city located at the intersection of two major highways and almost always centered on a mall, such as most of those in Figure 4–1; and (3) **greenfields,** a master-planned city by one developer on thousands of farmland acres, such as Irvine, California, and Las Colinas, near the Dallas–Fort Worth airport.

Because boomers, the most common form of edge cities, have grown so profusely throughout North America, urbanists identify three subcategories of them [see Figure 4–2 on page 110]. The strip boomer city is usually only a few hundred yards wide but extends for miles along a major highway. Most representative are the strips along Route 1 in Princeton, Route 128 near the Mass Pike outside Boston, and I-270 in Montgomery County, Maryland, in the Washington, D.C. region. All three suffer severe traffic congestion because of their extended shapes. The node boomer city is relatively dense and contained, such as The Galleria area near Houston, Tysons Corner in Virginia, and the Midtown–Yorkville and North York–North Yonge areas in Toronto. The pig-in-the-python boomer city is a cross between the previous two types. It is a strip that develops one or several nodes along it, such as the Lodge Freeway in Southfield, northwest of Detroit, or King of Prussia, Pennsylvania, northwest of Philadelphia. (Garreau 1991:115)

Evolving Middle-Class Centers

The majority of metropolitan North Americans now work, shop, and live in and around the 200-plus "new hearths of our civilization" (Garreau 1991:3). Shopping malls function as the village squares for these new urban centers. Adjacent are the hotels, office buildings, and corporate headquarters, whose tall buildings are not side by side as in a downtown, but instead are located on campuslike settings of grass and trees, gazing at one another at a respectful distance. Surrounding this broad center of employment and shopping are the single-family suburban homes whose occupants now outnumber those living next to the old downtowns.

The rise of edge cities is essentially a function of social class, not race. They are evolving in metropolitan areas with low black populations (Denver, Minneapolis, Seattle, Toronto) as well as in metropolitan areas with high black populations (Atlanta, Chicago, New York, Washington). In the latter, middle-class African Americans (presently about one-third of the total U.S. black population) are just as likely to be part of edge cities as are middle-class whites. Just as the skin of the middle-class North American comes in various hues—shades of brown, black, tan, and white—so too do edge cities reflect this reality.

The edge city, however, has been criticized as plastic and sterile, lacking in livability, civilization, community, neighborhood—in short, having little "urban soul." It is, however, an unfinished new city form and we do not yet know if, in its maturity, this ugly duckling will emerge as a splendid swan. Whatever their ultimate shape, we do know that our new cities have become the places in which the majority of North Americans "now live, learn, work, shop, play, pray, and die." (Garreau 1991:8)

And edge cities are appearing worldwide as well. They now mark the fringes of Bangkok, Beijing, London, Paris, and Sydney. Increased affluence, the desire for more individual transportation, greater use of computers and telecommunications requiring air climate control, and the existence of world financial centers are some of the important elements shaping the growth of edge cities in urban areas throughout the world.

Three Edge City Variations

Not all edge cities are alike, nor does their evolution occur for the same reasons everywhere. The following examples illustrate how a new city can serve as its own motivation, emerge as a solution to a problem, or simply become the problem.

Edge City as Motivator.   By 1990, Oshawa Centre, one of the oldest shopping malls in Ontario, Canada, was showing its age. Originally built for the town's blue-collar population, the place was dark and ugly, some of the stores had outdoor-facing windows and doors plastered with newspaper and cardboard, and its sales and rental value were declining. Not anymore. The Toronto-based Cambridge Shopping Centres purchased it in 1991 for $145 million. It did so because Garreau had written in *Edge City* that shopping malls usually function as the village

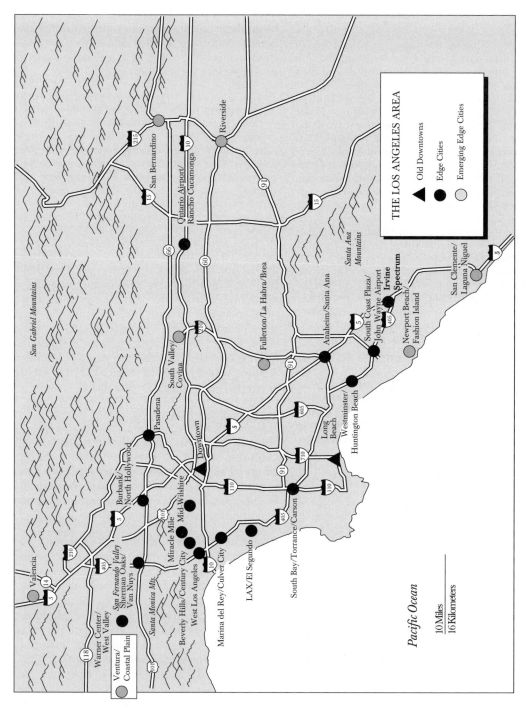

FIGURE 4–1A

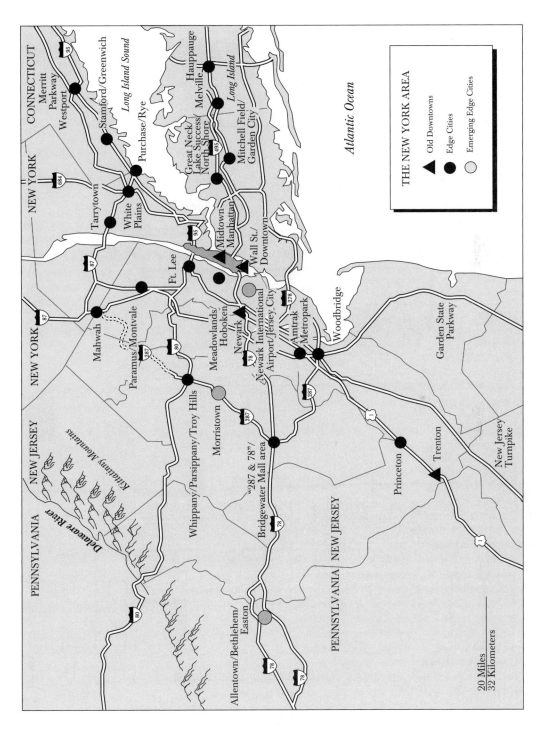

FIGURE 4–1B

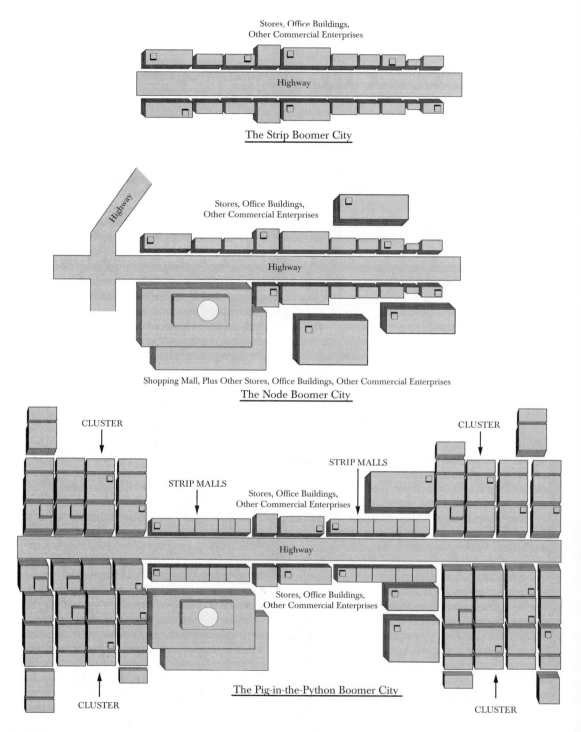

The Strip Boomer City

The Node Boomer City

The Pig-in-the-Python Boomer City

FIGURE 4–2

squares of the new urban centers. "So, taking that theory," said Ronald Charbon, Cambridge's director of strategic market information, "we said, 'Where are the next edge cities going to occur? Where is the next wave of growth going to occur in the greater metropolitan Toronto area? And are any of our shopping centres sufficiently located to capitalize on that growth?'" (cited in Berman 1997).

Using census tracts and surveys, Cambridge amassed a population profile of the area, discovering that areas surrounding Oshawa were white collar and that projections of the area's growth rate were almost three times that in the Greater Toronto Area. So the company took the gamble, invested $40 million in a major facelift, and recruited upscale stores. However, that was only one part of a sophisticated strategy to turn Oshawa Centre into the village square that Garreau described. Cambridge secured government approval to construct six modest-sized office towers over a 25-year period. The Oshawa Centre is thus in the midst of a massive transformation from a jerry-built suburban mall into a mixed-use development that includes retail, business, government, and community services, all inspired by Garreau's book.

Edge City as the Solution. Since incorporating in 1956, Schaumburg, Illinois, had been what Judy Pasternak (1998) called "the ultimate faceless postwar suburb." Located 26 miles northwest of Chicago, the town is home to nearly 74,000 people living in townhouses and subdivisions and shopping in one or more of the 65 shopping centers that line its streets. Along its expressway, glassy office towers provide a solid employment base. The one thing lacking in Schaumburg is that it had no center, no downtown, no place to walk to or for people to gather. In fact, it hadn't had a town center since 1875.

That is now changing. The local government tore down a faded strip mall on a 30-acre site to make way for a downtown center

Oshawa Centre, located in the Toronto metropolitan area, is a good illustration of the evolution of older, boxlike shopping centers containing only retail stores into upscale, architecturally stylish, mixed-use centers of business, commerce, and leisure activities. This transition is similar to what is occurring throughout North America: a reinterpretation of what constitutes an urban center.

called "Town Square." But this place is no small-town core like the downtowns of older suburbs that developed around train depots generations ago. There are no retail stores lining Main Street. In fact, there is no Main Street. Instead, a supermarket and a cluster of retail stores border a large parking lot, giving this area the look of a shopping center. Nearby are a new library, a brick clock tower, a green wrought-iron gazebo, a pond, curved benches, and a chain restaurant. "It's plastic," grumbled one store owner. Others, however, are more optimistic, hoping that this shopping area—with plenty of parking, strolling amenities, and mixed-use development—will allow community to blossom where none had existed before (Pasternak 1998).

Edge City as the Problem.   The more that Tysons Corner, Virginia—located eight miles west of Washington, D.C. and one of Joel Garreau's prime examples of an edge city—continues to grow and thrive economically, the more it remains an object of derisive commentary by architects, city planners, design critics, and urban scholars. Indeed, finding ways to "fix" Tysons Corner has been the goal of several planning studies sponsored by academic institutions, professional groups, and Fairfax County. Home to two massive shopping malls and an impressive array of high-tech firms and major corporations, Tysons Corner today is larger, in both geographic size and employment, than many U.S. central cities. Incredibly, only road transit exists and, during weekday rush hours and weekend shopping times, backups are horrendous. Clearly, mass transit would greatly alleviate the traffic congestion. Recommendations include creating an elevated rail system looping around Tysons Corner and introducing a link between Tysons and the regional Metrorail network.

This view of Tysons Corner, Virginia, shows the new edge city we now build. It has no defined borders or recognizable center, and its various buildings are not conveniently near one another. All the commercial activities and none of the charm of a city—the pedestrians, the architecture, the cultural attractions—can be found here. A car is a necessity in edge cities and, as a result, traffic congestion is unavoidable.

But much more is needed. Tysons is not pedestrian friendly, for there are few sidewalks or signalized crosswalks—critical for safely traversing the extraordinarily wide, traffic-choked roads—making walking around Tysons virtually impossible.

Even if traffic congestion could be reduced and pedestrian traffic encouraged, the aesthetic and visual deficiencies, the visual chaos and formlessness would still remain. In the interest of bringing a bit of visual order to Tysons Corner, a county task force developed a plan a few years ago to address streetscapes, pedestrian walkways, site planning of buildings, and open space. Still, Tysons has no civic focus, or heart, and so planners propose a "town center" as a way to "give Tysons more soul." Such an undertaking is still several years away, however. In the meantime, Tysons continues to be emblematic of how poorly we have planned, zoned, and developed much of the landscape girdling our cities since the end of World War II (Massing 2000).

GATED COMMUNITIES

Gated communities in the United States can be traced to the late 1800s, when upper-income gated developments in New York's Tuxedo Park and private streets in St. Louis sprang up, as wealthy citizens sought to "insulate themselves from the troublesome aspects of rapidly industrializing cities" (Blakely and Snyder 1997:4). However, these communities, and the fenced compounds built in the twentieth century by members of the East Coast and Hollywood aristocracies, were different from today's gated communities. They were unique places for unique people. Although a few other exclusive gated communities began to appear—such as Sea Pines on Hilton Head Island, South Carolina, in 1957—they remained rare until the late 1960s and 1970s, when master-planned retirement developments first appeared. These were the first places where average Americans could wall themselves off from the rest of society.

Beginning in the 1980s, gated communities increased rapidly—not only in retirement villages, but also in resort and country club developments, then in middle-class suburban subdivisions, setting off a quiet but important trend that continues today. In the mid-1980s, gated communities were rare on Long Island, New York, but by the mid-1990s they had become common, with a gatehouse included in almost every condominium of more than 50 units. Elsewhere, there are now entire incorporated cities that feature guarded entrances; one example is Canyon Lake, 60 miles east of Orange County in California.

About 6 percent of U.S. households—over 7 million—are in developments that are surrounded by fences or walls. About 60 percent of those households are in communities that also have controlled-entry systems such as guards and electric gates. Perhaps because the largest concentration of gated communities is in the West and Southwest, where there is a large Hispanic population, Hispanics are more likely to live in such communities than whites or blacks (U.S. Census Bureau 2004d). Although the greatest number of these developments is in suburban areas, older, inner-city neighborhoods are also experiencing this phenomenon. Many gated communities have been built in metropolitan areas across the country, including Los Angeles, Phoenix, Dallas, Houston, Chicago, New York, and Miami. This pattern is occurring in Canada as well. In Toronto, three older gated areas—Palmerston Avenue, Fairview Boulevard, and Wychwood Park—are city jewels that enjoy high real estate values.

Suburbanites, however, are gating just as fast as urbanites. In Southern California, for example, about 100 such communities were built in San Fernando Valley in the 1980s and, in that same decade, the number of gated communities doubled in Orange County. What makes gated communities different from typical twentieth-century suburbs, which usually also involve economic and social segregation?

Gated communities are actually defended by walls, with access control either by electronically operated gates or 24-hour guards, and grounds patrolled by private security forces. Residents enjoy their own pay-as-you-go services. They share responsibility for common areas and for enforcing the numerous rules and regulations, often through homeowner associations, rather than relying on conventional elected local governments for many common services.

Gated communities obviously segregate people living within their walls from others even more profoundly than the most exclusive suburban jurisdiction can, and they thus accentuate patterns of segregation. While there are a variety of approaches to living barricaded lives, the reasons residents choose gated communities usually center around fear of crime and attempts to produce economic and physical security, free from the problems of traffic and noise.

Types of Gated Communities

In their study of the development and social impact of this rapidly growing phenomenon, Edward J. Blakely and May Gail Snyder (1997) suggest that they fall into one of three categories: "lifestyle," "prestige," and "security-zone" communities. Although these categories are

helpful for analysis and understanding, there is actually much overlap between them, as each contains some elements of the others. Still, each caters to a different housing market and has a different approach to developing a sense of community within its walls. Moreover, each variety promotes a particular combination of four social values: the "sense of community" (preservation and strengthening of neighborhood bonds); "exclusion" (separation and protection from the outside); "privatization" (the desire to privatize and internally control public services); and "stability" (homogeneity and predictability).

> Where sense of community is a primary value motivating the residents of gated communities, it reflects all five aspects of community: shared territory, shared values, a shared public realm, support structure, and a shared destiny. Exclusion helps define shared territory by separating community members from outsiders. Privatization reflects a desire to protect a shared destiny through increased local control. Stability suggests shared values and support structures, and retaining stability is also a way of predicting shared destiny. (Blakely and Snyder 1997:122)

Gated communities, such as this one at Dana Point, California, are a rapidly growing phenomenon. Segregated from the outside world with walls, fences, electronically operated gates and/or 24-hour guards, residents essentially live barricaded lives. Such communities typically cater to a housing market emphasizing prestige, lifestyle, or security-zone neighborhoods that promise a sense of community, exclusion, private control of public services, and the stability of homogenization.

Lifestyle Communities. Lifestyle communities are an expression of conspicuous consumption and a new leisure class. They emphasize amenities and include retirement communities, such as the nationwide chain of Leisure Worlds, that offer senior citizens the chance to engage in a wide variety of activities close to their homes. Another type are golf and leisure communities, where the gates cordon off the leisure resources for the exclusive use of community residents. Blackhawk Country Club near San Francisco and Rancho Mirage in California's Coachella Valley cater to people with special interests, like golf or tennis. Lifestyle communities attract those who want separate, private services and amenities within a homogeneous, predictable environment.

Prestige Communities. Prestige communities are status-oriented enclaves, such as those in affluent Pacific Palisades or Marblehead in San Clemente, primarily containing the rich and famous, the affluent, the top one-fifth of Americans. These communities emphasize exclusion and image; the gates symbolize the eminent status of their residents. Prestige communities attract those seeking a stable neighborhood of similar people where property values will be protected. For these residents, concerns about separation and privatization of services are secondary.

Security-Zone Communities. Security-zone communities are "enclaves of fear" primarily concerned with protection and are a defensive measure reflecting a fortress mentality with walls, gates, closed streets, and various security systems. In these enclaves, often located in inner-city and lower-income neighborhoods, residents band together to shut out their neighbors in the hope that the gates will protect them from crime, traffic, and outsiders. Security-zone communities seek to strengthen and protect a sense of community, but their primary goal is to exclude the places and people their residents perceive as threats to their safety and quality of life.

A Sense of Community

For several decades, social observers have noted a loss of community in modern life—what Robert MacIver (1962) referred to as "the great emptiness." In *Habits of the Heart* (1985), Robert N. Bellah and his associates reported that traditional communities, where individuals have permanent emotional bonds, were yielding to "lifestyle enclaves," where relationships are often based on such superficial similarities as consumption style or leisure interests. Such enclaves diminish social life, say the authors, and all residents can do is compare their own material gains with those of their neighbors to piece together some idea of "how they are doing." Robert B. Reich (1991) expressed concern that wealth was rapidly polarizing society because the well-to-do were effectively seceding from society by walling themselves into privately policed fortress communities. In their study of gated communities, Blakely and Snyder also lamented the loss of community:

> The fabric of civitas, communal commitment to civic and public life, has begun to rip. . . . The borders of the gated communities are emblematic of the proliferation of boundaries being set and hardened as communities fragment, looking inward. (Blakely and Snyder 1997:176)

As communities turn inward, motivated by security and other social needs, do the residents find what they seek? Critics, including Blakely and Snyder, charge that they do not—that gated communities reflect the social fragmentation and civic atrophy currently plaguing society. Because these barricaded neighborhoods exclude the lower classes not only from living in these residences (through prohibitive housing costs) but also from even casually passing by, they limit social contact among different members and groups of society. Such class separation is often *de facto* racial segregation, and this social distance can weaken further the civic bonds among societal members. In his comprehensive look at the impact of gated communities, Andrew Stark (1998) noted that these self-governing private communities were redefining the grass-roots level of the boundary between public and private realms.

According to various studies, the quality of community does not improve in gated developments. Even though residents move to such places in the belief that they will find their nostalgic idea of community, they do not. In fact, these communities promote privacy within privacy; there are no front porches to induce interaction, and residents tend to stay in their own backyards and not visit one another. As a result, Blakely and Snyder found that gating often does not provide what people are seeking. Although residents often expressed some satisfaction about life within these enclaves, they also expressed much disappointment, especially about the lack of a sense of shared community. In comparison with nonresidents, members of gated communities do not find stronger ties with one another.

As to whether gated communities actually serve as a deterrent to crime, the statistics are mixed. Formidable fencing and gates, by design, restrict access and therefore provide both a physical and psychological barrier for criminals. However, the effectiveness of gates and fencing depends on the nature of the property and the people living in it. In the security-zone communities, crime declined right after closure of the gates, but no decline was sustained for more than a short time. Among lifestyle communities, Blakely and Snyder found that many had the same problems as other urban communities. In some cases, the gates fostered a false sense of security; police reported that crime was as likely to come from people living within the gates as from outside.

COMMON-INTEREST DEVELOPMENTS

Gated communities are often called **common-interest developments (CIDs).** However, not all CIDs are segregated communities (although many are), and not all gated areas are CIDs (although most are). There is a close relationship between the two phenomena, but they are not the same thing. CIDs—which require membership in a self-governing homeowners' association—include suburban planned-unit developments of single-family homes, urban condominiums, and housing cooperatives, and they have become familiar sights throughout North America. Moreover, the rapid spread of CID housing is the largest and most dramatic privatization of local government functions in North American history. Currently, over 250,000 of these developments exist in the United States, housing some 42 million people (Treese 1999).

Builders find CID housing profitable because it is a mass-produced commodity and enables them to concentrate more people on less land. Buyers are willing to accept smaller lots and narrower streets because the development contains open spaces and desirable amenities, including facilities owned in common by all residents—such as swimming pools, gyms, parks, golf courses, social centers, often even exclusive access to shopping centers and their own schools. Public officials are willing to issue building permits for these high-density, designed communities, with their private infrastructure, because they add taxpayers at minimal public cost.

Residents must belong to homeowner associations, pay monthly fees, and live under the rule of residential private governments. These governments perform functions for their residents that were once the province of local government, providing, for example, police protection, trash collection, and street maintenance and lighting. In one sense, this community design is a logical, evolutionary step in the suburban ideology of territorial control (housing-market segmentation, single-use zoning, inaccessibility to mass transit, cul-de-sacs). However, some critics think that the emergence of this new civic culture undermines the diversity and vitality of cities. The Critical Thinking box on page 117 takes a closer look.

In *Privatopia* (1996), Evan McKenzie wrote that millions of affluent homeowners were being "encouraged to secede from urban America, with its endless flux and ferment, its spontaneity and diversity and its unpredictable

CRITICAL THINKING

CIDs Threaten Urban Culture

For those who live outside CIDs, in America's beleaguered cities, the rapid spread of CIDs threatens to transform urban culture in ways some find deeply disturbing. This "secession of the successful," as Robert Reich calls it, deprives urban America of a vast amount of human and economic resources. It promotes a two-class society of haves and have-nots, the former enjoying a privatized set of what were formerly public services, and the latter struggling to survive in cities faced with increasing responsibilities and shriveling revenues.

The city, Lewis Mumford tells us, is "a structure specially equipped to store and transmit the goods of civilization." Cities are dense concentrations of a society's population, wealth and power—assets which, for 6,000 years, have enabled cities to create, reflect, amplify, and communicate whatever a society has to offer to the world.

Conservative scholar Charles Murray views CIDs as symbols of an emerging caste society in which the affluent, freed from dependency on public institutions, may come to regard cities as "an urban analog of the Indian reservation"—places of deprivation and dysfunction for which they feel no responsibility.

Urban theorist Mike Davis, in *City of Quartz,* paints the picture of a privatized Los Angeles, architecturally redesigned to physically separate the two classes and protect the rich from the rest. He saw in this separation the potential for "approaching Helter-Skelter," even before 1992 brought the most intense urban riot in American history.

CIDs are, in a sense, a privatized, master-planned version of the village-centered life that our species led for millennia, and that many romanticize today. For the rest of us, CIDs may speed the decline of cities as centers of cultural, political, and economic power. Cities may come to resemble the future Los Angeles of *Blade Runner*—desperate holding pens, struggling to provide mere physical security and unable to afford other social services to all. . . .

It is time to ask whether corporate builders should be allowed to continue spreading CIDs across the country, guided only by the calculus of private profit, or whether we should have an open, public discussion of the consequences—before the metropolis becomes a necropolis.

Source: Evan McKenzie, "Trouble in Privatopia," *The Progressive* 57 (October 1993), 30–36. Reprinted by permission from *The Progressive,* 409 E. Main St., Madison, WI 53709.

rewards and hazards" and "beckoned to a privatized, artificial, utopian environment where master-planning, homogeneous populations, and private governments offer the affluent a chance to escape from urban reality." However, said McKenzie, they pay a heavy price, for they surrender a good deal of their freedom and privacy. CID residents live under the rule of their corporate board of directors, an elected group of neighbors enforcing a set of restrictions created by the developer to ensure that the master plan will never be altered. This private government operates outside the constitutional limits that bind local authorities, because the courts often accept the legal fiction that CID restrictions are private, voluntary arrangements among individuals. In truth, they are nonnegotiable regulations, drafted by the developer's lawyers and imposed on all residents, as the Urban Living box on page 118 explains.

URBAN LIVING

CID Violations of Personal Freedom

The stories below, all reported in various news stories, do not merely reflect isolated neighborhood conflicts. They are examples of business as usual in walled, private, urban and suburban enclaves called common-interest developments (CIDs). For some, CID living means having to fight to defend a semblance of privacy and personal freedom, while the few residents who enforce the rules enjoy a degree of personal power over their neighbors that the Constitution denies to public officials.

- In Monroe, New Jersey, a homeowners' association sued a married couple because the wife, at age 45, was three years younger than the association's age-48 minimum for residency. The judge ruled in favor of the association, ordering the 60-year-old husband to sell or rent the unit, or else live there without his wife.
- In Ashland, Massachusetts, a CID board informed a Vietnam veteran that he could not fly the U.S. flag on Flag Day. He called the press, the story appeared on the front page of a local newspaper, and under public pressure, the board backed down.
- In Boca Raton, Florida, an association took legal action against a homeowner for having a dog weighing more than 30 pounds, in violation of association rules. A court-ordered weighing revealed that the dog was just an ounce over the weight limit. The association persisted with the suit nonetheless—determined to pay an attorney and use the courts to exclude the dog from the development for even that infraction.
- In Santa Ana, California, a condominium association issued a citation to a 51-year-old grandmother for violating one of its rules. Her offense? "Kissing and doing bad things" while parked one night in the circular driveway. She acknowledged kissing a friend good night, but retained an attorney and threatened legal action against this invasion of her privacy.
- In a development near Philadelphia, a couple bought a home and brought their sons' metal swing set with them. A year later, the association told them to take it down, despite the absence of any written rules on swing sets. When they challenged this order, the association passed a rule prescribing that all swing sets must be made of wood, in keeping "with what the overall community should look like." The family then submitted a petition from three-fourths of the homeowners supporting their swing set, along with data from the Environmental Protection Agency warning against the danger to children (theirs were aged two and four) from the poisonous chemicals found in pressure-treated wood used for outdoor swing sets. The association's response was to impose a daily fine of ten dollars until the set was removed, and to refuse offers to compromise, such as painting the swing set in earth tones.

Because CIDs contain relatively homogeneous groupings, some critics argue that such planned developments promote racial and economic segregation (Putnam 2001, Blakely and Snyder 1997). However, in a study of California CIDs, Tracy Gordon (2004) found their contributions to metropolitan segregation to be minor at this time, although their effect could be more pronounced if current trends continue.

Just as urban renewal frequently uprooted lower-income people from their homes, so too have CID developments. Perhaps the most publicized of these displacements occurred on Daufuskie Island, South Carolina, near Hilton Head. Here, amid the dirt roads crisscrossing the five-by-two-mile island, the black Gullah population owned land for generations. They lived in an open community with no property line restrictions, shared in each other's good fortune, and helped one another in bad times. In the 1990s, when developers came and made more than half the island off-limits to them, placing warning signs at nearly every fork in the road, a howl of protest arose. The National Council of Churches—with 25 million members—charged that the developers of Haig Point and Daufuskie Island Resort gated communities were committing "cultural genocide" by dislodging black residents. With the conflict publicized by national news shows and newspaper stories, the National Association for the Advancement of Colored People (NAACP) threatened to file a class-action suit against Beaufort County and the developers for driving black families off their land. A decade later, much of the island remains undeveloped, but the families are slowly dwindling in number and, in 2005, the Daufuskie Island Resort spent $10 million to build new luxury beach cottages and renovate existing ones (Parker 2005). Future development, however, is a virtual certainty, particularly after the resort was popularized as a romantic backdrop in a 2005 episode of *The Bachelorette* TV show.

As we have seen, then, how communities expand and evolve can have positive or negative consequences. Planners, sprawl opponents, and urban sociologists often cite Portland, Oregon, as a growing city that successfully controls its growth and development. Portland thus serves as an appropriate case study for the various themes and problems discussed in this chapter.

❖ *CASE STUDY* ❖
Portland, Oregon

Virtually all cities in western North America have undergone boom periods that gobbled up the land, strained the infrastructure, and resulted in congestion, dirty air, and tax-strained school systems. Yet Portland enters the twenty-first century as a healthy, vibrant city displaying few of the problems found in other urban places. Years ago, Portland determined to defy the boom mentality and set out to consciously plan its future. This effort reflects the city's long history of concern for urban quality of life and commitment to the common good (Egan 1996).

The Physical Setting

Portland stands in a choice location, surrounded by natural beauty and resources that greatly impressed its founders. Situated about 100 miles from the Pacific Ocean at the confluence of the Columbia and Willamette Rivers, Portland is surrounded by a combination of water and lush greenery rarely found in urban settings. Snow-capped Mount Hood, Oregon's highest point (11,235 feet), is 48 miles away, and Mount Rainier, Mount St. Helens, and Mount Adams in Washington are all visible from the city. Also nearby is the spectacular Columbia Gorge and Multnomah Falls (850 feet). The city thus offers cosmopolitan living coupled with a variety of nearby outdoor activities such as camping, canoeing, fishing, hiking, hunting, mountain climbing, and skiing.

Portland includes some of this outlying natural beauty within the city limits. Also known as "The City of Roses" for its large International Rose Test Gardens and the second-largest all-floral parade in the United States (after the Tournament of Roses Parade in Pasadena), Portland has a magnificent park system including some 200 green spaces. The city boasts the largest forested municipal park in the nation (5,000 acres) and the world's smallest dedicated park, Mills End Park (24 inches). Three other important areas are the elm-shaded South Park blocks in the downtown area, McCall Waterfront Park, and Washington Park, home of the Rose Test Gardens, where more than 500 varieties of roses bloom, as well as of the Oregon Zoo (known for its re-created African rain forest) and the Japanese Garden. Portland is also the only U.S. city to have an extinct volcano, Mount Tabor, within the city limits.

History

Several gold rushes drew immigrants along the Oregon Trail, stimulating Portland's early growth. Deep water and abundant natural resources soon made the settlement a popular and prosperous port and commercial center, handling the farm and forest produce of the Cascade Range, Willamette Valley, and Columbia Basin.

As with many Old West centers, Portland had its seamy side, with vice and violence figuring into its nineteenth-century scene. By the turn of the century, Portland became a tamer place, and the city eliminated most of the seedy activities of its busy waterfront. About this time Simon Benson, a teetotaling lumber baron, walked through one of his mills and noticed the smell of alcohol on his workers' breath. When he asked why they drank in the middle of the day, they replied that there was no fresh drinking water to be found downtown. To resolve this situation, Benson built 20 fresh-water drinking fountains in the downtown area, now known as Benson's Bubblers. Beer consumption reportedly fell by 25 percent after the fountains were installed. Those water fountains still bubble for locals and visitors alike along Portland's downtown streets. Yet Portlanders still love their beer: The microbrewery was practically invented here, long before the concept gained popularity in other cities, and today the city boasts several dozen microbrews from which to choose.

Urban Decline and the Planners' Response to Sprawl

In the 1960s, Portland fell victim to the same ills afflicting other U.S. cities. Its economy nose-dived as industries closed. Shuttered mills and empty warehouses dotted the waterfront. People began moving away, unemployment rose, and those who remained found their standard of living sliding downward. One after another, downtown stores went belly up as the central business district slipped into a serious economic decline. The bus system lost so much business that it, too, went bankrupt.

But the stage was set for Portland's revival when Republican governor Tom McCall signed a new state law in 1973 requiring all of Oregon's cities to devise plans to limit urban sprawl and to protect farms, forests, and open space. Portland responded with the strictest laws in the nation. Ignoring lawsuits and pressures from commercial and development interests, Portland's leaders drew a line around their metropolitan area, banning any development beyond that point (much as London had done during its post–World War II reconstruction). The plan's intent was to force jobs, homes, and stores into a relatively compact area served by light rail, buses, and cars.

Automobiles, of course, are a major cause of the urban sprawl besetting most cities. Portland bucked the trend by tearing up its downtown riverfront freeway, converting the area, along with abandoned warehouse sites, into one of the city's most-used parks, named for McCall. It also limited downtown parking spaces and created an award-winning mass transit system, with North America's first modern streetcar system, the MAX light rail and the TriMet bus system. The systems are fully intermodal, meaning that passengers can easily switch from one to the other. In the 10-block radius of downtown "Payless Square," travel is free.

A record 97,000 riders commuted daily on MAX in 2004–2005, more than in larger cities like Seattle and Denver. No Portlander is forced to ride MAX or Tri-Met buses, but 70 percent of those who own cars choose a public transit option instead. So successful has the MAX been that an 18-mile Westside extension was opened in 1998, a 5.5-mile extension in 2001, and a 5.8-mile line in 2004. Two additional lines—the 6.5-mile I-205 MAX and the Yellow Line along the Portland Mall—will soon be added (TriMet 2006). Portland is one of the few regions in the country where transit ridership is growing faster than vehicle miles traveled. The city also encourages bike travel, placing brightly colored bikes and bike racks throughout the city for anyone to use.

Portland also enacted a downtown development plan inspired by the ideas of Jane Jacobs, August Heckscher, William H. Whyte, and James Rouse (all of whom will be discussed in Chapter 14). All new buildings, including garages, must be people friendly at street level. Blank walls are banned in favor of stores, offices, and eating establishments. Further, Portland set aside 1 percent of public construction funds to enhance the physical attractiveness of the area through outdoor public art.

In 1996, Portland enacted an even stricter plan for its three-county metropolitan area to handle the anticipated 500,000 new residents—in essence, another Portland—in the existing urban boundaries of its 362-square-mile metropolitan borders within 20 years. This may mean more apartment buildings and townhouses in previously single-family neighborhoods. To keep "big box" stores from springing up in industrial areas, Portland's new plan limits retail outlets to 60,000 square feet and restricts the number of parking spaces a new store may have, in a further effort to encourage use of mass transit. As part of their ambitious crusade to stop sprawl by limiting job growth, Portland officials in 1999 imposed a $1,000-per-job "growth impact fee" on the Intel Corporation if its new jobs exceed an imposed limit (Hayward 1999).

In becoming "the reigning model for growth management in the United States,"

Portland followed the visionary guide set for it by Lewis Mumford back in 1938, when he declared, "I have seen a lot of scenery in my life, but I have seen nothing so tempting as a home for man than this Oregon country. . . . You have the basis here for civilization on its highest scale" (cited in Stephenson 1999).

Portland Today

In its transition from a timber town to a high-tech hub, Portland has become a model city. In 2000, *Money* magazine named it as the "Best Big City." Portland is one of the best job markets in the country. It is home to more than 1,500 technology companies, from Intel—the largest private sector employer with 11,000 workers—to Hewlett-Packard, Epson, NEC, and dozens of small software firms (Pachetti et al. 2000).

Portland has a dense downtown containing about twice the work force it had 20 years ago. Yet, despite its growth, Portland has retained its nineteenth-century small city block design, which yields a pedestrian-friendly city core. The central business district (CBD) is virtually a walker's paradise, beckoning strollers to pass along the tree-lined streets on brick walkways and to stop to enjoy fountains, benches, and small parks along the way. Pedestrians may shop at over 1,100 retail stores; enjoy many outstanding coffee houses and restaurants; visit one of the city's microbreweries; or browse in any one of the numerous bookstores—including Powell's City of Books, with the largest number of volumes (nearly 1.5 million) in the United States.

The city's economy is healthy, helped in large measure by the silicon forest of high-tech office campuses and factories—such as Intel, NEC, and Hewlett-Packard—that grew inside the metro area. Nowhere are there signs of the industrial or residential abandonment that scar cities elsewhere (Abbott 1995:3). Major department stores—Nordstrom's and Saks Fifth Avenue—enhance the central business district. Recreational activities include comedy clubs, ballet, opera, symphonies, modern dance, theater, a planetarium, hockey and

Portland's popular Tom McCall Waterfront Park attracts pedestrians at all hours of the day and is the site of numerous special events, such as the Rose Festival, Dragon Boat Races, and annual carnival. Many U.S. cities have rediscovered and revitalized their waterfronts, attracting residents and tourists alike, thereby enhancing the quality of life and ambience of the city.

baseball teams, and the Portland Trail Blazers professional basketball team.

In terms of aesthetics, amenities, economy, land use, and planning, most people applaud Portland as "a city that works," an appellation once only applied to Toronto. Another reason that Portland works is its effective, efficient, and rider-friendly transit system. As TriMet transportation planning director Ken Zatarain says, "In Portland, we try to make transit a livability choice. You can make public transportation a part of your lifestyle." In fact, many Portland areas developed *after* transit passed through. A good example is the Lloyd district, where housing, office towers, and businesses sprouted up after light rail began running through it. Zatarain calls the district a "complete community," meaning that the area is balanced with jobs and housing, and people can walk or bike. Portland, which now offers a rail link to the airport and other amenities, such as bike-friendly buses, will remain, its

leaders insist, a place for quality urban center living (Loehndorf 2003).

Will Portland, with a 2000 metropolitan population of 1.9 million, maintain its urban growth boundaries to protect the surrounding countryside? Although metropolitan Portland has grown by about 44 percent since 1980, the urbanized area has expanded by only 2 percent (O'Meara 1999:10). An anticipated population increase of 500,000 people in just 20 years will surely test both Portland's resolve and its ability to balance big-city excitement and small-town charm. But if the planners and city leaders have their way, the answer will be yes.

❖ ═══════════ ❖ ═══════════ ❖

SUMMARY

Four patterns of land development—sprawl, edge cities, gated communities, and common-interest developments—became so widespread by the end of the twentieth century that they will most likely affect both urban and suburban lifestyles for at least the first few decades of the twenty-first century.

Sprawl refers to low-density land development beyond the edge of services and employment. Sprawl uses up large tracts of land (even when cities decline in population), increases residents' dependency on automobiles, creates traffic congestion and pollution, and wastes natural resources. Solutions to sprawl include purchasing and preserving open space, setting urban growth boundaries, revitalizing existing cities and towns, and pursuing transit-oriented approaches.

The past three decades have seen the evolution of more than 200 new cities in North America and elsewhere, located at the fringes of older cities. Their sprawling land use and auto dependency stand in marked contrast to the compact land use of older "walking" cities. Not clearly marked by territorial boundaries but usually situated near two major highways, edge cities fall into three categories: uptown, boomer, and greenfield. Boomer cities are by far the most numerous and have three subcategories: strip, node, and pig-in-a-python. Essentially middle-class entities that cut across racial lines, edge cities have a shopping mall as their anchor point and provide more jobs, shops, and entertainment than older cities do.

Although gated communities first appeared in the United States in the late 1800s and a few other such exclusive locales came into existence in the 1950s, it was only in the late 1960s and 1970s, when retirement communities materialized, that average Americans began to wall themselves off from society. The 1980s marked a rapid increase in gated communities, both in urban and suburban locales, and now over 8 million people live in them. Categories of gated communities are lifestyle, prestige, and security zone. Critics charge that this residence pattern contributes to social fragmentation, does not really deter crime, and does not provide any real sense of community.

Common-interest developments (CIDs) may or may not include gated communities. These master-planned developments require monthly fees for shared amenities and membership in a homeowners' association, which has broad regulatory powers over residents— powers that critics charge invade both the privacy and the constitutional rights of individuals.

CONCLUSION

Although Canada has stronger central government controls over land use than the United States, both countries are experiencing sprawl, edge city development, and an increase in exclusive communities. Some areas have more successfully contained these growth patterns than others, but they predominate nonetheless. What do these popular choices bode for the future of older cities and for the social cohesiveness of Canadian and U.S. societies?

Generations ago, zoning and planning boards throughout Canada and the United States generated building and density code variances to preserve the position of the privileged; so economic and social segregation are by no means new social phenomena. However, gated communities go much further in their exclusivity, for they create physical entry barriers. Moreover, they privatize not only individual space, but community space as well. The common-interest developments do even more: They privatize civic responsibilities (police protection) and communal services (street maintenance, entertainment, and recreation). This new development creates a private world that requires residents to share little with their neighbors outside their barricades or even with the larger political system.

The recent evolution of edge cities and exclusive communities is still new, but already the dominance of these urban forms in North America suggests a need for further research. But this is only part of the urban picture. The next five chapters will examine how social scientists—sociologists, psychologists, geographers, anthropologists, and political economists—have come to analyze cities as living entities. Reading these chapters, you will discover that the urban story gets even more interesting.

KEY TERMS

Boomers
Common-interest developments (CIDs)
Edge city
Exurbs
Gated communities

Greenfields
Lifestyle communities
Prestige communities
Security-zone communities
Sprawl
Uptowns

CHAPTER 5

URBAN SOCIOLOGY
Classic and Modern Statements

❖ ━━━━━━━━━ ❖ ━━━━━━━━━ ❖

Once humans learned to harness the machine, the resulting social upheaval dramatically changed virtually everything. Nowhere were the changes more pronounced than in European cities. The emerging factory system drew in unheard-of numbers of people, with the result that the cities exploded with population. In 1816, for example, Germany had barely 2.5 million urbanites; by 1895 the number had passed 13 million. During the nineteenth century,

CITYSCAPE

Working-Class Manchester, 1844

Friedrich Engels, the son of a wealthy German manufacturer, went to Manchester, England, in 1842 to learn the textile business. During his early years there, he gathered material for his first book, *The Condition of the Working Class in England,* in 1844. This excerpt from that work vividly describes Manchester's appalling slum conditions.

Here one is in an almost undisguised working-men's quarter, for even the shops and beer-houses hardly take the trouble to exhibit a trifling degree of cleanliness. But all this is nothing in comparison with the courts and lanes which lie behind, to which access can be gained only through covered passages, in which no two human beings can pass at the same time. Of the irregular cramming together of dwellings in ways which defy all rational plan, of the tangle in which they are crowded literally one upon the other, it is impossible to convey an idea. And it is not the buildings surviving from the old times of Manchester which are to blame for this; the confusion has only recently reached its height when every scrap of space left by the old way of building has been filled up and patched over until not a foot of land is left to be further occupied.

. . . Right and left a multitude of covered passages lead from the main street into numerous courts, and he who turns in thither gets into a filth and disgusting grime, the equal of which is not to be found . . . and which contain unqualifiedly the most horrible dwellings which I have yet beheld. In these courts there stands directly at the entrance, at the end of the covered passage, a privy without a door, so dirty that the inhabitants can pass into and out of the court only by passing through foul pools of stagnant urine and excrement. . . . Below it on the river there are several tanneries which fill the whole neighborhood with the stench of animal putrefaction. Below Ducie Bridge the only entrance to most of the houses is by means of narrow, dirty stairs and over heaps of refuse and filth. . . .

The view from [Ducie] Bridge . . . is characteristic for the whole district. At the bottom flows, or rather stagnates, the Irk, a narrow, coal-black, foul-smelling stream, full of debris and refuse, which it deposits on the shallower right bank. In dry weather, a long string of the most disgusting blackish-green slime pools are left standing on this bank, from the depths of which bubbles of miasmatic gas constantly arise and give forth a stench unendurable even on the bridge forty or fifty feet above the surface of the stream. . . .

Passing along a rough bank, among stakes and washing-lines, one penetrates into this chaos of small one-storied, one-roomed huts, in most of which there is no artificial floor; kitchen, living and sleeping-room all in one. In such a hole, scarcely five feet long by six broad, I found two beds—and such bedsteads and beds!—which, with a staircase and chimney-place, exactly filled the room. In several others I found absolutely nothing, while the door stood open, and the inhabitants leaned against it. Everywhere before the doors refuse and offal; that any sort of pavement lay underneath could not be seen but only felt, here and there, with the feet. . . .

Enough! The whole side of the Irk is built in this way, a planless, knotted chaos of houses, more or less on the verge of uninhabitableness, whose unclean interiors fully correspond with their filthy external surroundings. And how

London grew from 861,000 to a monumental 6.5 million.

Imagine such radical change: Overwhelmed by incoming migrants, cities could not provide adequate food, safe housing, sanitary facilities, medical care, or enough jobs.

As a result, poverty, disease, malnutrition, and crime were on the rise. City streets no doubt seemed chaotic. This was the context in which urban sociology emerged. In the Cityscape box below, Friedrich Engels (1820–1895) vividly describes the appalling slum conditions

---

could the people be clean with no proper opportunity for satisfying the most natural and ordinary wants? Privies are so rare here that they are either filled up every day, or are too remote for most of the inhabitants to use. How can people wash when they have only the dirty Irk water at hand, while pumps and water pipes can be found in decent parts of the city alone? In truth, it cannot be charged to the account of these helots of modern society if their dwellings are not more clean than the pig sties which are here and there to be seen among them. The landlords are not ashamed to let dwellings like the six or seven cellars on the quay directly below Scotland Bridge, the floors of which stand at least two feet below the low-water level of the Irk that flows not six feet away from them; or like the upper floor of the corner-house on the opposite shore directly above the bridge, where the ground-floor, utterly uninhabitable, stands deprived of all fittings for doors and windows, a case by no means rare in this region, when this open ground-floor is used as a privy by the whole neighbourhood for want of other facilities!

As for the rest, the filth, debris, and offal heaps, and the pools in the streets are common . . . and another feature most injurious to the cleanliness of the inhabitants, is the multitude of pigs walking about in all the alleys, rooting into the offal heaps, or kept imprisoned in small pens. Here, as in most of the working-men's quarters of Manchester, the pork-raisers rent the courts and build pig-pens in them. In almost every court one or even several such pens may be found, into which the inhabitants of the court throw all refuse and offal, whence the swine grow fat; and the atmosphere, confined on all four sides, is utterly corrupted by putrefying animal and vegetable substances. . . .

Such is the Old Town of Manchester, and on re-reading my description, I am forced to admit that instead of being exaggerated, it is far

from black enough to convey a true impression of the filth, ruin, and uninhabitableness, the defiance of all considerations of cleanliness, ventilation, and health which characterise the construction of this single district, containing at least twenty to thirty thousand inhabitants. And such a district exists in the heart of the second city of England, the first manufacturing city in the world. If any one wishes to see in how little space a human being can move, how little air—and such air!—he can breathe, how little of civilisation he may share and yet live, it is only necessary to travel hither. . . .

Everything which here arouses horror and indignation is of recent origin, belongs to the industrial epoch. The couple of hundred houses, which belong to old Manchester, have been long since abandoned by their original inhabitants; the industrial epoch alone has crammed into them the swarms of workers whom they now shelter; the industrial epoch alone has built up every spot between these old houses to win a covering for the masses whom it has conjured hither from the agricultural districts and from Ireland; the industrial epoch alone enables the owners of these cattle sheds to rent them for high prices to human beings, to plunder the poverty of the workers, to undermine the health of thousands, in order that they alone, the owner, may grow rich. In the industrial epoch alone has it become possible that the worker scarcely freed from feudal servitude could be used as mere material, a mere chattel; that he must let himself be crowded into a dwelling too bad for every other, which he for his hard-earned wages buys the right to let go utterly to ruin. This manufacture has achieved, which, without these workers, this poverty, this slavery could not have lived.

Source: Friedrich Engels, *The Condition of the Working Class in England,* trans. by W. O. Henderson and W. H. Chaloner (New York: Macmillan, 1958).

that industrialization brought to Manchester, England.

THE EUROPEAN TRADITION: 1846–1921

Sociology was born in Europe, a child of the Industrial Revolution. Given its start by August Comte (1798–1857), it was nurtured by the sociologists who followed—including Karl Marx, Friedrich Engels, Ferdinand Tönnies, Emile Durkheim, Georg Simmel, and Max Weber—who sought to explain the great transformation wrought by urbanization and industrialization.

Karl Marx and Friedrich Engels: From Barbarism to Civilization

Karl Marx (1818–1883) spent most of his adult life in England during the heyday of the Industrial Revolution. Marx was among the first of the classical sociologists to offer an analysis of the transformation of European society.

Marx argued passionately that the economic structure of society is "the real foundation . . . [that] determines the general character of the social, political, and spiritual processes of life" (1959:49; orig. 1859). By this he meant that the economic system serves as the base on which the social institutions of family, religion, and the political system take form. Although he conceded many causes of social change (such as technological advances), Marx contended that societal transformation primarily results from *conflict* between those who control the process of economic production (capitalists) and those who supply the necessary labor (proletariat). Thus, to argue that social problems such as poverty and unemployment are the fault of individuals is a form of **false consciousness** since, as Marx saw it, the flaws of capitalism are the causes of these and other problems.

But Marx and his colleague Engels held that the city has special importance. People, they said, live as "generic, tribal beings" in preindustrial, traditional societies. Only with the rise of the city does productive specialization begin to free individuals to act on their own. It is in cities, then, that the state emerges so that people take on a political role as citizens, deliberately planning their own environment and using new scientific skills. Thus, to Marx and Engels, the rise of the city amounted to nothing less than a transition from barbarism to civilization:

> The greatest division of material and mental labour is the separation of town and country. The antagonism between town and country begins with the transition from barbarism to civilization, from tribe to State, from locality to nation, and runs through the whole history of civilization to the present day. . . . (1846:143)

However, Marx and Engels made it clear that not every city was liberating in this way. Under what they called "Asiatic modes of production" some cities remained chained to the bonds of the primitive community—with its limited division of labor, common property, and lack of individualism. As a result, these cities depended entirely on the agricultural surplus, and the functions of these cities—military, religious, or bureaucratic—lacked the dynamic drive of a commercial economy.

Even in industrial cities, however, Marx and Engels held that the social evolution of humans was not yet complete since a capitalist elite controlled the economy. Seeing firsthand the destructive aspects of early industrial capitalism, Marx and Engels believed that the historical process would further evolve with a worldwide anticapitalist revolution that would usher in socialism. Only in this final evolutionary phase would workers become aware of the real cause of their problems, unite, and act together to transform society into a new and just order.

Ferdinand Tönnies: From *Gemeinschaft* to *Gesellschaft*

In his masterwork, *Gemeinschaft and Gesellschaft* (1887), the German sociologist Ferdinand Tönnies (1855–1936) described two contrasting types of human social life: *gemeinschaft*, or "community," which characterized the small country village; and *gesellschaft*, or "association," which characterized the large city. Within the village, Tönnies maintained, social life forms a "living organism" in which people have an essential unity of purpose, work together for the common good, and are united by ties of family and neighborhood. Such is not the case in the city, in which social life is a "mechanical aggregate" characterized by disunity, rampant individualism, and selfishness, even hostility. Among city dwellers, a belief in the common good is rare; ties of family and neighborhood are of little significance.

The typology of *gemeinschaft* and *gesellschaft* has had a lasting influence on urban sociology because it was one of the first theories to understand human settlements by means of a continuum. At each "pole" of the continuum was a specific, "pure" type of settlement. Using such a formulation, one could classify any actual settlement at some point along the continuum as having a certain measure of *gemeinschaft* qualities and a certain degree of *gesellschaft* qualities.

In Tönnies's conceptions of *gemeinschaft* and *gesellschaft*, we can observe the influence of Karl Marx, a fact Tönnies openly acknowledged in citing "Karl Marx's masterful analysis of industrial development" (Tönnies 1887:64). In fact, Tönnies's idea of community finds its counterpart in the "primitive community" and "primitive mode of production" that Marx and Engels had written about 40 years earlier.

Gemeinschaft. Tönnies used the concept of *gemeinschaft* to characterize the rural village and surrounding land worked communally by its inhabitants. Social life was characterized by "intimate, private, and exclusive living together," and members were bound by common language and traditions. They recognized "common goods—common evils; common friends—common enemies" and carried within them a sense of "we-ness," of "our-ness." Thornton Wilder expresses this sense of village togetherness eloquently in his play *Our Town;*

Small-town America—such as here in Camden, Maine—is often idealized as today's closest approximation to a *gemeinschaft* society. In such locales Main Street is exactly that, a place where most of the area's commercial activity (banking, retail sales) occurs and where people are likely to encounter known others with whom they can easily engage in personal conversations.

see the analytical commentary about the play in the Cityscape box on page below.

Gesellschaft. In the character of the modern city Tönnies saw a wholly different style of life, in which the meaning of existence shifted from the group to the individual. Where *gemeinschaft* expresses a sense of "we-ness," *gesellschaft* is more rational, more calculating. By its very nature, *gesellschaft* conditions people to be primarily concerned with their own self-interest, to "look out for Number

CITYSCAPE

Our Town: *The Spirit of* Gemeinschaft

Thornton Wilder's play *Our Town* is an acclaimed classic for many reasons, including its poignant portrayal of "ordinary life-cycle events." However, to many people, its real charm lies in the insights provided into life in a typical small town, where people live in what we may appropriately call a *gemeinschaft* community.

The play opens with the "Stage Manager" telling the audience about "our town," Grover's Corners, a small village in New Hampshire. He asks the audience to imagine the layout of the town and the life of its inhabitants.

To orient us, he points out what first appear to be differences—where, for example, the Polish immigrants live. They migrated to Grover's Corners to work in the mill, he tells us, as did a few "Canuck" families. Next he tells us where the various churches are: Catholic, Congregationalist, Presbyterian, Methodist, Unitarian, and Baptist, in that order. He does not tell us that such differences may separate people's lives somewhat, but they by no means isolate them from one another. Almost intuitively we know this, however—a fact reaffirmed through our learning that everyone here knows quite a bit about almost everyone else. They don't necessarily like everyone, or always approve of certain people's behavior (such as excessive drinking, for example), but there is closeness, an intimacy, among the people nevertheless. This is how it also was in

the medieval city—Weber's ideal form of *gemeinschaft*—where class differences, disagreements, even conflict existed within a close-knit community dominated by traditional values and continuity.

To help us understand some of this tradition and continuity, the Stage Manager informs us that the town's earliest tombstones—dating back to 1670—are engraved with names such as Grover, Cartright, Gibbs, and Hersey. These are the same family names as among the townspeople in 1901, the year in which the play takes place. Emphasizing this theme of stable relationships in daily life, he tells us, "On the whole, things don't change much around here." He also offers bits of other information—the nonexistence of burglars and the daily visits by nearly everyone to the grocery store and the drug store on Main Street. These manifestations of mutual trust, daily routine, familiarity, and regular social interaction suggest a cohesiveness of community that is the essence of *gemeinschaft*.

As the play unfolds about this ordinary small town, one where "nobody remarkable ever come out of it, s'far as we know," we learn about more than just some events in the lives of George Gibbs and Emily Webb, or of their family, friends, and neighbors, both alive or deceased. We witness the way life once was in simpler times in North American small towns—a way of life that no doubt still exists in whatever small towns still remain. But for most of us—living in a *gesellschaft* environment—it is a bygone reality, not ours.

One," in contemporary terms. In *gemeinschaft* the "natural" social institutions of kinship, neighborhood, and friendship are predominant; in *gesellschaft* these forms of association tend to decline.

One way to distinguish easily the difference between *gemeinschaft* and *gesellschaft* is to consider, when people ask, "How are you?"—do they really want to know? Tönnies's communal relation—*gemeinschaft*—is built on broad concern for the other as a person, and such a question has significance beyond convention, beyond politeness. In the contrasting case—*gesellschaft*—each person is understood in terms of a particular role and service provided (as teacher, computer programmer, or butcher). In the city the question "How are you?" is usually asked only out of politeness: We don't know other people well and, what's more, we usually don't want to know them well.

Gemeinschaft **and** *Gesellschaft* **in History.** Tönnies believed that the study of European history revealed a gradual, and generally irreversible, displacement of *gemeinschaft* by *gesellschaft*. He saw the rapid rise of cities in Europe during the nineteenth century as the inevitable emergence of *gesellschaft* as the dominant form of social life. Although he thought it inevitable, Tönnies obviously did not think this transformation altogether good: For him, the unity and human concern of *gemeinschaft* was gradually lost in *gesellschaft*.

Tönnies's ideas contain the beginning of a sociology of the city. He was among the first to see urban life as distinctive and worthy of study. Moreover, his use of contrasting pure types is a pattern that numerous other urban sociologists followed.

Emile Durkheim: Mechanical and Organic Solidarity

Like Tönnies, the French sociologist Emile Durkheim (1858–1917) witnessed the urban revolution of the nineteenth century. He, too, developed a model of contrasting types: Mechanical solidarity and organic solidarity are analogous to Tönnies's *gemeinschaft* and *gesellschaft*.

Mechanical solidarity refers to social bonds that are constructed on likeness, on common belief and custom, on common ritual and symbol. Such solidarity is "mechanical" because the people who participate in it—people living in family units, tribes, or small towns—are almost identical in major respects and are united almost automatically, without thinking. Each family, tribe, or town is relatively self-sufficient and able to meet all life needs without dependence on other groups.

In contrast, **organic solidarity** describes a social order based on individual differences. Characteristic of modern societies, especially cities, organic solidarity rests on a complex division of labor, in which many different people specialize in many different occupations. Like the organs of the human body, people depend more on one another to meet various needs. A lawyer depends on other people—say, restaurant owners and grocers—to supply food, and is able to specialize in legal activity. Similarly, of course, the restaurant owner and the grocer need not study law, for the same reason.

In this complex division of labor, Durkheim saw the possibility of greater freedom and choice for all of society's inhabitants. Although Durkheim acknowledged the problems that cities might create—impersonality, alienation, disagreement, and conflict—he argued for the ultimate superiority of organic over mechanical solidarity: "[The] yoke that we submit to [in modern society] is much less heavy than when society completely controls us [as it does in rural society], and it leaves much more place open for the free play of our initiative" (1964:131; orig. 1893).

Durkheim and Tönnies: A Comparison. While Durkheim agreed with Tönnies's conclusion that history was characterized by a movement from an emphasis on one type of social order to another—from mechanical solidarity (or *gemeinschaft*) to organic solidarity (or *gesellschaft*)—there are important differences in their ideas. For instance, Durkheim took exception to labeling the tribal or rural environment alone as "natural." Rather, he asserted that "the life of large social agglomerations is just as natural as that of small groupings."

This assertion reveals that Durkheim did not share Tönnies's negative view of modern society. In fact, Durkheim reversed Tönnies's terminology and labeled *gemeinschaft* "mechanical" and *gesellschaft* "organic." Although Tönnies saw little hope for truly humane life in the city (he cited parents' admonition to their citybound children to beware of "bad *gesellschaft*"), Durkheim was more optimistic. Durkheim saw the increasing division of labor characteristic of modern urban societies as undermining traditional social integration and creating a new form of social cohesion based on mutual interdependence. Contractual agreements among individuals or groups clearly express this interdependence. Still, Durkheim cautioned, no society can exist entirely on the basis of contract: At the very least, there needs to be a moral foundation on which we agree about how to enter into and execute all contracts fairly.

Durkheim thus provides an important counterpoint to Tönnies. Although both theorists recognized that cities were associated with the growth of social differentiation and individuality, Tönnies feared the undermining of the very fabric of social life, whereas Durkheim saw the possibility of continuing social cohesion and greater human development. Yet the effects of the city on individuals extend beyond these two visions.

Georg Simmel: The Mental Life of the Metropolis

Both Tönnies and Durkheim described the broad societal processes that produced the modern city. Although they made passing reference to the mental characteristics of city dwellers—the city dweller was more impersonal, more rational, freer—they did not look systematically at the social psychology of city life. Another German, Georg Simmel (1858–1918), undertook that task.

Like his contemporaries, Simmel saw in the rise of the modern world a cause for concern: How was the individual to maintain a spirit of freedom and creativity in the midst of the city's "overwhelming social forces"? In his famous essay "The Metropolis and Mental Life," Simmel suggested that the personality would learn to "accommodate itself" to the urban scene (Simmel 1905, 1964).

The City's Characteristics.   To Simmel, the unique trait of the modern city is the intensification of nervous stimuli with which the city dweller must cope. Unlike the rural setting, where "the rhythm of life and sensory imagery flows more slowly, more habitually, more evenly," the city constantly bombards the individual with an enormous kaleidoscope of sights, sounds, and smells. To avoid being overwhelmed by such stimulation, the individual learns to discriminate carefully—to tune in what is important and tune out what is irrelevant. In time, urban people become more sophisticated and intellectual, more rational and calculating than their rural counterparts.

Such rationality means that urbanites are highly attuned to time. Cities, Simmel observed, are marked by the ever-present clock and wristwatch. "If," he continued, "all the clocks and watches in Berlin would suddenly go wrong in different ways, even if only by one hour, all economic life and communication of the city would be disrupted for a long time" (1964:413). In addition to the rational organization of time, Simmel saw the rationality of the city expressed in its advanced economic division of labor (here he echoed Durkheim). Social life in the city is the interplay of specialists.

But perhaps the most powerful means of conveying the message of urban rationality was Simmel's discussion of the importance of money. "The metropolis," he stated, "has always been the seat of a money economy." Why is money so important in urban life? One reason is that the advanced division of labor requires a universal means of exchange. Money performs this critical function. As Simmel wrote (1964:414), "Money is concerned only with what is common to all: It asks for the exchange value, it reduces all quality and individuality to the question: How much?"

The Individual's Response.   How, asks Simmel, is the urbanite to behave in the midst of such powerful stimulation and unending

Whenever we walk along a city street, we encounter an abundance of stimuli, far more than we can absorb. This intensification of nervous stimuli—from the many signs, sounds, movements, and crowds of people—forces us, says Simmel, to discriminate carefully, to tune in what is important and to tune out what is not.

demand for rational response? Or, on a more practical level, can you really stop to help everyone you see on the street who is in some sort of trouble? Simmel believed not. Consequently, he reasoned, the urbanite adapts to city life by developing what he called a "blasé" attitude, a social reserve, a detachment. Put simply, in the city we respond with our head rather than our heart. We learn to adopt a matter-of-fact attitude about the world around us. We simply don't care; we don't want to "get involved," as is shown dramatically in the examples in the Urban Living box on page 134.

Even worse, Simmel speculated that the cultivated indifference necessary to living in the city may harden into a measured antagonism. "Indeed, if I do not deceive myself," he wrote, "the inner aspect of this outer reserve is not only indifference, but, more often than we are aware, it is a slight aversion, a mutual strangeness and repulsion, which will break into hatred and fight at the moment of a closer contact, however

caused" (1964:415–16). Perhaps each of us can recall feeling some anger about the way someone unknown to us was behaving in a city— someone who broke into a line ahead of us, for example, or someone who approached us in a city park, demanding spare change.

Like Durkheim, Simmel could see freedom in the separateness fostered by city living. The urbanite, he thought, can transcend the pettiness of daily routine and reach a new height of personal and spiritual development. But Simmel also detected in the city's freedom a haunting specter. "It is obviously only the obverse of this freedom," he wrote, "if, under certain circumstances one nowhere feels as lonely and lost as in the metropolitan crowd."

Feeling like a cog in a giant machine, some people maintain their sense of individuality in a city by doing something "odd," by "being different" and thereby standing out. It is this sense of alienation that Simmel would use to explain the motivation for the graffiti craze in so many cities, a process that has defaced buildings,

URBAN LIVING

Urban Apathy: The Death of Kitty Genovese and Other Ignored Violent Attacks

On March 14, 1964, a grim item appeared in a tiny story on page 26 of the *New York Times.* It reported the murder of Kitty Genovese near her home in the Kew Gardens section of New York's Borough of Queens. What seemed at first to be a report of a crime without particular public significance exploded into a major controversy when the *Times* reported two weeks later that dozens of Ms. Genovese's "neighbors" had observed her attacker stab her repeatedly during a period of half an hour without coming to her aid or even calling the police until after she was dead! In an editorial the following day, the *Times* posed a frightening question: "Does residence in a great city destroy all sense of personal responsibility for one's neighbors?" The death of Kitty Genovese thus became symbolic of the argument that the city was an unhealthy setting that lacked even a rudimentary sense of human community.

But it didn't stop with Kitty Genovese. Hers is only the most celebrated case. On the night of November 30, 1984, the same thing happened in Brooklyn. A woman was attacked in the Gowanus Apartments, a New York City housing project. As she was beaten, she began screaming and continued her cries for 20 minutes. Many heard her—no one came to her rescue. Finally, her assailants dragged her into the lobby of a building and shot her dead. It was only then that someone deigned to call the police (*New York Times,* December 2, 1984).

The same year, the same indifference to the victims of urban crime surfaced again, this time in St. Louis. In one case a man was robbed at gunpoint while dozens of people looked on. When the man approached the onlookers afterward and asked why they hadn't helped him, they replied that they just "didn't want to get involved." In another incident three men attacked a woman at Busch Memorial Stadium during a Cardinals baseball game. She screamed for help. No one responded. She said later: "I was shocked more than hurt. I just sat there and screamed and not one soul stopped. I saw all these legs going by, and I thought about reaching out and grabbing somebody." Said Sgt. Frank Baricevic of the St. Louis Police of these disturbing incidents: "Police departments are only as good as the people they protect. If [people] don't want to get involved, if they don't want to cooperate, then we're in trouble" (*New York Times,* August 18, 1984).

Such incidents still happen, and not just in the United States. In 2003, a 14-year-old girl was raped in broad daylight on a busy street in Heide, Germany, by a drunken stranger despite her calls for help to several passersby. The girl was riding home when a 19-year-old male grabbed her bicycle and dragged her to the ground. Although she immediately called out to a female passerby, who apparently understood her plea for help, the woman walked on. Soon after, a group of four people walked by and also ignored her screams although the man had pressed her to the ground in front of a pharmacy and begun to rape her. The victim told police that at the same time, at least two men watched the attack from a nearby balcony and did not move to help. Only after she was able to free herself and her father arrived did a witness alert the police, who were able to locate and detain the rapist. Because he had no previous record of sexual attacks, he was released on bail. Police said his level of intoxication could serve as a mitigating factor and save him from conviction (News24.com 2003).

If you encountered this stranger lying unconscious on your campus or in a suburban mall parking lot, the probability is high that you would help him or get help. In the city, however, where sleeping vagrants, drunks, and addicts often abound, you might well ignore him and avoid getting involved, as several people here are doing.

signs, subway trains, and public monuments. For many of these vandals, their "tags" raise them out of their anonymity and shout out, "I'm not just another face in the project among a million others. I exist. I am here!"

In the end, then, Simmel appears to side more with Tönnies than with Durkheim in his evaluation of the city. Although he depicted the city as the setting where the great historical contest between true human liberation and alienation would occur, his analysis left little doubt that he believed the second option was likely to be victorious.

Max Weber: The Historical and Comparative Study of Cities

Tönnies, Durkheim, and Simmel all analyzed a single type of city. That is, they developed their theories by "reading" the main trends of European urban history and the main elements of life in the cities they knew.

German sociologist Max Weber (1864–1920) believed that any theory that took account of cities in only one part of the world at one point in time was of limited value. This concern proved to be his major methodological contribution to urban sociology.

Die Stadt. Weber demonstrated his approach in his famous essay "*Die Stadt*" ("The City"), which first appeared in 1921. Surveying cities of Europe, the Middle East, India, and China, Weber developed a definition of what he called the full urban community:

To constitute a full urban community, a settlement must display a relative predominance of trade–commercial relations, with the settlement as a whole displaying the following features: (1) a fortification; (2) a market; (3); a court of its

As Park suggested, urbanites typically respond to people's eccentricities with great tolerance, even to the point of ignoring them. This unusual scene (for many) depicts a man wearing his Rapid T. Rabbit character's costume on a subway train. He is one of the people known as furries (or fursuiters), who identify with animals or animal characters and dress up in their likeness.

own and at least partially autonomous law; (4) a related form of association; and (5) at least partial political autonomy. (1966:80–81)

This definition illustrates what Weber called an **ideal type,** a model constructed from real-world observation that highlights the crucial elements of some social phenomenon. Weber was well aware that many cities would not contain all of the elements in his definition. In such cases, the city simply would not be a "full urban community" in his sense. We shall examine the characteristics of such a community in more detail.

First, Weber's urban community is based on trade or commercial relations. In rural areas, people are more or less self-sufficient, growing their own food, providing their own clothing, and so on. Trade and commerce are of limited importance there. Not so in the city. Weber clearly agreed with Tönnies, Durkheim, and Simmel that economic self-sufficiency is nearly impossible in cities; people are economically interdependent, linked by Durkheim's organic solidarity. Indeed, the economic aspects of city life are so important that a distinct mechanism of exchange—the market—evolved to facilitate them.

Second, an urban community is relatively autonomous. Weber specified that a true city has a court and law of its own and at least partial political autonomy. It also must be militarily self-sufficient, having a fortification system and army for self-defense if and when necessary. Such autonomy is essential if urban dwellers are to identify the city as theirs, as a place demanding their allegiance in the way that the small town receives the allegiance of its inhabitants.

Third, Weber said that the urban community must have "a related form of association." By this he meant that city living must involve social relationships and organizations through which urbanites gain a sense of meaningful participation in the life of their city.

The "Full Urban Community" in History. Like Durkheim, Weber believed that cities could be positive and liberating forces in human life. Unlike Durkheim, however, Weber did not see much hope for twentieth-century cities. Indeed, he thought only the fortified, self-sufficient cities of the medieval period deserved the title of "full urban community." Only in these cities had there existed the commercial relations, autonomy, and social participation that he believed to be the defining characteristics of urbanism.

With the rise to preeminence of the nation as a political entity in the seventeenth, eighteenth, and nineteenth centuries, Weber claimed, cities had lost their military and, to a large extent, their legal and political autonomy—necessary elements for identifying with the city as a psychological "home." People came to identify with other units of society—the nation, country, business, or, as recognized by Tönnies and Simmel, with themselves alone.

By recognizing medieval cities as examples of the full urban community, Weber hoped to show that "the good life" had existed in cities and might flourish again. Yet, by suggesting that a pinnacle of urban culture had been realized before in history, Weber implied that history might not necessarily be progressive (Sennett 1969:6–10).

The City and Culture. Weber stood apart from his colleagues, who tended to see the city itself as the cause of the distinguishing qualities of urban life. In contrast, Weber's analysis, fueled by his broad understanding of cities in other cultures and at different points in history, suggested that cities are intimately linked to larger processes—to particular economic or political orientations, for example. If a society's character is different, the nature of its cities will be different. Thus, feudal or Chinese societies would not produce the same type of urban life that European industrial capitalism does.

The European Tradition: An Evaluation

The ideas of Marx, Engels, Tönnies, Durkheim, Simmel, and Weber form the core of classical urban sociology and have had an enormous impact on the field ever since. It is important, however, to balance their contributions with their limitations.

Contributions. Perhaps the most important contribution of the classical theorists was their insistence that the city is an important object of sociological study. Marx, Engels, Tönnies, and Durkheim all clearly analyzed the contrasts between rural and urban life. Simmel and Weber went a step further by actually developing theories of how cities worked.

Second, all six theorists recognized that *there is something distinctive about the city and the way of life it creates.* They all saw the city as increasing human choice, emphasizing rationality, being characterized by a complex division of labor, and creating a unique experience for its inhabitants. This concern with the city's unique qualities has been, as the next section will demonstrate clearly, a major focus of the discipline ever since.

Third, taken together, these theorists suggested the main concerns of the discipline. Marx and Engels emphasized economics and the problems of inequality and conflict. Tönnies, Durkheim, and Weber all considered the social structure of the city. Simmel suggested the importance of the urban experience.

Finally, all six Europeans made the evaluation of cities a fundamental element in their work. Each made quite clear what he thought beneficial and what he considered detrimental to the city's ability to produce a humane life for its population.

Limitations. Three generations later, we can easily see how the central ideas of these theorists were an outgrowth of the times and cities in which they lived. Cities were quickly replacing villages and countryside as the main arena of life. For all their excitement, one could hardly argue that these rapidly growing cities provided a good life for many of their inhabitants. Little wonder, then, that three of these theorists (Tönnies, Simmel, and Weber) saw the cities of their day as threats to long-cherished human values. Durkheim, Marx, and Engels had mixed responses to the changing cities. Durkheim acknowledged the problems of alienation and conflict in the cities but also saw the ultimate superiority of the new industrial age. Marx and Engels saw not the city, but the capitalist economy, as a social evil.

Of course, one can only speculate on how the theories of these men might have changed had they been able to witness the growth of suburbs, major efforts at urban planning, reforms in many of the most overtly exploitative practices of turn-of-the-century cities (such as child labor), the rise of labor unions, the civil rights movement, and the recent collapse of communism in an economically bankrupt Soviet Union and a fettered Eastern Europe.

Also, the theorists show some disagreement in their interpretations. The contrast between Tönnies and Durkheim is most instructive. Tönnies saw *gemeinschaft* as humane and *gesellschaft* as brutal. Using his terms of mechanical and organic solidarity, Durkheim reversed the interpretation: The tribal or country life was cloying, undeveloped; the life of the city, in contrast, was liberating and full of potential for development.

On another level, Simmel thought the social–psychological adaptations he studied were a product of the great city itself. He implied that all metropolises would produce similar mental processes. Weber disagreed. He argued that only certain historical and cultural conditions produced the type of city that Simmel observed (modern capitalist cities, for example) and that other historical and cultural conditions would produce very different types of urban social–psychological adaptation.

Similarly, Marx and Engels maintained that the human condition in cities was the result of the economic structure and that a different economic system would produce a different city with different social interaction patterns.

With the evidence available at the time, it was impossible to judge such contradictory claims, although later chapters will show that Weber's position on this issue was closer to the truth.

URBAN SOCIOLOGY IN NORTH AMERICA: 1915–1970

About the time of World War I, urban sociology began to develop in the United States. From the outset, the discipline's character was somewhat different from that in Europe, with U.S. researchers showing greater concern with actually going out and exploring the city. At the same time, many of the themes of the European tradition were carried into North American sociology.

The era in which this sociology developed is noteworthy. The early twentieth century in North America, as in Europe, was a period of industrialization and rapid urban growth. A mounting flow of immigrants— who mostly settled in cities—ensured that, by 1920, the United States would become a predominantly urban society. In short, the Grover's Corners of North America (as described in the Cityscape box on p. 130) were rapidly giving way to the expanding industrial metropolis.

No city typified this explosive growth better than Chicago. A crude outpost in 1830, by 1900 Chicago was approaching a population of 2 million and was expanding both upward and outward. The first steel-frame building— a marvel of the age—opened its doors in Chicago in 1884, towering an incredible ten stories above the ground! By the close of World War I, Chicago boasted a population of almost 3 million. Immigrants from Europe and migrants from the countryside were everywhere. Like hundreds of exploding North American cities, Chicago was billowing the black, smoky flag of prosperity, creating its share of severe problems as it went. It was in Chicago that the main elements of U.S. urban sociology took form.

Robert Park and Sociology at the University of Chicago

Although U.S. universities had offered courses in "social science" as far back as 1865, sociology first gained intellectual respectability when the University of Chicago invited Albion W. Small (then president of Colby College) to found a sociology department in 1892 (Faris 1967). Within the next 30 years the department attracted several notable scholars. One of the most outstanding was Robert Ezra Park (1864–1944).

Leaving a newspaper job in 1915 to join the department, Park established the first urban studies center in the United States. His interest in urban matters had both European and North American roots. In his early years he had studied with the Russian sociologist Kistiakowski (who held much the same view of social change as Tönnies) and with Georg Simmel. Park was also deeply influenced by *The Shame of the Cities* (1904), a book by U.S. journalist Lincoln Steffens suggesting that serious urban problems were everyone's responsibility. An excerpt from this critique appears in the Critical Thinking box on page 140.

Although he was aware of both the bad and the good, there can be no question that Park had an almost unbounded fascination with the city. Not only did Park guide several generations of students in explorations of all aspects of Chicago, but he served as first president of the Chicago Urban League. Dedicating his life to relentless personal exploration of the city, Park later wrote:

> I expect that I have actually covered more ground, tramping about in cities in different parts of the world, than any other living man. Out of all this I gained, among other things, a conception of the city, the community, and the region, not as geographical phenomenon [sic] merely, but as a kind of social organism. (1950, p. viii)

A Systematic Urban Sociology. Park presented the program he used to guide urban sociology at the University of Chicago in his classic article "The City: Suggestions for the Investigation of Human Behavior in the Urban Environment" (1967; orig. published 1916). First, he argued that urban research had to be conducted by disciplined observation, in much the same way that anthropologists studied other cultures. Second, he conceived of the city as a social organism with distinct parts bound together by internal processes. Urban life was not chaos and disorder (stereotypes of Chicago during the Roaring Twenties notwithstanding) but rather tended toward an "orderly and typical grouping of its population and institutions" (1967:1). He wrote:

> Every great city has its racial colonies, like the Chinatowns of San Francisco and New York, the Little Sicily of Chicago, and the various other less pronounced types. In addition to these, most cities have their segregated vice districts . . . their rendezvous for criminals of various sorts. Every large city has its occupational suburbs, like the stockyards in Chicago, and its residential enclaves, like Brookline in Boston, the so-called "Gold Coast" in Chicago, Greenwich Village in New York, each of which has a size and character of a complete separate town, village, or city, except that its population is a select one. (1967:10)

This notion of the city's orderliness led Park to urge his students to develop detailed studies of all segments of the city's population—industrial workers, real-estate officials, and VIPs, and also migrants, hobos, musicians, prostitutes, and dance hall workers. The conviction that all "parts and processes" of the city were linked was at the heart of Park's new social science, which he termed "human, as distinguished from plant and animal, ecology." Finally, Park also saw the city as a "moral as well as a physical organization" and carried evaluative judgments of urban living deep into his sociology.

Park's Image of the City. What was it about the city that so fascinated Park? First, like Weber, Park saw in the modern city a commercial structure that owed "its existence to the market place around which it sprang up." Like Marx, Weber, and Durkheim, he saw in modern city life a complex division of labor driven by industrial competition. With Tönnies, Park

CRITICAL THINKING

The Shame of the Cities: Who's to Blame?

When I set out on my travels, an honest New Yorker told me honestly that I would find that the Irish, the Catholic Irish, were at the bottom of it all everywhere. The first city I went to was St. Louis, a German city. The next was Minneapolis, a Scandinavian city, with a leadership of New Englanders. Then came Pittsburgh, Scotch Presbyterian, and that was what my New York friend was. "Ah, but they are all foreign populations," I heard. The next city was Philadelphia, the purest American community of all, and the most hopeless. And after that came Chicago and New York, both mongrelbred, but the one a triumph of reform, the other the best example of good government that I had seen. The "foreign element" excuse is one of the hypocritical lies that save us from the clear sight of ourselves. . . .

When I set out to describe the corrupt systems of certain typical cities, I meant to show simply how the people were deceived and betrayed. But in the very first study—St. Louis—the startling truth lay bare that corruption was not merely political; it was financial, commercial, social; the ramifications of boodle were so complex, various,

and far-reaching that one mind could hardly grasp them. . . .

And it's all a moral weakness; a weakness right where we think we are strongest. Oh, we are good—on Sunday, and we are "fearfully patriotic" on the Fourth of July. But the bribe we pay to the janitor to prefer our interests to the landlord's, is the little brother of the bribe passed to the alderman to sell a city street, and the father of the air-brake stock assigned to the president of the railroad to have this life-saving invention adopted on his road. We are pathetically proud of our democratic institutions and our republican form of government, of our grand Constitution and our just laws. We are a free and sovereign people, we govern ourselves and the government is ours. But that is the point. We are responsible, not our leaders, since we follow them. We let them divert our loyalty from the United States to some "party"; we let them boss the party and turn our municipal democracies into autocracies and our republican nation into a plutocracy. We cheat our government and we let our leaders loot it, and we let them wheedle and bribe our sovereignty from us. . . . The people are not innocent.

Source: Lincoln Steffens, *The Shame of the Cities* (New York: McClure, Phillips, 1904), pp. 2–3, 7–9.

believed that this market dominance would result in the steady erosion of traditional ways of life. The past emphasis upon "family ties, local associations . . . caste, and status" would yield inevitably to a *gesellschaft*-like system "based on occupation and vocational interests."

Second, Park perceived the city as increasingly characterized by *formal social structures,* best exemplified by large-scale bureaucracies

such as police departments, courts, and welfare agencies. In time, he reasoned, these would take the place of the more "informal" means (such as neighborhood interaction) by which people had historically organized their everyday lives. Similarly, politics would develop a more formalized tone. Park contended that

the form of government which had its origin in the town meetings and was well suited to the needs of the small community based on primary relations is not suitable to the government of the changing and heterogeneous populations of cities of three or four millions. (1967:33)

The city dweller, unable to take account of all the issues at stake in the operation of a complex city, would have to rely on "the organization represented by the political boss and the political machine or other civic organizations such as voter leagues."

As an ex-newspaperman, Park could hardly have been expected to omit the media from his description of the formalization of city life. The face-to-face oral network by which information flowed in the village ("gossip" is the more precise, if less scholarly, term) would be replaced by reliance on impersonal mass media. Such was the significance of the city newspaper, and, soon after that, radio and television and, eventually, the Internet.

The third dimension of Park's image of the city, showing the effects of his studies with Simmel, was his emphasis on the psychosocial dimension of urban life. Park suggested that life within the city would become *less sentimental* and *more rational*. Deep-seated sentiments and prejudices would give way to calculation based on self-interest. At the same time, however, Park was aware that the erosion of traditional sentimental ties in the city might give rise to new social bonds in the form of interest groups. In this, there is a clear Durkheimian quality to his argument: Ties based on likenesses (mechanical solidarity) gave way to bonds based on the interdependence of differentiated parts (organic solidarity).

Freedom and Tolerance in the City.   As a social reformer, Park recognized that the modern city revealed problem upon problem; but, like Durkheim, Park was fascinated with what he saw to be the possibilities for freedom and tolerance in the city. He wrote:

> The attraction of the metropolis is due in part to the fact that in the long run every individual finds somewhere among the varied manifestations of city life the sort of environment in which he expands and feels at ease; he finds, in

short, the moral climate in which his peculiar nature obtains the stimulations that bring his innate dispositions to full and free expression. It is, I suspect, motives of this kind which have their basis, not in interest or even in sentiment, but in something more fundamental and primitive which drove many, if not most, of the young men and young women from the security of their homes in the country into the big, booming confusion and excitement of city life. (1967:41)

In short, what Tönnies saw as steady disorganization, Park saw as potential for greater human experience. He continued:

> In a small community it is the normal man, the man without eccentricity or genius who seems most likely to succeed. The small community often tolerates eccentricity. The city rewards it. Neither the criminal, the defective, nor the genius has the same opportunity to develop his innate disposition in a small town that he invariably finds in a great city. (1967:41)

Summing up, we see in the ideas of Robert Park a new emphasis upon the doing of urban research and on-site investigation of the city quite unlike the more abstract theorizing of Tönnies, Durkheim, and Simmel, and unlike the historical work of Marx, Engels, and Weber. Park's main contribution was his demand that we get out there and see how the city actually works.

Louis Wirth and Urban Theory

If the European theorists produced a great deal of theory but conducted little actual research, early Chicago sociologists did just the opposite. During the 20 years that followed the publication of Park's urban studies program in 1916, Chicago sociologists produced a wealth of primarily descriptive studies. Not until 1938 was this imbalance rectified, when Louis Wirth (1897–1952) published his famous essay "Urbanism as a Way of Life," in which he identified **urbanism** as that "distinctive . . . mode of life which is associated with the growth of cities." To Wirth, the city worked its magic by forcing people to encounter one another in a special way: In the city, large numbers of heterogeneous people come into contact in dense settings, generating a new type of behavior and awareness—an urban way of life. City dwellers become rational, self-interested, specialized, somewhat reserved, and highly tolerant.

Wirth's great contribution to urban sociology was the patient and systematic organization of the insights of previous urban sociologists into the first truly sociological theory of the city. By a *theory* of the city, we mean that Wirth began his analysis by isolating several factors that he argued were *universal social characteristics* of the city. He then proceeded to deduce systematically the consequences of these factors for the character of urban social life. He said, in effect (as all good theorists do): If this condition is present, then that condition will result.

Wirth began with a definition of the city as a (1) large, (2) dense, permanent settlement with (3) socially and culturally heterogeneous people. Let us examine what conditions of urban social life follow from each of these elements.

Population Size or Scale. Wirth believed, first, that large population size alone produces great diversity in the cultural and occupational characteristics of a city. This diversity partly results from (1) the simple fact that larger numbers of people coming together logically increase the potential differentiation among themselves, and from (2) the migration of diverse groups to the city (as in Chicago, where Wirth was writing).

Second, the condition of cultural diversity produced by a large population has the additional effect of creating a need for formal control structures, such as a legal system. Third, a large, differentiated population supports the proliferation of specialization, and an occupational structure based upon differing occupations (artist, politician, cabdriver) emerges. Fourth, specialization organizes human relationships more on an "interest-specific" basis that Wirth described as "social segmentalization":

Characteristically, urbanites meet one another in highly segmental roles. They are, to be sure, dependent on more people for the satisfactions of their life needs than are rural people . . . but they are less dependent upon particular persons, and their dependence upon others is confined to a highly fractionalized aspect of the other's round of activity. This is essentially what is meant by saying that the city is characterized by secondary rather than primary contacts. The contacts of the city may indeed be face-to-face, but they are nevertheless impersonal, superficial, transitory, and segmental. (1964:71)

In other words, rather than understanding others in terms of who they are, the urbanite typically conceives of others in terms of what they do, in terms of their roles and what they can do to advance one's own ends. The qualities of rationality and sophistication are simply additional ways of suggesting that urban ties become, in essence, relationships of utility. Lastly, even with the stabilizing constraint provided by formal controls and professional codes of conduct, Wirth could not escape the conclusion that large population size carried with it the possibility of disorganization and disintegration, a fear shared by all the European theorists.

Population Density. The consequence of population density is to *intensify* the effects of large population size on social life. Rather than manifesting the quality of sameness one might associate with the countryside, the city becomes separated into a mosaic of readily identifiable regions or districts. (Here we can see the direct influence of Wirth's teacher, Park.) Both economic forces (such as differing land values) and social processes (such as attraction and avoidance based on race and ethnicity) tend to produce fairly distinct neighborhoods and districts.

For example, many U.S. cities have a predominantly Italian area (such as Boston's North End), a Chinatown (such as San Francisco's), and a high-income area (such as Chicago's North Shore). Similarly, major cities frequently have a garment district and a financial district (such as New York's Wall Street). Wirth called this process of separating the city into districts "ecological specialization." The more common term used today is **natural areas,** revealing that such places evolve as unplanned clusters.

Density also operates on the social–psychological level. Exposed to "glaring contrasts . . . splendor and squalor . . . riches and poverty," Wirth argued, city dwellers develop a mental shorthand, a mental mapping of the city, its regions, and its inhabitants. This insight (drawn from Simmel) helps us understand the urbanite's tendency to stereotypical and categorical thinking, and the reliance on grasping the city through visible symbols and uniforms (clothing, cars, fashionable street addresses). The implication is clear—population density fosters a loss of sensitivity to the "more personal aspects" of others—and suggests why people in the city sometimes seem "cold and heartless."

As suggested earlier by Durkheim and Simmel, Wirth contended that the "juxtaposition of divergent personalities and modes of life" results in a *greater toleration of differences.* Along with this, physical closeness tends to *increase social distance* among urbanites. Forced into physical proximity, city dwellers characteristically close off or tune out those around them. (On a small scale, this happens when people, busily chatting, enter a crowded elevator and abruptly become silent, staring up at the numbers on the elevator wall.)

Again echoing Simmel, Wirth suggested that high density might cause an increase in antisocial behavior. Wirth posited, "The necessary movement of great numbers of individuals in a congested habitat causes friction and irritation."

Heterogeneity. In completing his theory of urbanism, Wirth suggested several consequences of social difference, or heterogeneity. First, "social interaction among such a variety of personality types in the urban milieu tends to break down the rigidity of caste lines and to complicate the class structure."

Consequently, there tends to be a heightened social mobility in the city as the inertia of family background weakens under the force of personal achievement.

Second, physical movement typically accompanies social mobility. "Overwhelmingly the city dweller is not a homeowner and since a transitory habitat does not generate binding traditions and sentiments, only rarely is he a true neighbor." Remember Kitty Genovese in an earlier Urban Living box (p. 134)?

Finally, the concentration of diverse people leads inevitably to further depersonalization. Against a background of commercial mass production and consumption, personal relations are eroded by an emphasis on money. Thus, Wirth repeated Simmel's earlier view of the city as a "pecuniary nexus."

These three dimensions of Wirth's theory—size, density, and heterogeneity of population—interact to produce the unique way of life he termed "urbanism." Clearly, Wirth was pessimistic about urbanism as a way of life. He saw the city as an acid that, in time, dissolved traditional values and undermined the formation of institutions and meaningful relationships. Like Park, he touted the possibilities for greater freedom in the city, but he also worried that urbanism's positive aspects inevitably would be compromised by the disorganization he saw in turbulent Chicago. Only by massive efforts at urban planning, he imagined, could people create a humane urban environment.

As Wirth understood it, the essence of urban living was being *cosmopolitan*—literally, "belonging to all the world." Robert Merton (1968:447–53) drew a useful distinction between "localite" and "'cosmopolitan'" lifestyles. The life of the localite centers in the immediate area. Typically born in the area in which they live, localites are bound up within social relations and life commitments encapsulated within that specific territory. Cosmopolites, on the other hand, are more rootless and think in terms of wider possibilities. They are more likely to move on (perhaps to new jobs or a better home). Whether rich or poor, cosmopolites display a certain degree of detachment, have a somewhat blasé attitude toward their immediate surroundings, and show a sophistication in matters of taste and friendship not typical of localites. Although Merton acknowledged that cosmopolites and localites could exist anywhere, there is little doubt that the cosmopolitan attitude is found more frequently among city dwellers and the localite is more typical in small towns or rural areas.

But are cosmopolitanism and localism set off as clearly as Merton thought they were? For one thing, cosmopolitanism is found in many small college towns, such as Gambier, Ohio. Then, too, Chicago, Toronto, and most other large cities contain residential enclaves where localism abounds—Italian neighborhoods, Vietnamese communities, perhaps a Chinatown, or maybe an old upper-class area. If this is the case, then possibly the city doesn't produce a distinctive way of life at all. So argues Herbert Gans, the most outspoken critic of the Wirthian position.

Herbert Gans and the Urban Mosaic

Herbert Gans (1968) contended that the city is a mosaic of many lifestyles, only some of which resemble the cosmopolitanism described by Wirth. Further, he argued that Wirth's key variables—size of population, density, and social heterogeneity—cannot account for most of these lifestyles, nor does his macrosocial analysis explain how most city dwellers see their lives.

Exploring lifestyle diversity in North American cities, Gans identified four types of urban lifestyles: the cosmopolites, the unmarried or childless, the ethnic villagers, and the deprived or trapped. **Cosmopolites** are highly educated urban sophisticates who choose to live in the city because of its wide range of activities, experiences, and social contacts. They include intellectuals, artists, musicians, writers, and students. The second urban lifestyle, the unmarried or childless, frequently overlaps with the cosmopolite category. It includes single adults or couples without children,

and/or people whose children are grown up and on their own. The **ethnic villagers** show almost none of the so-called typical urban characteristics noted by Wirth. Instead, they sustain many rural life patterns in the city, claiming a local area, emphasizing traditional religious beliefs and family ties, and displaying suspicion of outsiders. Gans's remaining category of the trapped and deprived are the very poor, the handicapped, those in broken family situations, and those of nonwhite racial backgrounds who wish to move from deteriorating neighborhoods but lack the financial means to do so.

Wirth and Gans: A Comparison

We must not be too quick to accept the negative judgments from Wirth and other Chicago sociologists. Like their European colleagues, Chicago sociologists were responding to one kind of city, a North American city moving into the high gear of industrialization. Neglecting historical or cross-cultural comparisons limited the significance of their work. How would their evaluation of the urban environment have changed had they, like Weber, looked at cities in history or in cross-cultural perspective?

Chicago sociology may be skewed for yet another reason. Park's insistence on on-site study, coupled with his interest in urban disorganization and problems, led him and his colleagues to concentrate on the "seamy side" of city life. A glance at the group's classic publications, brilliant though many of them are, reveals this bias: Nels Anderson, *The Hobo* (1923); Ernest Mowner, *Family Disorganization* (1927); Harvey Zorbaugh, *The Gold Coast and the Slum* (1928); Frederich Thrasher, *The Gang* (1929); Clifford Shaw and Henry McKay, *Social Factors in Juvenile Delinquency* (1931); Paul Cressey, *The Taxi Dance Hall* (1932); Norman Hayner, *Hotel Life* (1936); and Edwin H. Sutherland, *The Professional Thief* (1937). Although there are many other aspects of city urban life that might be explored, Wirth based his theory heavily on the evidence supplied by such studies.

Limitations notwithstanding, the Chicago group made great contributions. Park deserves lasting credit for his rejection of armchair theorizing in favor of studying the city firsthand. The second key contribution was Wirth's first true urban theory, which became a persuasive document that dominated the field for the next 20 years. All in all, Chicago sociologists were almost solely responsible for the early growth of urban sociology in the United States (Lofland 1985; J. Thomas 1983).

Gans's contribution, on the other hand, was to call our attention to the complexities of urban life. Our discussion earlier of prominent urban "types" as discerned by Gans is only a partial list. Obviously, there are countless variations of all these lifestyles. And that is the point. So many urban lifestyles exist that it makes little sense to claim, as Wirth did, that the city produces a relatively uniform type of human being.

The rather hard-nosed, calculating person Wirth hypothesized as the typical urban dweller does appear—most frequently in the cosmopolite and unmarried or childless categories. But even among these people, Wirth's variables of population size, density, and heterogeneity appear to have limited effect. For instance, many cosmopolites can buy the space they need to fend off what they believe is excessive density, just as many ethnic villagers positively thrive in high-density neighborhoods. Population size or scale may increase the number of secondary or segmented relationships, said Gans, but most individuals maintain as many primary relationships as elsewhere because their social focus is on their neighborhood, family, co-workers, and co-religionists. With them, there is no increased social distance because of population density or increased depersonalization due to the heterogeneity, as Wirth maintained. Instead, said Gans, city residents function in smaller social worlds at home, work, and play, enjoying the same life satisfactions as others of their social class in other environments.

Thus, while cities do act on us in much the way Wirth claimed, we need to keep several limitations in mind. First, few urban lifestyles are found exclusively in the city; and, second, the determinants of these lifestyles are largely people's general social class characteristics rather than the city itself (an area we will fully explore in Chapter 10). That is, cosmopolites live as they do because they are relatively wealthy and highly educated; likewise, the lives of the deprived and the trapped reflect poverty, a lack of skills and schooling, and, often enough, racial or ethnic discrimination. We can make a similar argument for any other lifestyle on the list.

Wirth's mistake was in generalizing too much from the urban conditions of the time in which he lived. Observing the incredibly rapid growth of North American and European cities early in the twentieth century, Wirth became convinced that the city was a powerful force that would come to dominate human life. A generation later, Gans and others could see that this simply wasn't happening; urban diversity continued to flourish. Today, we can conclude that **urbanization**—the clustering of population in some areas—does not necessarily generate *urbanism*—a single, distinctive way of life.

THE CLASSIC THEORIES AND MODERN RESEARCH: MYTHS AND REALITIES

Is the city a heaven or a hell? Is it a place where the best attributes of human life emerge or a place where people inevitably "go bad"? The seventeenth-century English poet Abraham Cowley thought he knew the answer when he wrote: "God the first garden made, and the first city, Cain." But was he right? The weight of the classic tradition—European and North American—is on Cowley's side. Despite qualifiers and hopeful asides, only Durkheim was mostly optimistic. Wirth's theory symbolizes this verdict. On the one hand, he suggested that people in the city are more tolerant. But on the more negative side, he asserted that city people are impersonal and detached from meaningful relationships. He concluded that the city tends toward social pathology (crime, violence, mental illness), a tendency only made worse as urban density increases.

Are these observations correct? More than six decades have passed since the publication of Wirth's urban theory. Since then a great many social scientists have investigated cities and urban life to gather additional evidence.

Tolerance in the City

Early urban theory contended that the characteristic aloofness and social diversity of the city produced an atmosphere of tolerance that contrasted with the jealous parochialism of the village and small town. Indeed, for most of us, our urban experiences are linked somehow to the unusual and the unexpected, which we take in stride because, well, because we're in the city!

Most researchers who have looked closely at the relationship between urban life and tolerance conclude that this contention is only partially valid. Although greater tolerance of others' lifestyles and attitudes is more prevalent in cities than in rural areas, factors other than the city may account for this difference. For example, many city dwellers prefer anonymity and privacy, thereby encouraging a "live and let live" attitude (Fischer 1971; Karp, Stone, and Yoels 1991).

Another factor that may lend itself to greater tolerance in the city is migration. One research study found that tolerance increased among those moving to a city, regardless of the size of the destination community (Wilson 1991). Perhaps geographic mobility—moving to a more heterogeneous locale—enhances one's mental mobility as well in relating to strangers.

In summary, Wirth was only partly correct when he suggested that cities generate tolerant attitudes. People in cities do have more tolerant attitudes than people who live elsewhere; yet this difference appears to be declining with time and is partly a product of other factors, like wealth and regional differences.

Impersonality in the City

The dominant characteristics of urban relationships, concluded most of the classical theorists,

would be loneliness, indifference, and anonymity. At its most basic level, this argument is built on numerical logic. As the number of people interacting increases, attention becomes distributed more broadly so that impersonality inevitably must rise. Wirth summarized this argument by saying: "Increase in the number of inhabitants of a community beyond a few hundred is bound to limit the possibility of each member of the community knowing all the others personally" (1964:70).

Yet the "urban anonymity" thesis fails to recognize that many urbanites are not the lonely lot that Wirth and others implied. For example, as early as the 1940s, William F. Whyte's *Street Corner Society* (1943), a study of an Italian immigrant area in an eastern city, revealed the existence of strong family, neighborhood, and friendship ties. Soon after that, other studies (Bell and Boat 1957; Greer 1962; Bruce 1970) confirmed that primary ties were not incompatible with city living. Indeed, in some areas of the city—ethnic neighborhoods, for example—such ties appear to be as intense and intimate as any in rural areas. In a study of a Korean neighborhood in New York City, Ill Soo Kim (1981:319) found that urbanites who had yet to master English were forced to rely on one another, remaining a close-knit community.

Ethnicity is not the only bond among urban dwellers. Kinship, occupation, lifestyle, and other personal attributes also form the basis for group ties (Suttles 1972; Street et al. 1978; Fischer 1984). For example, many cities contain districts of college students, elderly people, homosexuals, artists and musicians, and wealthy socialites. More broadly, people with interests in common, wherever they may live, may remain in close contact with one another through an interactional network, utilizing the telephone, restaurants and bars, and special meeting places.

But perhaps these are the exceptions. What of the lonely crowd living in all those high rises, the people who don't know any of their neighbors? Doesn't Wirth's theory accurately describe them? Recent research suggests that this notion, too, may be exaggerated. The fact that one does not necessarily know (or want to

In a city we are almost never alone, but we may well be lonely. Most face-to-face contacts are impersonal, superficial, and segmental. However, research shows that although city dwellers have far more of these secondary relationships, they also have just as many meaningful primary relationships as nonurbanites.

know) one's urban neighbors does not mean that the urban dweller has no personal relationships. Indeed, what seems to be significant about the urban environment is not the lack of ties of attachment but how these ties vary. That is, cities seem to encourage alternative types of relationships more than other environments do.

The city, then, frees people from the often-stifling intensity of less dense settings. But it gives them many options for connecting with others. This is an exercise in the positive freedom Durkheim saw in the city.

Even the most "private" urban dwellers usually have meaningful personal relationships.

Karen Franck (1981) found that, although good friendships develop slowly in the city, urban friendships seem to become more intimate and more highly valued than those in rural settings. Friendship in the city also tends to be more varied, broadening people's perspectives and opportunities. Think of urban people you know. Most have friends and relatives, but not always in the same building or neighborhood. To expect urban friendship and intimacy to be localized, as they usually are in the village or small town, is to misunderstand urban living (Freudenberg 1992).

Other means for urban connectedness abound. The telephone, as well as e-mail, makes possible extensive contact without face-to-face interaction. Consider, too, the proliferation in cities in recent years of voluntary associations, such as film societies, singles bars, health and natural food centers, karate clubs, meditation and yoga centers, "stop smoking" groups, and physical fitness centers. Participants in such organizations, living throughout the urban area, often establish primary relationships with one another.

In *The Urban Neighborhood* (1968), Suzanne Keller suggested that urban "neighboring" varies markedly—from active and intense relationships to impersonal nods. While working-class people usually live in "tighter" neighborhoods, upper-middle-class people typically have networks of friends dispersed over a wide area. Similarly, people with children tend to be more "localized" in their orientation than single people "on the move." Here, Keller echoes Herbert Gans (1962b), who, in a stinging critique, concluded that the "impersonality" that Wirth saw in the city *as a whole* characterizes, at best, only the most poverty-stricken and down-and-out of the city's residents.

Even when coherent social networks are absent in low-income urban neighborhoods, they can develop. In Kalamazoo, Michigan, for example, the city's Building Blocks program generated street-level social capital by identifying small project areas and intensively using students as front-line organizers. The key to this program was organizing around inclusiveness through empowerment and use of the residents' "assets," and

Without question, the proliferation of cell phones has had a dramatic impact on our social interactions. By providing more frequent personal conversations without the constraints of access to a landline phone, cell phones enable greater connectivity among people. Such an enhancement of social networking is an important factor in negating the potential impersonality of the city.

straddling apparent divisions between self-interest and collective interest, self-help and cooperation. Initial success built on further success, and the trust, once established, also built on itself, leading eventually to an interactive community (Cummings, 2000).

Wirth's mistake, and that of other classic theorists, was to allow the most visible aspects of city life, its *public* demeanor, to become the basis of his theory about urban living in general. Although, following Park, he did acknowledge the neighborhood element in city life, he tended to focus his attention on "street behavior." Wirth saw, of course, the hustling, competing, apparently lonely crowd. By not examining more closely the *private* lives of the city's citizens, he inadvertently distorted urban life into a stereotype of impersonality.

We are led, then, to the conclusion that the early study of both rural and urban places suffered from what might be called a "misplaced

concreteness" (Cahnman and Heberle 1971). Early analysts took polarized constructions such as *gemeinschaft* and *gesellschaft,* or mechanical and organic solidarity, as synonymous with such real, concrete settings as actual villages and cities. While the overall social order of the city may place greater emphasis on *gesellschaft* characteristics, and while the village may tend more toward *gemeinschaft* characteristics, it is incorrect to assume that either *gemeinschaft* or *gesellschaft* exists in any absolute, concrete sense. There is an important difference between the statement that one commonly sees more strangers in cities and the statement that cities are impersonal. In some ways they are; in other ways, they most certainly are not.

Density and Urban Pathology

Perhaps the most provocative idea put forth by the classical theorists—particularly Simmel,

Park, and Wirth—was that human beings react to increasing population density with psychological disorder (such as mental illness) or antisocial behavior (crime or aggression, for instance).

One source of support for this hypothesis is our own common sense. Probably all of us have experienced some measure of frustration and aggression in crowded settings—trying to push our way through a turnstile at a football stadium, or fuming as thousands of cars coalesce in a massive traffic jam. It is easy to assume that the place where this occurs—the city—is responsible for our feeling. But are we reacting to the condition of urban crowding, or are we merely experiencing a sense of frustration not very different from what we might feel if our car broke down along a lonely country road?

A second source of the alleged linkage between density and pathology is research that appears to have some bearing on the quality of urban life. For example, John B. Calhoun (1962:139) found that high density in rat populations produced a reaction he termed a "behavioral sink"—an environment where aborted pregnancies, higher infant mortality, homosexuality, and cannibalism abounded. Although Calhoun made no attempt to suggest that human beings would respond in similar fashion to conditions of crowding, Edward Hall argued that such a connection is not only plausible but accurately describes urban life. "The implosion of the world population into cities everywhere," Hall wrote, "is creating a series of destructive behavioral sinks more lethal than the hydrogen bomb" (1966:155).

Hall realized that different groups of people—whites and blacks, for example—might have different cultural expectations about spatial behavior. Yet he appeared to believe that all of these different reactions have a biological basis, and that the human species, like rats, has a genetically given need for a certain amount of space. He asserted that if that built-in barrier is transgressed—in a crowded apartment or on a dense city block—pathology results.

There are at least two problems with this argument. First, no one yet has been able to locate any genetic code for spatial behavior in humans. Until such a linkage can be demonstrated, projecting onto human beings living in cities what we know about animal pathology and overcrowding is highly questionable. It may well be, for example, that people's perceived needs for space are entirely *learned* and that they react negatively to violations of their learned spatial expectations much as they would to an insult to their learned religious beliefs.

Second, as evidence for his thesis, Hall points to the high incidence of "social problems" (illness, crime) in densely settled areas of the city. Frequently, those cited are lower class and ethnic areas. But such associations may be spurious rather than causal. By this we mean that illness, crime, and crowding may appear together because all are caused by some other factor(s), such as poverty, unemployment, and racial discrimination. Moreover, subsequent research has shown that, when such factors are taken into account, there is little or no evidence that crowding has any of the negative effects posited by Hall (Michelson 1977; Fischer 1984; Bagley 1989; Lepore and Evans 1991; Rousseau and Standing 1995).

Urbanites do contend with crowded conditions, such as crammed elevators and subway cars; with rambunctious cabdrivers, the frustrations of traffic, and intense competition for parking spaces. However, people have one distinct advantage over rats: superior adaptability. First, we live and work on many levels, so we are not continually milling together on the ground. Second, we have codes of urban conduct that guide us to wait in line for the bus; keep to the right when walking; alternate merge or stop at red lights when driving. Cities have bicycle, foot, and horse paths connecting parks and open space that make movement safer and more pleasant. Freeways permit faster travel to and from downtowns, while traffic circles, one-way streets, and coordinated traffic lights ease the traffic flow in crowded areas.

Still, what of the fact that some researchers find that crowding does heighten aggression in some people? Perhaps an analogy with listening to music may explain the matter. When you listen to music that you like, turning the

For city residents, the streets are the "rivers of life," where people-watching and social interaction are the everyday norm. This privatization of public space—setting up crates or chairs on the sidewalk, sitting on front stoops or on a bench, playing games, or holding a street fair—is the urban equivalent to the suburbanites' front and back yards combined, and often a lot more interesting.

volume louder enhances the experience. However, if you don't like that music, an increase in the volume only makes the experience more unpleasant. For people with a good support system and a high level of life satisfaction, crowding has little effect, except perhaps temporarily affecting one's mood. On the other hand, if people are already in unpleasant circumstances, have aggressive tendencies, or feel alienated or frustrated, then crowding may well generate further negative reactions. The point is that crowding in and of itself does not result in pathological behavior, but rather other factors people bring to that situation may have that effect (Verbrugge and Taylor 1980; Aiello et al. 1983; Bonnes et al. 1991).

Finally, in global context we see that culture also mediates the experience of city living, influencing how we are affected by population density. For example, Mumbai (Bombay), India, has an extremely high rate of urban crowding but an extremely low homicide rate; to cite another example, Turks—whose cultural behavior favors closer interpersonal interaction—do not respond negatively to increased crowding conditions (Baldassare 1979; Bagley 1989; Rustemli 1992).

Urban Malaise

A last hypothesis put forth by most of the classical theorists concerned "urban malaise." They suggested that, conditions of density aside, the urban environment created loneliness, depression, and anxiety more readily than did other types of settlement.

This contention, too, was challenged by later research. Leo Srole (1972) questioned 1,660 New Yorkers in the 1950s and 695 people from the same group again in the 1970s.

Not only did Srole find that the mental health of New Yorkers was slightly better than that of rural residents; he also found that mental health, especially of women, had improved dramatically over the interval between the two samples. Other researchers reported similar results (Fischer 1973; Freedman 1978; Hackler 1979; Kadushin 1983).

In a review of global studies on the effects of cities on children, Thomas Weisner (1981) concluded that urban living does not subject children to more stress than do other types of environments. He noted that children moving to the city from the country did experience some increase in stress. However, such an increase in stress is regularly observed in people who have had other major catastrophic changes in their lives—such as the death of a loved one, the loss of employment, or moving from one place to another.

Apparently, then, the city doesn't create greater psychological distress. In fact, the higher population density of urban places may well have positive effects, such as making more people socially accessible to each other (Verbrugge and Taylor 1980). When it comes to city dwellers dealing with their environment, as the Urban Living box below suggests, it seems that the vast majority do quite well.

URBAN LIVING

How City Dwellers Cope—and Cope Well

How is it possible, given the fast pace and obvious stresses of urban life, that city residents can maintain mental health comparable to that of country folks? One explanation offered by experts: The relationship between stress and mental and physical pathology is dependent not so much on the nature of the stress as on the individual's perception of it. The brain has been called a stimulus-reduction system, a means to reduce, in order to comprehend, the nearly infinite number of stimuli that reach the senses at any given moment. It is an aspect of the brain that seems tailor-made for life in the city.

An out-of-towner caught in midtown Manhattan at rush hour, for example, may feel under enormous pressure and strain. But New Yorkers, with their stimulus-reduction mechanism operating at full steam, hardly feel any special stress at all. By the same token, the big-city residents may ignore the loud, the profane, the drunk, and the demented—phenomena that might compromise the mental equilibrium of the uninitiated.

And there are related statistics to support such thinking. Diala and Muntaner (2003) found rural men reported more mood and anxiety disorders than urban men, perhaps a function of diminishing resources (steady, high-paying jobs) or increasing financial strain particularly among whites, who comprise a majority of rural residents. No differences by place of residence existed among females. The National Center for Health Statistics (1997) conducted a national self-report survey of negative affect items related to anxiety, depression, and stress among city, suburban, and rural residents. The findings showed little difference in the negative affect prevalence in metropolitan areas (7.7 percent) and non-metropolitan areas (7.9 percent). A slightly higher negative affect prevalence occurred among city residents (8 percent) compared to rural residents (7 percent), but this is hardly sufficient to claim that urbanites experience more stress in their lives than those living outside the city.

Overall, little evidence supports many of the specific claims made by the classic theorists about urban living. The city is clearly not a heaven; but neither is it the hell some thought it to be. The city is more tolerant than other types of settlement, it is not as impersonal as many thought it was, and it does not produce greater rates of malaise or other pathologies. On the basis of what we now know, there is reason for more optimism than that shown by most classic theorists. The reality, in short, is both more complex and more hopeful than the myths.

The New Urban Sociology

All this research has produced a shift in the way many urbanists approach their subject matter. As we have just seen, the classical hypotheses about the city advanced by Simmel, Wirth, and others have not stood the test of careful scrutiny. Some have been shown to be false; others require serious modification. Such findings occasioned the creation of what John Walton (1981) called "the new urban sociology."

Instead of an emphasis on the role of technology or urban ecology, this newer approach directs attention to social conflict, inequality, and change as they affect cities, and does so within a global context. No single theory captures the new urban sociology, although neo-Marxists and conflict theorists predominate. We will explore this important approach later in Chapter 9.

❖ ━━━━━━ ❖ ━━━━━━ ❖

SUMMARY

The context in which urban sociology emerged was one of remarkable change. Indeed, it was ferment associated with the Industrial Revolution that was responsible for sociologists noticing the city as an object of study in the first place. What have we learned from them?

First, they suggested specific aspects of the city for urban sociologists to focus on; second, they attempted to analyze the nature of the

city in general. In the latter instance, they had successes and failures. On the positive side, they correctly saw in the city elements of social life not prominent elsewhere. They saw the city as having more specialized occupations, more formalized interaction patterns, more rationality, and a more rapid tempo of life. On the negative side, they erred in some of their specific claims about the nature of the city. They were right about greater tolerance, but they exaggerated the city's impersonality, and they seem, on the whole, to have been wrong about urban pathology. The context in which they wrote played a significant role in these misperceptions. Seeing cities growing by millions of inhabitants with seemingly unconquerable problems, they reasoned that the city itself must be the cause of these ills.

A second limitation is the narrowness of all early theory. Marx and Engels saw cross-cultural differences in how civilization evolved in Western compared with Eastern cities, but concentrated on the economic system as the basis for all attributes of an urban society. Tönnies and Durkheim employed the comparison of oppositional types but did not consider the city in concrete historical settings. Simmel added the social–psychological dimension, although he too considered only cities of one time and place. Weber argued for the importance of exploring cities in cross-cultural and historical perspective, but wrote little about the modern city (perhaps a subtle way of indicating that he—like all his colleagues except Durkheim—also saw it in a negative light).

Park and Wirth both provided breakthroughs. Park demanded that on-site city research be an integral part of urban sociology, thereby providing the mechanism for getting behind the surface impressions of the urban environment. Ironically, his focus on urban problems and his lack of a comparative historical frame led him to the same negative conclusions about the city as others. Wirth then tried to build a theory of the city by linking the suggestions of his colleagues. A major difficulty was that he built his theory on Park's skewed database and on the somewhat misleading evaluations of the European tradition.

Recent research has shown that many of the specific claims made by Wirth and his colleagues were incorrect. Early work saw the city as the cause of greater impersonality, poorer mental health, and various forms of stressful or pathological behavior. The new urban sociology, which has emerged in the wake of the classical urbanists' failing theories, sees the city as existing in a complex historical, cultural, and economic setting. All these elements play a role in how the city operates, and all must be carefully examined by systematic research.

CONCLUSION

What we take from the classical tradition is its interest in urban studies per se and its combined model of urban analysis. A useful urban analysis must (1) examine the city on both its social–structural and psychosocial dimensions, (2) study actual cities in historical and comparative perspective, (3) attempt to build an overarching theory of the city, and (4) evaluate cities in terms of the quality of human life. It will be the task of the remaining chapters to do justice to this tradition.

KEY TERMS

Cosmopolites
Ethnic villagers
False consciousness
Gemeinschaft
Gesellschaft
Ideal type
Mechanical solidarity
Natural areas
Organic solidarity
Sprawl
Urbanism

CHAPTER 6

SOCIAL PSYCHOLOGY
The Urban Experience

What makes cities so stimulating? Why do they pull from us reactions of either stout admiration or powerful aversion? Georg Simmel's answer was that the city is a tremendous concentration of buildings, images, and people that intensifies stimulation as no other form of human settlement does. Everywhere you turn—around a corner, breaking through a crowd, entering the subway—the city demands a response.

How do we make sense of this coming-at-you-from-all-sides, sometimes in-your-face creation that is the city? Simmel answered that we learn to categorize the city's elements, paying attention to some things and ignoring others. University of Chicago sociologist Louis Wirth agreed, suggesting that we mentally "map" the city. Unfortunately, neither theorist said much about how this mapping process works. But, drawing on later research, this chapter sketches the outlines of this process—the characteristic elements of the social psychology of the city.

THE PHYSICAL ENVIRONMENT

We react to the city in two ways—as a physical setting and as a social environment. First, we will consider how people perceive their physical surroundings and try to make sense out of them.

Kevin Lynch: The Image of the City

To explore how people made sense of the city's physical complexity, urbanist Kevin Lynch interviewed urbanites in Boston, Jersey City, and Los Angeles. In each city, Lynch showed his respondents a map of several square miles of the central city and asked them to describe it in their own terms. Most could offer a personal *image of the city* that Lynch defined as the individual's "generalized mental picture of the [city's] external physical world" (1960:4).

Before we continue, take a moment and think of the city you know best. On a piece of

To a great many people around the world, the New York City skyline is not only easily recognizable, but it is also a symbol of the power and lure of American life. To the residents of Jersey City living on the opposite shore of the Hudson River, the skyline is such a looming, overpowering presence that many residents mentioned it to Lynch as one of their landmarks.

paper, draw as detailed a map of it as you can, putting in everything of importance that you can recall. This exercise will make the following discussion far more meaningful.

Building an Image.   Most of Lynch's respondents developed their image of the city in a similar fashion. First, their images emerged as part of a two-way process: (1) They made distinctions among the various physical parts of the city, and (2) they organized these parts in a personally meaningful way.

For example, Figure 6–1 shows downtown Boston, where the large park known as the Boston Common and Public Garden separates various downtown districts from one another. To the west of the park is the residential Back Bay area, with its characteristic three- and four-story apartment houses. To the north is the wealthier Beacon Hill district, where one finds the State House. To the east and south is most of Boston's central business district, full of high-rise office buildings, stores, and entertainment facilities.

To a person living, say, in a small apartment house just west of the Garden and the Common, the park area may be the dominant element in an image of the city because the person may go there frequently for walks,

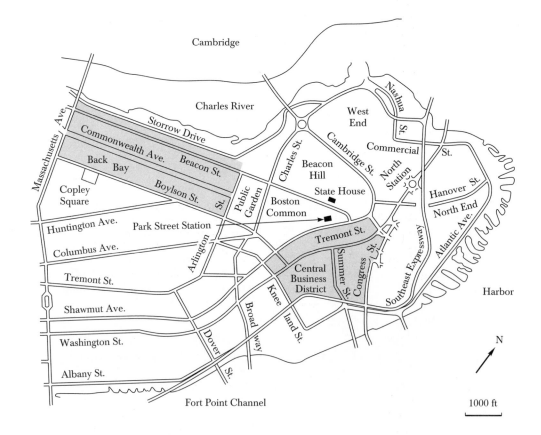

FIGURE 6–1   Downtown Boston [*Source:* Kevin Lynch, *The Image of the City,* 1960. MIT Press, Cambridge, Mass.]

getting to know every bench, fountain, and footpath. But this same individual may know little about the rest of downtown.

On the other hand, to another Bostonian living nearby, the park may have little significance. Working in the high-rise offices on the east side of the park, this person may have little desire to use the Garden. In this case, the distinct image might be of the downtown buildings, including where the good restaurants are, and of all the shortcuts for getting from one building or street to another.

Common Elements of Images.   Lynch discovered that people built their urban images from five common elements. **Paths,** he explains, are "channels along which the observer customarily . . . moves. They may be streets, walkways, transit lines, canals, railroads." **Edges,** the boundaries between two areas, include shores, walls, wide streets, or breaks between buildings and open space. **Districts** represent medium-to-large sections of the city. Examples in Boston that people commonly noted were "Back Bay," "Beacon Hill," "the Common," "the shopping district." **Nodes** stand as points of intense activity, such as a railroad terminal, a square, or a street-corner hangout. Nodes are often the places to which "paths" lead. Finally, Lynch's subjects built their images around **landmarks**—physical reference points including buildings, signs, stores, domes, gas stations, or hills.

At this point, look back at the map you drew a few minutes ago. Were you thinking in terms of Lynch's categories?

Lynch also found that most people incorporate many of the same elements in their images; that is, what is a path or edge to one person is a path or edge to many others. Looking back at Figure 6–1, virtually every Bostonian recognizes the Charles River as a major edge separating one large district of the city ("downtown") from another (Cambridge). Similarly, most people also mention "Mass. Ave." to the west and the Southeast Expressway to the east as key edges. Main paths are Beacon Street, "Comm. Ave.," and Boylston

and Tremont Streets. Commonly mentioned nodes include Copley Square (site of the "BPL," the Boston Public Library), North Station (a railroad and subway terminal), and Park Street Station. Although it is below ground, Park Street Station is another classic example of an urban node: The junction of Boston's three main subway lines is constantly abuzz with activity.

Although Lynch discovered that people in every city appear to use the same elements in constructing their images, he also found that some cities stimulate their residents to form more complex images than other cities do. In Boston, virtually everyone Lynch interviewed could identify *numerous* paths, edges, nodes, districts, and landmarks. In Jersey City, by contrast, even long-term residents could identify only a few such elements, often confessing confusion and uncertainty about what existed in different parts of their own city. Perhaps most illustrative of their weak image of their city was the residents' frequent mention of the looming, overpowering New York City skyline to the east as a landmark. In his summary findings about Jersey City, Lynch emphasized its nondescript character:

> When asked for a general characterization of the city, one of the most common remarks was that it was not a whole, that it had no center, but was rather a collection of many hamlets. The question: "What first comes to mind with the words 'Jersey City'?," so easy to answer for Bostonians, proved to be a difficult one. Again and again, subjects repeated that "nothing special" came to mind, that the city was hard to [characterize], that it had no distinctive sections. . . .

Many remarks came out about the indistinguishability of the physical scene:

> "It's much the same all over . . . it's more or less just common to me. I mean, when I go up and down the streets, it's more or less the same thing—Newark Avenue, Jackson Avenue, Bergen Avenue. I mean, sometimes they're more or less just the same; there's nothing to differentiate them." (1960:29–31)

In Los Angeles, Lynch found, residents have an even less sharp image of their city because of the great sprawl and uniformity of cross streets, which make it difficult to locate anything with confidence. Although the area studied was comparable in size to the other two cities, it included little more than a central business district. Those interviewed, most of whom worked there, could describe just a few landmarks in any specific detail: the "ugly" black and gold Richfield Building and the pyramid atop City Hall. The strongest element of all was Pershing Square,

> an exotically landscaped open space in the heart of the downtown, reinforced by its use as an outdoor political forum, camp meeting, and old people's hangout. Along with the Plaza–Olvera Street node (involving another open space), Pershing Square was the most sharply described element, with its immaculate central lawn, fringed first by banana trees, then by a ring of old people sitting in solid ranks on the stone walls, then by busy streets, and finally by the close files of downtown buildings. (1960:36–37)

Even so, many Angelenos were uncertain of the precise location of Pershing Square. Moreover, most residents of the city could identify only paths, and often confused one with another. When asked to describe or symbolize Los Angeles as a whole, residents found it hard to respond, simply describing their city as "spread-out," "spacious," "formless," or "without centers." Lynch offered one person's comment as illustrative of this diffused urban image:

> "It's as if you were going somewhere for a long time, and when you got there you discovered that there was nothing there, after all." (1960:41)

The "Imagability" of Cities.   Noting how his respondents differed in their precision about urban images, Lynch suggested that cities differ markedly in imagability. This concept is important for two reasons. First, a clear urban image gives people a working knowledge and emotional security about their city. (However, as the Urban Living box on page 159 reveals, recent terrorist acts make many people feel less secure in cities.) A strong urban image makes acquisition of knowledge relatively easy and sets people at ease emotionally. Second, a comprehensible urban environment "heightens the potential depth and intensity of the human experience" (1960:5). It invites us to experience more, to involve ourselves more in the life of the city. Lynch concluded that "imagability" is one of the essential aspects of a positive urban environment. Lynch's conclusions have been replicated in later studies of both large and small cities as well as in cities in other countries (Lynch 1984).

Stanley Milgram: More on Mental Maps

One of the most intriguing aspects of Lynch's work is his discovery that even people living in the same city construct very different mental images of their surroundings. Most people's maps mix details with distortions as well as large gaps. To understand why mental maps are so distinctive, psychologist Stanley Milgram explored how New Yorkers and Parisians understood their cities. In both cases, he found that people construct mental maps *based on their personal experience, their interests, and their knowledge of the socially recognized "important areas" of the city* (Milgram 1972; S. Duncan 1977; see also Thill and Sui 1993; Kulhavy and Stock 1996).

The Individuality of Mental Maps.   Figure 6–2 (pp. 160–161) presents drawings of two people's mental maps of Manhattan in 2006. New Jersey suburbanite Beth's Manhattan emphasizes details about access and parking for the artistic and cultural centers that draw her to the city's midtown. Virtually absent are details about the Upper West Side or lower Manhattan. In contrast, physical therapist Cara's Manhattan emphasizes the Upper West Side area where she lives. Featured prominently are restaurants, parks, and high-rise apartment

URBAN LIVING

Living with Terrorism

All of us have become sensitized to the vulnerability of cities to terrorist attacks. Masumoto City in 1994 and Tokyo in 1995 fell victim to chemical terrorism with use of the toxic gas sarin on defenseless civilians in subways. The 2001 attacks on the Pentagon in Washington, D.C., and on the twin towers of the World Trade Center in New York City, with their horrific losses of life and mass destruction, still reverberate in the minds of hundreds of millions of people worldwide. In March 2004, terrorists in Madrid killed 191 train passengers and wounded more than 1,400 others, while other terrorists in July 2005 killed 52 bus and train passengers in London, wounding an additional 700 people.

These and other incidents remind us all too often that urban centers attract terrorists. The large concentrations of people—as well as the tall buildings, symbolic monuments, and infrastructure of bridges and tunnels— are all tempting targets to those intent on inflicting maximum damage and deaths. People once avoided cities for fear of becoming victims of violent crimes. Now many fear not just being in major cities, but even living near one in the event of biological, chemical, or nuclear attack.

Seeing concrete barricades at many important locations and undergoing bag searches at concerts, sporting events, and airports are part of our new reality. For some, living or working in tall buildings, or viewing the cityscape from high-perched observation decks, holds little appeal. Others, refusing to allow their lives to be ruled by fear, continue their daily urban routines and lifestyles.

Whether they respond by avoidance or defiance, however, urbanites recognize that their world is a different one than the one that existed before September 11. That realization is also part of the psychology of urban life.

buildings. Missing, save for one or two items, are midtown and lower Manhattan.

No one, Milgram found, can re-create the complexity of the whole city. Moreover, everyone's images constantly evolve as urban experiences deepen or as the city changes. A relative newcomer to a city, for example, will typically draw a map of the center city that contains prominent landmarks but almost no detail at all. Often, the few areas noted are misplaced and distorted in size. Yet, for that same person living there just a few more months, the city usually comes alive, and she or he can offer far more detail, as well as greater geographical accuracy. In short, with time, most people succeed in comprehending the city and using it effectively.

Multiple Urban Realities. What all this suggests is that there are as many New Yorks or Seattles, for example, as there are people living there. More broadly, each of these active mental maps contributes to the larger urban dynamic that is the full New York City or Seattle.

But mental maps are not completely a matter of individual differences. Social class differences affect what people include in their cognitive maps (Lloyd and Hooper 1991). Race also plays a key part in how residents understand the city. Researchers have found

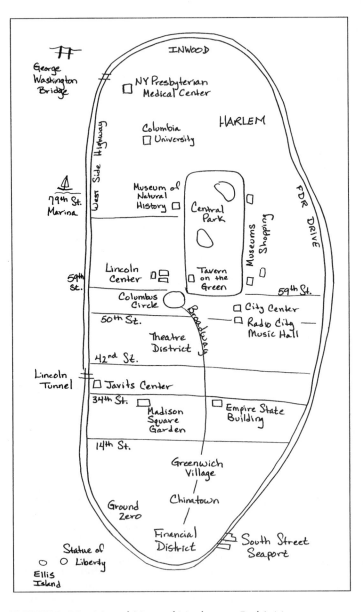

FIGURE 6–2A   Mental Maps of Manhattan: Beth's Map

that blacks' perceptions of community unde-sirability differ from that of whites. Generally, blacks rate most communities as more desirable than whites, often favoring communities in which they are the numerical minority. Whites often rate mixed-race communities as less desirable, particularly those with higher proportions of blacks, even when the latter are the numerical minority (Charles 2000; Sigelman and Henig 2001; Krysan 2002).

In sum, the city is a dynamic, creative, ongo-ing mixture of perceptions and experiences, as

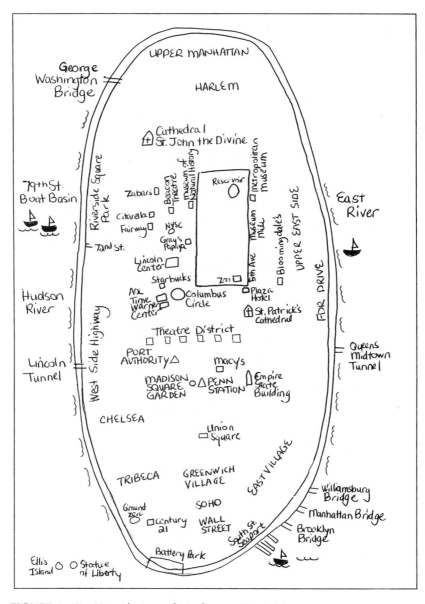

FIGURE 6–2B Mental Maps of Manhattan: Cara's Map

Chicago urbanist Robert Park (1916; 1967:1) eloquently stated:

> The city . . . is something more than a congeries of individual men and of social conveniences—streets, buildings, electric lights, tramways, and telephones . . . something more, also, than a mere constellation of institutions and administrative devices—courts, hospitals, schools, police, and civil functionaries of various sorts. The city is . . . a state of mind.

In the Cityscape box on page 162, novelist Alfred Kazin describes his return to his old

CITYSCAPE

The Streets of Brownsville

All my early life lies open to my eye within five city blocks. . . . On Belmont Avenue, Brownville's great open street market, the pushcarts are still lined on each other for blocks, and the din is as deafening, marvelous, and appetizing as ever. . . . When I was a boy, they . . . reached halfway up the curb to the open stands of the stores; walking down the street was like being whirled around and around in a game of blind man's bluff. But Belmont Avenue is still the merriest street in Brownsville. As soon as I walked into it from Rockaway, caught my first whiff of the herrings and pickles in their great black barrels, heard the familiarly harsh, mocking cries and shouts from the market women—"Oh you darlings! Oh you sweet ones, oh you pretty ones! Storm us! Tear us apart! Devour us!"—I laughed right out loud, it was so good to be back among them. . . .

Chester Street. . . . The way home.

On my right hand the "Stadium" movie house—the sanctuary every Saturday afternoon of my childhood, the great dark place of all my dream life. On my left the little wooden synagogue where I learned my duties as a Jew and at thirteen, having reached the moral estate of a man, stood up at the high desk before the Ark (Blessed Be He, Our Lord and Our Shield!) and was confirmed in the faith of my fathers. . . .

The block: my block. It was on the Chester Street side of our house, between the grocery and the back wall of the old drugstore, that I was hammered into the shape of the streets. Everything beginning at Blake Avenue would always wear for me some delightful strangeness and mildness, simply because it was not of my block, the block, where the clang of your head sounded against the pavement when you fell in a fist fight, and the rows of store lights on each side were pitiless, watching you. . . . [I recall] smelling the sweaty sweet dampness from the pool in summer and the dust on the leaves as I passed under the ailanthus trees. . . .

We worked every inch of it, from the cellars and the backyards to the sickening space between the roofs. Any wall, any stoop, any curving metal edge on a billboard sign made a place against which to knock a ball; any bottom rung of a fire escape ladder a goal in basketball; any sewer cover a base. . . . Our life every day was fought out on the pavement and in the gutter, up against the walls of the houses and the glass fronts of the drugstore and the grocery—in and out of the fresh steaming piles of horse manure, the wheels of passing carts and automobiles, along the iron spikes of the stairway to the cellar, the jagged edge of the open garbage cans, the crumbly steps of the old farmhouses still left on one side of the street.

Source: Alfred Kazin, *A Walker in the City* (New York: MJF Books, 1997), pp. 11–12, 17, 25–26, 30–31, 39–40, 83–84.

neighborhood in the Brownsville district of New York. Present in his image of the city are all of Lynch's visual categories, complex interpretations of sound and smell, as well as evidence of his own social background.

THE SOCIAL ENVIRONMENT: *GESELLSCHAFT*

Living in the city demands that we deal with more than the physical environment. We must also contend with large numbers of *people*, most of whom we don't know and probably don't want to know. How do we cope with what Ferdinand Tönnies (Chapter 5) called the city's *gesellschaft* characteristics—its vast numbers and characteristic anonymity?

The Pedestrian: Watching Your Step

Standing on the sidewalk during rush hour along Boylston Street in Boston; State Street in Columbus, Ohio; or Kearny Street in San Francisco, anyone can observe the "faceless crowd" of urbanites going about their daily business. Taking such a detached perspective, the city's people seem almost like sheep, an undifferentiated, robotlike herd. But is this really so?

Sociologist Erving Goffman (1980) believed city life is an orderly routine, one that allows people to meet their personal needs while surrounded by an unknown mass of others. He reminds us that people on the street are there for a reason. We travel the city to get to work, to enjoy a restaurant, to meet a friend, to catch a subway, or perhaps just to take a walk. Just because the observer cannot perceive such motives is no reason to think they don't exist.

Goffman then explains that pedestrians observe an intricate set of social rules. There is a traffic code for the sidewalks, just as there is a code for automobiles using the streets. Goffman notes that pedestrian traffic in U.S. cities sorts itself into two opposing streams, with the dividing line somewhere near the middle of the sidewalk. Within each stream, people "watch their step" in a variety of ways: First, they keep themselves at least slightly aware of obstacles, such as mailboxes, lampposts, or groups stopped on the sidewalk. Second, they casually note the speed of people in front of or behind them, gauging their own speed accordingly to avoid collisions. Third, to move faster or slower than the stream, people move to the outside of the lane. Fourth, people utilize various strategies to avoid collisions, perhaps making coughing noises or shifting packages to alert a careless walker to impending contact. Fifth, people scold one another

for breaking any of these rules. After someone brushes by, one pedestrian may loudly protest: "Why don't ya look where you're going?" Such reactions show us that people know the rules for pedestrian behavior and call others to task for any transgressions. In essence, a tacit contract exists among users of public space, who come to trust each other to act like competent pedestrians (Wolfinger 1995).

Rules of pedestrian traffic vary from culture to culture, of course. This variety can puzzle—and even intimidate—a traveler, as the Urban Living box on page 164 explains.

As Goffman suggested, pedestrians communally follow a sidewalk traffic code, creating two opposing streams, with the dividing line somewhere in the middle of the sidewalk. Within these two streams they share an intricate set of social rules that enable them to move easily at their own pace, without jostling or colliding with one another.

URBAN LIVING

Saigon: Learning to Cross the Street All Over Again

The first morning after we arrived in port, we left the ship early and made our way along the docks toward the center of Ho Chi Minh City—known to an earlier generation as Saigon. After looking us over—a family of U.S. visitors—the government security officers waved us through the security gates without so much as glancing at our papers. But we paused nonetheless, coming face to face with dozens of men crowded just beyond the gate, all operators of cyclos—bicycles with a small carriage attached to the front—which are the Vietnamese equivalent of taxicabs. "No, thanks," I stated firmly, breaking eye contact, and making a firm gesture with my arm. In New York, it is hard enough to find a cab; here, we spent the next twenty minutes fending off persistent drivers who cruised

alongside us pleading for our business. The pressure was uncomfortable.

Let's cross the street, I suggested. We turned to the traffic and immediately realized that there were no stop signs or signal lights. In fact, there was no break at all in the steady stream of bicycles, cyclos, motorbikes, and small trucks that rattled along the rough roadway. What to do? Then the answer came, in the form of a tiny woman who walked right next to us and plunged out into the traffic without so much as batting an eye. She simply walked at a steady pace across the street; drivers saw her coming and made room for her. To us, she appeared to part the waves of vehicles as if she had some mysterious power.

We took a deep breath. From several yards back, we walked right into the traffic keeping eyes straight ahead. Amazing! It worked. Such are the rules of the road in Vietnam.

Source: Based on travel by John Macionis to Vietnam, 1994.

Escalators represent another example of cultural variety. In the United States, passengers pile on all together, making passage by anybody behind almost impossible. In most European nations, however, escalator passengers ride on the right side, leaving a lane on the left for anyone wishing to pass. Taking their first ride on a European escalator, North Americans who place themselves on the left-hand side of a ramp are often a bit puzzled to hear people behind them asking them to please move over. Conversely, Europeans riding a North American subway escalator can be quite puzzled at the "rudeness" of locals who jam up the ramp so no one can pass.

Finally, even in that most dense and anonymous of urban worlds, the subway, people evolve mechanisms for ordering and

personalizing their experience. The second Urban Living box on page 165 offers a look at the subway at rush hour.

Together, these examples reveal that street behavior is not nearly as chaotic as it might appear at first glance. City dwellers may have to deal with larger numbers of people, often in crowded conditions, but urban life is not necessarily difficult or dehumanizing.

A World of Strangers

Besides coping with the city's sheer numbers, urbanites also must learn to deal with anonymity, since we live in what Lyn Lofland (1985) calls "a world of strangers." Lofland argues that we look for visual clues in order to classify strangers in much the same way

URBAN LIVING

The Subway at Rush Hour

A crowd of people surged into the Eighth Avenue express at 59th Street. By elbowing other passengers in the back, by pushing and heaving, they forced their bodies into the coaches, making room for themselves where no room had existed before. As the train gathered speed for the long run to 125th Street, the passengers settled down into small private worlds, thus creating the illusion of space between them and their fellow passengers. The worlds were built up behind newspapers and magazines, behind closed eyes or while staring at the varicolored show cards that bordered the coaches.

Source: Ann Petry, *The Street* (Boston: Houghton Mifflin, 1998), p. 27.

that we make sense of the city's physical environment.

Appearance and Location. First, we identify strangers in terms of their *appearance* and their *physical location* within the city. That is, we give strangers "the once-over," noting their clothing, hairstyle, jewelry, what they're carrying, and how they're walking. We also let location speak for people: For example, in a district of office buildings and expensive restaurants, we expect different types of people than in a district full of all-night movie houses or pornographic bookstores.

Lofland concedes that there is nothing uniquely urban about such tactics. Even in small towns, people judge each other by appearance and by "which side of the tracks" they call home. The point is simply that in big cities, our reliance on clues like appearance and location becomes essential. After all, the odds of running into someone one knows in midtown Manhattan or Chicago's downtown "loop" are small, indeed.

Worth noting is that using spatial location as a clue to people's identities is a modern practice. In pre-industrial cities, public spaces such as the town square usually had many uses: for schooling, religious services, parades, shopping, general loitering, and even

executions. In short, because virtually *anybody* might be found there, location provides few clues about who strangers are. In the part, then, citizens put great stock in appearance, as illustrated in the Urban Living box on page 166.

In modern industrial societies, however, the rules change. Although dress still plays a part in identifying strangers, costume is no longer the central clue it once was. Dress codes have relaxed and people from all walks of life, without fear of censure, wear almost any sort of clothing. There are important historical reasons for this change.

In the pre-industrial city, only the wealthy could afford clothes of silk and satin and jewelry made from gold and silver. With the Industrial Revolution, however, mass production made many types of dress much more affordable. Further, a rising standard of living allowed more and more people to purchase and display such goods. The film *Hester Street* (1975) offered an example: In one scene from this view of New York back in 1900, Jake, a Russian-Jewish immigrant, takes his family to Central Park. Making more money than he ever did in the old country, Jake is wearing a modestly priced but very fashionable suit. As he parades around the park, he exclaims proudly: "Look at me! I'm a real American! Who could tell if I was a Jew or a Gentile?"

URBAN LIVING

Clothes Make the Man

To a degree unknown to moderns, the resident of the preindustrial city literally "donned" his identity. The Roman citizen, for example, expressed the fact of his citizenship by wearing as decreed by law, the white toga. A "gentleman" in the Colonial cities of America was known by his "periwig." . . .

Urban elites everywhere struggled to differentiate themselves from their "inferiors" not only by the design of their dress, but by the materials as well. The cap of the medieval Frenchman was made of velvet for the elites, rough cloth for the poor. In Elizabethan England, [Gideon Sjoberg reported that] "Commoners were prohibited by law from wearing clothing fashioned from gold or silver cloth, velvet, furs, and other 'luxury' materials." Hair length also indicated status. Among the Franks, only the elite had long hair. . . .

The clothing of outcaste groups . . . was often regulated by law. . . . [T]he Parsi minority in the Persian city of Yezd were forced, until the 1880s, "to twist their turbans instead of folding them, [were] denied various colors, and [were] prohibited rings, umbrellas, and other items."

Occupation, too, was signaled by dress. The lawyers of medieval France, for example, were distinguished by their round caps . . . and the executioners of the period were forced to wear a special coat of red or gold so that they would be readily recognizable in a crowd. . . . Each of the various types of itinerant peddlers of Peking . . . wore a distinctive costume as did the clergy of twelfth century Europe and the members of religious sects in numerous preindustrial cities.

Source: Lyn H. Lofland, *A World of Strangers* (Prospect Heights, IL: Waveland Press, 1985), pp. 45–46.

If dress means less to us in modern cities, then, location means more. We recognize that industrial cities are composed of numerous distinct districts, for business, warehousing, residence, and entertainment. In business districts, we expect to encounter businesspeople and we expect them to act in a businesslike manner.

For example, Huntington Avenue marks the boundary between two major districts of Boston (look back at Figure 6–1). On the north side of the street are the upper-middle-class Back Bay and Fenway areas that include Symphony Hall, the Museum of Fine Arts, numerous expensive shops and art galleries. But just across the street begins the lower-class, predominantly African American Roxbury district, with run-down housing and down-scale shops.

To position oneself at the corner of Huntington and Massachusetts avenues near Symphony Hall when the Boston Symphony Orchestra is playing is a remarkable sociological experience. On one side of the street are men sporting formal black-tie dress and women decked out in ermine and pearls. Yet just 20 feet away are people in threadbare and tattered clothes. Strangers on both sides of the street are well aware that they inhabit two different social worlds, and few people move from one to the other.

Of course, such patterns don't mean that some people can't "work the system." We all know that it is possible for us to pass ourselves off as something we are not by manipulating the way we dress and act. A narcotics agent may infiltrate a drug ring, and a social scientist may live anonymously in an area in hopes of learning the inside story of people's lives. Sometimes people intentionally "perform": A sighted person may don dark eyeglasses, hold a sign saying "blind," and beg; sedate, middle-class suburbanites may come into the city to "swing" at night, retiring at evening's end to their normal routine.

Privatizing Public Space. Lofland (1985: 118–23) suggests that another way we reduce the vastness and complexity of a city is to transform areas into private or semiprivate space. People can claim a street corner as a hangout; a tavern (such as television's *Cheers*) can become a club to its regular patrons; and musicians can transform a section of a park into an outdoor performance arena. Such "home territories" are rarely intentional; usually, they result from unplanned, uncoordinated actions that end up spatially segregating certain types of people. The city is full of such

patterns: Yuppies appropriate plazas, skid row vagrants lay claim to benches and steam grates, gay people come to think of a neighborhood as "their own." Outsiders entering such spaces soon pick up cues of dress and behavior that indicate they are on semiprivate ground.

On a larger scale, whole urban districts can become home territory or "turf" to a specific group. Most residential neighborhoods have a dominant character, perhaps based on class, race, ethnicity, and age. Although cities are largely impersonal, they are also (in Robert Park's phrase) "mosaics of small worlds." Within *gesellschaft*, in short, the city reveals many *gemeinschaft*-like subsocieties.

Class, Race, and the Urban Experience

People have devised strategies for making sense of the city. But this hardly means that the

In a city many people share public space. Whether in small groups or alone, on a lunch or work break or resting from sightseeing, they gather wherever there is some pleasant sun and a place to sit. Steps and low walls are two popular choices, and there they either ignore others or else partake in that favorite urban pastime: people-watching.

Urban ethnic neighborhoods are often places to find examples of what Lofland calls the privatizing of public space. Here the street becomes a place to play stickball or wash a parked car, or use the sidewalk as a site for jump rope or hopscotch games, or for stores or street vendors to display their wares, or for people to sit to socialize or watch passersby.

urban experience is the same for everyone, since traits such as class, age, gender, race, and ethnicity shape our lives in the city as they do elsewhere.

The Cityscape box on pages 169–171 offers four very different urban experiences. In the first passage, Kathryn Forbes re-creates her "Mama's" image of turn-of-the-century San Francisco. Though by no means rich, Mama and her family were beginning to realize the dreams they had brought with them from Norway. Next, Jonathan Raban speaks about the difficulty he has in keeping from going "soft"—a bit crazy—"in a soft city." He writes as a "marginal man"—a freelance writer, unmarried, living alone, with few friends and no local family. Third, though she was poor, Clara Rodriguez tells of growing up in a stable and vibrant community, one that was largely cut off from the city as a whole. Eventually, she would witness the South Bronx collapse in urban decay—but her childhood memories convey a

far different reality. Finally, an African American migrant from the South, Lutie Johnson, struggled for years to free herself and her son from the grasp of the ghetto. Every time she made some progress, she saw it disappear in exploitation or cruelty. On this particular night she walks home and sees a robbery. She begins to realize that she may never get out and that life on the street amounts to a powerful barrier—built on race and class—that stands between her and her dreams.

The City as *Gesellschaft:* A Reassessment

Many early urban theorists feared that people could never cope with the city's sheer physical size, its large population, and its anonymity. Yet, we *have* learned to cope. We contend with physical size by creating our personal mental image of the city. We deal with the complexities of street life by observing codes of behavior and

CITYSCAPE

The Varieties of Urban Experience

Mama's San Francisco

In those days, if anyone had asked Mama unexpectedly, "What nationality are you?" I believe she would have answered without hesitation, "I am a San Franciscan."

Then quickly, lest you tease her, she would add, "I mean Norvegian, American citizen."

But her first statement would be the true one.

Because from the moment she was to step off the ferryboat, confused and lonely in a strange land, San Francisco was to become suddenly and uniquely her own.

"It is like Norvay," the Aunts and Mama had declared.

And straightaway she'd taken the city to her heart.

Mama learned so many things about San Francisco. She could tell you how to get to Telegraph Hill; what time the boats came in at Fisherman's Wharf; the names of the young boys who tended the teeming crab kettles along Bay Street; and where to find the blue and yellow lupines at Land's End.

The cable cars were an endless delight, and Mama's idea of a perfect Sunday afternoon was for Papa to take us riding on them from one transfer point to another.

Papa would tell of the time Mama took out her citizenship papers and astounded the solemn court by suddenly reciting the names of the streets. "Turk, Eddy, Ellis, O'Farrell," Mama had said proudly, "Geary, Post, Sutter, Bush, and Pine."

Papa said the clerk had quite a time making Mama understand that such knowledge was not necessary for citizenship.

And if anyone ever asked us where we were born, Mama instructed us we should say "San Francisco": Didn't copies of our birth certificates, neatly framed and hung on the wall of Papa's and Mama's room, testify to that proud fact?

"After all," Papa used to tease her, "after all, San Francisco isn't the world."

But to Mama it was just that. The world.

The Marginal Man

I live here on a corner of the square in a borrowed flat, without property, at haphazard. By comparison with the right family and neighborhood life of the small town, I have few attachments or continuities. My existence is lax and unshaven. I have no proper job, just an irregular series of commissions and assignments, the chores and errands of a middle class hobo. . . . Freelance writers . . . tend to drift to the peripheral fringe of things, habitual onlookers and overhearers. My flat is pitched on the western edge of my private version of London, a place to make forays from, scavenging eastwards for material and odd jobs. I am on the rim, both geographically and socially; and this marginal position suits me very well. . . .

Cities are scary and impersonal, and the best most of us can manage is a fragile hold on our route through the streets. We cling to friends and institutions, exaggerate the importance of belonging, fear being alone too much. The freedom of the city is enormous. Here one can choose and invent one's society, and live more deliberately than anywhere else. Nothing is fixed, the possibilities of personal change and renewal are endless and open. But it is hard to learn to live as generously as real citizenship demands. I spot in others the same mouselike caution which keeps me hugging the edge of the pavement, running from bolthole to bolthole, unequipped to embrace that spaciousness

(continued)

and privacy of city life which so often presents itself as mere emptiness and fog.

For me a city day is a succession of guarded moves, as if one was crossing a peat bog. . . . [We] need to hold on tight to avoid going completely soft in a soft city. So much of metropolitan life is just the slowing of symptoms of fright. In the city one clings to nostalgic and unreal signs of community, takes forced refuge in codes, badges and coteries; the city's life, surface and locomotion, usually seems too dangerous and demanding to live through with any confidence. The mad egotism of the man who stops you in Soho Square to tell you he is John the Baptist, or the weird rural delusions of another tramp nearby who fishes hopefully through a grating at the corner of Old Compton Street ("Caught anything?" "I had some good bites."), seem not unlikely consequences of the exercise of the freedom of the city. Its discontinuities give one vertigo; few people who aren't criminals or psychopaths will risk themselves on the rollercoaster ride of change and incongruity which the city offers. So much of city life is an elaborate process of building up defenses against the city—the self a fortified town raised against the stranger. We hedge ourselves in behind dreams and illusions, construct make-believe villages and make-believe families.

Life in the South Bronx

The South Bronx in New York City has always been home to me. As a young girl growing up there, I was surrounded by a stable family and a sense of community, even though the area was viewed as a place where only "the poorest of the poor" lived.

My earliest recollection of my neighborhood is of an energetic and alive community with a great deal of social interaction. I recall being wheeled with my sister in a huge baby carriage in front of what the *New York Times* would subsequently call those "solid, grimy five-story tenements." My parents would stop to converse with neighbors, part of a network of people who knew each other well and who helped each other.

My South Bronx had a richness of life, a dynamism and stability of relations that few other places have. However, as I matured, I came to understand that the world beyond my community's boundaries had a different view of us. That world saw us as "different" and poor and was often instinctively hostile or afraid of us. Yet, I never felt poor, deprived, or disadvantaged. I also never understood what inspired hostility toward those I held dear.

At an early age I came to puzzle over this contradiction, why the view from within was so different from the view from without; why hostility, fear, or disrespect should exist without cause. This developed in me a basic curiosity about the view of those affected and the factors that affected them.

The world within which I grew up was not all roses and pastels (a festive Puerto Rican dish). My childhood was as full of traumas, joys, and disappointments as the next person's. There were the usual struggles to survive that all people who have little money or who have strong differences of culture, color, and language experience. Life was hard, but life was manageable.

As I was growing up, I witnessed my community and others like it destroyed by forces over which we had little control: drugs,

seeking out clues to the identity of strangers. And, of course, our own social characteristics place us within some part of the city. While urban life may not always be pleasant, these factors work to make it meaningful.

THE SOCIAL ENVIRONMENT: *GEMEINSCHAFT*

Then, too, the city abounds with personal relationships. Only the most extreme of urban

urban renewal, and housing abandonment. . . . The dynamism and stability of the communities of the South Bronx [were] destroyed by external forces.

Not all Puerto Ricans fled; some fought to maintain their neighborhoods, fought drug dealers, and organized to get support from the city and federal governments. Currently, the decline has slowed and signs of revitalization have appeared. The South Bronx has bottomed out, but the history lived there will remain a bitter chapter for all concerned.

Lutie Johnson's New York

A man came suddenly out of a hallway just ahead of her—a furtive, darting figure that disappeared rapidly in the darkness of the street. As she reached the doorway from which he had emerged, a woman lurched out, screaming, "Got my pocketbook! The bastard's got my pocketbook!"

Windows were flung open all up and down the street. Heads appeared at the windows—silent, watching heads that formed dark blobs against the dark spaces that were the windows. The woman remained in the middle of the street, bellowing at the top of her voice.

Lutie got a good look at her as she went past her. She had a man's felt hat pulled down almost over her eyes and men's shoes on her feet. Her coat was fastened together with safety pins. She was shaking her fists as she shouted curses after the man who had long since vanished up the street.

Ribald advice issued from the windows: "Aw, shut up! Folks got to sleep."

"What the hell'd you have in it, your rent money?"

"Go on home, old woman, 'fore I throw somp'n special down on your rusty head."

As the woman's voice died away to a mumble and a mutter, the heads withdrew and the windows were slammed shut. The street was quiet again. And Lutie thought, no one could live on a street like this and stay decent. It would get them sooner or later, for it sucked the humanity out of people—slowly, surely, inevitably.

She glanced up at the gloomy apartments where the heads had been. There were row after row of narrow windows—floor after floor packed tight with people. She looked at the street itself. It was bordered by garbage cans. Half-starved cats prowled through the cans—rustling paper, gnawing on bones. Again she thought that it wasn't just this one block, this particular street. It was like this all over Harlem wherever the rents were low. . . .

And she began thinking of Pop unable to get a job; of Jim slowly disintegrating because he, too, couldn't get a job, and of the subsequent wreck of their marriage; of Bub left to his own devices after school. From the time she was born, she had been hemmed into an ever-narrowing space, until now she was very nearly walled in and the wall had been built up brick by brick by eager white hands.

Sources: Kathryn Forbes, *Mama's Bank Account* (Minneapolis: Sagebrush, 1999), pp. 39–40; Jonathan Raban, *Soft City* reprint ed. (London: Harvill Press, 1998), pp. 222–27, 230; Clara E. Rodriguez, "The Puerto Rican Community in the South Bronx: View From Within and Without," in Beth B. Hess, Elizabeth W. Markson, and Peter J. Stein, *Sociology* 5th ed. (Boston: Allyn and Bacon, 1996), p. 507; and Ann Petry, *The Street* (Boston: Houghton Mifflin, 1998), pp. 228–29, 324–25.

isolates—Jonathan Raban's "marginal man," perhaps—live according to the stereotype of *gesellschaft*. For most, interpersonal bonds provide a basis for social and psychological security in the city.

Urban Networks

The study of interpersonal ties is called *network analysis*. As we shall see, urban networks may or may not involve organized social groups, nor need they be defined by locality.

London Couples.   In an early study of networks, Elizabeth Bott (1972) examined the relationships of married couples in London. A key finding, illustrating the effects of social class on the urban experience, was that working-class partners each maintained their own networks, while middle-class spouses participated in a single network. Subsequent studies of the connection between conjugal role segregation and social networks suggest that other factors than absence of a kin network—such as the support system provided by the

network or even the availability of other groups—affect marital solidarity (Wimberley 1973; Dasgupta 1992). Such findings do not discount the role of class, however. The Urban Living box below offers a closer look at Bott's marriage networks.

Washington, D.C. Street-Corner Men.   Eliot Liebow (1967/2003) completed a classic participant observation study of poor African American men who frequented a street corner—"Tally's Corner"—in Washington, D.C. Most of these men, Liebow found, believed until their late teens that they would become adult breadwinners and husbands.

URBAN LIVING

Two Types of Marriage Networks

Segregated Marriage Networks

At one extreme was a family in which the husband and wife carried out as many tasks as possible separately and independently of each other. There was a strict division of labor in the household, in which she had her tasks and he had his. He gave her a set amount of housekeeping money, and she had little idea of how much he earned or how he spent the money he kept for himself. In their leisure time, he went to cricket matches with his friends, whereas she visited her relatives or went to a cinema with a neighbor. With the exception of festivities with relatives, this husband and wife spent very little of their leisure time together. They did not consider that they were unusual in this respect. On the contrary, they felt their behavior was typical of their social circle.

Joint Marriage Networks

At the other extreme was a family in which husband and wife shared as many activities and spent as much time together as possible. They stressed that husband and wife should be equals: all major decisions should be made together, and even in minor household matters they should help one another as much as possible. This norm was carried out in practice. In their division of labor, many tasks were shared or interchangeable. The husband often did the cooking and sometimes the washing and ironing. The wife did the gardening and often the household repairs as well. Much of their leisure time was spent together, and they shared similar interests in politics, music, literature, and in entertaining friends. Like the first couple, this husband and wife felt their behavior was typical of their social circle, except that they felt they carried the interchangeability of household tasks a little further than most people.

Source: Elizabeth Bott, *Family and Social Network,* 2nd ed. (New York: Free Press, 1972), pp. 52–53.

Driven by this ideal, many married and fathered children. Unfortunately, most of the men had few skills and little education and ended up with little more than menial jobs.

Many men came to hate the idea of performing degrading work. In time, many stopped working: Some were fired, some just quit. In any case, the men soon realized they could barely provide for themselves, much less a family. This failure was evident to their wives and children and a deep source of personal pain and family tension. To make matters worse, the government offered to provide public assistance to wives and children—but only if no father were living in the home.

Men crushed by their plight could find some comfort "hanging out" together. At Tally's Corner, people commiserated and didn't ask embarrassing questions. There, a man could forget failure and get by from day to day. Before long, most men were spending more time there than at home. The Urban Living box below explains that networks supplied the heart and soul of life on "Tally's Corner."

Boston Neighborhoods.   Many urban relationships are set in neighborhoods. Distinguished by physical or social boundaries, neighborhoods contain people who share important social characteristics such as social class, race, and ethnicity.

In a study of Boston's predominantly Italian West End neighborhood in the 1950s, Herbert Gans (1982) suggested that, despite the many differences among residents of an urban neighborhood, many *gemeinschaft*-like relations exist.

At the time of Gans's research in the 1950s, the West End was a low-income, low-rent district adjacent to the elite Beacon Hill area.

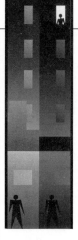

URBAN LIVING

The Networks of Street-Corner Men

[The most important people in a man's network are those] with whom he is "up tight": His "walking buddies," "good" or "best" friends, girl friends, and sometimes real or putative kinsmen. These are the people with whom he is in more or less daily, face-to-face contact, and whom he turns to for emergency aid, comfort or support in time of need or crisis. He gives them and receives from them goods and services in the name of friendship, ostensibly keeping no reckoning. Routinely, he seeks them out and is sought out by them. They serve his need to be with others of his kind, and to be recognized as a discrete, distinctive personality, and he, in turn, serves them the same way. They are both his audience and his fellow actors.

It is with these men and women that he spends his waking, nonworking hours, drinking, dancing, engaging in sex, playing the fool or the wise man, passing the time at the Carry-out or on the street-corner, talking about nothing and everything, about epistemology or [Muhammad Ali], about the nature of numbers or how he would "have it made" if he could have a steady job that paid him $60 a week with no layoffs.

So important a part of daily life are these relationships that it seems like no life at all without them. Old Mr. Jenkins climbed out of his sickbed to take up a seat on the Coca-Cola case at the Carry-out for a couple of hours. "I can't stay home and play dead," he explained, "I got to get out and see my friends."

Source: Eliot Liebow, *Tally's Corner,* 2nd ed. (Lanham, MD: Rowman and Littlefield, 2003), pp. 163–64.

Traditionally home to immigrants, over the years the West End had been dominated by various categories—including Italians, Jews, Poles, and Irish, as well as a handful of artists and bohemians.

Most casual observers of the West End concluded that it was a chaotic slum. Yet living in the area revealed a different—more accurate—picture. There, Gans found as much *gemeinschaft* as might be found in many nonurban environments, as the Urban Living box below suggests. This doesn't mean that everyone knew everyone else personally, but it does mean that most West Enders forged strong ties with family, neighbors, and friends.

Other researchers have reached similar conclusions after investigating other cities. For example, Gerald Suttles (1968) reported strong interpersonal ties among Italians in Chicago's Addams area, and Joseph Howell (1973) provided a similar description of life in an inner-city Washington, D.C. neighborhood. Finally, a complex study by Fischer et al. (1977) found important interpersonal networks operating throughout the Detroit metropolitan area. In sum, though they may be hidden to the casual observer, personal relationships may be every bit as important to urban neighbors as they are to people living in rural communities.

URBAN LIVING

Boston's Thriving West End

Everyday life in the West End was not much different from that in other neighborhoods, urban or suburban. The men went to work in the morning, and, for most of the day, the area was occupied largely by women and children—just as in the suburbs. . . . In the afternoon, younger women could be seen pushing baby carriages. Children of all ages played on the street, and teenagers would "hang" on the corner, or play ball in the school yard. . . . Many women went shopping every day, partly to meet neighbors and to catch up on area news in the small grocery stores, and partly to buy foods that could not be obtained in the weekly excursion to the supermarket. On Sunday mornings, the streets were filled with people who were visiting with neighbors and friends before and after church. . . .

On the whole . . . the various ethnic groups, the bohemians, transients, and others [lived together] without much difficulty, since each was responsive to totally different reference groups. . . . [For example] as Italians like to stay up late, and to socialize at high decibel levels, the bohemians' loud parties were no problem, at least to them. . . .

Many West Enders had known each other for years, if only as acquaintances who greeted each other on the street. Everyone might not know everyone else; but, as they did know something about everyone, the net effect was the same, especially within each ethnic group. Between groups, common residence and sharing of facilities—as well as the constant struggle against absentee landlords—created enough solidarity to maintain a friendly spirit. Moreover, for many families, problems were never far away. . . . Thus when emergencies occurred, neighbors helped each other readily; other problems were solved within each ethnic group.

For most West Enders, then, life in the area resembled that found in the village or small town, and even in the suburb.

Source: Reprinted with the permission of The Free Press, a division of Simon & Schuster Adult Publishing Group, from *The Urban Villagers* by Herbert J. Gans. Copyright © 1982 by Herbert J. Gans. Copyright © 1982 by The Fress Press.

Friendships. Yet many urban relationships do not involve neighbors. More affluent urbanites especially—many who move from city to city to establish their careers—are not linked to neighborhoods in any traditional sense. Yet friends they have. Such people typically forge friendships at work, with people with whom they have lunch or a drink and dinner, or with friends they meet more casually, say, at a concert or in the park. The point is that such friendships may be maintained among people who do not live near each other but with whom they share similar interests (Whitmeyer 2002; Gibbons and Olk 2003).

It was industrial technology that broke up the communities of old, with new opportunities pulling people away from the towns of their birth. Yet technology also provides new means to stay in touch: the land-line telephone served this purpose in the twentieth century, and the cell phone and e-mail heavily reinforce countless relationships in this century.

Scenes. One of the city's hallmarks is its diversity of people, meaning that not everyone has some traditional location—such as a neighborhood—in which to develop interpersonal ties. In fact, many people *invent* places where they get together. John Irwin (1977) called such places **scenes.**

Scenes include bars, clubs, discos, or areas of a city taken over by a group (much as San Francisco's Haight-Ashbury district was inundated by hippies in the 1960s or Bryant Park in New York City by yuppies in the late 1990s). Many who participate in scenes devote a considerable amount of time and energy to them.

Most scenes are part-time. They usually occupy the hours away from work (such as a favorite eatery for lunch, a coffee shop, or a health club/fitness center). Second, to "make the scene" suggests that participants are in some sense "on stage," emphasizing only one particular aspect of themselves—their ability

Many cities are filled with young adults for whom one of the most popular "scenes" is a bar or club where they can relax and enjoy themselves with friends, fellow students, or co-workers. Some places attract a particular lifestyle crowd—such as gays, musicians, or writers—while others are more open in attracting a wide range of customers.

to dance or their knowledge of literature, for instance.

Further, scenes are of four main types. Most cities have *lifestyle scenes* that attract writers, musicians, gays, political radicals, and other groups. On summer evenings in Toronto, for example, young people from all over the metropolitan area descend on Yonge Street, often remaining until the wee hours of the morning. On foot or in cars with stereos blaring, they eat, talk, yell, buy records, and generally hang out up and down a dozen city blocks.

The *local scene* is more exclusive. A local bar, for example, may attract a particular crowd and may even discourage "outsiders" from coming in.

The *open scene* is more fluid in terms of clientele, yet it too provides the opportunity for personal relationships. Bars without a well-defined clientele fall into this category. Such public drinking places provide opportunities for those present, whether acquainted or not, to engage others in conversational interaction in a setting that promotes the near-obligation to accept these extended overtures of sociability.

Finally, the *specialized scene* involves activities such as tennis, barbershop harmony, amateur theater, chess, skateboarding, and countless other activities. Like the local scene, these provide a sense of in-group solidarity with others who share some special interest. Yet specialized scenes have a degree of openness and population fluidity that local scenes cannot have.

Perhaps one of the best-known specialized scenes among college students, especially those attending a city college or university, are the clubs. These typically crowded gathering places have a DJ or band, a dance floor, a bar, and room to sit or stand. In Boston, for instance, some of the more popular clubs are Aria, Avalon, Club Nicole, Roxy, and the Sweetwater Cafe. Other clubs cater to different types of clientele, such as African Americans, Hispanic Americans, or yuppies. But all club people come to listen and dance to the music and, of course, to enjoy some good times with old or new friends.

Temporary Networks. Many urban dwellers use another type of network to make initial or short-term personal contact in the city. Examples of such networks are "lonely hearts" clubs, dating agencies, public ballrooms, call-in radio talk shows, dial-a-prayer, and suicide hot lines.

Sometimes such networks serve people who are extremely lonely or desperate. Just as frequently, they serve people who are quite happy with their lives. People who participate in late-night talk shows need not be lonely, after all; they may be working late, or just interested in speaking their mind.

Identifying with the City

The ability to know and identify with an entire city probably ended in the Middle Ages. With the dawning of the modern age, Western cities began a relentless increase in population, as well as an expanding division of labor, resulting in the large, diverse cities we find today.

Still, most people have some sense of knowing their city, although such knowledge often is based on clichés and stereotypical images that outsiders also may share. Thus, beer has made Milwaukee famous in the same way that sun defines Miami and the entertainment industry has elevated Los Angeles and Hollywood. St. Louis has its arch and Toronto its CN Tower ("world's tallest freestanding structure!"). And, while Stratford-on-Avon has its Shakespeare, Hannibal, Missouri, is proud to be the boyhood home of Mark Twain (Samuel Clemens).

In addition, identification with the modern city is fostered by sports teams ("Minneapolis–St. Paul—Home of the Twins, Vikings, and North Stars!") and by important local events (St. Patrick's Day in Boston, the Rose Parade in Pasadena, Inauguration Day in Washington, D.C.). One of the most famous urban rituals has been Mardi Gras, which practically defined New Orleans to many outsiders. This event's vital importance to residents of the city (not to mention its attraction for a million or so tourists each year) will no doubt return again once the city rebuilds after Hurricane Katrina (see the Urban Living box on pages 178–179).

Social researchers deflated the myth of urban alienation by documenting the pervasiveness of social networks among virtually all city dwellers, rich and poor alike. One does not need the formal trappings of social organizations to enjoy intimate ties with others. A street corner or public bench can easily serve to create a *gemeinschaft* environment.

Historical events—both negative and positive—also help to define the urban experience. The San Francisco earthquake of 1906 and the devastating aftermath from Hurricane Katrina in New Orleans in 2005 are examples of costly and tragic events that remain alive in people's minds, while the ride of Paul Revere through Boston and the First Continental Congress in Philadelphia are Revolutionary War events well known centuries later by most of the cities' present-day inhabitants.

The City as *Gemeinschaft:* A Reassessment

A wealth of research supports the conclusion that the vast majority of urbanites are "well-connected" in their cities. On the one hand, most are engaged in a variety of networks. Families, neighborhoods, friendships, scenes, and even temporary contacts are examples. Similarly, most city residents have a sense of identification with their city. We conclude, then, that, while they may not always be readily apparent, characteristics of Tönnies's *gemeinschaft*—personal relationships and a sense of belonging—do flourish in the city.

THE TEXTURE OF THE CITY

Most cities convey a unique impression—a look and feel that Gerald Suttles (1984) termed a "texture." New York is the "Big Apple," a city of energy, hustle, and fear; Boston is relaxed, "cultural," and intellectual; Los Angeles is "laid back," the heart of the "new America"; and New Orleans was (and will be again) "The Big Easy," where life is slower, simpler, and easy-going. While these are stereotypical impressions, many people share them.

URBAN LIVING

Great Urban Rituals

Cities, both large and small, have annual events that involve large segments of the population and serve as a means of sharing in an urban experience and thus identifying with the city. Here are just a few examples.

Each New Year's Day, weather permitting, about 1 million people line the streets of Philadelphia to watch the Mummers Parade. About 15,000 marchers, members of many Mummers clubs—capped and caped, in speckled and sequined costumes, literally strut to the music of a distinctive string band strum. They neither walk nor march, but instead cakewalk in a distinctive style that is difficult to imitate. It's a colorful, pleasant spectacle and famous city tradition.

In Boston the celebration of Patriot's Day (the third Monday in April) commemorates the events in that city that led to the American Revolution (the rides of Paul Revere and William Dawes, the battles at Lexington and Concord). Aside from reenactments of the rides and a traditional parade, the main attraction that day is the Boston Marathon. This oldest race in the United States, a marathon second only in age to the Olympics itself, attracts over 20,000 runners and more than a half-million enthusiastic spectators along the 26.2-mile route.

Cinco de Mayo festivals celebrate Mexico's victory over French forces in Puebla, Mexico, on May 5, 1862. Though celebrated in many major U.S. cities—including Austin, Chicago, Dallas, Houston, San Antonio, and St. Paul—it is in Los Angeles where hundreds of thousands of people gather in parks and on streets decorated in the Mexican colors (red, white, green) to enjoy the crafts, food, music, and dancing.

On Memorial Day weekend, Detroit hosts Movement, the largest electronic music festival in the world. More than 70 well-known acts perform on multiple stages in Hart Plaza

---

But to what extent are such images real? Suttles argues that a city's **texture** is grounded in its history, architecture, street names, and even the nicknames for certain parts of town. Together, these elements add up to an objective reality, not just one individual's impression.

A visitor to Hollywood, for example, can actually see the footprints and handprints of the stars in the cement in front of Grauman's Chinese Theater, use a map to visit the homes of the stars, and see the huge "Hollywood" sign overlooking the city. Who knows? If you're lucky, you might even end up face to face with a famed actor at a restaurant. Stars, money, and fame are all part of Hollywood's texture as "Tinsel Town."

Another city, Detroit, has been battling its negative image of urban decay and high crime for decades. With the decline of the automobile industry in the 1970s, the flight of affluent people to the suburbs, and the collapse of its center-city areas, Detroit gained a reputation as unsafe and unpleasant—a violent cultural wasteland. As both cause and effect, Detroit's population plummeted by 44 percent between 1950 and 1990, then lost another 77,000 people between 1990 and 2000, and another 52,000 people over the next five years. As a result, its population dropped from a peak of nearly 2 million in the early 1950s to below 900,000 for the first time since 1917 (Gray 2005).

for over 1 million fans. Held in the birthplace of techno music, the event integrates musical and visual artistry, creativity, diversity and state-of-the-art technology.

Atlanta hosts Music Midtown, one of the largest music festivals of its kind in the United States, with just about every musical genre included. The multiday spring extravaganza in central Atlanta includes over 100 well-known performers and attracts about 300,000 people.

Every summer since 1967, Toronto blazes with the excitement of calypso and elaborate masquerade costumes during the annual Caribana Festival. This two-week festival is the largest Caribbean festival in North America, attracting over 1 million participants, including hundreds of thousands of American tourists.

Among the many ethnic festivals in New York City, its oldest and most popular one that cuts across ethnic boundaries is the San Gennaro Festival in Little Italy, which runs for two weeks in mid-September. The street festivities—which include parades,

entertainment, food stands, and a cannoli-eating contest—attract over 1 million people annually.

Of the thousands of Oktoberfest celebrations in North America, Cincinnati's German heritage celebration is the largest, drawing over 500,000 people each year. Five downtown city blocks are transformed each September into Oktoberfest Zinzinnati with seven stages offering live entertainment and nearly 100 booths serving German food, wine, and beer.

We cannot end this section without mentioning Mardi Gras in New Orleans. Before Hurricane Katrina, there were two weeks of elaborate parades, at least one a day through Fat Tuesday, the day before the Christian season of Lent began. From the parade floats, riders in outrageous costumes threw beads and other trinkets to hundreds of thousands of spectators, many themselves dressed in costume during this fun-filled time. Hopefully, in the near future this city will once again be the scene for such traditional delight.

How does a city overcome such a reputation and population loss? City officials put more police on the streets and made concerted efforts to rebuild neighborhoods. Yet, by 2005, Detroit remained—for the sixth year in a row—the most dangerous large U.S. city, as measured by the six basic crime categories of murder, rape, robbery, aggravated assault, burglary, and motor vehicle theft. Overall, it ranked second among 327 cities among dangerous cities for its crime rate, behind Camden, New Jersey, which has 80,000 residents (Morgan Quitno 2005).

However, the city is also experiencing a cultural renaissance, with a restored Detroit Opera House and with appealing exhibits at the Henry Ford Museum, the Detroit Historical Museum, and the Museum of African

American History in the Detroit Cultural Center. In addition, the Detroit Institute of Arts is one of the nation's biggest art museums and contains exceptional Diego Rivera murals (Meredith 1996b).

Another recent innovation is the People Mover, an automated, elevated train system that takes riders on a 2.9-mile loop of the downtown Detroit. For just 50 cents, one can easily reach the numerous casinos, offices, restaurants, shops, nightlife, landmarks, and other attractions that are within walking distance of the People Mover's 13 stations and stops.

But perhaps the best indicator of Detroit's future potential to change its textural image is General Motors' 1996 purchase of the flashiest landmark in the city's skyline, the Renaissance Center. This downtown complex of

Ethnic pride parades and street fairs, such as the International Food Festival on Ninth Avenue in New York City, are popular means by which a city not only celebrates its diversity, but also provides a rich variety of activities not to be found in any other setting. Regardless of one's own background, such events are a source of interest and enjoyment.

30,000 square feet of meeting space, and about 70 high-end apartments that were converted to condominiums. In addition, Compuware's new $350 million world headquarters houses 4,100 employees and is located only a few blocks from the hotel. If it generates other businesses, Detroit's urban redevelopment may finally be realized.

Portland, Oregon (see case study in Chapter 4), already has a strong positive image, based on a revitalized downtown, new housing and businesses, and a rebuilt waterfront. Visitors take delight in strolling down tree-lined shopping streets, observing the many fountains, and traveling safely by bicycle. Portland is prospering as one of the vibrant new cities of the West: still, it effectively controls its growth, increasing in population by only 4,000 between 2002 and 2004 (U.S. Census Bureau 2005:34).

The "concrete canyons" formed by the tall buildings in midtown Manhattan create a different sense of place in the minds of visitors than, say, the streets of Boston's central business district, where few tall buildings abound, or the streets of San Francisco, with its many steep hills and cable cars.

In short, our senses do not deceive us when we get a different feeling from one city than from another. Although urban areas share many common elements, their individuality is quite real.

HUMANIZING THE CITY

People have devised ways to humanize life in today's urban environment, just as they did in the towns and villages of the past. Even when struggling with poverty, most people have found ways to maintain positive personal relationships (Henly et al. 2005). Although some homeless people live on the margins in almost complete isolation, most urban poor generate a social network to help them cope.

five glass towers—one soaring 73 stories and housing the 1,400-room Westin Hotel—has some 2.2 million square feet of office and retail space. GM's move back to the central city promises to spur the renewal of this troubled city, persuading other companies to locate downtown as well and to revitalize the urban economy.

Similarly, the renovation in late 2005 of the city's most famous grand hotel, the historic, 30-story Book-Cadillac Hotel, offers additional hope. It will be an upscale brand of Marriott International. Opened in time for the 2006 Super Bowl, it contains 386 hotel rooms,

Virginia Schein (1995) conducted in-depth interviews with 30 single mothers receiving public assistance. All were working or had some work experience. She found that, for many, a network of family, friends, and teachers provided both emotional support and resources, enabling the women to battle their fears and to struggle onward, despite many hardships in their daily lives. Arlene, a 34-year-old mother of three, had just earned an associate college degree in business administration and moved off public assistance benefits to start a job as a customer service representative. Never, she explained, could she have done so without family support:

> I told my sister when I graduated that I owed much of it to her. My sister helped me out with the baby-sitting. She would pick them up [my kids] from day care, feed them supper, and give them baths. Then she would bring them to my house, put them to bed, and wait for me to get home, usually around 9:30. (1995:102)

For others, support came from nonfamily members, as another woman explained:

> It was like a three-ring circus. I have the [two] children, five classes, driving back and forth. It was quite a struggle to juggle all of that. I realized that I couldn't do this all on my own. I could ask for help and not feel disgraced. . . .
>
>   I realized that there are people out there that care. They helped me. Then it got better. I knew there were people that I could call, that I had the support that I needed, that these people understood what I was going through. (1995:99)

Renata, a 37-year-old high school dropout and mother of two teenagers, spoke of the positive support she received from her church:

> I just got tired of trying to fix things and nothing would get fixed. Things would change and I couldn't change them back. I started going to church and I ended up going and going. I started going a year ago and am getting to know a lot of people. I was the type that stayed home all the time. I went to work, came home, went to work, came home. I didn't associate with many people on the block. I had one neighbor on one side and a girlfriend on the other and that was it. Now I go to church every Sunday, I sing in the choir, and I talk to people all day long.

> One woman said, "You look so good, you have a glow, it's your aura. I don't know what it is but you look so different." A little old lady that lives up the street also said, "You should have started going to church a long time ago—you look good." It all gives me a little more confidence each day. If I can make it this day, then I can make it the next day and the next one and the next one. (1995:102–103)

Carol Stack (1997) stressed the ingenuity of poor African Americans in the inner-city area of a large midwestern city. Most of the men, she learned, were recent migrants from the South whose search for better jobs had resulted, at best, in low-paying, menial jobs. Most of the women struggled to raise their children with no steady source of income. Despite the odds against them, Stack discovered, these poor people had responded to their plight by constructing a diffuse family structure that allowed them to maintain a stable community and meet everyone's basic needs.

The network was a means to respond to an immediate crisis, as people shared clothes, food, and rent money. But each time that help was given, a debt was incurred. The helping families and individuals, sure to be in need of assistance themselves in time, expected that those they had helped would assist them in turn. As these obligations spread, the residents established an extensive network of "cooperation and mutual aid" (1997:28–31). The expanding network became one extended family, a fact suggested by the common practice of referring to the community as "all our kin." In the Urban Living box on p. 182, Stack describes how one particular network evolved.

Residents, Stack found, shared virtually everything, from clothes to food to child care responsibilities. Sometimes fathers of children lived at home and sometimes, when they could not support their families, they did not. Even then, fathers frequently contributed what they could to the upbringing of their children. When mothers had to work, they turned to their own mothers or to neighbors for help with the children. Thus, an informal day-care system evolved that ensured that children

URBAN LIVING

Helping Each Other in the Ghetto

Cecil (age 35) lives in The Flats with his mother Willie Mae, his oldest sister and her two children, and his younger brother. Cecil's younger sister Lily lives with their mother's sister Bessie. Bessie has three children and Lily has two. Cecil and his mother have part-time jobs in a cafe and Lily's children are on aid. In July . . . Cecil and his mother had just put together enough money to cover their rent. Lily paid her utilities, but she did not have enough money to buy food stamps for herself and her children. Cecil and Willie Mae knew that after they paid their rent they would not have any money for food for the family. They helped out Lily by buying her food stamps, and then the two households shared meals together until Willie Mae was paid two weeks later. A week later Lily received her second ADC [Aid to Dependent Children] check and Bessie got some spending money from her boyfriend. They gave some of this money to Cecil and Willie Mae to pay their rent, and gave Willie Mae money to cover her insurance and pay a small sum on a living room suite at the local furniture store. Willie Mae reciprocated later on by buying dresses for Bessie and Lily's daughters and by caring for all the children when Bessie got a temporary job.

Source: Carol Stack, *All Our Kin* (New York: Basic Books, 1997), p. 37.

always would have the attention of at least one caring adult. Through this reciprocal aid system, people gave what was needed and expected that their kindness would be repaid later on. Or, as one woman put it,

> Sometimes I don't have a damn dime in my pocket, not a crying penny to get a box of paper diapers, milk, a loaf of bread. But you have to have help from everybody and anybody, so don't turn no one down when they come round to help. (Stack 1997:32)

Those who don't "play fair" by reciprocating are quickly sanctioned, as documented by other researchers, including Doug A. Timmer, D. Stanley Eitzen, and Kathryn D. Talley (1994), who conducted in-depth interviews of the homeless in Tampa, Denver, and Chicago. As one once-homeless woman explained:

> For six months I took [my sister] in my apartment without [the Housing Authority] knowin' about it and helped her out, fed her, bought things for her. We had holidays together. And I threw this in her face three weeks ago and told her, "This is the way it is, you know. I helped you and now you can't help me. Then you can forget about me." So we haven't called each other at all. And I won't call her. 'Til doomsday. I won't call her. Even if she comes lookin' for me, she won't find me. (Timmer et al. 1994:113)

Through this system of cooperation and mutual support, in spite of the conditions that hem them in, the people in study after study have invented ways to meet at least their basic needs and to soften the blow of their poverty. Such positive adaptation is a prime example of how people can make their urban experience, even under the harsh conditions of poverty, more humane.

❖ ━━━━━ ❖ ━━━━━ ❖

SUMMARY

Living in cities alters our perceptions. There is an urban experience because we react to the city as a physical and social environment. Such reactions represent a social psychology of the city.

We make sense of the city by ordering it. Kevin Lynch observed that we trace the physical landscape, identifying paths, edges, districts, nodes, and landmarks. In part, such distinctions arise from the physical form of the city itself (streets, after all, are "natural" paths) and, in part, from our personal needs and creativity (people invent "back street" paths to get from one place to another more quickly). To this basic insight, Stanley Milgram contributed a deeper understanding of the process of "mental mapping."

A similar ordering occurs as we respond to the city's social aspects. On the one hand, we cope with the city's *gesellschaft* characteristics (large numbers and high density) by inventing rules of behavior for riding the subway, standing in line, or walking in the street. We also size up strangers from their dress, demeanor, and location in the city. Nevertheless, despite many common strategies, we all react individually to the city. Our social characteristics—whether we are rich or poor, immigrant or native, mainstream or marginal—have much to do with the nature of our urban experience.

On another level, we have developed complex ways of establishing meaningful relationships in the city. Urban networks are a prime example. Personal networks take many forms, including kinship, neighborhood, street-corner friendships, or people frequenting some "scene." Most of us also identify with our city as a whole, merging traits of our particular city (a key industry, a winning sports team, or an important historical event) with our own personal urban experience. All these mechanisms lend a *gemeinschaft*-like character to the urban experience.

Next, there is the notion of urban texture. Recent research has shown that there is much truth in people's comments that, based on its history, architecture, location, and people, each city "feels" a little different.

Last, numerous investigations show how people, even those facing the most desperate conditions, can humanize the city and turn it into a meaningful experience.

Together, all these elements of the urban experience provide us with a sense of order and security in this largest of human agglomerations, and they make the city meaningful, usable, and often enjoyable.

CONCLUSION

The city is a big place. It has more people, more buildings, more paths, more nodes, more possibilities for interaction and relationship than any other form of settlement. As Georg Simmel argued many years ago, cities demand a lot of mental work from those who wish to make sense of them. In the end, such extra mental effort may be the unique element that creates the sophistication for which urban dwellers are noted.

KEY TERMS

Districts
Edges
Landmarks
Mental maps
Nodes
Paths
Scenes
Texture

CHAPTER 7

GEOGRAPHY AND SPATIAL PERSPECTIVES
Making Sense of Space

❖ ———————— ❖ ———————— ❖

If you happen to be endowed with topographical curiosity, the hills of San Francisco fill you with an irresistible desire to walk to the top of each one of them. Whoever laid the town out took the conventional checkerboard pattern of streets and without the slightest regard for the laws of gravity planked it down blind on an irregular peninsula that was a confusion of steep slopes and sandhills. The result is exhilarating. Wherever you step out on the street there's a hilltop in one direction or the other. From the top of each hill you get a view and the sight of more hills to the right and left and ahead that offer the prospect of still broader views. The process goes on indefinitely. You can't help making your way painfully to the top of each hill just to see what you can see. . . .

This one is Nob Hill. . . . Ahead of me the hill rises higher and breaks into a bit of blue sky. Sun shines on a block of white houses at the top. Shiny as a toy fresh from a Christmas tree, a little cable car is crawling up it. Back of me under an indigo blue of mist are shadowed roofs and streets and tall buildings with wisps of fog about them, and beyond, fading off into the foggy sky, stretches the long horizontal of the Bay Bridge.

Better go back now and start about my business. The trouble is that down the hill to the right I've caught sight of accented green roofs and curved gables painted jade green and vermillion. That must be in Chinatown. Of course the thing to do is take a turn through Chinatown on the way down toward the business district. . . .

> John Dos Passos,
> "San Francisco Looks West"

In a basic sense, cities are things—complex physical entities. Cities exist within geographic and climatic settings that naturally shape them. The hands and minds of human beings, of course, also play a part as people react to a city's physical setting. San Francisco is an excellent example—people started with an exciting geography and a pleasant climate and added a host of their own creations (diverse neighborhoods, clattering cable cars, a lively Chinatown, and bridges that span sparkling waters) to produce a particularly enticing urban experience. While San Francisco has its unique features, all cities have a distinct "personality," at least partly shaped by their physical layout. This chapter explores that interrelationship between a city and its physical setting.

URBAN GEOGRAPHY

Some cities, like San Francisco, straddle hills. Others, like St. Louis, Tucson, or Oklahoma City, stretch across flat plains. No matter what the topography of the land, however, a city's design reflects its physical environment.

Take, for example, Los Angeles, San Francisco's massive neighbor 500 miles to the south. Originally a Spanish mission outpost, for decades Los Angeles remained a series of scattered communities surrounded by mountains in the relatively flat, near-desert region of California's southwest.

In the 1920s, however, coincident with the rise of the movie industry, Los Angeles began to grow rapidly. As its population surged upward, the city became a bowl-shaped collection of outlying suburban communities. At first, public transport—electric trains and streetcars—linked the new settlements with Los Angeles. With the arrival of the mass-produced private automobile, public transportation ridership swiftly declined, as commuters preferred the convenience and privacy of driving themselves to and from the city. This heavy reliance on automobiles fostered ever-expanding urban sprawl throughout the region and gave us Los Angeles's incredible freeways. Says Jan Morris:

> These remain the city's grandest and most exciting artifacts. Snaky, sinuous, undulating, high on stilts or sunk in cuttings, they are like so many concrete tentacles, winding themselves around each block, each district, burrowing, evading, clambering, clasping every corner of the metropolis as if they are squeezing it all together to make the parts stick. They are inescapable, not just visually, but emotionally. They are always there, generally a few blocks away; they enter everyone's lives, and seem to dominate all arrangements. (Morris 2003:230)

As Los Angeles expanded, people settled the mountains themselves, with streets "forever ribbing and probing further into [the] perimeter hills, twisting like rising water ever higher, ever deeper into their canyons, and sometimes bursting through to the deserts beyond" (Morris 2003:229).

Ironically, the city's increasing population, its heavy reliance on the automobile, and its geography combined to produce an unexpected but monumental environmental problem: smog. Although it is by no means the only city beset by this threat to health, Los Angeles's smog problem has been particularly serious because the surrounding hills trap noxious fumes in the bowl-shaped region where most of the city's people live. Only recently has the problem lessened, thanks to California's "toughest in the nation" pollution laws. Despite its air quality problems, the Los Angeles area continues to grow—from about 3 million in 1980 to about 3.9 million in 2005—and the automobile continues to reign supreme.

The Location of Cities

Geography and climate, then, provide the physical conditions to which urbanites must adapt. In fact, certain physical characteristics usually determine whether an area becomes a city at all.

Look at Figure 7–1, which shows the geographical location of the 33 most populous urban areas in North America. All but a few are located on waterways. They are either seaports (Los Angeles, New York, Vancouver), lakeports (Chicago, Milwaukee, Toronto), or on major rivers (Cleveland, Memphis, Montreal). The advantage of such sites for stimulating trade is enormous. However, even cities not on important waterways (Dallas, Denver, Fort Worth, Phoenix) are where they are because, at least initially, there were enough streams and lakes to support their populations.

The sole exception to the waterway thesis is Atlanta. Yet its site, too, was determined by a geographical consideration: In the 1840s Atlanta was selected as the southern terminus of the Western and Atlantic Railroad because of its centrality to the rest of the South. Thus, even Atlanta illustrates that environmental considerations play a key role in locating a city. With this in mind, we can consider briefly the sites of five other cities: Houston, Miami, Montreal, Salt Lake City, and Washington, D.C. What products and activities do you associate with each?

FIGURE 7–1 Geographical Location of the 33 Most Populous North American Metropolitan Areas, 2004
[*Source:* U.S. Census Bureau, 2005, Table 26, pp. 29–31.]

Houston.   Located near the East Texas oil fields, this city has been booming since the 1950s. Its metropolitan population more than doubled between 1970 and 2005 to 5.2 million. Because of oil—every major oil company has offices in Houston—and cheap shipping of oil via the Gulf of Mexico, the city has the nation's second busiest port in the country (after New York) and the nation's largest port in international tonnage. Considered by many as the "energy capital of the world," Houston is home to more than 5,000 energy-related companies. It is also home to the largest medical center in the world and to 18 *Fortune* 500 companies (Houston 2005).

Miami.   Although it is a port, Miami is best known for tourism and as a mecca for retirement. The winter climate is ideal, with temperatures hovering near the 80s, nearly unlimited sun, and endless beaches. "Fun in the Sun" is the city's motto. In recent years, however, Miami has become a major market for specialized goods, thanks in large measure to its large Cuban American community. Because of the Cubans' economic success, the city has become attractive to wealthy Latin Americans. They fly to Miami, stay in or near Little Havana, speak nothing but Spanish, and buy numerous U.S. goods—clothes, computers, stereos—from Cuban merchants at prices much lower than they would pay at home. Such visitors are crucial to maintaining the city's economy (Miami 2005).

Montreal.   Built on and around a mountain slope located at the junction of the St. Lawrence and Ottawa River systems in the southwestern corner of Quebec, Montreal is North America's fifteenth largest metropolitan area, containing 3.6 million people (Statistics Canada 2004). Although Montreal has a strong, diversified industrial base, service dominates its economy. Many national and international service companies are headquartered there, especially in the banking, culture, finance, telecommunications, and transportation sectors. Montreal also accounts for one-fourth of all corporate research and development expenditures in Canada (twice its share by population). Long, cold winters have prompted an expansive and delightful underground network of shops, restaurants, and theaters that people enjoy year-round. Montreal also is home to four professional sports franchises, a ballet company, an opera company, and a symphony orchestra (Montreal 2005).

Salt Lake City.   Situated at the foot of a mountain range near the forbidding and barren Great Salt Lake in Utah, Salt Lake City might seem an unlikely urban site. Yet the Mormons thought otherwise. Migrating westward in the mid-nineteenth century, looking for a place where they could practice their religion freely, the Mormon leaders saw the Salt Lake region as the place God had set aside for them. In a sense, the region's remoteness was the key to its founding. But, as it turned out, the location is more hospitable than it appeared at first glance. Salt Lake City became a point of rest and departure for westward migration, and the salt proved to be a valuable resource, so the city became the only area within hundreds of miles able to support a large metropolitan population, numbering over 1 million in 2005 (Salt Lake City 2005).

Washington, D.C.   Here we have a very different case. Its founders did not look on Washington as an economic center. The issue was politics—wishing to avoid choosing between Philadelphia and New York as the permanent U.S. capital. In addition, Washington represented a symbolic link between two great regions: the North and the South. Once the Potomac River basin (water again!) became the site of the U.S. capital city, the nation's emergence as a world power generated a vast government bureaucracy, hundreds of foreign embassies, countless special interest groups, and a vast array of hotels, restaurants, and national landmarks that make this urban area unique. Its population, however, has steadily dropped, from 757,000 in 1970 to 554,000 in 2004 (Washington, DC 2005).

Geography has played a large role in Montreal's existence. The junction of the St. Lawrence and Ottawa rivers affected its location choice, and the sloping mountain terrain dictated the layout of its expansion. Its long, cold winters influenced the building of an extensive underground mall of shops, restaurants, and theatres as lively as any above-ground complex found elsewhere.

Why Cities Are Where They Are

Both environmental *and* social factors play a role in creating an urban area. On the environmental side, any setting, in order to become a city, must fulfill a number of basic conditions. First and foremost, it must be a *minimally hospitable environment*. It cannot be infested with disease-producing organisms, be subject to extreme heat or cold, or exist on a flood plain. In addition, any city has to have *access to adequate supplies of food, water, and building materials.* This is not to say that cities cannot overcome limitations in some sites, but settlers' ingenuity and technology must be up to the task. For example, gas and oil heat have made winter survival in northern cities possible for millions, just as air conditioning moderates the extreme heat of southern urban areas. Similarly, water and other resources can be imported. Las Vegas,

situated in the Nevada desert, is perhaps the best example of an "impossible" city brought to life by modern technology.

Once basic environmental conditions have been met, social factors come into play. We will discuss seven such factors, using the five cities just discussed as illustrations.

1. Some cities are situated at a **natural crossroads** for a region. Montreal, for example, is the most important port on the St. Lawrence River and Seaway, lying between the Atlantic Ocean to the east and the Great Lakes to the west. Other examples are St. Louis and Chicago, the latter nicknamed "the crossroads of the nation." Such crossroads facilitate the concentration of people, services, and, especially, trade goods.
2. Other cities develop because they are located at what economists call **break-of-bulk** points. These are locations where a good—the "bulk"—is transferred from one type of

CITYSCAPE

New Orleans: Paying the Price for Its Location

Its strategic location at the mouth of the Mississippi River allowed New Orleans to emerge as an important break-of-bulk city, making its port the fifth busiest in the country. Here, farmers in the Midwest send their crops down the river in barges, and the grains are then loaded onto 5,000 ships annually from 60 nations. As a result, the United States is the world's largest exporter of corn, soybeans, and wheat. However, it is not just agricultural exports that make New Orleans so important. The Mississippi River links into the Ohio, the Illinois, and the Missouri rivers, and manufacturers from across the Midwest depend on 50,000 inland river barges to carry chemicals, steel, rubber, and other cargoes to world export through New Orleans (Wikipedia 2005). Thus, the devastation to the city in 2005 as a result of Hurricane Katrina had a negative ripple effect on the economy and people far beyond the impacted area.

Moreover, the city's vulnerability to flooding—long known to government officials but never effectively countered—became painfully obvious to even the most casual observer. Although the older part of the city was built on higher ground, as the city expanded, development occurred elsewhere. As a result, major portions of the city are below sea level, protected by levees and sea walls designed to protect against storm surges about 20 feet high. However, it was not just much higher surges from the Gulf's waters that did the damage, but also from the waters of Lake Pontchartrain at the city's northern boundary. This oval-shaped lake is about 40 miles wide from east to west and measures about 24 miles from north to south. The heavy rains and winds were more than the lake's levees could withstand, and in several places they broke, flooding about 80 percent of the city. The loss of life, the struggles of the survivors, and the devastation of families, homes, businesses, and personal belongings were profoundly moving to people everywhere.

Water was the chief reason for the settlement, growth, and destruction of New Orleans. It will take years and billions of dollars, but the city will be rebuilt, because its strategic location demands that. However, the levees and walls protecting the new New Orleans will be made much stronger against the forces of nature so that, hopefully, the large bodies of water to the city's north and south cannot again wreak such havoc.

transportation to another, say, from truck to ship. Houston is a break-of-bulk point for oil. In such places, goods often are warehoused for a time or processed in some way to make the next leg of the trip more economical. When this happens, a city develops a set of subindustries that deal with storing or processing. In Houston, oil to be shipped from the city often is stored in huge tanks, later to be refined into gasoline or heating oil. James Heilbrun gives another example:

Probably the most often cited case of a city that has attracted industry because it is a transshipment point is Buffalo. An enormous flour-milling industry developed there because grain could be carried inexpensively across the Great Lakes from the grain belt of the North Central States, unloaded at Buffalo, the easternmost port that could be reached before the St. Lawrence Seaway was built, there milled into flour, and then

Though now known mainly by its devastation from Hurricane Katrina, and its annual Mardi Gras celebrations, New Orleans has long played a major role in the nation's economic welfare because of its strategic location at the mouth of the Mississippi River. This container ship with export grain is but one of thousands to leave this important break-of-bulk port city.

shipped by rail to the large East Coast markets. (1987:65)

Furthermore, the break-of-bulk function of cities is an enduring feature. The Urban Living box on page 191 describes two cases separated by more than a century. Note the striking similarities between Charles Dickens's description of 1860 London and Vincent Parrillo's comments about contemporary Seattle.

3. Another major reason for a city's location is access to some valuable *raw material*. Montreal's early history rested heavily on its colonial fur trade. Today, this city remains an important shipping center, handling the millions of gallons of petroleum processed each day by Montreal-Est refineries. Similarly, Houston and its refineries are near the East Texas oilfields; San Francisco boomed in the mid-nineteenth century because it was the closest port to the Sierra Nevada gold mines; and Pittsburgh's greatness was largely due to its proximity to coal mines that afforded cheap power for its steel mills.

4. Miami suggests another reason for a city location. Here we have an **amenity city** located in a particular place because it provides certain surroundings—sea, surf, sand, and sun—not easily available elsewhere. In its recent guise as "Latin America's supermarket," this predominantly Spanish-speaking city boasts a complete array of North American goods for sale. And much the same is true of Orlando (home of Disney World) and many other Florida cities. Similarly, Las Vegas offers the attraction of gambling to westerners, as Atlantic City does to people on the East Coast, and as Monte Carlo does to Europeans. Other amenity cities are Hot Springs, Arkansas, and Bath, England (both renowned for their hot mineral waters), and Innsbruck, Austria (a world-class skiing city).

5. Washington, D.C. is an example of an **administrative or political city,** a city established primarily for governmental purposes, as was Ottawa, Canada's national capital. Two recently constructed international examples are Canberra, Australia, and Brasilia, Brazil.

6. Closely related historically to the administrative function has been a city's *strategic military location*. That is, many cities have been situated in easily defensible spots (Athens, Quebec City), and others (London) have been sited because they offered military access into a whole region.

7. Finally, cities can be located for *religious or educational reasons*. Salt Lake City prospered as the home of Mormonism. In a similar way, Mecca in Saudi Arabia is the fountainhead of Islam, and Jerusalem is a focal point of no fewer than three major world religions: Christianity, Islam, and Judaism. University cities, such as Cambridge in England, Ithaca in New York (home of Cornell University), and Berkeley in California (site of one of the main campuses of the University of California), are

URBAN LIVING

Break-of-Bulk in Two Cities

In the following passage Charles Dickens describes London's River Thames in early morning, as seen from a small boat traveling downstream.

Nineteenth-Century London

Early as it was, there were plenty of scullers going here and there that morning, and plenty of barges . . . and we went ahead among many skiffs and wherries, briskly.

Old London Bridge was soon passed, and old Billingsgate market with its oysterboats and Dutchmen, and the White Tower and Traitor's Gate, and we were in among the tiers of shipping. Here, were the Leith, Aberdeen, and Glasgow steamers, loading and unloading goods, and looking immensely high out of the water as we passed alongside; here, were colliers by the score and score, with the coal-whippers plunging off stages on deck as counterweights to measures of coal swinging up, which were then rattled over the side into barges; here, at her moorings, was tomorrow's steamer for Rotterdam . . . and here tomorrow's for Hamburg, under whose bowsprit we crossed.

In the next passage, Vincent Parrillo describes a similar morning, only this time more than a century later and in a major U.S. port.

Late-Twentieth-Century Seattle

Even to the casual observer, the Port of Seattle is a busy place, filled with freighters, tugboats, barges, commercial fishing vessels, and pleasure craft. Geographically closer to Asia than any other major U.S. port, its natural deep-water harbor attracts commercial shippers from throughout the Pacific Rim. It is one of the largest U.S. container ports, one of the leading distribution centers on the West Coast, and the top U.S. port in container tonnage exports to Asia (over 6 million metric tons annually). Today ships from Japan, Singapore, and Taiwan are anchored at the docks, each by one of 28 commercial marine terminals.

At these terminals the container cranes transfer auto parts; bamboo baskets; electronic, household, and plastic products; foods; tools; and a variety of other products to an on-dock intermodal rail facility for direct shipment to inland destinations. Elsewhere, toplifts and forklifts transfer shipments to the 1.5 million square feet of warehouse storage space in the Terminal 106 Complex, to other outdoor storage areas, or to the waiting trucks at the 20 loading docks.

Everywhere the eye turns, one sees the bustling activity of workers: Longshoremen, stevedores, crane and forklift operators, grain terminal operators, truckers, railway men, foremen, and supervisors—are all unloading, storing, or loading the imports or exports passing through this port.

Source: Charles Dickens, *Great Expectations* (London: Chapman and Hall, 1860), from Chapter 54; and based on travel of Vincent N. Parrillo to Seattle, 1991.

cities that have achieved prominence for educational reasons.

A combination, then, of geographic–climatic conditions and social–economic factors explains why cities are where they are. Where many advantages come together, a city typically gains special importance. New York's prominence rests on its location as a natural port, an easily defended island, a gateway to a huge hinterland rich with raw materials, a natural break-of-bulk point, and a crossroads for people.

Finally, if the balance between a city's physical environment and people's social or economic needs and interests shifts, the city must adapt or else it will decline. History is strewn with the ruins of cities unable to adapt, including the ancient Egyptian capital of Luxor and the recently found Mayan city of El Mirador. On the other hand, cities sometimes survive great geographic–economic disasters. San Francisco is the best-known U.S. case, having recovered from the calamity of the 1906 earthquake to become one of the most vibrant U.S. cities.

THE SHAPE OF THE CITY

Once cities begin, what determines the form or physical shape they take? The answer depends on what the city's social and economic functions are.

To begin, consider that Athens is spread around the natural hilltop of the Acropolis; Edinburgh is sited around a massive outcropping in Scotland; and Paris and Mexico City are situated on islands. These examples suggest that defense was one of the prime interests of these city dwellers. Durham, in northern England, provides another example. Founded about 1000 C.E., Durham is situated atop a high, steep peninsula formed by the Wear River. The sides of the escarpment are extremely difficult to scale, even if one could get across the river. Naturally protected on three sides, the founders of Durham only had to defend the narrow fourth side, and so here they built their heavily fortified castle.

The Radiocentric City

The importance of defense prompted preindustrial people to build cities in the form of a great container, protected by natural geographic features (Durham's steep slope) and human constructs such as walls, moats, castles, or battlements. Urbanists characterize such cities as *radiocentric*, because they radiate outward from a common center.

A wonderful example of this urban form is preindustrial Baghdad, in Iraq (see Figure 7–2). Set within an outer wall with four fortified gates, the inner core of the city—containing

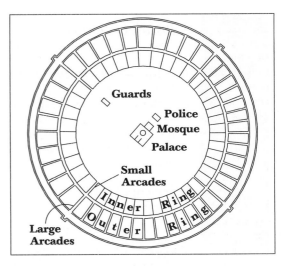

FIGURE 7–2   The Radiocentric City: Baghdad circa 146–762 C.E. [*Source:* From *An Urban Profile of the Middle East*, by M. Hugh Roberts. Copyright © 1979 by M. Hugh Roberts. Reprinted with permission of St. Martin's Press, LLC.]

the ruling caliph's palace and the mosque—was further protected by two rings of densely packed residential quarters where the city's poor people lived. Along the main access roads leading from the gates to the core, arcades or shops provided easy shopping access for Baghdad's inhabitants.

But not all **radiocentric cities** have a perfectly radial shape. Ming Peking (see Figure 8–1) was heavily walled and moated for defense, yet took the shape of a series of rectangles and squares attached to and within one another. These shapes reflect the Chinese cosmology of the 1400s, which led planners to arrange the city on the points of the compass—north, south, east, and west.

Other considerations encourage cities to develop a radial shape. As any city grows, people want to be as close to the center as possible to make travel easier. Because a circle places the most people closest to the center, many cities grow as subcommunities in a ringlike fashion around a central core. As anyone who has gazed out an airplane window at night knows, most cities look like huge wheels with central spokes radiating outward. The spokes—highways and rail lines—suggest another reason for the city's generally radial form. Because the shortest route to the center of a circle is a straight line, people build access roads to the city as directly as possible. That practice suggests the origin of one of history's best-known sayings: "All roads lead to Rome."

The Gridiron City

Despite the common radial pattern of most of the world's cities, the downtown areas of well-known North American cities—Atlanta, Chicago, Los Angeles, Montreal, New York, Philadelphia, Toronto, Vancouver—are not of a radiocentric design. Indeed, while radiocentric center cities are the rule in much of the world, that form is the exception in North America.

Closer to home, we find **gridiron cities,** composed of straight streets crossing at right angles to create many regular city blocks. This form is typical of cities built after the Industrial Revolution—because only then did cities place such importance on economic activity. A city gridiron plan facilitates the movement of people and products throughout the city. This form is also an efficient way to divide land—and sell it as real estate. Figure 7–3 shows William Penn's 1682 plan for selling lots in Philadelphia.

However, grid patterns do not always result from careful planning. Typically, when a settlement begins, merchants favor a main-street location that allows people to shop and move from one store to another along the street. Furthermore, open-ended streets serve business well because they allow room for growth as well as easy access to and from the shopping area. The U.S. and Canadian Midwest and West are full of such Main Street towns.

The lights of a city such as Toronto at night offer strikingly beautiful visual images while simultaneously illustrating its ongoing life and activities after dark.
Toronto's strategic location on the shore of Lake Ontario enhances its economic vitality, making this metropolitan area home to over 6 million people—one-fourth of Canada's total population.

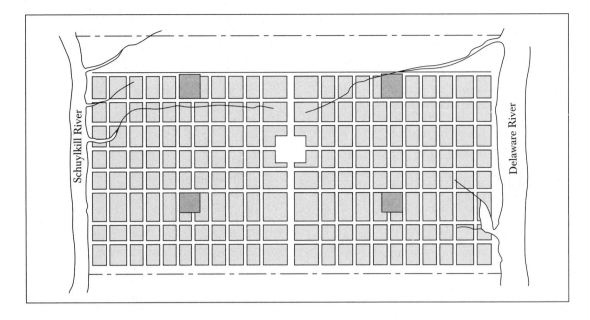

FIGURE 7–3 The Gridiron City: William Penn's Philadelphia Plan, 1682

If, in time, another major street crosses the original street, we see the beginnings of a gridiron around "four corners" that may well expand from there.

URBAN ECOLOGY: THE CHICAGO SCHOOL

As we discussed in Chapter 5, Robert Park and his fellow Chicago sociologists used cities as a laboratory to study social life. Their research generated the science of **human ecology,** a term coined by Park that focused on what he viewed as an orderly evolution of urban growth and development:

> There are forces at work within the limits of the urban community . . . which tend to bring about an orderly and typical grouping of its population and institutions. The science which seeks to isolate these factors and to describe the typical constellations of persons and institutions which the cooperation of these forces produce is what we call human, as distinguished from plant and animal, ecology. (Park 1984:1–2)

The Ecological Theory of Urban Development

Using the ecological approach that studies the relationship between living things and their environment, Park investigated how human beings live in their urban world. He believed that the evolutionary struggle for survival was evident in the everyday *competition for scarce resources* such as food, clothing, shelter, and land. Emerging from this competition were different clusters of activity that Park called **natural areas:** business districts, ethnic neighborhoods, skid rows, and rooming-house areas.

For Park, urban competition is not only economic; it is also about *power.* People compete for control of parks, streets, and ethnic districts—and above all for the prestige that comes from living in a fashionable neighborhood or having an impressive occupation.

Beyond competition, Park noted that large-scale *population movements* also influence urban development. Most of the immigrants who came to Park's Chicago and other growing North American cities a century ago had little education, few skills, and were exceedingly poor. With few options, they poured into overcrowded housing in the center cities and took low-paying jobs in factories. Marie Jastrow, recalling her father's arrival in New York, gives an illustration in the Cityscape box below.

CITYSCAPE

The New World—New York, 1905

My father crossed the Atlantic and landed on Ellis Island at the beginning of October 1905, well aware of the ordeal that awaited him. He had heard stories. The threat of deportation haunted every [poor] immigrant. . . .

Eyes, ears, chest—the entire person was scrutinized by doctors. Some were rejected. Those who were turned away fell into the depths of despair, waiting, without hope, for the first ship to take them back.

Hour after hour the examination went on. At last my father found himself on American soil, a silent, solitary figure. He had passed the inspection. Now, for the first time, he was alone, separated from his fellow travelers. It was a painful aloneness. . . .

A policeman walked by and stopped. What was this lonely figure doing in the cold afternoon, sitting in the park? An immigrant, no doubt, just off the ship. . . .

"Are you expecting anyone?" The officer spoke some German. My father shook his head. No, he expected no one, he knew no one. But he would appreciate help in locating a room.

"Can you pay?"

"Yes," Papa again shook his head. "But not much." He hesitated a moment. "The room has to be cheap."

The policeman smiled, writing something on a slip of paper.

"Go to this address. Tell them that Officer Schmidt gave you this." My father looked at the address he had just received. . . . He wondered how to get to the address he was holding in hand, but dared not ask.

Officer Schmidt was becoming impatient. "What is it? Can't you read?"

"Yes, I can read," said my father, "but, if you would be so kind to give me directions, I do not know this city."

"Of course, you just got in," laughed the officer. "I'll take you to the streetcar on that corner. You give this address to the conductor, he will let you off on the right street."

"Thank you," said my grateful father. "I shall never forget this—how you helped me on my first day in America."

. . . The Hester Street tenement where my father lived for the first few months stood in the midst of a heavily populated immigrant area. It was the first stopover for many Jewish families. No one arrived here with more than token funds. They had nothing, these people, but dreams and hopes for the better future this new land could offer. None spoke English, very few spoke any language but Yiddish. It is easy to see why they clustered together and found comfort in the nearness of their countrymen.

The six-story structures in that street were planned for thirty-six tenants, six to a floor. Actually, counting the boarders that were crowded into every available corner "to help pay the rent," no landlord knew how many people lived in his building. But no one counted, as long as the rent was ready on the first of every month.

Source: Marie Jastrow, *A Time to Remember* (New York: Norton, 1979), pp. 21–24, 36.

Jastrow's father and his family did not stay on lower Manhattan's Hester Street forever. With time, most immigrants learned skills, made money, and moved to better housing (Jastrow's family moved uptown to Yorkville in New York's fashionable East 80s). As they did in cities across the continent, immigrants or their descendants left their old neighborhoods to the next poor group to enter the city. The Chicago sociologists called this shifting of population **invasion-succession.**

The Concentric Zone Hypothesis

To Park, competition and population movement shaped and reshaped cities. The more economically successful selected the choice city locations for their businesses and homes, leaving the less desirable locations to the less successful. In this process, claimed Park, the city as a whole took on broad, spatial patterns characteristic of an economic hierarchy. In the mid-1920s, one of Park's students, Ernest W. Burgess, suggested that the city develops somewhat the way a tree does, growing outward in a series of concentric rings or zones over time.

Although Burgess assumed that economic competition was central to urban life, he, like Park, saw other social forces at work. Moving to a suburb, for example, is not just an economic consideration; it also confers prestige, suggesting that people have "made it."

Boston grew from a small, walled colonial city to an important city of commerce, annexing such adjoining municipalities as Brighton, Charlestown, Dorchester, Roxbury, and West Roxbury between 1868 and 1874. Today it is a large metropolis, utilizing its waterways to full advantage both commercially and recreationally.

Burgess described the city in terms of five main zones (see the right side of Figure 7–4). In his words:

This chart represents an ideal construction of the tendencies of any town or city to expand radially from its central business district—on the map "The Loop" (I). Encircling the downtown area there is normally an area in transition, which is being invaded by business and light manufacture (II). A third area (III) is inhabited by the workers in industries who have escaped from the area of

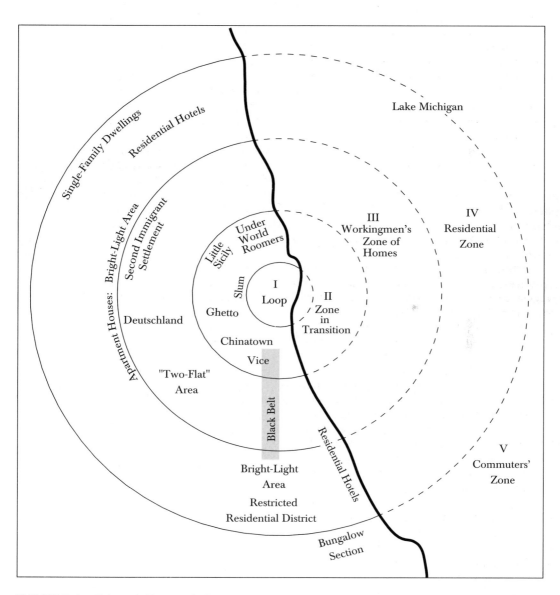

FIGURE 7–4   Chicago's Concentric Zones [*Source:* From "The Growth of the City," in Robert E. Park and Ernest W. Burgess, eds., *The City.* Copyright © 1967 University of Chicago Press, p. 55, chart II. Reprinted by permission of the University of Chicago Press.]

deterioration (II) but who desire to live within easy access of their work. Beyond this zone is the "residential area" (IV) of high-class apartment buildings or of exclusive "restricted" districts of single family dwellings. Still farther, out beyond the city limits, is the commuters' zone—suburban areas, or satellite cities—within a thirty- to sixty-minute ride of the central business district. (1984:50; orig. 1925).

Burgess illustrated his model by applying it directly to the Chicago of his day (the left side of Figure 7–4). Once we take the "halving effect" of Lake Michigan into account (the heavy line shows the city's edge by the lake), Burgess's theory did a creditable job in explaining the location of the city's districts. The most valuable land (Zone I) was contained within "The Loop" downtown, which was the exclusive preserve of business. In Zone II, the "zone in transition," stood factories and slums, the latter overflowing with down-and-out roomers and ethnic groups of various sorts including Italians (Little Sicily) and Chinese (Chinatown). The third zone, the "zone of workingmen's homes," was predominantly inhabited by second-generation migrants, the descendants of earlier Chicago immigrants who had taken the first step in escaping the inner city by moving out of the slums. Here, too, was the "two-flat" area, where two families occupied two-family houses, instead of the usual four or more families living in multihousing buildings in the inner city. Zone IV was the "residential zone," dominated by residential hotels, apartment areas, and, most important, single-family homes. In this zone, too, existed a relatively wealthy "restricted residential district," an area that excluded people with "undesirable" ethnic or racial traits.

Criticisms of the Chicago School

Although he based his model on Chicago, Burgess thought his zonal hypothesis would describe any city. But do other cities and towns conform to the concentric zone pattern? Certainly some do. One longitudinal study (1950–1980) of 318 U.S. metropolitan areas found such evolving patterns occurred among "industrially based, older, larger, more dispersed metropolitan communities" in the Northeast (Schwirian et al. 1990).

However, critics questioned the Chicago School's reliance on the concepts of unrestrained competition and large population movements. These vary in their intensity in different locales and time periods and, even then, may or may not play a key role in a city's growth and development. Other social forces—globalization, technological advances in production, communication, and transportation, for example—can impact on how a city's spatial development occurs.

Finally, some critics dismiss the ecological theory as "too biological." That is, the principles of plant and animal ecology do not do a very good job of explaining human activity. People, unlike plants, are thinking creatures who reflect and act creatively on their urban environment. Ecological theory pays little attention to the roles played by (1) choice, (2) culture in the city, and (3) community. In other words, this approach ignored important social considerations.

Such criticism has diminished the importance of Park's ecological approach and of Burgess's concentric zone model over time. In their place, a host of alternative theories and models suggest that the forces shaping land use are more complex than Park or Burgess suspected.

URBAN ECOLOGY: OTHER THEORIES

Soon after the emergence of the Chicago School, two other ecological growth theories achieved prominence. The sector and multiple nuclei theories addressed some of the shortcomings of the Park and Burgess approach.

The Sector Theory

Homer Hoyt (1939) was the first to modify the zonal hypothesis. He noticed that a fair number of city districts did not conform to the purely concentric model suggested by Burgess. Even in Burgess's Chicago (Figure 7–4), unusual areas like the "Deutschland Ghetto" (the home of German immigrants) and the "Black Belt" obviously cut across zones.

This observation led Hoyt to study, block-by-block, the residential patterns in 142 cities. The scope of Hoyt's study was a major advance over Burgess's work, which was based almost exclusively on Chicago. Hoyt also examined cities in three different time periods: 1900, 1915, and 1936, adding an important historical dimension. Figure 7–5 graphically presents Hoyt's findings concerning high-prestige, fashionable areas in three of his cities.

First, Hoyt found that upscale districts formed sectors of varying size. Second, although he noted a rough concentric shape to the cities, many sectors took a pie-shaped form rather than resembling an entire ring, as Burgess had suggested. Third, lower-income districts often abutted and sometimes even

surrounded fashionable districts. A classic example is Harlem's "Striver's Row" of the 1920s and 1930s, a wealthy, two-block oasis of pristine buildings (West 138th and 139th Streets between Seventh and Eighth Avenues), surrounded by buildings approaching utter collapse. Fourth, as time passed, Hoyt found a tendency for sectors to move out of the city radially, along a path begun by the sector in earlier years (Seattle provides a good example).

Fifth, in the later periods, cities revealed two or three fashionable areas in different places. Hoyt noted that factors other than competition and population movement influenced this process. For example, Hoyt observed that the wealthy neighborhoods in many cities stand on "high ground" (Boston's Beacon Hill, for instance), indicating a preference by the wealthy to be "above" the city's poorer residents. Elsewhere, he found

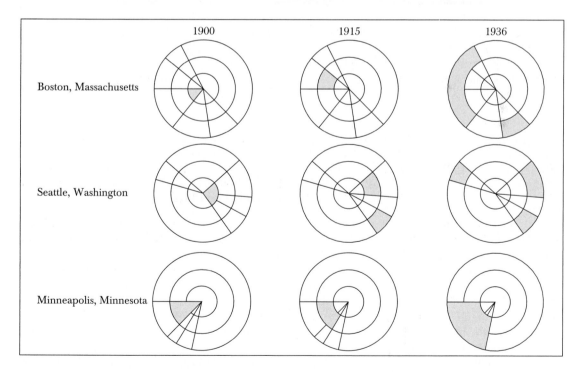

FIGURE 7–5 Shifts in the Location of Fashionable Residential Areas in Three American Cities, 1900–1936. Fashionable areas are indicated by shading. [*Source:* Adapted from Homer Hoyt, *The Structure and Growth of Residential Neighborhoods in American Cities* (Washington, DC: Federal Housing Administration, 1939), p. 115, figure 40.]

Paterson, New Jersey—the first planned U.S. industrial city—typifies an old manufacturing city. In classic sector theory patterning, many of its factories lined the railroad tracks, and its fashionable district moved eastward along Broadway to the high ground of Manor Hill. No longer thriving, the city struggles to maintain a solid economic base.

high-prestige sectors located for aesthetic reasons—on waterfronts, for example. In still other cities, he found such districts located along main transportation lines that facilitated easy access to the center city.

The Multiple Nuclei Theory

Although Hoyt's study was a major advance over the work of the Burgess model, it was limited by a focus on residential sectors. Hoyt imagined that industry, too, moved radially outward from the center city—upriver, or along railroad lines, for instance—but he never investigated this hunch.

In 1945 Chauncy Harris and Edward Ullman broadened Hoyt's findings with another theory of urban land use. They argued that as the contemporary city grew, it diversified, developing many distinct sectors of activity. They noted that modern cities typically have a major central business district (the CBD is sector 1 in Figure 7–6), but that there are also other districts generated by various historical, cultural, and economic factors specific to that city. For example, wholesale light manufacturing (2) might be near the CBD, with low-income residences (3) in various separate districts nearby. A medium-income residential area (4) might abut the CBD and give way on its outer edge to a high-income residential area (5). Between the two might exist a secondary business district (7) and, farther out, a completely separate residential suburb (8). Heavy manufacturing (6) might lie a relatively large distance from the CBD and evolve an industrial–residential suburb (9) nearby.

Cities experiencing their greatest growth during the automobile age have, like Houston pictured above, massive freeway approaches and interchanges as well as generally wider streets and more car-friendly services (parking, drive-in facilities) than older cities. They are typically situated in warm climes, on fairly level land, with port access less necessary.

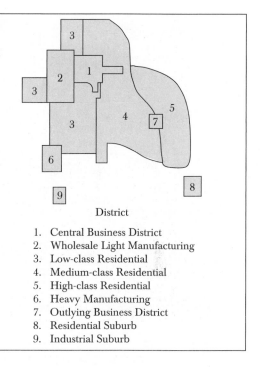

District

1. Central Business District
2. Wholesale Light Manufacturing
3. Low-class Residential
4. Medium-class Residential
5. High-class Residential
6. Heavy Manufacturing
7. Outlying Business District
8. Residential Suburb
9. Industrial Suburb

FIGURE 7–6   The Multiple Nuclei Theory [*Source:* From Chauncy O. Harris and Edward L. Ullman, "The Nature of Cities," *The Annals*, 242 (Nov. 1945), American Academy of Political and Social Science. Used by permission of American Academy of Political and Social Science.]

Why do multiple nuclei develop? First, certain types of activities require certain types of facilities. For example, heavy manufacturing requires a great deal of space. A century ago, space was plentiful downtown. In recent decades, however, space near the CBD became hard to find and expensive, and many modern factories required more floor space on one level. As a result, much heavy manufacturing moved from the CBD to outlying industrial areas where land was readily available and taxes were often lower. In Chicago, for example, heavy manufacturing once located in the CBD moved to the southeast, around Gary, Indiana.

Second, multiple CBDs can be the result of annexation. As the city absorbs a nearby municipality into its political domain, that preexisting CBD may evolve further as a secondary business district. This is particularly true of the so-called "spread cities" that have expanded greatly in the postautomobile age. As it becomes more time-consuming to travel into the central city's CBD for shopping, entertainment, or business-related activities, other CBDs emerge within the large cities' boundaries to accommodate those inconvenienced by a longer commute into the city center.

Perhaps the most important contribution of Harris and Ullman's theory is that it seriously questions the notion that urban land use is

Los Angeles is a spread city held together more by an intricate freeway system than a cohesive political system. Critics charge that actually neither works well. Local government is too fragmented and disorganized, while the densely populated area has the nation's worst traffic congestion, leading to the average driver wasting over 82 hours each year sitting in traffic.

predictable at all. Burgess's zonal hypothesis and, to a lesser extent, Hoyt's sector theory both implied certain inevitable patterns of land use. In contrast, Harris and Ullman's multiple nuclei theory suggests that a mix of historical, cultural, and economic situations shapes and continues to reshape every city. Even the core CBD might fall into decline, as it has in some smaller cities.

Social Area Analysis

Another technique to describe urban land use is comparing the social characteristics of urbanites living in different census tracts. A

census tract averages about 4,000 residents and typically contains relatively homogeneous units with respect to population characteristics, economic status, and living conditions. Using these social attributes social scientists can classify each census tract and then compare it to others to create a detailed profile of the larger urban community.

This approach began with the work of Eshref Shevky and Marilyn Williams (1949) in their study of distinctive social areas in Los Angeles:

> In the impersonal setting of the city . . . social standing does not rest on any intimate evaluation of persons nor any discriminating appraisal of differences within groups. Instead, certain easily recognizable traits, such as houses and possessions, become symbolic of rank. . . . As every occupation is evaluated and generally accorded honor and esteem on a scale of prestige in society, so every residential section has a status value which is easily recognized by everyone in the city. Even a casual visitor in Los Angeles could name a half dozen places representative of the exclusive sections on the westside and along the foothills of the Santa Monica and San Gabriel Mountains. (Shevky and Williams 949:61–62)

Shevky next partnered with Wendell Bell (1955) to classify **social areas** in Los Angeles and San Francisco in terms of their social characteristics, using a *social ranking index* (education, occupation, income); *family status index* (number of children, type of housing, whether the mother worked); and a *segregation index* based on the clustering of racial and ethnic groups. Such analysis, they suggested, would enable social scientists to describe and distinguish the social characteristics found among urban neighborhoods, since there were numerous variations that serve as the foundation of a community's social structure.

In San Francisco, for example, they found that groups in some areas measured low on social rank and family status but high on ethnicity. That is, people in this area typically had low prestige, lived in large families occupying multiple-dwelling housing, and were of identifiable ethnic or racial background. Conversely, people in other areas measured high on social rank and low on family status and ethnicity. These findings could then be mapped as an "illustrative application" to reveal the location of different social class neighborhoods or highly segregated ones.

Social area analysis proved to be a helpful statistical technique, not only for identifying social class, family status, and minority patterns in cities, but also in comparative studies that measure changes in these areas over time. In addition, this approach is most helpful in finding relationships between these social characteristics and any other measurable aspect of life, such as crime and mental illness rates or religious and voting behavior.

Like the other approaches we've discussed, social area analysis also has its critics. One problem is that this approach is not theoretical but merely gives a description of cities' areas. That is, social area analysis cannot predict where groups will settle or explain why groups settled where they did. In contrast, Park and Burgess noted the ecological forces of competition and population movements causing concentric rings to develop. Likewise, Harris and Ullman attributed the unique form of each city to historical, cultural, or economic factors.

In short, social area analysis also offers limited insights into urban land use. However, its usefulness as a systematic measurement of the complexities found in urban communities served as the springboard for a more sophisticated technique that came on the scene and provided some important results.

Factorial Ecology

Factorial ecology uses computer technology to sort through the many social traits of an urban population. This approach differs from social area analysis because, rather than beginning with a few preselected social characteristics (such as social rank), it analyzes *all* characteristics that might be important to urban life, including density and spatial arrangements (O'Brien and Roach, 1984). This analysis informs us which factors, in combination with one another, are most important.

What are some of the broader applications of factorial ecology in understanding cities? Wayne K. D. Davies (1984), who used various factorial techniques in his analysis of cities in western Canada, suggested three. First, this approach allows social scientists to create a systematic organization of areas based on shared attributes, which can then be studied more closely. Second, it identifies formal structures of urban systems to help explain both the character of cities and flow patterns among cities. Third, it identifies urban ecological patterns, allowing for comparative and interpretive analysis.

Basic Findings. An example of this approach was a study of the 22 census tracts of Whangarei, a city in New Zealand (Johnston 1976). Factorial analysis indicated that some areas of the city had high concentrations of male workers in professional or managerial occupations, who held university degrees and earned high incomes. These **socioeconomic status** traits were so strongly linked to one another that they paralleled the social ranking index of Shevky, Bell, and Williams discussed earlier. The second index, family status, was also important, as this study also found residential areas of the city that were home to unmarried people over age 16 living in rental housing. And, although of less importance, *ethnic factors* also played a part in determining where people lived in Whangarei. Taken together, these three factors—socioeconomic status, family status, and ethnicity—accounted for 86 percent of the residential patterning of this city.

Johnston's findings have been confirmed by others investigating cities. For example, in a study of the nature and amount of residential segregation by nonwhite Caribbean immigrants in New York City, Dennis Conway (1990) examined immigration and census data, indices of dissimilarity. and applied an intraurban comparative factorial ecology. He found socioeconomic status, family status, and population mobility—along with racism—to be key factors that explained these minorities' continued segregation.

A Synthesis Theory: Berry and Rees. Do these findings make earlier theories about concentric circles, sectors, and multiple nuclei obsolete? No, say sociologists Brian Berry and Phillip Rees (1969). In fact, factorial ecology shows that all these approaches have been partially correct. The problem was that no earlier theory captured the full complexity of what was going on with urban land use, which Berry and Rees depict in Figure 7–7.

They began by asking what would happen if each of the major social characteristics uncovered by factorial ecology—socioeconomic status, family status, and ethnicity—were the only force at work in the city. They concluded that if socioeconomic status were operating alone, cities would tend to divide themselves into sectors (Figure 7–7A). That is, of course, precisely what Homer Hoyt observed in his study as the pie-shaped outward movement of elite groups. But while Hoyt restricted his observations primarily to wealthy groups, Berry and Rees contended that this outward sectoring would characterize all urbanites, whether rich or poor.

Second, if family type were operating alone, differing demands for space would cause people to arrange themselves in concentric zones (Figure 7–7B), as Park and Burgess suggested. Single adults and those with few children would tend to cluster in the innermost circle, near their work and the attractions of the CBD (I). Those with more children (and fewer workers) would characterize the second circle (II), and groups with the most children and fewest workers would settle in the outermost circle (III).

Third, were ethnicity to operate alone, minorities (the shaded areas of Figure 7–7C) would tend to be segregated in various ethnic communities throughout the city—for example, in Chicago's South Side, New York's Harlem, San Francisco's Fillmore, and Miami's Little Havana, as the Cityscape box on page 206 explains.

In truth, of course, no social characteristic ever operates in isolation. Many influence one another, generating a complex land-use pattern. In Figure 7–7D, Berry and Rees show what might result from the effects of socioeconomic status, family status, and ethnicity working together. To take a few examples, beginning at the bottom right, you would be likely to find in the outermost area of a North American city white people of high socioeconomic status with a lot of children, and families with few working adults. (Thus the shorthand of "H III W," where "H" stands for a high income, "III" for numerous children, and "W" for white racial background.) In the next area, closer to the CBD, you also would be likely to find white people of high socioeconomic status, but this group probably would have fewer children and more working adults (H II W). Moving to the sector on the left, you would be likely to find, in the outermost district, white people of middle socioeconomic status with many children and few working adults (M III W). Moving toward the center-city area on the same sector, however, the next area might be a segregated African American neighborhood of low socioeconomic status (B). You could interpret the rest of Figure 7–7D in the same way.

Berry and Rees knew that particular minorities are often segregated from others and thus develop subsectors of their own, replicating the citywide pattern on a smaller scale. Figure 7–7E illustrates this process, showing, within the segregated area, the subgroups with low fertility and high number of working adults nearest the center city (I) and the subgroups with high fertility and fewest working adults farthest out (III).

As the city changes over time, as shown in Figure 7–7F, what Berry and Rees call **tear faults** develop. Given existing districts and neighborhoods within the city, however, the tear faults are not always symmetrical, resulting in the pattern shown in Figure 7–7G.

Finally, in time, new technology and competition for valuable CBD space produce multiple centers of industry and shopping districts away from the original downtown, as suggested by Harris and Ullman (Figure 7–7H). Also developing are suburbanized industrial workplaces (1), industrial satellites (2), and separate areas of heavy industry (3).

Figure 7–7I puts all these forces into play. It depicts sectors, inner circles, segregated areas (with their own inner circles), tear faults occasioned by city growth, and the decentralization of industry (symbolized by the

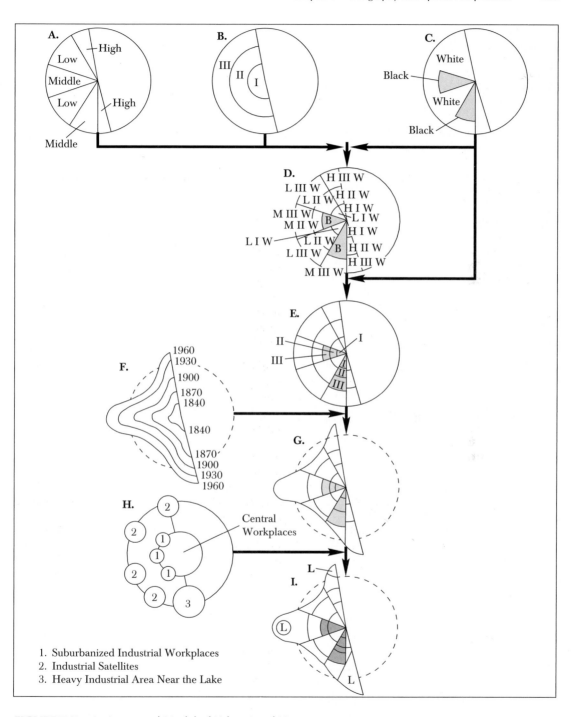

FIGURE 7–7   An Integrated Model of Urban Land Use [*Source:* Adapted from Brian J. L. Berry and P. H. Rees, "The Factorial Ecology of Calcutta," *American Journal of Sociology* 74 (March 1969), figure 13. University of Chicago Press. Reprinted by permission of the University of Chicago Press.]

CITYSCAPE

Miami's Little Havana

The center of Little Havana lies along 8th Street in Southwest Miami. It is one of several areas in Miami and its environs in which substantial numbers of Cuban Americans reside. As is typical in areas that served as initial enclaves for a particular group (Chinatown in San Francisco, for example) the current population of Little Havana is older and poorer than other, later Cuban concentrations in the Miami area. . . .

Along 8th Street, for a stretch of several miles, are homes and apartments occupied primarily by Cuban families. Many of the homes have characteristically Cuban features such as decorative Spanish tiles, Catholic shrines in the backyards, and fences enclosing the front yards. There are many Cuban-owned stores, restaurants, and financial institutions catering largely, but not exclusively, to co-ethnics. . . . Some shops offer special wearing apparel such as guayaberas: lightweight, short coats traditionally worn by Cuban men. There are a number of botanicas selling religious goods, including potions for recalling saints and spirits and aerosol cans whose contents are guaranteed to improve one's love life. Many small grocery stores sell Cuban food products and almost all the pharmacies in Little Havana have signs in their windows announcing that they send medicine to Cuba. Local churches offer masses in Spanish and English.

A dozen or more daily and weekly Spanish-language newspapers are available at Little Havana's newsstands or from coin-operated boxes. Some of the newspapers are primarily oriented to news about Cuba and the Cuban population in the United States, whereas others focus on Latin America as a whole. The area is also served by WQBA, one of several Spanish-language radio stations, but the one that has historically claimed to be La Cubanisma (the most Cuban). Little Havana also contains a number of outdoor cafes and outdoor tables, where a mostly elderly male clientele gathers during the day and evening to play cards and dominos under black olive trees. A focal point in Little Havana is Domino Park, where older men play dominos throughout the day, smoke cigars, and talk about the old days in Cuba.

A number of Little Havana's restaurants offer traditional Cuban dishes such as chicken and yellow rice. Some of the restaurants are inconspicuous neighborhood eateries, others are highly ornate. The most famous among the latter is probably the Restaurant Versailles, "the mirrored palace," which was designed to closely resemble several once-popular night spots in Havana. . . .

Walking down Southwest 8th Street gives a former Cuban a feeling of being transported back in time to the Havana of yesterday. Little Havana in Miami is, in many respects, a copy of Havana in Cuba. Murals of the latter, complete with street signs, decorate the walls of restaurants, keeping alive memories of life in Cuba.

Source: From *Urban Enclaves: Identity and Place in America* by Mark Abrahamson. Copyright © 1996 by Worth Publishers. Used with permission of W. H. Freeman and Company/Worth Publishers.

"L" areas that mark lower socioeconomic people "pulled out" from the center-city area to be near the industries for which they work).

Obviously, even Figure 7–7I is an idealized portrait that fits no actual city. Yet Berry and Rees contend that, once the additional effects of local geography (a mountain or lake may limit development in some direction) or history (a government grant may fund a low-income housing project in a place not accounted for by the model) are taken into account, this model can be applied to any city—at least in North America—and can provide an explanation for where types of people and business activities locate.

Criticisms of Factorial Ecology.   Although factorial ecology remains the "state of the art" approach in explaining urban land use, significant questions and problems remain. The reductionism resulting from distilling many variables into just a few by necessity eliminates some features that, though perhaps not the most important, are nonetheless elements that help us understand the complete picture. Moreover, this approach ignores the element of human choice (see the Critical Thinking box on p. 208).

Some critics question the method itself. For example, computers may distort (or even create) some of the patterns researchers find. Moreover, the census tracts used in factorial ecology are not always socially defined neighborhoods. Thus, people with particular traits in common (say, ethnicity) may see themselves as a community, a fact missed by researchers using government data that shows them living in different census tracts. Then, too, there are certainly errors in census data, known to miss significant numbers of migrants, homeless people, and poor people.

Other criticism focuses on how well this method may apply to cities around the world. Berry and Rees may have found similar processes at work in Chicago and Calcutta, but these cities have much technology and economic activity in common. Perhaps, factorial ecology works for Western cities and others that are undergoing Western-style "modernization." But what about more traditional cities shaped by cultural values unfamiliar to Westerners? There, perhaps socioeconomic status, family status, and ethnicity may play a smaller role, or even no role at all, in the urban ecology. For example, in a factor analysis of Rabat-Sale, an important metropolitan area in Morocco, Janet Abu-Lughod (1980) found that "social caste," a combination of ethnicity and social class characteristics, played the dominant role in determining where everyone lived in the city.

Similarly, in a study of Tel Aviv in Israel, Borukhov and his associates (1979) found that in addition to socioeconomic and family status, "religious orthodoxy" figures in where people live in that city.

Finally, rising in opposition to factorial ecology has been the Marxist-based school of radical urban geography. These geographers believe that urban land-use patterns in the modern era are mostly the result of capitalist market forces. They have been joined by scholars in the field of political economics and in what is called "the new urban sociology" to advance an alternative approach to the study of land use in cities. We examine their approach both in the following section and in Chapter 9.

THE LOS ANGELES SCHOOL AND POSTMODERNISM

Partly as a spinoff from the multiple nuclei theory, but more importantly as a rejection of the Chicago School, a new perspective—dubbed "the Los Angeles School"—emerged in the mid-1980s. Focusing on the five-county region of Southern California (Los Angeles, Ventura, San Bernardino, Riverside, and Orange counties), its emphasis is on multicentered, dispersed patterns of growth.

Perhaps the origins of this new perspective lie in the vivid depiction of the Los Angeles area by Rayner Banham (1973, 2001). He identified four basic "ecologies" that differed markedly from those advanced by the Chicago School. These were (1) *surfurbia* (the beach cities along the coast); (2) *the foothills* (the private enclaves of the privileged in such areas as Beverly Hills and Bel Air); (3) *the plains of Id* (the endless central flatlands); and (4) *autopia* (the freeways that exist as "a single comprehensible place" and "coherent state of mind"). Banham was partly harsh in his description of the "plains of Id," describing them as "gridded with endless streets, peppered endlessly with ticky-tacky houses clustered in indistinguishable neighborhoods, slashed across by endless freeways that have destroyed any community spirit that may have once existed."

Douglas Suisman (1990) reasoned that the city's boulevards, not its freeways, give form to its structure and communities. As surface streets—rather than the self-contained freeways with their on-off ramps—these boulevards connect different sections of the metropolis, provide an organizational framework for local travel destinations, and serve as a "filter to adjacent residential neighborhoods." For Suisman, boulevards are the defining element of the city's public space in its linkage between municipalities.

Edward W. Soja (2000) helped bring a postmodern perspective to this school of thought in his argument that Los Angeles is a decentralized metropolis with a fragmented power structure that is becoming increasingly pliant and disorganized. Although the center may hold as a strategic surveillance point for social control, radiating outward is a complex, highly fragmented mishmash of "wedges" and "citadels" separated by boulevards acting as corridors. With global capitalism serving as an underlying rationale, Soja views Los Angeles as resembling "a gigantic agglomeration of theme parks." Moreover, he suggests that the worldwide future of urbanism will resemble Los Angeles (Miller 2000).

Michael J. Dear, a leading advocate of the Los Angeles School, shares Soja's belief about the city serving as a prototype for fragmentation and social differentiation in a global economy and postmodern culture. He adds that, as a consequence of physical sprawl, the city's "decentered politics" is one way that the city serves as a herald of the future. He describes the L.A. region as "split in many separate fiefdoms, with their leaders in constant battle." With over 100 municipalities in Los Angeles County (total population nearly 10 million), there are many problems of political representation. These include city–county government disputes, slow-growth/no-growth movements, and the difficulties associated with minority-group political participation. As a result, many alliances—formal and informal, legal and illegal—form to press their claims. Either autocratic—even corrupt—power will result, or else there will be "polarization along class, income, racial and ethnic lines" (2000:14–15).

Are the postmodernists correct in saying that cities are developing in a way that is no longer rational or manageable according to the old logic of urban development advocated by the urban ecologists? Is the evolution of Los Angeles that they describe the wave of the future? Only time will tell. Yet, with the Census Bureau projecting the Los Angeles

CRITICAL THINKING

The New York City Skyline—A Cast of Thousands

No one could look at [the New York City skyline] without asking: "Who built it?" If you consult the library books, you'll be told that the Empire State Building was designed by Shreve, Lane & Harmon, and that Rockefeller Center was created by Corbet, Harrison & MacMurray, Hood & Foulhoux, Reinhard and Hofmeister. Yes, but who? What senior member of the firm drafting plans for the Lever Building said, "Suppose we used green glass?" . . . Who of the Seagram architects first said tentatively, "What about bronze?"

. . . Whose pencil drew the spectacular sweeping curve of 9 West Fifty-seventh Street? Who built it? Anon., that's who. Nobody built the New York skyline. Nobody by the thousands.

Source: Helen Hanff, *Apple of My Eye* (Mt. Kisco, NY: Moyer Bell Ltd., 1989), p. 54.

region to increase by another 6 million by 2020 (essentially by the size of three Chicagos), its ongoing growth and development as the second largest metropolitan area in the United States is more than just an academic question.

❖ ━━━━━━━━ ❖ ━━━━━━━━ ❖

SUMMARY

People founded cities at particular geographical sites that, at a minimum, supported a population's physical needs. Other human needs—political, religious, educational, and economic—also have played a role in locating cities.

Indeed, such factors helped forge two basic city shapes. Radiocentric cities have a tendency to emerge where religious and political forces are of central interest to a population; gridiron cities spring up when economic concerns predominate.

Robert Park and Ernest W. Burgess (the Chicago School) saw competition and population movement as responsible for shaping cities. Burgess's concentric zone model illustrates their ideas. But critics raised questions as to whether a biologically determined competition could explain people's behavior, and they pointed out numerous exceptions to the zonal hypothesis.

Recognizing the difficulties of the Chicago theory, Homer Hoyt suggested that many cities were organized in sectors, and that the prime cause of such sectoring was socioeconomic status. This was a helpful contribution but, like the Chicago model, it ultimately failed to account for the complexity of urban life.

An additional contribution was Harris and Ullman's multiple nuclei theory. This model abandoned any idea of a deterministic pattern of urban development: It held zones, sectors, and even the CBD as variable, with city form changing over time.

Social area analysis is an approach distinguished by its lack of theory. Its originators, Shevky, Bell, and Williams, simply examined the major social traits of the urban population.

While their technique produced accurate descriptions of who lived where in cities, it had no ability to explain why people lived where they did. With earlier explanations of urban land use (the concentric zone, sector, and multiple nuclei theories) discredited as being too simple, urban ecology was at an impasse until the arrival of factorial ecology. This technique analyzes the significance of all factors that researchers think might be influential in urban land use. Its major finding has been that the social characteristics initially examined by social area analysis— socioeconomic status, family status, and ethnicity—do account for most of the residential land uses in cities studied thus far.

This discovery led Berry and Rees to hypothesize that the earlier theories all held a part of the truth. Cities do take the shape of concentric zones, sectors, and multiple nuclei according to the socioeconomic status, family status, and ethnic traits of their residents. While the Berry and Rees model does seem to apply to most cities in the contemporary Western world, there is doubt that it can account for the full range of historical and cross-cultural urban life.

The Los Angeles School is a recently evolved approach that uses a critical spatial perspective and postmodern viewpoint to understand the spread-city phenomenon. Besides more accurately explaining urbanism in Southern California than the urban ecologists could, its emphasis on political fragmentation and social differentiation calls our attention to the problems of governance and community within a metropolitan area increasingly impacted by global capitalism.

CONCLUSION

Urban land use is extremely complex. This chapter has traced increasingly sophisticated efforts to capture this multifaceted reality. We can be pleased with major advances, particularly in our understanding of how cities in the Western or modernizing world organize space, but more needs to be done. While we certainly need to pursue all leads in the use of urban space, social scientists also need to consider the powerful influence that different cultural traditions and values have on city life. It is to this topic that we turn in the next chapter.

KEY TERMS

Administrative or political city
Amenity city
Break-of-bulk
Census tract
Factorial ecology
Gridiron cities
Human ecology
Invasion-succession
Natural areas
Natural crossroads
Radiocentric cities
Social areas
Socioeconomic status
Tear faults

CHAPTER 8

COMPARATIVE URBANISM
The City and Culture

❖ ▬▬▬▬▬ ❖ ▬▬▬▬▬ ❖

There is something rather ironic about the title of Louis Wirth's essay, "Urbanism as a Way of Life" (1938), which we discussed in Chapter 5. You will recall that he argued that their size, density, and heterogeneity make cities characteristically impersonal, transient, and anonymous. His negative overgeneralizations about cities and their impact on human behavior ignored the role of **culture,** which *is* the urban way of life and often has positive effects on the lives of city dwellers.

In this chapter we will examine the city and culture from two perspectives. First, we will look at the existence of what Daniel J. Monti (1999) calls **civic culture.** That is, in the urban way of life, the many different types of people have found an appropriate form of public behavior that enables them, mostly, to get along with one another. Through ceremonies, customs, and codes they have "worked out a way to be together in public and still carry on their private lives, peaceably and with at least a modicum of predictability" (Monti 1999: 103).

Second, *the city is not an entity unto itself.* All cities reflect and intensify the world's cultures. North American culture, with its emphasis on free enterprise and the nuclear family, creates cities such as Boston with skyscrapers downtown (which maximize trade advantages) and single-family dwellings all around the city. The culture of the Yoruba (the people who comprise the bulk of the population of Ibadan, Nigeria's second largest city) emphasizes personalized trade relations, handicrafts, and an extended family, and generates a city that is quite different in physical layout and social interaction. Cities are, after all, human creations that display the same variety as all human culture, and we can fully understand a city only by exploring the cultural patterns found throughout its larger society.

THE CITY AND THE COUNTRYSIDE

> . . . those that are good manners at the court are as ridiculous in the country as the behavior of the country is most mockable at the court.
>
> Shakespeare, *As You Like It,* III, 2

Interdependencies

Shakespeare noted something that everyone knows: Country and city ways are often quite different. Yet we must be wary of overgeneralization. For example, in Ibadan, with the city's fields so close by and farmers such a large part of the city's population, it is virtually impossible to distinguish between city and country ways (Lawal et al. 2004). Indeed, in any location, city and country are not independent of each other at all, but rather have a symbiotic relationship.

Consider this oft-forgotten connection: *Much of the population of the city initially came from the countryside.* Throughout history, the migration of people seeking a better life transformed city and country alike. To take but one example, during the great expansion of European cities in the nineteenth century, England changed from an almost completely rural society to a nation in which over 60 percent of the population lived in cities. Table 8–1 presents these population shifts in England and Wales during the second half of that century. In 40 years, the number of towns nearly doubled, the urban population more than doubled, and the rural population noticeably decreased.

The relationship between the city and its countryside involves much more than just the dynamics of migration, however. The resources that each supplies create a reciprocal

TABLE 8–1   Urban and Rural Population in England and Wales, 1851–1891

	Urban		Rural
	Number of Towns	**Total Population**	**Total Population**
1851	580	8,990,809	8,936,800
1861	781	10,960,998	9,105,225
1871	938	14,041,404	8,670,862
1881	967	17,636,646	8,337,793
1891	1,011	20,895,504	8,107,021

Source: Adapted from Adna Weber, *The Growth of Cities* (New York: Columbia University Press, 1899), Table XVIII.

Intimate open-air markets are common in many parts of the world. Much more frequently than in the urban Western world, city life—such as here at Bara Bazaar in northern India—is based on kinship and ethnic ties. While the men work their farms or produce their crafts, the women sell the products in the market place, often knowing just about everyone with whom they do business.

dependence. Because a large proportion of city dwellers (even in Ibadan) engage in specialized occupations other than agriculture, the countryside must supply the city's food. Many of the specialty occupations of the city—such as weaving or steel manufacturing—depend on the countryside's raw materials. Conversely, the countryside obtains many of its goods—the clothes made by weavers, tractors made with the steel—from the city.

But perhaps the most important link between city and countryside (Shakespeare notwithstanding) is the reciprocal shaping of lifestyles. Migrants who swell the city's ranks bring to the city their cultural traditions. The result is a living kaleidoscope of human behavior, ranging all the way from groups who devotedly try to continue living as they did in the "old country" (New York's Hasidic Jews, for example) to the various "hyphenated" Americans (Asian-Americans, Hispanic-Americans)

who maintain only some of the old ways in their new urban setting.

At the same time, other rural influences, including traditional folk music, art, and literature, are constantly altering the city's character. Country music, in fact, is exclusively played on at least one radio station in nearly every major U.S. city, and "country rock" is a peculiar rural–urban musical blend.

Very common in North American and European cities (less so in African cities like Ibadan) is the human cultural hybrid—the urban person who takes a little bit from numerous originally rural lifestyles existing in the city and integrates them into a new lifestyle altogether. Such a person was Mayor Fiorello La Guardia of New York, as described in the Urban Living box on page 214. Perhaps it would be fair to say that a little bit of La Guardia exists in most city dwellers today.

URBAN LIVING

Mayor Fiorello La Guardia of New York

To put it sociologically, La Guardia was a marginal man who lived in the edge of many cultures. . . . Tammany Hall may have been the first to exploit the vote-getting value of eating gefullte fish with the Jews, goulash with the Hungarians, sauerbraten with Germans, spaghetti with Italians, and so on indefinitely, but this unorthodox Republican not only dined every bit as shrewdly but also spoke, according to the occasion, in Yiddish, Hungarian, German, Serbian-Croatian, or plain New York English. Half Jewish and half Italian, born in Greenwich Village yet raised in Arizona, married first to a Catholic and then to a Lutheran but himself a Mason and an Episcopalian, Fiorello La Guardia was a Mr. Brotherhood Week all by himself.

Source: Arthur Mann, cited in E. Digby Baltzell, *The Protestant Establishment* (New York: Vintage, 1964), p. 29.

This influence works in two ways, however. Just as the city receives much from the countryside, it typically returns the favor, radiating outward an influence far beyond its borders. In fact, many sociologists think that this influence, in modern times, far outstrips the countryside's effect on urban affairs.

Urban Dominance

"I cannot see that London has any great advantage over the country," said Mrs. Bennett, "except the shops and public places. The country is a vast deal pleasanter, is it not . . . ?"

Jane Austen, *Pride and Prejudice,* 1813

Thus Mrs. Bennett, engaged in a verbal duel with some of London's high society, defended her rural environment in the early part of the nineteenth century. Her championing of the country was not well received. Everyone present—her own daughters included—subsequently told her that, like it or not, London had numerous advantages over the countryside, among them a greater diversity of people and, well, there was just so much more to do in London.

Right or wrong, Mrs. Bennett was wiser than she knew, for her allusion to what she saw as the city's one advantage—its shops and public places—suggests why the city's influence has spread so far beyond its physical boundaries. As Louis Wirth argued, the city's importance

. . . may be regarded as a consequence of the concentration on [it] of industrial, commercial, financial, and administrative facilities and activities, transportation and communication lines, and cultural and recreational equipment such as the press, radio stations, theaters, libraries, museums, concert halls, operas, hospitals, colleges, research and publishing centers, professional organizations, and religious and welfare institutions. (1964:63)

Indeed, North American cities have maintained cultural dominance over society far out of proportion to the number of city dwellers since the coming of European settlers in the seventeenth century. Moreover, as we described in Chapter 3, the importance of early eastern settlements, most notably Boston, Charleston, Montreal, Newport, New York, and Philadelphia, was supplemented by that of newer cities as the population moved westward to such places as Chicago, Kansas City, St. Louis, and Toronto. In the Far West, especially following the completion of the transcontinental railroad to San Francisco in 1869, towns and cities continued to stand at the center of social life. This fact was observed by Josiah Strong, who commented in 1885, "It is the cities and towns which frame state constitutions, make laws, create public opinion, establish social usages and fix standards of morals in the West" (p. 206).

North American growth is thus intertwined with the story of the development of cities. Cities—consistently the centers of an expanding market, the loci of advances in communication, and the sources of leadership in politics, fashion, and the arts—have a long linkage with cultural firsts: the first daily newspaper (Philadelphia, 1784), the first stock exchange (New York, 1792), and the first telephone system (Boston, 1877; linked to New York in 1884, to Denver in 1911, and to San Francisco in 1915).

Such a pattern of urban dominance over the broader society is hardly limited to North America. We find a description of the same phenomenon in Alexis de Tocqueville's historical account (1856/1955) of the French Revolution of 1789. Beginning in the 1600s as the feudal system weakened, French life increasingly became centralized in Paris. As a result, when the Revolution erupted in Paris, it quickly carried the rest of French society along with it.

Tocqueville noted that, in times past, Paris had been "no more than the largest town in France . . . [but by] 1789 things were very different; it [was] no exaggeration to say that Paris was France" (1955:72). The city controlled the nation's economic, intellectual, and political lifeblood. This urban dominance was also evident as one left Paris for the countryside. Inquiring as to the political climate of the outlying areas, English observer Arthur Young heard time and again: "We are only a provincial town; we must wait till Paris gives us a lead" (Tocqueville 1955:74).

By the late eighteenth century, Paris had established urban dominance over all of France in cultural, economic, and political matters. When Napoleon borrowed from ancient Roman tradition to build this massive triumphal arch at the western end of the Champs Elysées, it became a symbol of French patriotism, further strengthening the city's image as the "essence" of what is French.

That is exactly what Paris did. It is one of the remarkable facts of history that the cultural ideas ("Liberty! Equality! Brotherhood!") that transformed France and much of Western civilization, in conjunction with the American Revolution a decade earlier, were largely city born.

Urban dominance is thus a central pattern of the modern and historical world. Sometimes, however, urban influence is not so welcome, as the people of Grafton County, New Hampshire, have decided. Their views are described in the Cityscape box below.

In other instances urban dominance is understated, as in the case of "Springdale," a small town in upstate New York. With its quiet streets and surrounding rural countryside, it would seem a world apart from the city. The appearance is deceiving. While residents of the town displayed much pride in their traditions of independence and self-sufficiency—values they associated with small-town life—they also recognized that these sentiments were ebbing away. The average Springdaler, wrote sociologists Arthur Vidich and Joseph Bensman,

CITYSCAPE

The Invasion of the City Slickers

[What city people who move to the country] bring along is a series of unconscious assumptions. It might be better for rural America if they brought a few sticks of dynamite, or a can of arsenic.

Take a typical example. Mr. and Mrs. Nice are Bostonians. They live a couple of miles off Route 128 in a four-bedroom house. He's a partner in an ad agency; she has considerable talent as an artist. For some years they've had a second home in northern New Hampshire. The kids love it up there in Grafton County.

For some years, too, both Nices have been feeling they'd like to simplify their lives. They look with increasing envy on their New Hampshire neighbors, who never face a morning traffic jam, or an evening one, either; who don't have a long drive to the country on Friday night and a long drive back on Sunday; who aren't cramped into a suburban lot; who live in harmony with the natural rhythm of the year; who think the rat race is probably some minor event at a county fair.

One Thursday evening Don Nice says to Sue that he's been talking to the other partners, and they've agreed there's no reason he can't do some of his work at home. If he's in the office Wednesday and Thursday every week, why the rest of the time he can stay in touch by telephone. Sue, who has been trapped all year as a Brownie Scout leader and who has recently had the aerial snapped off her car in Boston, is delighted. She reflects happily that in their little mountain village you don't even need to lock your house, and there is no Brownie troop. "You're wonderful," she tells Don.

So the move occurs. In most ways Don and Sue are very happy. They raise practically all their own vegetables the first year; Sue takes up cross-country skiing. Don personally splits some of the wood they burn in their new woodstove.

But there are some problems. The first one Sue is conscious of is the school. It's just not very good. It's clear to Sue almost immediately that the town desperately needs a new school building—and also modern playground equipment, new school buses, more and better art instruction at the high school, a different principal. Don is as

. . . sees that the urban and metropolitan society is technically and culturally superior to his own community. He sees this in his everyday life when he confronts the fact that his community cannot provide him with everything he needs: almost everyone goes to the city for shopping and entertainment; large numbers of people are dependent on the radio and television; and everyone realizes that rural life would be drastically altered without cars and refrigerators. (1958:79)

It may be edge cities and not older cities that impact on many rural landscapes today, but this is merely a newer form of urban dominance. Nor are these the only links that bind the residents of Springdale to the larger urban society. Their lives are influenced by outside specialists from organizations such as the state agricultural extension service, as well as by their own college-trained professionals. Additional organizations that serve to "import" the culture of the urban society include such national organizations as the Odd Fellows and the Kiwanis Club. Perhaps more important, the economic and political life of the town is shaped more by state and federal agencies than by local entities. Taxes, education for the town's children, and the price of local farmers' milk are all increasingly subject to outside forces that are mostly city based. Vidich and Bensman concluded

---

upset as Sue when they discover that only about 40 percent of the kids who graduate from that high school go on to any form of college. The rest do native things like becoming farmers, and mechanics, and joining the Air Force. An appalling number of the girls marry within twelve months after graduation. How are Jeanie and Don, Jr., going to get into good colleges from this school? . . . Pretty soon Sue and Don join an informal group of newcomers in town who are working to upgrade education. All they want for starters is the new building ($2.8 million) and a majority of their kind on the school board.

As for Don, though he really enjoys splitting the wood—in fact, next year he's planning to get a chainsaw and start cutting a few trees of his own—he also likes to play golf. There's no course within twenty miles. Some of the nice people he's met in the education lobby feel just as he does. They begin to discuss the possibility of a nine-hole course. The old farmer who owns the land they have in mind seems to be keeping only four or five cows on it, anyway. Besides, taxes are going up, and the old fellow is going to have to sell, sooner or later. (Which is too bad, of course. Don and Sue both admire the local farmers, and they're sincerely sorry whenever one has to quit.)

Over the next several years, Don and Sue get more and more adjusted to rural living—and they also gradually discover more things that need changing. For example, the area needs a good French restaurant. And it needs a much better airport. At present there are only two flights a day to Boston, and because of the lack of sophisticated equipment, even they are quite often canceled. If Don wants to be sure of getting down for an important meeting, he has to drive. Sue would be glad of more organized activities for the kids. There's even talk of starting a Brownie troop.

In short, if enough upper-middle-class people move to a rural town, they are naturally going to turn it into a suburb of the nearest city. For one generation it will be a nice and truly rustic suburb, with real farms dotted around it, and real natives speaking their minds at town meeting. Then as the local people are gradually taxed out of existence (or at least out of town), one more piece of rural America has died.

Source: Text excerpt, "The Invasion of the City Slickers" reprinted from Noel Perrin, "Rural Area: Permit Required," in *Country Journal* (April 1980), pp. 34–35. Copyright © 1980 *Country Journal.* Reprinted by permission of *Country Journal* and Noel Perrin.

that, despite the desires and pretensions of the townspeople, most "plans and decisions that refer directly to the community are made from a distance by invisible agents and institutions" (1958:81). Thus, just as Springdalers now go periodically to the world of the city, the world of the city has subtly transformed, for better or for worse, Springdale and communities like it.

THE CITY AND CIVILIZATION

> Cities have always been the fireplaces of civilization, whence light and heat radiated out into the dark, cold world.
>
> Theodore Parker,
> nineteenth-century U.S. preacher

The reason for the city's increasing dominance in modern affairs, as we have hinted already, is that everything human—art, music, business, traditions, what we love and hate—converges there. The city does not create a way of life all its own but rather provides the setting where any way of life, any cultural tradition, can intensify and re-create itself in a manner not possible in other settings. For example, Socrates, Plato, and Aristotle all lived in Hellenic Athens, sharing ideas and challenging each other. This simply would not have occurred had they all lived in rural hamlets, cut off from one another.

Nowhere is this process of intensification represented more clearly than in the suggestion that the city encapsulates a whole culture. Throughout history, writers have seen the city as capturing the essence of human civilization. Indeed, Euripides, the classical Greek playwright, maintained: "The first requisite to happiness is birth in a great city." The Critical Thinking box on page 219 illustrates not only the connections among our most common words about cities and civilization, but also the linkage between city and culture as expressed in the writings of some of history's most important urbanists.

Is the city truly synonymous with civilization? To find out, let's examine in more detail the ideas of Oswald Spengler, Lewis Mumford, and Daniel J. Monti.

Oswald Spengler: The "Soul" of the City

Oswald Spengler (1880–1936) was a German philosopher who saw in cities the drama of the rise and fall of civilization. He contended that cities developed, ultimately dominated a society, and then declined, carrying with them the culture built over generations and centuries. The cyclical element in Spengler's theory (generally considered too simplistic by contemporary social scientists) is less important for our purposes than his belief that "all great cultures are town-cultures" and that "world history is city history."

Spengler believed strongly that human civilization takes on distinctive qualities in the city. At some point in its development, the "soul" of the city emerges: "Out of the rustic group of farms and cottages . . . arises a totality. And the whole lives, breathes, grows, and acquires a face and inner form and history" (1928/1969:65–66). Spengler believed that the countryside never has a soul in this sense; it is a "landscape" at most, never a "world."

Moreover, the city senses its own power and uniqueness:

> . . . it is a place from which the countryside is henceforth regarded, felt, and experienced as "environs," as something different and subordinate. From now on there are two lives, that of the inside and that of the outside, and the peasant understands this just as clearly as the townsman. . . . The new Soul of the City speaks a new language, which soon becomes tantamount to the language of the culture itself. (1969:66, 68)

Thus, we find the essence of ancient Egypt symbolized by Thebes, ancient Greece by Athens, the Roman Empire by Rome, Islam by Baghdad, and prerevolutionary France by Paris. Indeed, Spengler believed that whole periods of European civilization were manifest only in cities. Is it not true, he asked, "that the Renaissance style flourished only in the Renaissance city, the Baroque only in the Baroque city?" (1969:68).

CRITICAL THINKING

The City and Civilization

City Words

Those of us who live in the city should be grateful to our language, because the words that have to do with the city are usually flattering. We city dwellers, at least in ancient days, were supposed to be more *civil* in our manners and more *civilized* in our ways than others, for both of these words *civil* and *civilized* are the eventual children of the Latin term *civis* which meant "one who lives in a city." All city folks, you see, were regarded as automatically cultured and well housebroken. And from ancient Latin we have borrowed the word *urbs* which also meant city, and we used it to create the word *urbane* which describes the smooth manners that were presumed to be characteristic of *metropolitan* society. The Greek parts of the word *metropolitan* are *metro*, "mother," and *polis*, "city," so a *metropolis* is the "mother city" or the chief or capital city of a country, and he who lives in a *metropolis* is supposed to inherit the sophisticated ideas and manners that go with such a center. And from the

Greek *polis*, "city," we inherited our word *politic*. If you are *politic*, you are expedient, shrewd, discreet, and artful in your address and your procedure, which sounds dangerously like a city slicker!

City Culture

Just as the beginning of Western Civilization is marked by permanent settlement of formerly nomadic peoples . . . so the beginning of what is distinctly modern in our civilization is best signalized by the growth of great cities. (Louis Wirth, 1938)

The city is . . . the natural habitat of civilized man. (Robert Park, 1916)

[The city is] the most precious invention of civilization, second only to language itself in the transmission of culture. (Lewis Mumford, 1961)

All great Cultures are town-Cultures. . . . World history is city history. Peoples, states, politics, religion, all arts, and all sciences rest upon one phenomenon . . . the town. (Oswald Spengler, 1928)

Source: City Words extract: Wilfred Funk, *Word Origins* (New York: Bell, 1978), pp. 97–98.

Modern sociologists generally view Spengler's contribution to urban sociology as modest because few accept his cyclical ideas of historical change. Yet he correctly sensed the connection between city and civilization, an idea developed extensively by a U.S. urbanist whose work we will discuss next.

Lewis Mumford: The City as the Center of Civilization

Lewis Mumford (1897–1952) traced the cultural importance of cities through Western

history. Based on historical and comparative evidence, he argued that the city has indeed been at the very center of Western civilization from its beginnings.

Mumford believed that, of all creatures, only human beings seem to be aware of themselves as fundamentally distinctive. We can think, invent, and wonder about such things as life, death, sex, and god(s). In the course of human evolution, Mumford reasoned, people attached these thoughts to places. The earliest centers of this kind were probably caves and places of burial. These sites were symbolic centers to which wandering groups could return periodically to ponder the mysteries they wished to understand. Thus began civilization. "In the earliest gathering about a grave or a painted symbol, a great stone or a sacred grove, one has the beginning of a succession of civic institutions that range from the temple to the astronomical observatory, from the theater to the university" (Mumford 1961:9).

As time passed and technology improved, some people began living at these places permanently: The shrine became a camp, then a village, and finally a town. Mumford (like Spengler) suggests that, at a certain point, the cultural ideas, the people, and the place all jelled as the city emerged (see the Critical Thinking box below).

Thenceforth, the story of civilization became the story of urban history. Yet we must be careful here. We often assume that civilization automatically means progress—that what exists today is somehow a better form of what

---

CRITICAL THINKING

The Crystallization of the City

. . . This new urban mixture resulted in an enormous expansion of human capabilities in every direction. The city effected a mobilization of manpower, a command over long-distance transportation, an intensification of communication over long distances in space and time, an outburst of invention along with a large-scale development of civil engineering, and, not least, it promoted a tremendous further rise in agricultural productivity. . . . When all this happened, the archaic village culture yielded to urban "civilization," that peculiar combination of creativity and control, of expression and repression, of tension and release, whose outward manifestation has been the historic city. From its origins onward, indeed, the city may be described as a structure specially equipped to store and transmit the goods of civilization, sufficiently condensed to afford the maximum amount of facilities in a minimum space, but also capable of structural enlargement to enable it to find a place for the changing needs and the more complex forms of a growing society and its cumulative social heritage. The invention of such forms as the written record, the library, the archive,

the school, and the university is one of the earliest and most characteristic achievements of the city. . . .

What happened . . . with the rise of cities, was that many functions that had heretofore been scattered and unorganized were brought together within a limited area, and the components of the community were kept in a state of dynamic tension and interaction. In this union, made almost compulsory by the strict enclosure of the city wall, the already well-established parts of the protocity—shrine, spring, village, market stronghold—participated in the general enlargement of concentration of numbers, and underwent a structural differentiation that gave them forms recognizable in every subsequent phase of urban culture. The city proved not merely a means of expressing in concrete terms the magnification of sacred and secular power, but in a manner that went far beyond any conscious intention it also enlarged all the dimensions of life. Beginning as a representation of the cosmos, a means of bringing heaven down to earth, the city became a symbol of the possible.

Source: Excerpts from Lewis Mumford, "The Crystallization of the City" in *The City in History: Its Origin, Its Transformation, and Its Prospects.* © 1961 and renewed 1989 by Lewis Mumford. Reprinted with permission of Harcourt, Inc.

went before. Neither Spengler nor Mumford meant to suggest this notion of cultural evolution; rather, their idea was that the city was culture "writ large," the living embodiment of a society's or epoch's ideas. Cities did not inevitably progress. In them, as already mentioned, Spengler saw the rise and fall of civilization; and, like Max Weber before him (Chapter 5), Mumford believed that cities better than today's existed in the past—in Hellenic Athens, for example.

Daniel J. Monti: The Civic Culture of the City

Daniel J. Monti rejects the suggestion of some social scientists that cities have become "sinkholes of civic indifference," no longer possessing the cultural or moral vision that once motivated their residents (1999:378). Instead, he argues that cities continue to inspire both a public spirit and a civic mindedness among their inhabitants. Their ability to coexist and cooperate in the everyday routines of public habits and customs is the manifestation of a **civic culture.** Its elements borrowed from other cultures or adapted from earlier times, civic culture helps the many different peoples of a city to get along and make sense of each other's world.

Offering a detailed portrait of a civic culture is a difficult task. First, each city has its own distinctive style, temperament, and public rhythms, so generalizations are misleading. Second, civic culture is not static; it is continually changing and thus hard to pinpoint. Third, some of its elements may be better or less known to certain groups in the city, and therefore practiced unevenly or not at all in different parts of the city (Monti 1999: 103–104).

Despite the unevenness of some aspects of civic culture, other parts work well throughout the city because they are widely shared. These are found in the "ceremonies, customs, and codes for appropriate public behavior." Essentially, "they are expressions of how persons in that place have worked out a way to be together in public and still carry on their private lives, peaceably and with at least a modicum of

predictability" (Monti 1999:103). For example, urbanites typically line up awaiting the arrival of a bus in a single line, not in a cluster. This unspoken, untaught norm of civic culture is quickly learned, enabling strangers to accord one another a mutual respect and an orderly entrance once the bus arrives.

In this and countless other ways, urban public behavior reflects the shared values, norms, and practices of a civic culture that makes it possible for people—different and unknown to one another—to become part of an inclusive community. Essentially minding each other's business to behave appropriately in urban public space, rather than focusing only on one's own actions or rituals, city people develop a common view of the world and conceive better ways to be in it together (Monti 1999:104). This is a remarkable accomplishment, says Monti:

> The "good city" is not necessarily a fair city or a just city, and it is most certainly not an equal city. It is instead where a people creates a viable civic culture that makes sense to them and works. The civic culture of American cities is revealed to us as an interesting and even a paradoxical mix of conservative and liberal ways of "doing community." It works well, or at least a great deal better than we have been led to believe. The good news is that the rest of us share in the civic and cultural bounty of cities anyway. The bad news is that we do not see the urban way of life made in cities as part of our cultural inheritance, and we do not appreciate the contribution it has made to our lives. (Monti 1999:379)

THE CITY AND SOCIETAL CULTURE

From Mumford and Spengler we learn that, although the city and civilization are not precisely synonymous, the city definitely has a unique power to intensify and symbolize culture. From Monti we learn that the city also generates a civic culture that, to a greater or lesser degree, its residents share and practice. Another aspect of culture is that any city will dynamically and intensely reflect the

Monti suggests that civic culture in a city includes widely shared codes of appropriate public behavior that allow strangers to be together and act with a reasonable set of expectations from each other. Such practices as alternate vehicle merging or awaiting a bus in a single line allow fair and orderly movement through unspoken, untaught norms of mutual respect.

characteristics of its surrounding culture. However, because cultural patterns vary so widely, cities may be markedly different from one another. In the following case studies we will read about two cities, Peking during the Ming Dynasty (1368–1644 C.E.) and Hellenic Athens of the fifth century B.C.E.—capitals of vastly different civilizations and separated by more than 1,500 years.

❖ *CASE STUDY* ❖
Ming Peking

Situated on the northern seacoast, China's capital city is centered around the Forbidden City and Tiananmen Square, the world's biggest public square, with an area of 98 acres. Now a city of more than 15 million people, Beijing (formerly called Peking) has a 3,000-year history and contains fascinating remnants of its glorious past.

Established in northeastern China to protect the country from invaders from the north, Beijing grew into a city at least several centuries before the birth of Christ. During the thirteenth century C.E., when the Yuan (Mongol) emperor ruled China, Kublai Khan transformed Beijing into a capital city. Soon after the overthrow of the Yuan by the Ming Dynasty in 1368, the Emperor Yung Lo spared no expense in turning the city into a monument to all of Chinese culture and to himself as symbolic head of that culture. It was a massive job, including the transporting of large amounts of marble a distance of 1,500 miles not only to expand the palace but also to upgrade some of the city's roads and bridges (Mote 2003:617–20).

Physical Structure

The design, deliberately created to symbolize everything vital to Chinese life, arranged the whole city on a perfect north–south axis, around which were temples and altars. Perhaps no better example exists of Lewis Mumford's idea of the city as a physical container, for Ming Beijing literally revealed the city within the city, surrounding the all-important core where the emperor lived (see Figure 8–1).

The city was about 25 square miles in area and was composed of two major sections, each roughly rectangular in shape. Beijing's southern section, known as the Outer City or Chinese City, contained most of the city's population, probably about 320,000 people at the end of the thirteenth century (Chandler 1987:356).

The northern section, however, was of quite another character. Known by the name Tartar City or Inner City, this area was surrounded by a massive wall about 50 feet high and just as thick. Indeed, whereas in the West the words for *city* are linked to the words for *civilization* and *politics,* in Chinese the word for *city* literally means "wall," indicating in yet another way that the city was a container of major cultural significance (Murphy 1984:189). All city streets were arranged in a gridiron, with gates through the wall arranged symmetrically.

Centrally located within the walls of the Tartar City was another area, called the Imperial City. Protected by yet another wall, and including about 5 square miles of parklike land complete with artificially constructed lakes and hills, this was the focus of the political and religious power and splendor of Ming civilization. In the midst of this constructed urban tranquility, and surrounded by a moat and yet another defensive wall, were the palaces and residences—facing south—of the emperor. This was called the Purple City by the Chinese and later dubbed the Forbidden City by Europeans on their realization that access was gained only by the emperor's personal decree. Just to the north was a large, artificially constructed mound of earth, Coal Hill, on which stood temples prominently visible above the city.

Symbolism

Ming Peking was based on elaborate Chinese cosmology (Wright 1977). The temples and altars were religious symbols of the sun, earth, and, most important, heaven.

Chinese astronomers had discovered long before Peking was built that the center of the heavens was the North Star, around which everything revolved. On earth—the human universe—the Chinese believed that everything revolved around the "Son of Heaven," the emperor. As the northernmost major city of China, Peking thus became the emperor's capital. The importance of the north was also evident in the city's location on a north–south axis and by the fact that the emperor could be reached only by traveling north along the Great Processional Way. Even the name of the emperor's city, the Purple City, was chosen because the North Star gave off a purple hue in the night sky.

The symbolism did not stop there, however. The colors and height of all buildings had cultural meaning. Peasants, lowly and unimportant, were allowed only houses of one story and could paint their roofs only a dull gray. In the Imperial City various functionaries couldn't have houses of more than one story either, but to signify their higher status they were allowed roofs painted green, red, or purple, depending on their role. Only in the Forbidden City itself were buildings allowed to be more than one story. Their roofs were painted a bright gold-yellow, symbolizing the life-giving (sunlike) qualities of the emperor's rule. The emperor was the pivot of the world and, ruling with the mandate of heaven from the Forbidden City with the mandate of heaven, he harmonized the world, oversaw the calendar, and maintained order (Beguin and Morel 1997).

Given his importance, it is little wonder that the emperor had everything for the "good life" within a stone's throw. The construction of the Forbidden City was a marvel of urban design, as can be seen by carefully examining the buildings shown in Figure 8–2. Note especially the buildings in the center—the emperor's sole preserve. The first group, the buildings immediately to the north of the Supreme Imperial Gate, are buildings of state: The Hall of Supreme Harmony was reserved

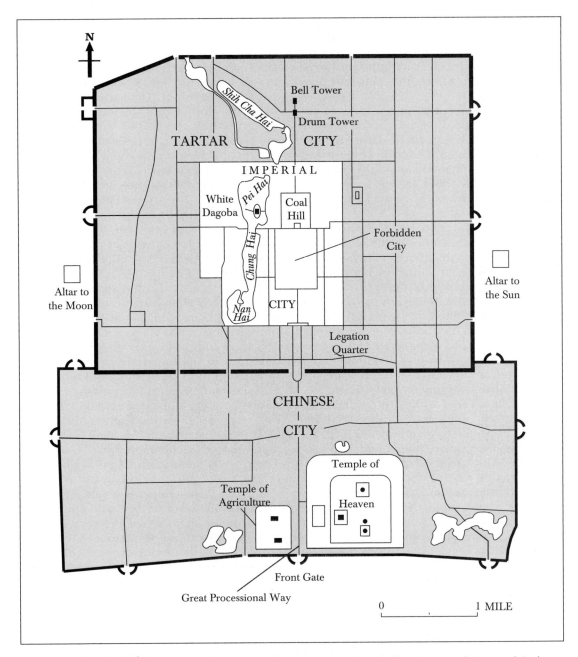

FIGURE 8–1   Ming Peking [*Source:* Adapted from Roderick MacFarquhar, *The Forbidden City* (New York: Newsweek Books, 1972), p. 46.]

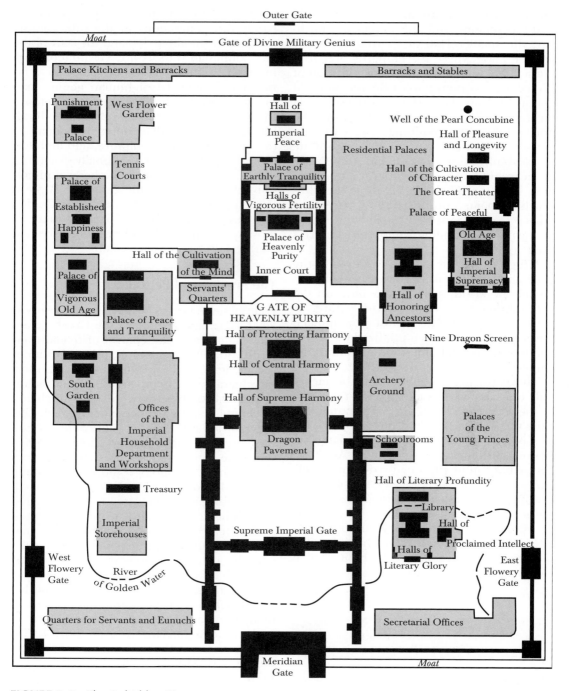

FIGURE 8–2 The Forbidden City [*Source:* Roderick MacFarquhar, *The Forbidden City* (New York: Newsweek Books, 1972), p. 73.]

for special state occasions, such as the New Year's ceremony and the emperor's birthday; the smaller Hall of Central Harmony was the place where the emperor prepared himself and waited for functions; the Hall of Protecting Harmony was for the reception of visitors and for day-to-day governance. The second group of central buildings—to the north of these state buildings—were the emperor's residences. Entering by the Gate of Heavenly Purity, one found the Palace of Heavenly Purity, the emperor's quarters; next was the Hall of Vigorous Fertility, which, its name notwithstanding, was where official seals were stored; finally, the Palace of Earthly Tranquility, where the empress lived.

Ming Peking is a striking example of the city's ability to intensify culture. Peking was a symbolic world, a whole city built on the cultural themes of harmony with nature, security (city within city), and power. Each "layer of the onion" reemphasized the whole and led to the vital, omnipotent center, the emperor.

This particular symbolism probably means little to us, but we can imagine what it meant to the Pekingese. In a similar manner, our cities transmit and magnify our culture. What is important in our culture is "writ large" in Boston, Birmingham, and Boise. We don't have cities within cities or predominant religious symbolism, like Peking. We have, as Dorothy McAllister saw as she flew over Boston on her way to Ibadan, commercial skyscrapers, fast-moving automobiles on superhighways, and private single-family houses. What might such constructions say about what is culturally important to us?

❖ CASE STUDY ❖
Hellenic Athens

There is small risk of exaggerating the differences between Ming Peking and Hellenic Athens, situated on the rocky northern coast of the Mediterranean. During a period of barely two generations in the fifth century B.C.E., between about 480 and the start of the Peloponnesian Wars in 431, a civilization took form which Mumford has described as "a far richer efflorescence of human genius than history anywhere else records, except perhaps for Renaissance Florence" (1961:167). Imagine an almost simultaneous development of the arts of painting, sculpture, and architecture; the realization of a rationally structured democracy; and the birth of a body of philosophy that remains at the center of Western thinking today. At the heart of this Golden Age was the city of Athens, leading to an almost synonymous identification of Athenian culture with Greek achievement.

The Preclassical Period

Four migrating tribes settled Athens as early as 2000 B.C.E., and eventually the Greek peninsula came under the control of feudal overlords who called themselves, perhaps with not the greatest modesty, the *aristoi* (or aristocracy; literally, "the best people"). By the eighth century B.C.E., these overlords were in charge of several hundred independent Greek city-states, or *poli* (the source of our contemporary word *political* and of the urban suffix *-polis*). Over the next two centuries the city-states grew rich, as technology and overseas trade improved and military conquests multiplied.

Ironically, it was this very success that led to the aristocrats' downfall. The improvement of trade created a wealthy middle class that began to demand participation in city rule, and the martial victories evolved a warrior class with both the skills and arms to take over the city-states. In a series of coups d'état between 660 and 550 B.C.E., they did just that in many trade and maritime city-states, earning in the process the name *tyrannos* (Burn 1970).

Tyrants or not, the preeminence of warriors during this period was to prove fortuitous. Early in the fifth century B.C.E., a series of Persian invasions threatened the Greek peninsula. Together, Athens and her rival city-state,

Athens today is strongly shaped by its culture and history. Even the physical environment reveals that social reality, as seen above. Looming above the city from its craggy hilltop site sits the Acropolis—built in the second half of the fifth century B.C.E. as the citadel of ancient Athens. Particularly prominent are the pillars of the Parthenon—the temple of Athena, patron goddess of the city.

the more militaristic Sparta, finally routed the invaders in 479 B.C.E., setting the stage for what many regard as the city's—and perhaps even Western history's—greatest moment.

The Golden Age

In the fifth century B.C.E., the city of Athens (about one mile square) and its surrounding villages had a population of perhaps 350,000 (Waterfield 2004:149). We can best understand Athenian life in the Golden Age as the celebration of human possibilities. "Men come together in the city to live," exclaimed Aristotle in a timeless salute to the human possibilities of city life, and "they remain there in order to live the good life." What was this "good life"? In his famous funeral oration in honor of Athenian victims of the Peloponnesian Wars, Athenian statesman Pericles conveyed its essence: The Greek ideal, he said, began with the principle of

democracy "which favors the many instead of the few."

The Athenian belief in democracy was grounded historically, for the city-states that preceded the Golden Age were independent units. Indeed, so independent were they that one cannot speak of one "nation," even at the apex of Greek culture. Each city-state pursued its own ends and believed that no one had the right to dictate otherwise.

This fierce sense of independence also characterized the Greek citizen. In 600 B.C.E., with dissatisfaction rife, Athens was on the verge of revolution. To avert this, Solon, an aristocrat, was chosen as arbitrator. He immediately proposed a reorganization of the Athenian constitution that allowed all "free citizens" (excluding women, slaves, and foreigners) a place in the city's governing body, the Assembly. He established the People's Council, numbering some 400, with the charge of preparing the Assembly's agenda. Members were chosen from the four main Athenian tribes (a hundred each), thereby preventing dominance by any one group. Finally, government officials were made accountable to the Assembly for their work each year. Political participation was mandatory for all citizens; without regard to "obscurity of conditions," each was required to take part in the public life of the city.

Athenian democracy was a brilliant innovation, affording all free citizens participation in government. It also allowed the citizen the right to live as one chose within that overarching system. Classical Athens did not stand as a monument to an all-powerful god or to a ruling family, but rather to all free citizens. In one of the great dramas of the age, Sophocles' *Antigone,* we find this statement (which could well serve as a critique of Ming Peking): "A city that is of one man is no city."

The ideals of human development and versatility were vital to Hellenic civilization. A primary cultural value was that all citizens should strive for refinement (although without extravagance) and pursue individual well-being—a fusion of the well-tutored body, mind, and spirit. Athenians developed the body through constant work, exercise, and sport, including the Olympic games, in which individuals from different city-states competed for the glory of their state. Continual dialogue provoked the mind. In their leisurely society citizens often spent much of the day talking about the deeper matters of life. Plato's dialogues between the great philosopher Socrates and his friends are an excellent example.

Athenians even managed the life of the spirit differently. For example, no system of formal or mystical religion placed the gods at great distance from the people of the city. In Peking the priests were "specialists" sequestered within the walls of the Forbidden City, but in Athens the "priest" was just another conscientious layman who made no prophecies and simply executed his religious duties as part of his civic duties. This ideal of participation meant that temples such as the Parthenon were always open to people, who typically marked their religious observances informally, frequently outdoors.

Indeed, as Greek civilization entered the Golden Age, the gods themselves became less abstract and more like human beings. They were the objects of jokes, criticism, and bargains, but—all the same—they were used as models for human development. The Olympian gods became the symbol of something nobler in human nature, something within the reach of human endeavor.

A tripartite focus on body, mind, and spirit was the unique combination that formed the crux of Athens's success. By developing serious interests in all three areas, the Athenian indirectly kept any one area from becoming all-absorbing. This focus kept more practical areas of life—politics or economics, for example—in check. Too much politics breeds overemphasis on power and control; too much economics cultivates obsession with wealth and material goods. For a brief period, the citizens of Athens avoided these pitfalls.

Behind the Glory

Athens's moment at the pinnacle of urban history was not to last; it was undermined eventually by the culture's own egocentrism and exploitative practices. The wealth and leisurely pace of Athens in its Golden Age rested in large measure on the goods and services of others. During its successful expansion before the fifth century B.C.E., Athens had conquered many other city-states and regions. From them Athens extracted tribute in materials, taxes, and people—many of whom became slaves; Waterfield (2004:149) estimated that about one-fourth of the city's population held this unhappy status, as the elite Athenian citizens benefited from the widespread use of such human servants. All women, however, were excluded from citizenship and relegated to household duties and supervision.

Elitism reared its head in yet another, more immediately destructive, way. The Athenians refused citizenship to 30,000 foreigners, many of whom, as traders, had become permanent residents. This robbed the citizenry of potentially invigorating new ideas, forcing the foreign population into an exclusive concern with economic matters. Demoralized, these traders devoted their energies to moneymaking and material consumption. In time, they became indifferent to government so long as they were free to make a profit. By the end of the fourth century B.C.E., profit making had become the center of city life, and the older idea that economic activity was simply a means to a more holistic life—so central to the health of the city—began to wane.

Into this setting came the Peloponnesian Wars, begun in 431 B.C.E. between Athens and Sparta. Soundly defeated, Athens surrendered in 404 B.C.E. In total confusion and in public contradiction of all their democratic ideals, in 399 B.C.E. the Athenians tried Socrates and condemned him to death for "undermining the state by his endless public questionings."

The handwriting was on the wall. In 338 B.C.E., the Athenians put up belated opposition to an invasion force led by Philip of Macedon. Their defeat at the Battle of Chaeronea has been called "the death of the free polis." After that, Athens became a satellite in the Macedonian Empire until the Roman overlords arrived in 148 B.C.E.

MING PEKING AND ATHENS: A COMPARISON

The culture that prevailed in classical Athens was of a radically different character from that of Ming Peking. Without doubt, the cities had certain parallels: substantial inequality; large areas of poor housing; crowded, winding streets; and important central monuments and public buildings. There were all-important differences, however. Chinese civilization rested on a fundamental cultural belief in a godlike emperor that gave an unmistakable stamp to Peking. Monuments and buildings dwarfed the common individual as they simultaneously magnified the pomp and majesty of the emperor and his elite. Indeed, what clearer indication of a distant, exclusive power structure could there be than a citadel in the form of Peking's Forbidden City?

Athens seems, overall, more humane in character. The Greek cultural ideals of citizen participation stamped that city with a human scale, encouraging openness, communication, and development among its free citizens. Such ideals can be seen in all Athens's public buildings—in the theaters (where, not by accident, the audience sat above the performers, not the other way around), in the public forums, in the temples, in the gymnasia, in the marketplace. These buildings were not monuments to an absolute emperor; rather, Athens was much more a celebration of the "good life," an ideal that was evident in spite of important failings in practice.

In comparing Hellenic Athens and Ming Peking, we see just how different cities in different cultures can be. But this comparison shows us more: Athenian success at encouraging citizen participation and in developing the very best in human nature by a process of dialogue and growth shows us what the city can be. We are prompted to ask, in other words, how or why one city might be better than another. If we agree, for example, that democracy, equality, and continual mental, bodily, and spiritual development are ideals for which human beings should strive, Athens provides us with a real-life case where those ideals were encouraged. What, then, might we do to encourage the further manifestation of positive cultural values in our own modern-day cities? (See the Cityscape box on p. 230 for a decidedly negative portrait.)

THE CULTURE OF CAPITALISM AND THE CITY

Nineteenth-century London certainly was not like either Ming Peking or Hellenic Athens. Dominated by feverish economic activity, it was the forerunner of the modern city described by U.S. urbanist Louis Wirth in Chapter 5.

But Friedrich Engels, who first saw London in 1842—the year he met Karl Marx and began their long collaboration—gave an interpretation radically different from that of Wirth. Whereas the Chicago urbanist imagined he was describing the essential characteristics of all large, modern cities, Engels was aware that he was looking only at a certain cultural setting,

CITYSCAPE

The Industrial City: 1850

London is unique, because it is a city in which one can roam for hours without leaving the built-up area and without seeing the slightest sign of the approach of open country. This enormous agglomeration of population on a single spot has multiplied a hundred-fold the economic strength of the two and a half million inhabitants concentrated there. This great population has made London the commercial capital of the world and has created the gigantic docks in which are assembled the thousands of ships which always cover the River Thames. . . . All this is so magnificent and impressive that one is lost in admiration. The traveller has good reason to marvel at England's greatness even before he steps on English soil.

It is only later that the traveller appreciates the human suffering which has made all this possible. . . . It is only when he has visited the slums of this great city that it dawns upon him that the inhabitants of modern London have had to sacrifice so much that is best in human nature in order to create those wonders of civilisation with which their city teems. The vast majority of Londoners have had to let so many of their potential creative faculties lie dormant, stunted and unused in order that a small, closely-knit group of their fellow citizens could develop to the full the qualities with which nature has endowed them. . . . Hundreds of thousands of men and women drawn from all classes and ranks of society pack the streets of London. Are they

not all human beings with the same innate characteristics and potentialities? Are they not all equally interested in the pursuit of happiness? And do they not all aim at happiness by following similar methods? Yet they rush past each other as if they had nothing in common. . . .

No one even thinks of sparing a glance for his neighbor in the streets. . . . We know well enough that this isolation of the individual—this narrow-minded egotism—is everywhere the fundamental principle of modern society. But nowhere is this selfish egotism so blatantly evident as in the frantic bustle of the great city. The disintegration of society into individuals, each guided by his private principles and each pursuing his own aims has been pushed to its furthest limits in London. [emphasis added]

. . . Here men regard their fellows not as human beings, but as pawns in the struggle for existence. Everyone exploits his neighbor with the result that the stronger tramples the weaker under foot. The strongest of all, a tiny group of capitalists, monopolise everything, while the weakest, who are in the vast majority, succumb to the most abject poverty.

What is true of London, is true also of all the great towns, such as Manchester, Birmingham and Leeds. . . . The observer of such an appalling state of affairs must shudder at the consequences of such feverish activity and can only marvel that so crazy a social and economic structure should survive at all.

Source: Friedrich Engels, *The Condition of the Working Class in England,* trans. by W. O. Henderson and W. H. Chaloner (New York: Macmillan, 1958), pp. 30–31.

a city intensifying the tremendous power of Western industrial capitalism. Note especially the passage in italics in the Cityscape box: What Wirth saw as a consequence of a large,

differentiated population, Engels interpreted as cultural forces at work.

Engels was mightily disturbed by what he saw. If Hellenic Athens with its cultural ideas of developing the whole person was the city's highest point, surely Engels believed nineteenth-century London to be its lowest point. Yet the characteristics of both cities reflect the dominant ideals and activities of the larger culture. In the same way that Greek culture produced cities in which economic activity was regarded as of decidedly secondary importance, Engels believed that Western culture under the influence of capitalism spawned cities where economic gain was an unrestrained obsession.

The Capitalist City

As a means of livelihood, capitalism is very old. A rich capitalist life flourished in the fifth century B.C.E. in Athens, and no doubt such activity is centuries older. Significant commercial activity aimed at the accumulation of profit also took place on an increasing scale in medieval Europe, especially after the eleventh century.

If capitalism itself was not new, the unparalleled energy with which the spirit of commerce and profit began to assert itself in the sixteenth century C.E. certainly was. Apparently, several factors prompted this change. First, the feudal order of the Middle Ages began to erode as merchants, primarily in cities, gained power. Desiring to broaden their market, these merchants established trade routes among cities all over Europe in the period between 1200 and 1500. Goods began to pour into these cities, and people in the countryside began to get wind that a better life—or at least a life with more material amenities—could be had in cities. Major urban population growth ensued and fueled increased economic vitality (Heilbroner and Milberg 2001).

Gradually, from the sixteenth century onward, the economic interests of life came to dominate Western European cities. Capitalism set the principal cultural theme, with the new order organized around a rather different set of economic relationships than its feudal predecessor. No longer bound to lords and manors, individual workers could sell their labor to whoever would pay the highest wages. Second, under these conditions economic

activity became increasingly competitive. Because everyone was striving for profits, workers had to outdo each other in some way to get the greatest economic benefits. When industrialization arrived in the mid-eighteenth century, capitalism's hold over Western cities was greatly enhanced.

The Industrial Revolution

Like capitalism, **industrialism**—the process of manufacturing goods in large quantities for mass consumption—had existed in Western society to a limited degree before the eighteenth century. However, it was only after the adoption of capitalism on a large scale that the influence of industrialism began to grow. For all intents and purposes, large-scale industrialism began in England about 1750.

One important reason that English society proved so amenable to industrialism was the penchant, particularly evident in the upper middle classes, for engineering and guiding economic activities by the most scientific methods available. If efficient methods were not available, the innovative British invented them. Perhaps the most famous example of an invention that changed the economic order was James Watt's steam engine. This machine, perfected by 1775, had literally hundreds of applications, from textile manufacturing to flour mills to the mass production of the common pin. Its ability to save hand labor and contribute to the mass production of items was nothing short of remarkable, and in very little time entrepreneurs put this invention into widespread use. By 1781, Matthew Boulton, Watt's partner in a steam-engine manufacturing company, was claiming that "the people of London, Birmingham, and Manchester [are] all 'steam mill mad.'" From then on, the Industrial Revolution was in full force. Other inventions, such as Arkwright's spinning jenny and Maudslay's automatic screw machine, revolutionized other areas of production. "The Revolution . . . fed upon itself. The new techniques . . . simply destroyed their handicraft competition around the world and thus enormously increased their own markets" (Heilbroner and Milberg 2001:75–77).

For the city dweller, the most important change was the invention of the factory.

> The factory may be singled out as the agent which gives [the industrial–capitalist] city its structural form and social purpose. By the word "factory" I mean more than an industrial enterprise: the factory is the locus of mobilized abstract labor, of labor power as a commodity, placed in the service of commerce as well as production. Accordingly, the term applies as much to an office building and a supermarket as to a mill and a plant. Once the factory becomes an element of urban life, it takes over the city almost completely. (Bookchin 1996:51)

With the domination of the factory, the very symbolism of the city changed. The city in feudal Europe had been, above all, a Christian city, symbolically dominating the region with its Gothic cathedral. (A striking example is Venice, spread out around St. Mark's Cathedral, built in 1176.) The capitalist era, as Mumford remarked, turned the culture of feudalism on its head, transforming "six of the seven deadly sins [gluttony, pride, covetousness, envy, lust, and anger] into cardinal virtues (sloth became perhaps an even greater sin)" (1961:346). The church declined as the focal institution of society; in the place of spires appeared smokestacks, and the public plaza became a growing central business district.

> If capitalism tended to expand the market and turn every part of the city into a negotiable commodity, the change from [small-scale handicraft] to large-scale factory production transformed the industrial towns into dark hives, busily puffing, clanking, screeching, smoking for twelve and fourteen hours a day, sometimes going around the clock. The slavish routine . . . became the normal environment of the new industrial workers. None of these towns heeded the old saw, "All work and no play makes Jack a dull boy." [They] specialized in producing dull boys. (Mumford 1961:446)

In short, the dominant capitalist cultural theme, in conjunction with industrial

A multi-story mirrored building in Toronto's city center towers above an old stone church. The size and positioning of these buildings suggest dominant cultural themes of past and present. Today, we see the relative importance of economics and religion in contemporary Western society, unlike previous centuries when church steeples were the highest visible points in cities.

mechanization, created a new emphasis in urban consciousness. In describing a typical schoolroom in "Coketown," a fictionalized English factory city of the nineteenth century, Charles Dickens explained the main ingredient of this consciousness, presented in the Cityscape box on page 233.

Urban Life as Economics

"You are never to fancy!" With this phrase Dickens summarized what so worried Engels about the capitalist city: It reduced everything in life to objective facts and quantity. Other

CITYSCAPE

"Nothing but the Facts, Ma'am"—Capitalist–Industrialist Consciousness

"Now, what I want is, Facts. Teach these boys and girls nothing but Facts. Facts alone are wanted in life. Plant nothing else, and root out everything else. You can only form the minds of reasoning animals upon Facts: nothing else will ever be of any service to them. This is the principle on which I bring up my own children, and this is the principle on which I bring up these children. Stick to Facts, Sir!"

The scene was a plain, bare, monotonous vault of a schoolroom, and the speaker's square forefinger emphasized his observations by underscoring every sentence with a line on the schoolmaster's sleeve. The emphasis was helped by the speaker's square wall of a forehead, which had his eyebrows for its base, while his eyes found commodious cellerage in two dark caves, overshadowed by the wall. The emphasis was helped by the speaker's mouth, which was wide, thin, and hard set. . . .

"Thomas Gradgrind, Sir. A man of realities. A man of facts and calculations. A man who proceeds upon the principle that two and two are four, and nothing over, and who is not to be talked into allowing for anything over. Thomas Gradgrind, Sir—peremptorily Thomas—Thomas Gradgrind. With a rule and a pair of scales, and the multiplication table always in his pocket, Sir, ready to weigh and measure any parcel of human nature, and tell you exactly what it comes to. It is a mere question of figures, a case of simple arithmetic. . . .

"Girl number twenty," said Mr. Gradgrind, squarely pointing with his square forefinger, "I don't know that girl. Who is that girl?"

"Sissy Jupe, Sir," explained number twenty, blushing, standing up, and curtseying.

"Sissy is not a name," said Mr. Gradgrind. "Don't call yourself Sissy. Call yourself Cecilia."

"It's father as calls me Sissy, Sir," returned the young girl in a trembling voice, and with another curtsey.

"Then he has no business to do it," said Mr. Gradgrind. "Tell him he mustn't. Cecilia Jupe. Let me see. . . .

"Give me your definition of a horse."

(Sissy Jupe thrown into the greatest alarm by this demand.)

"Girl number twenty unable to define a horse!" said Mr. Gradgrind, for the general behoof of all the little pitchers. "Girl number twenty possessed of no facts, in reference to one of the commonest of animals! Some boy's definition of a horse. Bitzer, yours. . . ."

"Quadruped. Graminivorous. Forty teeth, namely twenty-four grinders, four eye-teeth, and twelve incisive. Sheds coat in the spring; in marshy countries, sheds hoofs, too. Hoofs hard, but requiring to be shod with iron. Age known by marks in mouth." Thus (and much more) Bitzer.

"Now girl number twenty," said Mr. Gradgrind. "You know what a horse is. . . ."

["But Sir," said Cecilia Jupe, blushing] . . . "I fancy . . ."

"Ay, ay, ay! But you mustn't fancy," cried the gentleman, quite elated by coming so happily to his point. "That's it! You are never to fancy!"

Source: Excerpt from Charles Dickens, *Hard Times* (London: Oxford University Press, 1955; orig. published 1854), pp. 1, 3–5, 7.

aspects of life—subjectivity, quality, art, music, politics, religion, and creative thought—were downplayed or consciously eradicated.

This new consciousness not only transformed how city people acted; it transformed the physical structure of the city itself, thereby intensifying the capitalist theme even further. Land, once merely a place to live, became real estate:

> If the layout of a town has no relation to human needs and activities other than business, the pattern of the city may be simplified: the ideal layout for the business [person] is that which can be most swiftly reduced to standard monetary units for purchase and sale. The fundamental [urban] unit is no longer the neighborhood . . . but the individual building lot, whose value can be gauged in terms of front feet: this favors an oblong with narrow frontage and great depth, which provides a minimum amount of light and air to the buildings, particularly the dwellings, that conform to it. Such units turned out equally advantageous for the land surveyor, the real estate speculator, the commercial builder, and the lawyer who drew up the deed of sale. In turn, the lots favored the rectangular building block, which again became the standard unit for extending the city. (Mumford 1961:421–22)

So strong was this pattern in the physical form of the city after the sixteenth century that even cities with mountainous geography (such as San Francisco), which might have benefited from a switchback or zigzag pattern to facilitate moving up and down the terrain, were subjected to a grid pattern.

Murray Bookchin used even stronger language to suggest the extent to which the modern Western city has been shaped by the industrial–capitalist system:

> Every esthetic urban pattern inherited from the past tends to be sacrificed to the grid system (in modern times, the factory pattern par excellence), which facilitates the most efficient transportation of goods and people. Streams are obliterated, variations in the landscape effaced without the least sensitivity to natural beauty, magnificent stands of trees removed, even treasured architectural and historical monuments demolished, and wherever possible, the terrain is leveled to resemble a factory floor. The angular

and curved streets of the medieval city which at every turn delighted the eye with a new and scenic tableau, are replaced by straight monotonous vistas of the same featureless buildings and shops. Lovely squares inherited from the past are reduced to nodal points for traffic, and highways are wantonly carved into vital neighborhoods, dividing and finally subverting them. (1996:90–91)

Assets and Debits

On one level, the capitalist city has unquestionably been successful in generating a higher material standard of living for a larger proportion of its population than any other urban system in history. For example, 12.1 percent of the U.S. population in metropolitan areas was below the poverty line in 2003, compared with 14.2 percent in nonmetropolitan areas. Useful material goods and technological innovations are omnipresent, and, given the "hands-off-the-individual" value that is so central to capitalism, there is a very real degree of political freedom, and other kinds of freedom, too, for residents of such cities. They can vote, come and go as they please, and (if they have the money) live where they like.

But there are debits as well: Millions of poor families live in cities, and districts that are unprofitable have fallen into shocking decay. Within such areas, as we will see in later chapters, people suffer incredibly. Similarly, the dominant focus on material goods and technological innovations often means that many people are preoccupied with the newest MP3 or DVD player or the latest car, and less mindful of social and environmental needs that require attention.

Finally, even freedoms have their problematic side. The freedom to accumulate wealth, prestige, and power has meant, over the years, that some individuals in our cities have much more of these scarce resources than others. With wealth primarily in the hands of a few (the richest 5 percent of the U.S. population controls 59 percent of the wealth), there is a tendency for these people to control both the economic and political spheres of life to such a degree that others are effectively cut off from any true success or representation.

Problems such as these led to a reaction: a second type of modern city, established around and intensifying yet another set of cultural themes, those of communism.

❖ CASE STUDY ❖
Communist Beijing

To get a sense of the contemporary communist city, we return to Peking. The Urban Living box below gets us acclimated. It records the first visit to the city by Liang Heng, a young Red Guard supporter of Chairman Mao Ze-dong, during the turmoil of the Cultural Revolution of the 1960s.

Standing on the Meridian Gate of the old Ming Imperial City (see Figures 8–1 and 8–2), looking out over the millions assembled in Tiananmen Square, Mao established the People's Republic of China on October 1, 1949. It was on this historic spot that Liang Heng gazed in rapture as a dedicated revolutionary in the late 1960s.

Today, five decades after Mao made that fateful pronouncement, Peking is a different city. Its feudal and imperial past has been almost completely eradicated. Even its name has been changed—to Beijing (the old name, *Peking*, was a Western transcription of *Beijing*). On the site of the old dynasties has arisen what is the most important communist city in the world, now that communism no longer dominates Russia and eastern Europe.

Modern Beijing thus provides us with a final illustration of the consequences of different cultural themes in urban places. The great walls that protected the city and the emperor in the Ming period are gone. In their place is a city-encircling highway, while below ground the city's modern subway system provides 75 miles of track along four major lines. The Forbidden City is now a museum open to all, surrounded by great new buildings of state: the Great Hall of the People, the Historical Museum, and the Mausoleum that holds

---

URBAN LIVING

Peking! Home of the Glorious Revolution!

Peking was cold to my sneakered feet, and the wind was like knives, but to me it was heaven. The avenues seemed five or six times as broad as those in [my home city of] Changsha, the buildings cleaner and more splendid, if a bit austere. I immediately demanded to be taken to Tian An Men Square, and tired as they were, my friends took me, watching with amusement as I stared at everything that was legend—the Great Hall of the People, the Monument of the Heroes of the People, the Historical Museum. Like every other Red Guard coming to Peking for the first time, I took my oath in front of the huge picture of Chairman Mao, lifting my "Little Red Book" in my right hand, sticking out my chest and reciting proudly, "Chairman Mao, Liang Heng has finally come to your side. I will always be loyal to you. I will always be loyal to your Thought. I will always be loyal to your Revolutionary line." I could have stayed there all night. . . .

Source: Liang Heng and Judith Shapiro, *Son of the Revolution* (New York: Vintage, 1984), pp. 114–15.

Mao's remains. The many multistoried hotels in Beijing easily dominate the old buildings of the emperor. Replaced, too, are many of the old, sonorous names of the imperial years. For example, the Pavillion of Pleasant Sounds has given way to People's Road and Anti-Imperialist Street.

However, Beijing in the twenty-first century is significantly different from the "austere" city that Liang Heng mentioned. Three or four decades ago, a rigid communist government controlled almost all aspects of life. Everyone dressed alike in dark, uniform-like clothes. Individuals could not own their own businesses and residential relocation—whether from one city to another, or from outlying rural areas to the city—was not allowed. Economic stagnation was the norm and social use of public urban spaces was virtually nonexistent, especially at night. In contrast, Beijing today, along with other Chinese cities, has embraced capitalistic enterprise and city life flourishes with individual enterprises, colorful fashions and consumer goods, nightlife, and a booming economy.

The Emergence of Modern Beijing

The Communists did not gain control of China easily. Ironically, the expansion of capitalist nations and their cities in the nineteenth century made it possible.

In 1644, the Ch'ing Dynasty replaced the Ming rulers who had built Imperial Peking. Like their Ming predecessors, the Ch'ing emperors were not interested in contact with the outside world, despite the fact that the world was interested in China. In the late 1700s and early 1800s—not coincidentally the time of the industrial–capitalist revolution—various European countries made overtures to China in hopes of finding yet another trade market, for they desired China's silk, tea, and silver. When the emperor rebuked them, tensions grew. The Europeans became determined to find a way to open China to trade, and the

Modern Beijing is an energetic city in which capitalism and consumerism flourish, as partly indicated in this view of the Wangfujing shopping street by Oriental Plaza. A lenient government policy towards individual enterprise has generated more spending money to enable Chinese urbanites to purchase additional goods and enjoy a higher standard of living than in years past.

Chinese were just as determined to keep them out.

The denouement came in the mid-nineteenth century. For many years, the British had been smuggling India-grown poppies into China. Converted into opium and mixed with tobacco for smoking, the poppies gave rise to China's infamous opium dens, which served an estimated 2 million addicts by 1835. Finally, enraged, an imperial commissioner from Beijing seized and destroyed over 2.8 million pounds of opium in Canton in 1839. It was a fateful decision. Later the same year the English launched the so-called Opium War as a punitive action. They won hands down; the resulting treaty opened five Chinese ports to unrestricted trade and established the British colony of Hong Kong. In 1860 another war and treaty forcibly opened more Chinese ports to European trade.

Severely weakened, the ruling dynasty lost the Sino-Japanese War in 1895 and, during the antiforeigner Boxer Rebellion of 1900, fled Beijing. Chinese insurgents held Peking for 55 days against an eight-nation "relief force." The insurgents' inevitable defeat placed China almost completely under foreign domination. In 1911, Dr. Sun Yat-sen overthrew the remnants of the dynasty and proclaimed a Chinese Republic. Chiang Kai-shek succeeded him in 1927, but power struggles throughout the country meant that the government remained ineffectual.

Angered by the disadvantageous trade relations that the republic still tolerated with foreign countries, in 1934 China's fledgling Communist Party under Mao Ze-dong undertook the 6,000-mile Long March through China's countryside to escape Chiang Kai-shek's army. The Communists returned in 1948 and, after a six-week siege, occupied Peking and proclaimed the People's Republic the following year.

Urban Life as Politics

The Communists vowed to free China from centuries of domination of the many by the few and from exploitation by foreign countries. To do this they transformed nearly all of Chinese life into an expression of the new political ideas. The job of the state was to provide equally for everyone; the job of the individual was to contribute to the state's success by participating unselfishly in the state-linked neighborhood units, school classes, factories, and party committees. Only by collectivizing everything, the Communists believed, and by constantly reminding everyone of the dangers of backsliding into individualism, was true progress to be attained.

The key concept in all this was *tzu-li keng-sheng*—"self-reliance" or "regeneration through one's own efforts." In developing this concept, the party divided each city into districts (Beijing has nine), each district into neighborhoods, and each neighborhood into smaller residential areas. Each residential area developed its own "residents' committee," designed to link each individual with the city authorities and vice versa. It became the job of these committees to oversee local services—security, fire, and sanitation—and to keep political responsibility uppermost in peoples' minds (Whyte and Parish 1985:21–22).

Study groups developed unceasing political awareness in which all neighborhood residents participated (there also were study groups in schools and factories). The tasks of these groups were three: (1) to communicate to all citizens the importance of participation in all areas of life; (2) to chastise political trouble-makers of all kinds, such as "revisionists," "factionalists," "ultra-Leftists," "capitalists," and "imperialists"; and (3) to examine constantly through group self-criticism each individual's performance. The intent was to discourage individualism while encouraging both **groupthink**—conformity to opinions that supposedly reflect group consensus—and control through many eyes of each person's actions. It is difficult to imagine more contrasting views of city life than those outlined above and those held by people of contemporary Western cities.

The Difficulties of Urban Life

Beijing's population in 1949, the year of the declaration of the People's Republic, was less than 2.5 million. (Today it is over 7.7 million and bursting at the seams.) Successful in feeding and housing its people, China nevertheless remained saddled with a primitive industrial system and an inferior educational system that left it in desperate need of trained personnel (China was an almost entirely peasant society until the 1950s). Its standing as a world-class economic power remained elusive, and the nation was not able to provide widespread high-quality education.

To curb these problems, in 1959 Mao initiated the "Great Leap Forward," an unsuccessful crash program aimed at improving industry and production. He also launched the "Great Proletarian Cultural Revolution" in 1966 to eliminate "revisionism." Ironically, the overzealous youth movement associated with the Cultural Revolution, the Red Guards (of which Liang Heng was a passionate member), closed the universities, impaired production, and brought many Chinese cities to an almost dead stop until they were finally brought under control by the army.

Economic Reform

With Mao's death in 1976, a great power struggle emerged in Beijing for the control of the party—a struggle won by Deng Xiaoping and his followers. The new leaders de-emphasized the more extreme elements of Maoism and moved from a sluggish Soviet-style centrally planned economy to a more market-oriented economy, but one still within a rigid political framework of Communist Party control. To this end the authorities switched to a system of household responsibility in agriculture in place of the old collectivization, increased the authority of local officials and plant managers in industry, permitted a wide variety of small-scale enterprise in services and light manufacturing, and opened the economy to increased foreign trade and investment. The result has been a quadrupling of the gross domestic product (GDP) since 1978, making China the second largest economy in the world. China's economic reforms

have benefited hundreds of millions of people, giving them a better diet and better standard of living (Nationmaster 2004).

One long-term threat to continued rapid economic growth is the deterioration in the environment, with increasing air pollution and soil erosion and a steady fall in the water table, especially in the north. China continues to lose arable land because of erosion and economic development, but the government is spending on the infrastructure—such as water control and power grids. Presently though, China is home to 16 of the 20 most polluted cities in the world. It is now the world's second biggest generator of carbon dioxide emissions and could overtake the United States as the biggest source of greenhouse gases in three decades (Luard 2004).

A Rising Consumerism

Visitors to Beijing today find a city alive with energy. In one section of the city—just south of the old Forbidden City—is a shopping section for the capital's citizens. Beneath billboards advertising Toshiba TV sets are department stores filled with goods, with no shortage of lookers and buyers. One reason for this increasing consumerism is the additional spending money generated by the new policies encouraging individual enterprise. For example, in another part of the city is a farmers' market where workers from a local commune sell surplus vegetables not needed for the commune or for state consumption. They are allowed to keep the profits from such transactions. Some young people, selected by the government to go abroad to teach Chinese in a North American college, earn Western salaries—astronomical by Chinese standards. When they return to Beijing, they are allowed to keep the money they have saved and are thus able to afford better apartments in new sections of the city and to provide their families with a variety of consumer goods.

All this change—a movement "from Marxism to Mastercard"—has its critics. Many powerful Communist Party members see the revolution of Mao being "sold out," and, as an indication that the policies of Deng and his

Through the global economy and pop culture, cultural diffusion impacts on any city and its culture, yet few would think this is a scene anywhere in North America, not even in Chinatown. In Beijing, China, a delivery rider rests on his tricycle in front of a billboard promoting Pepsi, featuring pictures of pop singers Janet Jackson, Guo Fucheng, Wang Fei, and Ricky Martin.

successors are not all positive, they cite extensive evidence that corruption is now beginning to appear in many areas of Chinese life as people scramble for the accoutrements of a consumer society. They charge that the current policies generate self-centeredness and a kind of Western decadence. In fact, theft and prostitution, once virtually nonexistent, are now as common as in Western cities. Nonetheless, the open-door policy continues, and China and its cities once again are in the throes of major social change.

❖ ▬▬▬▬▬▬ ❖ ▬▬▬▬▬▬ ❖

SUMMARY

Ramona thought about the city.
—I have to admit we are locked in the most exquisite, mysterious muck. This muck heaves and palpitates. It is multidirectional and has a mayor . . . . Our muck is only a part of a much greater muck—the nation-state— which is itself the creation of that muck of mucks, human consciousness.

Donald Barthelme, *City Life,* 1978

The city does not exist by itself but is linked intricately to the broader society of which it is a part. Any city's physical and social forms are shaped by the cultural values of that society and by its historical epoch. For example, although there is some truth in the old idea that the ways of the country and the city are distinct and "ne'er the twain shall meet," recent research has shown that cities and their countrysides are bound together in a complex interdependence that allows each to have significant influence over the other.

Cities are not entirely synonymous with civilization. They are symbolic centers that concentrate, intensify, and re-create the cultural forces found throughout the society. Also, each city creates its own civic culture that makes it unique compared to other cities in the same society. In the cities we compared and contrasted in this chapter—Boston and Ibadan, Ming Peking and Hellenic Athens, nineteenth-century industrial–capitalist London and contemporary industrial–communist Beijing—we found significant differences. These differences attest to the importance of culture in shaping the social and physical environment of the city. Only by studying cities in a comparative manner can we understand this urban variability. As Brian Berry said, "The most fundamental axiom of . . . urban sociology is that the urban landscape is a mirror reflecting the society that maintains it" (1985:96).

CONCLUSION

If urban variety is so marked, what is left as distinctively urban? What do all the cities we've considered in this chapter have in common? To answer this question, we certainly must go beyond the factors of size, density, and heterogeneity proposed by Louis Wirth. We propose a new definition of the city, one that acknowledges the importance of the cultural dimension that Wirth neglected: In comparison with other types of permanent human settlement, *a city is a relatively large, dense settlement that has a civic culture and a complex social structure that greatly reflects, intensifies, and re-creates cultural values and forms.*

A few comments are necessary to clarify this definition. The first set of characteristics— "a large, dense settlement"—is Wirth's; he seems quite right about them. The next characteristic—"a complex social structure"—is from V. Gordon Childe (1950). You may recall that Wirth also suggested that the city is composed of "socially heterogeneous individuals." By this he meant that people of different racial, ethnic, and religious backgrounds tend to mingle in the city. Anthropological research has shown that this is more accurately descriptive of modern Western cities (to which people of different countries migrate) than it is of their nonindustrial counterparts (such as Ibadan and Beijing). Yet, even if social heterogeneity is not characteristic of all

cities, nearly every urbanist has noted that the city has a more complex division of labor and a more sophisticated political system (if only to handle the large numbers and density) than do other forms of human settlement. Such complexities are what we mean by "a complex social structure."

Finally, the idea that any city is a reflector, intensifier, and re-creator of cultural values and forms is a direct outgrowth of this chapter. In the final analysis, the nature of any city lies in its unique ability to interpret a particular set of cultural values in a distinctive form. By "cultural values" we mean those shared beliefs and ideas that characterize any social group of long duration. By "form" we mean the typical round of everyday activities and arrangement of urban space that characterize any city. Thus, because the cultural values of the Greeks during Athens's Golden Era (the fifth century B.C.E.) regarded moneymaking as secondary and a holistic life as primary, we found that the daily life of the city was dominated by dialogue, politics, recreation, and ritual. While the Greeks surely went to the agora (the market) to trade, they just as frequently went there to talk and relax. Even their buildings reflected this cultural emphasis. The Acropolis, where the most important buildings of Greek civilization were located (the Parthenon, the Erechtheum, the Propylea, the Temple of Athena Nike), sits on a hill overlooking the rest of the city. The agora, lesser in importance, lies at the bottom of the hill. All this appears reversed when we consider the form of contemporary capitalist cities such as those of North America. Here the round of daily activities focuses on the economic. Most people spend the bulk of their day getting and spending, and planning for more of the same. Dialogue, politics, recreation, and ritual come later—in the evenings, on the weekends, during the two-week vacation. The city's physical layout reflects this cultural priority. Streets are arranged on a grid for easy movement and buying and selling, and the most important buildings—at least those that dominate the skyline of any major North American city—are those of commerce.

In such comparative observations lies a crucial lesson about studying cities: Quite simply, if we don't understand the relationship between the city and culture, we can't properly understand the city. As alluded to in our discussion of the emergence of modern Beijing, we also need to consider the role of economic power in dictating quality of life and urban land use. It is to this perspective that we turn in the next chapter.

KEY TERMS

Civic culture
Culture
Groupthink
Industrialism
Urban dominance

CHAPTER 9

THE NEW URBAN SOCIOLOGY
The City and Capitalism

In the early 1970s, an alternative theoretical approach to urban ecology began to take form. In part, this development was a response to what its proponents saw as deficiencies of the earlier urban ecology model described in Chapter 7. But it was also a response to the turmoil of the times. The late 1960s and early 1970s were a period of upheaval in both the United States and Europe, prompting a more critical and political outlook on society. Not surprisingly, many scholars were led to reexamine the assumption that geography and technology were the main factors shaping urban life.

These "new" urbanists highlighted the distribution of wealth and political power in the city. They noted that the wealthiest people lived on the most desirable land and enjoyed the greatest access to the city's services. Is it any accident, they asked, that the city's best schools are situated in the city's richest neighborhoods? Or that new superhighways tear through old urban neighborhoods, with patent disregard for poor residents, to better serve the city's elite and those who have fled to the wealthy suburbs? Their answer was a resounding "No!" On the contrary, they concluded, "the structure of the city is to be explained by the pursuit of profit, which is the *raison d'être* of capitalist society, modified by the actions of the State, which has the functions of preserving and legitimizing this society" (Hall 1984:32).

This alternative approach has come to be known as "the new urban sociology" (Gottdiener and Hutchison 2000). In truth, however, most of its theoretical arguments are quite old, drawing heavily on the ideas of Karl Marx (1818–1883). What is new is their application to the city and, more specifically, to recent trends such as globalization of the economy, economic restructuring in the United States, and the proliferation of megacities and edge cities.

The heart of this new approach is a central reliance on *political economy theory* and its application to urban life. That is, urban life is to be understood in terms of the social structures and processes of change that benefit some groups at the expense of others (Gottdiener and Feagin 1988). Before we examine some of the major aspects of this new perspective—which has become the dominant view in the field—we will review some earlier contributions to political and economic analysis, which drew on the ecological model discussed in Chapter 7.

URBAN ECONOMICS: THE TRADITIONAL PERSPECTIVE

People who know cities often have an image of a vibrant downtown, a place where the action is, where the buildings are taller and the lights brighter. That is, indeed, an accurate image of North American, European, or "westernized" cities. Approaching a major city at night along a dark highway, one sees first the distant glow of the city lights even before making out the evening skyline. Barring an electrical blackout, large areas of the center city are never dark. Why? Why shouldn't the "action" be everywhere? Why should the tall buildings be concentrated in a single area?

Central Place Theory

To begin to answer these questions, realize that the city is the only place where everything human comes together. Compared with the fixed life of rural areas or the small town, the city's possibilities are practically limitless. Indeed, the city is the place where the mix of people and ideas makes the creation of new things easy. The city, by its very nature, promotes "interaction and fusion" (Mumford 1961:568).

Note, further, that as one approaches the center of the city, the level of human activity becomes more intense. The greatest action is, literally, in the center, where people contact each other more frequently. There, in the "downtown," one finds the greatest economic advantages that cities can offer.

The Economic Advantages of Cities.   Cities tend to be located where important *goods or services* are available in abundance (Winston-Salem, Raleigh, and Durham, North Carolina, are in the heart of tobacco-producing country) or where goods and services can be obtained easily (New Orleans is near the mouth of the Mississippi River). In either case, a prime location means that cities obtain, produce, and distribute their goods and services more cheaply than smaller settlements can. To ship heating oil to Albany, New York, costs a certain amount, but to further transport that oil to the small town of Ticonderoga, 100 miles away, adds additional transportation and handling costs.

Second, cities play host to what economists call **agglomeration industries.** Take Detroit, home of the automobile industry. Because the major U.S. car manufacturers have their home bases there, the city also attracts various subindustries to serve them—companies manufacturing car paints or engine pistons, for example. The Big Three automakers share these subindustries, which benefits everyone involved, including the customer, who ultimately buys the car for less. Other examples of famous agglomeration industries are the entertainment industry in Los Angeles and Hollywood, meatpacking in Chicago, country music in Nashville, and the fashion industry in New York. In each case, the presence of agglomeration industries keeps production costs lower than they might be in a smaller settlement.

A third economic advantage of cities, particularly those based on a free-enterprise system, is that *competition* among various producers works to keep costs down and quality up for various goods and services. Because so many businesses of the same type exist in cities, no business can charge a great deal more than its competitors for the same product. To do so, in a competitive environment, would simply mean that customers would go elsewhere to find a better deal, with predictable

Perhaps nowhere in North America is the global economy as visible as in the daily loading and unloading of container shipments onto or off trucks and ships at its seaports, such as here in Long Beach, California. While many import and export goods are finished products on their way to wholesalers, many others are parts destined for assembly in factories in nations other than the ones in which they were manufactured.

consequences for the company's future. For the same reason, if one business offers poor quality goods at the same price at which a competitor sells a better product, which firm will prosper?

But what about a business in a small town with little competition? There businesses typically offer less value to their customers, since it's too inconvenient and expensive for most local people to go to the city to get the lower price or the better product.

Competition also explains why so many businesses of the same type tend to cluster together in the city. In fact, most cities have entire districts devoted solely to the computer, furniture, camera, automobile, fashion, jewelry, or entertainment businesses. The reasons for such proximity are easy to understand. Businesses of the same type that are located near one another can (1) know what their competitors are up to by simply walking across the street; (2) provide a single locale where customers can easily engage in comparison shopping; and (3) share agglomeration services, thereby making the products cheaper for everyone.

Fourth and finally, cities can offer higher-quality products at lower prices because they stand amidst a *greater population*. This means that urban businesses have a larger available work force than do their rural counterparts; thus, other things being equal, they can hire the more qualified people. Just as important, urban companies benefit from a larger pool of customers.

For these four reasons, the city has marked economic advantages over the hinterland. Once established, a city may operate as a "magnet" or a "growth machine," becoming more and more productive as it draws raw materials and people from all around (Mumford 1961; Molotch 1976).

Within the city, economic advantages increase as one nears the city center; for this reason, people who stand to benefit from those advantages want to locate near there. This principle points up why we find at the city's center a **central business district** (CBD), and why, at the city's center, the action truly is greater, the buildings taller, and the lights brighter.

The Urban Hierarchy.   Basic economic advantages also help explain why some cities grow much larger than others. The largest cities are just more centrally located relative to important goods or services. Chicago is a major urban center because of its location at the southern end of Lake Michigan and also because of its centrality to the nation's population. A century ago, Chicago thrived as the ideal location for shipping goods from the heavily settled Northeast to all other regions of the nation. Similarly, Chicago was a natural stopover for people heading westward. In comparison, Milwaukee, another major Great Lakes port, is less centrally located. Therefore, as Chicago developed into a major city, Milwaukee evolved into a second-tier urban area.

That cities should arrange themselves into hierarchical order should come as no surprise. Common sense suggests as much—all Iowans know, for example, that Des Moines is a more important city than the college town of Fairfield. It was not until the 1930s, however, that German geographer Walter Christaller incorporated this pattern into what is known as **central place theory** (1966; originally published 1933). Christaller suggested that the more important a city's economic function to a region, the more its population will increase. In turn, the city's hinterland—smaller cities, towns, and rural areas—becomes dependent on the large city for many goods and services that their smaller populations cannot support. Of course, this makes the city grow even more.

Christaller also suggested that, all else being equal, cities (especially smaller ones) space themselves in order that they do not cut into each other's markets. That is, cities emerge at "distance intervals," so that each serves a local hinterland. The upstate New York area provides an example: Stretched along the New York State Thruway, at least 75 miles apart, are the major urban areas of Buffalo–Niagara Falls (2004 population: 1.2 million), Rochester (1 million), Syracuse (654,000), Utica–Rome (299,000), and Albany–Schenectady–Troy (845,000).

Over a fairly large geographical region then, we can expect cities to be distributed by size. Most numerous will be smaller, *local* cities (Geneva, New York, for example); next up the scale will be fewer but larger *regional* cities (such as Rochester); and, more significant, a smaller number of large, *national* cities (Pittsburgh and Philadelphia); and, finally, a very few, very large *world* cities like New York, Paris, and Tokyo. North America's world city, New York, is centrally located within the populous Northeast and affords easy access to the entire United States and Europe. There one can discover virtually anything from Indonesian restaurants to dozens of Broadway, off-Broadway, off-off-Broadway, and local theater groups. In smaller cities, of course, Indonesian restaurants are usually nowhere to be found and theatergoers must be content with pre-Broadway trial runs, post-Broadway tours, or small local theater offerings. This is why, over the last century or two, people have sometimes referred disparagingly to lower-order cities as "one-horse towns." Or, as essayist Alexander Woollcott put it back in the 1930s: "A hick town is one where there is no place to go you shouldn't be."

The General Pattern of Land Use

This vertical place is no more an accident than the Himalayas are. The city needs all these tall buildings to contain the tremendous energy there.

Edward Field

Imagine you are traveling through the countryside toward any North American city. At the beginning of the trip, there are fields and perhaps some scattered farms or houses. As you approach the city, built-up residential areas appear, increasing in density as you near the city's center.

A Theoretical Model.   Is this pattern typical of North American cities you know? If you think it is, economist William Alonso (1971) would say that this perception is no accident, as cities definitely use their land in a patterned way.

In building a model, Alonso described the ideal case, assuming that (1) the city existed in a completely flat, featureless place; (2) it had a single CBD; (3) efficient transportation existed in all directions; and (4) every person in the city was motivated by economic self-interest.

Alonso was well aware that, in real life, many of these assumptions might not hold. For example, San Francisco exists on hills, the Minneapolis–St. Paul metropolis has two CBDs, Philadelphia's subway system runs only to certain parts of the city, and the Mormons who founded Salt Lake City were hardly motivated by purely economic interests. Similarly, Alonso knew that other factors such as ethnic relationships, politics, and history all play a role in urban life. Nevertheless, Alonso's model helps us see how *economic concerns* shape city land use. Only those who can pay the most will locate in the city's center. This is why the downtown is primarily a business district, with whatever residential property exists there taking the form of smaller apartments typically piled high on a small amount of land.

Overall, Alonso's model suggests a city with two major districts: (1) a CBD in the middle occupied by businesses of various types (offices, industries, warehouses) and (2) the surrounding, mostly residential areas. Circling the residential district would be yet other rings, containing businesses that require even more land and where rents are even lower. In such urban fringe areas, we might expect to find junkyards, cemeteries, golf courses, and farmland. (If one ever found a CBD golf course, however, one could bet that the cost of going nine holes would be expensive, indeed!) Farther out still, as population dwindles away, we would begin to find little except farms.

Figure 9–1 summarizes Alonso's model of urban land use. As it shows, businesses pay the highest rents to be near the CBD. As the distance from the CBD grows, the number of businesses declines until, at some point, they cease altogether. This means that, despite the lower rents, it is not economically feasible to operate a business there since it requires giving up the trade advantages of being in or near the CBD.

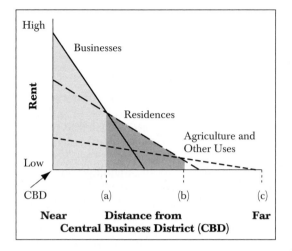

FIGURE 9–1   The Economics of Urban Land Use

Most residents cannot afford the high rents of the CBD and so they live some distance away. As distance increases, rents continue to drop, but, at some point, no matter how low the rent, transportation problems in terms of time and money become so great that virtually no city workers choose to live there. People engaged in agriculture and other land-intensive pursuits can least afford to pay CBD rentals; hence their businesses appear only a considerable distance from the CBD.

The Case of the Inner-City Poor.   At this point you may be agreeing with Alonso's general conclusions but wondering why most inner cities in North America also have many poor neighborhoods. If Alonso is correct, poor people, unable to afford high rents, should be living a long distance from the CBD.

Let's take a closer look. With little disposable income, poor people are unable to pay high rents. But they also cannot afford the high costs of travel from a remote area. Therefore, many poor people do pay higher rents than they would farther out, so they can live near the CBD. But to do so, they live in high-density housing, perhaps sharing an apartment with another family or assisted through a rent subsidy program. Also, the rents in

these neighborhoods are set at what the market will bear. If it is an undesirable poor neighborhood, landlords can only charge as much rent as low-income households can afford. However, if this neighborhood undergoes gentrification with more affluent residents moving in, the rents go much higher, forcing out those unable to afford them. Alonso's general conclusion then becomes applicable again.

On the other side of the coin, more affluent families can and do accept the higher cost of commuting from outside the CBD. But they do so mostly because they demand a great deal of space, which only a suburban neighborhood can provide within their budgets. And, no doubt, many find additional "value" in having few poor people as neighbors.

Criticisms of the Basic Theory

Some scholars, like Michael P. Todaro and Stephen P. Smith (2005), question whether free enterprise, in the sense assumed by the proponents of the economic theory we have just discussed, really exists at all. To them, consumers are too powerless to set the agenda for a society's economic production. The Critical Thinking box on page 248 takes a closer look at this question.

To illustrate this criticism, consider "Blackston," a pseudonym for a poor black area of a major eastern city. There, Betty Lou Valentine (1980) compared supermarket prices with those in surrounding, higher-income white neighborhoods. She found that poor African Americans paid *significantly higher prices* for their groceries in Blackston than more affluent whites living elsewhere did. Why? Supermarket owners in Blackston think of African Americans as "captured customers." Because of the expense and inconvenience of going to white neighborhoods (most black families in Blackston do not own cars) and because of the overt prejudice they encounter when they do, most blacks have little choice but to do their shopping locally. Knowing this, Blackston supermarket owners can charge more than storeowners whose customers can easily

CRITICAL THINKING

Does Free *Enterprise Really Exist?*

In economic theory, the basic questions of what and how much to produce are assumed to be determined by the aggregate preferences of all consumers as revealed by their market demand for different goods and services. Producers are assumed simply to respond to these "sovereign" consumer preferences and, motivated by the desire to maximize profits, they are assumed to compete with each other *on equal terms* in the purchase of resources and the sale of their products. . . . The ultimate rationale for the efficacy of this theory or model of economic activity is Adam Smith's famous notion of the "invisible hand" of capitalism, which postulates that if each individual consumer, producer and supplier of resources pursues his or her own self-interest, they will, "as if by an invisible hand," be promoting the overall interests of society as a whole.

Unfortunately, the facts of economic life in both the developed and the less developed nations of the world are such as to render much of [this] theory of negligible importance. . . . Consumers as a whole are rarely sovereign about anything, let alone with regard to questions of what goods and services are to be produced, in what quantities and for whom. Producers, whether private or public, have great power in determining market prices and quantities sold. The ideal of competition is typically just that—an "ideal" with little relation to reality. Finally, the so-called "invisible hand" often acts not to promote the general welfare of all, but to lift up those already well-off while pushing down that vast majority of the population which is striving to free itself from poverty, malnutrition, and illiteracy.

Source: Michael P. Todaro and Stephen C. Smith, *Economic Development,* 9th ed. (Boston: Addison-Wesley, 2005), p. 14.

---

climb in their cars and shop elsewhere. The point is that, to the extent that people cannot really choose where to shop, the free-enterprise system is an ideal rather than a reality.

Valentine's observation that people of color often encounter overt prejudice illustrates a second problem with Alonso's economic model: People do not live by bread alone. Important noneconomic factors also influence urban land use. People in some neighborhoods may actively resist any "undesirables" who seek to move nearby. This resistance often extends beyond personal attitudes, influencing zoning laws and the practices of real estate agents that can keep people from housing they may be able to afford. In an examination of the affluent suburb of Brookhaven on Long Island, Roger

Williams (1978) reported widespread resistance to a proposed low-income housing project that would allow some poor families to live in Brookhaven. This resistance, often tinged with racism, soon surfaced in local politics:

> In a local election campaign last fall, Bob Hughes, the Republican candidate for town supervisor, warned against the "teeming hordes" who would descend on Brookhaven if it provided low-income housing. "It's the pull-up-the-gangplank syndrome," says [a] county official. "I'm here, so don't let anybody else in—especially any of those people." (1978:18)

A third type of criticism points out that Alonso's economic theory applies to only a limited range of cities. For example, the capitalist–industrial city (on which the economic theory is based) is only *one* of at least five major city types that have existed historically. Other types include *regal–ritual* cities (with political and religious concerns at their core), *administrative cities* (with many government activities), *colonial cities* (that manage a colonial region for another nation), and *mercantile cities* (with trade as their principal concern). Of these, only the last operates on similar economic principles to the modern Western city. In the others, people are not making decisions based on the economic principles assumed by Alonso.

None of this is to say that Alonso's theory is wrong. But, clearly, it is limited in its utility and is but one model of how the free market makes use of land. Let's look at a different model of land use as a prelude to examining a newer, more dominant economic model, as delineated in the new urban sociology.

POLITICAL ECONOMY: THE "NEW" PERSPECTIVE

By the end of the 1960s, an increasing number of social scientists found that the traditional economic model, as well as conventional theories of urban ecology, no longer accounted for many important changes in cities. In North American cities, one had to look beyond the city itself to understand the dramatic decline in industrial jobs; the movement of millions of people from the cities to the suburbs; the movement from the Snowbelt to the Sunbelt; and the intensifying financial problems of so many cities. Some other model seemed necessary to explain the new urban realities, thus setting the stage for the political economy approach.

Several assumptions served as the foundation for the new approach. First, any city exists within the larger political structures of county, state, and nation. Beyond that, international political processes—such as oil embargos, trade agreements, hostilities—can affect urban life on a local level. Second, local economies do not operate independently but connect to one another to forge state, national, and international economic networks.

Most important, the new breed of social scientists began to discount the notion that "natural processes" shape the physical form and social life of cities in favor of the belief that political and economic institutions—including banks, governments, and international corporations—shape urban life.

One key focus is the role of investment decisions in shaping cities. Who makes decisions that direct a city's economy? And for what purposes? In addition, the political economy approach investigates how conflicts—between labor and management, between racial and ethnic populations, and between social classes—have shaped the physical and social character of cities.

The new political economy viewpoint drew together geographers and philosophers as well as sociologists specializing in the investigation of urban development. Drawing on the ideas of Karl Marx, such thinkers as Henri Lefebvre, David Harvey, Manuel Castells, and Allen Scott argued that urban changes must be understood in the light of historical economic and political forces.

Henri Lefebvre: Redefining the Study of Cities

French philosopher Henri Lefebvre (1902–1991) sparked the application of the critical and Marxian perspective to studying the city. Drawing from the writings of Karl Marx and his associate Friedrich Engels, Lefebvre (1970, 1991) applied the economic categories of capital, labor, profit, wages, class exploitation, and inequality to explain the unevenness of urban development. In doing so, he helped develop many ideas about cities to which Marx and Engels never devoted much attention. He thus became a seminal source of new thinking about the city, suggesting that urban development was as much a product of the capitalist economic system as was any manufactured good.

Two Circuits of Capital.   To advance his concept, Lefebvre made a distinction between two types of investment capital. He identified the commonly studied economic activity—investment to hire workers to manufacture a product to sell at a profit to be used for more investment—as the **primary circuit of capital.** Thus, in a capitalist system the main flow of money is from investors into materials and labor costs to create a manufactured good whose sale generates profits for still more manufacturing ventures. This continual circulation of manufacturing capital generates much wealth for investors but is also what pumps the national economy. Hence Lefebvre named this circular money flow the *primary* one.

To examine the unevenness of urban development, Lefebvre identified another important profit-oriented economic activity—real estate investment—as the **second circuit of capital.** Investment in land, he maintained, almost always leads to profit and serves as an important means for acquiring wealth. One buys property expecting it to appreciate in value or develops land for residential or commercial purposes—both of which yield a profit. The circuit becomes complete when the investor takes that profit and invests it in more land-based projects.

Within a city, he suggested, profit-seeking motives determine the stability, decline, or rejuvenation of various areas. Lefebvre's focus on real estate investment pushing city growth in certain ways was a turning point that influenced subsequent theories and analyses of the dynamics of urban development.

Space as Part of Social Organization. Lefebvre made a second important contribution with his assertion that space is more than just a social "container"; it is also closely linked to behavior. That is, we construct our surroundings to meet particular needs and objectives; our surroundings, in turn, affect our subsequent behavior. People thus organize their daily lives and actions—whether cultural, economic, educational, or social—within constraints or opportunities of the built environment. We need to think of planners and developers, then, as important architects of social life. Lefebvre added that comparable social systems organize space similarly, so that edge cities or suburbs in Australia, Canada, or

the United States, for example, closely resemble one another.

The Role of Government. Venturing further into territory uncharted by Marx, Lefebvre also considered the actions of government, from the national level down to the local level, as a critical factor shaping a city's use of space. Governments are empowered to make various decisions that affect city shape and urban life—decisions that range from condemnations of structures, claims of eminent domain, provision of funding, approving new roads or alterations to roads, supervising urban renewal, and responding to zoning appeals. The federal and state governments also collect taxes from, and distribute resources to, various lower-level political units (states, counties, and municipalities). The government also directly owns a great deal of urban land (fire, police, and government buildings; parks, roads) and exercises control over the rest (zoning, tax valuation). With all these forms of social control over space utilization, governments can strike deals to attract corporations to a certain locale or take many other actions to encourage development or redevelopment of an area.

Further, Lefebvre distinguishes between two definitions of space: **abstract space** and **social space.** The first is what businesspeople, investors, and government have in mind when they discuss the dimensions of size, location, and profit. The second is what individuals who live, work, and play in an area think about their environment. Often, Lefebvre claims, government and business talk about abstract space—plans, say, to build a shopping mall or construct a low-income housing project—paying little attention to the ideas of local people. The resulting conflict, continues Lefebvre, is much the same as (but not identical to) the class conflict discussed by Marx.

These three ideas of Lefebvre—two circuits of capitalism, space as a component of social organization, and the role of government in managing space—were highly influential in charting the course others would take. Most new theories in urban development trace their origins to this French philosopher, although many later theorists do not agree with all of Lefebvre's arguments.

Urban Areas as Themed Environments

An excellent example of Lefebvre's ideas is in the recycling of abandoned factories and docks into redeveloped areas that emphasize a heritage and leisure experience (Ward 1998). This transformation of public space into a packaged, themed environment has been a dominant land use pattern since the 1960s (Sorkin 1992; Gottdiener 2001). At the forefront of such efforts was developer James W. Rouse, who worked to rejuvenate dying downtowns by introducing so-called festival marketplaces, Fanueil Hall in Boston, Harborplace in Baltimore, and the South Street Seaport in Manhattan.

Although these themed public space areas are well known and prosperous, many other cities have also rediscovered their own waterfront areas. Seattle, Cincinnati, Cleveland, Louisville, and Memphis—to name just a few—have redeveloped them with parks, restaurants, stores, and various activities. Although each city's waterfront view may vary somewhat, one finds a generic similarity existing among all such areas in all cities. Similarly, historic districts—from San Diego's Gaslamp Quarter to Boston's Faneuil Hall marketplace—have their own unique charm, but their redevelopment to lure patrons to their shops, restaurants, and entertainment locales results in a somewhat homogeneous design.

Perhaps though, the epitome of themed urban space is not in the rebuilding of an old urban environment, but rather in the building of an artificial city environment as a theme park *away from* the city (such as Disney's Main Street). Built at a cost of $3 billion and opened in 1993, another such entity is CityWalk in Universal City, California. Originally intended to encourage traffic between Universal Studios' theme park and its Odeon Theatre to generate additional profits, it became not just a spectacular success in that regard, but its own destination as well for millions of visitors.

Promoted as possessing "all the glitz and excitement of an actual urban boulevard, but with none of the problems associated with real city life: no carjackers, no panhandlers, no grime, no graffiti, no hookers, no muggers—yet also with no mall roof to block out the sunny skies or night time stars," CityWalk claims that, "for once, walking outside in the 'city' is completely safe" (Wayne 2005). Designed by Jon Jerde, the same architect who created the massive Mall of America in Minnesota, CityWalk features outrageous architecture that uses every visual trick imaginable to wow the passing crowds, along with numerous street performers (mimes, magicians, musicians, and entertaining street vendors). In Orlando, Florida, Universal Studios offers a smaller CityWalk combination of shops, restaurants, cinemas, live entertainment, and nightclubs as a gateway between its two theme parks, Universal Studios and Islands of Adventure.

Whatever entertainment value private themed environments may have, critics warn of their dangers. Michael Sorkin (1992), for example, says that they are not benign imitations, but instead manipulative structures designed to maximize behavior control and eliminate authentic interaction as found in traditional public space. Mark Gottdiener believes that, in the aftermath of the cold, faceless public space left behind by the modernist era, the forces of capitalism have staged a "vengeful return of meaning and symbolism" to create "material space for the realization of consumer fantasies" through imitation and simulation (2001:34, 70). The problem with this is that we lose our reality as we buy into a visual theme, turning our landscape inside out, and becoming convinced that all places are the same in the built environment that excludes other forms (Zukin 1993).

David Harvey: The Baltimore Study

The prominent English geographer David Harvey (1992; 1973) illustrates Lefebvre's ideas in a Marxist analysis of how the capitalist real estate system operated in Baltimore, directly shaping many of the city's problems concerning social inequality. He divided Baltimore into real estate submarkets that included the inner city, white ethnic areas, the low- to moderate-income African American area of West Baltimore, areas of high turnover, middle-income areas in Northeast and Southwest Baltimore, and other upper-income areas. Each of these areas revealed a distinctive pattern of buying and selling, as reflected in the amount of up-front cash or investment through private loan transactions, bank financing, and government insurance. Each physical environment generated different levels of commitment by community banks, private financial institutions, and government agencies, which, in turn, influenced potential developers, speculators, homeowners, and renters.

Harvey's detailed analysis revealed that urban development is not a monolithic growth process. Instead, it occurs unevenly. This second circuit of capital varies in its investment arrangements from place to place, influenced by different combinations of social factors, profit potential, and conflict. For example, banks showed no interest in lending to the inner-city poor, who, of necessity, financed their housing transactions by cash payment, private loans, and/or government programs. White ethnics also had trouble securing bank financing; instead they financed their housing purchases through community-based savings and loans associations. Both inner city and white ethnic areas had difficulty obtaining Federal Housing Authority (FHA) or Veterans Administration (VA) insurance, unlike Baltimore's middle-income sections. People in more affluent sections rarely resorted to FHA guarantees and made far greater use of commercial and savings banks. Also, with their political and economic power, they could repel speculative incursions into their neighborhoods, unlike residents of poor or working-class neighborhoods.

Thus, Harvey demonstrated how discrimination by investment capitalists in the housing market affects the dynamics of buying, selling, and neighborhood transition. He also showed the role of government in shaping a city's use of space: West Baltimore rose above other poor areas in the city as a result of multiple government renewal programs. Essentially,

David Harvey's study disclosed how some Baltimore neighborhoods fared better than others because of priorities set by real estate investors and government programs. His conclusion was that these decisions, more than those by departing industrialists, are closely linked to decaying areas of a city, prompting abandonment and relocation to another area.

Harvey's Baltimore study disclosed how the priorities of the second circuit of capital, aided by government programs, link directly to central city decay and the suburbanization of the population. Actions by real estate investors—more so than actions by industrial capitalists, he maintained—lead to areas of the city becoming run-down and abandoned.

Urban change, claims Harvey, reflects the changing needs of a capitalist economy. That is, capitalists build a physical city appropriate to the city's needs at one point only to destroy it later, usually in the course of some crisis. Different segments of the urban population—investors (finance capital), store owners (commerce capital), manufacturers (industrial capital), financial analysts, as well as white- or blue-collar workers—have different priorities and goals. Capital interests, motivated by profit making, and labor, seeking to protect and enhance its standard of living, often engage "in a series of running battles over a variety of issues that relate to the creation, management, and use of the built environment" (Harvey 1992:268).

Unwilling, therefore, to risk their profits by granting too much power to workers, the capitalist class seeks government intervention to secure the type of urban development that serves its narrow interests. This strategy explains widespread urban blight; finance capital has little reason to invest in poor neighborhoods, preferring instead the greater profits found in high-rent districts. This reluctance to aid decaying urban areas, claims Harvey, is precisely why government intervention is so important. But public urban renewal projects seem to operate only to restore the area's profitability in order to attract finance and commerce capital once again, in the process doing little for the poor. Harvey's contribution, then, lies in revealing how the actions of finance capital (rather than industrial capital) affect a city's fortunes.

Manuel Castells: Updating Marx

Manuel Castells—while influenced by Lefebvre's writings—maintained a more orthodox Marxist approach to the study of cities. His special contribution (1982, 1985) was extending Marxist analysis beyond the traditional conflict between labor and capital to explicitly urban patterns. He also highlighted the conflict between local government and the working class arising from local administration of various social welfare programs. Although the federal government funds such programs as needs-based income, housing, and health care benefits for the poor, local or city governments typically administer them. City residents seeking these resources often become entangled in conflict with city agencies.

Welfare Capitalism. Castells views welfare capitalism—the government providing worker subsidies—as an important social movement affecting urban life. To him, key issues such as housing, education, mass transportation, health, and welfare make sense only within the context of disputes arising over their administration by city government agencies. Such government activity to provide resources to the working class, to Castells, represents an effort to "extend" capitalism and gives rise to new urban struggles and patterns of conflict unknown in Marx's time.

In one sense, changing economic conditions since the early 1980s have lessened the impact of Castells's analysis. The once expansive welfare states found in the advanced industrialized countries of the Western world are cutting back. Recessions, aging populations, tax revolts, budget deficits, and fiscal crises all have curbed government spending and, in some cases, have led to dismantling of welfare programs. Thus, local governments administer fewer subsidizing programs than they once did.

On the other hand, however, the 1996 welfare reform legislation in the United States empowered the states and local municipalities to set their own guidelines for administration of federal funds. Perhaps people's struggles to receive the more limited aid available under decentralized regulations may intensify the conflict between the working class and local government that Castells identified.

Modes of Development. Examining industrial growth in suburbs, Castells adapted one of Marx's concepts to fit the information age. Whereas Marx had stressed the **mode of production**—the things needed to produce goods and services, such as land, tools, knowledge, wealth, or factories—Castells (1991) introduced the concept of the **mode of development.** The key element in the industrial mode of development, he explained, was discovering and applying new sources of energy. In today's informational mode of development, however, the key element is developing new forms and sources of information. One obvious consequence of this shift is that corporate decisions about location no longer rest on proximity to raw materials or to a large, unskilled labor pool, as they once did.

Castells's focus was the differential effect of emerging high-tech businesses on segments of the urban region. Specifically, he found that high-tech production disproportionately occurred in suburban rather than central city communities. Such companies typically have facilities on the periphery of cities, thereby accelerating the pace of outward movement and sparking the rise of edge cities. Influencing choice of suburban locations is the need for large-batch production facilities combined with automated subsidiary plants, access to a freeway system, and the typically suburban locale of research and design centers and military installations for testing and marketing defense-related products.

Allen Scott: Business Location and the Global Economy

Another English geographer, Allen J. Scott (1980, 1988), offers additional non-Marxist insights into the impact of changes in the production process on urban space. His approach is not a comprehensive theory of the built environment but a study of the relationship between a city's fortunes and the globalization of the economy. Further, in rejecting the urban ecology approach, Scott suggests that the economic interests of powerful transnational corporations—not a biological model of species competition over territory—determine urban growth patterns.

Horizontal Integration

For most of the twentieth century until about 1970, cities evolved into metropolitan regions as corporations changed in their economic organization. Once, companies were small entities with all their functions centralized in one location. Gradually, many industries absorbed or consolidated with competitors, sometimes taking the form of an **oligopoly** (market domination by a few producers). Then they maintained headquarters in a major city with easy access to banking, marketing, and other necessary services—but located their production plants, distribution centers, and sales divisions elsewhere, in locales most advantageous to them. In time, many companies gained control over the manufacture of all parts that went into their final product, as when auto companies manufactured not just the engine, frame, and body of the automobile but also batteries, headlights, radios, upholstered seats, window glass, and bumpers as well. Some companies even obtained ownership of raw materials needed for the manufacturing process. With their separate functions thus spatially dispersed, companies maintained a national network of command and control to reduce costs and maximize profits. This economic structure is called **horizontal integration.**

One way to maximize profits is to minimize shipping costs in the total manufacturing process. Not surprisingly, when horizontal integration was predominant, the specialized production facilities were mostly located near the main assembly plant—virtually all auto parts plants were within 150 miles of "Motor City," or Detroit, the automobile manufacturing center. Close proximity of these subsidiary agglomeration industries not only kept shipping costs low but also created an economically interdependent metropolitan region. As the companies prospered, so too did the cities.

Vertical Disintegration. Beginning in the 1970s, large corporations, while still maintaining some horizontal integration (especially of manufacturing, marketing, and administration activities), began to unload their production support companies (**vertical disintegration**). In other words, instead of manufacturing materials or parts needed for the production process themselves, they awarded contracts to suppliers through a process of competitive bidding. Competitiveness among subcontractors resulted in lower costs because of the elimination of overhead costs in maintaining inventory stocks and offset concerns about shipping expenses. The advent of computer assisted manufacturing enhanced production coordination, enabling companies to keep track of all needs and to order "just-in-time" parts more easily.

A significant consequence of vertical disintegration was the creation of many new supplier companies locating where labor and energy costs were low, either in North America or abroad. Scott sees this last development as the climax of vertical disintegration: the ability of large companies to conduct business on a global scale. In short, businesses have become transnational or multinational, investing their capital and locating their manufacturing, marketing, and administration anywhere in the world that best suits their needs. Suppliers may now be anywhere: perhaps in the nonunionized, low-energy-cost Sunbelt or, better yet, in extremely low-wage countries in poor regions of the world.

How has this affected older industrial cities? For most of them, plant closings meant the loss of thousands of jobs, an out-migration of workers and their families seeking jobs elsewhere, and a depressed economy. Loss of an industrial base adversely affected the city's commercial base, as stores no longer had the same customers as before. In contrast, the Sunbelt exploded in industrial development and population growth. As virtually every northeastern U.S. city steadily shrank in population in the second half of the twentieth century, the fastest-growing cities were those in the Sunbelt (see Chapter 3).

No longer dominated by manufacturing, older cities have shifted to providing greater employment opportunities in business services. Most have not fully recovered and are still experiencing population decline. A few cities, however, such as New York, London, and Tokyo, now function as "highly concentrated command posts in the organization of the world economy." They are also important locations of finance, specialized service firms, and innovation sources, and serve as markets for the products and innovations produced (Sassen 2001:3–4).

New economic realities thus shape the production process and in turn affect urban growth patterns—a subject we will now explore further through two sociological approaches, one examining local conditions and the other viewing global conditions.

John Logan and Harvey Molotch: Urban Growth Machines

John Logan and Harvey Molotch (1987) employed political economy theory in an effort to identify *who* the central decision makers in North American cities are and to determine *why* they do what they do. In concentrating on the battles between pro- and antigrowth factions, their study is essentially an application of Lefebvre's categories of abstract space and social space that we discussed earlier.

Urban growth coalitions—typically made up of bankers, businesspeople, corporate property owners, developers, politicians, and investors—seek to spark population growth, increase the market value of land, and stimulate the city's economy through investment and development. To accomplish these goals, they pressure the city government to create a "good business climate" (cleanliness, safety, tax incentives, low-interest loans, relocation assistance). They also seek to enhance and promote the image of the city, promoting its attributes (such as cultural and recreational activities, sports teams, landmarks, and night life). Their focus on quality of life, however, only extends to what Lefebvre termed "abstract space" issues involving the high profits that accompany urban growth.

By contrast, most local residents have a "social space" view of their community, and they may oppose growth as being against their best interests. City residents may wish to protect the "character" of their neighborhood, preserve

An example of the global economy is the location of manufacturing plants of North American multinational corporations elsewhere, such as this garment plant in Cambodia. Benefiting from a cheaper, non-union labor force and generous tax incentives, companies willingly pay higher shipping costs to escape higher U.S. expenses for wages, employee benefits, and taxes.

older buildings, limit traffic flow, and maintain parks and other open spaces.

Advocates of urban growth point to its advantages—more jobs, additional tax ratables, increased economic activity—and they are often correct in doing so. What also accompanies growth, however, is environmental degradation, higher rents, more crime, greater traffic congestion, and an infrastructure unable to handle an increased population. Tensions in the growth machine materialize as community groups seek to block a proposal or at least to lessen its negative impact on their community and the environment.

Logan and Molotch also point out how the global economy influences many changes in the city. Local political action is less effective than it once was because the deindustrialization of North American cities has caused the flight of industrial capital. The "new international division of labor" may benefit some people (major corporations and their stockholders reap huge profits from the new global economy), but the loss of jobs hurts ordinary people in cities back home. Thus, local people have less power to oppose the corporate agenda, just as corporations have more power to get their own way.

At the heart of all contemporary urban land use, then, there is a focus on the most profitable use of materials and labor. The question that corporate executives ask is simply: "If we do this, will we make money?" Concerns for the welfare of the worker, the neighborhood, and the city's poor simply take a back seat (if they exist at all). This "profit-bias" has international roots and consequences, as Peter Hall explains:

In the modern world, newly industrializing countries undermine the traditional economic bases of older nations and regions. In the latter, skilled workers in declining industries lose their jobs and end up in unskilled service occupations. Entrepreneurs react to the threat of competition by closing older inner city plants and concentrating production in rural areas, where

Corporate headquarters once typically located in major North American cities, and many still do. In recent decades, however, some moved part or all of their operation to suburban campus locations, lured by local tax abatements and other economic incentives. This Hewlett-Packard office building—with its tree-lined courtyard, benches, and volleyball court—typifies this pattern.

unionization is weaker and wages are lower. Multinational enterprises centralize their control functions in a few of the world's cities, where they can displace other functions to other cities and suburbs. Because profit seeking and competition are inherent and incessant, this process of change is never ending. (1984:33)

In the end, urban political economy presents an alternative to what its proponents see as the biased approach of the older urban ecology model; in the newer model, there is an assumption that profit making and capitalism are the natural forces that shape cities.

THE GLOBAL ECONOMY

Economic forces always affect cities. As discussed in Chapter 3, for example, the Industrial Revolution redefined urban life and greatly increased city population size. At the midpoint of the twentieth century, the typical North American city was an industrial center. White-ethnic, blue-collar neighborhoods

peppered the urban landscape, built around the factories in which residents worked. In other parts of the city, its middle class resided. Then, in the 1950s and 1960s, the exodus of the middle class—soon followed by many businesses and industries—created a fiscal crisis from which some cities, especially smaller ones, have never recovered.

Deindustrialization

In the 1970s, U.S. manufacturers, particularly in the steel and auto industries, made profit-driven decisions to dismantle and disinvest in operations in the United States. They closed down factories to minimize labor costs and outsourced to Asia and Latin America, dramatically disrupting people's lives and the welfare of many urban communities (Bluestone and Harrison 1984). For example, Youngstown, Ohio—situated between Pittsburgh, Cleveland, and Chicago—had a robust blue-collar economy as the center of the steel industry.

When its famous Jeannette Blast Furnace was shut down in 1978, cutting the heart out of the local economy, 50,000 Youngstown workers lost their jobs and the city was rocked by economic devastation, from which it has still not fully recovered (Linkon and Russo 2003).

Other manufacturers—in appliances and electronics, for instance—quickly followed suit and by the end of the 1970s, manufacturing in virtually all fields was in decline nationwide, and the transfer of much economic production to other countries dramatically changed the older cities. Gone were most of the jobs that earlier migrants and immigrants used as a path to economic security. Gone too were the ties that bound central-city workers to their local employers. Also gone was a sizable portion of the cities' tax base.

Economic Restructuring

The 1980s and 1990s bore witness to **economic restructuring** and the globalization of the economy that spawned still other changes in metropolitan regions. Forced to restructure their economies away from manufacturing, North American cities evolved into service centers, specializing in advertising, corporate management, finance, and information processing. In particular, cities expanded those business services required by the finance capitalists heading up investment activity for the global economy (Sassen 2001).

Such changes are evident in the present-day character of the urban labor force. The demand for many of the entry-level factory jobs traditionally held by urban poor with limited education and skills dropped dramatically, countered by a rising demand for computer-literate workers with verbal and quantitative skills. The reason was that, although some corporate headquarters moved outside the central cities, the latter continued to provide a necessary concentration of firms and jobs necessary to run the more complex corporate economy (Sassen 2000:76).

This is an important point. Even though the evolution of a global economy prompted a new generation of cynics to sound the death knell for cities, cities still play an essential role in today's world. Those massive, globalization trends toward the spatial dispersal of economic activities at the metropolitan, national, and global levels ironically contributed to the demand for new forms of territorial centralization of top-level management and control functions. Insofar as these functions benefit from agglomeration activities even in the face of the electronic integration of a firm's globally dispersed manufacturing and service operations, they tend to locate in cities (Sassen 2002:3–4). The next Critical Thinking box further explains this reality.

This efficient agglomeration of specialized product services in central cities became a vital link in the evolving global economy, to which we now turn.

A World System

With its macrosocial view, the political economy approach to understanding cities' conditions fits nicely into a world-system perspective. This emphasis views capitalism as evolving through a long, historical process that draws increasing areas of the world into a single economic and political system (Wallerstein 1979; 1997). This system operates as a hierarchy so that countries at various stages of development constitute (1) the "core," (2) the "semiperiphery," and (3) the "periphery." Within that framework, cities occupy a place in the world urban hierarchy that greatly affects growth patterns within each city.

The Hierarchy of Countries.   The more economically developed countries (Canada, Japan, the United States, the nations of Western Europe) constitute the "core" of this world system and are home to the transnational corporations that dominate the global economy. The headquarters of transnational corporations, located in large cities within rich countries, carry out high-level decision making that guides the world's economic forces. Because so many employees are well-paid professionals, these cities benefit in the quality of housing and of economic and social enterprises that spring up to cater to their tastes.

CRITICAL THINKING

Cities and the World Economy

If cities were irrelevant to the globalization of economic activity, the center could simply abandon them and not be bothered by all of this. Indeed, this is precisely what some politicians argue—that cities have become hopeless reservoirs for all kinds of social despair. It is interesting to note again how the dominant economic narrative argues that place no longer matters, that firms can be located anywhere thanks to *telematics* [telecommunications and computer technologies that allow for instantaneous transmission of information over short and long distances], that major industries now are information-based and hence not place-bound. This line of argument devalues cities at a time when they are major sites for the new cultural politics. It also allows the corporate economy to extract major concessions from city governments under the notion that firms can simply leave and relocate elsewhere, which is not quite the case for a whole complex of firms. . . .

In seeking to show that (1) cities are strategic to economic globalization because they are command points, global marketplaces, and production sites for the information economy; and (2) many of the devalued sectors of the urban economy actually fulfill crucial functions for the center, [we should reemphasize] the importance of cities specifically in a globalized economic system and the importance of those overlooked sectors that rest largely on the labor of women, immigrants, and, in the case of large U.S. cities, African Americans and Latinos. In fact it is the intermediary sectors of the economy (such as routine office work, headquarters that are not geared to the world markets, the variety of services demanded by the largely suburbanized middle class) and of the urban population (the middle class) that can and have left cities. The two sectors that have stayed, the center and the "other," find in the city the strategic terrain for their operations.

Source: Saskia Sassen, *Cities in a World Economy* 2d ed. (Thousand Oaks, CA: Pine Forge Press), 2000, p. 124.

Countries in the "semi-periphery"—such as Argentina, Hungary, Poland, and South Korea—have close ties with the richest nations. These second tier countries are fast becoming key nodes in the global urban system, as information technology binds their cities together in dense networks. Yet, even though these cities in the midrange of the global hierarchy become integrated into the cross-border economic networks, these countries continue to play a secondary role in global economic matters (Sassen 2002). Most of the transnational corporate employees in these countries are lower middle class. For the most

part, their somewhat lower standard of living brings a less grand variety and quality of activities to the urban scene than found in the "core" countries' cities.

Countries in the "periphery" are the poor, less-developed countries in Africa, Asia, and Latin America. Jobs in these countries typically pay little and offer little opportunity to advance. These transnational corporate workers are typically rural migrants living in slums or shantytowns and struggling to survive. The impact of the global economy on the cities of "periphery" countries is more negative than positive. Although a small, affluent elite exists in virtually all cities, most urban residents of these third-tier countries live at the lower end of the socioeconomic scale. Their cities thus offer even fewer of the usual social amenities of a city, except for those catering to tourists or the small local elite. Integration into the global market encourages informal enterprises within local urban economies, but often at the cost of a serious erosion of wages and employment conditions. Essentially, the major impact of globalization on cities has been a strengthening of income inequality, an increasing vulnerability of their populations to poverty, and large-scale spatial segregation through the peripheral location of the poor (Portes et al. 1997:246; Roberts 2005).

Thus, the three tiers of countries in the world system are unequal yet interdependent. The system operates mostly in the interest of the richest nations, while providing far less to the majority of the world's people who live in less economically developed nations. The quality of urban life in each of the three tiers reflects this world-system hierarchy (see the Critical Thinking box below and also Figure 9–2 on page 262).

In recent years, many governments and non-profit organizations have taken action against one highly exploitative aspect of the global economy. Many northern hemisphere industries, such as in apparel and sporting goods, rely on low-wage labor in the third-tier countries in the southern hemisphere. Those companies' designers, researchers, executives, and other white-collar employees live and work in the large cities of the core countries and receive excellent salaries and benefits. In contrast, the workers who actually make the products live in the peripheral countries. There, young children and women

CRITICAL THINKING

The Impact of the Global Economy on U.S. Cities

[New York] was the preeminent city of the time; it housed the headquarters of major corporations and the nation's financial center and served as the country's locus of transportation and communication—it was the nation's major link to the rest of the world. Until the middle of the twentieth century, almost all of the United States' international flights arrived in and departed from New York, and the international publishing and financial institutions that were located in the United States were almost exclusively headquartered in New York.

The world economy has grown in the past fifty years or so, with the economy of each nation increasingly influenced by events occurring outside of its borders. Decisions that greatly affect millions of people are now routinely made in "global cities." These are the cities—such as London, Paris, and Tokyo—in which almost all of the world's economic activity is integrated and coordinated. The awesome efficiency of modern transportation and communication has made it possible for executives in the headquarters of a multinational corporation to control its production, sales, and marketing activities all around the world. The headquarters may be in London, production facilities may be in Taiwan, advertising may be centered in Atlanta, and the primary sales market may be Mexico City.

As ties between the United States and other nations have strengthened, the number of U.S. cities serving as important links to the world system has increased. In addition to New York, Los Angeles has become an important link to the Pacific Rim nations, Miami to the nations of South America, and so on.

work long hours for little pay in hot, crowded factories. Often, they are bonded laborers, meaning they have no freedom and are kept in confined areas when not working, receive only minimal amounts of food, and often suffer verbal and physical abuse. Some companies, like Adidas and Nike, have recently yielded to public pressure to end their allowing such conditions in their suppliers' factories. Passage of laws in the United States, Canada, Europe, and other countries against importing products made by child labor has reduced, but not eliminated, these practices.

The Role of Cities.   As mentioned earlier, cities serve as important nodes in the global network, linking together money (investment capital), people (human capital), production (industrial capital), and commodities (commercial capital). Instant communications,

electronic cash transfers, rapid transportation, and the relative ease of shipping by tankers or cargo jets make cities key elements of the global economy. As such, they are locked in a reciprocal relationship: They help shape the world system and, in turn, the world system shapes them. Today, it is the importance of a city's role in the world system that largely determines its prospects for growth and prosperity (Gugler 1996:2–4).

Cities are no longer independent entities whose fortunes rise or fall according to what happens in a limited, local region. The prevailing view is that place no longer matters—that modern technology allows firms to locate anywhere, making cities irrelevant to the globalization of economic activity. One expert, however, disagrees. Saskia Sassen (2000) argues that cities offer an infrastructure concentration and servicing that are key dynamics in providing the capabilities for global control.

In an apparent paradox, the rising pre-eminence of the local in the postmodern city has been facilitated by the appearance of a global capitalism. The emergence of post-Fordism [i.e., an increasingly flexible, disorganized regime of capitalist accumulation] has resulted in an accelerated flow of global capital, and an endless search for cheap labor supplies on an international scale. These trends have connected the local ever more effectively to the world-wide developments of post-Fordism; what happens in downtown LA tomorrow may result from yesterday's fluctuations in local labor markets in East Asia. At home, the consequences have been a rapid deindustrialization especially in the snowbelt, and (re)industrialization in the sunbelt. Los Angeles, in perhaps a typically postmodern way, is experiencing both simultaneously. Within its limits, the city has vestiges of a major automobile manufacturing industry, as well as in the glittering towers of corporate high- techdom. LA is an "informational city" with, at the same time, a

proliferation of minimum-wage, part-time service industry jobs (e.g., fast food outlets) and a massive informal sector (street vendors on freeway off-ramps; can recycling efforts from the backs of trucks; etc.). In social terms, the postmodern metropolis is increasingly minoritized and polarized along class, income, race and ethnic lines. The disadvantaged classes are overwhelmingly people of color. Their family lives are increasingly disrupted by the demands of a flexible, disorganized workplace (for example, the pressure on both parents to work, or the need for families to crowd together to be able to afford housing). These trends have been aggravated by the strong dose of privatism, as well as the practical effects of privatization, that emerged during the Reagan era and show few signs of abating.

Sources: From *Urban Enclave: Identity and Place in America* by Mark Abrahamson. Copyright © 1996 by Worth Publishers. Used with permission of W. H. Freeman & Co./Worth Publishers; Michael J. Dear, *The Postmodern Urban Condition* (Malden, MA: Blackwell, 2000), p. 15.

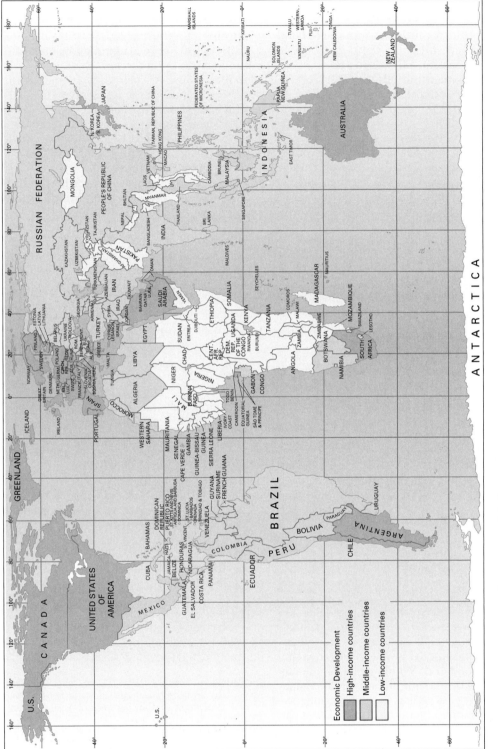

FIGURE 9–2 Economic Development in Global Perspective. [*Source:* From Macionis's *Sociology,* 10th ed. (2004), using data from United Nations Development Programme (1995) and The World Bank (2002). Map projection from *Peters Atlas of the World* (2002).]

Economic Development
High-income countries
Middle-income countries
Low-income countries

Potsdamer Platz, once a no-man's land of weeds and barbed wire between East and West, is the symbolic heart of modern Berlin. The 82-acre development is a cluster of a new mass transit system, sleek corporate high-rises, shopping malls, and theaters. The district was developed mainly with global capital from corporations such as Sony, Asea Brown Boveri (an international conglomerate), and DaimlerChrysler for the sites of their European headquarters.

Although some components of the financial district—notably in foreign currency markets—may exist in cyberspace, international cities such as New York, London, Paris, Sydney, Tokyo, and Zurich are examples of another aspect of the global economy: urban economic cores of banking and service activities. They are "transterritorial centers constituted via digital highways and intense economic transactions" within "a specific complex of industries and activities." Thus, these three cities stand at the apex of the global urban hierarchy because they are the financial capitals of the nations that dominate the world economy. On a smaller scale, Miami and Toronto—as significant regional sites—illustrate the locational concentration of certain industries and activities embedded in the new international corporate sector. Their financial districts are of recent vintage, their expansion a response to the dynamics of globalization.

The place of cities in the world economy, then, is as "command points, global marketplaces, and production sites for the information economy." Some intermediate sectors of the economy—the ones not geared to world markets but providing services to the mostly suburbanized middle class—may have left, but cities provide strategic terrain for the operations in a globalized economic system (Sassen 2000:124).

URBAN POLITICAL ECONOMY: FOUR PRINCIPLES

Although various urban political economists still emphasize different aspects of economic activity and mix the disciplinary viewpoints of economics, geography, political science, and sociology in one fashion or another, they all now agree on four principles as the foundation for studying and analyzing cities and urban life.

1. *A city's form and growth result not from "natural processes," but from decisions made by people and organizations that control wealth and other key resources.* Rejecting the ecological model, urban political economists view cities as benefiting or suffering from investment decisions made by financial and business organizations. Thus,

The global economy manifests itself in virtually all cities. It is practically impossible, for example, to go to any urban locale worldwide and not find McDonald's, Burger King, Pizza Hut, Kodak film, American cigarettes, Coke, or Pepsi. Foreign sales are an important part of all multinational corporate profits.

cities are products of broader economic forces and trends, as well as of the technologies employed by businesses.

2. *Urban forms and urban social arrangements reflect conflicts over the distribution of resources.* Urban life, claim political economists, is an ongoing struggle between rich and poor, between powerful and powerless, between management and labor, between the needs of vast businesses and the desires of local communities. As the Critical Thinking box on page 265 suggests, such ongoing confrontation often brings a sense of paralysis to people living within today's cities.

3. *Government continues to play an important role in urban life.* Local government plays a key role in allocating resources and mediating conflicts among various groups vying for support. Decisions about zoning, tax incentives, and spending priorities, for example, still have much to do with a city's (a) business locations, (b) housing and resident population types, and (c) public space activities. And, significantly, because cities exist within a larger society, the federal government—with its enormous resources and regulatory powers—is a key influence on urban life, both directly through its spending programs and

indirectly through its management of the prime interest rate for loans and its rules governing investors.

4. *Urban growth patterns significantly result from economic restructuring.* The globalization of the economy has changed the face of many North American cities as manufacturing has given way to service industries. Further, corporate mergers and takeovers have created vast conglomerates, in the process eliminating many medium-sized firms and the jobs they provided. Downsizing, by which corporations strive to achieve a leaner, less costly organizational structure, has also reduced the number of middle-management positions. Together, these dimensions of economic restructuring have dramatically reshaped cities, fostering growth or decline in metropolitan regions throughout North America and around the world.

THE URBANIZATION OF POVERTY

The world's poor once huddled mostly in rural areas, but no longer. Now, they live mostly in cities and, by 2020, about 2 billion

CRITICAL THINKING

Public Culture and Scarce Resources

[O]utright competition has dramatically changed the public sphere. Chronic fiscal crisis has so weakened public institutions and the members of their work force that their sense of mission has narrowed to saving their own jobs. Groups that interact in the same representative institutions, from city councils to boards of education, have radically different agenda that breed immobilism and distrust. The social practices of a public culture seem outmoded because they are "modern," along with the unquestioned hegemony of downtown and the pretended invisibility of class and ethnic cultures. The very concept of public culture seems old because it requires transcending private interests; it has been replaced by new rules of privatization, globalization, and ethnic separation. If every culture can set the rules—is individually hegemonic—it makes no sense to think of a transcendent common culture.

Yet what cities still do have in common is a "symbolic economy"—a continual production of symbols and spaces that frames and gives meaning to ethnic competition, racial change, and environmental renewal and decay. Despite the power of real estate developers, their architects, and members of public commissions, no single vision mobilizes this symbolic economy. Indeed, like the competing claims to embody "representations" of different cultures, the preeminence of culture since the 1970s has occurred despite the absence of vision, powerlessness of old elites to control the conditions of everyday urban life, and unprecedented debates over what should be built (or unbuilt) and where. A deep chasm lies between the post-1970s appreciation of visual culture and the absence of a master vision to control the chaos of urban life. This gap offers opportunities for both access and exclusion, for both elitism and democratization.

Source: Sharon Zukin, *The Cultures of Cities* (Cambridge, MA: Blackwell, 1995), p. 265.

---

people will live in already rapidly expanding urban slums (UN-Habitat 2004). This urbanization of poverty creates problems that affect the quality of life for all residents—problems that cities so far have been unable to resolve.

The Developing World

In virtually every less-developed country (LDC), poverty—once found primarily in the villages of traditional agricultural societies—has moved to the cities of those countries (see Figure 9–3). Significantly, however, the poverty of the world's poor is not in the same recognizable form found in industrialized countries. This new form of poverty traps these unfortunate people in nations that have solved the first economic problem (the production of

material goods), but not yet the second (the sufficient, if not equitable, distribution of the goods their industries produce). Food and consumer goods are not the only areas of deprivation. These cities lack sufficient housing, piped water, sewerage, public transportation, schools, police protection, doctors, hospitals, and other necessary amenities and defenses of urban life. See the Urban Living box on page 267 for one profile of urban poverty.

What is intimidating about the urbanization of poverty in LDCs is its scale. Between 1950 and 1990, as the first wave of industrialization came to poor, preindustrial countries, their cities expanded by 1 billion inhabitants, through migration from villages and through

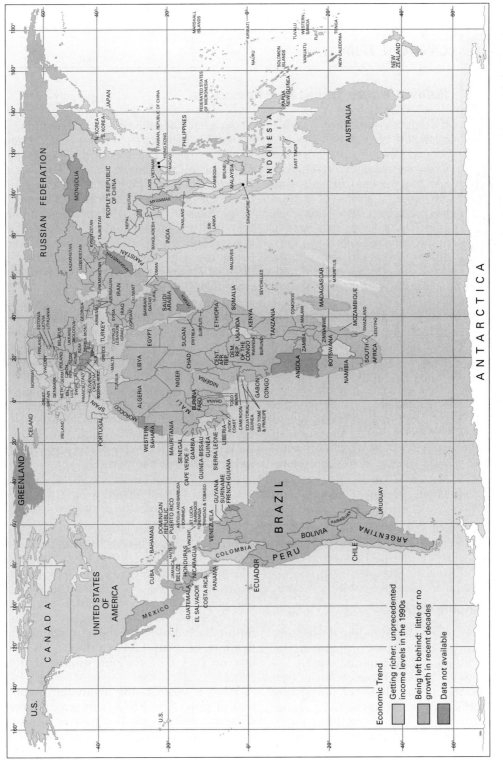

FIGURE 9–3 Prosperity and Stagnation in Global Perspective. [*Source:* United Nations Development Programme; updated in Macionis's *Sociology* (2004).]

Economic Trend

Getting richer: unprecedented income levels in the 1990s

Being left behind: little or no growth in recent decades

Data not available

URBAN LIVING

India: A Different Kind of Poverty

The statistics show that India is one of the poorest nations of the world, with a 2004 average annual income of $3,100. Unfortunately, India is home to one-third of all of Asia's poor people.

But statistics do not prepare North Americans to face the reality of poverty in India. Most of the country's 1.1 billion million people live in conditions far worse than do those we label as "poor" at home. A traveler's first experience of Indian life is sobering and sometimes shocking. Arriving in Chennai (Madras), one of India's largest cities with 4.2 million inhabitants, a visitor immediately recoils from the smell of human sewage that hangs over the city like a malodorous cloud. Untreated sewage also renders much of the region's water unsafe to drink. The sights and sounds of Chennai are strange and intense—as motorbikes, trucks, carts pulled by oxen, and waves of people choke the streets. Along the roads, vendors sit on burlap cloth hawking fruits, vegetables, and cooked food. Seemingly oblivious to the urban chaos all around them, people work, talk, bathe, and sleep in the streets. Tens of millions of homeless people fill the cities of India.

Chennai is also dotted by more than a thousand shanty settlements, containing about half a million people, many of whom have converged on the city from rural villages in search of something better. Shantytowns are clusters of huts constructed of branches, leaves, and discarded material. These dwellings offer little privacy and lack refrigeration, running water, and bathrooms. The visitor from the United States understandably feels uneasy entering such a community, since the poorest sections of our own inner cities seethe with frustration and, oftentimes, explode with violence.

But, here, again, India offers a sharp contrast because its people understand poverty differently than we do. No restless young men hang out at the corner, no drug dealers work the streets, and there is surprisingly little danger. In the United States, poverty often means anger and isolation; in India, even shantytowns are built of strong families—children, parents, and perhaps elderly grandparents—who extend a smile and a welcome.

In traditional societies like India, ways of life change slowly. To most Indians, life is shaped by *dharma,* the Hindu concept of duty and destiny that encourages them to accept their fate, whatever it may be. Mother Teresa, who won praise for her work among the poorest of India's people, went to the heart of the cultural differences: "Americans have angry poverty," she explained. "In India, there is worse poverty, but it is a happy poverty."

Perhaps we should not describe as "happy" anyone who clings to the edge of survival. But the sting of poverty in India is eased by the strength and support of families and communities, a sense that existence has a purpose, and a worldview that encourages each person to accept whatever life offers. As a result, the visitor comes away from a first encounter with Indian poverty in confusion: "How can people be so poor, and yet apparently content, vibrant, and so joyful?"

Source: Based on UN-Habitat data and John Macionis's field research in Chennai.

The *maquiladoras* system locates primary manufacturing in northern Mexico near the U.S. border to allow multinational companies to use cheap labor and ship finished goods back to the United States. Manufacturing inside the U.S. has declined, but there are presently about 100 U.S. owned and operated companies just south of the border, such as this automobile assembly plant.

natural increase. Already exceeding the total population of cities in industrialized countries, cities in poor countries will increase by another 2 billion in the next 15 years, according to the projections of demographers. These cities cannot now provide for the billion who have arrived during the past four decades, let alone the 2 billion yet to come. At present, 30 percent of households in Latin America lack piped water and sanitation. In the megacities of Asia, more than two-thirds of the urban poor do not have access to adequate sanitation, as is the case for about three-fifths of urban Africans (UN-Habitat 2004). When the predicted 2 billion new urban poor arrive, these percentages will no doubt increase.

Housing is no problem for most urban poor in LDCs, as they had previously built their own shelters in their villages. Since most city land already belongs to someone else, they build their makeshift dwellings in the less desirable locales—the lowlands and even wetlands around the city, or hillsides too steep for ordinary buildings. These shantytowns go by many names: *citas miserias, bustees, bidonvilles, geccondus, favelas,* and *pueblos jovenes.* With a stubbornness and resistance to bureaucratic oppression, the residents struggle to survive, and do so utilizing a reciprocal exchange system to help one another cope with extreme poverty. Others live an even worse existence as homeless city dwellers. Sadly, many of them are the young, as the Urban Living box on page 269 reveals.

The Developed World

Unlike the LDCs, the more-developed countries (MDCs) of Asia, Europe, and North America have maintained urban societies for generations, if not centuries. Although their cities have contained large numbers of poor

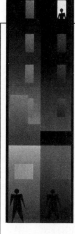

URBAN LIVING

Latin American "Street Children": Living on the Edge

Perhaps the greatest tragedy in Latin American cities has been the appearance of millions of "street children"—or *meninos de rua*. Like the tip of an iceberg, the presence of the street children suggests problems that run far deeper: poverty that stunts the lives of children who labor long hours each day, who work as prostitutes, or who fall victim to hunger and disease. The United Nations International Children's Emergency Children's Relief Fund (UNICEF) has estimated that there are 100 million street children worldwide, half of them in Latin America in virtually every country. Their greatest numbers are in Brazil, Colombia, Guatemala, Honduras, Mexico, and Nicaragua.

According to a study by the Casa Alianza (2004), 42 percent of the children on the streets are between six and eleven years old, and 49 percent are between ages 12 and 18. Many of these young people live in and around the cities' sprawling public markets, where it is easy to scavenge for food. A few work at shining shoes, cleaning windshields, or selling anything from candy to their bodies, but most beg or steal to survive. The average age of children at the garbage dump looking for items to reclaim and sell is ten. The average age for children involved in prostitution is 16, although 13-year-olds were also found in these activities.

The street children are orphans or come from broken or crowded homes where there is not enough to eat, and where physical and sexual abuse is commonplace. Just a couple of decades ago, the public looked on street urchins with a mixture of annoyance and affection. In Brazil they were known as *moleques,* that is, ragamuffins, scamps, or rascals. They were streetwise kids who were cute and cunning, sometimes sexually precocious, and invariably economically enterprising. Making themselves useful in a variety of ways, honest and otherwise, they were reminiscent of Aladdin, the Arabian Nights character portrayed by Disney. Today, however, most people look on them as public pests who should be forcibly removed from the urban landscape (Human Rights Watch, 2002).

Many cannot resist the temptation of cheap drugs to obliterate their hunger and cold. A few years ago, glue was the drug favored by street kids, but solvent and paint thinner are cheaper and easier to come by. A solvent-soaked rag, easily clenched in a palm, is also much more discreet than plastic bags of glue, which police have been known to seize and dump on the children's hair and clothes. All solvents have the desired effect: They stop the hunger pains and numb the physical and psychological effects of the brutality of the security forces. Inhaling the fumes produces hallucinations and escape, but the long-term effects are devastating: irreversible brain damage, paralysis, kidney or liver failure and, eventually, death. About 95 percent street youth in Latin America use drugs on a daily basis, most commonly solvents or show glue (Arms of Love 2002).

In other countries, the story is much the same. In the eyes of too many people, street children are not even human, and so they are dispatched in much the same way one would step on a cockroach. It's a form of social cleansing, ridding the streets of social vermin who lie amid the rubbish, or under parked cars, curled up inconspicuously on the concrete until someone comes along and kicks them. And people rarely stop to wonder why they are there in the first place.

people for that same period of time, only in recent years have greater concentrations of the poor clustered in urban areas than elsewhere. This pattern is more pronounced in Canada than in the United States.

Canada.   In a comparative demographic profile of poverty throughout Canada, the Canadian Council on Social Development reported that images of poverty as a rural phenomenon are out of date. Roughly seven out of every ten poor Canadians live in an urban area. Among Canada's largest metropolitan areas, Edmonton, Montreal, Toronto, Vancouver, Quebec City, and Winnipeg had the highest rates of poverty. Single-parent families are more likely to be poor in certain urban areas than in others. For example, in Calgary, Richmond, Gloucester, and Burlington, the proportion of poor single-parent families is much lower than in Cape Breton, Saint John, Montreal, and Hamilton. Also, the effect of unemployment on poverty rates varies in urban areas. Vancouver and Windsor, for instance, had similar unemployment rates, but the rate of poverty in Vancouver was 36 percent while in Windsor it was 26 percent (Lee 2000).

Similarly, the rate of poverty among senior citizens living in urban areas varies significantly. Less than 8 percent of elderly persons in Saskatoon, Gloucester, and Nepean live in poverty—less than in Burlington (21 percent) and Hamilton, Quebec City, Trois-Rivieres, and Winnipeg (15–16 percent). Reasons may be related to the cost of living in these different urban areas and to the source of income for seniors. In some urban centers, today's seniors are likely reaping the benefits of local economies that offered them good wages and benefits before they retired (Lee 2000). Furthermore, the number of homeless has increased to a level far beyond anything seen a generation ago (UN-Habitat 2004).

United States.   Central cities do not house the majority of the U.S. poor, as nearly two-fifths of the nation's poor live in suburban areas, another one-fifth live in nonmetropolitan areas, and the remaining two-fifths live in central cities (U.S. Census Bureau 2004b). However, central cities contain the highest concentrations of poverty, and their poverty rate has been above the national average since the early 1970s. About 3.5 million people are homeless (UN-Habitat 2004). Two major reasons account for this poverty concentration in the centers of large U.S. cities. First, many of the more affluent residents moved to the suburbs, leaving the poor behind. Second, as more jobs moved out to the suburbs, employment opportunities for city residents dwindled (Lichter and Crowley 2002:20–21). Douglas Massey (1990) sees this geographic (and social) segregation by income levels as intensifying in the coming decades. Furthermore, a growing concentration undermines efforts to prevent and reduce urban poverty.

Europe.   Many western European cities are beset with poverty problems, generated in large part by the influx of poor immigrants from developing countries who seek a better life. UN-Habitat (2004) reports that homelessness in Western Europe is at its highest level in 50 years. An estimated 3 million West Europeans were homeless in the winter of 2003, the largest numbers found in Germany and the United Kingdom. Over the last three decades, poverty has escalated throughout the European Union countries, with about 15 percent of EU citizens at risk of poverty. In the United Kingdom, the most extreme situation exists, with the number of poor children tripling in less than two decades (UN-Habitat 2004).

Poverty is thus increasing in the cities of many advanced economies throughout the world, the outcome of the uneven costs and benefits of economic globalization. The changing global economy has eliminated many low-skill jobs that once enabled the cities' poor to extricate themselves from poverty, and until policies are implemented aiming at causes, not symptoms, of urban poverty and homelessness,

CRITICAL THINKING

A Bold Initiative

While shelters can provide a clean and safe environment for a homeless family, the shelter system should not be simply a way station until permanent housing is secured. To address the needs of these families, shelters also must provide a variety of services and programs that enable families to build sound, independent living skills, complete their education, and obtain job training before moving to permanent housing. Not shelters, but rather Residential Education Training (RET) Centers—or American Family Inns—are required to deliver such a service intervention plan. Through RET Centers, desperately needed services such as health care, counseling, and substance abuse treatment can be economically and efficiently provided. Educational programs such as living skills workshops for adults or after-school accelerated learning programs for children are immediately accessible and responsive to the needs of parents and children. Homes for the Homeless has developed and has continued to refine the RET Center model over the past five years as a response to the changing characteristics of homeless families.

American Family Inns have proven to be a successful mechanism to start families on a secure path to independent living. *Approximately ninety-four percent of all families who have participated in the services offered by HFH's RET Centers have maintained their residences once placed in permanent housing.* When compared to New York City's return-to-shelter rate of fifty percent for formerly homeless families, RET Centers offer a successful solution by addressing the severe complexities of the poverty faced by homeless families.

The dramatic changes in the composition and characteristics of homeless families over the last several years highlight the emerging fact that homelessness is not simply a housing issue. Rather, the trends illustrate that homelessness is merely a symptom of a debilitating poverty affecting a very young and vulnerable population. Policymakers and service providers must meet the challenge of this complex issue with bold initiatives such as the RET Center model. Only then will it be possible to break the cycle of poverty and homelessness which is now plaguing the poor urban family.

Source: "A Bold Initiative" excerpted from *The Cycle of Family Homelessness: A Social Policy Reader,* Appendix B. Reprinted by permission of The Institute for Children and Poverty.

experts warn that the problem could get worse (Cohen and Tharp 1999). See the Critical Thinking box above for one approach to resolving this problem.

❖ ━━━━━━━━ ❖ ━━━━━━━━ ❖

SUMMARY

The conventional ecological analysis of cities and urban life highlights the advantages of particular locations and the various economic benefits cities offer over the hinterland. Living in cities allows people to get more goods of higher quality more cheaply. These economic advantages, economists like Alonso argue, are sufficient to explain recurrent patterns in urban land use: For example, businesses predominate at the center (the CBD), surrounded by residential areas and, farther out, agricultural areas. Even so, this theory may be descriptive only of Western (primarily North American) cities and, in any case, it ignores various noneconomic forces (such as race prejudice) that also affect urban land use.

By the 1960s, many social scientists came to the conclusion that the urban ecology model could not address changing patterns of urban life. French philosopher Henri Lefebvre was a major influence on the political economy perspective and contributed ideas about the primary and secondary circuits of capital, space as a form of social organization, and the role of government. David Harvey's Marxist analysis of Baltimore revealed that finance capital, not industrial capital, was the key shaper of neighborhood quality. Manuel Castells updated Marx by explaining welfare capitalism as a new form of class conflict probability and by discussing modes of development in lieu of modes of production. Allen Scott discussed horizontal integration and vertical disintegration as a basis for understanding business relocation in the global economy. John Logan and Harvey Molotch, drawing on Lefebvre's distinctions between abstract space and social space, examined the tensions arising between urban growth advocates and residents of the current built environment who may oppose the proposed new use of that space.

Economic restructuring changed older cities from a manufacturing base to a service industries base. Urban economic changes need to be understood in the context of an evolving world system of economic interdependence that places nations in a global hierarchy. This hierarchy consists of the "core" of highly developed countries, the "semi-periphery" of less-developed countries, and the "periphery" of the least developed countries. Within the ever-expanding global network, cities are locked in a reciprocal relationship, serving as important nodes linking together wealth (investment capital), people (human capital), production (industrial capital), and commodities (commercial capital).

Although political economists go in different directions, depending on their disciplinary viewpoints and areas of focus, they agree on four basic principles of political economy. First, decision makers controlling resources—not natural processes—shape city form and growth. Second, conflicts over distribution of resources also shape city form and social arrangements. Third, government continues to play a role in affecting urban patterns. Fourth, economic restructuring is a key influence in urban growth patterns.

Just as the world is becoming more urbanized, so too is poverty. In developing countries, poverty takes a different form than in developed countries, because the equitable distribution of goods does not match the production of material goods. The rapid growth of urban poor—1 billion over the past 40 years and a projected 2 billion in the next 15—creates a serious problem for developing world cities in attempting to provide both the necessities and amenities for this burgeoning population. Developed world countries, such as Canada and the United States, are experiencing greater geographic segregation based on income levels, placing greater burdens on their cities to cope with large concentrations of the poor. Poverty results in serious problems of homelessness in MDCs, while the wretched conditions in the many shantytowns in LDCs mark their housing problem.

CONCLUSION

The economic trends that have produced major changes in economic and employment opportunities in North American cities will continue. So will the increased integration of poor countries and their cities into the world economy. Globalization is a process that no one can stop or reverse. Therefore, an understanding of global political economy remains essential in any study of cities and urban life. This perspective addresses the rapid changes occurring worldwide and thus offers a comparative approach that is lacking in the ethnocentric U.S. urban ecology model.

Urban political economy, however, has two important limitations (Pahl 1989; Walton 1993). Large-scale concepts, such as Castells's modes of development, do not fully explain the differences between cities that are in the same mode of development. That is, global political and economic forces do not fully determine the character of all cities and neighborhoods;

local variations do exist. For one thing, individuals do not respond like a ball in a pinball machine, reacting to the force of a flipper by going in another direction. They reflect, interpret, and react on their own. One danger in the political economy approach is in ignoring the individual factor—something researchers now realize and are striving to overcome.

Peter Hall (1984:34) suggests further that urban political economy is as much defined by what it omits as by what it stresses. On the one hand, there is much to be recommended in the political economists' critique of urban ecology. On the other hand, the political economy approach does not deal very extensively or very deeply with cases where capitalist cities have been successful at raising the general standard of living of the city as a whole. Nor does it offer much insight as to the weaknesses of socialist cities in meeting the needs of many of their people. In the future, Hall sees both the conventional ecological and the new political economy approaches forming a critical dialogue that focuses on each other's strengths and limitations. In the end, of course, we can look forward to gaining an even more sophisticated understanding of urban land use.

Meanwhile, despite limitations, political economy has now become a dominant perspective in urban studies, inspiring many scientific investigations of cities throughout the world. These studies examine not only present-day patterns but also the future of cities—a subject we will turn to at the end of this book. Next, though, we will look at the variances in social stratification and social class, as reflected in the diversity of both urban and suburban lifestyles.

KEY TERMS

Abstract space
Agglomeration industries
Central business district
Central place theory
Economic restructuring
Horizontal integration
Mode of development
Mode of production
Oligopoly
Primary circuit of capital
Second circuit of capital
Social space
Vertical disintegration

CHAPTER 10

STRATIFICATION AND SOCIAL CLASS
Urban and Suburban Lifestyles

❖ ▬▬▬▬▬ ❖ ▬▬▬▬▬ ❖

What's your stereotype of a person from the city? How about describing someone from the suburbs? Most people find the second question much easier to answer, because conventional wisdom holds that cities are much more socially diverse than suburbs. Yet, as sociology often shows us, what people think is not necessarily true. Cities in the United States and Canada are home to people of various social classes, races, and ethnicities, and classes, and exploring any city will reveal both neighborhoods with a mix of people as well as many distinctive neighborhoods in which people have their own typical lifestyle. The same is true of suburbs. No large city or suburb is accurately described with any single stereotype.

In this chapter we investigate the diversity found in our cities and suburbs, highlighting the social class difference found within them. In Chapter 11, our attention will turn to the importance of race, ethnicity, and gender in creating urban and suburban diversity. These chapters are about social difference, but they are also about social inequality. As we examine the "structure" of the North American city, we shall see that some urbanites experience "the good life," but others contend with a host of problems. These urban problems, including inadequate housing, poor education, high levels of crime, are the focus of Chapter 12. We begin by investigating how social class differences create social diversity in both cities and suburbs.

SOCIAL STRATIFICATION

The United States, Canada, and all other countries are stratified societies. In every nation people are ranked in a social hierarchy that determines their quality of life. The social hierarchy involves access to jobs, income, schooling, and other resources, which, in turn, affects people's choices about where and how to live. Keep in mind that communities are not all the same in terms of social stratification. Some countries have more inequality than others. In addition, within any country rural communities with somewhat more homogeneous populations typically have fewer social levels than cities, where people differ more in terms of occupations, incomes, and schooling.

Two classical social theorists—Karl Marx and Max Weber—offered ideas about social stratification that still influence sociological thinking today. Drawing on the work of Marx, social-conflict theorists claim that inequality in wealth and power provides some people with so much greater advantages over others, that conflict between social classes is inevitable. Weber agreed with Marx that social stratification causes social conflict, but he saw Marx's two-class view of capitalists and workers as simplistic and suggested a more complex model. To Weber, economic inequality—the issue so vital to Marx—was indeed important, and he referred to this as **class** position. However, Weber viewed social class not in terms of two categories but as a continuum ranging from high to low. He also introduced the concept of **status,** or social prestige, as the second dimension of social stratification, with **power** as the third. With Weber's thinking in mind, most sociologists define **social stratification** as the *hierarchical ranking within a society of various social class groups according to wealth, power, and prestige.*

Further following Weber's concepts, sociologists use the term **socioeconomic status (SES)** to refer to *a composite ranking based on various dimensions of social inequality.* That ranking results from comparison of how many status symbol possessions one accumulates, such as how posh one's residence is and the expensiveness of one's car, clothing, eating habits, and vacations. Of particular interest is residence, for the ability to live in a particular place—whether voluntarily or involuntarily—is an excellent illustration of social stratification. This is not an issue of city versus suburban living, however, as people in all social class levels are living in both types of communities.

W. Lloyd Warner and his associates were the first to conduct a comprehensive study of social stratification in the United States in their examination of "Yankee City" in the 1930s. (It was actually Newburyport, Massachusetts, a small town of 17,000.) Combining objective criteria (such as income and occupation) with subjective input (using the **reputational method** in which people compared others to themselves in terms of status), Warner reported the existence of a six-tier class system (upper upper, lower upper, upper middle, lower middle, upper lower, and lower lower). Among his other findings was a significant relationship between an ethnic group's length of U.S. residence and its class status, a pattern that still holds true today for many immigrant groups.

Social Class Distinctions

Since Warner's seminal research, three generations of social scientists have studied the many manifestations of stratification and social class in all types of communities. The paradoxical coexistence of great poverty and wealth in our cities that they found is simply a condensed manifestation of what exists in society itself. Before we look at the social class segregation we find in our cities and suburbs, therefore, it would be helpful to describe the general characteristics found among the different layers of social strata in North American society. Although the two countries differ in their income and poverty definitions, what follow are a fairly definitive portrait of U.S. society and a close approximation of Canadian society.

Upper Class.   The main distinction between Warner's upper-upper and lower-upper classes was essentially that of "old money" and "new money," that is, of either multi-generational, inherited wealth (for example, Jay Rockefeller with a 2005 net worth of at least $82 million) or first-generation, self-earned wealth (for example, Bill Gates of Microsoft with a 2005 net worth of nearly $30 billion). The upper class constitutes about 5 percent of the total population, but whether they have "old" or "new" money creates a social divide between the two levels and they seldom have membership in the same clubs and organizations.

With their great wealth, the upper class lives ostentatiously in expensive neighborhoods, enjoys high prestige, and wields considerable political clout. They tend to be a fairly cohesive group, interacting with one another at the "right" social events, belonging to the same clubs and organizations, sending their children to the same private schools, supporting charities and the arts, and vacationing at the same elite resort areas. Upper-class women are in charge of hosting entertainments at home for guests and often do volunteer work for charitable and civic organizations, both locally and nationally; the men often are active in community service organizations (see the Urban Living box on p. 278).

Middle Class.   Constituting about 40 to 45 percent of society and more diverse racially and ethnically, this population segment is the one most often depicted in films and television, and most commonly targeted by advertisers. About half are upper middle class earning above-average income, typically in the range of $80,000 to about $170,000 annually. That income enables them to own an expensive co-op or townhouse in the city or a good-sized suburban home, participate in local politics, send their children to universities in preparation for careers in high prestige occupations and professions, and invest in stocks, bonds, and perhaps property. Upper-middle-class women may or may not work, as some are in professional careers while others prefer to be stay-at-home wives and mothers. Many will be active in local charitable, church, or civic organizations, as often are their husbands.

The other half of the middle class either work in less prestigious white-collar occupations as office workers, middle managers, and sales clerks, or else in highly skilled blue-collar jobs such as electrical work and carpentry. Their family income is comparable to the national average, about $40,000 to $80,000 annually. Generally, they build up a small nest egg for their retirement, and about half their children graduate from college, often at a state-supported school. To a lesser degree than the upper middle class, the women in this social stratum will also participate in local clubs and organizations, as will the men, who may also be active in fraternal organizations. Both middle class groups usually immerse

The high socioeconomic status enjoyed by members of the upper class partly rests, suggested Weber, on social prestige gained through the accumulation of prized status possessions. Among the measurable examples of such conspicuous consumption is a posh residence, along with expensive cars, clothing, eating habits, vacations, and other pursuits.

themselves in their children's activities, such as sports programs and scouting.

Working Class. Sometimes called the lower middle class, this population segment comprises about one-third of society and yields a family income below the national average, about $25,000 to $40,000 annually. This level of income gives them little means by which to acquire wealth, although about half of working-class families do own their own homes. However, they are especially vulnerable to financial crisis if they experience unemployment or serious illness. They are the classic Marxian model of workers in closely supervised jobs with little creativity and over which they have little control. Furthermore, these jobs offer fewer benefits, such as medical or dental insurance and pension plans, particularly if they are non-union jobs. About a third of the children in these families will go to college. In many working-class families, women

only work when single and become full-time homemakers once married. However, in many instances the high cost of living has obliged the women to work as well. Both genders are likely to restrict their outside activities to church-related activities or neighborhood associations. In addition, many men also enjoy participation in fraternal organizations and organized sports for themselves or their children.

Lower Class. About 20 percent of the population—poor whites, and poor racial and ethnic minorities—fall into this category. Some are the so-called working poor who hold low-prestige jobs with low incomes that nonetheless enable them to get by. Located in our inner cities and rural areas, about 40 percent own their own homes. Many have no medical insurance, so serious illness or long-term unemployment could easily send them into the need for government assistance. About 12–13

URBAN LIVING

The "Philadelphia Gentlemen"

E. Digby Baltzell, a sociologist born into the upper class, not only gave an excellent insider's view into the world of the elite, but he also provided probably the best study of this lifestyle in his excellent study, *Philadelphia Gentlemen* (1958). Although his in-depth portrait was of the Philadelphia elite, his analysis is applicable to most U.S. cities that have been home to a multi-generational, "old-money" constituency.

He described these "descendants of successful individuals" as a cohesive primary group who grew up together in the same exclusive neighborhoods, attended the same private schools, and vacationed in the same restrictive places, and so naturally became friends. Eventually, they intermarried, and in their adult lives continued their social bonding by living near one another, belonging to the same churches and clubs, and seeing each other frequently. With a strong sense of group identity and governed by social norms of what is "just not done," they maintained "a distinctive lifestyle and a kind of primary solidarity which [set] them apart from the rest of the population" (Baltzell 1958:7).

In describing the upper-class neighborhood in Philadelphia, Baltzell suggested a three-stage out-migration, which also approximates the pattern in other U.S. cities. From the colonial period through the first half of the nineteenth century, the city's elite lived in what is now the downtown business district; in Philadelphia this was the area around Independence and Washington Squares. Following the Civil War and until World War I, the upper-upper class shifted away from the increasingly busy, noisy, congested downtown to a quieter residential neighborhood nearby; in Philadelphia this was about 12 blocks west to the Rittenhouse Square district. In the third stage following World War I, in small and medium-size cities the elite moved out to the suburbs; large cities, however, were able to maintain their upper-income enclaves. In the Philadelphia metropolitan area, the elite continued their westward out-migration to the suburbs. We should also note that throughout all three periods, the city's elite typically maintained at least two residences, one in the city and another in the country (Baltzell 1958:179).

Source: Based on E. Digby Baltzell, *Philadelphia Gentlemen: The Making of a National Upper Class* (New Brunswick, NJ: Transaction Publishers, 1958/1989).

percent of the population receives such welfare assistance. Researchers have found distinctly separate social worlds of men and women living in these poor neighborhoods (Liebow 2003; MacLeod 2004). Women are more likely to be involved in organizational activities, usually the church, and interact in more confined areas, while the men will more often be out and about, congregating with friends to drink, talk, and enjoy sports.

Some urban neighborhoods have such extreme levels of poverty and unemployment that social scientists call them **hyperghettos** (Wacquant 1997). In Canada and the United States, the poverty rate currently hovers around 12 to 14 percent, but in hyperghettos more than 40 percent of the residents live in poverty. The unemployment rate in Canada has been about 7 percent and about 5 percent in the United States, compared to as high as 67 percent in hyperghettos. Other characteristics of these neighborhoods, which mostly contain rental units only, are low levels of education and job skills and high levels of single-parent households and social isolation. Because hyperghettos are almost always minority neighborhoods, we will explore this grim social phenomenon more fully in the next chapter.

Before we examine the different social class concentrations in our cities and suburbs, we will first examine in a larger context two of the best measurable indicators of social stratification: income and poverty.

Income Distribution Nationwide

The disparity between rich and poor is not simply a matter of difference in incomes (a normal fact in any competitive society), but in the proportionate share of total income each socioeconomic group possesses and in how each group's income situation changes from year to year. This information offers helpful insight into macrosocial factors relating to poverty.

If family income were distributed equally across the population, each quintile, or 20 percent segment, would receive one-fifth of the total. However, of all industrialized nations, the United States has the most unequal distribution of wealth (Philips 2003). As Figure 10–1 shows, in 2004 the top 20 percent of all U.S. households—those earning more than $88,029—earned 50.1 percent of all income. That is about as much as the remaining 80 percent of Americans combined! The top two-fifths earned almost three-fourths of all income, leaving the lowest 20 percent of households—those earning less than $18,500—drawing in only 3.4 percent of the total. Among Canadian households, the unequal distribution is also pronounced, though not to the same level of intensity. The top 20 percent of all Canadian households earned 41.5 percent of all income, while the lowest 20 percent of households earned 7.4 percent of the total.

A fur-coated woman passes a blanketed homeless person on East 51st Street in New York. Not uncommonly, we can find urban scenes like this one where ostentatious displays of affluence contrast with images of poverty. Such visual dichotomy is to be expected as part of the heterogeneity of cities, in which resides a mixture of people of all social classes.

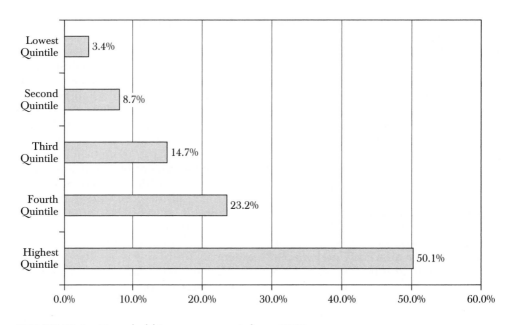

FIGURE 10–1   Household income, percent share, 2004. [*Source:* U.S. Census Bureau, 2005.]

Since 1968, the gap between the most affluent Americans and everyone else has been steadily widening, and by 1993, it reached its widest extent since the end of World War II in 1945. It widened still further by 2004 (U.S. Census Bureau 2005b). Similarly, the income gap has widened in Canada. In 1973, the richest ten percent of Canadian families made 21 times more than the poorest ten percent, but by 1996 they were making 314 times more (Yalnyzian 1998).

Incomes Within and Outside Cities

If we compare income data by residence, we find that those living outside central cities in metropolitan areas are better off than those living within central cities. As Figure 10–2 shows, the median money income of households in 2003 was $51,737 for those in suburban areas, compared to $37,174 in cities and $36,112 in nonmetropolitan areas (U.S. Census Bureau 2005). This difference of $14,653 between urban and suburban dwellers gives us an initial understanding of the greater financial resources available to many of those living beyond the city limits.

Poverty Nationwide

In 2004, the poverty threshold for a U.S. family of four was $21,623. The official poverty rate was 12.7 percent, a total of 37.0 million Americans. This was 10 percent lower than the poverty rate in 1959, the first year for which poverty data is available. In 2004, the poverty rates were: non-Hispanic whites 8.6 percent; blacks 24.7 percent; Hispanics 21.9 percent, Asians 9.8 percent. Of those living in poverty, 83.8 percent were native-born citizens, 3.6 percent were naturalized citizens, and 12.6 percent were foreign-born non-citizens (U.S. Census Bureau 2005).

In Canada, about 16 percent of its population was classified as low income in 2000. Those in this category included 14 percent of Canadian-born citizens and 20 percent of all immigrants. Length of residence was a factor, as 36 percent of all immigrants who lived in Canada less than six years were low income,

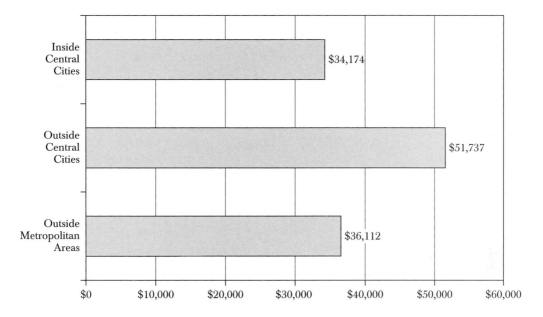

FIGURE 10–2   Median money income, 2003. [*Source:* U.S. Census Bureau, 2005.]

compared to 28 percent who were residents from six to ten years.

Poverty Within and Outside Cities

Poverty data offer an initial understanding of the greater strain put on cities' resources to assist those living below the poverty level. More U.S. city residents—17.5 percent or nearly one in six—lived in poverty than outside central cities where it was 9.1 percent (one in eleven). In nonmetropolitan areas, 14.2 percent (one in seven) lived in poverty (see Figure 10–3). In absolute numbers, this translated to 14.5 million in central cities, 13.8 million outside central cities, and 7.5 million in nonmetropolitan areas (U.S. Census Bureau 2004b).

We can partly explain the higher concentration of poverty in cities by the greater numbers of foreign-born residents. Throughout the history of Canada and the United States, cities have traditionally been home to many poor newcomers struggling to survive and improve their quality of life. That pattern continues

today. More than two-fifths of the foreign-born (44 percent) live in a U.S. central city. (Many of the remaining foreign-born have the financial means to live in the suburbs.) Of the 33.5 million foreign-born living in the United States in 2003, 10 percent of all naturalized citizens and 22 percent of all non-U.S. citizens, nearly double the national figure of 12.5 percent, lived in poverty (U.S. Census Bureau 2004b, c). Although studies show that the income for most immigrants improves with the passage of time, their early presence—particularly their large numbers—creates an ethnic underclass that competes with the long-term urban poor for socioeconomic well-being.

In Toronto, for example, while the number of families increased 15 percent between 1981 and 2001, the number of poor families increased by almost 69 percent. There was also a dramatic increase in the number of higher poverty neighborhoods from 30 in 1981 to 120 in 2001 (see Figure 10–4). This increase was particularly acute in the inner suburbs—in the former municipalities of Scarborough, North York, Etobicoke, York,

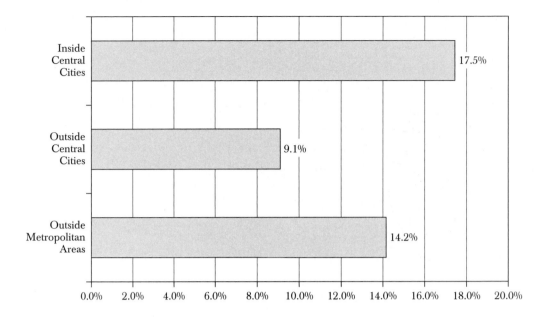

FIGURE 10–3   People in poverty by percent, 2003. [*Source:* U.S. Census Bureau, 2005.]

and East York. During this 20-year period, there was a 484 percent increase in the poor immigrant family population in these neighborhoods, from 19,700 to 115,100. Immigrant families accounted for two-thirds of the total family population living in higher poverty neighborhoods (United Way of Greater Ontario 2004).

New York City offers another example. In 2002, one out of five (20.5 percent) residents were poor, compared with less than one out of eight Americans (12.1 percent) nationwide. To appreciate the enormity of the first statistic, consider this: If New York City's 1.7 million poor resided in their own municipality, they would constitute the fifth largest city in the United States; only Houston, Chicago, Los Angeles, and the rest of New York would have a larger population. Not surprisingly, foreign-born residents are a significant component of the city's poor.

New York City is home to 2.9 million foreign-born residents (36 percent of the city's total population). The largest share comes from the Caribbean (25.6 percent), followed by Asia (24.3 percent), Europe (20.5 percent), and Latin America (18.9 percent) (Levitan 2003).

A Cautionary Note

It would be a serious mistake, however, to conclude from the foregoing information that the presence of immigrants translates to poor neighborhoods. Actually, hundreds of thousands of immigrants have the educational levels, job skills, and income to settle in middle-class suburban towns, not in low-income city neighborhoods. It would also be equally wrong to view cities as primarily the repositories of the poor and less affluent, while viewing suburbs as essentially the locales of the middle and upper classes. New York City, as

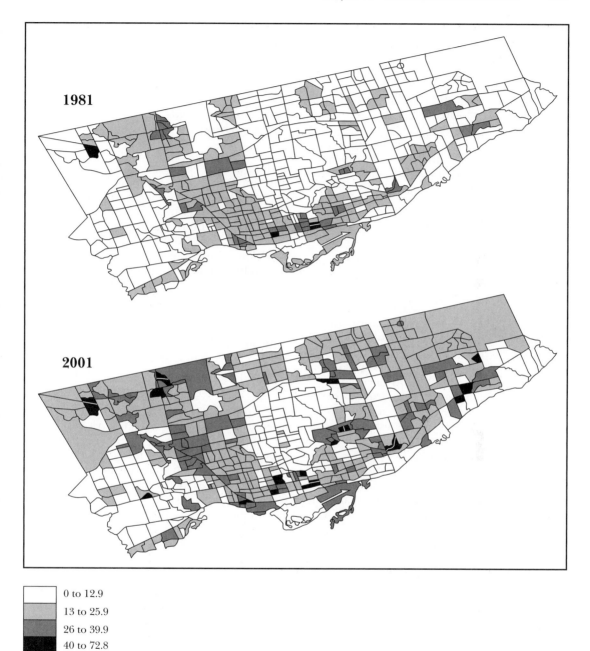

1981

2001

0 to 12.9
13 to 25.9
26 to 39.9
40 to 72.8

FIGURE 10–4   City of Toronto Family Poverty Rates, 1981 and 2001. [*Source:* City of Toronto.]

mentioned in the previous paragraph, has one in five residents living in poverty. That is a high proportion, to be sure, but this also means that four in five New Yorkers are not poor; instead, they are working-, middle-, or upper-class people. And remember, earlier we cited data that revealed one in eleven suburbanites lives in poverty. To understand more fully the socioeconomic diversity in all locales, we will first examine the social stratification layers among urbanites and then scrutinize the diversity found in suburbs.

URBAN SOCIAL CLASS DIVERSITY

Imagine sitting in Union Square in downtown San Francisco noting the different types of people who walk by. A well-dressed young woman carrying an attaché case hurries past, as if she is late for her next appointment. An old man, unshaven and in shabby dress, reclines on the grass enjoying the warm sun; occasionally he removes a brown bag from his coat pocket, unscrews the top of a bottle inside, and raises it for a quick drink. Nearby, four young men in Gap shirts and jeans engage in a serious discussion about the latest violence in Iraq. A short distance away, an African American woman plays a guitar as she offers Christian messages to anyone who will listen. For a moment, she attracts the attention of a group of Chinese American children, 10 or 11 years old, who playfully skip their way through the square. A middle-class couple emerges from Macy's department store carrying a large assortment of packages. They buy ice cream from a street vendor, stroll into the square, and collapse wearily but happily on the soft grass.

Similar scenes play out daily in all the major North American cities. This brief portrait suggests the essence of urban life: tremendous human variety, which is sometimes troubling, sometimes exhilarating, but always interesting. Clearly, urban people in North America lead very diverse lives. Although their lives may touch for a moment in a place like Union Square, different interests, experiences, and life circumstances propel them in different directions. We will now go in a few of those different directions as we explore the different types of social class neighborhoods found in our larger cities.

Upper-Class Urban Neighborhoods

The upper classes typically have several homes and alternate where they live at different times of the year. In the city they will live in the most fashionable neighborhoods, such as Nob Hill in San Francisco, or in luxury apartments or penthouses in the heart of the city, such as near Lincoln Center and Columbus Circle in Manhattan. Here they live securely and deliberately segregated from the rest of the population, protected by doormen, security guards, and controlled entrances. Their choice of transportation is mostly likely a door-to-door limousine service, whether to some cultural event (concert, opera, theater), social event (ball, fundraiser, private party), or shopping (in exclusive stores, often available by appointment only).

The Upper East Side.   Zip code 10021 is the most prestigious one in New York City, for it encompasses much of Manhattan's Upper East Side, the country's most affluent urban neighborhood, with some of the most expensive real estate in the United States. The Upper East Side runs from 59th Street to 96th Street, between Central Park and the East River. The majestic apartment buildings lining Fifth and Park Avenues offer the ritziest addresses in town—home to advertising and public relations managers, bankers, consultants, doctors, executives, lawyers, management analysts, Mayor Michael Bloomberg, and socialites of old wealth alike.

Although apartments closer to fifth or Madison Avenues are generally more expensive and more elegant, the entire Upper East Side neighborhood—all the way along the narrower side streets to the East River—is filled with beautiful buildings, well-maintained parks, and abundant places to eat, drink, and shop.

The elite neighborhoods in most North American cities vary according to a city's history and terrain. Some of these residential areas may contain high-rise luxury apartments, century-old mansions, or a combination of the two. Typically, they boast a special ambience at street level and often spectacular views, as here in San Francisco's Pacific Heights.

Separating the two wide residential avenues is the boutique-laden Madison Avenue, the area's shopping hub, where you can find everything from Prada to Picasso. This is the most expensive retail area in the world, with blue-chip art and antiques galleries, jewelry stores, expensive boutiques and restaurants. In addition to such stylish landmarks as Bloomingdale's, Tiffany's, and the Plaza Hotel are such nearby familiar stores as Henri Bendel, Chanel, Gucci, and Louis Vuitton. Also in the Upper East Side are the high-end auction houses, Christie's and Sotheby's. Also here are many custom boutiques that devote their entire staff solely to the shopping pleasure of one client one day or hour at a time (Beveridge, et al. 1996).

The appeal of this neighborhood extends beyond the elegant living spaces and retail establishments. The Upper East Side is also where you can find such world-class cultural institutions as the Metropolitan Museum of Art, the Guggenheim, and the Whitney, each located on or near New York's magnificent Central Park. Also here are the El Museo del Barrio, the Museum of the City of New York, and the Goethe Institut, a German cultural institution.

One of the biggest draws to the Upper East Side is, of course, Central Park. New York City's most famous green space borders the entire western length of the neighborhood, featuring boathouses, the Central Park Zoo and Children's Zoo, the Reservoir, and the Arsenal Building, original site of the Museum of Natural History. And for residents with children, this area is a huge draw for its spectacular public and private schools alone. The quiet, refined pace of life spells a perfect place to live or simply a place for nonresidents to escape the "rat race" of more hectic areas of the city.

Although not everyone who lives in the Upper East Side is wealthy, a great many are.

According to 2000 census data, the per capita money income in this neighborhood was $91,064, compared to the city per capita average of $23,389. Over one-third of those households in New York City who reported incomes of more than $200,000 lived in the Upper East Side, yet the area contains only 4 percent of all households in New York City.

Other Elite Neighborhoods. Chicago's Gold Coast is the second-wealthiest urban neighborhood in the United States, after New York's Upper East Side. Located on the city's North Side facing Lake Michigan, this premier residential area is considered the "old money" section of town. Luxury high-rise apartment buildings on Lake Shore Drive and rows of century-old multimillion-dollar mansions reside in quiet contrast to the lively stores, restaurants, and nightspots of Michigan Avenue, Rush and Division Streets. Historical landmarks and preservation districts mark much of the area, including the Astor Street Historic District.

Boston's Beacon Hill is one of the oldest historic districts in the United States. Boasting one of the most outstanding and intact collections of mid- to-late-nineteenth-century homes in the country, it features exceptional examples of Federal, Greek Revival, and Victorian architecture. In 2000, the median household income in this prestigious neighborhood was nearly twice that in all of Boston (U.S. Census Bureau 2003). Louisburg Square, known as the heart of Beacon Hill in Boston, has undergone a changing of the guard from the old elite of shipping and merchant banking descendants to a new elite of largely self-made millionaires from high-tech, financial, and other industries. In essence, the old Brahmin monopoly on financial and social power that controlled Louisburg Square has given way to something more open and complex. The change reflects the process of degentrification, in which meritocracy periodically wins out over breeding in forming an elite.

Another elite neighborhood can be found in the Pacific Heights area of San Francisco.

This privileged neighborhood, with its median household income well above average for the city, contains blocks of elegant Victorian mansions and impressive views of the Bay and the Golden Gate Bridge, making the area a perennial favorite with tourists. The nouveau riche of the late 1800s first colonized the neighborhood—loosely bordered by Van Ness and Presidio Avenues and Pine and Vallejo Streets—when the construction of a new cable-car line made the area accessible. That legacy of luxury has persisted, and the neighborhood remains generally quiet and residential, with the majority of its activity clustered around Fillmore Street. There shoppers purchase expensive women's clothing and luxury items, visit exquisite gift boutiques, bath-and-body shops and consignment stores, or else stop at a sidewalk café to engage in that favorite city pastime: people watching.

Middle-Class Urban Neighborhoods

Most of the middle class live in suburbia, not the city. However, even though the middle-class presence is not as proportionately high as it was two generations ago, it is nonetheless a significant reality in most large cities. Some city census blocks evolve as middle-class neighborhoods through the gentrification process, displacing the lower-income residents who can no longer afford to live there. The impetus for this change began in the 1970s as manufacturing declined in cities and their economies changed to corporate information-processing services, such as financial, legal, and marketing (Sassen 2001).

The rapid growth of the service sector generated well-paying professional positions that brought young (late twenties to early forties), urban professionals (**yuppies**) to the city, not only to work but also to live. While yuppies may be single or married, with or without children, a new term—**dinks** (dual income, no kids)—came into fashion to describe those young professional couples without children (see the Urban Living box on p. 287). Then, as a large number of African American college graduates

URBAN LIVING

DINKS Dine Out

Rich Parke, a patent attorney, and Liesbeth Severiens, associate publisher for two banking-industry magazines, are both in their mid-30s and have no children. The New Yorkers spend more than $20,000 a year eating out—and that doesn't include business meals. Dinner checks during their twice-a-week forays to five local restaurants average $65. On weekends, when they tend to dine with other couples and patronize trendy spots, the check is usually higher. Their weekly lunch expenses average $70, and restaurant breakfasts add $50 to their dining-out budget.

Mike and Judy Zeddies live in Chicago's upscale Lincoln Park neighborhood. He's a food broker; she's the art director at a local print shop. They're in their early 30s, too. The Zeddies guess they spend "a good $200" dining out each week. With dining patterns similar to those of Parke and Severiens, their grand total is about $12,000.

Bev Bajus is operating officer of the American Dietetic Association and its foundation. She lives in Chicago during the week. Her husband, Don, lives in Minneapolis, where he's a partner in a computer character animation studio. Both are over 50. They spend weekends together, generally alternating between the two cities.

"Dining out is a form of entertainment and adventure for Don and me," says Bajus. "Friends have similarly hectic schedules and dinner is often the only convenient time for socializing. Also, most of our friends share a similar love affair with food."

About 24 million married-couple households had no children living at home in 1995, and that number could top 30 million in 15 years, according to *American Demographics* magazine. It's a strong market for restaurateurs to pursue. While not all DINKs are affluent, they generally have more disposable income than their counterparts with children. . . .

"A lot of our dinner dining decisions revolve around the time factor," says Janet Janis, a Chicago bank vice president in her early 30s. "Cooking at home requires planning. You have to have gone to the store or gotten something out of the freezer. Around 8 o'clock, Dave and I look at each other and say, 'What are we going to do about eating?' And we sure aren't about to start cooking a meal at that time of the day. So we pick up the telephone, call a bunch of local restaurants and ask about the waiting times."

Source: Reprinted from Susie Stephenson, "DINKs dine out (advice on marketing restaurants to dual-income/no-kids couples)," *Restaurants & Institutions,* April 1, 1997, vol. 107, no. 8, p. 78(4). Reprinted by permission of Reed Publishing USA.

entered the urban labor market, another term emerged: **buppies**, to describe this new group of black, urban professionals (Sassen 2001). The yuppies, dinks, and buppies renovated brownstones and older loft buildings, upgrading the neighborhood. Moreover, their lifestyle prompted the opening of boutiques, fitness centers, specialty stores, new restaurants, coffee shops, bookstores, and other retail establishments, completing the gentrification process.

Not all middle-class urban neighborhoods are recently evolved entities. There are also older city residential areas that maintain their social-class character, sometimes despite outside forces that threaten their stability. We will look at examples of both types.

Many young urban professionals ("yuppies") find much in the city to enjoy. Eating out, shopping, going to a concert, the theater, or clubs are favorite pastimes. You'll also find many in the parks—biking, rollerblading, strolling, jogging, sitting and reading, or sunning themselves—as they enjoy "down time" in the public open spaces of the city.

Chicago.   Identified as low-income neighborhoods in 1990, Logan Square, West Town, the Near West Side, and the Near South Side experienced such significant growth in the 1990s that they are no longer low-income neighborhoods (see Figure 10–5). Once struggling neighborhoods, they are now among Chicago's most desirable residential areas. This change occurred because each of the neighborhoods became a destination for yuppies. Their arrival spurred further redevelopment, much of it through private developers not the

government. Mostly white, their arrival also coincided with a large exodus of blacks (the Near West Side) and Latinos (West Town). Displacement of low-income minorities did not occur on a significant scale in the Near South Side since the new development occurred on previously unoccupied land. Logan Square went through a changeover to better-educated, higher-income Latinos (Zielenbach 2005).

The population demographics give strong evidence of a higher social class taking over these neighborhoods. The four communities saw at least a 12 percent increase in residents aged 25 to 39, with 19 percent or greater increases in single-person households and sharp drops in the number of children. In addition, there were double-digit increases in the proportion of college graduates (Zielenbach 2005:5–6). This influx of highly educated, upwardly mobile individuals helped drive up the per capita income and property values, in turn driving out many low-income residents, thereby attracting still more middle class professionals. Although one might argue that these are actually mixed-income neighborhoods since pockets of low-income households remain, still developing patterns suggest that is a temporary phase and that these neighborhoods are evolving into middle-class entities.

Milwaukee.   On the northwest side, four miles from the city's downtown, is a culturally diverse, 30-block area known as Sherman Park, whose history dates back to the 1890s. At that time the upper class opted to remain closer to the central business district, living on the city's mansion-lined boulevards, but a steady stream of middle-class businesspeople and professionals—usually third- and fourth-generation German Americans—chose this area in which to build sturdy homes, noted for their ornamentation and high craftsmanship. Ever since, this neighborhood has remained a stable, middle-class residential area.

Today, the neighborhood remains one of Milwaukee's "most vibrant areas" (Curran 2003). Three of its streets have been designated as historic districts, but throughout the neighborhood, that craftsmanship and the variety of architectural styles (bungalows, Arts

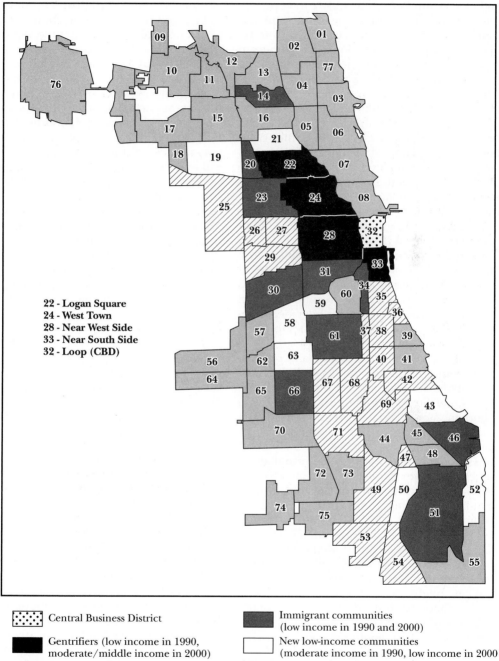

22 - Logan Square
24 - West Town
28 - Near West Side
33 - Near South Side
32 - Loop (CBD)

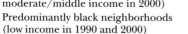 Central Business District

        Gentrifiers (low income in 1990,
moderate/middle income in 2000)

        Predominantly black neighborhoods
(low income in 1990 and 2000)

        Immigrant communities
(low income in 1990 and 2000)

        New low-income communities
(moderate income in 1990, low income in 2000

        Moderate/high income neighborhoods
(not included in analysis)

FIGURE 10–5   Gentrification in Chicago from 1990 to 2000. [*Source:* The Urban Institute.]

and Crafts, and Period Revival) attract people wanting to live in such fine homes on the wide, quiet streets. Property values thus remain high, but most residents are long-term residents and everyone knows everyone else.

In the 1970s, when "white flight" was occurring in Milwaukee as in many cities, the Sherman Park Community Association (SPCA) battled racially discriminatory real estate practices, landlord neglect, and crime. What was most distinguished about the SPCA was its embrace of racial integration, to encourage blacks and whites to live together. Today this neighborhood retains its racial diversity, although a black middle class is now the majority. Interracial couples also find a high comfort level here (Curran 2003).

Religious tolerance and integration also mark this neighborhood of large numbers of Catholics, Jews, and Protestants. One example is the Sherman Park Area Congregation, formed by clergy from all three faiths, which meets regularly to discuss neighborhood issues to reach consensus on how to tackle them.

While the neighborhood maintains residential stability, the stores along its main business thoroughfares—particularly Burleigh Street and Center Street—struggle to compete with suburban stores. Some progress has been made. The Burleigh Street Community Development Corporation, a non-profit coalition of local residents and business professionals, is dedicated to re-energizing the business district. Armed with government and private foundation funding, they replaced the vacant bowling alley and attached restaurant with a new business and community center. The $50 million St. Joseph Regional Medical Center is another welcome presence, and so are other new businesses attracted to this neighborhood.

What might have become a changing neighborhood has instead, thanks to the determination of its residents, remained a stable, middle-class urban neighborhood.

Working-Class Urban Neighborhoods

Often, though not always, a city's working-class neighborhoods are distinctive by the ethnic and racial minority groups who predominate. (The East End of Nashville, Tennessee, would be an example of a non-ethnic working-class neighborhood.) The many visual clues—signs, parallel social institutions (churches, clubs, stores, newspapers), and street activities—give a distinctive sense of place and they form an important part of the community's social life. The streets in such neighborhoods are, as William H. Whyte (1980) described, "the rivers of life" of the neighborhood. Here you will find people meeting and greeting one another, using the stoops and sidewalks as personal social space, as the public space of the street in essence becomes their front yard. Most importantly, such neighborhoods are a *gemeinschaft* community, with shared values, intimacy, a strong sense of belonging, and a strong support network. They remain what Herbert Gans (1962b) called **ethnic villages** (see the Urban Living box on p. 291).

Newark's Ironbound.   This working-class area in the East Ward of Newark, New Jersey, is one such example. It was brought to the attention of millions of moviegoers as the epicenter of the 2005 summer blockbuster, *War of the Worlds,* and is about four miles square and lies between the Passaic River and Newark Liberty International Airport.

The district's name derives from its being surrounded by railroad tracks. Once the industrial center of the city with many factories, forges, and breweries, it was first home to hundreds of impoverished laborers who toiled in the nearby factories during grueling 72-hour, six-day workweeks. In the 1920s Portuguese immigrants began to settle in the neighborhood, joining a mixture of blacks, Germans, Irish, Italians, and Polish already there.

With a more liberal immigration law passed in 1965, many Portuguese immigrants, driven by political unrest, joined their compatriots as other groups moved out. By the 1970s most of the factories and breweries in the Ironbound closed, but more Portuguese arrivals continued to settle here, because economic conditions were worse in their homeland but here jobs could be found nearby. Portuguese-speaking Brazilians arrived in the late 1980s and

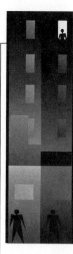

URBAN LIVING

The Ethnic Villagers

To most of the West Enders, the area had been home either since birth or marriage. Some were born in the West End because this was where their parents had settled when they first came to America or where they had moved later in life. Others came as adults in the Italian "invasion" of the West End during the 1930s. Many of them had grown up in the North End and had moved at the time of marriage in order to take advantage of better and larger apartments in the West End. In any case, almost all of the West Enders came to the area as a part of a group. Even their movements within the West End—that is, from the lower end to the upper—had been made together with other Italians at about the same time. . . .

. . . West Enders were in the West End because this is where they "belonged." . . . While they do want to be left alone, they are not averse to the aural or visual closeness of their neighbors. As everyone knows everyone else's activities and problems anyway, they know that it is impossible to hide anything by physical privacy. As one West Ender put it:

> I like the noise people make. In summer people have their windows open, and everyone can hear everyone else, but nobody cares what

anybody is saying; they leave their neighbors alone. In the suburbs, people are nosier; when a car comes up the street, all the windows go up to see who is visiting whom.

While the image of the suburb is overdrawn, it is true that in the West End, where people knew so much about each other, there was no need for prying. A feeling of privacy could be maintained in the midst of high density.

In addition, hearing and seeing their neighbor's activities gave the West Enders a share in the life that went on around them, which, in turn, made them feel part of the group. . . . West Enders, living mainly in the group, have an insatiable appetite for group experience. . . .

I was told by one social worker of an experiment some years back to expose West End children to nature by taking them on a trip to Cape Cod. The experiment failed, for the young West Enders found no pleasure in the loneliness of natural surroundings and wanted to get back to the West End as quickly as possible. They were incredulous that anyone could live without people around him.

Sources: Reprinted with permission of The Free Press, a Division of Simon & Schuster Adult Publishing Group from *The Urban Villagers* by Herbert J. Gans. Copyright © 1982 by Herbert J. Gans. Copyright © 1962 by The Free Press.

early 1990s, drawn by the low-cost housing, close-knit community, and convenient location. Brazilians now make up half the Portuguese-speaking population in the Ironbound, whereinitial tensions over cultural differences between mainland Portuguese and Brazilians have largely disappeared (Lawlor 2004).

Newark, in fact, has the largest Portuguese population of any city in the United States,

and the ongoing migration assures that Portuguese is often the first, sometimes the only, language spoken in many Ironbound shops (Stoneback 2005). *Luso-Americano*, the nation's largest Portuguese language newspaper, is published here and has a wide circulation.

The Ironbound is a mix of homes, stores and industrial buildings, with a vibrant commercial center of shops, ethnic restaurants, cafes, and clubs on Ferry Street, each offering

As with many vibrant, urban ethnic neighborhoods, Newark's Ironbound District serves a dual purpose. It is home to first-generation, working-class Americans (Portuguese-speaking in this case) and it also attracts many visitors, of the same or other backgrounds, who partake of its ethnic flavor in the stores and restaurants that line the streets.

different elements of the European lifestyle. Residents often speak of a strong sense of community, easily evident in daily walks and encounters with people they know.

> This closeness attracted many Portuguese immigrants to the Ironbound. Jobs were available in the many factories and there were people happy to help them find work and a place to stay. Today, there are some 20 Portuguese social clubs, most representing a single town or province of Portugal. The clubs help new immigrants, but mainly offer programs that keep the Portuguese traditions alive. (Lawlor 2004:5)

The clubs also sponsor soccer teams and the neighborhood parks are usually filled with adults and children playing soccer. In the bars and clubs, soccer is the spectator sport of choice and when Brazil won the World Cup, revelers took to the streets in the middle of the night (Lawlor 2004). In fact, World Cup soccer competition remains far more important in the Ironbound than the Super Bowl. During

soccer season the bars and restaurants are filled with fans rooting for their teams while having lunch or dinner (Stoneback 2005).

Apartment buildings of four or more units comprise about one-fourth of the housing. Demand exceeds the supply, so most tenants are found by word of mouth. Most housing (60 percent) is two- and three-family homes; single-family homes make up the rest. Housing demand has been high since the late 1990s, with 900 new homes built and prices tripling, causing a problem in increased taxes for older residents. The housing boom has led to overcrowding in the Ironbound's schools and the use of classroom trailers, and the city plans to build new schools in the neighborhood (Lawlor 2004).

More than 170 restaurants also attract many visitors, but it's not until 9 or 10 P.M. that they fill up with neighborhood residents who follow the Iberian pattern of late dining. On Thursday mornings the numerous seafood shops are their busiest, as Ironbound regulars line up to buy the fresh seafood that arrives each Wednesday evening from Portugal. From morning to night, this village-within-a-city "throbs with the accents of Portugal, Spain, and Brazil" (Corcoran 2003).

Other Ethnic Villages.   Virtually every U.S. city has one or more ethnic villages, where first-generation Americans cluster and re-create to some extent the world they left behind. The old European ethnic neighborhoods are fading, but new ones are taking their place with the concentrations of many African, Asian, and Hispanic immigrants. Of the thousands of examples, here are just a few. Toronto's Little India, found along Gerrard Street East between Greenwood and Coxwell Avenues, offers an active community life and array of ethnic stores. Koreatown, situated principally along Lawrence Avenue in the Albany Park neighborhood in Chicago's Northwest Side, remains a vibrant community although other groups are making inroads. The Dominican presence is so strong in New York's Washington Heights neighborhood in upper Manhattan that it is sometimes called "Quisqueya Heights." (*Quisqueya* is the informal nickname of the Dominican Republic.) Two of Miami's better-known, cohesive ethnic neighborhoods are "Little Haiti" in the old neighborhoods of Lemon City, Edison Center, Little River, and Buena Vista East, and "Little Havana" in Miami, located west of Brickell Avenue and along Southwest Eighth Street.

Many working-class neighborhoods have mixed ethnic populations. The urban neighborhood of Ridgewood in the Queens borough of New York City, for instance, is a high-density area known for its brick and stone two-story buildings. Once a German and Italian enclave, its newer immigrants are mostly from Central and Eastern Europe (especially Poland) and from Latin America. Archer Heights on Chicago's Southwest Side has mostly brick bungalows and ranches and is home to a large Polish population and growing Hispanic community. The Excelsior District of San Francisco is primarily a working-class neighborhood of Asian and Latino immigrant families.

Mixed-Income Urban Neighborhoods

In most cities there are urban neighborhoods that contain people from a mixture of income levels. These neighborhoods may result from intervention, such as public housing designed to reduce the concentration of poverty, or else planned gentrification programs, or simply the nonplanned result from the social dynamics of people opting to move. Whatever the cause, mixed-income neighborhoods can remain stable in their income diversity, as indeed many are. Otherwise, they may be in an early stage of gentrification with low-income people moving out and higher-income people moving in, or else they are deteriorating as the middle class moves out and more low-income people move in. The keys to the quality of life in a mixed-income neighborhood, then, are not only household income levels but also the desire/ability of residents to remain there.

Grand Rapids.   Located on the western side of Michigan, Grand Rapids is the state's second largest city, with a population in 2000 of nearly 200,000 within the city limits and over one million in its Metropolitan Statistical Area (MSA). It has a mixed economic base, with its largest employment providers in manufacturing (22 percent); educational, health, and social services (21 percent); and retail trade (12 percent). Median family income was $44,224 in 2000, compared to $54,118 in the Grand Rapids MSA. The percentage of city families with incomes below the poverty level was 9.2 percent. The city's non-Hispanic population declined from 74.9 percent in 1990 to 62.5 percent in 2000, as its racial minorities increased, reaching in 2000 20.4 percent black, 12.5 percent Hispanic, 1.6 percent Asian, and 6.6 percent other categories (U.S. Census Bureau 2002c).

June Thomas (2004) and her associates identified 11 of 131 census block groups as stable mixed-income neighborhoods, in that there was no significant change in the population from the lowest two income quintiles over a 10-year period. Unlike other block groups, these 11 had less vacant housing and lower proportions of families in poverty, as well as lower family median income than found in the MSA. In focus group interviews in three representative neighborhoods, the researchers were able to identify five stabilizing influences of these neighborhoods. First, strong religious communities, such as Catholic parishes, kept people in the neighborhoods. Positive feelings about the schools, with the ability of children to walk to local schools, along with strong social networks between and among neighbors were also important factors. Family connections to the neighborhood and well-organized, professionally staffed neighborhood associations completed the steadying elements.

At the same time, however, the researchers found fragility in these neighborhoods. Respondents were concerned about the increase in rental households, fearing poorly monitored property and renters who would cause noise, visible blight, and neighborhood change. They also were anxious about the decline in the quality of the public schools and the possible relocation of parochial schools. Many suggested that if the schools declined drastically, so would the neighborhood (Thomas et al. 2004).

Toronto.   The St. Lawrence neighborhood is a different example of a mixed-income area, one that was deliberately created through redevelopment of a large area previously used for warehousing and industrial activities (De Jong 2000). Now home to about 12,000 residents living in converted warehouses or new structures, it extends from Yonge Street east to Parliament and Queen streets south to the railroad tracks.

This thriving neighborhood effectively integrates people of all ages and different socioeconomic backgrounds living side by side.

The revitalized St. Lawrence neighborhood in Toronto is a mixed-income area, successfully integrating people of all ages and socioeconomic levels. What makes this area so successful is its mixture of different housing types in new structures, converted warehouses, and factories with a strategic intermingling of businesses, stores, restaurants, and theatres.

Planners achieved this social mix by strategic placement of a range of housing types that included condominium apartments (39 percent), nonprofit cooperatives (30 percent), private non-profit units (27 percent), and owner-occupied townhouses (4 percent). The three-story family townhouses stand on tree-lined interior roads, surrounded by seven- to ten-story apartments on busier streets. This mix nicely blends different levels of affordable housing, ranging from private ownership to rent-geared-to-income (RGI) apartments (Regent Park Collaboration Team 2003).

Complementing the successful mixture of people and housing types is vibrant economic activity that includes businesses, restaurants, stores, and theaters. Nearby St. Lawrence Market—site of the city's original market and still highly popular—offers a unique shopping destination, as do other businesses on Front Street and on the Esplanade. Adding to the mixed use of space and activities are a community center and a social network of civic organizations—a residents' association, seniors' group, school-based organizations, community center council, and various other youth and children's organizations.

All this helps reinforce residents' sense of commitment to stay in the area, a view reinforced by their sense of place. Experts further consider this a successful neighborhood because its excellent design ensured that the new buildings retained the character and scale of the older ones, and followed Toronto's nineteenth-century pattern of alignment along roads to encourage street-related activity. That deliberate design, augmented with excellent lighting, provides an active street life in this mixed-use neighborhood, which conveys a sense of safety to pedestrians (Regent Park Collaborative Team 2003).

All is not perfect, however. As in most mixed-income neighborhoods, there is an undercurrent of fear about possible negative changes. Some worried that neighborhood stability could be undermined if there is a high turnover rate in either the condominium units rented out for temporary lodging and in some of the rent-controlled units. Residents also expressed concern about the lack of play areas for children and recreational spaces for seniors (Regent Park Collaborative Team 2003).

Low-Income Urban Neighborhoods

Typically, we find neighborhoods with high poverty levels in a city's oldest districts. Many of these communities were once solidly middle-class, even upper-class areas that have fallen on hard times. Since these areas of high population density and substandard housing are most often located near the central business district, they came to be called **inner-city neighborhoods,** as well **ghettos** or **slums.**

For the trapped poor left behind in the inner city, the future is bleak. Lacking the necessary schooling and communication skills required for work in the service and information sectors of the economy, residents may experience unemployment rates as high as 80 percent (Kasarda 1993). High rates of substance abuse, single parents, infant mortality, violent crime, and welfare dependency also are common. These "truly disadvantaged," in the words of William J. Wilson (1990), are poor people who rely on welfare assistance and the underground economy to survive.

Unlike the immigrant poor of the past, today's poor inner-city residents face social isolation. The exodus of middle- and working-class two-parent families removes essential role models and reduces community resources. Furthermore, outsiders avoid these neighborhoods, leaving area residents to live virtually cut off from the larger society. Gary Orfield noted the magnitude of this isolation:

> To a considerable extent the residents of city ghettos are now living in separate and deteriorating societies, with separate economies, diverging family structures and basic institutions, and even growing linguistic separation within the core ghettos. (1988:103)

Current social indicators offer little cause for optimism, for such problems have structural causes that our society has yet to overcome.

Chicago. The city and its metropolitan region experienced significant economic growth in the 1990s, the city less so (4 percent) than its suburbs (16 percent). Still, the growth was strong enough to improve many of its low-income neighborhoods. In many of these communities, in fact, the improvement was greater than for the city itself. For example, per capita incomes in these low-income areas increased by 21 percent compared to 16 percent in the entire city, while unemployment fell by more than 4 percent compared to the city's decrease of 1.2 percent in the decade (Zielenbach 2005:4).

To illustrate how a neighborhood declines though, we will look at Gage Park, a new low-income Chicago neighborhood that was a moderate-income neighborhood in 1990. Most common here are 75- to 110-year old bungalows, along with Georgian-style homes from the 1940s, ranches from the 1960s and 1970s, and some more recently built Cape Cods. About 30 percent of the properties are two- and three-family houses (Steele 1998).

With a large foreign-born influx since 1990, primarily Hispanic, Gage Park experienced a 10 percent drop in its proportion of high school graduates by 2000, and many of the newcomers had difficulty speaking English. In fact, 36 percent of those aged 25 or more had less than a ninth-grade education, and another 18 percent had a higher level than that but were not high school graduates (U.S. Census Bureau 2002c). In this 10-year interval, per capita income in the neighborhood decreased by 31 percent. Another barometer—the overall index score that is a composite measure of per capita income, conventional home mortgage purchase rates, and median single-family property values—declined by 52 percent in relation to the city's overall score (Zielenbach 2005:5).

Los Angeles. One of the poorest and most densely populated neighborhoods in the city is Pico-Union, which gets its name from the key intersection of Pico Boulevard and Union Avenue. Originally developed as an LA suburb in the early twentieth century, its housing and building types give testimony to that original suburban character. Located west of the downtown district, that proximity made it an attractive residential locale for new immigrants, especially Scandinavian Lutherans, Russian Jews, and Greek Orthodox.

As suburbanization extended outward and residents relocated in the mid-twentieth century, Pico-Union became part of the "inner city." The shifting of economic and social resources away from the inner city and to the suburbs resulted in the decline of the physical appearance and service infrastructure of the area. Both housing and commercial buildings became run-down due to lack of maintenance. Landlords subdivided the large houses and rented out to accommodate the large number of low-income immigrant families. As a result, the neighborhood became a place characterized by overcrowding and substandard housing conditions (UCLA Department of Urban Planning 1998).

Pico-Union is now home to over 43,000 people, mostly Central Americans and Mexicans. The 2000 census revealed a population that was 82 percent Hispanic, 11 percent Asian, 4 percent non-Hispanic white, and 3 percent black (U.S. Census Bureau 2002c). As is so typical in immigrant neighborhoods, many community organizations and stores are tailored to the language, culture, and service needs of the population.

Persons living in poverty (44 percent) are twice that in the entire city. In 2000, per capita income was $8,690 compared to $20,671 in Los Angeles as a whole. Median household income and median family income were also less than half that of the city. Educational level offers another stark contrast; overall in the city 80 percent have a high school diploma or higher, but in Pico-Union only 32 percent do (U.S. Census Bureau 2002c). The low levels of education and the language barrier are reflected in employment patterns and corresponding rates of economic stagnation (Centro Latino de Educación Popular 2005).

Marred by graffiti and vacant stores, this neighborhood also suffers from a high crime rate. Gang activity is a serious concern, particularly by the 18th Street gang, which is involved in auto theft, drug trafficking, extortion, and murder (Valdez 2000). Both the police and community organizations attempt to make the area safer and have had some moderate success, but many problems remain.

The Homeless

Most of us encounter homeless people from time to time, perhaps sleeping on benches in parks or bus stations, standing in doorways along skid row streets, or panhandling on busy walkways. It is all too clear that they inhabit the edges of society, and we usually assume they are cut off from work and family, weeks away from their last job or even their last square meal—a familiar stereotype. However, the problem is much more complex and no stereotype gives a complete picture of the homeless.

Recent decades have seen a new type of homeless person. Efforts to revitalize cities with new construction on the edges of the central business districts or downtowns destroyed many of the old single-room occupancy hotels (SROs) that had provided housing to people living on the edge of poverty. Between 1970 and 1990, for example, Chicago and New York lost about 70 percent of their SROs and Los Angeles more than half (Hoch and Slayton 1989; Koegel 1996). In addition, the loss of low-cost housing due to urban renewal or rent increases in an area undergoing gentrification forced many out of their neighborhoods, thereby increasing the demand on remaining low-income housing, pushing up even those rents beyond what many could afford. Current estimates identify about 40 percent of all homeless as families with children, 41 percent as single men, and 14 percent as single women. Twenty-two percent are mentally ill, while 30 percent are substance abusers (U.S. Conference of Mayors 2005).

Particularly disturbing is the fact that one of the fastest growing segments of the homeless population is families with children. Each year over 800,000 children and youth experience homelessness, and at least one-fifth of them do not attend school (U.S. Department of Education 2005). The average age of the homeless child is six. Homeless children are three times more likely to repeat a grade and four times more likely to drop out of school than other children. Only four out of ten heads of these families have any work history and, even then, most jobs are either part-time or short-term, held less than six months. Also significant is that 68 percent of these parents lack a high school diploma (Whitman 1995:32). Limited schooling and little work experience are the all-too-typical attributes of the impoverished, but the added factor of homelessness denies these families any stability or community support (Institute for Children and Poverty 2005).

The situation is worsening. In 2005, requests for emergency shelter increased an average of 6 percent in the nation's cities. In 88 percent of the survey cities, emergency shelters were forced to turn away homeless families due to a lack of resources (U.S. Conference of Mayors 2005:59). The study also found that, while people remain homeless an average of eight months, the length of time people are homeless increased in 2005.

Clearly, lack of affordable housing is the leading cause of homelessness. The root causes of that inability to pay for a roof over one's head—lack of education, inadequate low-income housing, poverty, and unavailable jobs—are unlikely to go away soon. For many, the images connected with this small, unfortunate segment of a city's population distort their view of the social class diversity found in the total city population.

SUBURBAN SOCIAL CLASS DIVERSITY

Today's suburbs, particularly those closest to the city, no longer fit the white, middle-class, and family-with-kids stereotype. More and more, suburbs are home to minorities, the working class and poor, and the aged. Suburbs now vary widely in terms of average income, racial composition, average age, and length of residence.

Upper-Income Suburbs

A century ago, suburban residence symbolized the lifestyle of the well to do. Fabulous estates such as Lynnewood Hall—called the Versailles of America—clearly set off the lifestyle of early suburbanites from others. The idea was to emulate the country ways of European aristocracy, as Pierre Lorillard II did better than almost anyone. In 1886, Lorillard (heir to a tobacco fortune) inherited some 600,000 acres and, at a cost of $2 million, created a millionaires' colony north of New York. Tuxedo Park was "a kind of country club *cum* family resort where some two or three hundred of New York's Best People who were growing tired of resort hotels at Saratoga or Richfield Springs might come to hunt, fish, and skate" (Baltzell 1989:357).

> At Tuxedo Park Lorillard produced almost a caricature of the Victorian millionaire's mania for exclusiveness. In less than a year, he surrounded seven thousand acres with an eight-foot fence, graded some thirty miles of road, built a complete sewage and water system, a gate house which looked like "a frontispiece of an English novel," a clubhouse staffed with imported English servants, and "twenty-two casement dormered English turreted cottages." On Memorial Day, 1886, special trains brought seven hundred highly selected guests from New York to witness the Park's opening. (Baltzell 1964:122–23)

By offering his club members property within Tuxedo Park for purchase, Lorillard created, as Baltzell suggests, a sort of Levittown for aristocrats. Yet, as streetcar lines and automobiles kept increasing, new housing rippled outward from cities and, with it, a new image of the suburban lifestyle began to take hold among the masses. Its roots were the same—to live "the good life"—but the magnitude of the change ensured that the vision would be watered down.

Today's upper-class suburbs resemble the old aristocratic ones of yesteryear. They include Grosse Pointe Shores near Detroit and South Barrington near Chicago. Families have large houses on large properties, often with swimming pools, and center their social lives on churches or temples and exclusive country clubs, where golf and tennis are favorite leisure activities. This affluent lifestyle is marked by conspicuous consumption, symbols of high social status, and other attributes of class privilege.

The populations in these suburbs tend to be somewhat older, mostly white, highly educated, and with incomes significantly above the state average. Grosse Pointe Shores, for example, has a population of 2,800 within its one square mile who have a median age of 48, are 92 percent white, and 62 percent are at least college graduates, including 30 percent with advanced degrees. In 2000, the median household income was about $114,000, compared to a Michigan median household income of $45,000. South Barrington is larger, nearly seven square miles with a population in 2004 of about 3,900 that is 81 percent white and 13 percent Asian. The median household income in 2000 was $170,755 (in Illinois it was about $47,000), and 63 percent were at least college graduates, including 30 percent with advanced degrees (city-data.com 2005).

Although the older elite suburbs long resisted the entry of racial, ethnic, and religious minorities, the newer affluent suburbs—typically located at the outer suburban edges (such as South Barrington, which is 37 miles from Chicago)—accept anyone with the right-sized bank account. A good example of economic elitism prevailing over ethnic prejudice is Beverly Hills, California, where wealthy Arabs and rich Jews live harmoniously as neighbors—a far cry from their counterparts in the Middle East.

Middle-Income Suburbs

Darien, Connecticut, and Levittown, New York, closely resemble the suburban stereotype. Life centers on the family and child-centered activities. As Peter Muller describes:

> The management of children is a central . . . concern, and most local social contact occurs through such family-oriented formal organizations as the school PTA, Little League, and the Scouts. . . . Neighboring is limited and selective, and even socializing with relatives is infrequent. . . . The insular single-family house and dependence on the automobile for all trip making [accommodate the development of a] network of self-selected friends widely distributed in suburban space. (1981:72)

In suburbs such as these, few people are poor and almost everyone has at least finished high school. Once mostly white, these suburbs have become more racially mixed in recent years.

Solon, Ohio—profiled in the Urban Living box below—is an example of such communities, where affluent Asians, blacks, and non-Hispanic whites live harmoniously as neighbors.

URBAN LIVING

Comparing Working-Class and Middle-Class Suburbs

To many people who live in the inner city or in rural areas, all suburbs may seem the same. But suburbs differ in many ways, as portraits of two suburban Ohio towns close to the city of Cleveland show. The first, North Olmsted, is a working-class suburb. It is located 17 miles to the southwest of Cleveland, has a population of about 34,000 people and covers about 12 square miles of land. The second, Solon, is a middle-class suburb. It is 17 miles to the southeast of Cleveland, and has a far lower population density, with its 22,000 people spread over about 21 square miles.

As you might expect, the cost of housing differs in the two suburbs. In 2000, the median house value in North Olmsted was $142,300, compared to $217,000 in Solon. In Solon, there is much more new housing, with nearly half of its homes built since 1980. In North Olmstead, by contrast, just 13 percent of all homes were built since 1980. The age of homes matters, because newer homes typically are larger, with bigger rooms, and are more likely to have attached garages, and amenities like central air conditioning and perhaps even a swimming pool.

By and large, suburbs have a smaller share of minorities than central cities. But the middle-class community of Solon has more racial diversity than the working-class community of North Olmstead. In Solon, 87 percent of the people are non-Hispanic whites,

6 percent are African American, 4 percent are Asian American, 1 percent Hispanic, and 1 percent claim two or more races. North Olmsted, by contrast, is 93 percent non-Hispanic white, with African Americans making up just 1 percent of the population, Asian Americans 2 percent, Hispanic Americans 2 percent, and the remaining 2 percent of two or more races.

One of the biggest differences between the populations of these two suburbs involves schooling. Of Solon's adult population, 50 percent have earned at least a bachelor's degree, and 22 percent have a graduate or professional degree. In North Olmstead, just 27 percent of adults have a bachelor's degree and only 9 percent have a graduate or professional degree. Given this difference, it is no surprise that people in Solon have higher incomes: median household earnings in Solon in 2000 were $78,903, well above the $52,542 for North Olmsted. Unemployment is typically low in suburbs, but, here again, we see a difference: Solon's unemployment rate (1.6 percent) is half that in North Olmstead (3.1 percent).

As this comparison shows, suburbs display their own characteristic diversity, whether by casual observation of differences in property lot sizes and housing structures, or in analysis of socioeconomic data. Race and ethnicity thus appear to be less important attributes of social class differences between the two towns than educational level and income.

Source: Data from www.city-data.com. Accessed June 27, 2005.

Working-Class Suburbs

Working-class suburbs multiplied rapidly after World War II, when white ethnic, working-class families moved outward along with many industries. A generation later, Muller described the dominant interests of most:

> [Suburban] working-class, ethnic-centered neighborhoods are characterized by a broad social interaction of informal groups congregating at such local meeting places as the church, tavern, street corner, or door stoop. Local group acceptance and integration is the dominant social value, and communal life stresses the availability of a satisfying peer-group society, similar neighborhoods, maintaining easy access among people well-known to each other, and collective defense of neighborhood respectability. (1981:74–75)

Today, some of these older blue-collar suburbs are suffering from a loss of jobs as industries close or move factories abroad. With an eroding industrial and commercial tax base, these suburbs are deteriorating physically, and property taxes are on the rise. Not surprisingly, many of the more affluent residents are packing up and moving farther out. There, they hope to find a newer version of their dream home and, perhaps, a lower tax rate. However, other working-class suburbs remain healthy and are growing. One such town is the Cleveland suburb of North Olmsted, profiled in the Urban Living box on p. 299.

Suburban Cosmopolitan Centers

In marked contrast to the working-class suburbs (and different even from Darien and Grosse Pointe Shores) are communities like Princeton, New Jersey, home of Princeton University. Composed mainly of academics, professionals, writers, actors, artists, and students, these communities resemble the university areas, bohemian enclaves, and cosmopolite residential neighborhoods of central cities. Their population is usually deeply interested in "high culture," and theaters, music facilities, and elegant, unusual restaurants are found there in abundance.

Minority Suburbs

Minority suburbanization is most pronounced in metropolitan regions of 500,000 or more, where the minority population grew from 19 percent in 1990 to 27 percent in 2000. These suburbs are now 12 percent Hispanic, 9 percent black, and 5 percent Asian. The change is even more substantial in some areas. For example, blacks are now more than 20 percent of the suburban population in such areas as Atlanta, Fort Lauderdale, Miami, New Orleans, Richmond, and Washington, D.C. Hispanics exceed 25 percent of the suburban population in Miami, Los Angeles, Riverside, and San Diego (Lewis Mumford Center, 2001c).

Most suburbs are now racially diverse and becoming more so all the time. Even so, some suburban communities remain racially segregated, as some African Americans deliberately seek out predominantly black communities. Examples of these affluent African American suburbs that attract middle-class black families who prefer socializing in a racially homogeneous environment are Rolling Oaks near Miami; Brook Glen, Panola Mill, and Wyndham Park near Atlanta; and Black Jack, Jennings, Normandy, and University City near St. Louis. Similarly, black residents in suburban Prince George's County in Maryland, who comprise 63 percent of the county's total population, find comfort in living in affluent but predominantly black communities or subdivisions. Barron Harvey, professor of accounting at Howard University, explains moving from a white, upper-middle-income suburb in Fairfax County, Virginia, to Prince George's County:

> We always wanted to make sure our child had many African-American children to play with, not just one or two. We always wanted to be in a community with a large number of black professionals, and to feel part of that community. We never really felt like we were part of Fairfax. (Dent 1992:20)

More often, though, black suburbs result from invasion–succession. That is, after some

In the past two decades, many minority Americans, part of a growing middle class, have realized the American Dream by owning a house in suburbia. While some live in integrated neighborhoods, others prefer to live in mostly segregated communities, finding greater comfort for themselves and their children in a homogeneous racial setting.

minorities enter a community, whites begin to leave. Eventually most whites are gone, creating a segregated black suburban community analogous in many ways to its center-city counterpart, the black ghetto.

Muller (1981) distinguished three subtypes of black suburbs. The first is what he called the "spillover" community, such as Glenarden, Maryland, adjacent to Washington, D.C. These suburbs are direct outgrowths of center-city black ghettos that move, over time, beyond the center city. Significant spillover suburbs of blacks presently exist in Cleveland, St. Louis, Chicago, Atlanta, Miami, Los Angeles, and New York and are becoming more and more prevalent throughout the country. The income level of spillover communities is high relative to other black suburbs because, like whites who departed from the center cities, blacks

moving outward tend to be middle class, wishing to leave poorer neighbors behind.

"Colonies," such as Kinloch, Missouri (96 percent black in 2000), just outside St. Louis, represent a second type. Often these isolated communities originally arose as shantytowns outside the city proper and, in recent decades, white suburbs grew up around them. Colonies are poor areas with deteriorating housing and large numbers of people living below the poverty level (about 38 percent, in Kinloch's case). Few members of the community have much schooling, and most work in low-skill jobs. The outlook for them is as bleak as it is for center-city ghetto residents (see the Urban Living box about Robbins, Illinois on p. 302).

Only somewhat better off is the "satellite city," exemplified by Chester, Pennsylvania, about 10 miles downriver from Philadelphia.

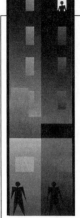

URBAN LIVING

Life in a Minority Suburb

Robbins, Illinois, is a small, minority suburb in decline. Its steadily declining population, now about 6,500 (95 percent black), is 3,000 less than in 1970. The town has as many people under age 18 as it does aged 65 or older (12 percent each).

Located 17 miles south of Chicago's Loop, Robbins is one of the oldest incorporated black municipalities in the United States. Largely farmland until 1910, it is characteristic of semi-rural black suburbs that developed during the Great Migration of the early twentieth century. The mostly working-class African Americans who settled here bought lots for as little as $90 each, many building their own houses and living without such amenities as electricity and indoor plumbing.

Outsiders derided the resulting makeshift landscape with its unpaved streets and called it a slum. Yet for the newly transplanted Southerners, Robbins offered numerous advantages: homeownership in a country-like environment; a safe location without risk of violence; a home near available factory jobs; and a tightly knit community. There were also work opportunities for the women, in domestic service or seasonal work in the city's canning and packing industries in Chicago. Moreover, many of the new residents could supplement their low incomes with garden produce and small livestock.

Over the next several decades, the population grew in size and population. Residents established a newspaper, the *Robbins Herald,* plus many churches and small stores. Robbins also became a popular recreation spot for black Chicagoans, who crowded its picnic grounds and nightclubs on summer weekends.

Because it was a blue-collar community with almost no commercial tax base, town officials could only undertake modest improvements, given the limited funds to upgrade services. As late as 1950, 22 percent of Robbins homes lacked indoor plumbing, and over 40 percent were considered substandard in 1960. In the 1960s, black developer Edward Starks opened the Golden Acres subdivision, which brought modern, suburban-style houses to the community. Paved streets and sewers came in the 1950s, but these costs—combined with plant layoffs in the 1970s—saddled the suburb with municipal debts. Although Robbins remained one of the few places in greater Chicago where African Americans with very limited resources could afford to buy a home of their own, lack of jobs in the area put the local economy into a tailspin.

With a median household income of just over $24,000 in 2000, other socioeconomic statistics offer little promise of a turn-around anytime soon. Two-thirds of the residents have a high school or higher level of education, but less than one in ten has a bachelor's degree or higher. One-fourth are married, one in ten are widowed, one in ten are divorced, and nearly half the eligible population has never married. New construction is a rarity; nearly one-fourth of its population is unemployed; and nearly one-third live in poverty.

Source: Adapted from Andrew Wiese, "Robbins, IL," *The Encyclopedia of Chicago* (Chicago: Chicago Historical Society, 2004) and from U.S. Census Bureau, 2000 Census Summary Files 1 and 3.

Originally an industrial city, Chester was a place of thriving shipbuilding and metal-working. No more. Both industries have fallen on hard times, leaving Chester and its black population—about three-fourths of the suburb's 37,000 residents—high and dry. Their unemployment rate is half that of Kinloch's, and the residents' outlook is only a bit brighter.

In 2000, 49 percent of all U.S. Hispanics lived in suburbs, up from 46 percent in 1990. The ten metropolitan areas with the most Hispanic suburbanites are in just five states: California (Los Angeles–Long Branch, Riverside–San Bernardino, San Diego, Orange County, San Francisco, Oakland); Florida (Miami); Texas (Houston); Arizona (Phoenix–Mesa); and Nevada (Las Vegas). Such cities now have what are in essence Hispanic suburbs (Lewis Mumford Center, 2001c).

Monterey Park near Los Angeles is an Asian suburb, its population over two-fifths Chinese American. This is the exception, however, because Asians—a diverse racial category of many cultures—typically move to predominantly white suburbs. As the most affluent U.S. minority group, with a median family income of $70,274 in 2003, more Asians (58 percent) live in suburbia than any other racial or ethnic category.

The continuing influx of Asian and Hispanic immigrants, together with the tendency of many to settle directly in the suburbs, suggests that suburbs will become more diverse in the years to come. Clearly the old stereotype about suburbia as a "white cocoon" no longer fits.

❖ ═══════ ❖ ═══════ ❖

SUMMARY

If stereotypes about urbanites contain some truth, they also contain distortions. Research points again and again to the existence of pronounced urban variety—a range of social class lifestyles that defies easy description. This is as true of the suburbs as it is of the center city. Proportionately, more residents in towns within the metropolitan region hold higher socioeconomic status than urban dwellers. However, if we look more carefully, we can find many examples of social class heterogeneity in both locales.

Ever since Marx and Weber offered their analyses about social stratification, sociologists have studied this aspect of community life, beginning with Warner's study of Yankee City in the 1930s, and continuing ever since. The middle class is the largest grouping in the United States (about 40 to 45 percent), followed by the working class (about one-third), the lower class (about 20 percent), and the elite upper class (about 5 percent). Each class has distinctive characteristics in wealth, power, prestige, and lifestyles, but not necessarily in choice of urban or suburban residence.

The gap between rich and poor is so pronounced that the United States has the most unequal distribution of wealth of all industrialized countries. The top quintile of the population earns about half of all income, as much as the remaining 80 percent combined, and the top 40 percent earns three-fourths of all income. The median household income is significantly higher in suburbia than in the city, and the city poverty rate is significantly higher than in suburbia. While this broad-brush portrait of city–suburb economic contrasts is accurate, sociologists use fine-brush analysis to see the details, intricacies, and inconsistencies of that broader portrait. Rather than upholding the simplistic stereotype of affluent suburbanites and nonaffluent urbanites, a much more complex picture evolves, as this chapter illustrated.

Our large cities are mosaics of differing social class enclaves: upper-, middle-, working- and lower-class neighborhoods. There are also mixed-income neighborhoods, some of them stable and others changing upwardly or downwardly. Cities do indeed have a high proportion of people living in poverty, but most city residents maintain a higher socioeconomic status. One poverty-struck population segment, the homeless, is a mixture of families (the fastest-growing element) and individuals, some of them mentally ill and/or substance abusers. They are a minute percentage of the urban population but form an indelible part of many people's image of the city.

Suburbs emerged in the late nineteenth century as country estates and small enclaves for the well-to-do—people anxious to escape the immigrant lifestyles and industrial commotion of the inner city. With the invention of the automobile in the twentieth century, however, a middle-class exodus accelerated, especially after World War II. The last three decades witnessed a marked increase in suburban diversity as large numbers of the working class and minorities moved to these outlying areas. This migration has produced a lifestyle complexity that rivals that of the central city. There is every reason to believe that this complexity and diversity will continue to increase throughout this century as immigration and decentralization continue.

Suburbs fall into recognizably distinct types. There are exclusive upper-income suburbs, middle-income suburbs, working-class suburbs, minority suburbs, and—increasingly in the South, Southwest, and West—Hispanic suburbs. Social class appears more significant than race and ethnicity in suburban settlement patterns as more and more African Americans, Asians, and Latinos move into the newer suburbs. Some suburbs have even developed into true cosmopolitan centers, offering all the goods, services, and entertainment that once drew people to the city's center.

CONCLUSION

Ultimately, what we have learned is that the manifestations of social stratification in North America are found *within both the city and the suburb*. Any simplistic socioeconomic comparison of the two ignores the lifestyle variations existing in each and really does a disservice to the many positive attributes that cities possess. Of course, central cities do have their problems, greatly intensified by the concentrated "critical masses" of diverse people. In addition to social class diversity, this chapter's topic, there is the diversity of race, ethnicity, and gender, to which we will turn in the next chapter.

KEY TERMS

Buppies
Class
Dinks
Ghettos
Inner-city neighborhoods
Power
Reputational method
Slums
Social class
Social stratification
Socioeconomic status (SES)
Yuppies

CHAPTER 11

RACE, ETHNICITY, AND GENDER
Urban Diversity

"I'm off to make a new life in the city!" Words such as these have echoed throughout history, in countless languages, throughout the world. Everywhere and always, cities have been immigrant-luring magnets. This basic fact explains why so many cities display striking diversity—in people, their neighborhoods, and their ways of life. Indeed, part of the excitement of a city lies in precisely this heterogeneity, the range of urban choices, the countless activities and opportunities.

Especially in the major immigrant-receiving nations—Britain, Canada, and the United States—racial and ethnic diversity has long been a common trait of cities. This chapter focuses on social diversity in North America and the ways in which race, ethnicity, and gender continue to play a vital part in shaping urban life.

CITIES AND IMMIGRANTS

In the United States, home to more immigrants than any other country on earth, cities remain mosaics of ethnic communities. At times, minorities even become the majority, as in Milwaukee back in 1850, when that city contained 6,000 Germans and 4,000 native-born citizens (Parrillo 2006:147). At the height of the "Great Immigration" between 1880 and 1910, roughly 1 million immigrants came to these shores annually, and seven out of ten of them settled in cities. Not surprisingly, in most cities in the northeastern United States, foreign-born people comprised two-thirds to three-fourths of the population. In 2000, by contrast, as seen in Table 11–1, the cities with the highest percentage of foreign-born residents were Miami at 59.5 percent, Los Angeles at 40.9 percent, San Francisco at 36.8 percent, and New York at 35.9 percent—proportions significantly higher than in 1990, but still far lower than those at the beginning of the twentieth century (U.S. Census Bureau 2002a).

Certainly their greater presence affects cities' economies, but are immigrants a benefit or a problem for cities? That question—whether on a national, state, or local level—is a fiercely debated one. A two-year study published by the National Academy of Sciences for the U.S. Commission on Immigration Reform found that immigrants add about $10 billion annually in net economic output due to the increased supply of labor and resulting lower prices, and that a typical newcomer pays $80,000 more in taxes than he or she receives over the course of a lifetime. However, immigrant households are costly at first because they tend to be younger and have school-age children using the public schools. Even illegal immigrants make a positive contribution. The Cato Institute reported that they pay approximately 46 percent as much in

TABLE 11–1 Racial/Ethnic Population in Metropolitan Areas, 2000 (by percent)

City	Asian	African American	Hispanic	Foreign-Born
Boston	5.5	7.2	5.9	25.8
Chicago	5.2	19.0	17.1	21.7
Dallas	4.6	15.2	23.0	24.4
Detroit	2.8	23.3	2.9	4.8
Houston	5.9	17.5	30.0	26.4
Los Angeles	13.5	9.9	44.6	40.9
Miami	1.9	20.0	57.3	59.5
New York	10.1	23.7	25.1	35.9
Philadelphia	3.8	20.3	5.1	9.0
San Francisco	25.1	5.6	16.8	36.8
Washington, D.C.	7.7	26.6	8.8	12.9

Source: U.S. Census Bureau, 2000.

taxes as American-born citizens but only receive 38 percent as much from the government (National Center for Policy Analysis 2002).

Critics argue that some states and urban centers receive the lion's share of immigrants, and their concentrated presence strains a community's social fabric and places an economic burden on those areas in education, health, and welfare costs (McCarthy and Vernez 1997; Clark 1998). George Borjas (2001) maintains that, while immigrants in general may enrich the nation, their high numbers and the growing proportion of poorly educated, low-skill workers have negative consequences that require a reexamination of our immigration policy objectives.

Ethnic Enclaves and Ethnic Identity

When we take account of the racial and ethnic variation of the U.S. population, today's cities display highly visible racial and ethnic diversity that is actually increasing. Like the European immigrants of previous generations, the new immigrants create their own ethnic enclaves and distinctive social institutions. The very size of cities allows for large concentrations of ethnic peoples. Cities thus continue to be mosaics of small worlds, abuzz with different sights, sounds, and smells reflected in ethnic celebrations, parades, restaurants, street fairs, stores, and other cultural activities. For some people, of course, cities—or at least certain neighborhoods in cities—are to be avoided precisely because of these differences, which they equate with danger and disorder.

The shifting pattern of ethnic and racial immigration underlies much of the complexity of today's cities. Table 11–2 shows that, from 1861 to 1960, the vast majority of legal immigrants to the United States were white people from Europe and Canada. During this period, differences between immigrants and people already in this country were mostly ethnic. That is, various whites—say, the Irish, Italians, and Jews—differed in cultural traditions but not in race. Since 1960, however, the bulk of our legal (and illegal) immigrants have been people of color from Asia and Latin America. Racial diversity, as well as ethnic differences, compounds the problems of acceptance and rejection.

Ethnic Change

A city's spatial structure reflects ethnic subcultures as immigrants arrive and, through a process known as **chain migration,** settle near friends and relatives. A vibrant ethnic community evolves—with leaders, institutions and organizations, stores, clubs, and same-language media—to help newcomers put down roots and "make it." At the same time that this pluralism manifests itself, however, the forces of assimilation also take hold. Immigrants seek to be part of their adopted country and try to become "American." Despite the challenges of learning a new language and, for some, barriers based on skin color, virtually all immigrants gradually identify more and more with their new country, where they expect to spend the rest of their lives.

Herbert Gans (1962b, 1982) noted that tight "ethnic villages" built by first-generation

TABLE 11–2   Legal Immigrants to the United States, 1861–2000 (by percent)

Region of Birth	1861–1900	1901–1930	1931–1960	1961–1990	1991–2000
Europe	90	79	58	18	15
Canada and Newfoundland	7	11	16	5	2
Asia	2	3	5	31	31
Latin America	0	5	17	34	38
Africa	—	—	1	2	4
Other	1	2	3	10	10

Source: U.S. Office of Immigration Statistics, 2000.

European immigrants did not always hold up when members of the second and third generation moved from the "old neighborhood" in the central city to leafy (and less ethnic) patches of the suburbs. Of course, such out-migration makes room for new immigrants, an invasion-succession process that refreshes urban pluralism even as assimilation draws others into the mainstream.

New York City.   For most of the nation's history, New York has stood as a symbol of racial and ethnic diversity. More than a generation ago, E. Digby Baltzell noted:

> Even today [New York's] citizenry, almost half of whom are foreign born or the children of foreign born, includes more blacks than most cities in Africa, a greater concentration of Jews than at any other time or place. . . . More Puerto Ricans than any other city outside of San Juan, more persons of Italian descent than most cities in Italy, and more [Irish] than Dublin. (1964:ix)

URBAN LIVING

The Multicultural City and Food

Each ethnic group has its own cuisine, and part of the fun of recalling your heritage or of widening your ethnic experiences is to taste the foods associated with other groups. As any urbanite will tell you, one of the great pleasures of the city is to partake of the great variety of foods available during the numerous cultural celebrations or at the many ethnic eateries and restaurants found everywhere. And there is yet another intriguing aspect of eating these ethnic foods, brought on by the **invasion-succession** process of one group replacing another.

With the decline of new French, Irish, Italian, Japanese, and Jewish immigrants, and their children moving into professional fields, Asian and Hispanic newcomers are replacing the old chefs in cities throughout North America. The new arrivals learn how to prepare the other culture's foods and take over established locales, popular for their original cuisine. Some of these changes seem an easy transition because of the old countries' proximities and histories. In New York City, for example, it is not unusual to find Bangladeshis running Indian restaurants or Albanians operating Italian restaurants.

However, New York also offers more radical examples. For instance, there's a pizza maker on Second Avenue and 80th who is Tibetan. Down on West 48th Street, a sushi chef at a popular Japanese restaurant is Mexican. At a French restaurant on West 55th Street, the pastry chef is Ecuadorian. A Chinese immigrant from Hong Kong, who learned his culinary art at a famous Jewish restaurant, now has his own place and serves smoked salmon and sturgeon to appreciative Jewish customers. And that wonderful nectar of the old Jewish neighborhoods, the egg cream (a wonderful, frothy drink that blends seltzer, milk, and chocolate) is served in the East Village by an Asian Indian who learned the secret recipe from the previous owner, an Italian, who learned it from the original storeowner, a Jewish immigrant.

So this is the multicultural face of the city: many different peoples serving many different kinds of food, not necessarily from their own homeland. A Central American may well have made that Middle Eastern *falafel* you get, or your Greek *moussaka* may be coming your way thanks to the efforts of a Peruvian. The city! Even its ethnic varieties have variety!

Source: Drawn from the experiences of Vincent N. Parrillo, his family, and friends.

New York still holds first place as the nation's leading destination of immigrants and is truly a multicultural city (see the Urban Living box on p. 308). In 2000, about 86,000 immigrants entered New York City, compared with about 71,000 coming to Los Angeles (U.S. Office of Immigration Statistics 2002:59). At present 36 percent of New Yorkers are foreign-born. Brighton Beach, Brooklyn, is known as "Little Odessa"—a place where tens of thousands of Russians live in the largest Russian immigrant community in the world. New York City also has this nation's largest concentration of Haitians, most of them living in the Brooklyn neighborhoods of La Saline, Flatbush, Bedford-Stuyvesant, Bushwick, and East New York.

Dominicans were the single largest immigrant category coming into the city during the 1980s and 1990s, at a rate of about 20,000 a year, pushing their total numbers in the city to over 406,000. Other Caribbean immigrants include Jamaicans and Guyanans. About a third of the Guyanans are of Asian Indian descent, but most Guyanans are of African ancestry and tend to live in culturally mixed neighborhoods.

The Asian Indian community in Queens, numbering over 110,000, may be the largest in the country. Indians have the highest median income of any new ethnic group, probably because 80 to 90 percent are professionals who spoke English before arriving. Lower Manhattan's Chinatown is five times the size it was in 1965, both in size and numbers, and is now home to about 100,000 people. Chinatown has now all but swallowed up New York's Little Italy, with more than two-thirds of the buildings on the Little Italy stretch of Mulberry Street now Chinese-owned. More than 90 percent of the independent greengroceries in New York City are Korean-owned, as are over 15,000 small businesses, including import–export companies, manicure shops, gift shops, and fish markets. Over 86,000 Koreans now live in New York City, and they are typically highly educated professionals from urban areas such as Seoul.

Park called the city a "mosaic of small worlds" and it still is. In every major city you can find a patchwork of communities in which the lives of individuals are embedded. Yet, even as these different cultures coexist in semi-isolated worlds, they also collide with one another in the city itself, as does this multi-ethnic group of people in a Queens, New York Arabic neighborhood.

Los Angeles.   Dubbed the "Ellis Island of the 1990s," Los Angeles increased its population by 17.4 percent from 1980 to 1990, and by an additional 6 percent between 1990 and 2000, mostly due to foreign immigration (U.S. Census Bureau, 2005). Today, nearly half of all residents in Los Angeles city are Hispanic, and almost two-thirds of these are Mexican Americans. The city now has more people of Mexican ancestry than any other city in the Western Hemisphere except for Mexico City and Guadalajara. Salvadorans and Guatemalans are two other heavily represented populations.

African Americans comprise 11 percent of the city's population, followed by Asians at 10 percent. Included among the Asians are 63,000 Chinese, 101,000 Filipinos, 92,000 Koreans, 37,000 Japanese, 25,000 Asian Indians, and 20,000 Vietnamese. In addition, 13,000 Native Americans represent 0.4 percent of the Los Angeles population. Found there also are tens of thousands of Iranians.

RACIAL AND ETHNIC MINORITIES

Cities have been home to racial and ethnic minorities almost as long as cities have existed. In past generations, particular cities were home to fewer different groups than they are today. Once a city might be known primarily for its black or Mexican or Irish or Italian concentrations, for example, but now virtually any major North American city is a multicultural place, with dozens of immigrant groups from all parts of the world.

The early history of people of color in North American cities is primarily the story of people of African descent living in the United States. Their influx into Canada occurred in small numbers in the nineteenth century, but increased significantly as more and more people from the Caribbean and the United States moved north during the twentieth century. Interestingly, in the United States, most blacks call themselves African Americans, but in Canada blacks refer to themselves as black Canadians (Fabbi 2003). Native peoples in both Canada and the United States have

seldom lived in the white people's cities, and an Asian presence did not become significant in most locales until the second half of the nineteenth century. The Muslim presence is a more recent social phenomenon.

African Americans

From the time of the first census in 1790 until the beginning of the twentieth century, about 90 percent of the U.S. black population lived in the South, mostly in rural regions. Overall, just one in four African Americans lived in an urban area. A few southern cities had sizable black populations (ranging from 25 to 50 percent of the total) in the late 1800s, a time that the black population of northeastern cities had yet to reach even 5 percent.

The Lure of the North.   The promise of schooling and better work lured black migrants to the North after 1900. By 1910, 10 percent of the African American population lived in the North. Full implementation of the segregationist Jim Crow laws in the South, economic hard times, and the boll weevil's destruction of cotton crops prompted many more to head north in the next decade, raising the northern black population from 850,000 in 1910 to 1.4 million in 1920.

Hostility to labor unions in the North and **de facto segregation** (unequal treatment of people based on social customs and traditions) created a dual society there, just as **de jure segregation** (unequal treatment established by law) had done in the South. But northern blacks were an urban people, some poor, others working class or even middle class. Black churches formed the bedrock of the segregated racial community. Although African Americans did earn more money in the North, in 1914 their earnings did not exceed four-tenths of white earnings (Higgs 1980:125).

The Great Migration.   World War I and the restrictive legislation that followed it put an end to the Great Immigration from Europe, initiating the Great Migration from the South. As cities such as Chicago, New York, and Boston grew into industrial metropolises,

African Americans saw greater opportunity there than in the agricultural South. The **push–pull factors** spurring migration included the decline of southern agriculture as well as farm mechanization on the one hand, and northern industries' shortage of labor and active recruitment of black workers from southern states on the other.

During the 1920s, the net black out-migration from the South amounted to almost 1 million people. Slowing during the Great Depression of the 1930s, the massive relocation of blacks accelerated once again as industrial production rose during World War II. Migration remained high until the 1970s, when urban decentralization and minority movement to the suburbs slowed the process. Note, for example, in Table 11–3, that Baltimore, Washington, D.C., St. Louis, Atlanta, Los Angeles, San Jose, and San Francisco experienced a decrease in their African American populations between 1990 and 2000. Most other cities showed only modest gains. The dramatic increase in New York City was primarily the result of a large influx of Dominican, Haitian, and Jamaican immigrants.

In Baltimore, Detroit, Atlanta, and New Orleans, blacks are the majority population,

TABLE 11–3 African American Population in Selected U.S. Cities

Region	City	1990	2000	2000 as Percent of Total Population
Northeast	Boston	157,234	175,921	20.2
	New York	1,185,340	2,830,010	25.4
	Philadelphia	674,126	698,380	43.7
	Baltimore	444,910	432,860	63.0
	Washington, D.C.	424,202	376,117	45.1
Midwest	Cleveland	251,143	265,237	44.0
	Detroit	812,812	818,434	71.3
	Indianapolis	171,821	213,225	25.3
	Chicago	1,138,970	1,143,232	33.7
	Milwaukee	191,102	227,384	34.4
	St. Louis	239,894	228,411	42.0
	Kansas City, MO	181,920	195,941	27.3
South	Atlanta	262,113	256,251	61.5
	Jacksonville, FL	159,358	214,898	29.2
	New Orleans	308,631	329,241	64.5
	Houston	464,087	507,389	24.7
	Dallas	311,439	337,285	23.1
	San Antonio	69,768	78,363	6.6
West	Denver	56,747	63,876	11.5
	Phoenix	59,980	89,913	4.3
	San Diego	104,924	105,794	7.7
	Los Angeles	565,105	529,121	12.0
	San Jose	43,961	40,407	3.3
	San Francisco	76,944	62,677	8.1
	Seattle	54,106	58,938	7.7

Source: U.S. Census Bureau, 2000.

as is the case in other cities including Birmingham, Alabama (73.5 percent); Gary, Indiana (84.0); Jackson, Mississippi (70.6); Macon, Georgia (62.5); Memphis, Tennessee (61.4); Newark, New Jersey (53.5); Richmond, Virginia (57.2); and Savannah, Georgia (57.1). While it is conceivable that blacks may achieve a majority in other major cities as well, the fact that African Americans represent about 13 percent of the total U.S. population makes it statistically improbable that black majorities will appear in most other major cities. In fact, in Inglewood, California, and Washington, D.C., blacks were a majority in 1990, but were not in 2000 (U.S. Census Bureau 2004b).

To some, the city seems a dangerous place where only the strongest and most calculating survive. That image applies only to certain sections of cities, and in those locales, as explained in the Urban Living box below, being "streetwise" is a valuable asset.

URBAN LIVING

Street Wisdom

Typically, those generally regarded as streetwise are veterans of the public spaces. They know how to get along with strangers, and they understand how to negotiate the streets. They know whom to trust, whom not to trust, what to say through body language or words. They have learned how to behave effectively in public. Probably the most important consideration is the experience they have gained through encounters with "every kind of stranger." Although one may know about situations through the reports of friends or relatives, this pales in comparison with actual experience. It is often sheer proximity to the dangerous streets that allows a person to gain street wisdom and formulate some effective theory of the public spaces. As one navigates there is a certain edge to one's demeanor, for the streetwise person is both wary of others and sensitive to the subtleties that could salvage safety out of danger.

The longer people live in this locale, having to confront problems on the streets and public spaces every day, the greater chance they have to develop a sense of what to do without seriously compromising themselves. Further, the longer they are in the area, the more likely they are to develop contacts who might come to their aid, allowing them to move more boldly.

This self-consciousness makes people likely to be alert and sensitive to the nuances of the environment. More important, they will project their ease and self-assurance to those they meet, giving them the chance to affect the interaction positively. For example, the person who is "streetdumb," relying for guidance on the most superficial signs, may pay too much attention to skin color and become needlessly tense just because the person approaching is black. A streetwise white who meets a black person will probably just go about his or her business. In both cases the black person will pick up the "vibe" being projected—in the first instance fear and hostility, in the second case comfort and a sense of commonality. There are obviously times when the "vibe" itself could tip the balance in creating the subsequent interaction.

Source: Excerpt from Elijah Anderson, *Streetwise.* Copyright © 1990 by University of Chicago Press. Reprinted with the permission of the University of Chicago Press.

Residential Segregation Patterns. Most African American migrants, like earlier European immigrants, typically settled in the least desirable central-city neighborhoods. For the Europeans, this **residential segregation** reflected mostly lower resources and group preferences (Lieberson 1963; Douglas Massey 1985; Lieberson and Waters 1988). As these immigrants gained education and income, they assimilated and moved out of these traditional ethnic enclaves.

Unlike the Europeans, however, many African Americans have remained confined and isolated in racial ghettos, particularly in the Northeast and Midwest, where 36 percent of all African Americans live. Through a variety of individual and institutional actions, a persistently high level of black–white segregation remained throughout the twentieth century, revealing the extent of racial stratification in U.S. society (Massey 1999; St. Clair and Clymer 2000).

Between 1870 and 1920, segregation in the cities of the North was slight. By 1965, Karl and Alma Taeuber's classic study of racial segregation revealed a dramatic climb in the segregation index. To measure that segregation, the Taeubers developed what they called an **index of dissimilarity,** which they applied to each neighborhood. Their index ranged from a low of zero, meaning the neighborhood reflected the same proportion of blacks and whites as in the entire city, to a high of 100, meaning that no racial mixture was found. Overall, in 1960, the average segregation index for 207 large cities was 86.2, with scores ranging from a not-so-low 60.4 (San Jose, California) to 98.1 (Fort Lauderdale, Florida).

Since the Taeubers' research findings, other researchers have used the index of dissimilarity to track trends in residential segregation. Since the 1970s, racial residential segregation has slowly but steadily decreased in the United

Although racial residential segregation has slowly decreased since 1970, it still remains fairly high among blacks and whites in both cities and suburbs. Most of the ten most segregated metropolitan areas are in the North, while the ten least segregated metropolitans areas are in the South. Even so, the 2000 Census showed high segregation levels in Atlanta, Miami, and New Orleans.

States. In 1980, the black–white metropolitan segregation index was 73.9, and it dropped to 65.1 in 2000. However, it still remains fairly high between blacks and whites in cities and suburbs. In 2000, the average white person in metropolitan America resided in a neighborhood that was 80 percent white and 7 percent black. In contrast, the typical black individual lived in a neighborhood that was only 33 percent white and as much as 51 percent black (Lewis Mumford Center 2001a).

Of the 50 metropolitan areas with the largest black populations, the ten with the highest levels of segregation (in descending order) were Detroit (see Figure 11–1), Milwaukee, New York City, Chicago, Newark, Cleveland, Cincinnati, Nassau–Suffolk (N.Y.), St. Louis, and Miami. All but New York and Miami experienced modest segregation declines since 1990, and most are "Rustbelt" metro areas where black–white segregation has been particularly resistant to change. At

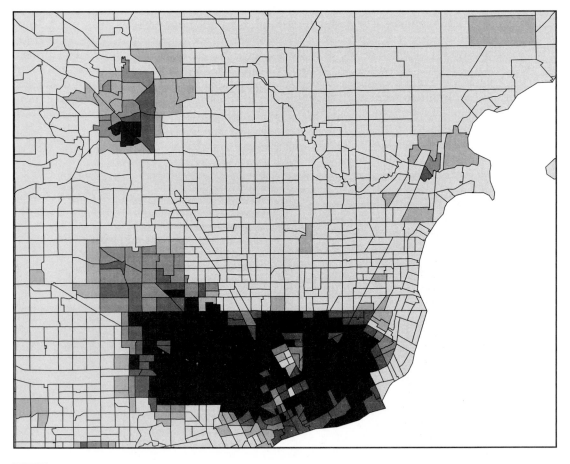

0 to 9.9
10.0 to 34.1
34.2 to 64.1
64.2 to 86.2
86.3 to 100.0

FIGURE 11–1   Percent of Persons Who Are Black in Detroit, 2000. [*Source:* U.S. Census Bureau.]

the other end, the ten metro areas with the least black–white segregation were all Sunbelt regions in North and South Carolina, Florida, California, and Virginia. Despite signs of progress in the South, several cities in this region also display persistent segregation. For example, Pre-Katrina New Orleans was above the national average, and segregation in the city of Atlanta has risen in the past 20 years and is much higher than the national city average (Lewis Mumford Center 2001a).

In recent decades, as the black middle class moved out of central cities into mostly inner-ring suburbs, they left behind an isolated black poor concentrated in decaying neighborhoods of high crime and unemployment (Wilson 1990). Researchers have long known that ethnic and racial residential segregation interacts with social class and the family life cycle to shape the entire urban area (Shevky and Bell 1955). Many social scientists, particularly those using the political economy model, emphasize the economic roots of racial segregation (Logan and Stearns 1981; Logan and Molotch 1987; Jargowsky 1996).

Still, beyond economic differences, racial prejudice also plays an important role as many whites flee a neighborhood when blacks move in. Similarly, African American preferences for moving to mostly black suburbs also contribute to segregation. Evidence also points to active, if unacknowledged (by the white community at least) attempts to keep blacks from buying homes in white urban neighborhoods.

Prior to the civil rights and open housing laws of the 1960s and 1970s, realtors included in their code of ethics a regulation that prohibited selling homes to buyers not sharing the racial and ethnic characteristics of neighbors (Helper 1969). Most whites believe that passage of fair housing and antidiscrimination laws mostly eliminated institutional discrimination in housing (Farley et al. 1993). However, recent studies show that, even now, African Americans stand a one-in-two chance of being discriminated against in a rental and a one-in-five chance of being discriminated against in the sale of a home (Galster 1990, 1996).

A common method is **steering,** in which rental or real estate agents direct, for example, an African American couple to a city area populated by others of their race or else refrain from telling them about available property in a white area. Another strategy to discourage the African American buyer is asking a much higher rent or purchase price than a white family would pay (Downs 1982). Such subtler forms of discrimination occur much more frequently than the highly publicized but infrequent instances of vandalism or firebombing of a home newly acquired by people of color in a white neighborhood.

Whatever the circumstances, such practices combine to create a *dual housing market.* White resistance to housing desegregation results in practices that make housing differentially available to people based on their race. Despite the continued increase in income of the growing black middle class, racial segregation persists for most African Americans.

The Truly Disadvantaged.   For the trapped African American poor left behind in the inner city, the future is bleak. Among those lacking the necessary schooling and communication skills required for work in the service and information sectors of the economy, unemployment rates may be as high as 80 percent (Kasarda 1993). These "truly disadvantaged," in the words of William J. Wilson (1990), are poor people who rely on welfare assistance and the underground economy to survive.

Unlike the immigrant poor of the past, today's poor inner-city residents face social isolation. The exodus of middle- and working-class two-parent black families removes essential role models and reduces community resources. Furthermore, outsiders avoid these neighborhoods, leaving them plagued by massive unemployment, crime, and schools that do not promote achievement. Consequently, area residents—women and children on welfare, school dropouts, single mothers, and aggressive street criminals—live virtually cut off from the larger society. Gary Orfield noted the magnitude of this isolation:

> To a considerable extent the residents of city ghettos are now living in separate and deteriorating societies, with separate economies, diverging family structures and basic institutions, and even growing linguistic separation within the core ghettos. (1988:103)

Besides being isolated, the ghettoized poor have poor quality schools, limited medical care, high infant mortality, and high rates of substance abuse and violent crime. Current social indicators offer little cause for optimism, for such problems have structural causes that our society has yet to overcome.

Asian Americans

Like Hispanics, Asians in North America reflect a wide range of distinctive cultures. They are a highly urban population, with 96 percent living in metropolitan areas in 2000, compared with 81 percent of the total population (see Figure 11–2). However, they are more likely than African and Hispanic Americans to live in suburbia; almost half do so, in fact. Most numerous are the 2.7 million Chinese Americans, followed by the 2.4 million Filipino Americans, 1.9 million Asian Indians, and the 1.2 million each Vietnamese and Koreans (Lewis Mumford Center 2001b). Most of the newer immigrants from these ethnic groups reside in larger cities such as Los Angeles, New York, and Chicago (described further in the Case Study at the end of this chapter).

Chinese Americans. Since their initial arrival on the West Coast around 1850, Chinese immigrants gradually moved eastward in both Canada and the United States. Usually, they banded together in low-rent urban enclaves, often situated near major means of transportation (shipping docks or railroad terminals). These became the Chinatowns that, even today, still attract immigrants. In these enclaves, the Chinese pooled their resources to provide economic assistance to one another even as they faced formidable social barriers from mainstream society. Kept within the limits of racial ghettos by prejudice and discrimination, many Chinese never learned to speak English, further limiting their opportunities.

Since 1965, the Chinese American population has quintupled. Chinatowns—such as those in Los Angeles, New York, San Francisco, and Vancouver—are, paradoxically, both tourist attractions and slum communities. Filled with overcrowded, dilapidated buildings and troubled by the problems of youth gangs and high rates of tuberculosis, they nonetheless retain historical, picturesque, and commercial importance. The streets mark off the sections of regional origins and dialects of their residents,

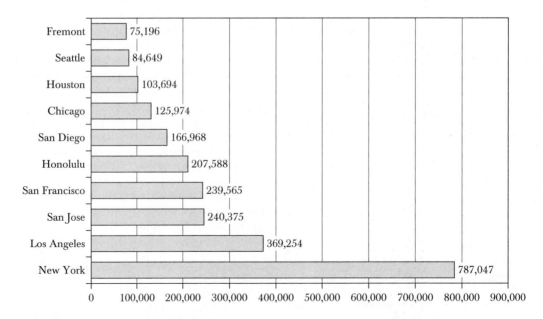

FIGURE 11–2 U.S. Cities with largest Asian populations, 2000. [*Source:* U.S. Census Bureau.]

Asians have become a more visible presence in many North American cities due to their continuing migration to Canada and the United States and their almost universal choice to live in an urban area. Koreans have become especially evident outside of Asian communities because of their partiality for operating supermarkets, grocery stores, and fruit stands.

much as in any early twentieth-century Little Italy. In New York, the largest Chinese enclave in the Western Hemisphere, Burmese Chinese concentrate on Henry Street, Taiwanese on Centre Street, Fukienese on Division Street, and Vietnamese Chinese on East Broadway (Kwong 1996).

Chinese Americans currently present a bipolar occupational distribution. About 30 percent are in professional and technical positions, twice the rate among whites. However, the Chinese are also over-represented as low-skilled, low-paid service workers, with 24 percent in this category compared with 7 percent of the white labor force. Although median family income among Chinese Americans is above the national average, they are likely to have more wage earners in the family. That fact accounts for most of the difference, rather than a greater proportion of higher-paying positions.

Japanese Americans. With low annual immigration, Japanese Americans represent a steadily declining share of Asian Americans and now number about 800,000. Most are U.S.-born and have high educational and income levels, higher even than white people. Outgroup marriage now exceeds 50 percent, making Japanese Americans the most structurally assimilated nonwhite group (Zia 2001; Fu 2001).

Korean Americans. In metropolitan Los Angeles, where about 200,000 Korean Americans now live, 40 percent of adult males operate their own businesses (Awanohara 1991a:36). Nationwide, Korean self-employment is higher than in any other racial or ethnic category, including whites: 1 in 9 Korean Americans is a business owner, compared with 1 in 15 among whites and 1 in 67 for African Americans (Yoshihashi and Lubman 1992:A1). So deeply entrenched is self-employment in the Korean immigrant ethos that one survey reported that 61 percent of South Koreans planning to emigrate to the United States expect to go into business for themselves even though few had done so in their homeland (Awanohara 1991a:36–37).

In Los Angeles, Korean Americans have cornered the wig and liquor businesses. In Washington, D.C., Philadelphia, and New York City, Koreans are especially visible as grocery-store owners and fruit-stand operators. Korean greengrocers now sell more than three-fourths of New York City's produce (Min and Kolodny 1994).

Asian Indians. The Asian Indian presence in North America has increased dramatically in the past several decades. Census tallies reported about 300,000 Asian Indians in Canada in 2001 and 1.9 million in the United States, twice the number a decade earlier. With overpopulation a serious problem in India (one in six of the world's people live there!), high migration rates are likely to continue.

Hindi speakers constitute the largest group of Asian Indian immigrants, followed by Gujarati, Punjabi, and Bengali speakers. Asian Indian immigrants also arrive from East Africa and Latin America, particularly from the Caribbean and Guyana, where earlier generations had first gone as indentured plantation laborers (Awanohara 1991b:35). Almost three-fourths of the immigrants are in professional or managerial occupations; the remainder most often operates convenience stores, gas stations, and family-managed hotels and motels. Consequently, most Asian Indians settle in large metropolitan areas, most significantly in Chicago; New York; San Jose; Washington, D.C.; and Central New Jersey (U.S. Office of Immigration Statistics 2002).

Vietnamese Americans. Barely noted by the Census Bureau in 1970, over 1.9 million Vietnamese lived in the United States and over 110,000 in Canada in 2000. They are the largest Asian group in Texas; but by far the largest concentration of Vietnamese—some 150,000 people—is in "Little Saigon" in Orange County, California, where the language, signs, shops, offices, and music all convey a distinctly Vietnamese character. Similarly, Anaheim, California, now has its own Little Saigon (Matsuoka 1990:341; Lee 1998). San Jose is home to over 105,000 Vietnamese Americans, and the Houston–Galveston–Brazonia megalopolis contains another 64,000 (U.S. Census Bureau 2002a).

The "Model Minority" Stereotype. Despite their cultural diversity, many Asian Americans have a record of educational achievement, high income, and overall success in Canadian and U.S. metropolitan areas. Dubbed a "model minority" because of their accomplishments, Asian Americans often display success in a variety of occupational roles: Chinese engineers, Japanese financiers, Filipino nurses, Korean entrepreneurs, and Vietnamese restaurateurs abound, reinforcing this positive stereotype. Yet the reality is not entirely favorable:

> Beneath a thick crust of scientists, professionals, and entrepreneurs are thicker layers of struggling families—peddlers and waiters and office cleaners and sweater stitchers who eke out a bare living by dint of double jobs and the presence of multiple wage earners. (Chua-Eoan 1990:33)

Many Southeast Asian refugees remain on welfare, hampered by language difficulties, poor education, and weak job skills. Not all Asian students perform well in school. The criminal activities of Asian drug rings, extortion gangs, and youth gangs are often a brutal menace.

In short, there is some truth to the "model minority" stereotype; but, like other generalizations, it conceals as much as it reveals about a complex category of people.

Hispanic Americans

By far the fastest-growing nonwhite category in the United States is Hispanics—Mexicans, Puerto Ricans, Cubans, Central and South Americans, and others of Spanish origin—and they now constitute the nation's largest minority. In the majority of U.S. cities with a population exceeding 100,000, Hispanics outnumber African Americans. These cities include Albuquerque, Dallas, Denver, Houston, Las Vegas, Los Angeles, New York, Phoenix, Salt Lake City, San Diego, San Francisco, and Tucson. In 12 other large cities, Hispanics are a majority of the population, outnumbering all other categories combined (see Table 11–4).

TABLE 11–4   Hispanic Majorities in Selected Cities of 100,000 or More—Percent of Total City Population, 2000

Brownsville, TX	91.3	Miami, FL	65.8
Corpus Christi, TX	54.3	Oxnard, CA	66.2
El Monte, CA	72.4	Pomona, CA	64.5
El Paso, TX	76.6	Salinas, CA	64.1
Hialeah, FL	90.3	San Antonio, TX	58.7
Laredo, TX	94.1	Santa Ana, CA	76.1

Source: U.S. Census Bureau, 2000.

Many first-generation Hispanic Americans, who can be of any race, cluster in urban ethnic neighborhoods, repeating a centuries-old pattern of earlier immigrants. Here they create a community support network through **parallel social institutions** (clubs, churches, organizations, stores), where they can share the commonality of language and culture. Hispanic residential segregation is less than that for blacks, but higher than for Asian Americans. Hispanics tend to be as segregated from blacks as they are from whites, although this pattern is declining. The degree of segregation varies by ethnic group. The Cubans and South Americans are far less segregated than are Dominicans, Central Americans, Puerto Ricans, and Mexicans. By far, Dominicans are the most segregated of the Latino groups. See Figure 11–3 for a depiction of the heavy Dominican concentration in New York's Washington Heights and of other Hispanics, especially Puerto Ricans, in the Bronx.

The Census Bureau term *Hispanic* wrongly suggests a single category of people. In truth, Hispanics differ in their race, cultural backgrounds, social class, and length of residence in North America. Some—most often Mexican Americans—live in rural areas, particularly in the U.S. Southwest. Others, such as Cuban Americans not living in Miami, often live in suburbs. In terms of residence, many Central and South Americans have been in North America for only a few years, while others, notably Puerto Ricans and the *Hispanos* of the U.S. Southwest, have lived all their lives on the U.S. mainland. Although Hispanics live in all 50 states and in all Canadian provinces, many categories tend to cluster in one geographic area. Florida is home to over 70,000 Nicaraguans and about three-fourths of all Cubans. Almost two-thirds of all Puerto Ricans live in the Northeast (primarily New York and New Jersey); California and Texas, by contrast, are home to three-fourths of all Mexican Americans (Lewis Mumford Center 2001a). We now take a closer look at Hispanic diversity.

Puerto Ricans.   As U.S. citizens, Puerto Ricans enjoy open migration privileges between their island and the mainland. Before World War II, the poor living conditions on the island offered strong push factors that impelled people to migrate:

> If someone had looked around at the potential sources of new [urban] immigration . . . his eye might well have fallen on Puerto Rico . . . in the middle 1930's [it was] a scene of almost unrelieved misery. (Glazer and Moynihan 1970:86)

After 1945, postwar prosperity and regular air flights to the mainland brought as many as 50,000 Puerto Ricans per year to the United States. Most came to New York. Why? Anthropologist Elena Padilla explained in 1958:

> For years now Puerto Ricans have been hearing about New York City, have read about it in the local papers, heard about it on the radio, and seen some of its scenery in the movies. . . . New York is regarded as a place where many Puerto Ricans live and where they have improved their conditions of life, their health, and their general welfare. Many . . . have known New York migrants who have returned to Puerto Rico and boasted of their "good life" in New York. (1958:21–22)

Glazer and Moynihan (1970) noted that often men migrated first, leaving their wives and children in Puerto Rico until they secured enough resources to support the entire family. (This is a common pattern in all poor nations, as Chapter 13 explains.) In other cases, women, often with children (but unmarried or separated), moved from the island, hoping for work or at least welfare support until they could find employment.

Upon a newcomer's arrival, friends and extended kin provided support services to help

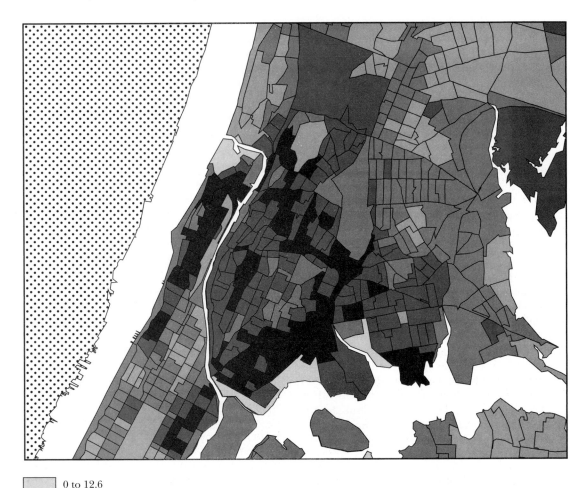

	0 to 12.6
	12.7 to 26.7
	26.8 to 45.2
	45.3 to 65.3
	65.3 to 100.0

FIGURE 11–3 Percent of Persons Who Are Latino in Upper Manhattan and the Bronx, New York, 2000.
[*Source*: U.S. Census Bureau.]

ease the adjustment to mainland city life. Despite this, life in New York was significantly different from Puerto Rican life and created particular hardships. Padilla (1958) suggests that this "culture shock" involved unfamiliar patterns of behavior, differing attitudes and values, and, perhaps most significantly, unexpected individualism. Often expecting others to make sacrifices to aid them, many migrants were disappointed at the degree of individualistic self-interest shown in the city.

By 1960, some 900,000 Puerto Ricans lived within the continental United States, about 600,000 residing in New York City. The center of the New York Puerto Rican community became East Harlem, also known as Spanish

Harlem (97th Street to about 125th Street between Third and Fifth Avenues). Until the late 1970s, however, continuous shuttle migration (migrants returning to the island and new arrivals coming to the mainland) inhibited an organized community life. Hometown clubs—voluntary organizations based on one's place of birth—offered social opportunities to celebrate life cycle events (birthdays, first communions, confirmations, weddings). But because they drew members from scattered New York neighborhoods, they did not operate as community centers. Only the annual Puerto Rican Day parade, begun in 1958, served as a focal point of group identity. By the late 1970s, greater neighborhood organization was evident, as more people put down roots in the city.

In the 2000 census, over 3 million people living on the mainland United States identified themselves as Puerto Rican. New York City, where most Puerto Ricans once lived, now is home to only one in four. New York State's Puerto Rican population—64 percent of the mainland total in 1970—fell to 34 percent in 2000, as members of this group continued their migration into other states. Those other states with large shares of the Puerto Rican population are Florida (16 percent), New Jersey (12 percent), Pennsylvania (8 percent), Massachusetts (7 percent), Connecticut (6 percent), with Illinois and California at about 5 percent each (U.S. Census Bureau 2002a).

Migration has brought limited success to Puerto Ricans. About 30 percent earned family incomes exceeding $50,000 in 2001, while 27 percent earned between $25,000 and $50,000. These statistics are a marked improvement over previous years, yet more Puerto Ricans live in poverty than all other Hispanics, as shown in Table 11–5. Furthermore, like African Americans, Puerto Ricans experience racial discrimination and are, after blacks, the category most segregated from whites. The reason, Massey and Bitterman (1985) argue, is racism. Since a significant percentage of Puerto Ricans have dark skin, they tend to live in cities near blacks. Since whites often shun blacks when choosing residences, "Puerto Ricans become bystander victims of [whites'] racial prejudice, leading to their residential segregation in society" (Massey and Bitterman 1985:306).

Another factor contributing to Puerto Rican poverty is a high level of female-headed families. In recent years women have headed over one in three Puerto Rican families, compared with one in five Mexican-American families. Yet nearly two-thirds of Puerto Rican youths graduate from high school, a share higher than the one in two for Mexican Americans (U.S. Census Bureau 2002a). Perhaps as educational attainment improves (13 percent now graduate from college), future earnings for this group will also improve.

Mexican Americans.   Over 20 million Mexican Americans lived in the United States in 2000, with most living in the West (57 percent) and South (33 percent). Mexican Americans make up 30 percent of the Los Angeles

TABLE 11–5   Income Levels of Hispanic Americans, 2000

	All Hispanics	Mexicans	Puerto Ricans	Cubans	Central and South Americans	Other Hispanics
Median family income	$31,663	$31,123	$30,129	$38,312	$33,105	$34,935
Percent of families in poverty	20.2	21.2	23.0	15.0	16.3	18.1
Percent of persons in poverty	22.8	24.1	25.8	17.3	16.7	21.6

Source: U.S. Census Bureau, 2000.

population, 27 percent of Houston, 21 percent of San Diego, and 18 percent of Chicago (U.S. Census Bureau 2002a).

Although most are new arrivals, Mexican Americans have been a significant presence in the United States for over 150 years. Generally accorded greatest prestige are the *Hispanos,* descendants of families who resided in the Southwest prior to the Mexican American War in 1848. Immigration from Mexico picked up around the turn of the century, and descendants of these more "recent" residents occupy a middle status. Below them are the most recent arrivals, many of whom prefer to be called *Chicanos,* a name that implies both a political consciousness and cultural pride in their Mexican heritage.

New arrivals typically live in crowded urban barrios in California and Texas. Poverty is common, although life is better than the destitution they left behind in Mexico. Aiding their adjustment is the Mexican American tradition of family support, which continues (although somewhat weakened) in large cities. Today's urbanites tend to follow nuclear family instead of extended-family residence patterns and to have less male dominance, higher intermarriage rates, and more diverse occupations (Parrillo 2006:403).

The fertility rate for Mexican American women is nearly twice as high as for the non-Hispanic population. This higher fertility rate, together with high levels of migration by mostly young people, suggests further significant population increases in the urban Mexican American population. However, women of Mexican ancestry born in the United States show much lower fertility rates than do women born in Mexico, illustrating the effect of cultural assimilation on family size. This pattern holds true for all foreign-born and American-born Hispanic women (McFalls 2003:9).

Mexican Americans face a number of disadvantages. Discrimination in employment and housing, coupled with a lack of English language skills, limits opportunities for many. Some adolescents, with little hope for the future, turn to street gangs for a sense of belonging and importance. The Urban Living box on pages 324–325 shows what gang membership means to *Chicana* women in East Los Angeles.

Despite the challenges, about 45 percent of Mexican Americans have made it into the middle class, with annual family incomes exceeding $35,000. Over one-third are working class, and the remainder are poor (U.S. Census Bureau, 2002a). Most in poverty live in central cities, where school dropout rates run as high as 45 percent and drug use and gang violence are everyday realities (Lichter and Crowley 2002; Mayer 2004). For them, urban life is a far cry from the opportunities many hoped for when they came.

Central and South Americans. Over 120,000 immigrants from Central and South America enter the United States each year, almost one-third of them from El Salvador and Colombia (U.S. Office of Immigration Statistics 2005). Nearly 700,000 Central Americans live in the Los Angeles–Long Beach metropolitan area, over 200,000 in the Washington, D.C. region, and nearly that number in Miami. New York and Houston each contain over 150,000 Central Americans. With a population of about 650,000, Salvadorans constitute the majority of Central Americans in most cities, followed by Guatemalans, who number about 370,000. From the Caribbean, Dominicans are another significant urban presence, particularly in New York, where they are the second-largest Hispanic group, numbering over 400,000 (Parrillo 2006:420). Most are working-class people living in central cities.

Since 1981, more than 330,000 Colombians also have settled in the United States. Although they are dispersed throughout the country, sizable Colombian communities exist in New York, Miami, and Los Angeles. Colombians are a mixture of educated professionals and low-skilled peasants seeking a better life in North America's cities.

Muslim Americans

For more than 100 years, Muslim immigrants have settled in U.S. cities. Cedar Rapids, Iowa, is the home of the oldest mosque still in use. Back in the late 1800s, Quincy, Massachusetts, on the outskirts of Boston, attracted Muslim immigrants to jobs in its shipyards. In the early twentieth century, work in the auto industry brought Sunni and Shi'ite Muslims from many parts of the Middle East to Dearborn, Michigan, outside Detroit. Together with Middle Eastern Christians, these Michigan Muslims today constitute the largest Arab American settlement in the country.

Similarly, New York City has experienced the visible presence of Muslim Americans for over a century. Its Muslim population has included merchant seamen, tradesmen, entertainers, white-collar professionals, and owners of major businesses. New York Muslims represent a broad spectrum of nationalities from virtually every country in the world. Mosque-building activity has flourished in New York in recent years. National Islamic organizations, a large number of elementary and upper-level Islamic schools, and Muslim stores and businesses have sprung up all over the city (Smith 2005).

In the early 1900s, Chicago may have had more Muslims in residence than any other U.S. city. Today more than 40 Muslim groups from the Middle East, India, Central and South Asia, and many other parts of the world call this city home. Likewise, in Los Angeles and San Francisco, Muslims represent many areas of the Muslim world, most recently Afghans and Somalis and citizens of other African countries. The Islamic Center of Southern California is one of the largest Muslim entities in the United States (Smith 2005).

These are difficult times for Muslim Americans, particularly those living in cities. Almost all of them follow the non-violent teachings of their religion, but the attacks by Muslim radicals on 9/11 and the 2004 Madrid and 2005 London bombings have heightened prejudices and/or suspicions among non-Muslim urbanites. Muslims were killed in all those attacks as well, but this group finds itself the frequent target of **racial profiling,** both in anti-terrorist law enforcement actions and in stereotyping.

Native Americans

Throughout their history right up to about 1950, few Native Americans lived in cities. Most resided in rural areas, on or near reservations. In recent decades, however, a steady migration to cities has brought more than half of all Native Americans to urban areas.

The largest groups of natives are the Cherokee (281,000) and the Navajo (269,000). Census data indicate there were 2.5 million Native Americans in 2000, up from 800,000 in 1970. Some of this increase is due to a birth rate almost twice the national average, and some is due to the fact that more people now claim Native American ancestry on census forms.

About 43 percent of U.S. natives reside in the West and another 31 percent in the South, although several hundred thousand live in various metropolitan areas across the country. Table 11–6 provides population totals for native peoples living in major Canadian and U.S. cities.

As always, migration to cities is prompted by the desire for a better life—most reservations are economically depressed, offering few jobs, little schooling, and insufficient services provided by the two federal governments. Yet for most natives the city has not delivered much, although the situation is somewhat better in Canada.

TABLE 11–6   Native American Population Living in Metropolitan Areas, 2000

Albuquerque	17,444	Omaha	2,616
Boston	2,365	Ottawa	13,485
Calgary	21,915	Philadelphia	4,073
Chicago	10,290	Phoenix	26,696
Cleveland	1,458	Portland, OR	5,587
Dallas–Fort Worth	6,472	San Antonio	9,584
Detroit	3,140	San Diego	7,543
Denver	7,290	San Francisco	3,458
Edmonton	40,930	Saskatoon	20,275
Houston	8,568	Seattle	5,695
Jacksonville	2,474	Toronto	20,300
Los Angeles	29,412	Tucson	11,036
Minneapolis	8,378	Tulsa	18,551
Montreal	11,085	Vancouver	36,860
New York	41,289	Victoria	8,695
Oklahoma City	17,743		

Source: Statistics Canada and U.S. Census Bureau, 2000.

URBAN LIVING

Women in the Gangs of Los Angeles

In the traditional Mexican culture, it is undesirable but certainly more acceptable for boys to be out roaming the streets; it is never appropriate behavior for females. Therefore, Latinas who either join a gang or in any way affiliate themselves with the *cholo* lifestyle, are subsequently stigmatized by the more traditional Mexican community. . . . In the present field investigation, parents and members of extended family who were interviewed had nothing but negative remarks concerning the "*Cholas*"—the gang girls.

On the other hand, the young women had completely rejected the hardworking ethic, the good wife and mother role model so common among Hispanic women, for the *Cholo* lifestyle. They, in turn, had nothing positive to say about the more traditional women either. . . .

There has been historically and frequently a good deal of bad blood between barrio residents and law enforcement. Then if there is also friction at home, the gang subculture is skillful at socializing many youths to their value system. For many of these teens—not just the females—their Mexican self-concept has already been altered. They recognize that they do not belong to the mainstream Anglo culture, but they know they do not belong to the Mexican culture either. Those who have ever traveled to Mexico to visit grandparents and other relatives have soon learned that they are considered outsiders in their ancestral land as well. Their speech is ridiculed and they are called "*pochos.*" Thus, Mexican values about home and family do not carry very much weight for some youngsters.

Different individuals experience varying degrees of cultural conflict. Those who experience severe marginalization are easy targets for the gang paradigm, especially if parental influence is lacking or not respected by the youngster. Young women living on the margins of both cultures are easy prey.

Frequently such young women are confronted with a double standard at home. In many Mexican culture homes, it is normal for boys to be treated more leniently than girls, enjoying more privileges, being allowed to stay out later, and even dominating their sisters who must often iron their shirts to perfection and wait on them at the dinner table. In the traditional Mexican family, the joys of motherhood and family security are highly prized. Typically, Mom always seems happy and both she and Dad are primarily concerned with providing for the children. The family is sacred. In the traditional Mexican family, Mom also stays at home and cooks

Although not living in ghettos, about three-fourths of urban Native Americans in the United States do live in poorer neighborhoods. Those lacking schooling and job skills generally experience the same poverty they left behind but without the tribal support system. Research suggests that Native Americans who migrate to cities are more likely to earn higher income than those who remain behind on the reservations, but this is partly due to their higher educational attainment (Larriviere and Kroncke 2004).

Some urban migrants experience culture shock in their unfamiliar environment. Aware of their standing as a minority, newcomers may seek out other Native Americans, usually of the same tribe, often by frequenting a local bar. Drunkenness is as serious a problem in the cities as it is on reservations. The problem is a cultural clash: Native peoples find that their and sews—even today with the economy virtually forbidding this practice any longer. In some Mexican homes, Mom has to work; nevertheless, she returns to the nest and puts in another shift cooking, washing, ironing, and nurturing.

Many young women are fed up with this double standard and expressed their exasperation vociferously. Given a few other displeasures and grumblings about home, and with the pressures provided by poverty-stricken environments, they become likely targets for gang recruitment. In addition, in many of the homes, Dads were not always present and if they were, they were not necessarily able to provide very much of anything for their children. Some Moms were not at all happy with cooking and sewing. Others were themselves in gangs at one time.

Many of these youngsters have witnessed or experienced beatings, and a number of forms of parental violence.

Connie: "Mom always got between me and my Dad and she'd catch the belt in her hand sometimes so it wouldn't hit me again. Sometimes my Dad would get so mad he'd start swinging at both of us. One time my older brother beat me up till I was black and blue."

In the traditional Mexican family, "spare the rod; spoil the child," is still very much in style. The gang girls often reported other kinds of abuse as well.

. . . In this investigation, Latina gang and non-gang affiliated seemed to function in large measure as auxiliary, or as accomplices to males, going along with criminal activity committed by the males. Girls' crimes appeared to be still largely "traditionally female" prostitution, shoplifting, running away, fighting with other girls, and drug-related crimes. Actual scuffles among these young women involved knife assaults and/or scratching and kicking types of fights which reportedly occurred frequently sometimes against other women and often against males as well. . . .

In the current research, most gang girls came from less conventional Mexican families. They seemed to be from more dysfunctional families, sometimes from *cholo* families. Many of their parents were at one time themselves gang-members, or associates of one kind or another. Other gang-affiliated females came from homes with parents who have given up, or who never cared very much in the first place. . . .

Much of the current study concurs with older studies. The gang has been and still appears to be a welcome source of support for *cholas*. Ironically, in view of the ill treatment, the infidelities and abuses the women receive at the hands of the males, it is surprising that so many women, gang as well as non-gang affiliated, found the gang members so appealing. . . .

Source: Francine Garcia-Hallcom, *An Urban Ethnography of Latino Street,* 1999. Accessed at www.csun.edu/~hcchs006/gang.html on August 1, 2005.

emphasis on consensus, equality, and communal use of property do not fit with the competitive life of North American cities. With few role models to point the way, some gravitate to skid row and an existence centered around the bottle and the bar. Others gradually adapt to urban living, but often holding a low-paying job. Only those who manage to gain economic security are likely to move from the central city into a racially mixed suburb. Even there, most natives try to preserve their ethnic identity, and they tend to interact little with non-natives (Weibel-Orlando 1999).

WOMEN AND URBAN LIFE

Women's lives in the city have always reflected the gender stratification of the larger society. Prior to women's liberation, the differentiated roles that men and women played in the home, school, workplace, and community resulted in what Daphne Spain (1992) called **gendered spaces.** By this she meant how differences in gender status resulted in the organization of space to reflect and reinforce those unequal distinctions. For example, women were once excluded from college altogether, and then secluded in women's colleges before finally being permitted to attend coed schools, at which point the gender stratification system began to change for the better (Spain 1992:4–5).

The workplace also revealed the division of labor, both in terms of occupation and place. Men and women performed different tasks that split along gender lines (for example, domestic service and teaching for women compared to medicine and law for men) and usually did so in segregated spaces. In fact, when women first entered the labor force, their doing factory or clerical work became controversial because both sexes were occupying the same spaces (Spain 1992:14).

A clear distinction also existed in the use of public and private space. Men had the freedom to use public space at any time, but genteel women did not venture alone onto the streets without a male or female companion. Only prostitutes or poor working women used urban public space, and then only in certain areas of the city. Public space was essentially a male domain and a woman's "place" was the private space of her home.

For the city's middle and upper classes, life in that city home—typically a two- or three-story brownstone or mansion—followed gender-specific guidelines in the use of physical space. Men rarely ventured into the kitchen, leaving that room to the women and servants. The parlor (a room designated for the reception of guests) and dining room were used by both sexes, but after dinner, the men would "retire" to the study or billiard room for cigars and brandy while the women "withdrew" to the drawing room for tea and perhaps biscuits. That social segregation of private space in one's house extended to the downtown district, where exclusive men's clubs enabled the city's "wheelers and dealers" to dine, drink, socialize, and talk business in comfortably furnished male domain.

In the second half of the twentieth century, as women's rights and social interactions increased during society's evolution toward greater gender equality, so too did the use of private and public space, at home, work, and in the public sphere. Homes became more open, with fewer inside doors shutting off kitchens, dining, and living rooms. Family rooms, shared by all, became common instead of separate men and women's relaxation areas. With men and women working side by side, adjustments in the work environments occurred, from the obviousness of rest rooms to what could or could not be done or displayed to avoid what legally came to be defined as a **hostile environment.**

In short, the changing times and values led to greater life opportunities for women in all facets of life, which in turn prompted new spatial arrangements in both cities and suburbs. We now turn to these considerations.

Work

As both Canada and the United States industrialized, poor women, mostly from immigrant families, went to work in urban factories in low-skill jobs for low wages. In fact, women were the main workforce in many textile mills and garment factories.

In the mid-nineteenth century, millions of Irish flocked to North American cities to seek their fortunes. The number of Irish households headed by women was high, approaching 20 percent, often because many husbands died from industrial accidents. In such cases, women commonly expanded their households to include other relatives or boarders to help meet living expenses. Then, too, of some 2 million Irish who came to the United States between 1871 and 1910, most were women, unlike the common pattern by which males migrated first. Many unmarried women migrated to U.S. cities, primarily to seek domestic work as maids or jobs in textile mills (Diner 1983:73–74). For Irish women, then, the city was a place of continual hard work and economic security.

Most other immigrant women also sought work in cities. In Chicago, the needs of immigrant women and their families prompted

Jane Addams to found Hull House, beginning the U.S. settlement home movement. The case study of Chicago at the end of this chapter looks more closely at her role in improving women's lives.

A very different story centers on middle and upper class women, usually born to prosperous U.S. merchants and industrialists. Men placed them on a pedestal, as towers of moral strength and refinement, as if to balance their own competitive world of work. Prevailing values in the nineteenth and early twentieth centuries held that the nature of women was to please and the nature of men was to achieve. By the 1920s, the expanding number of middle-class families only reinforced the notion that a woman's place was as housewife and mother, as keeper of home and hearth (Ryan 1979; Freeman 2000).

For the most part, this attitude prevailed among the middle class until World War II, when a labor shortage drew women into the work force, filling factory positions vacated by men now in uniform. From 25 percent in 1920,

the percentage of women working increased to 36 percent during the early 1940s. But a postwar recession and soldiers returning to their former jobs resulted in the firing of 2 million women within 15 months after the war ended. Then, as the suburban decade of the 1950s ensued, the "Ozzie and Harriet" generation (named after the popular sitcom) resumed the pattern of women's lives' being confined to the house.

By 1970, however, change was under way, due to the increasing costs of a middle-class lifestyle (including the soaring costs of sending children to college), along with a wide range of new employment opportunities for women in the city's information and service economy. The dual-career family became the norm. By 2004, the female labor force participation rate reached 66 percent, way up from 46 percent in 1980. Mothers, too, joined the labor force: In 1975, 45 percent of mothers of children under age 18 with a husband at home worked for pay; by 2004, that share was 68 percent (U.S. Census Bureau 2005).

Railroad commuters are a familiar part of any large city's work force. Once their ranks were mostly male but, with almost half the labor force now female, so too is the proportion of commuters. The greater presence of women has led to changes in the texture of urban space and in services and activities catering to their needs.

Urban Space

A key focus of recent feminist urban research is the extent to which cities use space to meet the needs of women (Mazey and Lee 1983; Spain 1992; Garber and Turner 1994). For example, how does the urban environment support the needs of today's working woman? One answer is that a host of specialized services have emerged, providing child care, household cleaning, lawn care, and shopping assistance to the working woman.

One dimension in the progression of gender equality is in the greater use by women of urban public space. This scene at the Chelsea Piers sports complex in New York City is one such example. Not only does this facility provide an unconstrained and safe environment, but it also enables women to experience such previously male-dominated activities as rock climbing.

Moreover, fast food and takeout restaurants, laundries, and dry cleaners carry out tasks for which she often has little time. Large merchandising stores and supermarkets, as well as malls and mini-malls, make shopping efficient by minimizing time spent going from store to store.

Another issue concerns the allocation of public space. In a male-dominated society, planners typically allocate most open space to male-oriented activities such as sports, giving little consideration to the needs of women. More attention needs to be given to creating safe environments to protect children at play, providing less-constrained places for women to walk or jog, and creating housing that promotes more contact with neighbors, especially for children. Finally, researchers suggest that spatial arrangements should not segregate the sexes, thereby reinforcing traditional ideas about gender, but should allocate space to help all individuals' lives (Doreen Massey 1994).

The Public Sphere

More women than ever before hold elected public office; tens of thousands now serve as mayors or members of city councils across North America. Among major cities where women have served as mayor are Chicago, Phoenix, Portland, Oklahoma City, San Antonio, San Francisco, San Jose, and Mississauga, Ontario. As women become more active and visible in the public arena, they seek to shape and redirect policies affecting women's daily lives in the city. Now that major cities have a large share of women who make extensive use of urban facilities and services—including transportation and child care—an urban policy responsive to women's needs is imperative.

To date, even though many women now participate in decision making, they have had limited success in putting on the political agenda key issues that challenge male dominance. As the number of women leaders increases, however, this situation is likely to change.

In concluding this chapter, we present a case study of what was, for a century, the "second city" of the United States—its greatest inland metropolis, Chicago. Chicago's development illustrates all the issues raised in this chapter. As Robert Park and the University of Chicago sociologists (Chapter 5) found out, Chicago has been a city in which class, race, ethnicity, and gender have played a central part in people's lives.

❖ *CASE STUDY* ❖
Chicago, "City of the Big Shoulders"

Hog Butcher for the World,
Tool Maker, Stacker of Wheat,
Player with Railroads and the Nation's Freight
  Handler;
Stormy, husky, brawling,
City of the Big Shoulders:
They tell me you are wicked and I believe
  them, for I have seen your painted women
  under the gas lamps luring the farm boys.
And they tell me you are crooked and I
  answer: Yes, it is true I have seen the
  gunman kill and go free to kill again.
And they tell me you are brutal and my reply
  is: On the faces of women and children I
  have seen the marks of wanton hunger.
And having answered so I turn once more to
  those who sneer at this my city, and I give
  them back the sneer and say to them:
Come and show me another city with lifted
  head singing so proud to be alive and
  coarse and strong and cunning.
Flinging magnetic curses amid the toil of
  piling job on job, here is a tall bold slugger
  set vivid against the little soft cities;
Fierce as a dog with tongue lapping for
  action, cunning as a savage pitted against
  the wilderness,
    Bareheaded,
    Shoveling,
    Wrecking,
    Planning,
    Building, breaking, rebuilding,
Under the smoke, dust all over his mouth,
  laughing with white teeth,
Under the terrible burden of destiny
  laughing as a young man laughs,

Laughing even as an ignorant fighter laughs
  who has never lost a battle,
Bragging and laughing that under his wrist is
  the pulse, and under his ribs the heart of
  the people,
    Laughing!
Laughing the stormy, husky, brawling
  laughter of Youth, half-naked, sweating,
  proud to be Hog Butcher, Tool Maker,
  Stacker of Wheat, Player with Railroads
  and Freight Handler to the Nation.

Carl Sandberg, "Chicago"

Carl Sandberg captures much of the flavor of turn-of-the-century Chicago in this poem he wrote in tribute to the city in 1916. Not everyone, of course, shared his enthusiasm. Visiting Chicago in the 1850s, Swedish novelist Frederika Bremer decried it as "one of the most miserable and ugly cities," a place where people come "to trade, to make money, but not to live" (cited in Glaab and Brown 1967:85–86). Rudyard Kipling, visiting the Chicago of the Gay Nineties, was more direct: "Having seen it," he wrote, "I urgently desire never to see it again. It is inhabited by savages" (cited in Rakove 1975:22).

What is it about Chicago that draws such powerful and divergent responses from observers? Perhaps it is that the most powerful themes in the United States concern wealth, prestige, power, and the drama by which they are gained or lost. Chicago, which rocketed to prominence in barely 50 years, clearly exhibits such themes. This "city of the big shoulders," at once brash and breathtaking, is a magnifier of U.S. wealth and poverty without equal.

Early Chicago

In 1673, the future site of Chicago, where the Chicago River joins Lake Michigan, caught the attention of early explorers Jacques Marquette and Louis Joliet as a possible water link between Lake Michigan and the Mississippi.[1] The

---

[1]Much of the history of Chicago that follows is based on Harvey M. Mayer and Richard C. Wade, *Chicago: Growth of a Metropolis* (Chicago: University of Chicago Press, 1973).

Chicago's skyline offers a striking array of architectural styles that enhance its visual appeal. Within the city itself, as in all cities, a population also rich in diversity often grapples with problems of housing and crime that affect quality of life and satisfaction with urban living.

area remained under Indian and French control for almost a century until the English took charge in 1763. Shortly thereafter, it passed into the hands of the new United States of America. Early in the next century, Native Americans vacated the area and the U.S. Army erected Fort Dearborn amidst a sprinkling of settlers' cabins. Another generation passed before, in the shadow of a fort, the settlement of Chicago began in earnest.

In 1830, a century of spectacular growth was under way. Starting with just 50 persons, the new city (incorporated in 1833) boasted 4,000 residents by 1837. As the Erie Canal stimulated regional trade, Chicago became a boomtown. A building lot that sold for $100 in 1830 brought $15,000 by 1835. The population soared—growing by 50 percent or more between 1840 and 1900. So great was the demand for housing that the city emerged as a center for innovative architectural techniques, a tradition it has maintained. "Balloon frame" housing—assembled quickly with machined lumber rather than heavy timbers—was an early Chicago strategy to provide homes for waves of new arrivals.

The key to the economic success of the city was its position in the growing urban trade network. Chicago was linked to the East by the Great Lakes and the Erie Canal; to the South by river and canal to the Mississippi River; and, by midcentury, to the West by the railroad. On November 20, 1848, a locomotive carried the first load of wheat into the city. Although it was a trip of only 10 miles, the significance was clear: With the railroad, Chicago became the center for the entire Midwest, a break-of-bulk point for goods shipped in all directions.

By 1855, 96 trains a day entered and left the city. In the 1850s, the McCormick Reaper Company made Chicago a center for farm machinery. The famed stockyards developed during the Civil War and, with the making of steel rails, Chicago also took its place as a manufacturing center. In short, "Chicago had become Chicago" (Mayer and Wade 1973:24).

In the following decades, Chicago's wealth and influence continued to grow. Railroad lines converged on the city from all directions, and water traffic expanded as lumber, grain, and livestock trade increased dramatically. Factories proliferated, forming new industrial districts. Many industrialists became rich beyond imagination: Cyrus McCormick with his reaper and other agricultural inventions; Henry B. Clarke in hardware; and Archibald Clybourne, Gustavus Swift, and Philip Armour in beef and meat packing. By 1885, Armour employed some 10,000 workers in his meatpacking business. Prosperity seemed to be everywhere:

The old boundaries could no longer contain the burgeoning commerce and industry. . . . Lumber yards, factories, [grain] elevators, warehouses, docks, and depots lined the river and pushed north and south along the banks of both branches; commercial facilities steadily expanded at the city's center, forcing residential construction to move out to the edge of town. . . . urban displacement. . . . had begun. (Mayer and Wade 1973:54)

Industrial giants such as McCormick, Clybourne, Clarke, Swift, and Armour became the city's first elite. As the rich did elsewhere, these men displayed their new wealth with spectacular homes away from the city's center that contrasted sharply with the working people's squalid settlements near Packingtown and other industrial areas. Further enriching the lifestyle of the privileged residents was the opening of an opera house and art gallery in 1850 and, a decade later, of Marshall Field's, the nation's first modern department store.

The Burning and Rebuilding of Chicago

According to Chicago lore, on the night of October 8, 1871, near the corner of 12th and Halsted Streets, Mrs. O'Leary left her cottage to milk her cow in the small barn in the back. But the cantankerous old cow kicked over her lamp and started the fire that burned down the city of Chicago. Fanned by a stiff southwest wind, the fire swept northward along the lake, consuming 1,700 acres within 24 hours. As in London in 1666 and Atlanta in 1864, the destruction was virtually total. In a day, 100,000 Chicagoans were rendered homeless, and the heart of the city's business district lay in ashes.

However, the forces that had created Chicago—the quest for commercial and industrial success—were very much alive. The new Chicago became more of a "growth machine" than ever before. In 1884, the city opened the age of the urban skyscraper with the construction of a ten-story steel building. By 1890, Chicago's population passed the 1 million mark. Pushing its borders outward, the nation's second-largest city once again dominated the Midwest.

Jane Addams and Hull House

In 1889, Jane Addams—suffragist, activist, and the first woman to win a Nobel Peace Prize—founded Hull House in an old mansion at the corner of Halsted and Polk Streets amid Chicago's West Side slums. Her house was a refuge for displaced people to "aid in the solution of social problems engendered by the modern conditions of life in a great city" and to help her neighbors "build responsible self-sufficient lives for themselves and their families" (Addams 1910).

Immigrant Aid

Hull House was situated in an ethnically diverse section, astride Italian, Bohemian, Greek, Jewish, Polish, and Russian neighborhoods. To build pride and respect for ethnic heritage, Addams implemented the Hull House Labor Museum, which portrayed the labor of immigrant parents in their native countries and connected it to the jobs held by young adults in Chicago. Unlike most of her contemporaries, Addams recognized the unique problems of African Americans and became a pioneer in the fight against racial discrimination (Addams 1930).

In *The Spirit of Youth and the City Streets* (1909), Addams voiced concern over the breakup of the sense of community caused by industrialization, which tended to segregate social classes as well as immigrants, and even the generations within the same social class. Gifted as a speaker and writer, she often addressed the issue of respecting diversity in others:

> Possibly another result of our contemptuous attitude toward immigrants who differ from us is our exaggerated acceptance of standardization. Everyone wants to be like his neighbors, which is doubtless an amiable quality, but leading to one of the chief dangers of democracy—the tyranny of the herd mind. (1930:330)

Through it all, Hull House remained the center of her activism.

Hull-House expanded to include many buildings. Eventually 70 people experienced collective living and more than 2,000 others crossed its doorway daily. It became a community center for all of Chicago; there was an art museum, a theater, a boys' club, a music school, a coffee house, meeting rooms for discussion clubs, a gymnasium, an employment bureau, a lunchroom, a library, apartments for working women and their children, a kindergarten, and much more. Scholars from the universities, leaders from Chicago society, and international leaders came to observe and learn. (Lundblad 1995:662)

Social Activism

Addams's social activism included successfully lobbying the Illinois state legislature to pass strong child labor laws and laws protecting women. She conceived of and helped create the juvenile court system, set up school playgrounds, demanded enforcement of housing and sanitation laws, worked for woman's suffrage, advocated for the legal protection of immigrants, and much more. Among Hull House firsts were:

- the first public swimming pool in Chicago;
- the creation of four labor unions (Women Skirt Makers, Women Cloak Makers, Dorcas Federal Labor Union, Chicago Women's Trade Union League);
- the nation's first private venture capital fund for neighborhood business development;
- the first domestic violence court in Chicago in conjunction with the Chicago Metropolitan Battered Women's Network (Domestic Violence Court Advocacy Program);
- the first infant care facility in a Chicago high school;
- the first community-based foster care program of its kind in the country (Neighbor to Neighbor).

Early Feminism

Equally important, Addams believed that dramatic changes could be made in U.S. society and, to that end, she provided a forum where people of all classes, races, and genders could speak together (Deegan 1991). An especially important feature of Hull House was its role as a nurturing, fertile arena for women to engage in intellectually stimulating debates with men. With Hull House as a model, scores of settlement houses sprang up in slum neighborhoods in other cities. Everywhere, settlement houses served as a breeding ground for feminism and activism. At least half the women residents went on to lifelong careers in some branch of social service.

Jane Addams was a close associate of George Herbert Mead, who gave lectures at Hull House. Her contributions to the founding of the science of sociology and to the first department of sociology at the University of Chicago are pivotal intellectual achievements. The noted educator John Dewey was also an associate and a good friend of Jane Addams; Dewey modeled his classes at the Laboratory School, University of Chicago, after the children's activities at Hull House. Clearly, Jane Addams was a major force not only on the Chicago urban scene, but at the national and international levels as well. Her achievements, contributions, and humanitarian efforts still shape our lives today.

Chicago in the Early Twentieth Century

> Chicago . . . offered a world of hope and opportunity to the beginner. It was so new, so raw; everything was in the making . . . the youth, the illusions, the untrained aspirations of millions of souls. . . . Chicago [at the turn of the century] meant eagerness, hope, desire. It was a city that put vitality into almost every wavering heart. It made the beginner dream.
>
> Theodore Dreiser

Chicago plunged into the new century with clear title as the metropolis of the Midwest. The city shot upward as a towering skyline took form. Immigrants from Europe swelled the city's population: Germans, Swedes, Irish, Poles, and Italians. For many, life in Chicago's poorest neighborhoods was often brutal, unsanitary, and exceedingly crowded. An estimate at the turn of the century revealed that if all of Chicago "were as densely populated as its worst slums [900 people per acre], the whole of the Western Hemisphere could have been housed in Chicago" (Felter, as cited in Mayer and Wade 1973:256).

Over time, however, the dreams of many working-class Chicagoans became a reality. More and more sons and daughters of immigrants moved outward from the old crowded neighborhoods into newer middle-class housing. This outward flow spilled into newly annexed developments on the city's edge.

But success did not come to all. African Americans had an especially hard time. Drawn to Chicago in ever-increasing numbers in the early 1900s, blacks settled primarily on the city's South Side. There, unlike many others, they experienced little prosperity, and few migrated outward. The black ghetto simply expanded to the north and west of the city. Periodically, too, racial violence erupted. On July 27, 1919, after a confrontation on a local beach, a black youth drowned, leading to five days of rioting in the South Side ghetto. Damage was extensive, and many blacks suffered death and injury at the hands of white mobs.

By the 1920s, when the sociologists of the University of Chicago began studying their city intensively, they found Chicago shaped by a complex social stratification system based on race, ethnicity, occupation, and income. Soon, organized crime asserted itself in the form of "gangsters," fed by the public's thirst for alcohol despite Prohibition. Nowhere did guns speak louder than in the smaller city of Cicero, adjacent to Chicago, where Johnny Torrio, Al Capone, and "the mob" had their headquarters. To consolidate his control of the city, Capone launched a campaign of terror on Election Day in April 1924. This represented urban political corruption at its peak of power, and the mob's victory gave gangsters control of much of the city. Still, some people fought back and, by 1931, Capone was convicted of income tax evasion, and he spent the rest of his life in prison.

Then came the Depression, which cut deeply into Chicago's economic life. Unemployment soared, construction stalled, and even the city's second World's Fair in 1933 couldn't conceal the widespread social injury. Homeless Chicagoans sleeping in public parks or milling about street corners became commonplace. Only with World War II did the economy finally recover.

The Postwar Period

Post–World War II growth took place largely beyond Chicago's city limits. A familiar pattern changed the social character of Chicago as the more affluent population moved out, leaving behind the growing ranks of minorities and the poor. By 1960, with people demanding more services as the economic base continued to contract, some began speaking of the "death of the city." Chicago fought back under the leadership of a Mayor, Richard J. Daley, whose long and controversial record lasted from his election in 1955 until his death in 1976.

The Chicago Machine

An old saying about Chicago holds that "the Jews own it, the Irish run it, and the blacks live in it" (Rakove 1975:32). This is partly incorrect—the greatest wealth in the city is controlled by white Anglo-Saxon Protestants—but the Irish have controlled the politics of the city for most of its history, although they now face a growing political challenge from blacks and Hispanics, who constituted 63 percent of the city's population in 2000 (U.S. Census Bureau, 2005).

The Chicago political machine of the Democratic Party came to power in the 1930s, later than in many other cities, and did not reach its greatest strength until Richard J. Daley became the undisputed city boss. Political life in Chicago under Daley carried the tone of the immigrant political machines of the late nineteenth century. Its leaders, from block captains to the mayor himself, tried to meet the needs of their constituents and, in return, they expected people's votes.

Daley focused on maintaining the quality of the central business district—the Loop. Centered along State Street, the Loop is the economic heart of the city, of vital concern to the city's powerful business interests. In addition, the city revitalized the lakefront to make Chicago attractive and exciting both to visitors and to Chicagoans themselves. The record of improvements was uneven, however. While all residents of the city benefited to some degree from better lighting, street cleaning, and snow removal, poorer neighborhoods got the short end of the stick. A political opponent of Mayor Daley observed:

> Get off the subway anywhere in the central business area and you won't find a broken city sidewalk. Get off the subway almost anywhere else, and you will. Between the central business area and the outskirts lie large, almost uninterrupted grey areas of urban dry rot. This is where most Chicagoans live. (Leon Despres, cited in Rakove 1975:78–79)

Chicago also boasts three of the five tallest buildings in the nation—including the Sears Tower, one of the tallest in the world—yet commitment to improving housing for the poor has been lacking until recently, a topic highlighted in the next chapter. Especially for African Americans, segregation remains all too evident, prompting a greater political voice from the black community (now 36 percent of the population). Hispanics, too, are a growing political force (27 percent of the city's people).

Since Daley's death in 1976, the Irish-dominated machine has held on in Chicago, although with considerably less power. Soon after Daley's death, Jane Byrne became the city's first woman mayor, followed by Harold Washington, Chicago's first black mayor, elected in 1983 following a divisive racial campaign. Presently, Richard Daley, son of the late mayor, is Chicago's leader.

Ordered Segmentation

Race and ethnicity are thus fundamental parts of the social organization of Chicago, as Gerald Suttles (1968) discovered through a participant-observer study of the Addams area on Chicago's West Side. Most observers considered this area, once prime turf for the Capone mob, little more than a disorganized slum. Suttles's most important finding was that while some housing was surely dilapidated and many people were poor, the area was far from "disorganized." Rather, Suttles found a marked social order he termed **ordered segmentation** based on race and ethnicity.

How did it work? Back then, four categories—African, Italian, Mexican, and Puerto Rican Americans—made up the bulk of the area's population. Each had its own distinctive way of life, claimed its own "territory," and had its own ideas about all the others who lived nearby. Suttles found the Italians very closely knit and trusting of one another. African Americans, in contrast, seemed alienated from each other, typically distrustful, and very poor. The Mexican Americans and Puerto Ricans fell somewhere in between. They were somewhat better off than the blacks economically and had more of a sense of community.

Contacts across racial and ethnic lines were rare. Most people kept their distance from others who, according to local stereotypes, were different and best avoided. The positive irony here is that such divisiveness allowed most people to establish community ties with those whom they did trust. By avoiding African Americans, Italians, and Mexican Americans, in other words, Puerto Ricans could form a sense of identity and community among themselves, thereby providing some defense against a hostile outside world. Suttles concluded:

> For all its shortcomings . . . the moral order they have developed includes most, if not all, of their neighbors. Within limits, the residents possess a

In the 1990s, Chicago experienced both a renaissance of its older commercial streets and a building boom along Michigan Avenue at the edge of Lake Michigan. Navy Pier—with its mix of amusements, exhibitions, restaurants, shops, theaters, and touring boats—is a year-round attraction for hundreds of thousands of residents and visitors each year.

way of gaining associates, avoiding enemies, and establishing each others' intentions. In view of the difficulties encountered, the [ordered segmentation] of the Addams Area has provided a decent world within which people can live. (1968:234)

Chicago Today

Despite corruption scandals in 2005 involving some city officials accepting bribes to award trucking contracts or illegally doling out patronage jobs, the news from Chicago these days is mostly positive. Across the city, remarkable changes are under way—physically, economically, and among its residents. Its trademark skyline now includes more rooms with a view than ever before, as high-rise

residences continue to sprout up throughout the downtown area and nearby neighborhoods. In 2005 alone, 4,500 new condo units were built and quickly purchased by young professionals, aging suburban empty nesters, and speculators. Three new condominium high-rises are in the works, including Donald Trump's 90-story hotel and condominium tower. Despite an increase in office vacancies—caused primarily by corporate mergers and layoffs—new commercial development downtown continues, punctuated by the newly opened 48-story Hyatt Center and 51-story 111 South Wacker Drive next door. Nearly 4 million additional square feet of office space was under construction in 2005 (Widholm 2005).

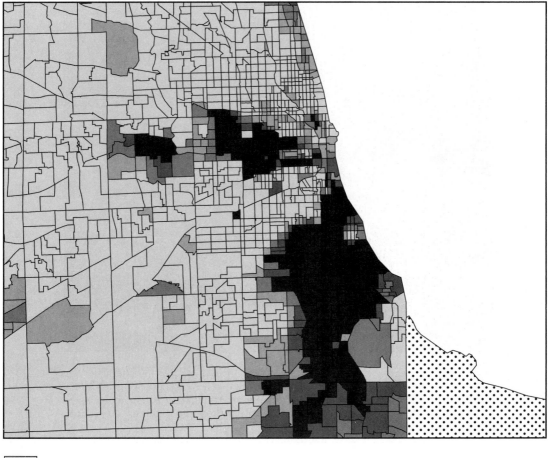

0 to 9.1

9.2 to 25.7

25.8 to 50.5

50.6 to 81.3

81.4 to 100.0

FIGURE 11–4A Percent of Persons Who Are Black in Chicago, 2000 [*Source*: U.S. Census Bureau.]

New theater venues and restaurants in the Loop have brought additional vitality to the downtown. Moreover, the city's new, nearly half-billion-dollar lakefront park completes the third element of its catch phrase since 2000 of "live, work, play." The highlight of this leisure area is the 3,000-foot-long Navy Pier—a mix of year-round entertainment, shops, restaurants, exhibition facilities, and attractions, including a 525-seat Shakespeare Theater, a 440-seat IMAX theater, a 150-foot Ferris wheel, and a stained glass window museum—attracts hundreds of thousands of visitors annually (Bruno 2001; Widholm 2005).

Another significant change is in Chicago's population composition. Since 1980, the

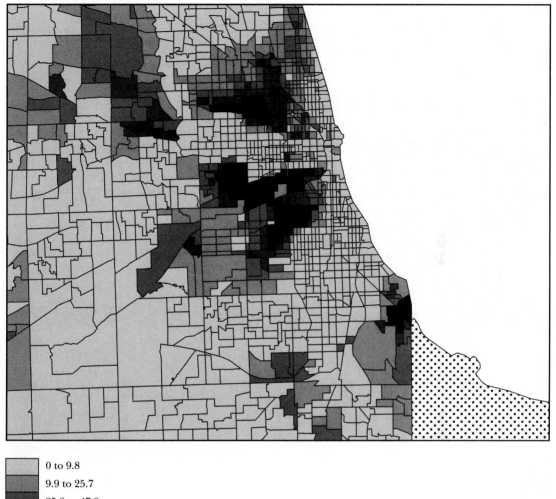

	0 to 9.8
	9.9 to 25.7
	25.8 to 47.8
	47.9 to 71.6
	71.7 to 100.0

FIGURE 11–4B   Percent of Persons Who Are Latino in Chicago, 2000. [*Source*: U.S. Census Bureau.]

city's black and white populations have been declining, as new immigrants introduce fresh dimensions of social diversity. As recently as the 1970s, most immigrants were Europeans; today, however, the European-born population of Chicago has fallen to less than 8 percent. In their place are now Hispanics, whose numbers tripled since 1970 to more than 753,000 by 2000, and Asians, who total about 126,000 (U.S. Census Bureau 2005). As mentioned earlier, Chicago has one of the nation's highest levels of black residential segregation, but its Hispanic residents are not as intensely segregated (see Figure 11–4).

In the Chicago of today, neighborhoods that once contained Germans, Poles, and Czechs bustle with African, Filipino, Korean, Mexican, Puerto Rican, and Vietnamese Americans, and many other ethnic groups. Within each category, of course, there is greater diversity still. Some new immigrants come to Chicago with wealth, extensive schooling, and bilingual fluency. Others, by contrast, are poor. Like immigrants throughout history, they come with little, seeking something more. As one might expect, those with the greatest social advantages tend to spread most widely throughout the city; most of Chicago's new immigrants from India, for example, are professionals and are widely dispersed. On the other hand, those with the fewest social advantages are re-creating the racial and ethnic enclaves that have existed in Chicago throughout its history, evident in the clusters of signs marking Mexican, Korean, and Chinese neighborhoods.

Most of the new racial and ethnic communities in Chicago are still too small to have a marked impact on the political scene. Yet, in the heyday of the Irish-dominated political machine, probably few could have imagined that the city would ever elect a black mayor. But as new performers step to the stage in the twenty-first century, the leaders of this large and complex city will need to have big shoulders indeed.

❖ ══════ ❖ ══════ ❖

SUMMARY

Cities are marked by social diversity. Throughout history, one characteristic of the city has been its ability to generate more opportunity for its people than rural living can. Seeking this opportunity, billions have streamed into cities. Certainly this was the wheel driving the Great Immigration to North American cities that occurred between 1880 and 1920. By and large, people found much of what they were hoping for. As time passed, many immigrants and many more of their descendants moved from poverty into relative affluence.

But this was not true for all. North American cities also became home to an impoverished class. Historically, the worst off have been the city's newest arrivals: northern Europeans until 1830, southern and eastern Europeans until 1920, "new minorities," including African, Asian, Hispanic, and Native Americans since then.

Women with few privileges have typically worked out of necessity. Middle-class women, though, have moved in and out of the labor force over time. Today, most women work for pay, a fact that shapes the city by fostering various support services to meet the needs of dual-career families and single parents. Moreover, as women become better represented in decision-making positions, we can expect further change in how cities use space.

Finally, our case study of the Windy City, Chicago, illustrates all these themes. From its beginnings as the Midwest's regional center to its emergence as this nation's "second city," Chicago (like any other North American city we might have studied) exhibits a clear-cut stratification system based on differing amounts of wealth, prestige, and power. At the top were such industrialists as the Armours and the McCormicks. At the bottom were, first, poor European immigrants; somewhat later, African Americans; and, most recently, immigrants from Latin America and Asia.

Out of the Great Depression of the 1930s arose the Democratic Party machine that reached its culmination in the 21-year administration (1955–1976) of Mayor Richard J. Daley. Like machines elsewhere, this one benefited some people and largely ignored others. Among the latter were various racial and ethnic minorities, such as those who lived in the Addams area on Chicago's West Side. It was here that Jane Addams founded Hull House and centered her highly productive career of social activism. In his later study of this district, Gerald Suttles noted the persistence of racial, ethnic, and territorial divisions, an organization pattern he termed "ordered segmentation." As European immigrants organized themselves within urban neighborhoods in decades past, so do many of the "new immigrants" today in a city that is experiencing a building boom in new residential, commercial, and leisure space.

CONCLUSION

The larger insight from Suttles's work is that prejudice always works to distinguish some **ingroup** from some **outgroup.** Looking around them, people conclude that "they" simply don't look, think, or act the way "we" do. Kenneth Clark (1980) suggested that such prejudice and the resulting discrimination are the heart of the disadvantages faced by African Americans, a visible minority based on skin color. Much the same applies to people with a different language, who are also set apart as different and become easy targets for discrimination. Thus, some of the success experienced by white ethnics is due to their ability, over time, to "pass," that is, to assimilate into the dominant urban culture. The same opportunity is not as easily afforded others with more clearly identifiable differences.

This pattern reminds us that cities do not exist in a cultural vacuum, for the values, norms, and stratification that shape the broader society also shape cities. Thus the unequal distribution of wealth and power that characterizes North America, as well as structures of prejudice and discrimination, play out most clearly in our cities.

KEY TERMS

Chain migration
De facto segregation
De jure segregation
Gendered spaces
Hostile environment
Index of dissimilarity
Invasion-succession
Ordered segmentation
Parallel social institutions
Push–pull factors
Steering

CHAPTER 12

HOUSING, EDUCATION, CRIME
Confronting Urban Problems

❖ ━━━━━━━━ ❖ ━━━━━━━━ ❖

I am an optimist about the possibilities and a pessimist about the probabilities.

Lewis Mumford

We did not all come over in the same ship, but we are all in the same boat.

Bernard Baruch

With four out of five North Americans living in cities, we are unquestionably an urban people. But most of us recognize that urban living involves not just opportunities and excitement, but also various problems. Indeed, troubles such as poor housing, poor education, and crime seem more intense in cities than elsewhere.

A close look at such problems reveals that most do not exist in isolation. On the contrary, many connections exist among such problems as poverty, poor housing and education, crime, and racial and ethnic tensions. Focusing on any one alone not only hinders understanding but also frustrates any efforts at solutions. Urban problems are part of a "package," partly a product of cities but also a product of the structure and values of society itself.

Urban living is the search for a high quality of life. Three aspects of good living are adequate shelter, a good education, and physical and emotional security. How well, then, do our cities provide housing for everyone, including the poor? How well do they educate our children? How well do they offer safety for all citizens? This chapter explores the issues of housing, education, and crime, three key issues that define the quality of our urban lives.

HOUSING: A PLACE TO LIVE

Chapter 10 explained that the lifestyles of the urban population are strikingly diverse, a fact that is clearly evident in people's choice of housing. Some urbanites prefer the life of a downtown apartment; others desire the liveliness of row houses in an ethnic neighborhood; still others are drawn to a spacious single-family suburban home. Of course, housing and neighborhood are not simply matters of personal choice. Differences in wealth set the range of choices available. Also important are past and present economic forces that have created the city, and the cultural factors that set many of our personal priorities.

Adequate Housing: Who Has It?

To define housing as either "adequate" or "substandard" is, of course, somewhat arbitrary. It is also culturally variable, because even the worst housing in the United States is of far better quality than that which commonly exists in poor nations of the world (Chapter 13).

Still, we can all agree that housing characterized by structural defects; inadequate plumbing, heating, or sanitation; or lead paint easily ingested by children poses a threat to the health and safety of those who live there. Millions of people do live in such substandard housing, and most of them live in our cities. Since most North Americans never have any direct experience with such housing, we might well be shaken if we were to confront the daily reality of the worst-housed members of our society.

Like everything else of value, quality housing is distributed quite unequally in urban North America. Not surprisingly, the worst housing is concentrated in areas occupied by the poor and minorities who are subject to discrimination—in short, people who have the fewest social choices. Such people's options have been further reduced by changes in the housing market itself: a steady decline in the number of low-rent housing units and a corresponding increase in the number of higher-rent housing units. Beginning about 1980, the U.S. government reduced its funding for low-income housing, pushing the number of available units downward even as demand rose. Small wonder, then, that some critics claim that the combination of declining stock of low-cost housing and the constant need for such housing is a key cause of today's homelessness.

Housing Problems: A Brief History

To better understand current housing problems, we need to look to their roots in the past. Many of the older cities' tenements are nineteenth-century structures that present some of the same problems today that they did back then.

Nineteenth-Century Housing Problems. Housing problems in North America are hardly new. In fact, in the great metropolises of the nineteenth century, housing conditions were far worse than they are today. In an examination of conditions in New York in 1870, James D. McCabe, Jr., recorded the following impressions:

> If the people [housed in tenements] are sufferers, they at least live upon the surface of the earth. But what shall we say of those who pass their lives in the cellars of [these] wretched buildings . . . ?
>
> [Most] have but one entrance and that furnishes the only means of ventilation . . . and . . . the filth of the streets comes washing down the walls into the room within. The air is always foul. The drains of the houses above pass within a few feet of the floor, and as they are generally in bad condition the filth frequently comes oozing up and poisons the air with its foul odors.
>
> . . . The poor wretches who seek shelter here are half stupefied by it, and pass the night in this condition instead of in a healthful sleep. (1970:405, 406, 409)

Despite such horrors, for generations government leaders made little effort to regulate housing. For their part, private builders, concerned mainly with profits, did little on their own. Indeed, only the collapse of the U.S. economy in the 1930s forced the government to enact a housing program—part of President Franklin Roosevelt's "New Deal."

A New Deal.   Under the Roosevelt administration, the federal government became more involved in everyday life than ever before. Officials argued, first, that inadequate housing was so widespread that it amounted to a serious social problem and, second, that only governmental intervention was likely to lead to a solution.

Under the New Deal, federal housing programs had four specific goals. First, government directed federal funds to encourage the construction of new housing. Second, since some 500,000 families had lost their homes due to inability to pay their mortgage debts, agencies offered assistance to homeowners faced with foreclosure by banks. Third, the Federal Housing Administration (FHA) guaranteed construction loans to increase the housing supply. Fourth, the Public Works Administration, begun in 1938, hired

unemployed people to build low-rent public housing in 30 cities.

Taken together, these programs rapidly improved urban housing. According to the housing census of 1940, however, about 40 percent of urban housing in the United States still had at least some serious defect (such as a lack of running water or other inadequate plumbing).

Postwar Programs.   All housing construction, public and private, slowed for the duration of World War II. Soon afterward, however, the United States faced a great housing shortage as military personnel returned home and families began having children (the "baby boom"). This shortage, along with the continued need to improve the overall quality of housing, led government to devise several new strategies.

One was a broadening of federal mortgage guarantees through the FHA and the Veterans Administration (VA). The latter agency, created under the Servicemen's Readjustment Act of 1944 (popularly known as the GI Bill of Rights), provided federally backed loans to military personnel and veterans. These programs greatly enhanced the home-buying ability of moderate-income families.

Another major initiative was passage of the Housing Act of 1949. This program provided a two-pronged attack on urban decline by launching major efforts at slum clearance and the construction of new housing.

The program, called **urban renewal**, rested on local governments' ability to seize a decaying area through the right of **eminent domain** and sell the property to a private developer who would rebuild it. Of course, developers sought *profitable* redevelopment, so the new construction was seldom affordable to the low-income residents who had previously occupied the neighborhood. Most often, urban renewal projects created new housing for the middle class. A classic example is Boston's once-thriving Italian West End. Declaring it in need of renewal in 1953—despite the fact that the outwardly aging buildings were, on the inside, extremely well kept by residents—the city bought up the area between 1958 and

1960, evicted its residents, and let the developers have a go at renewal. The personal trauma of such relocation was often enormous. Said one evicted West Ender,

> I wish the world would end tonight. . . . I wish they'd tear the whole damn town down . . . damn scab town . . . I'm going to be lost without the West End. Where the hell can I go? (Gans 1982:331)

What was built in the "new" West End were high-rise luxury apartments, beyond the reach of virtually all of the area's earlier residents. As this pattern was repeated throughout the 1960s, critics often charged that urban renewal meant "poor or Negro removal." Many of the displaced poor had no choice but to crowd into other low-grade housing that they could afford. The resultant overcrowding only hastened the decay of those buildings; thus, ironically, "slum clearance" actually created more slums.

Urban renewal often made the housing crisis worse in another way, since many redevelopers did not build as many housing units as had been destroyed. The predictable result was fewer homes and thus more competition and more overcrowding. Today there are about 2.3 million subsidized rental-housing units in the United States, but that is not enough to meet the need (U.S. Census Bureau 2002b).

Public Housing

Public housing has never been very successful in the United States. Our cultural orientation has long viewed private home ownership as the foundation of a virtuous life and a stable social order (Bellush 2000). Therefore, people tend to judge those living in publicly supported rental housing as somehow deficient. Add to this the fact that public housing is almost exclusively the preserve of poor minorities, and we see why such a stigma is attached to housing projects. Instantly they become ghettos, places to be avoided, out-of-the-way reservations designed to contain an unwanted segment of society.

Originally conceived as incorporating exciting housing innovations, too many of these high-rise projects turned into unmitigated human disasters, plagued by crime, low income, overcrowding, and terrible sanitary conditions. Even poor people soon looked on them as residences of last resort. People in almost every major city can tell of such a high-rise housing project nightmare. One of the most infamous of cases is St. Louis's Pruitt-Igoe project, described in the Cityscape box on page 344.

Some later housing projects—notably Philadelphia's Society Hill—overcame the mistakes of these first programs. Still, the failures far outnumber the successes. Scott Greer suggested that, in the light of the dismal results, we could justly call the program one of "minimal charity" (1966:16).

Exactly why life in public housing is often so bad is a matter of bitter disagreement. Urban critics such as Edward Banfield (1970, 1974) suggested that residents themselves are largely to blame, since many do not work, have children they cannot afford, and generally act in irresponsible ways. Architectural critics (as we'll discuss shortly) point to the design of such structures, condemning high-rise buildings as anonymous spaces vulnerable to crime and vandalism (Newman 1972, 1996). Others, such as Ronald Utt (1996) and Lee Rainwater (1970), point to the pathologies of concentrated poverty—not the people themselves—as the fundamental cause of public housing's rather dismal record.

Different Approaches. In the climate of criticism and social reform that characterized the late 1960s, the federal government renewed efforts to ensure a "decent home for every American," the elusive goal first put forth in 1937 and reaffirmed in 1949.

The Housing Act of 1968 provided for the construction or rehabilitation of 26 million housing units, targeting 6 million of them for low- and moderate-income families. Even then, experts acknowledged, meeting this objective would not entirely end the housing crisis (Pynoos 1980:7).

An important innovation of the 1968 legislation was its attempt to place home ownership within reach of more families through loan guarantees and direct subsidies. Ideally,

CITYSCAPE

Pruitt-Igoe: Symbol of a Failed National Solution

It sounded so promising in 1951—a public housing project designed to improve the lives of thousands in a badly run-down area of East St. Louis. Taking advantage of the 1949 Housing Act, local officials sought to break through the "collar of slums which [was] threatening to strangle [the] downtown business section" (*Architectural Forum* 1951:129).

Three years later, residents fully occupied the 2,762 apartments in 33 innovative high-rise buildings. But by 1959, Pruitt-Igoe "had become a community scandal" (Rainwater 1970:8). Crime, dirt, and accidents were rampant; the project became "a concrete shell where anarchy prevailed" (Green 1977:179). Essentially a concentration of poor, welfare-dependent African American families (57 percent were female-headed households with children), Pruitt-Igoe's population declined as more and more residents could not bear to remain. The history of Pruitt-Igoe came to a dramatic close in 1972 when the St. Louis Housing Authority dynamited the buildings into oblivion. Soon high-rise housing projects would meet the same fate in other U.S. cities.

Since the dynamiting of Pruitt-Igoe in 1972, a similar fate befell other high-rise public housing as city governments attempted to correct past mistakes (not considering social as well as physical factors) with low-rise replacements. This photo shows the implosion of one of three remaining 13-story buildings of the Scudder Homes complex in Newark, New Jersey in 1996.

this program provided an alternative to public housing and helped to improve neighborhoods by increasing the number of families who had a long-term stake in the area as homeowners. To succeed, the program depended on the cooperation of real estate and government personnel. Too often, however, this didn't materialize: The program provided unscrupulous real estate speculators and public officials with opportunities that would have delighted corrupt urban politicians of a bygone era.

The basic plan was laudable: Low-income families would pay only 20 percent of their income toward the home; the government would pick up the rest. This was a major step toward extending to the poorest people the federal assistance already made available to middle-class families by the earlier FHA program (Green 1977). However, while the government labored to protect the investments of developers and lending banks, it overlooked protecting the homebuyers as well. Often, purchasers ended up with an overpriced house in need of extensive repairs that they could not afford to maintain. The result was foreclosure. But the banks then received full payment from the government, leaving the "owners" back on the street. In the end, the government owned more and more undesirable houses.

By the early 1970s the handwriting was on the wall and the program was cut back. By 1975 over $4 billion had been spent and the government was saddled with 100,000 bad houses. "With hindsight," Green concluded, "it can safely be said that private concerns [investors, developers, banks] were given too much rope, and with it, they hung the poor" (1977:181).

An alternative approach, begun in 1974 and still active, is the Section 8 Program, which provides rent subsidies to low-income tenants in private housing. This assistance program enables tenants to choose where to live instead of forcing them into a public housing project. The program offers subsidies to developers to build or rehabilitate rental housing. Developers then set aside a certain portion of the units for low-income

families and—in a subsidy contract with the government—receive 30 percent of the rent from the tenant and the rest from the government. Although Section 8 and other rental assistance programs have increased the stock of low-cost rental housing, the program is severely underfunded. Waiting lists can run into the years, and many local housing authorities frequently close their waiting lists and stop accepting applications because their lists are too long.

Evaluation.   Even this brief history makes clear that federally supervised urban housing programs fell well short of their lofty goals. Some specific problems are worth highlighting.

First, did the urban housing programs prior to the 1990s help the poor? Because of the deep involvement of private banking and construction industries in renewal programs, for many, profit overshadowed any sense of social responsibility to help the poor. Furthermore, the design of some redevelopment projects was intended for more affluent buyers, at prices out of the reach of those who originally lived there. Scott Greer charges that the original intention of urban housing programs of the 1930s—to improve the housing of the poor—was "slowly transformed into a large-scale program to redevelop the central city," usually with economic interests predominating (1966:32). Thus, Greer (1966) and Lowe (1968) concluded that, while urban renewal created "tall towers and green malls," these programs actually reduced the total amount of low-cost housing across urban North America.

A second problem is that, given the tendency of investors and developers to pursue profit rather than assist the poor, local residents had little voice in the decision-making process. Herbert Gans studied the redevelopment of Boston's West End, claiming that local residents were unorganized and lacked understanding of the programs that seemed to "attack" them. Thus, for many, renewal was a bitter experience.

A similar fate befell the residents of Poletown, a mostly ethnic but racially integrated neighborhood in Detroit, whose 465 acres contained over 1,300 homes and apartments, 143 businesses, 16 churches, 2 schools, and a hospital. In 1981, anxious to keep a new General Motors plant and 6,000 jobs in the city, municipal leaders exercised their right of eminent domain to take over Poletown, razed it (at a cost exceeding $200 million), and sold the land to GM (for $8 million) to build its new plant. Residents—joined by consumer advocate Ralph Nader and Gray Panthers leader Maggie Kuhn—futilely tried to stop the forced uprooting and destruction of their homes, churches, and businesses. To this day, much bitterness remains among those dispossessed people.

Third, Gans and other critics like Jane Jacobs argued that redevelopers didn't even try to see that many areas subject to redevelopment were actually healthy, safe neighborhoods. In effect, many development programs reflected the bias of middle-class planners against the lifestyle of low-rent areas. Somehow, such areas just weren't what the planners considered "normal."

> Reformers [who] have long observed city people loitering on busy corners, hanging around in candy stores and bars and drinking soda pop on stoops . . . have passed a [class-biased] judgment, the gist of which is: "This is deplorable! If these people had decent homes and a more private . . . outdoor place, they wouldn't be on the street!" [Such a judgment] makes no more sense than to drop in at a testimonial banquet in a hotel and conclude that if these people . . . could cook, they would give their parties at home. (Jacobs 1961:55)

At present, we find some promise for public housing, even as the U.S. government seeks to reduce funding severely. We will discuss the bright spots in both public and private housing shortly. First, though, we will discuss housing troubles in the private sector that also plague the cities.

Deterioration and Abandonment in the Inner City

Picture this: block after block of empty, dilapidated buildings, many burned, as if the area had collapsed under a full-scale bomb attack. Do such urban "ghost towns" really exist in the United States? Especially in the older, industrial inner cities of the Midwest and Northeast, the answer is, sadly, yes.

As the economic activity of cities spread outward after World War II with the decline of older industries and the globalization of trade, the older central cities fell on hard times. Without the resources necessary for repairs and improvements, many inner-city neighborhoods declined in population and deteriorated sharply, in some cases falling victim to extensive vandalism and arson. Estimates then placed the number of abandoned buildings in U.S. central cities at 2 million (W. Conway 1977). Although some were later torn down and others rehabilitated, the number of additional abandoned buildings grew some 150,000 yearly well into the 1980s. In the 1990s, the numbers dropped considerably, thanks to the economic revitalization in many cities and the gentrification process. Still, in 2000, Baltimore had as many as 40,000 abandoned buildings, while Detroit had 36,000, Philadelphia 21,000, and St. Louis over 6,000 (Cohen 2000).

Why would people simply walk away from otherwise usable buildings in cities where housing was in short supply? The answer is a complex vicious circle of decline. Faced with the mounting expenses of taxes, insurance, heating fuel, and repairs due to vandalism, not to mention the loss to the suburbs of middle-income renters, and often constrained by rent control caps, some building owners reduce or entirely eliminate routine maintenance and repairs in an effort to retain some profit. Angered tenants often withhold rent, which, in turn, encourages owners to withhold more services to obtain rents. If the building eventually represents more costs or trouble than rental income warrants, some owners simply default on their mortgages or cut off the utilities. In some cases buildings are deliberately "torched" in an effort to secure payment of insurance claims. As desperate ex-tenants scatter in search of other housing, vandals and looters seek whatever of

The South Bronx in the 1980s looked like a war zone and its violent crime rate made it feel like one. Arson and abandonment led to the loss of 30,000 buildings in the 1970s, leading to scenes such as this one. By the mid-1990s though, urban homesteading and gentrification programs had transformed this area into a safe, pleasant area to live and raise children.

value remains (including sinks, bathtubs, and plumbing). First the building, then the block, and then eventually the whole neighborhood succumbs to the process. In the end, just hollow buildings remain: giant headstones marking the grave of a now-dead urban neighborhood.

Other developments in the private sector are more encouraging. In recent years, housing in the South Bronx as well as throughout New York City and in other major cities has vastly improved. Although much more needs to be done, notable progress is clearly evident, as we shall now explain.

The Inner City Today: A Revival?

When a city begins to grow and spread outward
   from the edges, the center which was once
   its glory . . . goes into a period of desolation,
   inhabited at night by the vague ruins of men.

. . . Nearly every city I know has such a dying mother of violence and despair where at night the brightness of the street lamps is sucked away and policemen walk in pairs. And then one day perhaps the city returns and rips out the sore and builds a monument to its past.

John Steinbeck, *Travels with Charley*

Although the success of public programs has surely been limited, efforts by private groups to rebuild certain inner-city areas have achieved significant results in the past few decades. Two trends deserve attention: urban homesteading and gentrification.

Urban Homesteading. In 1973, the city of Wilmington, Delaware (burdened with some 1,200 abandoned homes) revived the mid-nineteenth-century Homestead Act that gave away land and mules to pioneers if they built on vacant land in the West and lived on it for five years. The city offered buildings it acquired through default of tax payments for a token fee of a few hundred dollars to people agreeing to rehabilitate them and stay there a minimum of three years. Wilmington's success in restoring tax ratable properties encouraged many other cities to initiate their own homesteading programs, often transferring houses to people at the top of long waiting lists for Section 8 rental housing who were willing to become "urban homesteaders"—pioneers in rebuilding an urban area.

In New York's ravaged South Bronx, where over 30,000 buildings were abandoned in the 1970s (an average of eight a day), local citizens' groups such as the People's Development Corporation stood up against seemingly impossible odds to return deteriorating inner-city buildings to life. With little capital to invest, such groups could rely only on their own physical efforts to be successful; their collateral was not future earnings or other property but their own sweat, giving rise to the term "sweat equity." The Cityscape box on page 349 captures some of the 1970s spirit that inspired people to accept the challenge of building something out of almost nothing.

Ramon Rueda and Danny Soto were just a few of the thousands who reclaimed the South Bronx. Nonetheless, urban homesteading has had only limited success, because too many abandoned homes have deteriorated and been vandalized beyond rehabilitation. Others stand amid so much ruin and desolation that they are not worth salvaging. Furthermore, both the cost of repairing the building to meet occupancy code standards and the difficulty of getting rehabilitation loans eliminates most urban poor from participating in urban homesteading.

Demand far outstrips supply, however. A few years ago, for example, over 2,000 people lined up in Washington, D.C., to participate in a housing lottery for 68 boarded-up buildings that were offered for $250 each, a pledge to renovate them to bring them up to housing code standards and to live in them for five years. The mostly three- and four-bedroom houses and a few small apartment buildings had been vacant for more than a decade, with the exception of occasional visits by drug dealers, prostitutes, and the homeless. Now they are part of the city's good housing stock (Fleishman 1999).

Another form of urban homesteading requiring sweat equity of incoming homeowners, but overcoming some of the obstacles just mentioned, is Habitat for Humanity. Habitat is a nonprofit organization that utilizes volunteer labor and some donated materials from area churches and organizations to build new housing for low-income families. Those screened to become homeowners pay interest-free, low mortgage loans and must work to build their house along with the volunteers. Since its founding in 1976, Habitat has built over 50,000 houses across the United States, most in areas of massive urban blight, ultimately transforming many places into attractive, stable neighborhoods. The organization now has over 1,700 local affiliates in all 50 states, plus another 550 active affiliates in 100 countries, where it has built more than 200,000 homes (Habitat for Humanity 2005).

Gentrification.   Unlike urban homesteading, which is limited to the reclamation of just a few buildings or blocks at a time, gentrification is a broader process. The word **gentrification**, coined by the wealthy "landed gentry" in the nineteenth century to describe the renovation of run-down London homes, today refers to the movement of more affluent North Americans back into older, often decaying areas in the city. Virtually every major city in Canada and the United States is experiencing this spreading urban renaissance, following a path taken by Paris and London years earlier.

Today's gentry, like those of the past, are a rather select group of people. They are usually the cosmopolites or unmarried and childless groups discussed in Chapter 10. Or, to put it another way, they are frequently the "yuppies" we spoke of at the end of Chapter 3.

CITYSCAPE

Sweat Equity in the South Bronx

Ramon Rueda and Danny Soto, two Puerto Rican friends living in the South Bronx, are certainly familiar with tenements. Yet this one—at 1186 Washington Avenue—is very special to them and unusual to anyone: It was rehabilitated through the labor of a group of mostly poor young blacks and Puerto Ricans trying to improve their own neighborhood. This is the process of "sweat equity"—which simply means that people invest their own labor rather than money in a residence. And labor, in the strongest sense of the word, is what is involved.

In 1976, this was just one of many abandoned buildings with no heat or water, where a few squatters camped. Forming an organization known as the People's Development Corporation (PDC), with Ramon, then 26, as its director, Danny, then 21, and a few others bought this building for one dollar from the city, which had seized it for tax arrears. Then, with no financial assistance, they worked—in the extremes of climate—at the somewhat dangerous demolition of a structure suffering from several decades of abuse and neglect. First, they cleaned and gutted the rotting six-story structure. This was a daunting task, as rubble, rats, excrement, and dead animals seemed everywhere. Worst of all was the basement with its knee-deep mud, unbelievable kinds of refuse, and fleas that embedded themselves in the workers' hair and clothing.

Slowly they restored the structure, including all the necessary plumbing, wiring, and carpentry. The work was time-consuming and difficult, but the group had an evident sense of spirit driving them on. They had a dream of creating a self-sufficient community with enough businesses, services, and jobs to keep money circulating in the neighborhood.

At 1186 Washington Avenue are two rather interesting elements, at the bottom and top. In the basement is a worm farm, with over a million worms, part of its Bio-Eco-Solar-System (BESS). The worm castings are used to fertilize the vegetable gardens and some of the worms are used to feed the fish. On the top floor, below the five gleaming, rooftop solar panels, is Garden Terrace, a common room flooded with sunlight through an enormous skylight. From there the core group of PDC now living there can look out at the dozen-plus buildings they have rehabilitated over a nine-block area, as well as "Unity Park," a cleared-out lot at the corner of Washington Avenue and 168th Street.

Sweat equity is not likely to become popular with people who have the money to buy a fashionable home, but it is one option for the poor who have the skills and strength to undertake such a monumental task. In some of the poorest neighborhoods of many cities, people like Ramon and Danny try to turn housing that is all but falling down into livable homes for themselves and other local residents. The benefits of sweat equity are very real—this one building became 28 apartments—but, just as important, a project of this kind brings neighborhood residents together with a sense of common purpose. Urban homesteading projects are still quite rare and hardly likely to eliminate the massive housing problem in the United States. Yet people like Ramon and Danny are optimistic that they can make a real change in at least a small piece of their city.

Source: Partially adapted from Roger M. Williams, "The New Urban Pioneers: Homesteading in the Slums," *Saturday Review,* July 23, 1977, pp. 9–14; Judith Levine, "Cooperative Enterprise," *Manas Journal* 33 (1980): 12.

More to the point, they are people with enough money to buy a brownstone in Manhattan, a Society Hill townhouse in Philadelphia, a brick cottage in the German Village of Columbus, Ohio, or a Victorian house in San Francisco's Haight-Ashbury district. However, sometimes working-class neighborhoods undergo gentrification while retaining their socioeconomic group identity, as in several of Baltimore's row-house districts.

Why, though, would middle-class people *choose* central-city neighborhoods when the trend for the last century has been to escape to the suburbs? The reasons vary, but certainly many find that the central city still has the greatest amount of variety and stimulation. Theater, music, and chic stores—all flourish in the greatest concentrations downtown. Second, as we noted in Chapter 9, economic restructuring increased the number of administrative and professional jobs available in central cities. The well-paid "gentry" taking these jobs need a place to live, and central-city living eases the time and costs of getting to

work. Third, as more women enter the work force (in 2004, 68 percent of women worked for pay) and as two-career couples become common (61 percent of all married couples in 2003), the time needed to maintain a single-family suburban house often makes it too burdensome (U.S. Census Bureau 2006). Fourth, suburban housing is expensive, and, while some central-city housing is extremely costly (brownstones in Manhattan often top $1.3 million), one can still find bargains, particularly in districts where the average income is low. Fifth, and finally, remember that much central-city housing built from about 1880 to 1910 (except tenements) has a level of craftsmanship and quality—with details like solid oak floors and stained-glass windows—rarely found in today's suburbs.

Indeed, the fact that deteriorating housing eventually might become a bargain for someone with cash and energy is what caused critics like Edward C. Banfield to look hopefully on inner-city decay. Earlier studies suggested that, with the exception of local sweat-equity

Habitat for Humanity is a nonprofit organization that builds new low-income family housing. It has built more than 125,000 homes around the world to date through church fundraising, volunteer labor, and donated materials, as here in Washington, D.C. How do urban homesteading projects, such as Habitat for Humanity and gentrification, offer alternative solutions to problems of urban housing?

projects, gentrification of deteriorating neighborhoods usually displaced the previous poorer inhabitants by causing tax assessments and rents to rise (DiGiovanni 1984; LeGates and Hartman 1986:194–97; Zipp and Cook 1999:1). However, two recent studies found that lower-income and less-educated households were more likely to remain in gentrifying areas than those living elsewhere in the city. The best explanation for these surprising results is that these families value the neighborhood improvements and make greater efforts to stay, even if it means more of their income spent on rent (Vigdor 2002; Freeman and Braconi 2004).

Political economy theorists see gentrification as a logical flow of investment capital. Beginning in the 1950s, investment capital moved out of the cities into the suburbs, where profit rates were higher. Later, with the emergence of a "rent gap" (profits above costs) in the inner city, capital returned to make greater profits there, as low-valued property rose in value (Smith and LeFaivre 1984; Zipp and Cook 1999). This return to the inner city certainly contradicts the predictions of an ever-outward migration of the affluent made by Ernest W. Burgess in the 1920s (Chapter 7). The Critical Thinking box on p. 352, however, explains why these predictions still hold true in Canada.

The New Urbanism

Perhaps the best-known critique of public housing came from Jane Jacobs in *The Death and Life of Great American Cities* (1961), a still-influential book on urban form and function. Critical of conventional planners, Jacobs wrote:

> One of the unsuitable ideas behind projects is the very notion that they are projects, abstracted out of the ordinary city and set apart. To think of salvaging or improving projects, as projects, is to repeat this root mistake. The aim should be to get that project, that patch upon the city, rewoven back into the fabric—and in the process of doing so, strengthen the surrounding fabric also. (1961:392)

One of the most encouraging developments in restoring the vitality of older cities has been an approach in urban design called the **New Urbanism,** which includes sociological principles in physical planning. Initially a response to the perceived lack of community in sprawling suburbs, the New Urbanism caused a rethinking of the entire city. Some of the principles of the New Urbanism are walkability, connectivity, mixed use and diversity, mixed housing types, and a traditional neighborhood structure with public space at the center. Today, in both central cities and suburbs, the goal is creating spaces that encourage people to socialize and watch out for each other.

Seaside, Florida, offers one example. Built in the mid-1980s in Florida's Panhandle, this planned community has codes mandating that houses have front porches close to the sidewalk so that residents sitting outside can converse easily with pedestrians. The town boasts corner stores that serve a function more important than providing provisions. It is a place where friends frequently come to chat with one another over a cup of coffee.

Far more impressive is what architects and planners influenced by the New Urbanism are accomplishing in old, problem-infested neighborhoods.

Columbia Point/Harbor Point.   In Boston, a government-funded housing project known as Columbia Point—built in 1953 on a small, swampy peninsula near the first suburbs of Dorchester and Roxbury—long stood as evidence of the insensitivity of urban planners. There, architects originally laid out 28 bland, institutional-style buildings three and seven stories high, a full mile from the closest subway stop. And the surrounding water and lack of roads isolated residents even more. With few stores in the area, shopping became a major effort, more expensive and more time-consuming than for other city residents nearer the mainstream of Boston life.

Eventually, the 1,502-unit development fell victim to the same problems that plagued public housing nationwide. By the 1970s

CRITICAL THINKING

Gentrification and the Burgess Concentric Zone Model

A look back at Figure 7–4 will remind you of Ernest Burgess's concentric zone theory, which argued that progressively wealthier residential areas would be located at an increasing distance from the CBD. How valid is that model today, with so much gentrification occurring to attract affluent singles and families? According to two Canadian researchers who conducted a 20-year longitudinal study of 14 Canadian cities, the Burgess model is still a valid one. Here is their explanation as to why:

> Our analysis shows that changes in urban development in the last several decades, such as urban renewal, gentrification, mass transit systems, as well as other demographic and social changes such as occupational composition and female labour force participation have not invalidated the association found between SES [socioeconomic status], family size and concentric zones. Though the original description by Burgess of the character of the zones should be re-examined in modern-day Canadian cities, the gradient pattern itself not only persists but may have intensified as far as socio-economic status and family size are concerned. This is especially evident for medium-sized cities on SES, but the intensification has occurred for all sizes for family size. The relationship with family size remains stronger than that with SES.
>
> We speculate that there are two basic factors which explain the durability of these patterns. First, the norm of owning a single-family,

detached dwelling is so embedded in North American culture, that those who can afford the time and cost of transportation continue to opt for locations with more of this type of housing, which increase with distance from the center of cities. This is especially true for those who today have families with children. Smaller families and an increase in marriage dissolutions have not eroded this value. Instead, they have intensified the contrast between two sharply divergent styles of life: the one devoted to singlehood, childlessness, freedom from family commitment and often oriented to cosmopolitan participation in the amenities of the inner zones of refurbished cities; the other devoted to traditional family life, yet attempting to provide a full range of educational opportunities for children, often relying on dual or multiple wage earners to meet the rising scale of expenses, and living in the suburbs.

Second, though mass transit systems are not widely used in Canada except in Toronto and Montreal, the development of freeways and other roads within cities has been effective enough to enable extensive use of the automobile for the journey to work. In spite of the increase in the area and population size of the metropolitan areas in Canada, for most Canadians the journey to work has not increased proportionately. The majority can still commute comfortably in less than an hour. Therefore, for one with the economic resources, the motivation to move from the centre continues to be strong.

Source: T. R. Balakrishnan and George K. Jarvis, "Is the Burgess Concentric Zonal Theory of Spatial Differentiation Still Applicable to Urban Canada?" *Canadian Review of Sociology & Anthropology* 28:4 (November 1996), 526–39. Used by permission of the publisher.

crime was so rampant in Columbia Point that even ambulances refused to enter the project without a police escort. By 1984, only 350 families wanted to stay on when, encouraged by the U.S. Office of Housing and Urban

Development, the Boston Housing Authority leased the land for 99 years at $1 a year to a partnership of the remaining tenants and a private developer. Architects for the project decided to redesign Columbia Point, modeling it after some of Boston's active, thriving neighborhoods. Also influencing their design was the New Urbanism idea that cities are enriched by the creation of a "public realm" that highlights amenities such as waterfront views. Architects thus set down a new street pattern so that all residents would have a view of both the harbor and the Boston skyline.

Reopened in 1990, what is now called Harbor Point is a mixed-income complex that appeals to people from all ethnic backgrounds and social classes, which ensures the diversity and stability of this revitalized community (Roessner 2000). Housing is a mixture, with two-thirds market-rate apartments and one-third low-income housing, but with no physical distinctions between the two types of apartment buildings. Moreover, architects designed a variety of building types: blue and gray townhouses with wood clapboard siding as well as red and brown brick apartment houses. They kept ten of old Columbia Point's flat-topped residential buildings, but peaked roofs, decoration, and a reddish stain made them indistinguishable from the new buildings. To free Harbor Point completely from the stigma of public housing, they added other visual subtleties such as rounded and pointed rooftop gables. Still other amenities were added, including a health club, swimming pool, tennis courts, and ample parking.

Along the harbor, where thieves used to dump stolen cars, is a 6-acre landscaped park where a visitor hears not gunshots but screeching sea gulls and water coursing over rocks. Slicing through the center of the complex is a 1,000-foot by 199-foot grassy mall with old-fashioned street lamps, benches and tennis courts patterned after Boston's Commonwealth Avenue. . . .

Narrow by design, the streets are tightly framed on each side by apartment buildings and townhouses in contrast to the open spaces and freely placed structures of tower-in-the-park urbanism. Front doors face the streets. Most apartment windows look directly at the streets. The arrangement eliminates unsupervised

The new urbanism design of Harbor Point, which replaced Columbia Point, was based on thriving Boston neighborhoods, such as Back Bay. Mixed building types are set close together along narrow streets canted at a 45-degree angle to the water's edge, which opens views of the harbor and Boston skyline to all residents.

pockets of dead space where drug dealing and other illicit activities can occur. (Kamin 1995)

Fully leased, Harbor Point is now among Boston's safest neighborhoods. Yet some wonder whether this safety is the result of a security fence and a guard station at the main vehicular entrance to keep away outsiders. In short, Harbor Point seems to work, but is it "rewoven back into the [city's] fabric," as Jacobs urged? Critics claim that it remains physically isolated from the rest of Boston.

> Today . . . Harbor Point seems too much like a world apart, a residential complex that has adopted the forms of the city without the functions, like corner bars, that fill neighborhoods with life. Harbor Point, in short, has mixed incomes but not the mixed uses that make cities hum. Its architecture, while free of cloying postmodernism, still has the contrived variety of a planned community. (Kamin 1995)

Hopefully, someday soon greater linkage will occur. Still, many view Harbor Point as a success model of urban revitalization. It stands as a successful alternative to an urban nightmare and offers vivid testimony to the extraordinary transformations that the New Urbanism can achieve.

Water as an Amenity. Just as Harbor Point's architects redesigned its grid to enable all residents to enjoy the view of surrounding water, so too has the New Urbanism enabled many cities to rediscover the aesthetics and social use possibilities of public space at water's edge (Whyte 1980). Baltimore's Inner Harbor and New York's South Street Seaport are thriving, rebuilt areas enjoyed by tourists and natives alike. Chicago, Cleveland, Cincinnati, Louisville, and many other cities have converted decaying piers and waterfront properties into park areas and mixed-use sites. San Antonio converted what was essentially a narrow and dirty drainage canal into the charming 2.5-mile cobblestone River Walk—with lush green lawns, flowering shrubs and trees, and a view of paddleboats—where one delights in many interesting shops, restaurants, and night clubs. Here and at many other renovated

water's edge locales, cities have successfully merged social and commercial activities into a vibrant urban atmosphere.

Replacing High-Rises. As Harbor Point demonstrates, the New Urbanism is transforming public housing, as the "superblocks" of giant high-rises come down, replaced by modest townhouses and low-rises that don't "look like projects."

> Imagine leveling whole blocks of decaying, crime-ridden slums in one great sweep, and building in their stead modern apartments with plenty of light and fresh air and high-rise views. Think about replacing crowded streets and decrepit playgrounds with paths for pedestrians and bicycles, winding between wide lawns. (Adler and Malone 1996:70)

Many cities are addressing the failure of high-rise public housing by blowing up the buildings. Scudder Homes, seven high-rises built in 1963 in Newark, New Jersey, to house 1,800 low-income families, are gone, replaced by 150 single-family townhouses. In place of the 1,206 units in that city's seven hulking 13-story Stella Wright homes are townhouses for low- and moderate-income residents. In Atlanta, a developer demolished over 1,000 housing units in Techwood Homes—the first U.S. public housing project, completed in 1935—to build a mixed-income "village," with new stores, community facilities, schools, and apartments. Today this once predominantly black enclave has been transformed into Centennial Place, a residential complex of 900 units that is host to a variety of races, ethnicities, and income levels. In Chicago, the Housing Authority has been demolishing the Cabrini-Green high-rise project buildings and redeveloping its 65 acres through construction of 2,000 units of new, low-rise housing units; a new Town Center; a 145,000-square-foot shopping center; new schools; an East Chicago District police headquarters; and a library. Half the housing units are sold at market prices, with another 20 percent reserved as "affordable" units for less-affluent working families. Some of the original low-income tenants living at Cabrini remain in the new housing units, thereby creating a mixed-income site similar to Harbor Point and totally unlike the all-low-income site Cabrini-Green once was (Gallun 2005). The designs of all three developments—in Newark, Atlanta, and Chicago—use grid patterns to link them to the surrounding neighborhoods rather than setting them apart, minding Jacobs's recommendation that housing projects be rewoven into the urban fabric.

These rebuilding programs seek to achieve two key goals of the New Urbanism. First, don't isolate the poor by themselves. Instead, create a mixed-income housing complex to integrate all strata of society. Second, create an environment that is physically attractive and facilitates walking and social interaction, fostering a sense of control and community among residents.

Limitations.   As promising as the New Urbanism may be, three major problems prevent its broader impact. First, in every case noted, there are now fewer low-income housing units than there were before. As with post–World War II urban renewal, displacement of the poor has occurred in these redevelopment projects as well. Of course, one might argue that at least some poor people are better off living in safer and more vibrant communities, but what of the rest of the displaced poor?

Second, weaving a housing project into the surrounding area is enormously difficult in the midst of extensive, nightmarish ghettos. If little more than empty lots or bombed-out buildings are nearby, for example, reorganizing a public housing project as an inward-facing enclave may be the only strategy, at least in the short run.

Finally, even at its best, the New Urbanism cannot, by itself, address the extensive poverty that makes public housing such a problem in the first place. For instance, in San Francisco, the Robert Pitts Plaza development project replaced a notorious, dangerous high-rise called Yerba Buena Plaza West. The new 203-apartment, neo-Victorian complex in no way looks like a public housing development. Its architecture blended in with neighboring apartment buildings and included projecting cornices and pastel shades of blue—a far cry from the high-rise "boxes" so common in public housing. Completed in 1991, it contained other amenities such as an internal rectangular courtyard with lush sod, bushes, and neat lines of trees, and a colorful playset for children in a sand playground.

Three years later, though, broken glass lay everywhere. Gone were the sod and sprinkler heads; gone too were the bushes and plants, ripped out by vandals. Profane graffiti covered concrete seating ledges. Burglar bars shielded ground-floor windows following a rash of burglaries suspected to have been committed by residents. Wire mesh covered many other windows, suggesting an escalating sense of fear. The problem is poverty, and all that goes with it:

> Standing in the courtyard, the on-site manager of the complex, Ken Babb, explained the mess by saying that the tenants—less than a quarter of whom work—did not have an ownership mentality. . . . (Kamin 1995)

A Comparison.   Fortunately, the situation at Robert Pitts Plaza has since improved. This building complex is but one part of a 19-block redevelopment area of Yerba Buena that is a successful mixture of a wide variety of housing, cultural facilities, and open space. The lesson to be learned here is that new architecture and even new planning strategies such as the New Urbanism don't work if they have limited application. Robert Pitts Plaza reveals that simply replacing high-rise buildings with low-rise buildings, even if wonderfully designed, is not enough. A more comprehensive approach is necessary. Harbor Point is a good example of at least the beginnings of connecting low-income housing to its surroundings—through a return to traditional urban forms that promote interaction *and* a mix of income groups to eliminate public housing's isolation. In short, any successful approach to improving urban life must take account of not only local planning considerations but also broader structural concerns that include social stratification and the region's economy.

EDUCATION: THE URBAN CHALLENGE

Schools in urban settings face a variety of challenges, often more daunting than school districts elsewhere face. These difficulties include overcrowded schools, discipline and violence, high dropout rates, and issues of quality education and student learning outcomes. Add to this mix the fact that cities attract large numbers of immigrant families and children with limited English proficiency, greater concentrations of low-income families, and a weaker tax revenue base, all of which place a heavy burden on the schools to educate, fully and effectively, the students they serve.

Meeting the "No Child Left Behind" Challenge

The landmark No Child Left Behind Act of 2001 dramatically increased the role of the federal government in guaranteeing the quality of public education for all children. Its main provisions are increased funding for poor school districts, higher achievement for minority and poor students, and new measures to hold schools accountable for their students' progress. Significantly, it requires the annual administration of standardized tests in reading and math to all students in grades 3 through 8, with the results publicly reported according to poverty, race, ethnicity, disability, and limited English proficiency. These results will be compared to an independent benchmark called the National Assessment of Educational Progress (NAEP).

Learning Outcomes.   Prior to this legislation, most urban schools had a policy of **social promotions,** moving children through grades with their age peers regardless of their actual learning achievement. Whatever merit this practice

Magnet schools—such as this one in Schenectady, New York—enable cities to overcome residential segregation patterns by offering special programs and facilities to raise students' scholastic achievement. Despite their success, critics complain that they are expensive, have limited appeal, and that their elitism relegates most urban students to "mediocre" schooling.

had, it led to a watering-down of course content because of the gradual but steady lowering of general class ability. As a result, it produced graduates deluded into thinking they had received an education when, in reality, many lacked even basic skills. No more. Published test results will identify schools whose students are not doing well on the tests. Those schools that fall behind may be subject to various "school improvement," "corrective action," or "restructuring" measures imposed by the state.

Language Proficiency.   Immigration remains primarily an urban phenomenon, although it affects suburban and rural schools and communities as well, and students' language proficiency plays an important role in academic achievement. Nearly half of all immigrants now choose to live in just a dozen metropolitan areas: New York; Los Angeles; Miami; Chicago; Washington; D.C.; Orange County, California; Houston; San Jose; Boston; Oakland; San Francisco; Fort Lauderdale; and San Diego (U.S. Office of Immigration Statistics 2002:73). Urban schools in these and other cities, therefore, must accommodate a large influx of immigrant pupils, and it is not unusual for a third or more of a school's population to lack proficiency in English (Zhou 2003). This creates the need for hiring a greater number of bilingual or English-as-a-Second-Language (ESL) teachers, in addition to teachers of regular subjects. The schools must also deal with other cultural adjustment issues, such as clothing, food, religious observances, role behavior, and parents whose own language and educational deficiencies may limit support for at-home study.

Environment.   Whether immigrant or native-born, many students come from home environments where poverty, family instability, or poor health may limit educational success. Other dangers or obstacles that can work against educators' goals are (1) conflicting values in the student's home or on the street about the importance of education; (2) the lack of positive, academically successful role

models; and (3) the presence of gangs, street crime, drugs, and violence. In 2003, 21 percent of students aged 12 to 18 reported street gang presence at school, a 3 percent increase from 1999 (U.S. Department of Education 2004).

Funding.   Further undermining academic achievement in many city schools is the lack of funding. Unlike affluent communities, cities lack the tax base to provide adequate per-student expenditures, even with additional state aid. As a result, students in urban schools are more likely to enter older, dilapidated buildings, where they face overcrowded classrooms with limited supplies, poor discipline, insufficient libraries and labs, and often a shortage of qualified teachers. It remains to be seen if the additional funding through the No Child Left Behind Act will be sufficient to overcome the urban–suburban disparity in school funding.

Political Clout.   Cities actually have limited control over their affairs, whether in education or other areas such as mass transit and poverty. Until the 1970s, cities lacked political power in the rural-dominated state and federal legislatures, despite their higher overall population. By the time the Supreme Court ruled in favor of one-person, one-vote reapportionment to balance legislative district representation, the majority of the population had shifted to the suburbs. Added to the rural–suburban bias against cities is the frequent political split between Democratic-controlled city governments and Republican-controlled state legislatures, further hindering efforts to solve urban problems.

Cities across the country are struggling to meet the federal government's demand to improve their schools. Some modest gains have occurred, but enormous challenges remain. For example, Chicago has been making a concerted effort to improve its educational system since passage of the Chicago School Reform Act in 1988. Notable improvements have occurred since then, yet fewer than half of all high school students graduate, barely half were on track in their freshmen year, and the dropout rate remains above 40 percent (Miller et al. 2002). Hopefully, with continued improvement at the elementary level, as mandated by the No Child Left Behind Act, Chicago and other cities will also see progress at the secondary level as well. However, it will take more than wishful thinking to make this a reality.

A deepening dissatisfaction with traditional public schools has engendered several innovations to give parents other options for educating their children, thus providing competition to force all schools to do a better job. Three of the most popular programs to improve urban education are magnet schools, a school voucher system, and charter schools.

Magnet Schools

Magnet schools (schools offering special programs to attract students from many districts to achieve integration) began as an alternative to mandatory busing, but their success in raising students' scholastic achievement gained them even more popularity. They offer special facilities and programs to promote educational excellence in a particular area, such as computer science, foreign languages, science and mathematics, or the arts. Parents can choose the school best suited to a particular student's talents and interests, enabling these advanced programs to attract talented students from beyond traditional neighborhood boundaries. This permits magnet schools to overcome residential segregation patterns to create a more diversified student population.

About 20 percent of U.S. students living in or around cities attend one of the nation's more than 5,000 magnet schools. However, about 21 percent are partial-site magnet schools (a mixture of traditional and special programs), resulting in desegregated buildings that have racially segregated classrooms. The drawbacks to magnet schools becoming more widespread are that (1) they are expensive to operate; (2) they have limited appeal; and (3) critics charge they are "elitist" in luring the best students and teachers, thereby relegating the majority of students to the "mediocrity" of ordinary city schools (West 1994).

Howe is one of four magnet schools in Schenectady, New York, one of the nation's oldest cities. With over 300 enrollees in grades K–5, its global curriculum and emphasis on cultural diversity combines basic New York State curriculum standards with a wide variety of multicultural learning activities through a nurturing and challenging educational environment.

School Vouchers

Another choice option in some school districts is to give parents a **school voucher** equal to the state's share of the cost of educating a child (usually about 90 percent of the average private school's tuition). Parents can then use this voucher to place their child in a public or private school of their choice. The program is limited at present because there are not enough private-school spaces to meet demand; usually a lottery determines who goes to choice schools in such cases. Among the cities utilizing a school voucher plan are Cleveland, Indianapolis, Milwaukee, and Minneapolis. Critics (including teachers' unions) charge that this approach siphons off much-needed public education funding, thus undermining the nation's commitment to public education, and does little to improve central-city schools where the need is greatest (Martinez et al., 1995; Gorman 2003).

Because many of the private schools are church-affiliated, voucher opponents charge that this system violates the First Amendment provision concerning the separation of church and state. At the state level, recent court decisions gave mixed signals on this issue. Arizona, Ohio, and Wisconsin supreme courts ruled that voucher programs did not violate the state or federal constitution by including religious schools. In contrast, the supreme courts of Vermont and Maine, as well as a federal appellate court in a separate Maine case, ruled against religious schools on constitutional grounds. After years of conflicting lower court opinions about Cleveland parents using vouchers at private schools, the U.S. Supreme Court ruled in 2002 that they could do so. Experts believe this ruling may be as significant as the 1954 *Brown v. Board of Education* decision on school desegregation, as it gives the green light nationwide to this program (Brokaw 2002).

Charter Schools

Charter schools are a recent alternative to traditional public schools and, in cities where a voucher plan exists, a major beneficiary of such payments. Charters are private schools that operate with less state regulation so that teachers and administrators can try out new teaching strategies. Unlike public schools, however, they are held accountable for achieving educational results. If a school fails to meet the terms of its charter with the local school board or state, the charter can be revoked and the school closed. In essence, then, a charter school receives greater autonomy to operate in return for greater accountability for student performance. Nationwide, charter schools enroll 1.5 percent of all students (Hoxby 2004).

Perhaps more important than numbers are the types of learning environments being cultivated within these schools. According to *The State of Charter Schools: Fourth Year Report* (U.S. Department of Education 2000), small school size appears to be a principal reason for the high demand for charter schools. The median enrollment of charter schools in the study was 137, compared with a median enrollment of 475 students in the regular public schools in the same states. Smaller classes afford teachers the space to be more creative with curriculum and the time to provide more individualized instruction. Some charter schools have been founded with a particular type of student in mind. Whether for the arts-oriented or the at-risk, these schools provide assistance to students who are otherwise underserved by the public school system.

Supporters of charter schools hope that local educators, ministers, parents, community members, school boards, and other sponsors will provide new models of schooling and exert competitive pressures on public schools that will improve the current system of public education. Others fear, however, that charter schools, at best, may be little more than escape valves that relieve pressure for genuine reform of the whole system and, at worst, may add to centrifugal forces that threaten to pull public education apart.

In fact, some charter schools are no better than their public school counterparts. Critics say that many have weak curricula and teaching, substandard buildings, and a surprising prevalence of financial abuses. Basic classroom supplies are often lacking, labs and libraries are rare, and staff turnover is high among the low-paid, inexperienced teachers. Also, the segregation of many charter schools along ethnic, racial, and religious lines has created church–state conflicts in conjunction with the voucher controversy (Toch 1998).

It is too soon, though, to assess the success of magnet schools, vouchers, or the charter school reform movement. Only time will tell whether or not they are an improvement. The Urban Living box below gives a further insight into these innovations.

CRIME: PERCEPTION AND REALITY

The problems of poor housing and poor education affect only part of the urban population.

But, surveys suggest, almost everyone expresses concern about the extent of crime. Often, people living in outlying areas point to fears about personal safety as the primary reason they chose not to live in the city. And many city people conclude that a higher risk of crime is just part of the price one pays for the advantages of urban living. But are such perceptions correct? Is crime worse in the city than elsewhere? Is there more crime in bigger cities than in smaller ones? Are visitors to the city more likely than residents to fall victim to crime?

Urban crime gets extensive media attention and influences public perception. Yet the public's fear about crime overlooks the important fact that the U.S. crime rate has actually dropped each year since 1991. From 1994 to 2003, the violent crime rate (for murder, rape/sexual assault, robbery, assault) plummeted from 51.2 per 1,000 people to 22.3. Similarly, the property crime rate (for burglary, motor vehicle theft, property

URBAN LIVING

The New Urban Schools

On a typical morning, just north of Milwaukee, at the Marva Collins Preparatory School of Wisconsin, 180 students—kindergarten through the fifth grade—neatly dressed in their uniforms, enter an old building and climb three flights of stairs to their school on the top floor. A few miles to the east, next to a busy freeway and across from a clinic for the homeless, the 360 students at Messmer High School file in. In the hallways of this Roman Catholic institution hang portraits of Dr. Martin Luther King, Jr., Abraham Lincoln, and Jesus. Closer to the heart of the city, the 600 students in grades K–5 at the Elm Creative Arts School learn through an arts-driven curriculum. Today, while many are

away performing at a concert downtown, a group of fifth graders—divided into small teams—is sprawled out on a classroom floor piecing together colorful math games while big-band music plays on the class stereo.

Welcome to public education, Milwaukee-style. These three schools, scattered throughout the city and featuring vastly different educational settings and philosophies, have one thing in common: public tax dollars.

One is a charter school adopted by the City Council; one is a private, religious school; and one is a magnet school operated by the school district. All three are part of a growing roster of alternatives available in a city that is ground zero for the school choice movement nationwide.

The definition of public schooling in the United States has changed dramatically in theft) dropped from 310.2 per 1,000 people to 163.2. As a result, overall criminal victimization rates are at their lowest levels in two decades (U.S. Bureau of Justice Statistics 2005).

Except for an increase in 2003, crime in Canada has been falling since its peak year in 1991. In 2004, its crime rate was 12 percent lower than a decade earlier. In contrast, its homicide rate rose 12 percent in 2004, after hitting a 36-year low the year before (Canadian Centre for Justice Statistics 2005). A 2004 survey revealed that 94 percent of respondents said they felt safe from becoming a crime victim, up from 91 percent in 1999. Among women ages 15 to 24, 79 percent said that they felt safe walking alone in their neighborhoods at night (Statistics Canada 2004).

Public Perception of Crime

The American public has grown less pessimistic about the severity of the nation's crime problem,

reflecting the actual decline in the crime rate in recent years. However, broad concern remains. An ABC News/*Washington Post* poll found that 36 percent of respondents called the crime problem "very bad," while another 44 percent called it "bad," for a total of 80 percent. Perception about crime affects how people live their lives; 57 percent of adults said so in 2002, a 9 percent increase from a similar poll four years earlier (ABC News 2002). And the poor worry most of all: 71 percent of people earning over $50,000 but just 48 percent of those earning less than $20,000 felt very safe in their neighborhoods. When controlled for race only, 54 percent of blacks and 61 percent of whites said they felt safe in their neighborhoods (U.S. Bureau of Justice Statistics 2005).

In light of the facts, why do so many of us think we are living in a high-crime period? Part of the answer lies in more extensive news reporting of violent crime. An ABC News poll

---

recent years, and nowhere is it changing faster than in Milwaukee. The city's long tradition of forward-looking views on government and politics has provided fertile soil for experiments and innovations in its public schools.

Here, in one place, are schools based on ideas that not too long ago were unheard-of in a U.S. school district: students attending religious schools with public money, a private school that has essentially been hired by the district to become a public school for a year, and a city government that has bypassed the local school board to create its own charter schools.

Yet Annette Williams, a Democratic state representative and author of the state's voucher legislation, has concerns. Williams, an African American, says she originally intended the voucher program to help mainly

black-run schools and low-income students. But today, she contends, vouchers and charter schools mainly benefit white churches, white-run private schools, and white students. "Affluent folks are going to take it all on as their own," she says. "Yuppies who have choices are going to be the beneficiaries now."

Others fear in Milwaukee the emergence of a dual private and charter school system, one black, one white, and a community whose loyalty to schools is divided along racial and socioeconomic lines. Only time will tell whether or not the alternative school programs are an improvement over traditional efforts or simply another form of racial segregation in the schools.

Source: Adapted from Kerry A. White, "Ahead of the Curve." Reprinted with permission from *Education Week* Vol. 18, No. 18, January 13, 1999.

revealed that 82 percent of Americans said their perception of crime is based on what they read or see in the news; only 17 percent based their views on personal experience (ABC News 2000). One study found nearly 1,800 acts of serious violence reported over a two-week period, 80 percent of them on broadcast television and 20 percent on cable programs (Center for Media and Public Affairs 1999). In addition, the frequent "promos" of upcoming violent crime stories, the popularity of "reality-based" cop shows, and tabloid sensationalism spread the image of crime well beyond the news programs themselves.

Another frightening fact is that, despite a decline in the murder rate, an increasing share of killings is stranger-on-stranger homicides. Also, drug-related shootings sometimes result in stray bullets killing innocent people, even in their homes or blocks away from the source. Moreover, alarmingly, there is a steady involvement of children in deadly violence. As one analyst explains,

> Crime now seems more "senseless" because deadly acts are carried out by people too young to realize the implications of their decisions. Altercations that twenty years ago would have ended in a fistfight and a bloody nose now terminate with a corpse riddled by twenty-two-caliber bullets fired from an automatic machine pistol. (Douglas Massey 1995:1204)

The homicide victimization rate for youths aged 14 to 17 increased almost 170 percent from 1985 to 1993. Since 1993, victimization rates for teens and young adults have declined, but they still remain considerably higher than the levels of the mid-1980s (U.S. Bureau of Justice Statistics 2005).

Attitudes about crime, then, are a mix of facts and fears. To gain a more accurate sense of crime in the city, we need to look at additional statistics.

Crime and City Size. Most violent crimes take place in cities, often growing out of street, school, or social club altercations. Indeed, the negative attitudes of non–city dwellers and their reluctance to enter cities stems in large measure from their fear of becoming an urban crime statistic. But are cities really more dangerous? Table 12–1 compares crime in various types of communities.

Note the steady decline in crime in mostly all locales. Violent crime rates are higher in large metropolitan areas than in smaller cities outside metropolitan areas and, especially, in rural areas. Such data would seem to support the conclusion that large cities are dangerous places. However, property crime rates are higher in those smaller cities than in the metropolitan regions.

Louis Wirth, whose theory of urbanism was central to Chapter 5, might claim that the size, density, and social heterogeneity of cities are to blame. Perhaps. But if this were true, we would expect the largest metropolitan areas to have the highest crime rates, which is not the case. As Table 12–2 shows, the highest crime rates occur in smaller, third-tier cities (under 500,000) and in second-tier cities (500,000 to 999,999 population).

TABLE 12–1 Crime Rates per 1,000 Residents by Type of Community, 1980, 2000, and 2004

	Property Crime			Violent Crime		
	1980	2000	2004	1980	2000	2004
U.S. Total	53	36	35	5.8	5.1	4.7
Metropolitan Areas	61	39	37	7.0	5.6	5.1
Cities Outside Metro Areas	50	41	41	3.5	4.0	3.8
Rural Areas	21	17	17	1.8	2.1	2.0

Source: Federal Bureau of Investigation, *Crime in the United States—2004.* Accessed at www.fbi.gov/ucr/cius_04/documents/CIUS2004.pdf?file.

TABLE 12–2   City Size and Crime Rates, 2004

Population Size	Violent Crime	Property Crime
1,000,000 or higher	9.2	40.2
500,000–999,999	9.1	59.0
250,000–499,999	9.7	56.4
100,000–249,999	6.0	48.2
50,000–99,999	4.7	39.8
25,000–49,999	3.8	36.4
10,000–24,999	3.0	34.0
Under 10,000	3.3	37.0
Suburban Areas	3.2	28.2
Rural Counties	2.2	17.4

Source: Federal Bureau of Investigation, 2005.

These data point to the conclusion that, although cities have higher crime rates than other types of communities, city size by itself does not explain crime rate. How else can we explain the fact that New York, the nation's largest city, has less crime per capita than all other U.S. cities with 1 million or more population? On a per capita basis, New York City has less than half the crime of such cities as Albuquerque, Miami, Memphis, New Orleans, Oklahoma City, Phoenix, and Tucson. Put differently, in 2004 New York City ranked 221 out of 240 cities across the nation in its crime rate.

Before going further, however, a warning is in order. Crime statistics are notoriously imperfect. For example, many crimes are not discovered, or reported to police, or recorded carefully. All the statistics in Tables 12–1 and 12–2 reflect official police records. Many criminologists argue that a more accurate portrait of crime comes from the Census Bureau's semiannual random population survey. By questioning people (rather than police), the victimization survey uncovers many unreported crimes missed in the crime index and crime rate calculations. While such studies confirm the decline in crime over time, they suggest that the actual number of crimes may well be twice the level of the official statistics.

Further, criminologists agree that, as with other problems, the amount of crime varies throughout the urban area. The greatest concentration of offenses occurs in inner-city districts with poverty-stricken minority populations. In 2003, for example, members of the poorest U.S. households, with incomes under $7,500, were twice as likely to be assaulted and four times more likely to be robbed than those of more affluent households with incomes over $75,000 (U.S. Bureau of Justice Statistics 2005). Urbanists at the University of Chicago first identified this pattern back in the 1940s, and it holds true for both the inner city and the suburbs.

The Race Issue.   In the United States, discussions of crime almost always raise the issue of race, because many people link crime to nonwhite minorities. In truth, however, two-thirds of the arrests police make for serious crimes involve white people. Even so, relative to population size, African Americans are more likely to be arrested than whites.

Keep in mind, too, that crime is largely intra-racial. To illustrate, 91 percent of single-offender violent crimes committed in 2003 by blacks were against black victims, and 84 percent of such crimes committed by whites involved white victims (FBI 2005).

Moreover, the crime problem is worst in overwhelmingly black urban ghettos, where homicide is at a crisis level. Blacks are six times more likely to be murdered than whites, and 94 percent of all black victims are killed by blacks (U.S. Bureau of Justice Statistics 2005). Nationwide, the leading cause of death by far for black males between the ages of 15 and 24 is homicide (U.S. Census Bureau 2004d). In 2003, blacks killed 2,864 blacks—only 153 fewer killings than of whites by whites, who outnumber blacks by more than six to one (FBI 2005).

Explaining High-Crime Areas

Why are some communities terrorized by crime? We know that the highest crime rates occur in the poorest sections of cities. Why? Social scientists offer a variety of theories to explain concentrations of urban crime. Four of the main causative explanations involve (1) cultural patterns; (2) lower intelligence;

(3) persistent racial inequality and prolonged poverty; and (4) residential segregation. As we shall see, each position has both advocates and critics.

Cultural Patterns. Edward Banfield (1970, 1974) claimed that crime flourishes in urban areas steeped in a lower-class culture, where people share a "present-time orientation," have low aspirations, and are generally morally irresponsible. Under such conditions, he contended, people victimize anyone who seems an easy mark, including one another.

Moreover, parents pass these cultural patterns on to their children, which explains the persistence of crime in some neighborhoods for decades. Rather than learning values and skills that ease their way toward success, children too often learn apathy, resignation, and fatalism; indifference toward schooling; a desire for immediate gratification; and a distrust of authority. In such an environment, crime simply thrives. Add to this the fact that high-crime neighborhoods tend to have high levels of single parenting; this means that children have less supervision, especially from fathers.

Critics, such as Charles Valentine (1968), responded that such cultural patterns should be viewed as the *consequences,* not the causes, of poverty. Among people who have few opportunities to work, are forced to live in crowded, run-down housing, and must contend with the worst schools a city has to offer, we should not be surprised that crime rates are high. Only structural changes that alleviate societal inequality are likely to bring about changes in the vicious circle of poverty and crime.

Lower Intelligence. In perhaps the most controversial effort to explain concentrations of crime and other social problems, Richard Herrnstein and Charles Murray asserted that criminality is concentrated in areas where average intelligence is low. In their book *The Bell Curve,* they suggested that crime—like poverty, welfare dependency, and illegitimacy—is strongly related to low IQ (1994:338–39). It is because the more talented people have long since left the inner cities, these researchers continued, that the plight of those who are left is worse than ever. And, given the cause, there is little that even a compassionate public can do about it.

Critics attacked this book on many fronts, suggesting that intelligence tests are unfair to begin with and that it is far from clear what intelligence really is (Willie and Taylor 1995; Fischer et al. 1996). More specifically, numerous studies show that low-income people test lower on IQ tests and that scores typically improve along with achievement of a higher socioeconomic status (Sowell 1977:57).

Persistent Racial Inequality and Poverty. There is far broader support for the idea that the primary problem with crime lies in social structure, including our definitions of crime itself. Manuel Castells (1979, 1982) contends that capitalism's unceasing orientation toward profit defines "crime" and "criminals" largely in terms that protect the interests of the rich. People in capitalist societies do not believe that causing people to suffer a life of poverty is criminal, but rather that taking another's *property* is—especially if the victim is somebody "important." In a society in which most wealth and power lie in the hands of the few, high rates of criminality among the more deprived are simply to be expected because of how those in power define crime and enforce the law.

Other social scientists also maintain that racial and economic inequalities breed high crime rates (Fajnzylber et al. 2002). After studying 125 large metropolitan areas, Judith and Peter Blau suggested that, insofar as a city concentrates people of highly unequal incomes, those with less than others see themselves as unjustly deprived. Therefore, even in the absence of **absolute poverty,** a city with significant **relative poverty** would still breed resentment and crime. In other words, Blau and Blau argue, African Americans and other poor people engage in more crime as offenders—and suffer more as victims—only because they are heavily represented among the economically deprived.

In contrast to the assertions by Banfield, Herrnstein, and Murray that poor people are *themselves* to blame for criminality, this approach sees the poor as victims of injustices within society itself. Judith and Peter Blau sum up:

> Thus, aggressive acts of violence seem to result not so much from lack of advantages as from being taken advantage of, not so much from absolute deprivation but from relative deprivation. In a society founded on the principle "that all men are created equal" economic inequalities rooted in ascribed positions [such as being born black or impoverished] violate the spirit of democracy and are likely to create alienation, despair, and conflict. (1982:126)

More recent research, however, challenges the idea that economic and racial inequality is a causal factor in crime. Some researchers found that changing structural conditions (neighborhood demographics, competition, and racial inequality) can lead to differing rates of violence (McCall and Parker 2005). Eric Neumayer (2005) argues that the link between income inequality and crime is a misleading one, because it varies from one country to another, making cultural norms a more important factor. Other researchers suggest that the relationships between economic factors and black interracial homicide might be explained for a financially motivated crime such as robbery, but not necessarily for other crimes (Wadsworth and Kubrin 2004). We can conclude that there may be some connections between racial inequality and crime, but not always. The Urban Living box on pages 366–367 offers a glimpse into one such interplay of joblessness, poverty, and crime.

Residential Segregation. A fourth factor noted by social scientists to explain the high rate of African American crime is that residential segregation—from slavery times to the present—makes the black situation unique. Douglas Massey and Nancy Denton coined the term **hypersegregation** to describe this extensive segregation existing on many geographic dimensions simultaneously (1989: 373). Since then they identified 20 hypersegregated metropolitan areas that contain nearly 40 percent of the total U.S. African American population (Massey and Denton 1993).

In another study, researchers Ruth Peterson and Lauren Krivo (1993) examined the relationship between black segregation and black homicide in 125 metropolitan areas. They found that black–white segregation far exceeded other variables such as income inequality and poverty, as well as several others, in explaining intercity variations in the black murder rate. In addition, they found that segregation had no bearing on homicide within families but clearly had an effect on acquaintance killings and homicides involving strangers. That is, the impact of segregation on the homicide rate manifested itself in public space, not in the home.

As Massey puts it, "Any social process that concentrates poverty also concentrates crime and violence to create an ecological niche characterized by a high risk of physical injury, violent death, and criminal victimization" (1995:1207). Rejecting the notion that black urban crime is simply a product of individual failings, he views such crime as "an inevitable outgrowth of social conditions created by the coincidence of racial segregation and high rates of black poverty." Believing that only federal policy initiatives could bring an end to the legacy of American apartheid, Massey is pessimistic. He predicts that many urban black communities will continue to deteriorate, with all of us paying a heavy economic and social price for a shameful "retreat from American democratic ideals" (1995:1231–32).

A modest decline in racial segregation occurred during the 1980s in many U.S. metropolitan areas. Analysis of 2000 census data shows very slow change since 1980 in residential segregation of African Americans (see Table 12–3). In some smaller and newer metropolitan areas, their segregation from whites declined markedly, but in the larger places where most African Americans live, segregation has remained high. Segregation of Hispanics and Asians has not changed in the last two decades (Lewis Mumford Center 2002a).

Effects of Crime on Everyday Life

The toll of crime extends far beyond its immediate victims. For one thing, nothing pulls

URBAN LIVING

Poverty, Drugs, and Crime

West Adams Street is in the Austin District of Chicago, location of the Cabrini-Green housing project. This is just one story of thousands, a tragic commonality in our inner cities.

Nigel McKinney lived and died on West Adams. He was 11 when he was shot down in early October, perhaps involved in drug dealing, perhaps not. In this landscape, the culture of drugs is so pervasive, it becomes hard to tell if anyone is really untouched. . . .

Baby-faced drug dealers and teenage killers aren't unique to West Adams; nor is the neighborhood's distrust of police; both are a numbing reality in poor, minority communities.

But on West Adams these traits have a particular intensity, revealing in stark terms the dynamics that can turn members of the Vice Lords street gang into community leaders and police officers into the enemy, even if they're African-Americans.

It's an easy place for a child to lose his way, lose his life, or begin compiling a long police record. Though Nigel's murder has long since faded from the news, it remains a source of tension in Austin and has become an emblem of why the typical rules just don't apply here. . . .

Though there are undoubtedly some families on West Adams who live quietly and are disdainful of the drug trade, many families have someone who has dealt drugs, used drugs, or benefited from their sale.

"A lot of parents will not admit their kids are involved . . . because they are benefiting

---

down property values like a high crime rate (Taylor 1991). Owners lose equity in their investment, face high homeowners' insurance premiums, and lose neighbors or renters who otherwise would provide stability and community role models. If large numbers of people

TABLE 12–3   Most Segregated Metropolitan Areas, Black and White, 2000

Metropolitan Area	Index of Dissimilarity
1. Detroit, Michigan	85
2. Milwaukee, Wisconsin	82
3. New York, New York	82
4. Chicago, Illinois	81
5. Newark, New Jersey	80
6. Cleveland, Ohio	77
7. Nassau–Suffolk, New York	74
8. Cincinnati, Ohio	75
9. St. Louis, Missouri	74
10. Miami, Florida	74

Source: Lewis Mumford Center for Comparative Urban and Regional Research, 2001a.

move out and cannot be replaced, owners may well abandon buildings they cannot sell, eroding the city's tax base. The vicious circle grinds on and on.

The fear of crime also reduces our use of public space. As William H. Whyte (1980) observed, "Streets are the rivers of life of a city. We come to partake of them, not to escape them." Certainly, in areas where people feel safe, extensive use of streets, parks, plazas, and other public places provides enjoyment for people at all hours of the day and night. Such urban areas contain the social dynamics and all the variety and excitement the city can offer. However, crime (and merely the fear of crime) restricts the use of public spaces. Another vicious circle is thus set in motion, since empty streets, plazas, and subway stations are unprotected and become ever more dangerous. In some communities, "take back the streets" campaigns have had some success, but the bitter reality remains that urbanites' enjoyment of public space is more limited than it once was, especially after sunset, in too many areas.

from the money that the children are bringing in," said Thomas J. Stewart, principal of Piccolo Middle School. "You are going to throw your own son out of the house? Nine (times) out of 10, a mother will not do it."

Those who don't turn a blind eye try to justify the illicit drug lifestyle by saying there are few, if any, other options. Drugs, they say, put food on the table, clothes on their children's backs, a new television in the living room, and a functioning car on the street. . . .

Police have recorded nearly 100 crimes this year on the [two-block] stretch of West Adams, from assaults and burglaries to car thefts and drug arrests.

In late October, police arrested two 11-year-old boys who lived in the neighborhood, but not on West Adams, for allegedly bringing

three silencers, 12 bullets, and 56 packets of crack cocaine to class with them at Nash Elementary School, just a few blocks north of West Adams. One of the boys told police he stole the loot from an uncle. . . .

Nigel's brother has been a bona fide gang member since the age of 12. Now 15, Derris has been arrested for alleged drug dealing. He lives on his own and is recovering from three gunshot wounds he sustained in August while playing basketball in a West Side park.

Asked to explain why he was shot, the short, slim youth with a tough demeanor said simply that the gunman, a rival gang member, was "jealous."

Source: Jerry Thomas and Andrew Martin, "Notorious Block's Deadly Legacy," *Chicago Tribune,* Web-posted November 23, 1996.

What Is the Solution?

Can high crime rates in urban places be reduced? Is there a way to make our cities safe so that people can walk through a park in the daytime (let alone at night!) without fear? Here, again, a number of proposals are noteworthy.

Urban planner Oscar Newman (1972, 1996) maintained that building design plays an important part in controlling crime. High-rise apartment blocks, Newman explains, serve to encourage crime because they isolate inhabitants from each other, creating many unwatched places where crime can easily occur. Newman argues that crime can be reduced if

> designers can position windows, and entries, and prescribe paths of movement and areas of activity so as to provide inhabitants with continuous natural surveillance of the street. (1972:15)

Where designs create what Newman calls **defensible space,** people can protect their own communities naturally as they go about their

daily lives rather than relying on security guards and police for protection.

To support his argument, Newman compiled crime data from various low-income public housing projects, first in New York, then in other cities in a subsequent study. Some of his key findings are as follows:

1. The average crime rate is higher in taller buildings (over six stories) than in lower ones. Tall buildings with many (over 1,000) living units are worst of all and appear to encourage isolation, stigmatization, apathy, neglect and withdrawal, the latter two first on the part of the residents, then by housing management, and finally by the municipal agencies that service the project: police, education, parks and recreation, refuse collection, and social services (1996:28).

2. In larger, taller buildings, crime occurs mostly in public areas (for example, elevators, halls, and lobbies), which are the places residents cannot easily monitor. Crime in such spaces is far less frequent in low-rise buildings, where residents can more easily supervise their surroundings.

3. In a comparison of two low-income projects in New York—low-rise Brownsville and high-rise Van Dyke—that had comparable residents but different architecture, Newman found rates of crime and vandalism to be significantly higher in the "less defensible" Van Dyke project.

We can conclude, then, that improving the physical design of buildings is a partial solution to the urban crime problem. But, regardless of architectural design, residents of a building must be motivated to notice and respond to potentially criminal situations. There is evidence, for example, that neighborhoods in which there is a greater sense of community will be the locales where greater crime prevention and deterrence will occur (Clarke 1992; Cochrun 1994).

Another crime-fighting strategy, advocated by Curtis Sliwa of the Guardian Angels, a volunteer crime patrol group, is street patrols by local citizens. Patrols, as well as Neighborhood Crime Watch organizations, sensitize community members to the problem as they involve everyone in watching for suspicious behavior. Studies have found that both do reduce neighborhood crime (Belkin 1983; Weillisz 1983).

Another approach, suggested by urban critic Roger Starr (1985), is that cities adopt a "get tough, no nonsense, this has gone far enough!" approach. Specifically, he proposed that (1) cities target vulnerable areas—subways, for example—and make special efforts to control crime there; (2) cities create citizens' boards (with racially and ethnically mixed membership) to fight for more jails, more police, and to pressure legislators to reform the laws that let many criminals slip through with little or no punishment; (3) cities adopt a policy of tougher punishment, increasing the severity of the jail sentences for each subsequent offense; and (4) cities ask parents and educators to commit themselves to instilling in children and students a sense of

A recent form of community policing measures to reduce crime in many North American cities has been the utilization of police officers on bike patrols, such as this multiethnic trio in Los Angeles. Using bicycles provides greater mobility and coverage of territory than covering a beat on foot, yet allows closer observation and interaction than in a car.

social responsibility so that fewer young people will be drawn into crime.

Proposals such as these have already yielded important positive effects. Still, one wonders whether any of them can produce real, long-term results. Frequently, communities mobilize against, say, drug dealing and succeed in getting the dealers, pushers, and addicts off the streets. But once the vigilance weakens, drug traffic reappears, suggesting a need for broader changes.

At present, New York City is boasting a remarkable drop in crime. A few years ago, city officials enacted stronger community and strategic policing measures, as well as a "get tough" approach. **Community policing** is an approach that increases interaction and cooperation between law enforcement agencies and the people and neighborhoods they serve. **Strategic policing** is an aggressive tactic of deploying increased patrols, decoys, and sting operations in locales identified as high-crime areas through frequent computer analyses. As a result, violent crime dropped almost in half, and the city became a model for other cities. Homicides, for example, dropped from 2,245 in 1990 to 565 in 2003, compared to 445 in Chicago, a city about one-third New York's size. This is a truly remarkable achievement. As some critics see it, however, "get tough" approaches do little to solve the root causes of crime; rather, they deal only with the consequences.

Ultimately, achieving long-term reductions in crime probably depends on increasing economic opportunity in poor communities. Doing so may involve providing greater mobility for inner-city residents so they are able to reach jobs on the metropolitan periphery, or providing job training and economic incentives through government to encourage businesses to locate in economically depressed areas. In addition, of course, community efforts at policing the streets, greater involvement by churches and local community groups, and efforts at upgrading neighborhoods (such as Habitat for Humanity) all will help. Fortunately, many city leaders recognize these needs and are taking steps to improve living and employment conditions.

❖ ━━━━━━━━━━ ❖ ━━━━━━━━━━ ❖

SUMMARY

Poor housing, substandard education, and crime are three significant problems plaguing our cities. Certainly, there are others, including environmental pollution, inadequate public transportation, and governmental corruption. This chapter highlighted housing, education, and crime because they seem to be the issues of greatest concern to the public as a whole.

All urban problems are closely linked to the state of a city's economy and, especially, to the extent of urban poverty. Thus, we can see that urban problems are complex, inter-related issues (consider the links among poverty, crime, and drug abuse) with roots that extend beyond a particular city to society as a whole.

In the 1930s, as part of Franklin Roosevelt's New Deal, the federal government first enacted public housing policies. Financial assistance to homeowners and builders, together with public works programs, quickly improved urban housing. Even so, by 1940, some 40 percent of U.S. urban housing still lacked amenities such as adequate indoor plumbing. The Housing Act of 1949 launched urban renewal programs and initiated the construction of more public housing. However, private developers never provided anywhere near as many low-income housing units as were torn down, resulting in the displacement of the poor. Moreover, high-rise public housing stigmatized and isolated the poor and created unsafe neighborhoods. Rent subsidies were a better idea, giving families choices other than public housing.

Rising taxes and increased maintenance costs, coupled with rent levels limited by local policy and the inability of tenants to pay, eventually resulted in hundreds of thousands of landlords abandoning buildings. More recently, urban homesteading, gentrification, and the New Urbanism are improving the urban scene. Each approach, however, has limitations and none can solve all the cities' housing problems.

Beset by problems of old buildings in need of repair, limited funding, a growing minority student population with limited English proficiency, a shortage of qualified teachers, and inadequate teaching resources, the nation's urban schools face serious challenges in their efforts to provide a quality education. A deepening dissatisfaction with the failure of urban schools to do their job has led to alternative approaches. Magnet schools, vouchers, and charter schools become more popular each year, but they also have their critics. Charges of elitism, violation of church–state separation, and the siphoning off of much-needed funds for urban public schools are controversies that surround these innovations.

Rates of serious crime are going down (although still rising among juveniles). Media coverage and the increase of stranger-on-stranger violence has raised public worries about crime. The greatest concentration of crime is in poor inner-city neighborhoods. Various explanations of the existence of high-crime areas highlight cultural patterns, alleged intellectual deficiencies, persistent racial inequality and poverty, and residential segregation.

Crime victimizes everyone by eroding property values, increasing insurance premiums, and generating a climate of fear. Crime also reduces use of parks, streets, and mass transit, denying urbanites free use of their city.

Trying to build "defensible spaces" is a partial solution to the crime problem, as are "get tough" policies that target vulnerable areas for extra police protection. Yet neither approach can ultimately solve the problem of crime. Strengthening families in order to provide good adult role models for young people, as well as generating jobs for adults and building a sense of community through churches and other local organizations, are also needed.

CONCLUSION

While there is ample reason for pessimism and concern, recent decades have witnessed positive signs of improvement in urban life. For example, New York City has dramatically curtailed violent crime. Many other cities have also reduced crime, but whether such a trend will persist remains to be seen. Similarly, time will tell whether or not the recent innovations in housing and education improve the quality of life and life chances for all segments of the cities' population. As cities convert the failed high-rise projects to more livable, mixed-income housing complexes that no longer isolate and stigmatize the poor, they are being guided by important lessons learned at mid-century. But what is happening to cities in developing countries? Are they learning from Western mistakes or is their situation even worse? In the next chapter we will discuss Latin American, African, Middle Eastern, and Asian cities to learn the answers.

KEY TERMS

Absolute poverty
Charter schools
Community policing
Defensible space
Eminent domain
Gentrification
Hypersegregation
Magnet schools
New Urbanism
Relative poverty
School voucher
Social promotions
Strategic policing
Urban renewal

CHAPTER 13

CITIES IN THE DEVELOPING WORLD

❖ ═══════════ ❖ ═══════════ ❖

When most of us think of large cities, we usually imagine towering New York City or sprawling Los Angeles. However, São Paolo, Brazil, with a population exceeding 10 million, is the largest city in the Western Hemisphere. Mexico City follows close behind with a population of 8.6 million. The 10 million inhabitants of Shanghai easily surpass New York City's 8 million, while the 12 million people in Mumbai (Bombay) are more than three times the population of Los Angeles (3.8 million).

These major cities, and many others throughout Africa, Asia, Latin America, and the Middle East, have an urban history unlike that of Canada and the United States. That past partly explains their present situation. All of these regions had indigenous cities that fell under the control of colonizers but eventually gained their political independence. Today, these areas are in the midst of rapid and far-reaching urban transformation and are growing at a startling rate, as vast numbers of people pour into their cities. Furthermore, the economic well-being of these cities (as well as of those in Canada and the United States) is linked to the changing global economy, which is dominated by the more-developed countries (MDCs). So, for the most part, the past, present, and future of cities in less-developed countries (LDCs) are interrelated with the fortunes of the MDCs.

Mexico City symbolizes in many ways the current state of poor cities around the globe. Pouring in are tens of thousands of people who must compete for extremely limited resources. Not surprisingly, those meager resources have not been shared equally. Nowhere in sub-Saharan Africa is there a city approaching the size of Cairo (at 10.8 million it is the continent's megacity), but large cities are numerous throughout Africa. Kinshasa, Congo (formerly Zaire) boasts 4.7 million inhabitants, while Capetown, South Africa, is home to 2.7 million people, Durban has 2.4 million, Johannesburg has about 1.7 million, and Pretoria has about 1.3 million residents. Most of the other sub-Saharan nations have at least one city with 1 million or more residents.

Moreover, **primate cities** (principal cities that are extremely large in comparison with other cities in the country)—appearing only in the last half of the twentieth century—dominate virtually all African countries as they do in Latin America. In many cases, a single city is home to more than half a country's urban population.

This chapter explores the development of cities throughout the developing world, with an eye to what they have in common, how they vary, and how they compare with Canadian and U.S. cities. This is a formidable task. Africa and Asia are vast continents of striking geographic and cultural contrasts. Africa has over 1,000 spoken languages and Asia has four major cultural traditions (in China, India, Japan, and Southeast Asia). Latin America, although it mostly shares a Spanish heritage, nonetheless varies significantly from one country to another in its population composition, resources, and economic development (see Figure 13–1). The Middle East is a region where countries (and their cities) vary considerably in economic development, political structure, and quality of life. Still, many common elements exist in the global urbanization we are witnessing.

HISTORICAL CONTEXT

At a basic level, cities seem to be relatively large, dense agglomerations of socially heterogeneous people characterized by a complex division of labor and a multifaceted set of interactions and experiences. Beyond this, cities are shaped by their cultural and historical context. Each of the developing world cities discussed in this chapter is working out its own version of the urban story. Nevertheless, a few common themes emerge when we compare how their histories impact on their present condition.

Latin American Cities

Most of the cities we think of as Latin American—Rio de Janeiro, Brazil; Buenos Aires, Argentina; Bogotá, Colombia; Santiago, Chile;

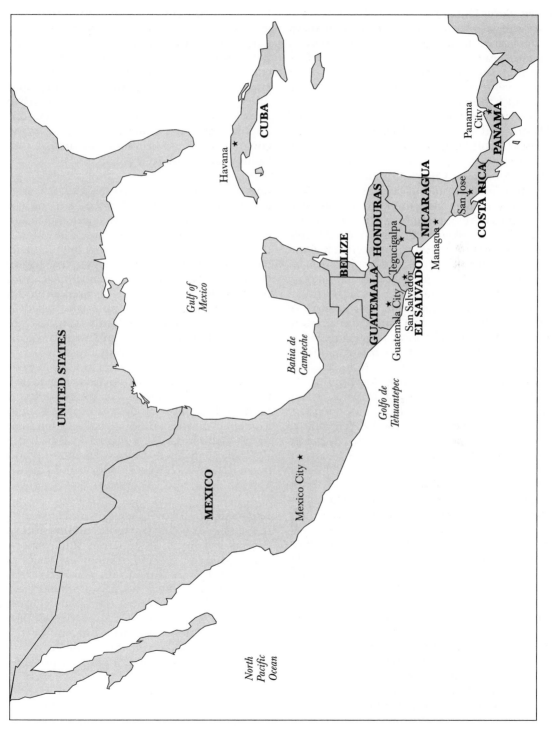

FIGURE 13–1 Map of Major Central American Cities

Lima, Peru; La Paz, Bolivia—did not exist before the sixteenth century. They, and many others, are the products of **colonization** by Spanish and Portuguese conquerors. Before the founding of such cities, however, other urban centers existed. The most outstanding examples were the capitals of the Mayan and Aztec civilizations in Central America and Mexico and the Inca Empire on the western coast of South America.

Pre-Columbian Cities. Teotihuacan, the Mayan capital located in central Mexico, was primarily a religious center. It reached the peak of its development between 450 and 650 C.E., when its population was about 200,000. For reasons still unclear, its streets fell silent in about 750 C.E.

The Inca Empire in Peru reached its peak of development somewhat later, between 1430 and 1525. Containing a population of over 6 million and stretching from present-day Ecuador into northern Argentina with a land area of over a million square miles, its center was the city of Cuzco, home of "the Inca," the absolute ruler of the civilization.

During the same period in Mexico, another mighty yet completely independent empire thrived. In 1325 the Mexica, one of several tribes now known as the Aztecs, settled in the Texcoco Lake basin and, on an island, established the city of Tenochtitlan, 30 miles southwest of the old city of Teotihuacan. The site was remarkably favorable—easily defensible in war and providing trade access to the surrounding region. Within 100 years, bolstered by conquests and commercial prosperity, the city controlled a population of between 5 and 6 million. The Cityscape box on page 375 describes its awe-inspiring splendor.

Tragically for Tenochtitlan, the Aztec king, Montezuma, respectfully but cautiously welcomed Cortés and his officers. He invited the Spaniards into the city, housed them in a great palace, and gave them gifts of gold—in retrospect, a serious mistake. As Miguel Leon Portilla, who was present, later wrote: The Spaniards "picked up the gold and fingered it like monkeys: they seemed transported with joy, as if their hearts were illuminated and made new . . . they hungered like pigs for that gold" (quoted in Cottrell et al. 1979:46). This experience foreshadowed what was about to happen in all of Latin America. Cortés and other European explorers did not come to live in peaceful coexistence with the indigenous populations. They came to conquer and become rich. They were about to destroy pre-Columbian civilization.

European Domination. In April 1521, Cortés and his forces encircled Tenochtitlan and cut off its food and water for three months. In August, overcoming the last resistance, he entered the city victorious. To ensure that the remnants of the proud Aztec Empire never rose again, Cortés utterly demolished Tenochtitlan and, on its rubble, erected a city focused around a completely European culture. He called it *Ciudad Imperial de Mexico*—Mexico City. To complete his domination, the surviving Mexicans were made to serve their conquerors.

In the conquest of the Inca Empire in Peru about a decade later, Francisco Pizarro followed the same pattern. He conquered and destroyed the Inca cities and replaced them with Spanish cities. Although a pre-Columbian urban civilization did not exist in Brazil, the Portuguese invaders established cities up and down that country's coast (Morse and Hardoy 1993).

Exploitation. All over Latin America, new colonial cities were constructed as administrative centers for local domination and export-oriented trade. Inland settlements such as Mexico City were linked with port cities such as Vera Cruz. Where no important port existed, the Europeans built one; Lima (Peru), Valparaiso (Chile), Buenos Aires (Argentina), and Rio de Janeiro (Brazil) are examples (see Figure 13–2). However, the "trade" of these cities was a one-way operation, with precious gold, silver, tobacco, and coffee shipped to Spain and Portugal. Served in this way, these relatively poor and weak nations in Europe hoped to become rich and powerful.

CITYSCAPE

The Magnificent City of Tenochtitlan

The Aztec rulers built Tenochtitlan into a city of incredible magnificence. While London was still a backwater of Europe and New York was nonexistent, Tenochtitlan was probably, after Rome, the world's greatest city. Here are two brief descriptive accounts:

Half city and half floating garden, its profile etched by dozens of temples dominated by the Pyramid dedicated to the worship of Huitzilopochtli and Tlaloc, [Tenochtitlan] rose majestically above the lake and green groves of trees. The setting was imposing: snow-covered peaks, cultivated slopes, and the densely populated fertile valley. (Hardoy 1975:12)

An island-metropolis, Tenochtitlan was set like a radiant jewel amid the clear, calm turquoise of saline Lake Texcoco, linked to mainland suburbs by three great paved causeways. Elegant palaces and pyramid temples, interspersed with broad plazas and exotic gardens, gleamed spotless white in the brilliant crystalline air more than 7,000 feet above sea-level. (Cottrell et al. 1979:37)

In 1519, the Spaniard Hernan Cortés and his men gazed with disbelief on this city. Cortés later described it as "the most beautiful city in the world," and one of his soldiers, Bernal Diaz, described the Spanish reaction this way:

We were amazed. . . . [I]t was like the enchantments they tell of in the legend of Amadis, on account of the great towers and [temples] and buildings rising from the water, and all built of masonry. And some of our soldiers even asked whether the things that we saw were not a dream. . . . I do not know how to describe it, seeing things as we did that had never been heard of or seen before, not even dreamed about. Some . . . among us who had been in many parts of the world, in Constantinople, all over Italy, and in Rome, said that so large a market and so full of people and so well-regulated and arranged, they had never beheld before. . . . (1956:218–19)

Commerce was the lifeblood of the city:

Everything consumed by the Aztec capital was imported daily by bearers who traveled the highways linking the city and the lake's edge, or was unloaded from canoes. Tenochtitlan and Tlatelolco procured goods from the provinces by means of tribute imposed after successful military campaigns or the threat of military occupation. Their artisans, among them specialists in luxury articles, found sure buyers for their work in the city and among the local merchants who controlled regional trade. Tenochtitlan based a large part of its economic strength, which was unrivaled in Mesoamerica after the mid-fifteenth century, upon commerce and tribute. (Hardoy 1975:12)

The strategic location of most of these cities in relation to the hinterland also allowed colonists to dominate the native population. Ensconced in fortifications on the coast, the Europeans could defend themselves from internal attack and receive supplies from the sea. Such battlements also protected them from an external enemy—pirates—who lusted after the wealth these cities harbored.

Military might alone, however, did not ensure European dominance of the new cities and their hinterland. One of the most tragic aftermaths of the conquest was the literal decimation of the indigenous population. Anthropologists and historians estimate the loss of native human life in Central America in the sixteenth century at roughly 95 percent. This means that, in scarcely a

FIGURE 13–2   Map of Major South American Cities

single century, the Indian population plummeted from more than 25 million to perhaps 1 million. There were many reasons for this frightening loss of life, chief among them the brutal wars with the colonists and the toll taken by European diseases, such as measles and smallpox, against which native Latin Americans had no biological defense.

Cultural Impact. Imposing European culture on Latin America had other long-lasting effects. Decreeing a set of principles called the "Laws of the Indies," the Spanish constructed all their new cities along very similar patterns, resulting in the breakdown of local cultural patterns. Although local geography and earlier customs brought some variations, most colonial cities were constructed around a grid plan with a central plaza—the *plaza mayor.* At one end of the plaza was an imposing Catholic church. On the other three sides were government offices, residences of the wealthy, and some businesses. Such a design established the dominant institutions of European culture—the church, the state, the power of the elite, and commerce—at the very heart of the city.

Around the city center, in a second district, were the residences of the city's middle class: artisans, government clerks, and small merchants. Further out still, in a third zone, were the much more dilapidated residences of the city's poor. Finally, on the outskirts, were large parcels of land originally called *encomiendas,* given in trust to the local elite by the Spanish government. After independence in the nineteenth century, many of these large parcels of land became part of the equally exclusive *hacienda* system: large farms or ranches run by elites and worked by serfs.

Although physically similar to European cities, these preindustrial colonial cities were even more exclusive, favoring only a small and extremely powerful elite of European descent. Under normal circumstances, native Latin Americans could never become members of

Throughout Latin America the Spanish influence manifests itself in both architecture and urban design. One common feature is a large church or cathedral, as well as a government palace, adjacent to or dominating a central plaza in the heart of the old city area. Illustrating this pattern is Murillo Plaza in La Paz, Bolivia.

the elite. Although remnants of pre-Columbian culture remained—particularly in rural communities—the dominance of colonial cities in Latin America ensured the dominance of European culture in most areas of life (Skidmore and Smith 2004).

Independence and Urban Growth. By the early 1800s, the willingness and ability of the European colonists to maintain Latin American outposts was waning. They had long ago taken most of the easily extracted raw materials. Then, too, local insurgents, such as Simón Bolivar, were mounting more frequent challenges to colonial governance. Soon after a series of wars of independence (1816–1825), most Latin American nations gained their freedom.

With colonial restrictions removed, many Latin American cities began to prosper through trade with cities in England, France, and the United States. At the same time, populations began to increase. For example, between 1797 and 1914, the population of Buenos Aires jumped from 30,000 to 1.5 million, and between 1800 and 1900, Rio de Janeiro's population climbed from 43,000 to 800,000 (Boyer and Davies, 1973:33). Similar patterns appeared in Mexico City, Montevideo, Caracas, Santiago, Lima, and Havana. Indeed, by the early twentieth century, these few cities had grown so much that they dominated all other cities in their respective countries, becoming what urbanists call **primate cities**, as the Critical Thinking box below explains.

Not all of the growth of primate cities resulted from rural migrants seeking greater economic opportunity in the city; some was attributable to foreign immigration. Between 1860 and 1930, Latin America absorbed millions upon millions of Jews, Russians, Poles, Italians,

CRITICAL THINKING

The Evolution of Primate Cities

A primate city is one that grows in population and influence far beyond other cities in a nation or region. In many poor countries, the largest city may have several times the combined population of the next-largest two or three cities. Primate cities thus resemble, to use Alejandro Portes's metaphor, "gigantic heads on dwarfish bodies" (1977:68), absorbing an enormous portion of the available labor, trade, and population.

The extent of the dominance of a primate city in its own country can be shown by a **primacy ratio,** computed by dividing the primate city's population by the population of the second-largest city in the country. In the following table are some examples.

Note that, with the exception of four cities, the primacy ratios for the largest Western cities (Prague, Moscow, New York, Rome, Tokyo, and Berlin) are relatively low. This suggests that primacy is linked to more than a good location and established trade patterns.

Selected Developing World Cities in 2005*		Selected Developed World Cities in 2005*	
Bangkok	16.8	Paris	7.1
Lima	9.8	London	7.0
Santiago	9.3	Vienna	6.9
Managua	8.7	Copenhagen	4.9
Beirut	5.5	Prague	3.1
Mexico City	5.2	Moscow	2.2
Havana	4.9	New York	2.1
Nairobi	3.2	Rome	2.1
Jakarta	3.2	Tokyo	2.3
Cairo	2.0	Berlin	2.0

*All ratios computed from populations reported in "Nations of the World," 2005 *Britannica Book of the Year* (Chicago: Encyclopaedia Britannica, 2005).

Swiss, and Germans. Because of their generally higher level of education and greater familiarity with business, these immigrants soon came to control much of the medium-scale commerce of Latin America's primate cities, dominating such areas as construction, small industry, workshops, artisan and craft activities. As a result, immigrants occupied many middle-class jobs at the expense of the impoverished indigenous population that also was streaming into the cities (Gwynne 1985).

African Cities

African urbanization is uneven, with most contemporary African cities located on or near the continent's coastlines. The greater urbanization on Africa's north coast is a historical legacy of trade, both with Europe and with the Islamic countries of the Middle East. To reach Europe, Africans transported their goods from the interior, crossing the forbidding Sahara Desert, then loading them onto ships that plied the Mediterranean or sailed Europe's west coast. Established during the seventeenth- and eighteenth-century European colonization to facilitate exports (including slaves), cities on Africa's west and east coasts soon became the most technologically and economically developed settlements on the continent.

Early African Cities.   Though unknown to most Westerners, complex civilizations, complete with highly developed urban centers, existed in Africa as early as 3000 B.C.E. One such civilization, Kush, with its core cities of Meroë, Musawarat, and Naga, was centered about 100 miles north of the modern city of Khartoum. According to unearthed archaeological evidence, these Kushite cities, originally imitators of the ancient cities of Egypt,

---

Recent research suggests that primate cities develop more frequently (1) in small countries—Copenhagen and Vienna are clear examples; (2) in countries that, for historical reasons, have only one or a few cities with anything approaching modern facilities—certainly true of poor countries around the world; and (3) in countries that were once or still are under foreign control either politically or economically—colonial cities, for example.

Some urbanists argue that primate cities are helpful to a region's urban development. They speed up the evolution of a modern urban facility, which, in time, makes possible the "trickling down" of advanced urban technology and economic vitality to smaller cities. These urbanists point to this process in the more-developed countries. Historically, for example, London was England's primate city. With the advent of industrialization, however, large numbers of modern middle-level cities emerged in England: Birmingham, Manchester, Leeds, and Sheffield.

Other theorists are much less optimistic. They argue that cities in highly industrialized nations are not comparable with those in poor regions. Rich countries, like the United States and England, were, at the time of the emergence of their middle-level cities, much more economically advanced and politically stable than most poor countries today. In the latter, because the rest of the country is so poor, people flock to the primate city as the only chance to better their lives. This hampers the development of a series of middle-level cities and ensures that, if growth goes unchecked, then the primate city itself will become overwhelmed with migrants. Thus, the only way to prevent overgrowth is to strictly limit further population growth in the primate city and to build middle-level cities that will drain off some of the population (Kasarda and Crenshaw 1991).

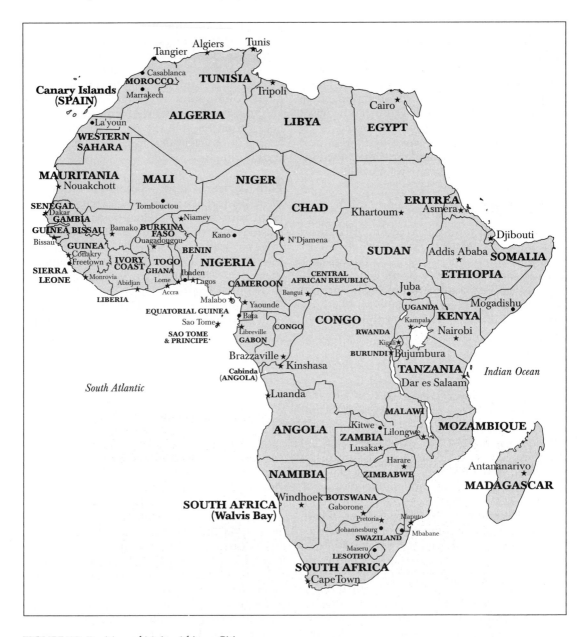

FIGURE 13–3 Map of Major African Cities

were highly sophisticated. By 590 B.C.E., Meroë traded extensively with Saharan and Mediterranean peoples in slaves, gold, ivory, iron, and copper (Wenke 2005). In fact, Meroë's trade in copper was so extensive that

great slag heaps from the manufacturing process are still evident in the city's ruins.

Other early African cities, particularly those in the sub-Saharan region, served as capitals of indigenous African empires, as craft or manufacturing centers, or as break-of-bulk points on major trade routes. Gao, in present-day Mali, was built in the seventh century C.E. as the capital of the Songhai Empire. More impressive was Kumbi, capital of the Empire of Ghana around 1000 C.E. Backed by a large army equipped with iron weapons, Kumbi had an estimated population of 30,000, supported by a rural population numbering in the hundreds of thousands. Trade in gold and ivory—as well as in salt, kola nuts, slaves, and iron weapons—provided the empire's economic base (Wenke 2005).

As Wenke suggests, trade was crucial to these cities. In the eighth century C.E., shortly after the establishment of Islam as a major religion, cities based on trade with Arab countries and the East began to appear throughout Africa—cities such as Mogadishu in Somalia and Mombasa in Kenya. As exchange became more lucrative, the Muslim traders conquered the North African cities in the name of transforming them into major shipping centers to

Europe. Their trade networks linked these cities to dozens of inland, sub-Saharan cities to the south. One such city was Kano, founded in 999 C.E. Another was the legendary Timbuktu, founded in 1100 and the intellectual capital of western Sudan, with its stone palaces, many-windowed homes, city university, and bustling marketplace.

All these early African cities were typical preindustrial cities with a walled enclosure, narrow and winding streets, and daily life organized around religion, crafts, and the crown. Residence was often determined by craft—for example, metalsmiths might cluster together—or by tribal or religious affiliation. There was nothing resembling the modern Western pattern of a CBD surrounded by residential rings determined by income. Rich and poor, commercial and residential uses all intermingled.

European Domination. The isolation of African cities did not continue forever, however.

Taroudannt, Morocco, is a city of 30,000 that traces its origins to the eleventh century. Its sixteenth-century, 23-foot fortified walls are in excellent condition and still define three-fourths of the city's borders. Walled cities once existed on all continents except Antarctica as a defensive measure and those that remain offer vivid testimony to how cities once defined their boundaries.

Although this period of empire building, trade, and urbanization (from approximately 500 B.C.E. to 1500 C.E.) was modern Africa's formative period, in which the dynamics of growth and change produced uniquely African cultures and civilizations, all became progressively submerged in the coming centuries. Looking for an easy passage to the East, the Portuguese arrived in the late 1400s. Other European colonists—the French, British, Danish, and Dutch—were not far behind (Davidson 2001).

The First Wave.   The initial opening of Africa by Europeans stimulated one of history's most wretched practices: slavery. Although the use of slaves has a long history—ancient Egyptians, Greeks, and Romans, for example, regularly subjugated those they conquered—the slave trade between 1500 and 1850 is second to none in barbarity. The Spanish and Portuguese secured African slaves (often with the help of other black Africans) and exported these human beings to Latin America to replace the decimated Indian population. For their part, English and U.S. traders joined in shipping vast numbers of slaves to the New World to do the backbreaking work of building a new country. Other European countries participated as well. All enlisted the aid of a cadre of professional slave traders—Europeans, Muslims, Africans—to bring the "black gold" to market at Daka in Senegal, Elmina on the coast of Ghana, Zanzibar in Tanzania, and other slave-trade towns established up and down the continent's coasts.

The first European invasion also upset many of the delicate economic, political, and interpersonal linkages of precolonial Africa. The Portuguese demolished the east coast cities and destroyed the trade alliances that linked these cities to the Persian Gulf, India, and the Far East. In other parts of Africa, Europeans destroyed many of the political allegiances that had kept African tribes and empires in balance with one another. Added to this was the incalculable confusion and suffering brought about by the slave trade, which forcibly separated husband from wife,

brother from sister, mother from child. In the wake of such practices, much of African society was brought close to collapse.

The Second Wave.   The character of urban Africa changed radically in the nineteenth century when Europeans arrived in force. No longer looking for a passage east, and with the slave trade waning, the rapidly industrializing colonizers now eyed Africa with much the same plundering eye that Cortés and Pizarro had cast upon Latin America more than three centuries before. After all, Africa is a source of almost incalculable raw materials. And so they swarmed like locusts over the continent, trying to claim as much land and other wealth as they could.

Between 1862 and 1915, Europeans established city after city. Where no previous cities existed, they built them. Where indigenous urban centers were in place, they "Europeanized" them. Among those established or transformed during this period—some easily betraying their colonial origin by their European names—were Dar es Salaam (1862); Accra (1876); Leopoldville (1881)—now Kinshasa; Brazzaville (1883); Johannesburg (1886); Salisbury (1890)—now Harare; Kampala (1890); Nairobi (1899); Stanleyville (*c.* 1900)—now Kisangani; Jos (1903); Elisabethville (1910)—now Lubumbashi; and Albertville (1915)—now Kalima.

Unlike Latin America, where the "Laws of the Indies" produced a continent of similar cities, the presence of many European nations in Africa resulted in a variety of different policies for urban areas. The British, for example, subscribed to a policy of indirect rule, content to let local African rulers maintain their positions as long as they bowed to the colonial government. The French, on the other hand, insisted on the eventual assimilation of Africans into the French way of life. To promote this they dismantled indigenous governments, taught only French in public schools, and encouraged the local population in total identification with French culture.

In still other instances, where prominent African settlements had existed prior to the coming of the colonizers, dual cities appeared. In cities like Kano, Ibadan, and Kampala, the Europeans paired the African city with a new city of their own next to it. The contrast was striking: An African city constructed of mud bricks and organized around its religious life and craft associations would coexist with a European city built of stone and organized around a growing CBD.

In all cities, however, a policy of racial segregation prevailed—a form of **apartheid** (the practice as it came to be known in South Africa) by which Europeans dominated the local people. Obviously, such a system imposed tremendous economic, political, and social hardships on Africans while enriching the Europeans. Racism was at its worst in southern Africa—particularly in the then Union (now Republic) of South Africa and in Namibia—where only recently have black majorities gained power. In more northerly parts of the continent, different colonizers and different urban traditions allowed the races some contact, and thus mitigated the racism somewhat. Thus, although racial tensions remain in West, East, and North Africa, conflict has been greatest in the south in the Republic of South Africa, Namibia, and Zimbabwe, where rigid racial segregation and stratification ended only in the 1990s.

Middle Eastern Cities

Chapter 2 highlighted early Middle Eastern cities. In this region the world's first-known city—Jericho—developed nearly 10,000 years ago. It was followed by other early cities such as Catal Hüyük and Eridu and, beginning in the fourth millennium B.C.E., by the domination of the Persian and Egyptian empires. As these empires faded—a process hastened by the invasions of Philip of Macedon, Alexander the Great, and the Romans in the last four centuries before the birth of Christ—they left behind established sites on which more modern cities would flourish.

A second period of city building occurred after Alexander's conquest in 334 B.C.E. Seeking to bolster his empire through trade, Alexander established a string of colonies

from present-day Syria all across the coast of northern Africa. As Romans followed Greeks, additional cities, typically military outposts, were added, including Tangier, Algiers, Tunis, and Carthage. After 300 C.E., the declining fortunes of Rome, plus soil erosion and overgrazing, led to the eclipse of some of these coastal cities. Many ruins remain to this day, stark reminders of long-faded cultures.

Islamic Cities. The prophet Muhammad died in 632, unleashing a religious movement that swept over the entire Middle East, into Europe via Spain and the Balkan states, across some of sub-Saharan Africa, and, eventually, as far east as Pakistan, India, Indonesia, and the southern Philippine Islands. As it spread, Islam generated an impressive array of cities. Even as European cities contracted during the Middle Ages, Islamic cities along the coast of North Africa were entering their greatest period. The Muslims' status as among history's greatest "middlemen" helped assure the success of these cities, as traders utilized the Middle East's geographic location to become the link between Europe and the Far East and, in the case of North Africa, between Europe and the sub-Saharan region.

But the inland cities were probably Islam's greatest triumph. For centuries, as nomads and overland traders, the people of the Middle East had learned how to live and prosper across vast distances of inhospitable terrain. As trading centers, they established Mecca, Riyadh, Baghdad, Tehran, and Kabul, among others.

All the Islamic cities had a similar form, as described in the Cityscape box. By and large, the Muslim city reflected the power of the city's royal and religious elites, and many find these the most beautiful of all the world's cities. The following passage, excerpted from Robert Byron's writings on his travels in the Middle East in the 1930s, describes Isfahan in Iran:

> The beauty of Isfahan steals on the mind unawares. You drive about, under avenues of white tree trunks and canopies of shining twigs; past domes of turquoise and spring yellow in a sky of

CITYSCAPE

The Islamic City

In the typical Islamic city, environmental and cultural elements dominant in the Middle East combined to produce a unique urban place. The surrounding wall, for example, served a dual function, first as a defense against marauders, and equally important, as a barrier to dust-laden winds coming from a variety of directions depending on the time of day or season of the year. When bush shrubs were planted along the wall, the effect on wind and dust was that of an almost total barrier, and with strategic planting of vegetation within the settlement, wind and dust could be kept aloft and away from inhabited areas across the whole extent of the settlement.

The bustle and intensity of activity on the main thoroughfares were a notable feature of the Islamic town. The animated nature of its commercial sections and the awareness of a rich texture of human contact and activity were, and in some cases still are, the very life force of Islamic urbanism. In sharp contrast to the harsh desolation and silence of the desert, the *sugs* or bazaars provided access to a multitude of goods and services. . . .

Turning away from the main thoroughfares, a further contrast was encountered as the traveler ventured into the residential quarters on either side. Here the streets were much narrower, with walls often within touching distance on either side. The intimacy and semi-private atmosphere of these streets were borne in on the visitor as the shade provided by the dense building pattern created cool conditions in which to linger. The noise of the main streets was quickly cut to a distant murmur as the traveler moved further into the quarter. . . .

On gaining entry to a private house, yet another contrast was unveiled as the anonymous faces of the outsides of houses presented to the street were transformed by the wealth of detailed internal decoration, apparent in even

liquid violet-blue; along the river patched with twisting shoals, catching that blue in its muddy silver, and lined with feathery groves where the sap calls; across bridges of pale toffee brick, tier on tier of arches breaking into piled pavilions, overlooked by lilac mountains, by the Kuh-I-Sufi shaped like Punch's hump and by other ranges receding to a line of snowy surf; and before you know how, Isfahan has become indelible, has insinuated its image into that gallery of places which everyone privately treasures. (1982:166).

But this image is misleading, for enduring internal conflict often characterized Islamic cities. Given the division of the city into multiple residential quarters—sixteenth-century Damascus contained no fewer than 70 quarters in the city itself and 30 more in the suburb of al-Salihiyyah—ingroup solidarity often led to surging outgroup hostility, particularly when central religious values were at stake:

So intense was neighborhood communal solidarity that at times faction fights broke out between quarters. . . . [It was] a society where economic grievances could seldom be articulated without group violence. Political communication with the ruling . . . caste was limited. Food shortages or abusive taxation provoked street demonstrations, assaults on officials, pillage of shops and the closure of markets. . . . [Youth gangs, associated with different quarters] preyed upon the quarters, running protection rackets, pillaging, and murdering. (Costello 1977:15–16)

Islamic cities reached their zenith during the Middle Ages. Thereafter, like their Persian, quite modest homes. Houses were usually built on the courtyard principle with rooms opening onto a central space, often embellished with a fountain. This space provided the chief communal living area for the family. In keeping with the modesty of Islamic tradition, rooms of one part of the house were used only by women and the overall layout catered for the entertaining of guests without their need to encounter all members of the household.

The courtyard principle provided the ultimate achievable protection of private open space from the extremes of temperature, dust and wind outside the settlement. In an almost cell-like structure the town was set within its walls as a first line of protection from the environment. The residential quarters, often within their own walls, were then located close together in a pattern which afforded mutual protection of each building by all the others. The building density did nothing to compromise the privacy of individual houses orientated inwards as they were, so that a third and final line of protection between courtyard and residential street was afforded by the house itself. . . .

Moving finally towards the centre of the town, the traveler was confronted with the mosque. These were originally built not so much as houses of God but as a means by which to exclude unbelievers from regular prayer ceremonies. The addition of minarets, though partly only ornamental, was made to project the muezzin's call to prayer, with other mosques built once the call was out of earshot in an expanding city.

The more recent urban settlements in the Middle East often lack the high degree of unity and atmosphere found in the still-existing, specific features of the older Islamic towns. The flavor of these old urban communities, in complete contrast to the desolation all around them, was at once intimate, intricate and intense. Thus, cities such as Baghdad, Cairo, Fez, or Tehran—situated in one of the harshest environments in the world—could provide comfortable living conditions for populations running into the hundreds of thousands.

Source: From *An Urban Profile of the Middle East* by M. Hugh Roberts. © 1979 by M. Hugh Roberts. Used with permission of W. H. Freeman and Company/Worth Publishers.

Egyptian, Greek, and Roman predecessors, they began to slide into decline. Again, the land near the cities became overgrazed and the topsoil depleted, leading to evaporation of precious water supplies and increasing dust and erosion. This, in turn, triggered a loss of timber, a crucial raw material any preindustrial society consumes for heat, artifacts, houses, ships, and tools (Costello 1977:18).

City populations plummeted. For instance, in the sixteenth century Baghdad dropped to a population of less than 100,000, one-tenth of its former size. In Syria, Egypt, Iran, and Saudi Arabia, cities were reduced to shadows of what they had been. Even in the largest cities such as Alexandria and Aleppo (in Syria), trade slowed to a trickle.

European Domination.   Not until the nineteenth century, under European influence, did urban growth begin once more. Europeans saw in the Middle East waiting markets for their goods, a potential source of raw materials, and, in some areas such as Suez, strategic locations for military affairs.

But the Europeans never viewed the Middle East as the valuable prize that Latin America and Africa were. Thus, they made limited efforts at colonization. Britain administered Egypt as a protectorate from 1882 to 1914 but otherwise was content to trade. But trade with outsiders was sufficient to weaken the centuries-long Islamic pattern. Despite efforts by many Muslims to bar nonbelievers and their way of life (including books, telephones, and automobiles), their world was changing.

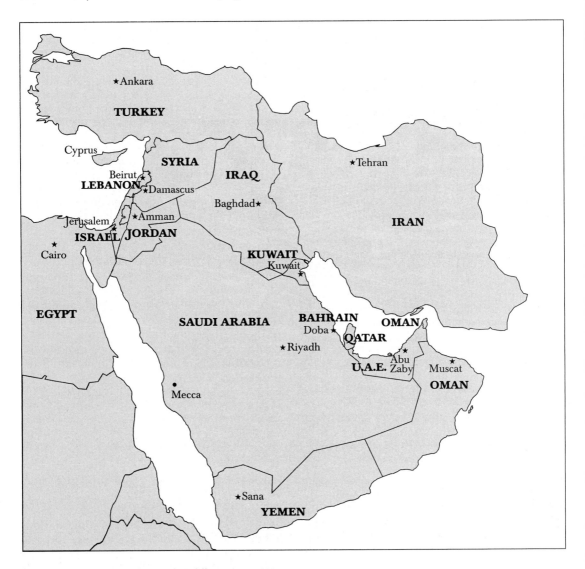

FIGURE 13–4   Map of Major Middle Eastern Cities

As European influence spread across the region, new urban patterns emerged. For example, the French textile industry in Egypt after 1830 sparked urban growth throughout the rest of that century. From Cairo to Beirut to Tehran, suburban districts swelled beyond the quarters of the old cities, and new, wider roads were routinely clogged with motor vehicles (Cleveland 2004).

The real change, however, went deeper than the physical level. Foreign traders ventured into rural areas to make better deals for agricultural products, thereby passing up the ancient bazaars. Foreign investors opened businesses and factories in Middle Eastern cities and began undercutting the prices of the traditional guilds. In sum, new competition altered the face of the entire region's

The Islamic world is one rich in art, architecture, culture, history, and tradition. Religion is the centerpiece of that world and its ornate mosques dominate each cityscape, much as Christian cathedrals dominate older cities in Europe. A Muslim example is the Masjed-e-Jame mosque, in Isfahan, a city of 1.3 million people in central Iran.

economy. Where local sheikhs had administered land communally and restricted the open-market sale of goods, now people began to sell land, goods, and skills to the highest bidder. The ultimate cost was a weakening of traditional authority and an erosion of long-established communities. Before long, Middle Eastern cities had begun to alter their earlier self-sufficient subsistence economies, becoming export-oriented and dependent on the economies and needs of Europe and North America. Of course, this process only accelerated with the discovery of the new "black gold" of the region: oil.

Asian Cities

The richness and complexity of Asian culture forces us to be highly selective. Indeed, of all global regions, Asia provides the greatest challenge because it encompasses almost 30 percent of the earth's land area and is a region of many sharp contrasts: Japan is a highly industrialized, rich nation, with one of the world's lowest birth rates. China is poorer but with a rapidly growing economy and the largest urban population of any country in the world. Southeast Asia stands out as having no real tradition of indigenous cities at all; yet, despite this history, major cities now are growing at a startling rate. Despite some gains, India is still struggling to address urban problems as serious as those anywhere in the world. We begin there.

India.   Chapter 2 revealed that the Indus Valley region of India and Pakistan had thriving cities such as Moenjo-Daro and Harrappa as early as 2500 B.C.E. And in antiquity, the fabled opulence and beauty of ancient India and China held nearly mythical fascination for westerners. These myths enticed that most famous of world travelers, Marco Polo, to set out from Venice in 1271 to find an easy route to the East.

Early Contact.   The published tales of Marco Polo further fired the European imagination.

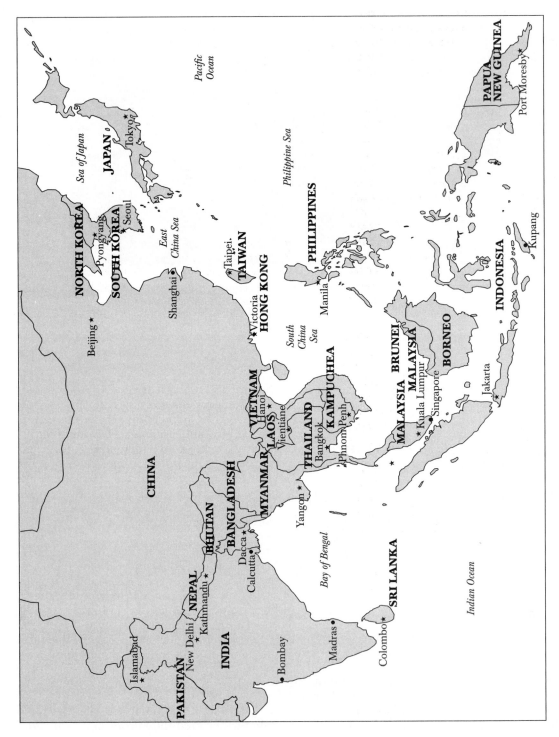

FIGURE 13–5 Map of Major Asian Cities

Yet his stories also chronicled the enormous difficulties of reaching India and China via an overland route. So the Europeans had no recourse but to take to the sea. Beginning in the early 1400s, the Portuguese moved down the west coast of Africa, establishing outposts as they went. By 1460, they reached Sierra Leone, and by 1488, the Cape of Good Hope. Eleven years later, after moving up the east coast of Africa, Vasco da Gama made the leap across the Indian Ocean and arrived in India. By 1534, the Portuguese had outposts at Goa and Diu along India's west coast. The passage, however, was hardly easy, for between India and Europe lay more than 10,000 miles of ocean. Consequently, when the riches of the New World were discovered in the early 1500s, Portugal turned its attention to the considerably closer continent of South America.

European Domination.   A century later, the British began the colonization of India in earnest. In 1639, they established George Town (later to become Madras) at the mouth of the Cooums River on India's southeast coast. By 1661, the British gained control of Bombay Island from the Portuguese and in 1690 they established the city of Calcutta. As in Latin America and Africa, such cities had a dual purpose: as centers of political control and as bases for economic exploitation.

Where cities already existed, as in the case of Delhi, the British simply constructed a second settlement next to it, in this case New Delhi. This pattern of separation was nearly identical to the dual-city African settlements described earlier, resulting in a striking contrast between the indigenous part and the Anglicized part. One typical distinction would be a congested urban center in the old section and carefully planned, often-spacious sections nearby dating from the British period.

The older area (the original city) typically has a form much like that of the Islamic cities described in the last section. Crowded into a central market or bazaar, numerous small retail shops offer a vast range of goods, including foods, cloths, hardware, and jewelry. Surrounding the marketplace is a residential area strictly divided into quarters, dividing Muslims from Hindus and separating Hindus according to their caste position. Brahmins and other high castes are usually in the best-built residential areas in or near the center of the old cities. The laboring castes and the menial outcastes of lowest socioeconomic status occupy the poorest houses and tend to be located in the outskirts rather than the center. The British part of the city, on the other hand, is very Western in form, with broad streets, often arranged in a grid pattern. At the center is a trading and manufacturing area, with a railroad leading outward.

China.   Like India, China is a land of ancient cities. Beijing (Peking), as profiled in Chapter 8, has long stood as a magnificent center of Chinese culture. Today, some of traditional China remains, although much has been changed, as our historical account will explain.

Foreign Domination.   From the mid-nineteenth century until the end of World War II, China was subjected to foreign control, first by Europeans and then by the Japanese. Invaders occupied the cities, particularly the so-called treaty ports opened to them by the Treaty of Nanking, which ended the Opium Wars in 1843. From Shanghai to Canton, Europeans remade parts of Chinese cities. Hotels, parks, tennis courts, and residential areas emerged, all catering to non-Chinese. To oversee European control of the area's economy, each city had a European-style CBD, complete with banks, corporate headquarters, and docks equipped to handle Western ships. As always, the Europeans imagined themselves on a "civilizing" mission. Said J. H. Wilson in 1887:

> Progress has planted her foot firmly on the banks of [Shanghai's Wusung River] and from her safe and abiding place in the foreign city is sure, slowly but inevitably, to invade and overcome the whole vast empire.

Despite such arrogant pronouncements, European-style "progress" apparently had little need of the Chinese themselves. Placed at the entrances to Shanghai's foreign-built park, one sign summed up the matter: "No Dogs or Chinese Allowed." Similarly, Shanghai's European merchants routinely recruited unsuspecting Chinese laborers for work on ships bound for far-off ports. Thus did the idea of being "shanghaied" come into our language.

Communist Anti-Urbanism. Not surprisingly, the Chinese people resented such treatment. Thus, when the People's Republic was established in 1949, Mao Zedong and his followers made a concerted effort to eradicate all aspects of European influence and privilege from China's cities. Moreover, believing cities to be by their very nature destructive of revolutionary ideals, Mao encouraged China's citizens to remain in their rural villages and transform the country from there.

More extreme action was also taken. During the 1970s, the highly regimented and often brutal Maoist system forced perhaps 25 million urbanites from large cities into small towns and rural villages. Despite these efforts, however, China's urban population continued to grow. Although reliable data are hard to come by, only about 10 percent of the Chinese population was urban in 1950, while the urban share had increased to 38 percent by 2002 (*Britannica Book of the Year* 2005:547; Davis 1969, 1972).

Japan. The urban roots of the country extend back at least to the eighth century C.E., when ruling elites established a series of provincial capitals. A warrior caste (the *samurai*) protected these capitals, which were weakly linked to an emperor living in the capital city of Kyoto. Within this feudal structure, local elites kept the citizenry in subjugation over the next few centuries while they warred with each other for control of various regions.

At the end of the sixteenth century, a samurai named Ieyasu emerged victorious over the warring elements. The emperor named Ieyasu *shogun* (leader and protector of Japan), and Ieyasu established his capital at the city of Edo (now Tokyo). Ieyasu and his successors set about reorganizing the administrative system of Japan, putting greater emphasis on cities. By the eighteenth century Edo had a population of nearly 1.5 million, making it the largest city in the world (London at the time had a population of 900,000). Osaka and Kyoto had populations of over half a million.

Over the centuries the growth of Japanese cities produced, as it had in Europe and North America, a wealthy and powerful middle class. By the mid-1800s, these merchants controlled the purse strings of the country, and the power of the shogun declined considerably. When Commodore Perry of the United States and representatives of various European interests (British, French, Russian, Dutch) arrived in the 1850s, intent on opening Japan to Western trade, the shogun had little power to resist.

Amid cries for revolution, the shogun stepped down in 1868. The new 16-year-old emperor, Meiji, urged his country to end centuries of economic isolation and become a modern nation strong enough to resist attempts at colonization. The Japanese responded. In less than half a century, Japan became a world power economically, technologically, and militarily. As people flocked to the cities, a transformation occurred. The following passage from an 1881 guidebook to Tokyo expresses this change:

> A great change has taken place since 1868 in the outward appearance of many parts of the city which were formerly covered with the *yashiki* or mansions of the territorial nobility. Many of these have been pulled down to make room for new official buildings. At the same time the disappearance of the two-sworded men [*samurai*], the displacement of the *palanquin* [an enclosed carriage, carried by people] by the *jin-riki-sha*, the adoption of foreign dress . . . and the European style of wearing the hair, now almost universal, have robbed the streets of the picturesque aspect which was formerly so great an attraction to the foreign visitor. (Quoted in Maraini 1977:84)

Industrialization proceeded throughout the twentieth century. Japan's lack of the natural resources needed to run its industrial machine, as well as its own imperialistic ambitions, led the country into foreign expansion and finally into the disaster of World War II.

Common Legacies

With the exception of some parts of the Middle East, Southeast Asia, and Japan, all of the regions covered in this chapter were colonized. Although the specifics of such colonial control varied (it lasted for a longer period in Latin America than in Africa; it destroyed indigenous culture more thoroughly in Latin America than in Asia), its legacy has been much the same.

Economic Legacies. Colonization left behind an urban system with an underdeveloped economy. As we have seen, in most instances it was a process established for the benefit of a ruling elite and the citizenry of the mother country. Most colonial cities specialized in exports and showed little interest in generating wealth or opportunities for the bulk of the local population or in developing industrial capabilities. Thus, they prospered only to a point and remained relatively small. For example, in 1780, a full two centuries after its founding, Buenos Aires was a city of only 25,000 with few roads and virtually no contact with other cities. Compare this with the postcolonial cities of the United States. Freed of their ties with England, they exploded in population and wealth as they forged links with each other and the westward frontier. However, when independence came for developing countries in the twentieth century, they found their cities well behind Western cities in competitive advantage and without the technical know-how or capability to catch up. Despite their efforts, most are still unable to provide enough jobs or wealth for their populations.

Even in areas of the developing world never colonized directly, economic underdevelopment remains the rule rather than the exception. In noncolonial Southeast Asia (Thailand, for example), urban industrial capacities lag far behind those of the West, primarily because there is no tradition of vital indigenous cities and also because of disadvantageous export-oriented trade agreements with Western countries. In the noncolonial Middle East, the situation is much the same. Although indigenous cities have long existed, the insular policies of Islam and foreign domination of trade in the last century produced cities unable to provide for the growing needs of their populations. (This situation is changing in some countries as oil money continues to pour into the region.)

The only exceptions to this pattern are Singapore, Hong Kong, and Japan. Singapore, by means of its rigid politics, controls its population growth and maintains a steadily rising standard of living. Hong Kong, no longer a British colony, has accomplished the latter goal (though not for all of its people by any means) but not the former. Japan has done both, and this makes Japan unique among these countries. Yet Japan's history is markedly different: It has a tradition of vital indigenous cities, no colonization, a strong commitment to industrialization a century ago, a basically stable political system, and a social structure flexible enough to allow most of its people the chance to improve their standard of living.

Political Legacies. Colonization also left political instability in its wake in many areas of the developing world. The leadership vacuum created by departing elites left the rule of the country either to a foreign-trained native elite or simply "up for grabs" between competing factions. Foreign-trained elites (as in much of Latin America) have typically re-created the limited-opportunity social structure of colonial days—advantageous to the few, difficult for the many. Competing factions (in much of Africa) have typically generated continued violence and unrest in urban areas. All these conditions have further retarded economic growth. What business corporation wants to invest heavily in a city where a coup may cause the loss or nationalization of its entire investment? Ironically, when corporations do invest, often another negative reaction follows. Many regard this type of investment as a contemporary form of colonialism—an alliance between multinational corporations and government elites—and see it as a continuing strategy to exploit the people.

National Boundaries. A third consequence has to do with how little the national boundaries established by the European colonizers related to the territorial boundaries of indigenous populations. The Spanish and Portuguese carved up Latin America in terms of what they were able to conquer, without concern for any native group's natural homeland. As a result, many peoples previously separated by political, linguistic, and other cultural factors for centuries became citizens of a single, newly constructed country. In the same way, the new national boundaries arbitrarily separated some groups who, traditionally sharing a given territory, now found their lands split by the European conquerors. (European powers enforced a similar but much more severe carving-up process in Africa.) When political independence came, many nations had yet one more barrier to rapid entry into the modern world: a local citizenry divided against itself by an artificial historical boundary. (Many analysts see this situation as still contributing to the political instability in many African nations today.)

THE MODERN ERA

The crisis of developing world cities goes beyond economic dependency on other nations. All over the globe, poor countries are experiencing a demographic transition based on falling death rates, with predictable consequences for population size.

Latin American Cities

Most Latin American cities have not followed the pattern of rapid industrialization typical of Europe, Canada, and the United States. Despite a century and a half of independence, in terms of wealth and productive capacity Latin American cities lag far behind the cities of these other regions.

Why? First, from the outset, most Latin American cities were export-oriented. Their valued products or raw materials—gold, silver, cattle, coal, oil, grains, coffee, fruits, wool—were sent to other countries, not consumed by their own populations. The demand by other nations for these goods did not change after independence, and Latin American cities continued such one-way trading. The problem is that selling raw materials generates far less money than processing and marketing finished products. As a result, Latin American cities generated much less wealth than cities that engaged in processing and distributing goods to consumers.

Second, with raw material exports as their primary source of wealth, most Latin American cities never developed much of an industrial base. Modern cities without major industries not only develop fewer jobs for their populations, but also cannot compete on numerous levels (skilled labor, investment opportunities) with cities that have them. Consequently, export-oriented cities simply fall further behind their industrialized counterparts, leading to a worsening gap between "the rich nations" and "the poor nations."

This disadvantageous situation is not simply the result of poor investment policies and lack of foresight on the part of Latin Americans. Many urbanists argue that rich nations and their corporations have contributed significantly to the problem (Geisse and Sabatini 1988; Morse and Hardoy 1993; Greenfield 1994). Still seeking raw materials and cheap labor in Latin America, these countries and corporations have thrown their aid and political support to Latin American governments that favored export over local development. Many Latin American business and government elites have become rich "playing ball" in this way, but this pattern has done little for the overall development of their countries. Thus the old colonial pattern of external domination is preserved in another guise.

Some Latin American countries—particularly Argentina, Brazil, and Mexico—have benefited somewhat by gaining the industrial operations that have been closed down in deindustrializing rich nations such as the United

States. The *maquiladoras* program—creating enterprise zones in which multinational corporations control production and marketing, employ cheap labor, and often receive subsidies from the host nations—has brought some industrialization into these nations' economies. However, the extensive use of female and child labor helps perpetuate a culture of paternalism. Further, automation, together with other modern technology and production techniques, results in these companies' not generating many skilled jobs. Industrial development, therefore, is not creating enough employment opportunities to keep pace with the rural migration to the cities, so shantytowns on the cities' perimeters grow despite industrial development (Fernandez-Kelly 1991).

African Cities

During the colonial era, most African cities grew slowly, hampered like their Latin American counterparts by one-sided trade policies (exporting raw materials at low prices). Only a few cities—coastal ports or mining cities, for example—grew more swiftly, because of their location or because of their special wealth. The post–World War II era ushered in a major change. Four factors coincided, leading to the independence of African nations. First, the oppressive systems of racial segregation and political and economic inequality began to spawn nationalist opposition movements. Second, such movements encouraged the revival of each country's precolonial heritage, long suppressed by Europeans. Third, Africa became a confrontation site for world ideologies. Siding with the Africans in most cases were leftist or Communist countries, prominent among them the former Soviet Union, China, and, later, Cuba. Such countries often equipped local insurgents with arms to fight the colonizers. Finally, colonies were becoming very costly to maintain, both economically and politically, and Europeans were having second thoughts about the whole business.

In the 1960s, 32 former colonies in Africa gained their freedom. In 1960 alone—dubbed the "African Year"—more than 3 million square miles and 53 million of Africa's people saw an end to colonialism (Herskovits 2004). This success only further fueled independence movements, with the result that the retreating colonizers became more and more eager to let go.

In some cases, the aftermath of rapid withdrawal was debilitating political disorder. For decades, Africans had had little experience with political rule, so freedom often unleashed tribal warfare and a succession of military coups. For example, after the hurried Belgian retreat from the Congo in 1960, that country endured five years of bloody civil war as factions warred for control. The civil war and horrendous slaughter in the mid-1990s between the Hutu and Tutsi tribes in the former English colony now known as Rwanda is partly attributable to the same legacy.

In global perspective, Africa is still the least urbanized continent, but it has the highest rate of increase in urbanization. Just 15 percent of the African population lived in cities in 1950, but by 2000, that proportion had more than doubled to 37 percent. Demographers estimate that the number of African urbanites will reach 53 percent by 2030 (U.N. Population Division 2004).

This increase is due to in-migration from the hinterland as well as to natural population increase. Some nations—including Zambia, Zimbabwe, Gambia, Botswana, Kenya, Madagascar, Mauritania, Namibia, and Tanzania—have had success in bringing down fertility rates. Ethiopia, Nigeria, and the Congo, in contrast, have not. Nigeria is presently one of ten countries with over 100 million people, a level that Ethiopia and the Congo will reach within the next 50 years. Tragically, the AIDS epidemic is worst in sub-Saharan Africa, where about two-thirds of the world's HIV infections (30 million cases in 2003) currently exist. In some nations, including Botswana, Lesotho, Swaziland, and Zimbabwe, more than 30 percent of the population is HIV-infected (Dixon 2005). Despite this tragic epidemic, projections are for a sub-Saharan population growth from 752 million in 2005 to 1.1 billion in 2025 (Population Reference Bureau 2005).

Together these factors help explain why Africa is a continent in severe crisis. Aside from Africa's health crisis, much of its population is starving. An example is Niger, a vast land-locked country in central Africa that is twice the size of France. One of the poorest countries in the world, Niger's people have a life expectancy of 46 years. In 2005, about 3.5 million people—more than a third of its total population—experienced dramatic food shortages. No statistic better captures the stunning reality of such poverty than the chilling fact that, across central Africa—from Mauritania in the west to Ethiopia and Somalia in the east—poor children in Africa are twice as likely to die before age five than poor children in the Americas (World Health Organization 2005).

Middle Eastern Cities

The main effects of economic development in the Middle East have been (1) to increase the prominence of coastal cities, downplaying the significance of inland urban areas, and (2) to spark a major migration to all cities. Urban migration, as we have seen in Latin America and Africa, has the effect of taxing the city's capacity to provide for its people. Iran's urban population, for example, increased tenfold—from 4.6 million to 48 million—between 1950 and 2005. More than two-thirds of Iran's 71 million people now live in cities, compared to 27 percent in 1950. The urban population in Syria also grew dramatically in the same time period, going from 1 million to 9.4 million, and from 31 percent to 51 percent of the total population (U.N. Population Division 2003).

Another change has been that the free market economy has created in the Middle East, as elsewhere, a relatively large middle class of affluent entrepreneurs. By and large, this middle class has settled in new and exclusive suburbs outside the old cities.

Finally, rapid urban growth has established a primate-city pattern for the entire region. Tehran, for instance, has outdistanced all other Iranian cities in size, market strength, and problems. In similar fashion, Baghdad, Kuwait City, Damascus, Beirut, Amman, and Cairo dominate their countries. As elsewhere in poor regions, some urbanists see the existence of such primate cities as curbing the growth of other cities and creating virtually insoluble problems.

In short, contemporary Middle Eastern cities are in a period of intense social change. Most are no longer the pure Islamic cities of the past millennium, yet they are not likely to become fully westernized. Like the cities of Latin America and Africa, these cities are in the process of forging a new and complex urban tradition. The emphasis here is on the word *complex*. As Janet Abu-Lughod has argued: "If, at some previous point in time, it was possible to generalize about cities in the wide region encompassed by Arab-Islamic culture, it is clear that such generalizations are no longer realistic" (1984:116).

Abu-Lughod identifies five urbanization patterns in the Middle East. These she calls (1) *neo-colonial,* typified by cities in Tunisia and Morocco; (2) *state socialist,* the urban pattern in Algeria, Iraq, and Syria; (3) *charity cases,* exemplified by cities in countries such as Jordan, Egypt, and Lebanon that are supported by other countries; (4) *oil and sand,* including cities in Libya, Saudi Arabia, and Kuwait; and (5) *fourth world,* cities in countries that are astonishingly poor such as the Republic of Yemen and the Sudan. Such a varied pattern, Abu-Lughod contends, follows from countries and cities of the Middle East being so deeply enmeshed in world economics and politics. In a sense, then, their urban development is not of their own making and is not likely to change drastically in the near future (1984:117).

Asian Cities

As previously mentioned, the complexity of Asian history and culture negates a generalist approach, and so in this section we focus on India, China, Southeast Asia, and Japan.

India.   India's rate of population increase (about 1.7 percent annually) leads demographers to project that its 2005 population of 1.1 billion may grow to more than 2 billion before the increase ends, and that within 30 years India will pass China to become the world's most populous nation. In Uttar Pradesh state (by itself, this region's population of 166 million would make it the sixth largest country in the world), the average woman has five children (U.N. Population Division 2004).

India produces enough food to feed its people—if the food were distributed equally to everyone. But this is not the case. Thus, poverty pushes people off the land and cities pull them in with the promise of a higher standard of living. But many of the urban migrants end up in *bustees,* India's version of the shantytowns we have seen in other poor countries. Here living conditions are often appalling, with people crowded into huts, without heat, safe water, electricity, sewerage, or other normal amenities, and offering inadequate protection from the elements.

Kolkata (Calcutta). Although Kolkata is favorably located for trade in northeastern India, its land slopes away eastward and westward from the Hooghly River to marshes and swamplands, thereby confining the metropolitan area to a strip three to five miles wide on either bank. Reclamation projects, however, have allowed some expansion. With the exception of the grid pattern in the central area where Europeans formerly lived, the narrow roads have a haphazard character. With Kazi Nazrul Islam Avenue as the only express highway and few river crossings, Kolkata's transportation system—like its utilities and municipal facilities—is heavily overburdened. Most of the city's heavily used roads are in poor repair. The 17-mile subway system, completed in 1998, carries an estimated 25 percent of Calcutta's 7 million commuters an alternative to the older trams and buses.

Kolkata remains the world's largest producer of jute, but the city also operates as a port, shipping coal, iron, manganese, mica, petroleum, and tea from its hinterland. However, with a river channel, Kolkata handles

Like many Asian and Middle Eastern cities, Delhi, a city of over 7 million people, suffers from growing pains, as India's growing population increasingly worsens traffic congestion. Streets are typically jammed with some cars, but mostly pedicabs and bicycles, throughout each day as traffic moves at a snail's pace through the many intersections.

only a small share of India's imports and exports. Although it is set in one of the poorest and most overpopulated regions of India, Kolkata's artistic, cultural, and intellectual life thrives. Home to three major universities and known as the "cultural capital" of India, Kolkata is unmatched among Indian cities in the volume of people who flock to its art exhibitions, book fairs, and concerts. But never very far away are hundreds of *bustees,* which contain fully one-third of the city's 11 million residents. Worse off still are the hundreds of thousands of Kolkata's people who are entirely homeless and sleep on the streets or wherever they can find temporary shelter. People dump all manner of human and other refuse into open sewers. Needless to say, disease is widespread.

Mumbai (Bombay).   Not only is Mumbai, a port city on India's west coast, unable to care for its people now, but legions of newcomers continue to stream in from the countryside, where life is even worse. Such migration—the primate-city pattern—depletes the rural areas of people and creates huge cities that are unworkable.

About two-thirds of Mumbai's 15 million residents are concentrated on an island, giving this city one of the highest population densities in the world. Mumbai has another distinction, that of being India's most culturally and religiously diverse city. More than half its residents are Hindu, with the remainder divided among Muslims, Christians, Parsis, Buddhists, Jains, and Sikhs. To make matters more complex, Mumbai's people speak three major languages: Marathi, Gujarati, and Hindi.

The surrounding Black Cotton Soils, India's greatest cotton-growing area, has made Mumbai one of the largest cotton textile centers in the country. This industry employs almost half of Mumbai's factory workers. Most of the rest are employed in the production of silk, artificial fibers, chemicals, and glassware and in the dyeing, bleaching, and printing industries. However, most rural migrants are illiterate and lack industrial skills. Unable to find factory work, they get by as best they can, typically living in deplorable conditions. Perhaps 40 percent of Mumbai's people lack an adequate diet, and virtually everyone contends with an unsanitary environment.

Outlook.   The long-run picture for India's cities may be somewhat brighter. Some real progress has been made in recent years against hunger. In addition, transportation, electricity, and schooling are more widely available than ever before. Some rural areas—notably the Punjab in the north—have become self-sufficient; and smaller cities (under 100,000 people) seem to be faring better than the major cities like Mumbai, Delhi, Kolkata, and Madras. Real economic growth in the 1980s and 1990s permitted a small but significant rise in average living standards.

Production, trade, and investment reforms since 1991 have provided new opportunities for Indian businesspeople and for an estimated 100 to 200 million middle-class consumers. The economy has posted an excellent average growth rate of 7 percent since 1994, reducing poverty by about 10 percentage points. India is capitalizing on its large numbers of well-educated people skilled in the English language to become a major exporter of software services and software workers. Negative factors include the desperate poverty of about one-fourth of the population and the impact of the huge and expanding population on an already overburdened environment. Whether the positive trends and hopes can finally eradicate the urban horrors remains to be seen.

China.   In the 1970s, China introduced major reforms aimed at curbing population growth and stimulating economic growth in order to help Chinese cities "catch up quick." Its controversial "one-child" policy, applying both incentives and pressures to prevent couples from having more than one child, led its leadership in 1995 to boast of great success in reducing its birth rate. Even so, China's 1.3 billion population 2005 may still increase to 1.4 billion before 2020. On the economic front, China allowed cities to introduce private enterprise in an attempt to create a flexible, market-driven economy but one that remained under one-party, centralized political control. As a result, China's gross domestic product has quadrupled since 1978. China now stands as the second largest economy in the world after the United States, although in per capita terms the country is still poor (CIA *World Fact-book* 2005).

Special Economic Zones.

One radical innovation was the establishment of so-called Special Economic Zones, such as the fairly new city of Xiamen in southern China. Xiamen, with a population of 2 million, is so liberalized from the old policies that it seems almost capitalist. The city is a free-trade zone where China's manufacturers can wheel and deal with their Western counterparts without the restrictiveness that characterized the Mao regime. Chongqing, a city with a 4.2 million population, serves as another example. The Beijing government gave the city free rein to make deals with foreign companies and encouraged Chongqing's citizens to use their ingenuity to find ways to make the city more productive. Another city, Guangzhou (4.7 million), is alive with Deng's new spirit of free enterprise. With glittering window displays of cosmetics, fashions, and video appliances, major streets like Dongfanglu look more like Nathan Road in Hong Kong than like anything previously seen in China. On the side streets, private stalls selling clothes, stir-fried food, and household commodities line block after block. Along with Guangzhou's surging economic energies, however, have come some elements that worry hard-line Maoist conservatives. These "evil winds," as the Maoists call them, include open gambling, pool halls, prostitution, a thriving smuggling operation that deals in China's antiquities, and crime. Even if significant economic progress is made, they ask, will the price be too great? Will China's cities exchange one "evil" for another, gaining wealth at the

expense of a citizenry divided against itself—rich against poor, law-abiding against law-breaking—the very divisions the Communist revolution was fought to eliminate? Only time will tell.

Hong Kong.

In 1997, Hong Kong came once again under Chinese sovereignty, returned by Great Britain, which had forced China to cede the 380 square miles after the First Opium War (1840–1842). Located on the southeast coast of mainland China just 80 miles southeast of Canton, Hong Kong has 6.9 million residents, giving it a population density of over 16,000 people per square mile, double that of Los Angeles (U.N. Population Division 2004).

Not surprisingly, overcrowding is omnipresent. Shantytowns, which have virtually disappeared from the People's Republic, house some 15 percent of the city's population, despite determined efforts to provide public housing. Other, particularly older, housing is bursting at the seams. Even the port itself has become a kind of slum, housing hundreds of thousands of the city's poor on Chinese-style boats called junks. In some areas one can literally walk across much of the harbor by simply stepping from one moored junk to another. On one level Hong Kong has been and continues to be very successful. It has become the most important trade port on the China coast other than Shanghai and has generated an industrial machine that is the envy of much of the world, replacing a number of other major manufacturing points. That industrialization, however, together with high population density, has resulted in serious pollution problems. For generations, Hong Kong filtered, but did not chemically treat, its sewage, which was pumped out into Victoria Harbor near the main container terminals. Years of industrial sewage as well as human waste turned the city's "fragrant harbor" both toxic and foul. However, in the late 1990s Hong Kong finally built a real sewerage treatment system in which wastewater is collected from points around Hong Kong's urban center and

Hong Kong, as viewed from Victoria Peak, could easily be mistaken for a North American city from a distance. But even this highly successful city, now under Chinese communist rule after 150 years of English control, contains shantytowns. Some poor residents live in shacks on the city's outskirts while others live in the harbor in Chinese-style boats called "junks."

chemically treated before being dumped back into the sea.

On another level, however, Hong Kong has problems well beyond density and pollution. Many of the city's migrants are extremely poor, and an adequate number of jobs to absorb them is not on the immediate horizon. Perhaps as a result, crime is rampant and growing. Robbery, often accompanied by violence, is commonplace; youth gangs terrorize many of the city's communities; and public and private corruption is rife. If one is not careful to shop in the government-controlled stores, one can easily be sold counterfeit or damaged goods. And an unwary shopper may find in his bag a cheaper item than the one he thought he had bought. Nonetheless, Hong Kong is one of the most successful urban areas in Asia and so far under Chinese Communist control is remaining what it was under British rule.

Southeast Asia.   Unlike India and China, Southeast Asia has little tradition of large indigenous cities. Most of its urban areas are the product of Chinese or European influence within the past few centuries. However, the principal cities of the region— Yangon, formerly Rangoon (in Myanmar, formerly Burma), Bangkok (in Thailand), Ho Chi Minh City (formerly Saigon, in Vietnam), Manila (in the Philippines), Jakarta (in Indonesia), and Singapore (Republic of Singapore)—essentially reflect the themes we have encountered throughout Asia. A few portraits will illustrate.

Singapore.   Situated at the southern end of the Malay Peninsula, Singapore is the largest port in the region and the fourth largest in the world. Despite a dearth of natural resources, it prospers as a center of East–West trade. In 2004, Singapore had a population of 4.2 million, about 77 percent Chinese, 14 percent Malayan, and 8 percent Indian. Eighty-five percent of these people live in the city itself, on 28 square miles of land. Density (15,712 people per square mile) is thus a problem

(U.N. Population Division 2004). To reduce congestion and pollution, the government bans cars from the city center during working hours; only those few with an expensive entry permit may drive into the CBD in the daytime.

As population increased throughout the twentieth century, shantytowns (*kampongs*) and squatter settlements appeared on Singapore's periphery. To alleviate the situation, the government took a novel, if heavy-handed, approach: It ripped up old neighborhoods, constructed thousands of high-rise apartment buildings, and literally forced the city's population into them. Importantly, most residents own or are in the process of purchasing their apartments through a government-incentive program. The process has transformed an old Asian city into an ultramodern one. From a distance, today's Singapore appears Western, with a clearly recognizable downtown and apartment high-rises almost as far as the eye can see. The high-rises have absorbed over four-fifths of the city's population, and each group of well-maintained buildings boasts its own school, parking lot, community center, social facilities center, and lush landscaping. Singapore thrives with its open market–based economy, strong service and manufacturing sectors, and excellent international trading links derived from its history as a **break-of-bulk** port. The manufacturing, financial, and business services sectors dominate economic growth. Exports are booming, led by the electronics sector, particularly U.S. demand for disk drives. In applied technology, per capita output, investment, and labor discipline, Singapore is becoming Southeast Asia's financial and high-tech hub (CIA *World Factbook* 2005).

Significantly, Singapore's population growth is under control. Its growth rate of about 1.6 percent a year is much lower than in almost all other developing world cities. Its success in population control is the product of an all-out attack: Singapore's government made contraceptives and abortion readily available, decreased taxes for families with fewer children, increased educational and housing benefits for small families, and raised hospital costs to families for each additional child.

All of this progress comes at a price: Singapore has a highly autocratic government. For example, residents or businesses in a district marked for redevelopment have no choice but to accept government compensation and leave. Although past practices of suppressing political opposition have ended and the first popular election of a president occurred in 1993, rigid social regulations control people's lives. Violators receive harsh punishments, even for minor offenses—littering is punishable by a heavy fine, and the punishment for drawing graffiti is caning. Singapore thus is a tightly controlled society, but its citizens accept the regimentation and prosper.

Jakarta. Indonesia, lying along the equator between the Asian mainland and Australia, consists of 17,000 islands, of which only 6,000 are inhabited. As the fourth most populous country in the world, Indonesia is the largest Muslim nation. Nearly 80 percent of the country's total population (growing from 79.5 million in 1950 to 223 million in 2005) resides on the three islands of Java, Madura, and Sumatra. As a primate city, Jakarta on the island of Java, with its 9.5 million residents, has a population density of 5,222 persons per square mile, but in Java as a whole the population density is 2,070 persons per square mile (U.N. Population Division 2004). To reduce the strain on severely crowded areas of the archipelago, Indonesia initiated a voluntary transmigration program through which poor, landless families in overpopulated areas move to underdeveloped regions and begin a new life with a house, land, and technical assistance. Since the program started in 1950, more than 12 million Indonesians have relocated, half of them without government sponsorship.

Until surpassed by Singapore in the nineteenth century, the Indonesian capital, Jakarta, was unquestionably the most important city in Southeast Asia. Today, it is a primate city par excellence, with a growing number of high-rise buildings and monumental traffic jams. People migrate to Jakarta for the same reasons they trek to all cities: They want a better life, and the city's booming economy is an attractive lure. Per capita income is $3,500, classifying

Indonesia as a middle-income economy. In 1965, more than 60 percent of Indonesians lived in poverty. By 2000, that figure was about 27 percent. Indonesia has made significant improvements in education, health care, nutrition, and housing over the past quarter century. Another indicator of the potential for improving the quality of life in Jakarta and its hinterland is that, between 1985 and 2005, the total fertility rate dropped from 4.1 to 2.4, thereby bringing Indonesia's population more under control. Although Indonesia remains a poor country in most respects, its rising levels of education and literacy, combined with falling fertility, may help accelerate socioeconomic development and bring greater prosperity to Jakarta and its people (CIA *World Factbook* 2005)

Bangkok.   Like Jakarta, Bangkok is relatively typical of Southeast Asia's cities and serves as the capital of Thailand, a country never colonized. Currently with a population of 6.3 million, the city has more people than all 118 other Thai municipal areas combined. It is also over 16 times as large as Samut Prakan, the country's second-largest city, making Bangkok the premier primate city of the world.

A few figures illustrate the predominance that such primacy causes in Thai affairs. Bangkok contains over three-fourths of the nation's telephones and half its cars, consumes over four-fifths of its electricity, holds three-fourths of all commercial bank deposits, and generates two-thirds of its construction. All automobile roads, railroads, and airplane routes converge on the city (so much so that to go from one place to another you have to go through Bangkok, even if it is out of your way); most Thai universities are in Bangkok, as are all the country's television stations; the city has about 20 daily newspapers (a few other cities have one); and it is the seat of the federal government.

With such advantages, people are still drawn to the city by the millions, further strapping its meager resources. A massive "riverboat culture," much like that in Hong Kong,

A new apartment high-rise building towers over old Thai houses by a lake in central Bangkok. Rapid growth fueled by foreign investment has changed the face of the once-sleepy Thai capital as the country emerges as one of Asia's most vibrant countries. This stark contrast of old and new is a common sight throughout the Asian continent.

houses many of the city's poor. About 20 percent of the city's population—1.3 million—live in slum communities. Population density in the inner city is over 11,000 persons per square kilometer, which is less than the 15,270 reported in 1987. Farther out, but within the city, are about 1,300 persons per square kilometer, and that number is increasing (Bangkok Municipal Administration 2001). Bangkok thus is a city of contrasts. Its population growth intensifies further its over-crowding, traffic jams, and pollution. Yet the city's cultural, economic, and educational opportunities attract many tourists, business leaders, and students.

Comparative Review.   Southeast Asia remains one of the least urbanized areas of the world (see Chapter 1, Table 1–2), yet its urban growth rate is incredible. In the past 20 years Jakarta, Kuala Lumpur (Malaysia), and Hanoi (Vietnam) tripled their populations. In the same period Surabaja (Indonesia), Yangon, Manila, and Ho Chi Minh City doubled theirs. This pattern of overurbanization is not likely to stop, as natural population increase and in-migration continue for the foreseeable future.

Only Singapore seems an exception, both in population growth and in economic self-sufficiency. But this exceptional status is easily explained: Singapore is a city-state in a small area (248 square miles) and it draws population from a limited hinterland. In all other cases, primate cities cannot keep up with staggering growth nor meet obvious needs. Unlike Singapore, they draw population from the whole geographical spans of their countries. For example, people from all over Thailand (almost 200,000 square miles) flock to Bangkok. As a result, overurbanization is rampant, causing a scarcity of jobs and services.

This situation may be typical of Southeast Asia and the developing world generally, but Japan, where we turn next, provides a sharp contrast to the rest of Asia.

Japan.   The economic success of contemporary Japanese cities is remarkable. Government–industry cooperation, a strong work ethic, mastery of high technology, and a comparatively small defense allocation (roughly 1 percent of GDP) helped Japan advance with extraordinary rapidity in the past several decades to become one of the most powerful economies in the world. Another reason for Japan's success lies in its unique combination of the spirit of free enterprise and a collective orientation, where employees hold great loyalty to their companies.

Japan's economic growth, however, has a down side. Exorbitant land costs and expensive housing either force urbanites to live in small-sized dwellings with wall-to-wall lots without any traditional Japanese gardens, or else to commute long distances by subway or commuter rail lines. The typical commuter, forced to live in a satellite town because of high city housing costs, travels $1^1/_2$ hours each way to and from work. During rush hour, commuter lines operate at 250 percent of capacity, necessitating the employment of "pushers" to force additional passengers into overcrowded cars. Heavy automobile traffic clogs the city streets, including the express roads built above the streets because of space limitations.

On the positive side, Japan has established an exemplary health care system, and life expectancy (81.2 years) is among the world's highest. The Japanese have made great gains in reducing crime, unemployment (only 4.7 percent in 2004), and slums. They have set the strictest air pollution standards in the world and, perhaps most important, have controlled their population growth. Japan's success in establishing a high-quality urban life also impresses Western visitors, who express amazement at the tidiness of urban facilities, the reliability of public transportation, and the quality of restaurants.

Thus, the cities and urban life of Japan stand in marked distinction to most of Asia. Their familiar neon lights and thriving central business districts place Japanese cities solidly in the center of society. Indeed, the first-time visitor to Japan, even a visitor from the United States or western Europe, is bedazzled: Tokyo's Ginza district alight at night makes New York's Great White Way and London's Piccadilly Circus seem tawdry in comparison. In Asia, only Hong Kong and Singapore provide partial parallels.

What makes Japan such an exception to the overurbanization–underdevelopment pattern so common elsewhere in the nonindustrial world? At least four factors seem crucial. First, Japan was never colonized. It was thus spared the social indignities and exploitation-oriented urban economy characteristic of so many other regions.

Second, without colonization, Japan was able to generate, maintain, and revitalize numerous urban centers (controlled by different warlords) over the centuries. Although Tokyo–Yokohama is a major primate city, it is only twice the size of the Osaka–Kobe–Kyoto complex and other vital urban centers (Hiroshima and Nagasaki, for example) that exist elsewhere in Japan. All have industrialized effectively, spreading wealth and opportunity throughout the country. This keeps "overload" on a single city to a minimum.

Third, as already mentioned, encouragement of and opportunity for individual and collective advancement within the Japanese social structure is common. Although not everyone is rich, through hard work most Japanese can better their lives economically and socially. This is not the case in urban areas and countries still regulated by caste (India, for example) or by rigid ethnic boundaries. Nor do elites so tightly control access to the higher reaches of the status system that the less fortunate can never hope to better their situation.

Finally, despite past major population increases, Japan's current demographic pattern is distinctly different from patterns in the rest of Asia. Its multi-year low birth rate and current 1.4 total fertility rate means that its total population is shrinking. Because of this, despite its current economic slump, Japan has been able to provide jobs for its citizens and keep the lid on the massive shortage and pollution problems that bedevil many other cities throughout the world.

Common Problems

We have now completed our examination of cities and urban life in those areas in which most of the world's urban population lives. Perhaps the first comparative lesson is that these cities vary enormously from the Western cities with which we are most familiar. The diversity of history, cultural traditions, religion, and politics accounts for these differences.

Thus, Islamic cities of the Middle East are in many respects radically unlike cities of the United States. Equally important, the cities of the developing world—Latin America, Africa, the Middle East, and Asia—vary tremendously among themselves. No brief formula can ever grasp the diversities existing among La Paz, Kano, Kolkata, and Tokyo. However, these diverse cities do share some common concerns.

Spiraling Populations.   Latin America—much more urbanized than Asia or Africa—had a population equal to that of North America as recently as 1950. By 2005, though, the total population in Latin America and the Caribbean had skyrocketed to 559 million, far more than the 329 million people in North America. The growth rate in Latin America dropped from 2.0 percent in 1994 to 1.6 percent in 2005. Still, this level of growth increase (which will increase the population to 805 million by 2050) is considerably higher than the annual percentage increases of Canada (0.3) and the United States (0.6). Throughout Latin America and the Caribbean, the **total fertility rate** or TFR (the average number of children a woman has during her lifetime) was 2.6 in 2005, versus 1.5 in Canada and 2.0 in the United States (Population Reference Bureau 2005).

Should the AIDS epidemic now rampaging through Africa be stopped, population growth (now about 2.3 percent annually) will only increase that much faster, given its 2005 total fertility rate of 5.1, by far the highest in the world (PRB, 2005). In 1990, only six African cities had a population exceeding 1 million; but by 2020 some 30 cities will reach this level. Between Benin City and Accra, demographers anticipate a region containing 25 million inhabitants, with five cities of 1-million-plus people. Accommodating these burgeoning urban populations is a challenge that will require massive investment in infrastructure and social services, as well as wise, talented, and patient leaders (Brockerhoff 2000)

As for Asia—where three-fifths of the world's population live—demographers project that its

2005 population of 3.9 billion, at its present 2.5 TFR, will increase by 1.3 percent annually and reach 4.8 billion by 2025. The growth rate is higher in the Middle East (2.0 percent), where the present TFR of 3.6 will result in its population of 214 million in 2005 increasing to 303 million by 2025 (PRB 2005). By 2030, the urban population will reach 72 percent in the Middle East, 55 percent in Asia, 85 percent in Latin America and the Caribbean, and 54 percent in Africa (United Nations 2004).

In the future, demographers fear, population totals in less-developed countries will soar further. In most of these nations, one-third or more of the population is under the age of 15, so they have not yet entered their childbearing years. Another factor promoting a strong population increase in the LDCs is that scientific advances and technological improvements (vaccinations, better sewage systems, and the like) have brought death rates down sharply. Although this is good news in a basic sense, it also contributes to a bigger problem of overpopulation as time goes on.

Quality of Life. As the cities in poor countries swell in size, they are less and less able to provide sufficient employment and even basic services in water, sanitation, waste removal, gas, electricity, and police and fire protection. In Latin America alone, where only one city exceeded a million people in 1930, 50 cities reached that level by 2000. Most of these cities include large numbers of poverty-stricken people. In 2002, the National Center for Policy Analysis estimated that, over the past two decades, the number of impoverished Latin Americans had increased by 3 percent. In the 1990s, impoverished Latin Americans increased from 200 to 211 million, or roughly 40 percent of the region's population. This poverty is increasingly visible. Almost all Latin American cities are surrounded by *cinturones de miseria,* large belts of extreme poverty often lacking the most basic comforts, infrastructure, and social services. Similarly, in Africa, Asia, and the Middle East, cities struggle with street congestion, overcrowding, an inadequate infrastructure, and pollution.

Many of the less-developed countries are extremely poor—so much so that they simply cannot generate the wealth they need to solve their cities' problems at this time. Chronic underemployment and unemployment characterize many cities—a legacy of historical dependency on one or two trade goods and the lack of a diversified industrial base. One way many nations attempt to improve this situation is by encouraging tourism. A mixed blessing, tourism brings the world's richest citizens into contact with its poorest, a contrast only the most myopic tourists fail to see.

Finally, political corruption, crime, and urban violence are everywhere on the rise. For example, in Lagos, Nigeria, one of Africa's most economically and technologically advanced cities, violent crime is a constant risk and many streets have become so dangerous that few people go out at night. In the Caribbean, Latin America, Africa, and Asia, one can easily become a crime victim in almost any city.

Shantytowns. One of the major problems accompanying rapid urbanization has been the growth of city slums or squatter settlements and shantytowns on the periphery of the cities, as mentioned throughout this section (see the accompanying Urban Living box). They have many names: *bidonvilles* ("tin-can cities") in former French African colonies, *bustees* in India, *los villas miserias* ("cities of the miserable") throughout Latin America, and other names elsewhere. They also take many forms: mud and cardboard shacks outside Seoul, Korea; junks moored in Hong Kong harbor; shacks in Africa and Latin America made from castoff lumber and tin. Their varying names and forms, however, are incidental to one underlying truth: They are the locales of abject poverty, malnutrition, poor sanitation, and disease. A quiet determination, strong family ties, and steadfast hope are often their positive counterparts as the inhabitants cling to the edge of survival, but these shantytowns nonetheless constitute the worst side of urban life in the developing world.

URBAN LIVING

Shantytowns Throughout the World

Africa

The hut was made of corrugated metal set on a concrete pad. It was a 10-by-10 cell. Armstrong O'Brian, Jr. shared it with three other men.

Armstrong and his friends had no water (they bought it from a nearby tap owner), no toilet (the families in his compound shared a single pit latrine), and no sewers or sanitation. They did have electricity, but it was illegal service tapped from someone else's wires and could power only one feeble bulb.

This was Southland, a small shanty community on the western side of Nairobi, Kenya. But it could have been anywhere in the city, because more than half the city of Nairobi lives like this—1.5 million people stuffed into mud or metal huts, with no services, no toilets, no rights. . . .

Outside a mound of garbage formed the border between Southland the adjacent legal neighborhood of Langata. It was perhaps 8 feet tall, 40 feet long, and 10 feet wide, set in a wider watery ooze. As we passed, two boys were climbing the Mt. Kenya of trash. They couldn't have been more than 5 or 6 years old. They were barefoot, and with each step their toes sank into the muck, sending hundreds of flies scattering from the rancid pile. I thought they might be playing King of the Hill. But I was wrong. Once atop the pile, one of the boys lowered his shorts, squatted, and defecated. The flies buzzed hungrily around his legs.

When 20 families—one hundred people or so—share a single latrine, a boy pooping on a garbage pile is perhaps no big thing. But it stood in jarring contrast to something Armstrong had said as we were eating—that he treasured the quality of life in his neighborhood. For Armstrong, Southland wasn't constrained by its material conditions. Instead, the human spirit radiated out from the metal walls and garbage heaps to offer something no legal neighborhood could: freedom.

Asia

In the Bangladesh capital Dhaka, three million people—one-third of the city's population—live in slums. The working poor, who are most of the slums' inhabitants, earn their living as construction or factory workers, lorry drivers, rickshaw pullers, or work in informal sectors as domestic helpers or trash pickers.

One shantytown, named No. 2 Pura Basti or Burned Slum after it was damaged in a fire 15 years ago, is a cluster of tin and bamboo shacks that line narrow cobbled lanes flanked by open gutters. The shacks have electricity, but no running water or gas supply. The women cook food over wood-fired earthen stoves outside their shacks.

❖ ━━━━━━━ ❖ ━━━━━━━ ❖

SUMMARY: WORLD URBANIZATION IN PERSPECTIVE

In decades past, social scientists debated whether economic growth was preferable to the preservation of local urban traditions. People taking the preservationist position usually argued, quite convincingly, that "creeping Westernization" by way of industrialization and foreign-oriented trade was rapidly obliterating ancient urban traditions, valuable not only to their peoples but also to the world as

Just a few years ago, the only sources of water for the slum's 500 families were wells and an intermittent supply from an illegally connected tap to the city's water utility. For drinking water, the women and children had to wait in line for up to two hours to collect a pitcher or bucket of water from a local market or nearby houses where they often had to bribe guards and caretakers, or pay exorbitant prices. Today they use water from wells dug behind their shacks for bathing and washing, but for drinking and cooking, they get "safe" water from the slum's "water point"—two hand pumps that draw water from an underground reservoir that is filled with piped water supplied by Dhaka's water utility.

About four years ago, the Dhaka city corporation, which owns the land, paved the slum's dirt lanes and installed some community toilets. But these basic latrines, which are concrete rings set in the ground without any water or flushing facilities, drain into an open gutter, which in turn is linked to a nearby pond. The area reeks of garbage and human waste. Nearly 200–300 people, carrying pots of water, wait in long queues to use the toilets each morning, and children and the elderly, who cannot make it on time, defecate in the gutters outside their homes.

Latin America

In severely overcrowded Mexico City, one-third of its residents lack such essential services as electricity and sewage facilities. Most are squatters who live anywhere they can: in abandoned boxcars or shacks teetering on hillsides, in public parks, in roadside hovels. About a quarter-million people live illegally in 360 shantytowns built on property they don't own. Or at least, they don't own it yet, since Mexican law gives squatters property ownership rights after five years' occupancy.

Squatters often live without drainage, with frayed electric cables hooked illegally into the city's electricity grid, and drinking water from buckets or leaky rubber hoses. A fire apparently sparked by illegal electric hookups swept through about 100 shacks in "The Last Hope" squatters' camp in an industrial area of downtown Mexico City in 1998. No serious injuries were reported. Most area residents didn't even know the tarpaper shacks had been built between two factories until the squatters' burned possessions were shoveled into the street.

The problem isn't confined to the capital. A fire, also resulting from an illegal electric hookup, swept through a shantytown in Juarez in 2003, killing four women. Another similarly caused fire swept through a public market in Durango in 2004.

Sources: Adapted from numerous sources, including Robert Neuwirth. *Shadow Cities: A Billion Squatters, A New Urban World.* London: Routledge, 2004, pp. 3, 5; Mallika Wahab, "Bangladesh Slums Demand Access to Clean Water," *International Journal of Humanities and Peace* 19 (2003): 46–47; Chris Hawley, "Trying to Exorcise Mexico's 'Little Devils'," *Arizona Republic* (December 20, 2004).

examples of the alternative forms that the urban process could take.

Although the preservation argument has lost none of its appeal today, the simple fact is that most cities in the developing world are inundated with so many people that they cannot provide adequately for their populations without major advances in economic vitality and technological efficiency. Already—as we have seen perhaps most dramatically in Kolkata—millions upon millions of the world's urban dwellers are suffering tremendous deprivation. Moreover, some of the large cities in developing nations have become so crowded

African shantytowns, like their Latin American counterparts, typically exist through-out the continent on the outskirts of cities. These *bidonvilles* have a different name from similar places elsewhere but they are still squatter settlements and pose the same health, economic, and psychological problems found in other slum settle-ments in the developing world.

and polluted that they are straining carrying capacity of their environment.

Once again, the city is literally transform-ing our world, as it has twice before. In Chapter 2 we spoke of the first and second urban revolutions—the first occurring when people moved into cities in large numbers for the first time, from approximately 8000 to 2000 B.C.E.; the second occurring during the capitalist and industrial revolutions, which began around 1700 C.E. and continued through the first half of the twentieth century. This second urban revolution was responsible for a demographic transition—an unprece-dented growth in population, made possible by the city's ability to provide a higher level of income, technological efficiency, and health care than rural areas. Now, once again, the city is fostering a demographic transition, only this time with two differences: (1) The greatest

population growth is not in the developed world but in developing countries, and (2) the magnitude of the change makes the demo-graphic transition of the 1700–1950 period look meager by comparison. This is the third urban revolution. No one ever expected the kind of growth we are seeing now.

Consider this: A generation or two ago, one correctly thought of more-developed countries as the locales of the world's largest metropolitan areas, or **urban agglomerations** as they are sometimes called. No more: Rapid growth and urban migration already have moved numerous developing world cities into this category, as the first column of Table 13–1 shows. The shift to developing world dominance becomes even more pro-nounced when we consider the longer term (Table 13–1, right-hand columns). The only Western city in the top ten is New York and

TABLE 13–1   The World's Ten Largest Urban Agglomerations, 2003 and 2015

2003		2015	
Urban Area	**Population**	**Urban Area**	**Population**
Tokyo, Japan	35,000,000	Tokyo, Japan	36,200,000
Mexico City, Mexico	18,700,000	Mumbai (Bombay), India	22,600,000
New York, USA	18,300,000	Delhi, India	20,900,000
São Paulo, Brazil	17,900,000	Mexico City, Mexico	20,600,000
Mumbai (Bombay), India	17,400,000	São Paulo, Brazil	20,000,000
Delhi, India	14,100,000	New York, USA	19,700,000
Kolkata (Calcutta), India	13,800,000	Dhaka, Bangladesh	17,900,000
Buenos Aires, Argentina	13,000,000	Jakarta, Indonesia	17,300,000
Shanghai, China	12,800,000	Lagos, Nigeria	17,000,000
Jakarta, Indonesia	12,300,000	Kolkata (Calcutta), India	16,800,000

Source: United Nations Population Division, *World Urbanization Prospects,* 2003.

by 2015 the projections are that it will drop from third to sixth place. Next, look at the magnitude of the urban areas in the 2015 column: The smallest one is larger than five of the top ten cities in the 2000 column. These will truly be **megacities,** unprecedented in human history.

CONCLUSION

Thus we come, at the end of this overview of global urbanization, to no single solution to the problems we have encountered. Scholars themselves are divided about the causes and the most efficient solutions.

One conclusion, however, seems certain. Whatever is done, most cities of the developing world are going to continue to grow at enormous rates for the foreseeable future. With this growth will come, inevitably, greater problems, including congestion, pollution, and major shortages of basic necessities. As each country copes with its crises, perhaps one, or a combination of two or more, of the solutions we have discussed will emerge as clearly superior, thereby lightening the load on other overburdened cities some decades hence.

It is no small task. Millions of poor people in less-developed countries are unable to advance greatly because, given the ever-increasing population, there simply will not be enough jobs, houses, or health services to go around. The evolution of developing world cities thus provides a marked contrast to that of European and North American cities. Perhaps the most remarkable aspect has been the speed at which their modern development has taken place—in decades compared with more than a century in Canada and the United States. So-called *overurbanization* in the developing world may well get a good deal worse before it gets better.

The evolving cities throughout the developing world each have their own complex cultural traditions and unique histories. Previously we discussed how Herbert Gans stressed the primacy of culture over space in detailing the variety of lifestyles *within* a city (Chapter 10), and how cultural values shape a city's physical and social form (Chapter 8). In this chapter we saw how cities throughout the developing world may share some common legacies and problems but are also different in many ways from one place to another. The expanding global economy and telecommunications networks will link these cities more closely to one another than ever before, but they will also evolve through varied patterns of development, each nation's cities with its own distinct characteristics.

KEY TERMS

Apartheid
Break-of-bulk
Colonization
Megacities
Primacy ratio
Primate cities
Total fertility rate
Urban agglomerations

CHAPTER 14

PLANNING THE URBAN ENVIRONMENT

As we have seen, cities do not always work well. Occasionally a city may approach its potential as a "pinnacle of human civilization" (some historians say this about Hellenic Athens, for example), but, typically, cities struggle with various problems like those detailed in the last four chapters.

In this chapter we will introduce the work of individuals who responded to the shortcomings of cities with bold and provocative plans for improvement. Some tackled urban problems at the neighborhood level; others imagined radically transforming the entire city—or even society as a whole.

As anyone would expect, such plans have been controversial, frequently challenging cherished cultural beliefs or clashing with vested economic interests. However, only by giving these ideas serious consideration can we keep all the possibilities alive in the urban debate.

VISIONS

In the late 1800s, what a vision Ebenezer Howard had! Deeply influenced by Edward Bellamy's novel *Looking Backward* (a utopian vision of the year 2000 in which all the problems of the city had been solved), Howard dedicated his life to realizing Bellamy's goal in Britain. As Howard saw it, the industrial city was a virtual nightmare: People streamed to these overcrowded cities, leading only to misery and despair.

Howard conceded that the city had advantages—opportunity, entertainment, diversity—but he asked why cities should deny people the best of the country—a healthful environment, low densities, and a sense of freedom. Thus, Howard set out to solve this dilemma by creating what he called the "Garden Cities of Tomorrow." In 1898, he wrote:

> The two magnets must be made one. As man and woman by their varied gifts and faculties supplement each other, so should town and country. The town is the symbol of society—of mutual help and friendly co-operation, of fatherhood, motherhood, brotherhood, sisterhood, of wide relations. . . . The country is the

symbol of God's love and care. . . . All that we are and all that we have comes from it. Our bodies are formed of it; to it they return. We are fed by it, clothed by it, and by it we are warmed and sheltered. . . . It is the source of all health, all wealth, all knowledge. . . . Town and country must be married, and out of this joyous union will spring a new hope, a new life, a new civilization. (1898; 1965:48)

Celebrating the "marriage of town and country," Howard worked out the details of his **garden cities** plan and hoped to convince others that realizing his plan was not only desirable but entirely possible. The specific outline of his vision is illustrated in Figure 14–1 and described in the Critical Thinking box on page 412.

Unfortunately, Howard's vision was a vision that many of his contemporaries could not understand. It struck conservatives as outlandish and liberals as too complex. Said the ultraliberal *Fabian News:*

> Mr. Howard proposes to pull [our cities] all down and substitute garden cities, each duly built according to pretty colored plans, nicely designed with a ruler and compass. . . . We have got to make the best of our existing cities, and proposals for building new ones are about as useful as would be arrangements for protection against visits from Mr. [H. G.] Wells' Martians [a reference to Wells's novel *The War of the Worlds,* which depicts a Martian invasion of earth]. (Quoted in Osborn 1965:11)

Undaunted, Howard pushed on. In 1903, in conjunction with a group of businessmen, he established his first garden city, Letchworth, about 35 miles from London. A second city, Welwyn (pronounced "well-en"), sprang up nearer London in 1919. On balance, both were quite successful. Still, until the 1940s, they remained Britain's only attempts at "planned" towns.

The entire history of urban planning is in many ways evident in the story of Howard's new towns. As the *Fabian News* noted, to alter established cities would be a massive, expensive, and disruptive undertaking. Cities are not only bricks and mortar, they are people's

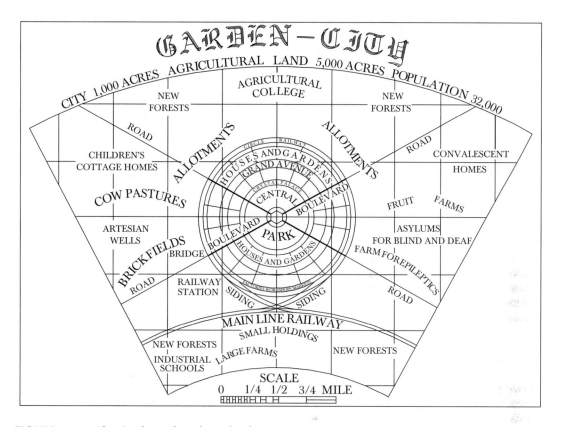

FIGURE 14–1   The Garden Belt and Rural Belt. [*Source:* Ebenezer Howard, *Garden Cities of To-Morrow* (Cambridge, MA: MIT Press, 1965), p. 52. Reprinted by permission of MIT Press.]

lives, and rest on historical traditions, entrenched power relationships, and vested economic interests. No one should be surprised that plans for urban redesign have typically been greeted with suspicion. Moreover, given the consequences of *bad* city planning, this is not a task to be undertaken lightly.

CITY PLANNING IN WORLD HISTORY

Ebenezer Howard was hardly the first to undertake urban planning on a large scale. Moenjo-Daro, the Indus River Valley civilization of 2500 B.C.E. discussed in Chapter 2, had streets laid out in a grid pattern, broad thoroughfares, and individual houses designed for comfort and efficiency. Even more impressive were the Mexican cities of Teotihuacan around 700 C.E. and Tenochtitlan around 1500 C.E. Both capitals were large and richly symbolic. Expansive plazas, massive temples, and elaborate gardens were central features of these cities. Finally, recall the case study in Chapter 8, where we discussed the tightly controlled plan of Ming Dynasty Peking. Here we saw planned city within planned city, all connected to convey key themes of China's culture.

Western cities too show a long history of planning. The Greeks planned Hellenic Athens, just as the Romans planned much of the pomp and majesty of Imperial Rome. Even towns of the Middle Ages show some planning, especially in the walls built for

CRITICAL THINKING

Sir Ebenezer Howard's Garden Cities of To-Morrow

Howard's Garden City was to cover about 1,000 acres at the center of a 6,000-acre tract. Figure 14–1 shows the idealized layout of the whole municipal area.

Six magnificent boulevards—each 120 feet wide—traverse the city from centre to circumference, dividing it into six equal parts or wards. In the centre is a circular space containing about five and a half acres, laid out as a beautiful and well-watered garden; and, surrounding this garden, each . . . in its own ample grounds, are the larger public buildings—town hall, principal concert and lecture hall, theatre, library, museum, picture-gallery, and hospital.

The rest of the large space encircled by the "Crystal Palace" is a public park, containing 145 acres, which includes ample recreation grounds within very easy access of all the people. Running all round the Central Park (except where it is intersected by the boulevards) is a wide glass arcade called the "Crystal Palace," opening on to the park. Here manufactured goods are exposed for sale, and here most of that class of shopping which requires the joy of deliberation and selection is done. The space enclosed by the Crystal Palace is, however, a good deal larger than is required for those purposes, and a considerable part of it is used as a Winter Garden—the whole forming a permanent exhibition of a most attractive character, whilst its circular form brings it near to every dweller in the town—the furthest removed inhabitant being within 600 yards.

Passing out of the Crystal Palace on our way to the outer ring of the town, we cross Fifth Avenue—lined, as are all the roads of the town, with trees—fronting which, and looking on to the Crystal Palace, we find a ring of very excellently built houses, each standing in its own ample grounds; and, as we continue our walk, we observe that the houses are for the most part built either in concentric rings, facing the various avenues (as the circular roads are termed), or fronting the boulevards and roads which all converge to the centre of the town. . . . [T]he population of this little city may be . . . about 30,000 in the city itself, and about 2,000 in the agricultural estate. . . .

On the outer ring of the town are factories, warehouses, dairies, markets, coal yards, timber yards, etc., all fronting on the circle railway, which encompasses the whole town, and which has sidings connecting it with a main line of railway which passes through the estate. This arrangement enables goods to be loaded direct into trucks from the warehouses and workshops, and so sent by railway to distant markets, or to be taken direct from the trucks into the warehouses or factories; thus not only effecting a very great saving in regard to packing and cartage, and reducing to a minimum loss from breakage, but also, by reducing the traffic on the roads of the town, lessening to a very marked extent the cost of their maintenance. The smoke fiend is kept well within bounds in Garden City; for all machinery is driven by electric energy, with the result that the cost of electricity for lighting and other purposes is greatly reduced.

Source: Ebenezer Howard, *Garden Cities of To-Morrow* (Cambridge, MA: MIT Press, 1965), pp. 50–56.

protection as well as in the various "zones" set aside for specific activities. There were planned markets, squares, residential quarters, and, always, the medieval church at the city's center.

Still later, during the Renaissance, there arose a veritable boom in urban planning, with careful efforts to achieve efficient traffic circulation and also to provide fortification against invasion. It was at this time that planners designed the radial boulevards of Paris—roadways as beautiful as they are practical.

Why Plan?

Early city planners sought, first, *to solve specific urban problems.* They planned underground sewage lines for health reasons, walls for protection, parks for leisure hours, and thoroughfares to facilitate movement.

Second, we know that the motives of city planners in Rome, Teotihuacan, Tenochtitlan, and Beijing were also *to glorify those in power.* Thus, the Emperor Augustus and his successors, declared gods by the Roman Senate in the first few decades of the Christian era, were "immortalized" by buildings, parks, plazas, and innumerable statues. City planners had a good reason to glorify the ruling elite: These people, after all, employed them. City planning, in short, often proceeds "from the top down." To ask "Why plan?" then, we also need to keep in mind another question: "For whom are cities planned?"

A third focus of urban planning is often the *glorification of important cultural values.* Ming Peking was not only a monument to the all-powerful emperor, but also a reminder to

everyone of beliefs central to the Chinese way of life. Centuries later, during the Renaissance, the residency of the pope was reestablished in Rome. To showcase the Church as the wealthiest and most important institution in the Western world, Pope Julius decided to replace the old St. Peter's Basilica with the greatest cathedral and piazza in Christendom. The result was the large, grand Piazza of St. Peter. A long processional way leads the visitor to a massive circular area before the cathedral, which leads to the cathedral itself. The faithful find a powerful religious experience in this setting; everyone is awed by the size and magnificent design of St. Peter's. Both reactions were important to the piazza's designers.

Something different is symbolized in Figure 14–2, showing Sir Christopher Wren's plan for the rebuilding of London after the Great Fire of 1666 (see the Chapter 2 case study). Here, although the magnificent St. Paul's Cathedral (B) is a dominant focus, major roads lead not to the cathedral but to the city's stock exchange (A). The dominant feature of the plan (which ultimately was not adopted) was the financial and trade element of the city's life. London at the time was fast becoming the most powerful economic center in the world. City planning thus reflected this change.

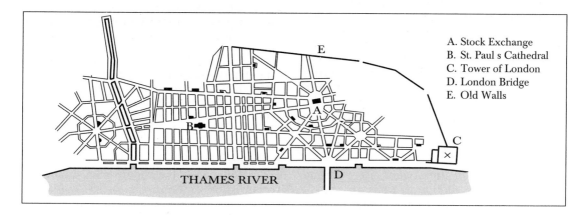

FIGURE 14–2 Sir Christopher Wren's Plan for the Rebuilding of London, 1666 [*Source:* Arthur B. Gallion and Simon Eisner, *The Urban Pattern,* 4th ed. (New York: Van Nostrand, 1980), p. 43. Reprinted by permission of Van Nostrand Reinhold.]

Three concerns, then, appear again and again in the history of urban design. People plan their cities, or parts of them, (1) to solve specific problems, (2) to serve the interests of those with wealth and power, and (3) to reflect and intensify cultural ideals.

Planning in the Industrial Era: 1800–1900

Ebenezer Howard shared many concerns about the overcrowded industrial cities with the classical sociological theorists—Tönnies, Durkheim, Weber, Marx, Simmel, Park, and Wirth—whom we discussed in Chapter 5. Howard saw little hope for the industrial city, which he believed was a monument to greed and to the interests of the few rather than the many. Effective city planning, he believed, could never exist in cities of such size.

In many ways, he was right. Planning on a citywide scale did not exist in early cities. While quite a few industrial towns were built during the 1800s—Manchester and Birmingham in England and Paterson, New Jersey, and Falls River, Massachusetts, in the United States (see Chapter 3) are good examples—by and large the underlying concern was limited to profit and efficiency.

Back in the early 1600s when the Dutch settled New Amsterdam at the tip of Manhattan Island, street development evolved more or less haphazardly, as in medieval European cities. But as the city expanded northward two centuries later, city leaders in 1807 adopted a rigid gridiron plan that they applied to the entire island regardless of topography. Profit and efficiency carried the day: "Straight-edged and right-angled houses," reported the city commission, when adopting the gridiron plan, "are the most cheap to build and the most convenient to live in" (Eisner, Gallion, and Eisner 1993:49).

In the new trade-dominated city, tradition counted for little. Buildings went up only to be torn down as commercial interests dictated. Builders adopted architectural styles, such as Greek facades, "for show," and not for their deeper symbolism of a revered historic tradition (Goldberger 1989:xiv). With the major (and wonderful) exception of Central Park, the profit motive fundamentally shaped all of New York. The Boston Commons park in midtown Boston is another notable exception.

The "City Beautiful" Movement

In the United States, some architects, planners, and civic leaders had other ideas. The first significant innovation in U.S. city planning grew out of the 1893 Chicago World's Fair, which showcased architect Daniel Burnham's "White City" (a vision opposing grimy, sooty industrial cities). Burnham proposed a city built around monumental civic centers, with careful zoning and active citizen participation groups. Inspiring a **City Beautiful movement,** Burnham's ideas had considerable influence among urban planners across the country. Chicago, Cleveland, Detroit, Los Angeles, Minneapolis, St. Louis, San Francisco, and Washington all initiated City Beautiful projects after the fair.

Yet the costs of this movement soon led even advocates to scale back their plans. Moreover, some private interests, especially businesses, resisted compromising their narrow objectives. Before long, the City Beautiful movement simply went away.

"TILL WE HAVE BUILT JERUSALEM": THE NEW TOWNS MOVEMENT

> I will not cease from mental strife,
> Nor shall my sword sleep in my hand,
> Till we have built Jerusalem
> In England's green and pleasant land
>
> William Blake

This stanza from the great English poet and artist William Blake opens Sir Ebenezer Howard's book *Garden Cities of To-Morrow*. Howard's belief that his New Town movement would solve all of urban society's ills influenced many others both in and beyond his native England.

A Socialist–Feminist New Town

Howard greatly influenced Alice Constance Austin, an upper-class radical from Santa Barbara, California. Convinced that women were greatly oppressed, Austin proposed in the early 1900s a series of new towns based on communal living and kitchenless houses. Only a "Socialist City," she maintained, could relieve women "of the thankless and unending drudgery of an inconceivably stupid and inefficient system, by which her labors are confiscated. . . ." (1935:63).

With help from co-investors, Austin founded her new town, Llano del Rio, in California. But, like Howard, she soon found that such a venture was fraught with difficulties. After a brief tenure, the Llano group folded in 1917. Although they later resettled in New Llano, Louisiana, Austin's Socialist City movement never attained further success (Hayden 1978:286–87).

Later New Towns in Great Britain

The devastation of London during World War II created a desperate housing shortage and renewed interest in Ebenezer Howard's vision. In 1946, Britain passed the New Towns Act, providing for government sponsorship of new urban communities to draw population away from London and other cities. New communities—complete with industrial, housing, and commercial areas—were built at some distance from larger cities.

Another central goal of the New Towns Act was to limit London's increasing sprawl by surrounding the city with a **green belt**—an idea taken directly from Howard. The new towns were to be built beyond the green belt.

In all, Great Britain built 34 new towns, their success in large measure assured because of deep government involvement. The first group of new communities—called the Mark I towns—adhered closely to Howard's ideas and were modeled after Letchworth and Welwyn. Mostly single-family houses organized in neighborhoods, these communities of about 30,000 residents each were completely self-sufficient

centers of industry, housing, education, and transportation facilities.

A second wave of new towns—the Mark II group—was begun in the 1950s and 1960s and deviated rather significantly from Howard's original plan. Typified by Cumbernault, outside Glasgow, Scotland, these towns reflected the government's concern that small cities of just 30,000 would do little in the long run to alleviate population problems in the larger cities. A second concern was that too many small towns would eat up too much of what Britain had too little of—land. Thus, the Mark II towns, with population projections of 80,000, began to sacrifice greenery for density and to emphasize central (rather than neighborhood) shopping and recreational facilities. The most recent new towns are larger still. One example, Milton Keynes, lies 50 miles north of London with a population of about 178,000 living in its 120 square miles, and it is expected to grow to 300,000 by 2030.

Britain's **new towns,** Howard's "marriage of the city and country," proved eminently successful at providing decent housing and sufficient jobs. On other levels, however, the new towns fell short. With their small number (34) and limited size, they have not had much impact on the large populations of Britain's large cities. Moreover, most of these towns are socially rather cliquish, with the same ethnic and class prejudices encountered in most large cities. Some critics claim that homogeneity is a product of the planning process itself, with its emphasis on neighborhoods. As sociologists often note, ingroup solidarity (which neighborhood living facilitates) often creates a corresponding sense of outgroup hostility.

Another problem has been the inflexibility of many new-town plans. Rather than recognizing that cities are dynamic entities that must adjust to changing human needs, many new towns stuck rigidly to their original plans. The result often has been a sense of inefficiency and even oppression that, as we will see, crops up again and again in city planning efforts.

Although London suburbs often contain single detached houses in close proximity to one another, these locales usually also contain a mixture of building types, such as this block of rowhouses, or else a high-density area with multiple-family dwellings. Such combinations of housing are in keeping with the new towns concept of comprehensive planning of a community.

New Towns in Western Europe, Australia, and Brazil

To some degree, early British new towns were anti-city. They were small towns, their limited size suggesting a distinct dislike of large urban areas. They were also anti-growth, strictly limiting population in the belief that more was always less. Bigness was equated with disorder and the destruction of a delicate ecological balance between people and the environment. Several more recent new towns, however, take a very opposite view. In France, the Netherlands, and Spain, new-town development attempted to stimulate the growth of an entire urban region. Creating jobs around a cluster of industries, the new communities draw population from the countryside while also luring away

people from nearby established cities. In the mid-1960s, for example, France developed five new towns near Paris, and others near Lille, Lyon, Marseille, and Rouen, in an effort to collect the population in the immediate area and lessen migration into those older cities.

Sweden. The Scandinavian countries, particularly Sweden, look on new towns as a form of "suburb control." Stockholm, like many European and North American cities, had a problem with suburban sprawl in the 1950s. In an effort to curb decentralization, the Swedish government planned a series of satellite cities linked to the central city and to each other by efficient transportation. The five cities, known as the Vallingby Complex, are distinct entities but look to the larger city for goods, many services, and jobs. Each of these small cities has about 10,000 people living in low-density housing within 300 yards of a subway-station/plaza complex.

As in Britain, the Swedes also built higher-density new towns. Instead of low-rise brick buildings that promote a sense of community and allow open space, the newer towns contain physically parallel rows of unattractive, look-alike, concrete-slab buildings of six to eight stories. These drab structures look much like sterile, low-income housing projects in the United States. Not surprisingly, these developments repel the middle class; only impoverished immigrants or low-income natives concentrate in them. Such places can also be found in France, Germany, and Italy, and there, as well as in Sweden, crime, drugs, and welfare dependency are common.

Australia. Australia presents us with a different new town, one designed to be the core of a new urban region and home to the national government. Located in the outback (isolated rural area), Canberra is some 180 miles from the seacoast metropolis of Sydney. Settled as early as 1912, Canberra was to be a new, inland city that would not only house the Australian government but would also develop the Australian hinterland. This was no simple task. Canberra was far from Australia's normal trade routes and had no major resources (mineral deposits or cheap water power) to attract investors. Thus, government and planners were in complete control, which might well have pleased Ebenezer Howard.

The result is a physically beautiful city with a population now exceeding 353,000. Economically, however, the city has suffered because of its off-track location, unavoidable over-reliance on a single activity (government services), and the implementation of relatively rigid plans that often put off business-people. For example, the government retains control of all land, so that businesses do not cluster near the center but are scattered throughout the city—a pattern that many find inefficient.

Canberra's widely dispersed single-family dwellings have also hindered the development of a sense of community. Similarly, the city's dependence on one major employer—the government—essentially created an upper- and middle-class city. Because of the high cost of living, most low-income families simply cannot afford to live there.

Brazil. Brasilia, the inland capital of Brazil, presents a contrasting case. Conceived in the 1950s as a showcase for a modernizing Brazil, the city is about 600 miles from the coastal megalopolis of Rio de Janeiro. As with Canberra, Brasilia's location helped develop the nation's interior, with the intent of siphoning off population from the country's older cities.

An artificial lake surrounds much of the city and separates it from the suburban towns to the north. The cross-shaped plan of the central city, designed by the Brazilian architect Lúcio Costa, utilizes the North–South Axis, Brasilia's main transportation artery, and the East–West, or Monumental, Axis, lined by federal and civic buildings.

With just 12,000 people in 1957, Brasilia grew to more than 500,000 by 1970 and now exceeds 2 million. Expanding faster than anticipated as people streamed into the city looking for construction jobs, Brasilia abandoned or modified many parts of the original plan. As elsewhere in poor nations, migrants unable to find adequate housing constructed their own out of anything they could find. Thus Brasilia evolved huge *favelas* or squatter shantytowns filled with working-class and poverty-stricken people and lacking waste removal, water, and electricity. Ironically, then, this "model" Brazilian city reflects all the problems that beset other Latin American cities.

All the new towns and cities considered so far were government sponsored, with limited involvement of private investors. During the early history of the United States, government-planned communities were not unusual and included Williamsburg; Washington, D.C.; Indianapolis; Raleigh, North Carolina; Tallahassee, Florida; and Austin, Texas. However, except for one program in the 1930s, U.S. new towns in the past 100 years relied on a nearly complete dependency on the ideals, plans, and investments of private businesses.

When first conceived and built in the 1950s, Brasilia was a stark example of modern architecture lacking in people-friendly usage and, for that matter, even people, as few chose to live there. Now its population exceeds two million, much of its original plan has been scrapped, and squatter settlements ring this "model" city now exhibiting many of the urban ills found elsewhere.

New Towns in the United States

We begin with the exceptions to the rule. Only three government-built new towns exist, all with their origins in the Great Depression of the 1930s, when millions of Americans were out of work.

In 1935, President Franklin Delano Roosevelt signed the Emergency Relief Appropriation Act and the National Industrial Recovery Act. One of the provisions of these acts was a federally sponsored project called "Greenbelt Towns." As its name implies, the project was deeply influenced by Ebenezer Howard. Its stated objectives:

1. To give useful work to men on unemployment relief;
2. To demonstrate in practice the soundness of planning and operating towns according to certain garden city principles;
3. To provide low-rent housing in healthful surroundings, both physical and social, for

families in the low-income bracket. (Stein 1957:119)

The three towns constructed as part of the project were Greenbelt, Maryland (13 miles northeast of Washington, D.C.); Greendale, Wisconsin (7 miles from Milwaukee); and Green Hills, Ohio (5 miles north of Cincinnati). Planners had high hopes that these towns would help to solve big-city problems and create the jobs needed to help end the Depression.

But the hopes faded. Unlike new towns in Great Britain, these settlements never attracted their own industry. Built before the age of superhighways, they simply did not provide enough economic incentive for major industry to relocate there. Then, too, soon after the towns were started, World War II intervened, diverting funding to military objectives. And by the time the war was over, the Cold War was upon us, leading many to charge that government-sponsored towns smacked of "communism." By 1949, government began selling off the new towns to private interests. The Greenbelt Towns became, and remain, more like suburbs of the large cities nearby than like the independent small cities they were envisioned to be.

After World War II, architects and private developers created more than 100 new urban environments in an attempt to follow Howard's approach. Among them were Baldwin Hills (now part of Los Angeles); Park Forest and Park Forest South near Chicago; Jonathan, Minnesota; and St. Charles, Maryland. However, most of the so-called American garden cities—despite containing elements of Howard's vision, such as shared public space—lack their own industry and so are essentially middle-class suburban developments, not "new towns" as Howard proposed.

What might have been a new town fitting the Howard model—Soul City, North Carolina, championed by civil rights activist Floyd McKissick—became an unrealized dream when the federal government withdrew financial support and the economic recessions of the 1970s dissuaded major industries from locating in a rural community. Nevertheless, Soul City foreshadowed the New Urbanism movement discussed in Chapter 12 in designing "unified, mixed-use urban spaces that include multicultural neighborhoods, and that cater to families of differing economic backgrounds" (Strain 2004:70).

Among the best known U.S. "new towns" are Radburn, New Jersey; Reston, Virginia; Columbia, Maryland; Irvine, California; and Celebration, Florida.

Radburn.   Developed by architect and planner Clarence Stein (see his classic *Toward New Towns for America* published in 1957), Radburn—about 20 miles west of New York City—was a direct attempt to adapt Ebenezer Howard's garden city to the United States. Radburn is laid out using what Stein called "superblocks," each surrounded by a green space. Radburn also attempted to completely separate pedestrian and automobile traffic. Stein and cofounder Henry Wright planned

access roads only for service purposes and built houses facing the inner green areas. In 1929 Geddes Smith described Radburn as follows:

> [It is a] town built to live in—today and tomorrow. A town "for the motor age." A town turned outside-in—without any backdoors. A town where roads and parks fit together like the fingers of your right and left hands. A town in which children need never dodge motor-trucks on their way to school. (As quoted in Stein 1957:44)

Like so many new towns, however, Radburn ran into financial difficulties as the years passed and was never completed as originally planned. About 670 families live in Radburn today, creating a population of about 3,100 within the New Jersey borough of Fair Lawn. On the other hand, Reston and Columbia, both near Washington, D.C., overcame economic crises to achieve moderate success as separate entities.

Reston.   Twenty-five miles from downtown Washington, in suburban Virginia, Reston is the brainchild of developer Robert E. Simon, with a name made from his initials. He planned his "quality urban environment" around two town centers linking seven villages of approximately 10,000 residents each in a beautiful, contemporary design replete with trees, lakes, and pathways. He intended Reston to be economically self-sufficient and diverse, with mixed-income housing (high-rise luxury apartments side by side with single-family homes). Now owned by Westbrook Communities, Reston is home to 2,000 businesses and nearly 57,000 residents, about 9 percent of whom are black, 9 percent Asian, and 10 percent Hispanic. However, Reston has become mostly an affluent community, with a median family income exceeding $80,000. Its housing includes single-family homes, townhouses, condominiums, waterfront homes, homes on the golf courses, and homes that back up to woods and nature paths. The price of more than 70 homes is over $1 million. One of Reston's main focal points is Town Center, which includes high-rise offices, a Hyatt Regency hotel, boutiques, national retailers, and restaurants. Town Center has a covered outdoor ice-skating rink that doubles as a concert and events shelter during the rest of the year (city-data.com 2005).

Columbia.   Columbia, Maryland, was also designed as a money-maker. James Rouse, the town's developer, intended "to create a social and physical environment which works for people and nourishes human growth and to allow private venture capital to make a profit in land development and sale" (as quoted in J. Bailey 1973:16). To apply the best thinking available to the execution of his city, Rouse employed a host of specialists in the planning phase, including government employees, family counselors, recreationalists, sociologists, economists, educators, health specialists, psychologists, and transportation and communications experts.

Larger than Reston, with current population exceeding 88,000, Columbia does have low-to-moderate-income housing. A racially integrated community (one-fifth of its residents are African American), Columbia successfully scattered its several hundred subsidized units throughout the city. Covering over 14,000 acres with a planned population total of 110,000, the new town is composed of communities of 800 to 900 homes, each with its own elementary school, neighborhood center and convenience store, swimming pool and recreational facilities. The plan then groups four neighborhoods into villages (of which there are nine), each with a middle school, meeting hall, supermarket, and some other shops clustered around a small plaza. In the town center are office buildings, large department stores, and a larger shopping center. Enhancing the town in its variety of programs is Howard Community College. Columbia has 5,300 acres of permanent open space, including 144 tot lots (children's playgrounds), 227 pedestrian bridges, the 40-acre Symphony Woods, 3 lakes, 19 ponds, and natural open space areas interlaced with more than 78 miles of pathways for walking, biking, and jogging. There is also a vast network of plazas, picnic areas, public areas, tennis courts, and two par-course fitness trails.

Irvine.   Also begun in the 1960s, Southern California's Irvine is the largest planned community in North America, set on 58 square miles, and is headquarters for more than 100 major corporations. It is also home to a 15,000-acre campus of the University of California. An upper-middle-class city, with a city population exceeding 172,000, its median household income in 2000 was $70,057. Its racial–ethnic breakdown is 57 percent white, 1 percent African American, 30 percent Asian American, and 7 percent Hispanic (city-data.com 2005).

Celebration.   A still-developing project is the Walt Disney town of Celebration in central Florida, near Walt Disney World Resort. Planned through the collaboration of nine of the nation's leading architects, this community is the most visible example of the New Urbanism. Celebration, say Disney officials, is "sustainable and holistic," demonstrating that development can be responsive to environmental issues. It is a normal community, not an exclusive, gated enclave.

Disney began the project by building the downtown—a lively mix of retail shops, restaurants, offices and apartments, town hall, post office, grocery store, and cinema—situated along a wide promenade circling the lake in the center of town. Most notable is the Art Deco–style movie complex and a cylindrical post office. More than 3,000 people call Celebration their home, with an eventual total population planned to reach approximately 12,000. Homes are designed in six varying architectural styles: Victorian, Classical, Colonial Revival, Coastal, Mediterranean, and French. Oversized porches and verandas encourage old-time neighborhood socializing, and the community is surrounded by a 4,700-acre protected green belt with miles of walking paths.

The tallest point in Celebration neighborhoods will not exceed three stories. There is a model school, kindergarten through twelfth grade, run by the county school system but with

Celebration, Florida, is a planned community that is anticipated to have about 12,000 residents on 4,900 acres surrounded by a 4,700-acre protected green belt. Designed as a pedestrian-friendly place to live, work, and play, the new town has a lake adjacent to its traditional retail and business district, a 109-acre office park, miles of walking paths and nature trails, village parks and recreational areas, and an 18-hole public golf course. [*Source:* Used by permission from the Celebration Company © Disney Enterprises, Inc.]

the best equipment that a $9 million cash boost from Disney can buy. There is a 60-acre "health campus"—a cross between a full-service gym and a hospital—where people can keep in shape downstairs to avoid the medical wards upstairs. Unlike the average "designer suburb," where all the houses carry a similar price tag, Celebration's nearly three-dozen $1 million estates coexist with many other lower-priced homes, including terrace homes starting at $175,000, as well as with about 350 rental apartments, to form a social mix not often seen in the United States anymore.

Celebration is clearly an attempt to return to the pedestrian-friendly, compactly built town of the past, as compared with what the New Urbanists describe as the car-dominated suburban sprawl of freeways, malls, and widely dispersed single-family homes. Admired by many, Celebration also receives criticism from others who call it a retreat to a dreamworld of the past that only appeals to a small segment of the population.

Failure Elsewhere.   Encouraged by the partial success of Columbia and Reston, in 1970 the federal government instituted the New Communities Program, directing money toward building 13 more new towns (including Soul City). The program was a near disaster. It was reduced to a salvage operation by 1974 and completely shut down in 1983, when 12 of the 13 communities were unable to meet their financial obligations (Rodwin and Evans 1982). Except for Irvine and Celebration, the new-town movement in the United States is now all but dead. Why has such an appealing idea fared so poorly? To find out, we need to critically review the major goals of the global new-town movement.

Have They Worked?: Criticisms of New Towns

Many new towns have been built worldwide since Ebenezer Howard sounded the clarion call in 1898. Yet just a few dozen (particularly in Europe and Israel) have been successful; most have not. Why?

One major goal of most new towns was to spread population more broadly. Howard and his followers viewed big cities as destructive of human well-being. Congestion bred inefficiency and anonymity, they argued, and a city's economic dominance sapped vitality from the rest of the region.

Critics point out that new towns really haven't done much along these lines. Even in Britain, after decades of new-town development, barely 1 percent of the population lives in them. It is doubtful that governments could raise the tax money needed to build new towns on a much larger scale. And even if they could, there is little reason to think that a large share of any country's population would

CRITICAL THINKING

What Will the "New" New Orleans Be Like?

The devastation of New Orleans in the aftermath of Hurricane Katrina in 2005 was so widespread that a massive rebuilding effort became necessary. With large sections of the city uninhabited and billions pledged to rebuild the city, leaders had a unique opportunity—one virtually unknown since colonial and frontier days—to envision, on a large scale, the creation of a beautiful and well-functioning city. Bruce Babbitt, former Secretary of the Interior, even called for a national commission of scientists, engineers, and planners to draw up a regional land plan and recommend a realistic course of action (Babbitt 2005).

Obviously, the first step was to secure the city against future flooding. As the flood waters receded in the weeks after the hurricane, there was no shortage of ideas on how to rebuild the city. Universal agreement occurred for constructing better sea walls and levees to hold back future high waters. Most experts also advocated action to rebuild the delta and coastal barriers to enable nature to assist in the city's defenses against future storms.

For the city itself, geographers and urbanists offered a variety of ideas. A more radical proposal was to convert New Orleans into an island, surrounded by miles of open water, with an island infrastructure of relocated streets, highways, and utilities to achieve an "American Venice" (Babbitt 2005). Another bold proposal was to bring in massive amounts of earth to raise the low parts of the city above sea level, as Galveston, Texas, did after a storm surge in 1900 killed more than 6,000 residents (Petroski 2005). In contrast, another suggestion was to create higher-density neighborhoods to allow the return of those lowest-lying parts of the city (where the flood waters stood deepest) to the wetlands they once were. This would restore the marshland to absorb Lake Pontchartrain's overflow and protect the rest of the city (Colten 2005).

Standing on higher ground, the historic buildings in the French Quarter were spared. Other unique appealing architecture in the Bywater District, where many buildings were stunningly restored after a flood in 1965, suffered only minor flood damage this time. These areas should form centerpieces for the city's renewal. In contrast, the public housing built in the 1970s in the eastern part of the city was hardest hit and needed replacement. Some feared their replacement with high-end housing and businesses would displace the poor, as occurred in other cities through the dynamics of gentrification. An alternative could be recreating the city's original development pattern want to live in one. A better idea may be the improvement of already-existing center city, and the need to rebuild New Orleans offers an opportunity to do so (see the Critical Thinking box below).

New towns were also to be centers of employment and economic activity. But here again, few of them attracted much industry or other business. The problem is largely economic: At a distance from major cities, new towns present businesses with added costs for materials and transportation. Thus, especially in North America, new towns have ended up with a strong suburban flavor—bedroom communities for people who, by and large, work elsewhere.

The collapse of the New Communities Program of 1970 reflected these issues. First, the costs of building new towns are enormous, and years go by before any profits are returned. Second, government never made more than a halfhearted commitment to such programs. New towns are the dream of a few—some city planners, a few public officials, architects, builders, and mayors. But others think these efforts could be more effectively

With much housing rendered uninhabitable by the floodwaters from Hurricane Katrina, New Orleans neighborhoods face a massive rebuilding effort. The challenge is to avoid piecemeal efforts and instead to develop and implement a comprehensive plan that incorporates the best ideas of urban planners and overcomes the segregation and poverty problems that existed previously.

on the east side, just as it already exists on the west side. Here grand houses line large boulevards and avenues while the interior and side streets contain more modest residences. Such a mixed-income arrangement, found in successful new towns worldwide, would defuse racial tensions by keeping the races in close proximity to one another (Crutcher 2005).

As this book goes to press, how New Orleans will be rebuilt has yet to be determined. Planners and engineers stand ready to come up with whatever it takes, perhaps even to build the "City Beautiful" or "New Jerusalem." However, it will be the politicians who decide what approach—comprehensive or piecemeal—to take and how much to invest.

placed elsewhere—in inner-city development, for example, or in the elimination of slum housing. The overall result is that the New Communities Program is dead in the United States, and there is little likelihood that any such program will take its place in the foreseeable future.

This is not to ignore the many contributions of the new-town idea. Columbia's developer, James Rouse, and Reston's developer, Robert E. Simon, both demonstrated broad social concern and purpose in undertaking projects of such economic magnitude and social audacity. We might also direct such tribute to Ebenezer Howard, who aspired to so much in his new-towns vision. Nevertheless, no one yet has built "Jerusalem." Moreover, the new town is not the magic potion to cure all urban problems. There are other visions to consider.

UTOPIA UNLIMITED: ARCHITECTURAL VISIONS

> The possible will be attempted only because we have postulated the impossible.
>
> Goethe

An irony marks Ebenezer Howard's ambition— to change all of society through building cities that were very small. Some visionaries argue that solving the city's problems demands not outlying new towns, but completely new *central cities*—more efficient, more humane, and for *everybody*. Here we examine three large-scale "visions of the street." Each is the work of an architect; each is refreshingly different.

Le Corbusier: The Radiant City

Among the most important figures of modern architecture, Le Corbusier was also an influential urban planner. In his books *The City of Tomorrow* (1927) and *The Radiant City* (1933), Le Corbusier, like Howard, condemned modern cities and outlined a vision of a new urban society. But his solution was the very opposite of Howard's. Rejecting widespread decentralization, Le Corbusier saw obvious benefits to

concentrating people in tall, architecturally magnificent buildings surrounded by huge open spaces. Such mammoth structures, Le Corbusier reasoned, allowed keeping 95 percent of available land free from any building at all. Le Corbusier's plan for a "Contemporary City" is shown in Figure 14–3.

A second innovation was doing away with the typical Western city's central concentration "by substituting virtually equal densities all over the city. This would reduce the pressure on central business districts, which would in effect disappear. Flows of people would become much more even across the whole city, instead of strong radical flows into and out of the center which characterize cities today" (Hall 2002:51).

Decentralization with density, concentrated living and open space, administrative efficiency and spontaneity, organization and individuality—many such oppositions are intentionally built into Le Corbusier's work. To him, the city should be a place where human paradoxes could be explored and exploited.

Although no such **urban utopia** was ever built, Le Corbusier's influence on city planning was great. One classic example is the

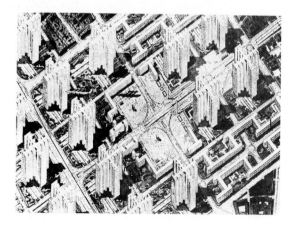

FIGURE 14–3   Le Corbusier's Contemporary City
[From *The Radiant City* by Le Corbusier translated by Derek Coltman. Translation copyright 1967 by Grossman Publishers, Inc. and Faber & Faber Ltd. Used by permission of Viking Penguin, a division of Penguin Putnam, Inc. © 2003 Artists Rights Society (ARS), New York/ADAGP, Paris/FIC.]

Alton West estate in Roehampton in southwest London, built after World War II. A second example of a Le Corbusier–influenced project is Manhattan's Stuyvesant Town. Red brick buildings stand between wide walkways and lawns in this parklike setting constructed in 1947. Although Stuyvesant Town has been controversial because of its isolation from the surrounding neighborhood, architecture critic Paul Goldberger (1989) believes that its successes outweigh its problems. Still, Goldberger concedes that the satisfaction felt by residents may be as much a function of their comfortable income as it is of the project itself.

Le Corbusier expressed his vision to its fullest extent in his 1953 design of Chandigarh, India, which calls itself "the city beautiful." Structurally, Chandigarh is a very modern city, with a population exceeding 900,000. Each of the city's 49 sectors is a block about one square kilometer in size with markets, shopping centers, and schools to limit people's need to travel. Citywide transportation (buses, auto-rickshaws, and taxicabs) links the sectors. Chandigarh is best known for its outstanding modern and folk architecture. The State Library, Super Market, Sukhna Lake, Gulab Bag (rose garden), Shanti Kunj, the Art Museum, the High Court, Bidhan Sabha (secretariat), and the Punjab University are each a wonderful example of modern architecture. One factor Le Corbusier was unable to control was population density; as India's sixth most densely populated city, with 7,902 people per square kilometer, its density is four times what Le Corbusier wished.

Frank Lloyd Wright: Broadacre City

Frank Lloyd Wright, the most famous of all U.S. architects, viewed Le Corbusier's urban vision as a nightmare. Such high-density living should be avoided at all costs, Wright maintained, and he championed instead what he called "organic architecture"—the living union of architectural design with the natural environment. He reasoned that if homes could be constructed in an "organic" way, why couldn't the same be done for entire cities?

Like both Howard and Le Corbusier, Wright accepted the integral role of modern technology. Unlike them, however, he sought to increase vastly the space occupied by his utopian city to lower greatly its density. He thought a city might easily spread over 100 square miles or even more. With automobiles (or even airplanes), he contended, people could live on their own acres of land and still easily reach neighbors and shopping facilities.

Figure 14–4 depicts Wright's vision of Broadacre City. A central structure (the tall building in the background) is the local administrative center. At its foot, on the shores of the lake, lies a stadium. In the foreground, the circular building with the spires is a cultural center. Interspersed throughout the area are agricultural fields and dwelling complexes—an idea very much like Howard's. Roads link these areas, and overhead whirl the personal helicopters of Broadacre residents.

Broadacre City was a fusion of what Wright saw as the ideals of Jeffersonian democracy (fundamentally, extensive personal freedoms), the North American dream of plenty of land for personal use, and modern technology. He believed as well that people should pay no rent for land; rather, a "single tax" would support all urban costs. After that, people were on their own (Fishman 1982).

Broadacre City never was more than a dream, of course. The plan met with massive criticism during Wright's lifetime (1867–1959). Critics dismissed Broadacre City as too expensive, too expansive, and far too radical. Although stung by the negative reaction, Wright never gave up on his ideas. He rewrote his Broadacre treatise, *The Living City*, for the fourth time at age 90.

Paolo Soleri: The Arcology

One of Wright's students was a young Italian named Paolo Soleri. Like many genius students of other geniuses, Soleri both respected and rebelled against his master's teaching. He accepted Wright's central notion of organic architecture, but he rejected entirely his teacher's vision of Broadacre City.

FIGURE 14–4   Frank Lloyd Wright's Broadacre City reflected an ideal fusion of urban and rural, where agricultural fields and residential areas intermingled, with proximity to sports complexes and cultural centers. It was a place where everyone developed multiple abilities in farming, mechanics, and intellectual pursuits, and enjoyed great freedom of choice and movement. [Frank Lloyd Wright, Living City, drawing 5825.002, Air View MOMA#266. Height: 35 1/4, Width: 42 1/4, Media: sepia. The drawings of Frank Lloyd Wright are Copyright © 2000 The Frank Lloyd Wright Foundation, Scottsdale, AZ. © 2000 Artists Rights Society (ARS), New York.]

Siding with Le Corbusier, Soleri advocated a dense concentration of people in an urban area. But his vision is even more extreme: a completely self-contained unit housing up to half a million people in a structure many times larger than the Empire State Building, occupying just the space of a few city blocks!

Soleri calls such cities **arcologies** or architectural ecologies—environmentally safe, architecturally beautiful, and totally efficient. His key idea was to make the city "in the human image," concentrating and intensifying everything human. Because, to him, cities were vital elements of human evolution, dispersed concepts like Broadacre City did not apply.

Babel.   Soleri's Babel IIB, designed for a population of 520,000, contained underground industrial and commercial areas; the city center at ground level; a public area and a promenade on the first level; a neighborhood and a park (both outdoors) on the second level; gardens, a community area (for recreation), and a living–working area on the third level (about 1,500 feet high!); and housing at the very top. All service facilities—elevators, heating, and exhaust systems—are contained in the central core of the city.

Structures like these (Soleri designed dozens) are so audacious, even in the history of utopian urban planning, that few take them seriously. Critics dismiss the arcologies as gigantic beehives. Soleri counters by claiming they are "miniatures" compared with today's cities. They occupy a fraction of the land, free up the surrounding countryside for enjoyment, and allow that countryside a chance to return to nature. Imagine, he suggests, the population of Los Angeles, which now sprawls over 470 square miles, contained in 10 to 12 well-dispersed Babels. Everywhere else: no freeways, no smog, just beautiful Southern California. No doubt, however, such structures would be astronomically expensive, and no one came forward to finance constructing one.

Arcosanti.   Undaunted, Soleri proceeded on his own. Rising out of the desert at Cortez Junction in Arizona, about an hour's ride north of Phoenix, is Arcosanti, Soleri's "urban laboratory" prototype to demonstrate the viability of his vision fusing architecture, ecology, and urban planning. Arcosanti, shown in model form in the illustration, is planned to be completely self-sufficient and has been under

construction since 1970. When complete, Arcosanti will house approximately 7,000 people, providing an urban infrastructure with workplaces, cultural centers, and service facilities while allowing easy access to the surrounding natural environment. As of 2005, though, Arcosanti is less than 1 percent completed, although more than 6,000 people have participated in its construction.

To Soleri, Arcosanti serves to (1) maximize the interaction and accessibility associated with an urban environment; (2) minimize the use of energy, raw materials, and land, as well as environmental pollution; and (3) allow ready access to the surrounding natural environment. The "city," including an array of large-scale solar greenhouses, will occupy only 30 acres of a 4,060-acre preserve and will serve as a research and study center for the social, economic, and ecological implications of its

Arcosanti, Soleri's vision of the integration of architecture, ecology, and urban planning, is presently home to only 1 percent of its planned 7,000 inhabitants. This model shows Arcosanti in its planned final form. Intended to occupy less than 30 acres of the 4,060-acre preserve, it will serve as a research and study center for the social, economic, and ecological implications of its architectural framework.

architectural framework. More than 30 years after its inception, Arcosanti presently consists of eight various mixed-use buildings and public spaces, and construction is progressing at a very slow pace. Each year its 70 residents host 50,000 visitors in the Gallery, Café, and Bakery, produce nearly 15,000 windbells in the Foundry and Ceramic Studios, and conduct educational seminars for over 400 people (Arcosanti 2005).

Utopia's Limitations: A Critique

Planned utopias, like those of Le Corbusier, Wright, and Soleri, share many of the limitations found in the New Town movement. First, as Arcosanti amply demonstrates, they are financially impractical. Second, each is a rigid vision developed by a single person who assumed that everyone would see the basic logic of his vision and support it. To his credit, Paolo Soleri has been more flexible than other planners in this respect, changing his designs frequently after dialogue with others. Third, such plans seem sociologically naive. As Peter Hall (2002) notes, these utopians are all *architects* who believe that altering the physical world will automatically alter the social world as well. But, of course, beautiful designs do not necessarily do away with social problems, such as racial prejudice or poverty.

Yet, in the final analysis, society needs utopian thinkers. They are, by their work, natural consciousness raisers. They challenge our thinking about cities, point to obvious problems, and prod us to consider visionary solutions that we "on the street" barely understand.

MEANWHILE . . . DOWNTOWN: MORE FOCUSED URBAN PLANNING

The problem with utopian planners is that their schemes are simply too grandiose and impractical. A city is simply *too complex a phenomenon* to be controlled as though it were a programmable computer. Other planners argue that urban planning only works when it is focused on a limited segment of city life—say, a neighborhood

or park. We may never be able to manage the city as a whole, but we can handle the urban scene one segment at a time.

Sidewalks, Neighborhoods, and Local Initiative

Since the 1960s, the trend has been away from comprehensive visions such as those of the utopian city planners. Leading this reaction was Jane Jacobs, author of *The Death and Life of Great American Cities* (1992/1961). To Jacobs, the greatest value of the city is its diversity; the city's "life" lies in its countless interactions and the multiple uses of its streets, parks, sidewalks, and neighborhoods. Hence, anything that diminishes this quality (as does comprehensive planning, by definition) leads cities to their "death." Put otherwise, urban living is never *planned* in any broad sense. People of the city *invent* their lives, as they meet their own needs and solve their own problems.

Consider sidewalks. In any vital city, a sidewalk has uses far beyond easing the passage of pedestrians. Front steps facing the sidewalk are places for neighbors to sit and visit, just as corners are places to "hang out." Second, sidewalk street life serves as a means of public surveillance, through which people come to know each other and to identify strangers. Jacobs points out that, in areas where street life abounds, crime rates are low. Third, sidewalks are environments where children explore their neighborhood, test themselves, and grasp the rules of urban social life. Finally, street life brings a sense of community to a neighborhood. South Philadelphia, New York's Lower East Side, New Orleans's French Quarter (before Hurricane Katrina in 2005), and San Francisco's Haight-Ashbury district all maintain a positive identity based on their street life.

In general, then, Jacobs supports local planning initiatives but loathes grandiose designs. What city planners should do, she says, is facilitate diversity and vitality and let local people do the rest. The best planning, then, is sometimes the least planning. The Critical Thinking box on page 429 outlines Jacobs's suggestions to a city planning board.

Open Spaces: Squares, Parks, and Architecture

Not everyone who shares the belief in more focused city planning, of course, goes as far as Jacobs. While agreeing that holistic city planning is undesirable, some argue that good planning can be more comprehensive than Jacobs allows.

August Heckscher spent two years studying cities such as Omaha, Dallas, Cincinnati, Buffalo, Rochester, and Milwaukee. To Heckscher, the vitality of a city was fundamentally a matter of how well it organized its space:

Each city is a place of its own, its uniqueness determined in large measure by patterns created by the alternation of structure and void, of buildings and spaces between. The large green spaces, parks and parkways, river banks and waterfronts, give to a city a coherence that allows the urban dweller to have a feeling of the whole. . . . What is expressed in open spaces is the essential quality of urban life—its casualness and variety, its ability to crystallize community feeling. (1978:4)

Heckscher noted that the spatial organization of cities reflects deep cultural values.

CRITICAL THINKING

Jane Jacobs: Planning for Vitality

Consider, for a moment, the kind of goals at which city planning must begin to aim, if the object is to plan for city vitality.

Planning for vitality must stimulate and catalyze the greatest possible range and quantity of diversity among uses and among people throughout each district of a big city; this is the underlying foundation of city economic strength, social vitality and magnetism. To do this, planners must diagnose, in specific places, what is lacking to generate diversity, and then aim at helping to supply the lacks as best they can be supplied.

Planning for vitality must promote continuous networks of local street neighborhoods, whose users and informal proprietors can count to the utmost in keeping the public spaces of the city safe, in handling strangers so they are an asset rather than a menace, in keeping casual public tabs on children in places that are public.

Planning for vitality must combat the destructive presence of border vacuums [vacant land at the edges], and it must help promote people's identification with city districts that are large enough, and are varied and rich enough in inner and outer contacts to deal with the tough, inescapable, practical problems of big-city life.

Planning for vitality must aim at unslumming the slums, by creating conditions aimed at persuading a high proportion of the indigenous residents, whoever they may be, to stay put by choice over time, so there will be a steadily growing diversity among people and a continuity of community both for old residents and for newcomers who assimilate into it.

Planning for vitality must convert the self-destruction of diversity and other cataclysmic uses of money into constructive forces, by hampering the opportunities for destructiveness on the one hand, and on the other hand by stimulating more city territory into possessing a good economic environment for other people's plans.

Planning for vitality must aim at clarifying the visual order of cities, and it must do so by both promoting and illuminating functional order, rather than by obstructing or denying it.

Source: Jane Jacobs, *The Death and Life of Great American Cities* (New York: Random House, 1961), pp. 408–459.

Grounded in the values of individualism, freedom, and material success, U.S. cities typically adopted a grid pattern. With a grid, vistas open up; people can look down whole streets, thus introducing regularity and suggesting control. Curved streets and irregular building patterns (as found in medieval towns), by contrast, are enclosing, limiting, unpredictable, not future-oriented.

Heckscher highlights the value of squares, parks, architecture, and artwork to urban life. These are especially important in cities—like those in North America—dominated by economic concerns. They prompt people to remember that there are "other things" to city life. Squares provide small, natural meeting places, as well as settings for more formal occasions such as political rallies and concerts. They provide a vital physical and psychological break in the city's structure. New Orleans's Jackson Square, located in the French Quarter, has been one such vital square. Others include Fountain Square in Cincinnati, Union Square in San Francisco, City Hall Square in Toronto, Rittenhouse Square in Philadelphia, and Washington Square in New York.

Parks are equally important. Roy Rosenzweig (1998) speaks for many in celebrating New York's Central Park, 843 acres on the upper half of Manhattan Island, which preserves a bit of country in the city. Although perhaps not as well known as Central Park, a similar public space is found in virtually every major North American city where residents delight in recreation and informal activities of all kinds. Atlanta has Piedmont Park (185 acres), Chicago has Grant Park (305 acres), and San Diego has Balboa Park (1,158 acres). There is Schenley Park in Pittsburgh (456 acres), Stanley Park in Vancouver (1,000 acres), and Griffith Park in Los Angeles (4,063 acres). Philadelphia boasts the largest city park in the world, Fairmount Park (4,079 acres).

Architecture, too, is a crucial source of a city's flavor and excitement. Buildings provoke human *feelings*. Frank Lloyd Wright's Guggenheim Museum in New York always demands a response, as do San Francisco's brightly painted Victorian houses. Walking through the world's great cathedrals—St. Paul's in London or Notre Dame in Paris, for example—creates a powerful reaction, much the same as gazing on the New York skyline from the Brooklyn Bridge. It is for this reason, no doubt, that many advocate protecting a city's architecture as the means of preserving a city's soul.

In a study of urban spaces, William H. Whyte found that many people simply thrive on the streets. Observing the Seagram Plaza in midtown Manhattan, he wrote that "On a good day, there would be a hundred and fifty people sitting, sunbathing, picnicking and schmoozing—idly gossiping, talking 'nothing talk'" (1980:14). Moreover, claims Whyte,

> [People] go to the lively places where there are many people. And they go there . . . not to escape the city but to partake of it. . . . The multiplier effect is tremendous. It is not just the number of people using these small urban places, but the larger number who pass by and enjoy them vicariously, or the even larger number who feel better about the city center for knowledge of them. For a city such places are priceless, whatever the costs. (2001:100–101)

Rouse Revisited: The Middle Ground

Later in his life, James Rouse, the creator of Columbia, Maryland, shifted his attention to midsize projects of urban regeneration. Most of these have been spectacularly successful. These are neither comprehensive, all encompassing visions like Columbia, nor small-scale, local efforts like those championed by Jane Jacobs. They are in between—the middle ground. While such planning takes account of the needs of the whole city, it targets a small portion of the city's space. The most well-known of Rouse's mid-sized efforts are the Faneuil Hall complex in Boston, New York's South Street Seaport, Baltimore's Inner Harbor, and the Grand Avenue Mall in Milwaukee.

All of these projects reclaimed portions of deteriorating central cities in the 1950s and 1960s that Rouse sought to reverse. He was concerned that Americans had lived so long with grim, congested, worn-out inner cities and sprawling, cluttered outer cities, that they subconsciously accepted such conditions as inevitable and unavoidable. He worried that people no longer realized that cities can be beautiful, humane, and truly responsive to the needs and yearnings of their people (Olsen 2004).

So he set to work. Before Rouse began, the Faneuil Hall area of Boston had become as tawdry as one could imagine. The site of the city center in Revolutionary War days, the area abounded with old, dilapidated warehouses that abutted on the harbor. No one lived there and only a few businesses remained. With a generous spirit, one would have called the locale "down and out."

Today, it is transformed. The old warehouses have been outwardly maintained, but the inner cores have been thoroughly modernized. Faneuil Hall has been revamped in the same manner. Inside, food shops run its football-field length. On either side of the Hall are pedestrian areas with benches, outdoor eating areas, and places where street musicians play. The refurbished old warehouses on either side are now the place of business of high-quality shops. On any summer day, the place is teeming with people—locals, tourists, and visitors from the suburbs. Looking at the project from the vantage point of one of the high-rises in the area or from the harbor, one sees how Rouse's vision works: The new buildings mimic or harmoniously blend with the old buildings of the area. Perhaps most important, the businesses in the project are profitable, and the success of the Faneuil Hall project subsequently stimulated development

The diversity in cities is also found in its variety of architectural styles. For example, this Boston cityscape spans the centuries of design and function, from the eighteenth-century structures of the revitalized Faneuil Hall and Quincy Market area, to the Gothic Revival buildings over 100 years later, to the sleek, modern skyscrapers from the mid- to late-twentieth century.

throughout Boston's downtown. Much the same happy story applies to Baltimore's Inner Harbor and, on a smaller scale, to New York's South Street Seaport.

Critics charge that Rouse's successes pander to the wealthier elements of urban areas and do little for the poor. There is truth in this accusation. Still, Rouse's changes have helped turn around one stunning problem by replacing collapsing inner-city districts with thriving, vibrant urban places.

THE REALITIES OF URBAN PLANNING

Whatever the philosophical stance one ultimately takes about urban planning, shaping the city always forces us to contend with traditions, vested interests, and environmental conditions. Such realities operate both as barriers and as opportunities.

Economics and Politics

Radical alterations in the urban landscape have hardly ever gotten far off the ground. Even Ebenezer Howard could establish only two garden cities. Even with government support, the British new-town effort has been quite limited. In the United States, Stein's Radburn, New Jersey, fell victim to financial troubles, while Columbia and Reston went through dire straits for the same reason. Partially because of expense (and partially because of its audacity), Paolo Soleri's Arcosanti has barely taken form, and Frank Lloyd Wright's Broadacre City was never even started. The stark reality is that, in a free-market economy, urban planning rarely strays very far from the interests of business.

Local politics, too, swirls around city planning, as interest groups contend with each other to achieve their various goals. Sometimes the complexities of even projects that are small in scale lead to challenges that intimidate elected officials not wanting to alienate voters.

The Difference That Values Make

In the final analysis, urban planning is always a question of values: which ones and whose are the key issues. Throughout this chapter, we have seen that city planning has always reflected cultural values. In Catholic Rome we found planning that glorified the Church; in monarchic France we found planning that celebrated the king; in nineteenth- and twentieth-century New York, we found planning that augmented the pursuit of the almighty dollar.

Values also permeate, explicitly or implicitly, the work of urban planners. In a review of Jane Jacobs's *Death and Life of Great American Cities,* sociologist Herbert Gans (1962a:170–75) pointed out that Jacobs is a typical product of her society. She complains that, too often, city planning has not been left up to the people. What could be more Western, more North American, Gans asks, than a complaint that we need more emphasis on the individual, and should make way for local initiative?

Of course, the values implicitly criticized by Jacobs appear in virtually all U.S. city planning. Even planners like Columbia's James Rouse, who have tried to improve people's lives in cities, do so with the expectation of being well paid for it. Said Rouse in an interview:

> The business mentality today is that the pursuit of profit is the purpose of life, and that people come second or third. I think that's deplorable. It's why development has such a bad name and why cities suffer from so much ugliness. What should be important is to produce something of benefit to mankind. If that happens, then the profit will be there. (Pawlyna 1981:64)

Similarly, because most of us are deeply committed to the values of individuality and personal initiative, we are put off by the all-inclusive plans of Le Corbusier, Soleri, or Wright that seem to demand submission to the group. Indeed, perhaps the characteristic element of North American urban planning has been the lack of comprehensive planning. From the 1600s on, most U.S. and Canadian cities developed with very limited intervention by any governmental agency. There are notable exceptions, such as Portland, Oregon, and Toronto. Mainly though, the United States has no overall plans or policies for its cities because its population does not want

Prefabricated concrete apartment buildings built throughout the old Soviet Union and Eastern European communist countries resulted in a sterile look of uniformity. This is the Nibelungen-Ring housing complex in Leipzig in eastern Germany, with other apartment buildings in traditional rows in the upper left. In most socialist cities, these gray buildings created a drab, somber look for the first-time visitor.

them. If private investors, like Jim Rouse, can't make our cities better, then most people seem content to live with the consequences. French and Hamilton sum up well:

> State intervention and control [in cities] in Western countries is aimed at, and can only hope to achieve, the amelioration of the inadequacies of the existing system because planning has to operate within the limits imposed by private ownership of land and buildings, private control of investment, and the greater freedom of choice and action *possessed* by the individual, even when such action may not be in the public interest. (1979:19; emphasis added)

In recent years a growing number of scholars and practitioners have become interested in private, market-based programs to address urban economic and social ills. As explained in *The Voluntary City: Choice, Community, and Civil Society* (Beito 2002), many areas of civic and commercial life do not necessarily require government involvement. Various authors of this edited volume offer numerous examples of the non-government sector effectively providing for roads and bridges, education, housing, social welfare, land-use planning, commercial law, even policing and criminal prosecutions. The private, self-governing enclaves and large-scale industrial communities with complex physical infrastructure and services (such as Chicago's Manufacturing District) are examples that challenge the orthodoxy that government alone can improve community life. So perhaps the private sector can play a greater role in urban planning and policy.

Some Canadian and U.S. cities already illustrate the vitality wrought by good government planning. Among them are Portland, San Francisco, Seattle, and Vancouver, locales frequently cited in public opinion polls as the "best" cities. Another city fulfilling all of these qualifications is Toronto, Ontario, whose planning successfully addresses the challenges of urban diversity and urban sprawl. We will examine Toronto as a model of good urban planning in our final case study.

Toronto is a Great Lakes port and, through the St. Lawrence Seaway, an ocean port as well. With 5.2 million people living in the region in 2004, Toronto is the most populous metropolitan area in Canada. About one in six Canadians live there and it continues to attract newcomers, as illustrated in an 8.5 percent population growth between 1997 and 2001 (Statistics Canada 2004). The Toronto region has the nation's major concentration of industrial jobs and serves as the commercial and financial center of the country. The central area, downtown Toronto, is the predominant regional center, encompassing major government, financial, medical, and education services.

Although it contains a large industrial base, Toronto has not experienced the problems of crime and population loss that plague another nearby industrial city, Detroit. Toronto attracts a large number of immigrants from the developing world and has an increasing number of people requiring welfare assistance, but its school system and financial stability are stronger than those of many U.S. cities in a similar situation. Although Toronto faces suburban and edge city development as do other cities, its central city remains strong, the region's growth patterns are not wasteful of environmental resources, and the transportation systems are more efficient, with greater reliance on mass transit. What makes Toronto more successful in these areas than its sister cities elsewhere? The answer lies in a metropolitan approach to governance and policy-making that enables Toronto to address spatial development and quality-of-life issues in a more comprehensive manner and with greater resources at its disposal, as we will discuss shortly.

The Physical Setting

Situated on the northern shore of Lake Ontario, Toronto is almost entirely flat, except 3 to 4 miles inland where the land sharply rises about 40 feet at the shoreline elevation of the former glacial Lake Iroquois. Streets are in a grid design except for the diagonal roads along the shoreline. Railroad tracks and an expressway separate the lakefront from the downtown area. The central business areas are around Bloor, Queen, and Yonge streets, while the central financial district is south of the old city hall in the vicinity of King and Bay streets. The CN Tower (1,815 feet) dominates the city skyline—along with the Toronto-Dominion Centre, Commerce Court, and First Canadian Place—all of which are more than 50 stories high.

North of the central business district lies a fashionable shopping area. The Ontario Parliament Buildings and the University of Toronto rise south of Bloor Street in a section with tall shade trees and grassy areas known for its park-like atmosphere. One of the most attractive residential areas in Toronto is Rosedale, an older neighborhood of distinguished homes set on winding, tree-lined streets quite close to the downtown center, which itself contains many attractive streets of modest, well-designed houses.

History

Inhabited first by the Seneca and later by the Mississauga Indians, the area that was to become the city of Toronto was first established as a trading post in the seventeenth century because of its strategic location at the crossing of ancient Indian trails going west to the Mississippi and north to Lake Simcoe and the vast wilderness beyond. The French built three small forts there in the eighteenth century, which were subsequently destroyed after the English defeated the French in 1759. During and after the U.S. War for Independence, about 40,000 loyalists fled the United States and settled in this region.

In 1787, Lord Dorchester, the Canadian governor-in-chief, peacefully negotiated the purchase of 250,000 acres from three Indian chiefs for the future capital of Ontario. Its name was changed from Toronto to York in 1795, and U.S. forces temporarily occupied the small settlement of about 700 residents during the War of 1812. By 1834, the population had grown to 9,000 and its original name was restored.

The coming of the Grand Trunk and Great Western railways in the 1850s sparked rapid development. As a break-of-bulk port city, Toronto flourished, shipping agricultural products, minerals, and timber from the surrounding region. Industrialization further spurred growth, as the city and its environs soon produced more than half of Canada's manufactured goods. Through annexation of adjacent villages and towns, the city doubled in area by 1900, then doubled again by 1920. In 1930, the metropolitan area included the central city, four towns (Leaside, Mimico, New Toronto, and Weston), three villages (Forest Hill, Long Branch, and Swansea), and five townships (Etobicoke, East York, North York, Scarborough, and York).

Creation of a Metropolitan Government

The Great Depression of the 1930s caused severe financial problems for the city, and these still remained at the end of World War II in 1945. Already having difficulty finding funds to provide water and sewage systems to outlying areas, Toronto saw its municipal burden increase further with a rapid rise in population at that time. After investigating various options, the Ottawa Municipal Board in 1953 recommended that the 13 municipalities (named in the previous paragraph) create a federated form of government unique in North America. Passage that year of the Municipality of Metropolitan Toronto Act united the metropolitan area, and the 25-member Council of Metropolitan Toronto began its task of finding ways to deal with such common concerns as revenues, education, transportation, and urban

growth. This combined form of government offered greater credit than each individual municipality had, thereby enhancing financing for various public projects. A significant feature of this metropolitan government system was that council members were appointed to it by virtue of their election as mayors, aldermen, or controllers of a particular municipality, which ensured good communication and a high level of coordination between the central body and the local municipalities.

The Metropolitan Council worked well. It authorized construction of new schools and renovation of older ones and also introduced a regional system of parks in an attempt to control future development. It greatly improved transportation by upgrading or building new roads and expressways and by constructing an excellent subway and a new airport terminal building. Toronto's transit system now consists of a grid network of streetcars, buses, three underground rapid transit lines, and a light rail transit system that together account for two-thirds of all trips to the central city. This transportation network is integrated with the multicentered urban structures located along the rapid transit lines and brings workers from the surrounding regions to the downtown area.

In 1967, the Corporation of Metropolitan Toronto reorganized. It reduced its 13 municipalities to six and increased from 25 to 33 the number of seats on the Council. The Council also considerably extended its responsibilities in education and social services and added others, such as ambulance and library services, urban renewal, and waste disposal. The reorganized council subsequently succeeded in resolving many of the difficult sewage and water problems to create effective systems for both.

Essentially, Toronto functioned with a two-tiered government, with local government focus on neighborhood issues and metropolitan focus on issues facing the metropolitan region. Regional government has thus enabled Toronto to consolidate its resources and to develop a coordinated plan for the growth of both its urban and suburban schools. In a 1990 comparison of Toronto and Detroit, which are about 230 miles apart, *The Economist* reported that the Toronto region avoided many of the problems that plagued Detroit in the areas of crime, education, and social services because it could evenly control use of space and distribution of resources throughout the metropolitan area. As a result, the Council has been credited with contributing substantially to shaping Toronto into "one of the most effectively planned metropolitan areas in North America" (United Nations Development Programme 1995).

> Major achievements have included a strong industrial base, a successful mass transit system providing 70 percent of trips to an enlarged central area, concentration of office employment near subway stations, and provision of housing for an additional 1 million residents, well-located with respect to public transport. In addition [the Municipality of Metropolitan Toronto] has upgraded the road system to provide improved access to industrial and commercial employment throughout the metropolitan area and provided an effective water supply and sewerage system. (United Nations 1995:256)

Two Phases of Urban Planning

In a provocative book, *City Form and Everyday Life: Toronto's Gentrification and Critical Social Practice* (1994), Jon Caulfield described two distinct planning phases—modern and postmodern—that Toronto experienced in its inner-city development. The first of these began in the 1950s and lasted until the early 1970s and was characterized by an all-out prodevelopment attitude and adherence to the principles of modernist planning. This approach emphasized intense specialization of land use, massive infrastructure (particularly urban expressways), and the redevelopment of older areas (Filion 1995).

In Toronto, city officials identified a number of districts within the city as blighted and obliterated them to make room for expressways, public housing projects, private high-rise apartment developments, or an expansion of downtown's commercial functions. With little regard for existing neighborhoods in these designated areas, the wrecking ball and bulldozer razed some of the city's architectural gems and destroyed communities in such places as Alexandra Park, Rusholme Road on the east side, St. Jamestown, and Regent Park. These old neighborhoods were seen as an inconvenience between two modernist sectors: the suburbs and a rapidly redeveloping central business district (Caulfield 1994:7).

Alexandra Park exemplifies the outcome of the modern planning approach found in many other North American cities as well. Once it was an area of mixed use, consisting of old residential houses and commercial activities linked with the rest of the city. Now it is an area reflecting simplification, segmentation, withdrawal, and a land use that is segregated from the day-to-day activities of the rest of the city. Most people living in Alexandra Park these days need public assistance, and the area has become an isolated, virtually impenetrable ghetto (Caulfield 1994:11–13).

Toronto officials and local developers continued to raze prominent architectural landmarks and stable working-class neighborhoods, replacing them with modern, "efficient" structures, until local activist groups began to fight city hall's urban renewal plans. The reformers pointed to the decay of U.S. inner cities and argued that Toronto could avoid their mistakes if it remained "people-oriented" and emphasized neighborhood preservation. Their arguments were persuasive; they succeeded in preserving such areas as Rusholme Road on the west side, Old City Hall, Toronto Island, Church of the Holy Trinity, Union Station, and Trefann Court. This "cultural resistance," suggests Caulfield, played an important role in the introduction of the second phase of planning: postmodern inner-city development. Postmodern urbanism is a celebration of traditional urban form and of social and cultural heterogeneity (Caulfield 1994:97).

From the late 1960s onward, the postmodernist movement—overlapping the modernist movement for a few years before emerging as the dominant force—found sufficient support in Toronto's Metropolitan Council to halt modernist redevelopment of most inner-city neighborhoods. Echoing the antimodernist perspectives of Jane Jacobs and Lewis Mumford, planners began emphasizing the benefits of a diversified, small-grained urban texture and the importance of preserving older buildings. Ironically, the preservation and upgrading of the built environment led to the loss of its social diversity, as middle- and upper-income people—seeking easy downtown access and a more stimulating environment than was available in the suburbs—displaced the working-class and ethnic populations previously there (Sewell 1993).

Toronto Today

In 1998, Toronto restructured its municipal government once more, merging its six local governments into one entity. At the same time, the city's responsibilities, revenues, and property tax base were reformed, all without disruption of city services to residents and businesses. Although the new Toronto government centralized its administration, the city still maintains community councils to deal with purely neighborhood matters, and its various local civic and social services remain in local communities, with the six former city halls now functioning as "municipal civic centres" (Toronto 2005).

As a result of its planning reforms and metropolitan governance, Toronto has emerged into a dynamic city with one of the world's safest urban environments. It is, as Jane Jacobs remarked, "a city that works." *Fortune* magazine in 1996 named it "the best global city for business." It is Canada's number one tourist destination, the financial center of Canada, and the fourth largest financial center in North America. The city has one of the highest percentages of fiber optic telecommunications cables installed and more wireless phones per capita than anywhere else in North America. It also contains the continent's largest continuous underground pedestrian system, connecting 1,200 stores and restaurants, 50 office towers, 6 major hotels, and several entertainment centers (Toronto 2005).

Toronto is also one of the world's most multicultural cities, as nearly half of all Canada's immigrants come to the Greater Toronto Area. Not surprisingly, then, half the city's population are immigrants, a much higher proportion than anywhere else in North America. The 315,000 immigrants who settled in Toronto between 1990 and 1996 were equivalent to a city the size of Victoria or Halifax. With the exception of Oceania (the countries of the Pacific and South Pacific), every part of the world has sent at least 10,000 emigrants to Toronto in recent years. During the 1990s Asia supplied about 60 percent of all immigrants arriving in Toronto. The leading countries were China, Hong Kong, the Philippines, Vietnam (East Asia); India and Sri Lanka (South Asia); and Guyana, Jamaica, Trinidad, and Tobago (West Indies). Italy and the United Kingdom remain the top two countries of origin for all immigrants living in Toronto but, if present migration patterns continue, that will change in a few years. The postwar suburbs of North York, Scarborough, and York have become the main immigrant settlement areas as the central city, as mentioned earlier, has proven an attractive locale for middle- and upper-income residents.

Toronto is also an important cultural center, with a rich fare of ballet, concerts, films, opera, and theater offerings. In fact, it is the third-largest English-language theater center after London and New York. It is home to the Toronto Symphony Orchestra, three major theaters, and many small experimental theaters, as well as the Art Gallery of Ontario, the Royal Ontario Museum, the Ontario Science Centre, and a zoo. Often called "Hollywood North," it ranks third in TV and film production. Its institutions of higher learning include the Ontario College of Art, Ryerson Polytechnical Institute, the University of Toronto, and York University. The Toronto Maple Leafs (ice hockey) and Argonauts (football) are professional sports teams that add to the city's excitement and vitality. Like any vibrant city, Toronto also offers an appealing array of restaurants, boutiques, movie theaters, festivals, exhibits, and recreational and social activities (Toronto 2005).

Toronto is not entirely free of problems. Increased traffic congestion, a shortage of

CITYSCAPE

Toronto Plans Its Future

Following are introductory excerpts from an official master plan—developed, publicly discussed, and adopted in 2002—in which the city of Toronto designed its evolution over the next 30 years.

Building a successful Toronto means that we have to make sustainable choices about how we grow. We have to see connections and understand the consequences of our choices. We have to integrate environmental, social and economic perspectives in our decision making. We have to meet the needs of today without compromising the ability of future generations to meet their needs.

There is no such thing as an isolated or purely local decision. Each of us makes choices every day about where to live, work, play, shop and how to travel. They seem like small choices, but together and over time the consequences of these choices can affect everyone's quality of life. That's why planning matters. . . .

This Plan is about the basics of successful city-building. Holistic and integrated thinking is a fundamental requirement for planning a modern city like Toronto. Integrated thinking means

seeing, understanding and accounting for all the connections as we go about our decision making. Sometimes it means thinking differently about solutions. Always it means searching for outcomes that demonstrate integration, balance and interdependence and that earn social, environmental and economic benefits. . . .

Toronto cannot plan in isolation or expect to stand alone in dealing with the effects of urban growth. Our view of the quality of urban life tends to be based on the local conditions in our own neighbourhoods. These conditions are in turn affected by events happening in the larger region. The quality of the air, water, services and region-wide transport systems all affect the quality of life in our neighbourhood, where we work and where we play. The way in which growth and change are managed in Toronto must mesh with that of our neighbours because we are integrally linked in many ways. . . .

Building a successful city means making choices that improve our quality of life. As our City grows and matures, we can create a more beautiful environment, healthy and vibrant communities and greater prosperity. . . .

In order to remain economically competitive in today's global economy, a city must be more than functional. It has to work well, but it also must be beautiful, vibrant, safe, and inclusive.

---

affordable housing, and a need for more waste disposal sites are three of its main concerns. Following the consolidation of its six municipalities, the city set about developing and implementing a new Official Plan—a vision of how Toronto will change and grow in the new millennium—by setting priorities for social, environmental, and economic development (see the Cityscape box above). The plan's aim is to (1) protect the best of what it has; (2) invest in areas that are aging and need revitalizing; (3) ensure that new development is consistent with the existing character of the area; and (4) convert former industrial lands into uses that fit into the surrounding neighborhoods and add to community vitality

(Toronto 2005). Facing its future, Toronto's leaders recognize that good, people-oriented planning is essential to its continued vitality as "a city that works."

SUMMARY

Ancient, medieval, and modern cities have usually evolved through the planning of their physical layout and structure, if not in their entirety, then certainly at least in part. Such planning addressed urban problems (protection, water supply, sanitation, traffic, and leisure activities);

Great cities do not happen by accident—they are designed and orchestrated so that individual private and public developments work together to create cohesive blocks, neighbourhoods and districts. Good urban design is not just an aesthetic overlay, but an essential ingredient of city-building. Good urban design is good business and good social policy.

Civic pride is infectious. The City and the private sector should work together as partners in creating a great city and achieving Toronto's architectural and urban design potential. The City can play its part by organizing, designing, maintaining and improving the streets, parks and public buildings. The private sector can do its part by building the structures and landscapes that define and support these public places. This Plan demands that both the public and private sectors commit to high quality architecture, landscape architecture and urban design.

Beautiful, comfortable, safe and accessible streets, parks, open spaces and public buildings are a key shared asset. These public spaces draw people together, creating strong social bonds at the neighbourhood, city and regional level. They convey our public image to the world and unite us as a city. They set the stage for our festivals, parades and civic life as well as for daily casual contact. Public space creates communities.

This Plan recognizes how important good design is in creating a great city. Great cities are judged by the look and quality of their squares, parks, streets and public spaces and the buildings which frame and define them. People flock to the world's great cities not just to enjoy the culture, but to wander the streets, to explore their parks and plazas, to enjoy the street life, to shop and to people watch. The same characteristics and qualities that make these cities great places to visit also make them great places to live. What do these places share in common? All are very urban, high density, mixed use, mixed income, transit and pedestrian oriented vibrant places.

Great cities not only have great buildings—but the buildings work together to create great streets, plazas, parks and public places. Great cities inspire and astonish. Whether it's a bustling shopping street lined by vibrant shop windows and sidewalk cafes, an intimate, residential, tree-lined street, or a public plaza in the central business district—everywhere you look there is evidence that the place has been designed. The buildings, both public and private, work together to create the "walls" for the city's great outdoor "rooms."

Source: Toronto Urban Development Services, *Toronto Official Plan* (May 2002). Accessed online at http://www.city.toronto.on.ca/.

glorified the ruling elite (statues, buildings, plazas, parks); and reflected cultural ideals (such as the scale of religious or commercial structures or direction of processional routes).

In the late nineteenth century, two urban visionaries influenced many architects and planners. David Burnam's work at the 1893 World's Fair in Chicago inspired the "city beautiful" movement throughout the United States. In England, Ebenezer Howard gave action to his concept of "garden cities" by building Letchworth and Welwyn in the early twentieth century. An early example in the United States of a planned new town is Radburn, New Jersey; though never completed, it served as a model for other new towns worldwide. As centers of residence, employment and leisure activities, new towns have been more successful in countries with a strong tradition of central government planning, than in the United States with its greater emphasis on individualism and home rule.

Architectural visions of a new central city—such as Le Corbusier's "radiant city," Wright's "broadacre city," and Soleri's "arcology"—are simply impractical utopias, but they do challenge our thinking about cities and prod us to consider bolder solutions to the cities' ills. The rebuilding of New Orleans has provided a unique opportunity for a complete makeover of the city's design to improve the quality of life there, but it appears unlikely that any bold initiatives will take place. Instead, the emphasis so far has been in strengthening the levees and rebuilding residences and businesses as once before.

Elsewhere, urban planners have been focusing on smaller sections of the city—its neighborhoods, open spaces, water edges, and historic sections—to revitalize tourist, leisure and economy activity while making the city a more attractive locale. Economics, politics, and values are extremely significant factors in influencing what does or does not happen in urban planning. Although most cities attempt to control their destinies through good government planning, Toronto serves as a particularly impressive model for a comprehensive plan for its future.

CONCLUSION

Can we honestly say that one type of city planning has been spectacularly more effective than any other? Our review suggests a number of conclusions.

First, all the evidence suggests that changing a city's physical form does not automatically reshape social life. In new towns the world over— from Ebenezer Howard's Letchworth to James Rouse's Columbia to Lúcio Costa's Brasilia— new structures have become home to many old problems, including harmful prejudices, class antagonism, and environmental pollution. So we may conclude that changing the city physically, while sometimes necessary, is not sufficient to realize the idealistic environment envisioned by planners. The best planning blends good sociology with dramatic architecture.

Second, all of the planning experiments of the last century have fallen short of their goals. New towns have not solved the problems of large cities, nor have they been able to solve many of their own troubles. Utopian designs intrigue us but offer few real solutions. Finally, small-scale efforts, such as those proposed by Jane Jacobs, August Heckscher, William H. Whyte, and James Rouse, are helpful but often leave untouched the larger problems of the city—such as racial prejudice and desperate poverty.

Third, we always must bear in mind that urban planning occurs within a framework of certain unbending realities. Economic and political considerations limit the scope of any plan. If it costs too much, it won't be done. If sponsored by the rich, it probably won't be much help to the poor. What some people want, others are sure to resist. Urban planners, if they are to have any chance to work their craft, must become skillful politicians.

Surely, planning is vital to the future of our cities. But we must merge two often-contradictory forces—the planners' desire to shape the urban environment, and a free people's need to choose. We must also overcome the tendency to think in purely local terms and recognize instead the need for a regional, integrated view of metropolitan regions. Cities and suburbs do not exist independently of one another; their fates are inextricably linked, for many of the issues and problems that affect quality of life transcend municipal boundaries. Further, to ensure the vitality of cities in the twenty-first century, planners and the public need to gain an understanding of both the problems and the possibilities of urban life. And, yes, even try to learn from some of the utopian thinkers of the past.

As cities struggle to define their futures, people must ask some hard questions of themselves and of their leaders. Why should we plan in the first place? What are the issues that planners can address better than the people themselves? Whom does any plan really benefit? Guiding the discussion that such questions provoke, we also suggest, must be a fundamental commitment to the health and welfare of all people who live in the city. With such a dedication—evident today in the urban life of Toronto's people—it is possible that, in time, we will generate a vision of the street that perhaps all citizens can understand.

KEY TERMS

Arcologies
City Beautiful movement
Garden cities
Green belt
New towns
Urban utopia

REFERENCES

ABBOTT, CARL. 1995. "Portland: People, Places, and Politics." *Urban Affairs,* Winter.

ABC NEWS. 2000. "Crime Fears Linger." Accessed online at http://abcnews.go.com/sections/politics/DailyNews/poll000607.html on September 23, 2002.

———. 2002. "Poll: Crime Worries Running High." Accessed online at http://abcnews.go.com/sections/us/trDailyNews/crime_poll010604.html on September 23, 2002.

ABRAHAMSON, MARK. 1996. *Urban Enclaves: Identity and Place in America.* New York: St. Martin's Press.

ABU-LUGHOD, JANET. 1980. *Rabat: Urban Apartheid in Morocco.* Princeton, NJ: Princeton University Press.

———. 1984. "Culture, 'Modes of Production,' and the Changing Nature of Cities in the Arab World." Pp. 94–119 in *The City in Cultural Context,* edited by John A. Agrow, John Mercer, and David E. Sopher. Boston: Allen and Unwin.

ADAMS, ROBERT MCC. 1966. *The Evolution of Urban Society: Early Mesopotamia and Prehistoric Mexico.* Chicago: Aldine Publishing Company.

ADDAMS, JANE. 1909. *The Spirit of Youth and the City Streets.* New York: Macmillan.

———. 1910. *Twenty Years at Hull House.* New York: Macmillan.

———. 1930. *The Second Twenty Years at Hull House.* New York: Macmillan.

ADLER, JERRY, AND MAGGIE MALONE. 1996. "Toppling Towers." *Newsweek,* November 4, pp. 70–72.

AIELLO, J. R., J. S. VAUTIER, AND M. D. BERNSTEIN. 1983. "Crowding Stress: Impact of Social Support, Group Formation, and Control," paper presented at the 91st annual convention of the American Psychological Association, Anaheim, California.

ALONSO, WILLIAM. 1971. "A Theory of the Urban Land Market." Pp. 154–59 in *Internal Structure of the City,* edited by Larry S. Bourne. New York: Oxford University Press.

AMERICAN FARMLAND TRUST. 2005. "Farming on the Edge: Sprawling Development Threatens America's Best Farmland." Accessed at www.farmland.org/farmingontheedge/major_findings.htm on June 20, 2005.

AMERICAN LUNG ASSOCIATION. 2000. *State of the Air 2000.* Accessed at www.lungusa.org/air2000/sota_table2.html on August 4, 2002.

AMERICAN PLANNING ASSOCIATION. 2005. "Paying for Sprawl." Accessed at www.planning.org/viewpoints/sprawl.htm on June 20, 2005.

ANDERSON, ELIJAH. 1990. *Streetwise: Race, Class, and Change in an Urban Community.* Chicago: University of Chicago Press. *Architectural Forum.* 1951. "Slum Surgery in St. Louis." April, pp. 128–36.

ARCOSANTI. 2005. www.arcosanti.org. Accessed September 4, 2005.

ARMS OF LOVE INTERNATIONAL. 2002. *What We Do: Street Children.* Accessed at www.armsoflove.org/what_street. htm# on July 29, 2005.

ARMSTRONG, REGINA BELZ. 1972. *The Office Industry.* Cambridge, MA: MIT Press.

ASBURY, HERBERT. 1940. *The Chicago Underworld.* New York: Ace.

AUSTIN, ALFREDO LOPEZ, AND LEONARDO LOPEZ LUJAN. 2001. *Mexico's Indigenous Past.* Norman: University of Oklahoma Press.

AUSTIN, ALICE CONSTANCE. 1935. *The Next Step.* Los Angeles: Institute Press.

AWANOHARA, SUSUMU. 1991a. "All in the Family." *Far Eastern Economic Review* 151 (March 14): 36–37.

———. 1991b. "Political Indian Summer." *Far Eastern Economic Review* 151 (May 25): 35.

BABBITT, BRUCE. 2005. "How to Rebuild New Orleans: Make It an Island," *New York Times* (September 9), p. A17.

BAGLEY, CHRISTOPHER. 1989. "Urban Crowding and the Murder Rate in Bombay, India." *Perceptual and Motor Skills* 69 (August): 1241–42.

BAHR, H. 1973. *Skid Row: An Introduction to Disaffiliation.* New York: Oxford University Press.

BAILEY, JAMES, ed. 1973. *New Towns in America.* New York: Wiley.

BALDASSARE, MARK. 1979. *Residential Crowding in Urban America.* Berkeley: University of California Press.

BALTZELL, E. DIGBY. 1964. *The Protestant Establishment.* New York: Vintage.

———. 1980. *Puritan Boston and Quaker Philadelphia.* New York: Free Press.

———. 1989/1958. *Philadelphia Gentleman: The Making of a National Upper Class.* Reprint ed. Philadelphia: University of Pennsylvania Press.

BANFIELD, EDWARD C. 1970. *The Unheavenly City.* Boston: Little, Brown.

———. 1974. *The Unheavenly City Revisited.* Boston: Little, Brown.

BANGKOK MUNICIPAL ADMINISTRATION. 2001. *Profile of Bangkok City.* Accessed at www.rrcap.unep.org/reports/soe/ bangkok_profile.pdf on August 9, 2005.

BANHAM, RAYNER. 2001. *Los Angeles: The Architecture of Four Ecologies.* Berkeley: University of California Press. (Orig. edition 1973, Viking Penguin).

BARTHELME, DONALD. 1978. *City Life.* New York: Pocket Books.

BAUDER, H., AND E. PERLE. 1999. "Spatial and Skills Mismatch for Labor-Market Segments." *Environment and Planning* 31:959–77.

BEGUIN, GILES, AND DOMINQUE MOREL. 1997. *The Forbidden City: Heart of Imperial China.* London: Thames and Hudson, Ltd.

BEITO, DAVID T., PETER GORDON, AND ALEXANDER TABARROK (eds.). 2002. *The Voluntary City: Choice, Community, and Civil Society.* Ann Arbor: University of Michigan Press.

BELKIN, LISA. 1983. "Jersey Town: A Feeling of Community." *New York Times*, September 14, p. B1.

BELL, WENDELL, AND MARION BOAT. 1957. "Urban Neighborhoods and Informal Social Relations." *American Journal of Sociology* 62:391–98.

BELLAH, ROBERT N., RICHARD MADSEN, WILLIAM M. SULLIVAN, ANN SWIDLER, AND STEVEN M. TIPTON. 1985. *Habits of the Heart: Individualism and Commitment in American Life.* New York: Harper & Row.

BELLUSH, J. 2000. *Urban Renewal: People, Politics, and Planning.* Garden City, NY: Doubleday.

BERGER, BENNETT. 1960. *Working Class Suburb.* Berkeley: University of California Press.

BERMAN, DAVID. 1997. "Shopping on the Edge." *Canadian Business*, October 31, pp. 72–79.

BERRY, BRIAN J. L. 1985. "Islands of Renewal in Seas of Decay." Pp. 69–98 in *The New Urban Reality*, edited by Paul E. Peterson. Washington, DC: Brookings Institution.

BERRY, BRIAN J. L., AND PHILIP H. REES. 1969. "The Factorial Ecology of Calcutta." *American Journal of Sociology* 74:445–91.

BEVERIDGE, ANDREW A., SUSAN WEBER, AND CHARIS NG. 1996. "Stroll the Upper East Side for Lifestyles of the Elite," *Footnotes* 24:3 (March). American Sociological Association.

BLAKELY, EDWARD J., AND MARY GAIL SNYDER. 1997. *Fortress America: Gated Communities in the United States.* Washington, DC: Brookings Institution Press.

BLUESTONE, BARRY, AND BENNETT HARRISON. 1984. *The Deindustrialization of America: Plant Closings, Community Abandonment, and the Dismantling of Basic Industry.* New York: Basic Books.

BONNES, MIRILIA, MARINO BONAIUTO, AND ANNA PAOLA. 1991. "Crowding and Residential Satisfaction in the Urban Environment: A Contextual Approach." *Environment and Behavior* 23 (September): 531–52.

BOOKCHIN, MURRAY. 1996. *The Limits of the City.* 2nd rev. ed. Toronto: Black Rose Books.

BORJAS, GEORGE J. 2001. *Heaven's Door: Immigration Policy and the American Economy.* Princeton, NJ: Princeton University Press.

BORUKHOV, ELI, YONA GINSBERG, and ELIA WERCZBERG. 1979. "The Social Ecology of Tel Aviv." *Urban Affairs Quarterly* 15: 183–205.

BOSS-BICAK, SHIRA. 2004. "Cut Red Tape to Ease Shortage," *Crain's New York Business* 20 (February 16-22): 24.

BOTT, ELIZABETH. 1972. *Family and Social Network.* 2nd ed. New York: Free Press.

BOYER, R. E., AND K. A. DAVIES. 1973. "Urbanization in Nineteenth Century Latin America: Statistics and Sources." *Statistical Abstract of Latin America.* July supplement.

BRADBURY, CATHERINE, ANTHONY DOWNS, AND KENNETH SMALL. 1982. *Urban Decline and the Future of American Cities.* Washington, DC: Brookings Institution.

BRIDENBAUGH, CARL. 1964. *Cities in the Wilderness.* New York: Capricorn Books.

Britannica Book of the Year. 2005. Chicago: Encyclopaedia Britannica.

BROCKERHOFF, MARTIN. 2000. "An Urbanizing World." *Population Bulletin* 55 (September).

BROKAW, TOM. 2002. NBC News, June 27.

BROOKS, VAN WYCK. 1936. *The Flowering of New England.* New York: Modern Library.

BRUCE, J. M. 1970. "Intergenerational Occupational Mobility and Visiting with Kin and Friend." *Social Forces* 49:117–27.

BRUNO, PAT. 2001. "Dinner and a Show: New Theaters Draw Diners Downtown." *Chicago Sun-Times*, September 7, p. 16.

BUCKLAND, ROBERT. 1968. *Share My Taxi.* London: Michael Joseph.

BUREAU OF JUSTICE STATISTICS. 1999. *Criminal Victimization 1998: Changes 1997–98 with Trends 1993–98.* Accessed at www.ojp.usdoj. gov/bis/pub/ascii/cv98.txt on December 26, 1999.

BURGESS, ERNEST W. 1984. "The Growth of the City." Pp. 47–62 in *The City*, edited by Robert E. Park and Ernest W. Burgess. Chicago: University of Chicago Press.

BURN, A. R. 1970. *Greece and Rome.* Glenview, IL: Scott, Foresman.

BUTTERWORTH, DOUGLAS, AND JOHN K. CHANCE. 1981. *Latin American Urbanization*. New York: Cambridge University Press.

BYRON, ROBERT. 1982. *The Road to Oxiana*. New York: Oxford University Press.

CAHNMAN, WERNER, AND RUDOLF HEBERLE. 1971. *Ferdinand Tönnies, On Sociology: Pure, Applied and Empirical*. Chicago: University of Chicago Press.

CALDWELL, WILLIAM A., ed. 1973. *How to Save Urban America*. New York: Signet.

CALHOUN, JOHN B. 1962. "Population Density and Social Pathology." *Scientific American* 206:139–48.

CANADIAN CENTRE FOR JUSTICE STATISTICS. 2005. *Juristat*.26. Ottawa.

CASA ALIANZA. 2004. *Street Children and Juvenile Justice in Nicaragua*. Accessed at www.streetchildren.org.uk/ reports/Nicaragua on July 29, 2005.

CASTELLS, MANUEL. 1979. *The Urban Question*. Cambridge, MA: MIT Press.

———. 1982. *City, Class, and Power*. New York: Palgrave Macmillan.

———. 1985. *The City and the Grass Roots*. Berkeley: University of California Press.

———. 1991. *The Informational City*. Malden, MA: Blackwell.

CAULFIELD, JON. 1994. *City Form and Everyday Life: Toronto's Gentrification and Critical Social Practice*. Toronto: University of Toronto Press.

CENTER FOR MEDIA AND PUBLIC AFFAIRS. 1999. *Merchandizing Mayhem: Violence in Popular Culture*. Accessed online at www.cmpa.com/archive/viol98.htm on September 23, 2002.

CENTRAL INTELLIGENCE AGENCY. 2005. *World Factbook*. Accessed at http://www.odci.gov/cia/publications/ factbook/index.html on February 17, 2006.

CENTRO LATINO DE EDUCACIÓN POPULAR. 2005. "Pico-Union: A Community Profile." Accessed at http://www. centrolatinoliteracy.org/overview/overviewneighbor-hood.htm on July 12, 2005.

CHANDLER, MITTIE O. 1988. *Urban Homesteading: Programs and Policies*. Westport, CT: Greenwood Press.

CHANDLER, TERTIUS. 1987. *Four Thousand Years of Urban Growth*. Lewiston, NJ: Edwin Mellen Press.

CHANG, KWANG-CHIH. 1977. *Archaeology of Ancient China*. New Haven, CT: Yale University Press.

CHARLES, CAMILLE Z. 2000. "Neighborhood Racial-Composition Preferences: Evidence from a Multiethnic Metropolis," *Social Problems* 47: 379–98.

CHILDE, V. GORDON. 1950. "The Urban Revolution." *Town Planning Review* 21:3–17.

CHRISTALLER, WALTER. 1966. *Central Places in Southern Germany*. Englewood Cliffs, NJ: Prentice Hall.

CHUA-EOAN, HOWARD G. 1990. "Strangers in Paradise." *Time*, April 9, pp. 32–35.

CIARDI, JOHN. 1990. *How Does a Poem Mean?* 2nd ed. New York: Random House.

CITY-DATA.COM. Accessed September 4, 2005.

CITY OF NEW YORK. 2005. "Mayor Michael R. Bloomberg and NYC & Company Announce City Tourism to Hit Record Levels in 2004." Press release, January 10.

CITY OF SPOKANE PLANNING SERVICES DEPARTMENT. 2003. "City of Spokane's Comprehensive Plan." Accessed at www.spokaneplanning.org/history.htm on June 20, 2005.

CLARK, KENNETH. 1980. "The Role of Race." *New York Times Magazine*, October 5, pp. 25–33, 90–91.

CLARK, WILLIAM A.V. 1998. *The California Cauldron: Immigration and the Fortunes of Local Communities*. Guilford, CT: Guilford Press.

CLARKE, R.V. 1992. *Situational Crime Prevention*. Albany, NY: Harrow and Heston.

CLEAN WATER ACTION COUNCIL. 2005. *Land Use & Urban Sprawl*. Accessed at www.cwac.net/landuse/ on June 20, 2005.

CLEVELAND, WILLIAM L. 2004. *A History of the Modern Middle East*. 3rd ed. Boulder, CO: Westview Press.

COCHRUN, STEVEN E. 1994. "Understanding and Enhancing Neighborhood Sense of Community," *Journal of Planning Literature* 9: 92–99.

COHEN, JAMES R. 2000. "Abandoned Housing: Implications for Federal Policy and Local Action," paper presented at a Lincoln Center of Land Policy conference at Ithaca, New York, on September 8–9.

COHEN, WARREN, AND MIKE THARP. 1999. "Fed-up Cities Turn to Evicting the Homeless." *U.S. News & World Report,* January 11, pp. 28–30.

COLTEN, CRAIG E. 2005. "How to Rebuild New Orleans: Restore the Marsh," *New York Times* (September 9), p. A17.

COMMUNITY SERVICE SOCIETY OF NEW YORK. 2004. *Poverty in New York City, 2003*. Accessed at www.cssny.org/pdfs/ PovertyNYC2003.pdf on June 18, 2005.

CONGDON, PETER. 1995. "Socioeconomic Structure and Health in London." *Urban Studies* 32 (April): 523–49.

CONNOR, TIM. 2001. *Still Waiting for Nike to Do It*. San Francisco: Global Exchange.

CONWAY, DENNIS. 1990. "Non-White Immigration, Residential Segregation, and Selective Integration in a Restructuring Global Metropolis, New York City." Paper presented at the annual meeting of the International Sociological Association.

CONWAY, WILTRAM G. 1977. "People Fire in the Ghetto Ashes." *Saturday Review,* July 23, pp. 15–16.

CORCORAN, DAVID. 2003. "Restaurants: Unbound in Ironbound, *New York Times,* July 20, p. NJ10.

COSTELLO, VINCENT F. 1977. *Urbanization in the Middle East*. New York: Cambridge University Press.

COTTRELL, JOHN, AND THE EDITORS OF TIME-LIFE. 1979. *The Great Cities: Mexico City*. Amsterdam: Time-Life.

COX, HARVEY. 1965. *The Secular City*. New York: Macmillan.

CRUTCHER, MICHAEL E. 2005. "How to Rebuild New Orleans: Build Diversity," *New York Times* (September 9), p. A17.

CUMMINGS, KIM C. 2000. "Regenerating Social Capital in Urban Neighborhoods: A Case Study." *Journal of Applied Sociology* 17:56–68.

CURRAN, DAN. 2003. "Sherman Park Still One of Milwaukee's Most Vibrant Areas." Accessed at www. onmilwaukee.com/visitors/articles/shermanpark.html on July 8, 2005.

DANA, RICHARD HENRY. 2001. *Two Years Before the Mast*. New York: Random House Modern Library; originally published 1862.

The Dark Side of the American Dream. 1998. At www.sierraclub.org/sprawl/report98/report.asp. Accessed on January 9, 2003.

DASGUPTA, SATHI. 1992. "Conjugal Roles and Social Network in Indian Immigrant Families." *Journal of Comparative Family Studies* 23:465–80.

DAVIDSON, BASIL. 2001. *Africa in History: Themes and Outlines*. 4th. ed. London: Orion Publishing Company.

DAVIES, WAYNE K.D. 1984. *Factorial Ecology*. Aldershot, England: Gower Publishing.

DAVIS, KINGSLEY. 1969, 1972. *World Urbanization, 1950–1970*. Vols. 1, 2. Berkeley, CA: Institute of International Studies.

DEAR, MICHAEL J. 2000. *The Postmodern Urban Condition*. Malden, MA: Blackwell.

DEEGAN, MARY JO. 1991. *Women in Sociology: A Bio-Bibliographical Sourcebook*. Westport, CT: Greenwood Press.

DE JONG, IAIN. 2000. "Devolution Hits Housing in Canada," *Shelterforce Online*. Accessed at www.nhi.org/online/issues/113/dejong.html on July 8, 2005.

DEMAREST, MICHAEL. 1981. "He Digs Downtown." *Time*, August 24, pp. 36–43.

DENT, DAVID J. 1992. "The New Black Suburbs." *New York Times Magazine*, June 14.

DIALA, CHAMBERLAIN C. AND CARLES MUNTANER. 2003. "Mood and Anxiety Disorders Among Rural, Urban, and Metropolitan Residents in the United States," *Community Mental Health Journal* 39: 239–52.

DIAZ, BERNAL. 1956. *The Discovery and Conquest of Mexico*. New York: Farrar, Straus, and Cudahy.

DICKENS, CHARLES. 1853. *Bleak House*. London: Chapman and Hall.

———. 1955, orig. 1854. *Hard Times*. London: Chapman and Hall.

———. 1860. *Great Expectations*. London: Chapman and Hall.

DIGIOVANNI, FRANK F. 1984. "An Examination of Selected Consequences of Revitalization in Six U.S. Cities." *Urban Studies* 21:245–59.

DIIULIO, JOHN J., JR. 1995. "Comment on Douglas S. Massey's 'Getting Away with Murder.'" *University of Pennsylvania Law Review* 143 (May): 1275–84.

DINER, HASIA R. 1983. *Erin's Daughters in America: Irish Immigrant Women in the Nineteenth Century*. Baltimore: Johns Hopkins University Press.

DIXON, PATRICIA. 2005. *AIDS in Africa: In-Depth Report*. Accessed at http://www.globalchange.com/aidsafrica.htm on August 8, 2005.

DOBRINER, WILLIAM. 1963. *Class in Suburbia*. Englewood Cliffs, NJ: Prentice Hall.

DOS PASSOS, JOHN. 1969. "San Francisco Looks West." Pp. 484–89 in *City Life*, edited by Oscar Shoenfeld and Helen MacLean. New York: Grossman; essay originally published 1944.

DOWNS, ANTHONY. 1982. *Neighborhoods and Urban Development*. Washington, DC: Brookings Institution.

———. 1985. "The Future of Industrial Cities." Pp. 281–94 in *The New Urban Reality*, edited by Paul E. Peterson. Washington, DC: Brookings Institution.

DUNCAN, BEVERLY. 1956. "Factors in Work–Residence Separation: Wages and Salary Workers." *American Journal of Sociology* 21:48–56.

DUNCAN, SUSANA. 1977. "Mental Maps of New York." *New York*, December 19, pp. 51–62.

DUNLAP, DAVID W. 1999. "Filling in the Blanks at Battery Park City." *New York Times*, February 7, p. RE2.

DURKHEIM, EMILE. 1964. *The Division of Labor in Society*. New York: Free Press; originally published 1893.

EGAN, TIMOTHY. 1996. "Portland's Hard Line on Managing Growth." *New York Times*, December 30, p. A1.

EIESLAND, NANCY L. 2000. *A Particular Place: Urban Restructuring and Religious Ecology in a Southern Exurb*. New Brunswick, NJ: Rutgers University Press.

EISNER, SIMON, ARTHUR GALLION, AND STANLEY EISNER. 1993. *The Urban Pattern*. 6th ed. New York: Wiley.

ENGELS, FRIEDRICH. 1958. *The Condition of the Working Class in England*, trans. by W. O. Henderson and W. H. Chaloner. New York: Macmillan.

FABBI, NADINE. 2003. *Early Black Canadian History*. Accessed at http://jsis.artsci.washington.edu/programs/canada/edumodules/Early%20Black%20Canadian%20History.pdf on July 30, 2005.

FAJNZYLBER, PABLO, DANIEL LEDERMAN, AND NORMAN LOAYZA. 2002. "Inequality and Violent Crime," *The Journal of Law & Economics* 45 (April): 1–40.

FARIS, ROBERT. 1967. *Chicago Sociology: 1920–1932*. Chicago: University of Chicago Press.

FARLEY, REYNOLDS, ET AL. 1993. "Continued Racial Residential Segregation in Detroit: 'Chocolate City, Vanilla Suburbs' Revisited." *Journal of Housing Research* 4(1):1–38.

FEDERAL BUREAU OF INVESTIGATION. 2005. *Crime in the United States—2004*. Accessed at www.fbi.gov/ucr/cius_03/pdf/toc03.pdf on June 18, 2005.

FEDERAL RESERVE SYSTEM. 2000. *Federal Reserve Bulletin*. Washington, DC: U.S. Government Printing Office.

FERNANDEZ-KELLY, M. 1991. "Labor Force Recomposition and Industrial Restructuring in Electronics." Paper presented at symposium: "Crossing National Borders: Invasion or Involvement." December 6, Columbia University.

FILION, PIERRE. 1995. "City Form and Everyday Life: Toronto's Gentrification and Critical Social Practice." *Journal of the American Planning Association* 61 (Spring): 281–82.

FISCHER, CLAUDE S. 1971. "A Research Note on Urbanism and Tolerance." *American Journal of Sociology* 76:847–56.

———. 1973. "Urban Malaise." *Social Problems* 52:221–35.

———. 1975. "Toward a Subcultural Theory of Urbanism." *American Journal of Sociology* 80:1319–41.

———. 1984. *The Urban Experience*. 2nd ed. Orlando: Harcourt Brace Jovanovich.

———. 1991. "Ambivalent Communities: How Americans Understand Their Localities." Pp. 79–90, in *America at Century's End*, edited by Alan Wolf. Berkeley: University of California Press.

FISCHER, CLAUDE, R. M. JACKSON, C. A. STUEVE, K. GERSON, AND L. M. JONES. 1977. *Networks and Places.* New York: Free Press.

FISCHER, CLAUDE S., ET AL. 1996. *Inequality by Design: Cracking the Bell Curve Myth.* Princeton, NJ: Princeton University Press.

FISHMAN, ROBERT. 1982. *Urban Utopias in the Twentieth Century.* Cambridge, MA: MIT Press.

FLEISHMAN, SANDRA. 1999. "Abandoned Housing Is Now Hot Property." *Washington Post,* September 1, p. BO1.

FLORIAN, ELLEN. 1999. "Oh, No, It's Spreading." *Newsweek,* July 19, pp. 24–25.

FORBES, KATHRYN. 1999. *Mama's Bank Account.* Minneapolis: Sagebrush.

FRANCK, KAREN. 1981. "In Cities, Fast Friends Come Slowly." *Psychology Today,* (April), pp. 32–33.

FREEDMAN, JONATHAN. 1978. *Happy People.* New York: Ballantine.

FREEMAN, JO. 2000. *The Politics of Women's Liberation: A Case Study of an Emerging Movement and Its Relation to the Policy Process.* Reprint ed. New York: David McKay.

FREEMAN, LANCE AND FRANK BRACONI. 2004. "Gentrification and Displacement," *Journal of the American Planning Association* 70:39–52.

FRENCH, R. A., AND F. E. IAN HAMILTON. 1979. "Is There a Socialist City?" Pp. 1–22 in *The Socialist City,* edited by R. A. French and F. E. Ian Hamilton. New York: Wiley.

FREUDENBERG, WILLIAM R. 1992. "Addictive Economics: Extractive Industries and Vulnerable Localities in a Changing World Economy." *Rural Sociology* 57 (3):305–22.

FREY, WILLIAM H. 1998. "Black Migration to the South Reaches Record Highs in 1990s." *Population Today,* (February): 1–2.

FU, VINCENT K. 2001. "Racial Intermarriage Pairings," *Demography* 38:147–59.

FUNK, WILFRED. 1978. *Word Origins.* New York: Bell.

GALLUN, ALBY. 2005. "Cabrini's Green," *Crain's Chicago Business* 28 (May 16): 3, 8.

GALSTER, GEORGE. 1990. "Racial Discrimination in Housing Markets during the 1980s: A Review of the Audit Evidence." *Journal of Planning Education and Research* 9(3):165–75.

———. 1996. *Reality and Research: Social Science and U.S. Urban Policy since 1960.* New York: Urban Institute Press.

GANS, HERBERT. 1962a. "City Planning and Urban Realities." *Commentary* 33:170–75.

———. 1962b. *The Urban Villagers.* New York: Free Press.

———. 1968. "Urbanism and Suburbanism as Ways of Life: A Re-evaluation of Definitions." Pp. 34–52 in *People and Plans.* New York: Basic Books.

———. 1982. *The Urban Villagers: Group and Class in the Life of Italian Americans.* New York: Free Press.

GARBER, JUDITH A., AND ROBY TURNER, eds. 1994. *Gender in Urban Research.* Thousand Oaks, CA: Sage.

GARCIA-HALLCOM, FRANCINE. 1997. *An Urban Ethnography of Latino Street.* Accessed at www.csun.edu/~hcchs006/gang.html on August 1, 2005.

GARREAU, JOEL. 1991. *Edge City.* New York: Doubleday.

GEISSE, G., AND F. SABATINI. 1988. "Latin American Cities and Their Poor." Pp. 322–27 in *The Metropolitan Era,* edited by M. Dogan and J. Kasarda. Newbury Park, CA: Sage.

GEORGANO, G. N. 1973. *A History of the London Taxicab.* New York: Drake.

GIBBON, EDWARD. 1932. *The Decline and Fall of the Roman Empire.* New York: Modern Library; originally published in London, 1879.

GIBBONS, DEBORAH AND PAUL M. OLK. 2003. "Individual and Structural Origins of Friendship and Social Position Among Professionals," *Journal of Personality & Social Psychology* 84:340–51.

GIOVANNINI, JOSEPH. 1983. "I Love New York and L.A., Too." *New York Times Magazine,* September 11, pp. 145, 147–49.

GIRARDET, HERBERT. 1994. "Keeping Up with Capital Growth." *Geographical Magazine* 66 (June): 12–15.

GLAAB, CHARLES N. 1963. *The American City: A Documentary History.* Homewood, IL: Dorsey Press.

GLAAB, CHARLES N., AND A. THEODORE BROWN. 1967. *A History of Urban America.* New York: Macmillan.

GLAZER, NATHAN, AND DANIEL P. MOYNIHAN. 1970. *Beyond the Melting Pot.* 2nd ed. Cambridge, MA: MIT Press.

GOFFMAN, ERVING. 1980. *Relations in Public.* New York: HarperCollins.

GOLDBERGER, PAUL. 1989. *City Observed: New York.* New York: Vintage.

GOLIBER, THOMAS J. 2002. "The Status of the HIV/Aids Epidemic in Sub-Saharan Africa." *Population Bulletin* (July).

GORDON, TRACY M. 2004. "Moving Up by Moving Out? Planned Developments and Residential Segregation in California." *Urban Studies* 41 (February): 441–61.

GORMAN, S. 2003. "Labor Pain," *Washington Monthly* 35 (September): 20.

GOTTDIENER, MARK AND RAY HUTCHISON. 2000. *The New Urban Sociology.* 2nd ed. New York: McGraw-Hill.

———. 2001. *The Theming of America.* 2nd ed. Boulder, CO: Westview Press.

GOTTDIENER, MARK, AND JOE FEAGIN. 1988. "The Paradigm Shift in Urban Sociology." *Urban Affairs Quarterly* 24:163–87.

GOTTMANN, JEAN. 1961. *Megalopolis.* New York: Twentieth Century Fund.

GRAY, KATHLEEN. 2005. "Declining Numbers Give Detroit Image Problem," *Detroit Free Press,* February 8, p. 1.

GRAY, ROBERT. 1986. *A History of London.* London: Dorset Press.

GREEN, CONSTANCE. 1957. *American Cities.* Welwyn Garden City, England: Broadwater Press.

GREEN, ROBERT L. 1977. *The Urban Challenge: Poverty and Race.* Chicago: Follett.

GREENFIELD, GERALD M. 1994. *Latin American Urbanization.* Westport, CT: Greenwood Publishing Group.

GREENGARD, SAMUEL, AND CHARLENE M. SOLOMON. 1994. "A City Rebuilds Its Symbol—and Rejuvenates Itself." *Personnel Journal* 73 (February): 64–65.

GREER, SCOTT. 1962. *The Emerging City.* New York: Free Press.

———. 1966. *Urban Renewal and American Cities.* Indianapolis: Bobbs-Merrill.

GUGLER, JOSEF. 1996. *The Urban Transformation of the Developing World: Regional Trajectories.* New York: Oxford University Press.

GWYNNE, ROBERT N. 1985. *Industrialization and Urbanization in Latin America.* Baltimore: The Johns Hopkins University Press.

HABITAT FOR HUMANITY. 2005. *Habitat for Humanity Fact Sheet.* Accessed at www.habitat.org/how/factsheet.html on December 27, 2005.

HACKLER, TIM. 1979. "The Big City Has No Corners on Mental Illness." *New York Times Magazine,* December 19, p. A1.

HALL, EDWARD. 1966. *The Hidden Dimension.* Garden City, NY: Doubleday. Chap. 13.

HALL, PETER. 2002. *Urban and Regional Planning.* 4th ed. London: Routledge.

———. 1984. "Geography." Pp. 21–36 in *Cities of the Mind,* edited by Lloyd Rodwin and Robert M. Hollister. New York: Plenum.

———. 1988. *The World Cities.* London: Orion Publishing Rave Macmillan.

HAMBLIN, DORA JANE. 1973. *The First Cities.* New York: Little, Brown.

HANDEL, MICHAEL. 2003. "Skills Mismatch in the Labor Market," *Annual Review of Sociology* 29:135–65.

HANFF, HELENE. 1989. *Apple of My Eye.* Mt. Kisco, NY: Moyer Bell Ltd.

HARDOY, JORGE E. 1975. *Urbanization in Latin America.* New York: Anchor Books.

HARRIS, CHAUNCEY D., AND EDWARD L. ULLMAN. 1945. "The Nature of Cities." *Annals* 242:7–17.

HARVEY, DAVID. 1992. *Social Justice and the City.* Malden, MA: Blackwell; original ed. Baltimore: Johns Hopkins University Press, 1973.

HAWKES, JACQUETTA. 1973. *The First Great Civilizations.* New York: Knopf.

HAWLEY, AMOS. 1981. *Urban Society.* 2nd ed. New York: Wiley.

HAWLEY, CHRIS. 2004. "Trying to Exorcise Mexico's 'Little Devils'," *Arizona Republic* (December 20). Accessed at http://www.azcentral.com/specials/special03/articles/1220electricity.html on August 9, 2005.

HAYDEN, DELORES. 1978. "Two Utopian Feminists and Their Campaigns for Kitchenless Houses." *Signs: Journal of Women in Culture and Society* 4:274–90.

HAYWARD, STEVEN. "The Scourge of New Jobs." *New York Times,* June 12, 1999, p. A15.

HECKSCHER, AUGUST. 1978. *Open Spaces: The Life of American Cities.* New York: Harper & Row.

HEILBRONER, ROBERT L., AND WILLIAM S. MILBERG. 2001. *The Making of Economic Society.* 11th ed. Englewood Cliffs, NJ: Prentice Hall.

HEILBRUN, JAMES. 1987. *Urban Economics and Public Policy.* 3rd ed. New York: Palgrave Macmillian.

HEILPRIN, JOHN. 2005. "Groups: Sprawl Threatens Plants, Animals." Associated Press (January 11).

HELPER, ROSE. 1969. *Racial Policies and Practices of Real Estate Brokers.* Minneapolis: University of Minnesota Press.

HENG, LIANG, AND JUDITH SHAPIRO. 1984. *Son of the Revolution.* New York: Vintage.

HENLY, JULIA R., SANDRA K. DANZIGER, AND SHIRA OFFER. 2005. "The Contribution of Social Support to the Material Well-Being of Low Income Families," *Journal of Marriage and Family* 67:122–40.

HERBERT, WRAY. 1996. "Rock and Roller Coasters: Hit Cleveland's New Museum and Cedar Point's Rides for Thrills, Then Chill Out on Lake Erie's Isles." *U.S. News & World Report* 120 (April 15): 71–74.

HERRNSTEIN, RICHARD J., AND CHARLES MURRAY. 1994. *The Bell Curve: The Reshaping of American Life by Differences in Intelligence.* New York: Free Press.

HERSKOVITS, MELVILLE J. 2004. *The Human Factor in Changing Africa.* London: Routledge.

HEVESI, DENNIS. 2001. "East New York: A Neighborhood Reborn." *New York Times,* June 10, pp. RE1, 10.

HIGGS, ROBERT. 1980. *Competition and Coercion: Blacks in the American Economy, 1865–1914.* Chicago: University of Chicago Press.

HOCH, CHARLES, AND ROBERT A. SLAYTON. 1989. *New Homeless and Old: Community and the Skid Row Hotel.* Philadelphia: Temple University Press.

HOHENBERG, PAUL M., AND LYNN HOLLEN LEES. Reprint ed. 1996. *The Making of Urban Europe, 1000–1950.* Cambridge, MA: Harvard University Press.

HOLMES, GEORGE (ed.). 2002. *The Oxford History of Medieval Europe.* New York: Oxford University Press.

HOLUSHA, JOHN. 2002. "Strong Demand for Store Space in Manhattan." *New York Times,* July 28, pp. RE1, 6.

HOUSTON. 2005. Accessed at http://www.houstontx.gov/abouthouston/houstonfacts.html on July 17, 2005.

HOWARD, EBENEZER. 1965. *Garden Cities of To-Morrow.* Cambridge, MA: MIT Press.

HOWELL, JOSEPH T. 1973. *Hard Living on Clay Street.* Garden City, NY: Anchor.

HOXBY, CAROLINE M. 2004. "The Charter Advantage," *The Wilson Quarterly* 29 (Winter): 93–94.

HOYT, HOMER. 1939. *The Structure and Growth of Residential Neighborhoods in American Cities.* Washington, DC: Federal Housing Administration.

HUMAN RIGHTS WATCH. 2002. "Street Children." Accessed at www.hrw.org/children/street.htm on July 29, 2005.

HUNG, KWING, AND SHARON BOWLES. 1995. "Public Perceptions of Crime." *Juristat* 15 (January): 1.

INSTITUTE FOR CHILDREN AND POVERTY. 1998. *The Cycle of Family Homelessness: A Social Policy Reader.*

———. 2004. *Reports and Statistics.* Accessed at www.homesforthehomeless.com on February 17, 2006.

International Social Development Review. 1969. "Growth of the World's Urban and Rural Population: 1920–2000."

IRWIN, JOHN. 1977. *Scenes.* Beverly Hills, CA: Sage.

JACKSON, K. 1973. "The Crabgrass Frontier: 150 Years of Suburban Growth in America." Pp. 196–221 in *The Urban Experience: Themes in American History,* edited by R. Mohl and J. Richardson. Belmont, CA: Wadsworth.

JACOBS, JANE. 1992/1961. *The Death and Life of Great American Cities.* New York: Random House.

JARGOWSKY, PAUL A. 1996. "Take the Money and Run: Economic Segregation in U.S. Metropolitan Areas." *American Sociological Review* 61 (December): 984–98.

JOHNSON, KIRK, AND THOMAS J. LUECK. 1996. "Region's Economy in Fundamental Shift." *New York Times,* February 19, p. A1.

JOHNSTON, R. J. 1976. "Residential Area Characteristics." Pp. 193–235 in *Social Areas in Cities.* Vol. I, *Spatial Processes and Form,* edited by D. T. Herbert and R. J. Johnston. New York: Wiley.

JONES, DEL. 1999. "Employers Battle Urban Sprawl Issues." *USA Today,* June 14, p. 1B.

JUBILEE LINE EXTENSION. 1997. "Archaeological Excavation at London Bridge." www.jle.lul.co.uk/arch/index.htm.

KADUSHIN, CHARLES. 1983. "Mental Health and the Interpersonal Environment." *American Sociological Review* 48:188–98.

KALISH, SUSAN. 1995. "Spotlight: China." *Population Today* 23 (September): 7.

KAMIN, BLAIR. 1995. "Unifying Cities." *Chicago Tribune,* June 19, p. B1.

KARP, DAVID A., GREGORY P. STONE, AND WILLIAM C. YOELS. 1991. *Being Urban: A Sociology of City Life.* New York: Praeger.

KASARDA, JOHN D. 1993. "Inner-City Concentrated Poverty and Neighborhood Distress: 1970 to 1990." *Housing Policy Debate* 4(3):253–302.

KASARDA, JOHN D., AND EDWARD CRENSHAW. 1991. "Third World Urbanization: Dimensions, Theories, and Determinants." *Annual Review of Sociology* 17:467–501.

KAZIN, ALFRED. 1997. *A Walker in the City,* reprint ed. New York: MJF Books.

KELLER, SUZANNE. 1968. *The Urban Neighborhood.* New York: Random House.

KELLY, JOHN. 2005. *The Great Mortality: An Intimate History of the Black Death, The Most Devastating Plague of All Time.* New York: HarperCollins.

KEMP, BARRY J. 1992. *Ancient Egypt: Anatomy of a Civilization,* reprint ed. New York: Routledge.

KEMPER, ROBERT V. 1977. *Migration and Adaptation.* Beverly Hills, CA: Sage.

KENNEDY, RANDY. 2002. "Study Finds Airport-Related Business in New York Hit Hard by 9/11." *New York Times,* October 25, p. B3.

KIM, ILL SOO. 1981. *New Urban Immigrants: The Korean Community in New York.* Princeton, NJ: Princeton University Press.

KING, S. 1974. "Suburban Downtowns: The Shopping Centers." Pp. 101–104 in *Suburbia in Transition,* edited by L. Masotti and J. Hadden. New York: New York Times Books.

KOEGEL, PAUL, ET AL. 1996. "The Causes of Homelessless." *Homelessness in America.* Washington, DC: National Coalition for the Homeless.

KOMROFF, MANUEL, (ed.). 1964. *The Travels of Marco Polo.* Norwalk, CT: Heritage.

KRYSAN, MARIA. 2002. "Community Undesirability in Black and White: Examining Racial Residential Patterns through Community Perceptions," *Social Problems* 49:521–43.

KULHAVY, RAYMOND, W., AND WILLIAM A. STOCK. 1996. "How Cognitive Maps Are Learned and Remembered." *The Annals of the Association of American Geographers* 86 (March): 123–45.

KUNSTLER, JAMES. 1996. "Home from Nowhere." *Atlantic* (September): 43–66.

KWONG, PETER. 1996. *The New Chinatown.* Rev. ed. New York: Hill and Wang.

LAO, SHE. 1979. *Rickshaw.* Honolulu: University of Hawaii.

LARRIVIERE, JAMES B., AND CHARLES O. KRONCKE. 2004. "A Human Capital Approach to American Indian Earnings: The Effects of Place of Residence and Migration," *The Social Science Journal* 41:209–24.

LAURENTI, LUIGI. 1960. *Property Values and Race: Studies in Cities.* Berkeley: University of California Press.

LAWAL, NIKE S., MATTHEW N.O. SADIKU, AND ADE DOPAMU (eds.). 2004. *Understanding Yoruba Life and Culture.* Trenton, NJ: Africa World Press.

LAWLOR, JULIA. 2004. "The Ironbound: A Home Away From Home for Immigrants," *New York Times,* January 11, Section 11, p. 5.

LE CARRÉ, JOHN. 1978. *The Honourable Schoolboy.* New York: Bantam.

LE CORBUSIER. 1967. *The Radiant City.* New York: Grossman-Orion. Originally published 1933.

———. 1971. *The City of* New York: Architectural Press. Originally published 1927.

LEE, KEVIN K. 2000. *Urban Poverty in Canada: A Statistical Profile.* Canadian Council on Social Development. Accessed at www.ccsd.ca/pubs/2000/up/index.htm on July 29, 2005.

LEE, SHARON M. 1998. "Asian Americans: Diverse and Growing." *Population Bulletin,* June.

LEFEBVRE, HENRI. 1970. *La Revolution Urbaine.* Paris: Gallimard.

———. 1991. *The Production of Space.* Malden, MA: Blackwell.

LEGACY, JAMES. 2000. Review of *Hoodwinking the Nation. Knowledge, Technology & Policy* 12 (Winter 2000): 94–95.

LEGATES, RICHARD, AND CHESTER HARTMAN. 1986. "The Anatomy of Displacement in the U.S." In *Gentrification of the City,* edited by N. Smith and P. Williams. Boston: Allen & Unwin.

LEPORE, STEPHEN J., AND GARY W. EVANS. 1991. "Social Hassles and Psychological Health in the Context of Chronic Crowding." *Journal of Health and Social Behavior* 32 (December): 357–67.

LEVINE, JUDITH. 1980. "Cooperative Enterprise," *Manas Journal* 32:12–13.

LEVITAN, MARK. 2003. "Poverty in New York, 2002: One-Fifth of the City Lives Below the Federal Poverty Line." http://www.cssny.org/pubs/special/2003_09 poverty.pdf. Accessed June 27, 2005.

LEWIS MUMFORD CENTER FOR COMPARATIVE URBAN AND REGIONAL RESEARCH. 2001a. "Ethnic Diversity Grows, Neighborhood Integration Lags Behind." Albany: State University of New York. Accessed at http://mumford1.albany.edu/census/WholePop/WPreport/MumfordReport.pdf on February 17, 2006.

———. 2001b. *From Many Shores: Asians in Census 2000.* Accessed at http://mumford1.albany.edu/census/Asian Pop/AsianReport/AsianDownload.pdf on February 17, 2006.

———. 2001c. *The New Ethnic Enclaves in America's Suburbs.* Accessed at http://mumford1.albany.edu/census/suburban/SuburbanReport/SubReport.pdf on February 17, 2006.

———. 2002a. *Metropolitan Racial and Ethnic Change—Census 2000.* Accessed at www.albany.edu/mumford/census/ on September 21, 2002.

———. 2002b. *Hispanic Populations and their Residential Patterns in the Metropolis.* Accessed at http://mumford1.albany.edu/census/HispanicPop/HspReportNew/MumfordReport.pdf on February 17, 2006.

LICHTER, DANIEL T., AND MARTHA L. CROWLEY. 2002. "Poverty in America: Beyond Welfare Reform," *Population Bulletin* 57 (June).

LIEBERSON, STANLEY. 1963. *Ethnic Patterns in American Cities.* New York: Free Press.

LIEBERSON, STANLEY, AND MARY WATERS. 1988. *From Many Strands: Ethnic and Racial Groups in Contemporary America.* New York: Russell Sage Foundation.

LIEBOW, ELIOT. 2003. *Tally's Corner* 2nd ed. Lanham, MD: Rowman & Littlefield.

LINKON, SHERRY LEE, AND JOHN RUSSO. 2003. *Steeltown USA: Work and Memory in Youngstown.* Lawrence: University Press of Kansas.

LLOYD, ROBERT, AND HARTWELL HOOPER. 1991. "Urban Cognitive Maps: Computation and Structure," *Professional Geographer* 43:15–28.

LOEHNDORF, S. 2003. "Getting on Track." *E: the Environmental Magazine* 14 (November/December): 23–25

LOFLAND, LYN. 1985. *A World of Strangers: Order and Action in Urban Public Spaces.* Prospect Heights, IL: Waveland Press.

LOGAN, JOHN, AND HARVEY MOLOTCH. 1987. *Urban Fortunes: The Political Economy of Place.* Berkeley: University of California Press.

LOGAN, JOHN, AND LINDA STEARNS. 1981. "Suburban Racial Segregation as a Nonecological Process." *Social Forces* 60:61–73.

LOWE, JEANNE R. 1968. *Cities in a Race with Time.* New York: Vintage.

LUARD, TIM. 2004. "Paying the Price for China's Economic Growth." Accessed at http://news.bbc.co.uk/2/hi/asia-pacific/3743332.stm on July 24, 2005.

LUECK, THOMAS J. 1995. "Taking Heart in New York City." *New York Times,* October 8, p. A5.

LUNDBLAD, KAREN SHAFER. 1995. "Jane Addams and Social Reform: A Role Model for the 1990s." *Social Work* 40 (September): 661–69.

LYNCH, KEVIN. 1960. *The Image of the City.* Cambridge, MA: MIT Press.

———. 1984. "Reconsidering the Image of the City." Pp. 151–61 in *Cities of the Mind,* edited by Lloyd Rodwin and Robert M. Hollister. New York: Plenum.

LYNE, JACK. 2005. "New York Bulks Up Aid for Big Apple Manufacturers," *Site Selection* 50 (March): 180.

MACIONIS, JOHN J. 2004. *Sociology.* 10th ed. Upper Saddle River, NJ: Prentice Hall.

MACIVER, ROBERT. 1962. "The Great Emptiness," in *Man Alone: Alienation in Modern Society,* edited by Eric and Mary Josephson. New York: Dell Laurel.

MACLEOD, JAY. 2004. *Ain't No Makin' It* expanded ed. Boulder, CO: Westview Press.

MACMANUS, SUSAN, AND CHARLES BULLOCK. 1995. "Electing Women to Public Office." In *Gender in Urban Research,* edited by Judith A. Garber and Robyne S. Turner. Thousand Oaks, CA: Sage.

MAGEE, PETER. 2005. Excavations at Tepe Yahya, Iran, 1967–1975: The Iron Age Settlement. Cambridge, MA: Harvard University Press.

MARAINI, FOSCO. 1977. *Tokyo.* New York: Little, Brown and Company.

MARQUAND, JOHN P. 1943. *So Little Time.* Boston: Little, Brown.

MARSHALL, LEON S. 1969. "The English and American Industrial City of the Nineteenth Century." Pp. 148–55 in *American Urban History,* edited by Alexander B. Callow, Jr. New York: Oxford University Press.

MARTINES, LAURO. 1979. *Power and Imagination: City-States in Renaissance Italy.* New York: Knopf.

MARTINEZ, VALERIE J., R. KENNETH GODWIN, FRANK R. KEMERER, AND LAURA PERNA. 1995. "The Consequences of School Choice: Who Leaves and Who Stays in the Inner City." *Social Science Quarterly* 76 (September): 485–501.

MARX, KARL. 1859. "A Contribution to the Critique of Political Economy." Excerpted in *Marx and Engels: Basic Writings on Politics and Philosophy,* edited by Lewis S. Feuer. Garden City, NY: Anchor Books.

MARX, KARL, AND FRIEDRICH ENGELS. 1846. *The German Ideology.* New York: International Publishers, 1976.

MASSEY, DOREEN. 1994. *Space, Place, and Gender.* Minneapolis: University of Minnesota Press.

MASSEY, DOUGLAS S. 1984. "Processes of Hispanic and Black Spatial Segregation." *American Journal of Sociology* 89:836–73.

———. 1985. "Ethnic Residential Segregation: A Theoretical Synthesis and Empirical Review." *Sociology and Social Research* 69:315–50.

———. 1990. "American Apartheid: Segregation and the Making of the Underclass." *American Journal of Sociology* 96:329–54.

———. 1995. "Getting Away With Murder: Segregation and Violent Crime in Urban America." *University of Pennsylvania Law Review* 143 (May): 1203–32.

———. 1999. "America's Apartheid and the Urban Underclass," pp. 125–39 in Fred L. Pincus and Howard J. Ehrlich (eds.), *Race and Ethnic Conflict: Conflicting Views on Prejudice, Discrimination, and Ethnoviolence.* Philadelphia: University of Pennsylvania Press.

MASSEY, DOUGLAS S., AND BROOKS BITTERMAN. 1985. "Explaining the Paradox of Puerto Rican Segregation." *Social Forces* 64:306–31.

MASSEY, DOUGLAS S., AND NANCY A. DENTON. 1989. "Hypersegregation in U.S. Metropolitan Areas: Black and Hispanic Segregation Along Five Dimensions." *Demography* 26:373–91.

———. 1993. *American Apartheid: Segregation and the Making of the Underclass.* Cambridge, MA: Harvard University Press.

MASSING, MICHAEL. 2000. "Stalled in Paradise." *American Prospect* 11 (May 22):22–27.

MATARRESE, LYNNE. 1997. History of Levittown, New York. New York: Levittown Historical Society.

MATOS, EDUARDO M. 1990. *Teotihuacan, The City of Gods.* New York: Rizzoli.

MATSUOKA, JON K. 1990. "Differential Acculturation Among Vietnamese Refugees." *Social Work* 35 (July): 341–45.

MAYER, HAROLD M., AND RICHARD C. WADE. 1973. *Chicago: Growth of a Metropolis.* Chicago: University of Chicago Press.

MAYER, MIRA. 2004. "The Dropout Rates of Mexican Students in Two California Cities," *Research for EducationalReform* 9:14–24.

MAZEY, MARY ELLEN, AND DAVID R. LEE. 1983. *Her Space, Her Place: A Geography of Women.* Washington, DC: Association of American Geographers.

McCABE, JAMES D., JR. 1970. *Lights and Shadows of New York Life.* New York: Farrar, Straus and Giroux; originally published 1872.

McCALL, PATRICIA L, AND KAREN F. PARKER. 2005. "A Dynamic Model of Racial Competition, Racial Inequality, and Interracial Violence," *Sociological Inquiry* 75:273–93.

McCARTHY, KEVIN F., AND GEORGES VERNEZ. 1997. *Immigration in a Changing Economy: California's Experience.* Santa Monica, CA: Rand Corporation.

McFALLS, JOSEPH A., JR. 2003. "Population: A Lively Introduction," 4th ed., *Population Bulletin* 58 (December).

McKENZIE, EVAN. 1993. "Trouble in Privatopia." *The Progressive* 57 (October): 30–36.

———. 1996. *Privatopia: Homeowner Associations and the Rise of Residential Private Government.* New Haven: Yale University Press.

McLARIN, KIMBERLY J. 1995. "Poverty Rate Is the Highest in 16 Years, a Report Says." *New York Times,* July 14, p. A3.

McLAUGHLIN, JEFF. 1999. "Where Do We Grow from Here?" *Boston Globe,* June 20, p. 1.

McMAHON, EDWARD T. 1997. "Stopping Sprawl by Getting Smarter." *Planning Commissioners Journal* 26 (Spring): 4.

MEREDITH, ROBYN. 1996. "G.M. Buys a Landmark of Detroit for Its Home." *New York Times,* May 17, p. 12.

MERTON, ROBERT K. 1968. *Social Theory and Social Structure.* New York: Free Press.

MIAMI. 2005. Accessed at www.ci.miami.fl.us on July 17, 2005.

MILGRAM, STANLEY. 1972. "A Psychological Map of New York City." *American Scientist* 60:194–200.

MILLER, D.W. 2000. "The New Urban Studies," *Chronicle of Higher Education,* August 18, pp. A15–16.

MILLER, DAVID. 2002. *The Regional Governance of Metropolitan America.* Boulder, CO: Westview Press.

MILLER, SHAZIA R., ELAINE M. ALLENSWORTH, AND JULIE R. KOCHANEK. 2002. "Student Performance: Course Taking, Test Scores, and Outcomes," *The State of Chicago's Public High Schools: 1993 to 2000.* Chicago: Consortium on Chicago School Research.

MIN, PYONG GAP, AND ANDREW KOLODNY. 1994. "The Middleman Minority Characteristics of Korean Immigrants in the United States." *Korean Journal of Population and Development* 23:179–202.

MITCHELL, JERRY. 2001. "Business Improvement Districts and the 'New' Revitalization of Downtown," *Economic Development Quarterly* 15 (May): 115–23.

MOLOTCH, HARVEY. 1976. "The City as a Growth Machine." *American Journal of Sociology* 82:309–33.

MONTI, DANIEL J. 1999. *the American City: A Social and Cultural History.* New York: Blackwell.

MONTREAL. 2005. Accessed at www.frommers.com/destinations/montreal/0018010001.html on July 17, 2005.

MOORHOUSE, GEOFFREY. 1979. *Great Cities San Francisco.* Amsterdam: Time-Life.

MORENO, SYLVIA. 1997. "Cabbies Threaten Strike in Alexandria." *Washington Post,* December 31, p. B4.

MORGAN QUITNO. 2005. *11th Annual America's Safest (and Most Dangerous) Cities.* Accessed at www.morganquitno.com/cit05pop.htm on September 7, 2005.

MORRIS, JAN. 2003. *The World: Travels 1950–2000.* New York: W.W. Norton & Company.

MORSE, RICHARD J., AND JORGE E. HARDOY, eds. 1993. *Rethinking the Latin American City.* Washington, DC: Woodrow Wilson Center.

MOSLEY, MICHAEL E. 1975. "Chan Chan." *Science* 187: 219–25.

MOTE, F.W. 2003. *Imperial China 900–1800.* Cambridge, MA: Harvard University Press.

MULLER, PETER O. 1981. *Contemporary Suburban America.* Englewood Cliffs, NJ: Prentice Hall.

MUMFORD, LEWIS. 1961. *The City in History.* New York: Harcourt, Brace and World.

MURPHY, RHODES. 1984. "City as a Mirror of Society." Pp. 186–204 in *The City in Cultural Context,* edited by John A. Agnew, John Mercer, and David E. Sophen. Boston: Allen and Unwin.

MUSCHAMP, HERBERT. 2002. "Don't Rebuild. Imagine." *New York Times Magazine,* September 8, pp. 46–60, 63.

NASH, GARY B. 1979. *The Urban Crucible.* Cambridge, MA: Harvard University Press.

NATIONAL CENTER FOR HEALTH STATISTICS. 1997 *Negative Mood and Urban Versus Rural Residence.* Washington, DC: U.S. Government Printing Office.

NATIONAL CENTER FOR POLICY ANALYSIS. 2002. *Immigrants, Welfare, and Work.* Accessed at www.ncpa.org on August 9, 2005.

NATIONMASTER. 2004. "Asia: China Economy." Accessed at www.nationmaster.com/country/ch/Economy on July 24, 2005.

NEUMAYER, ERIC. 2005. "Inequality and Violent Crime: Evidence from Data on Robbery and Violent Theft," *Journal of Peace Research* 42:101–12.

NEUWIRTH, ROBERT. 2004. *Shadow Cities: A Billion Squatters, A New Urban World.* London: Routledge.

NEWS24. 2003. "Girl Raped on Busy Street," March 6. Accessed at www.news24.com/News24/World/News/ on July 17, 2005.

NEWMAN, OSCAR. 1972. *Defensible Space.* New York: Macmillan.

———. 1996. *Creating Defensible Space.* Washington, DC: U.S. Department of Housing and Urban Development.

NOBLE, JEANNE. 1996. "Spotlight on Indonesia." *Population Today* 24 (June–July): 7.

O'BRIEN, DAVID J., AND MARY J. ROACH. 1984. "Recent Developments in Urban Sociology." *Journal of Urban History* 10:145–70.

OLSEN, JOSHUA. 2004. *Better Places, Better Lives: A Biography of James Rouse.* Washington, DC: Urban land Institute.

O'MEARA, MOLLY. 1999. "How Mid-Sized Cities Can Avoid Strangulation." *Public Management* 81 (May): 8–15.

ORFIELD, GARY. 1988. "Ghettoization and Its Alternatives." In *The New Urban Reality,* edited by Paul E. Peterson. Washington, DC: Brookings Institution.

ORFIELD, MYRON W., AND DAVID RUSK. 1998. *Metropolitics: A Regional Agenda for Stability and Community.* Washington, DC: Brookings Institution.

OSBORN, FREDERICK J. 1965. Pp. 9–28, "Preface" to Ebenezer Howard, *Garden Cities of To-Morrow.* Cambridge, MA: MIT Press.

PACHETTI, NICK. 2000. "The Best Places to Live." *Money* 29 (December): 148–59.

PADILLA, ELENA. 1958. *Up from Puerto Rico.* New York: Columbia University Press.

PAHL, R. E. 1989. "Is the Emperor Naked? Some Questions on the Adequacy of Sociological Theory in Urban and Regional Research." *International Journal of Urban and Regional Research* 13:709.

PARK, ROBERT E. 1950. *Race and Culture.* Glencoe, IL: Free Press.

———. 1984. "The City: Suggestions for the Investigation of Human Behavior in the Urban Environment." Pp.1–46 in *The City,* reprinted, edited by Robert E. Park and Eugene W. Burgess. Chicago: University of Chicago Press, originally published 1916.

PARKER, JIM. 2005. "Daufuskie Island Vacation Spot Undergoes $10 Million Face-Lift, New Construction." *The Post and Courier,* February 26, p. 12G.

PARRILLO, VINCENT N. 2006. *Strangers to These Shores.* 8th ed. Boston: Allyn and Bacon.

———. 2005a. *Diversity in America.* 2nd ed. Thousand Oaks, CA: Pine Forge Press.

———. 2005b. *Contemporary Social Problems.* 6th ed. Boston: Allyn and Bacon.

PASTERNAK, JUDY. 1998. " 'Edge City' Is Attempting to Build a Center." *Los Angeles Times,* January 1, p. 5.

PAWLYNA, ANDREA. 1981. "James Rouse, a Pioneer of the Suburban Shopping Center, Now Sets His Sights on Saving Cities." *People,* July 6, pp. 63–71.

PEDERSON, DANIEL, VERN E. SMITH, AND JERRY ADLER. 1999. "Sprawling, Sprawling. . . ." *Newsweek,* July 19, pp. 23–27.

PERRIN, NOEL. 1980. "Rural Area: Permit Required." *Country Journal,* (April): 34–35.

PETERSON, RUTH D., AND LAUREN J. KRIVO. 1993. "Racial Segregation and Black Urban Homicide." *Social Forces* 71.

PETROSKI, HENRY. 2005. "How to Rebuild New Orleans: Raise the Ground," *New York Times* (September 9), p. A17.

PETRY, ANN. 1998, orig. 1946. *The Street.* Boston: Houghton Mifflin.

PHILIPS, KEVIN. 2003. *Wealth and Democracy: A Political History of the American Rich.* New York: Broadway Books.

PICOT, GARNETT AND FENG HOU. 2003. "The Rise in Low-Income Rates Among Immigrants in Canada," *Analytical Studies Branch Research Paper No. 18.* Ottawa: Statistics Canada.

PIRENNE, HENRI. 1980. *Medieval Cities: Their Origins and the Revival of Trade.* 2nd ed. Princeton, NJ: Princeton University Press.

PLOEGER, NANCY. 2002. "Six Months Later." New York: Manhattan Chamber of Commerce.

POPULATION REFERENCE BUREAU. 2005. *World Population Data Sheet: 2005.* Washington, DC.

PORTER, ROY. 1994. "Curtains for the Capital." *New Statesman & Society* 7 (November 11): 30–31.

PORTES, ALEJANDRO. 1977. "Urban Latin America: The Political Condition from Above and Below." Pp. 59–70 in *Third World Urbanization,* edited by Janet Abu-Lughod and Richard Hay, Jr. Chicago: Maaroufa.

PORTES, ALEJANDRO, CARLOS DORE-CABRAL, AND PATRICIA LANDOLTS, eds. 1997. *The Urban Caribbean: Transition to the Global Economy.* Baltimore: Johns Hopkins University Press.

PRISTIN, TERRY. 1999. "Harlem's Pathmark Anchors: A Commercial Revival on 125th Street." *New York Times,* November 13, p. B1.

PROKESCH, STEVEN E. 1985. "U.S. Companies Weed Out Many Operations." *New York Times,* September 30, pp. A1, D5.

PUBLIC PURPOSE. 1999. Accessed at http://publicpurpose. com/dm-nyc.htm on December 11, 1999.

PURDUM, TODD S. 1999. "Suburban 'Sprawl' Takes Its Place on the Political Landscape." *New York Times,* February 6, pp. A1, A12.

PUTNAM, ROBERT D. 2001. *Bowling Alone: The Collapse and Revival of the American Community.* New York: Simon & Schuster.

PYNOOS, JOHN. 1980. *Housing Urban America.* 2nd ed. Chicago: Aldine de Gruyter.

RABAN, JONATHAN. 1998. *Soft City,* reprint ed. London: Harvill Press.

RAINWATER, LEE. 1970. *Behind Ghetto Walls.* Chicago: Aldine.

RAKOVE, MILTON L. 1975. *Don't Make No Waves, Don't Back No Losers.* Bloomington: Indiana University Press.

REGENT PARK COLLABORATIVE TEAM. 2003. *Lessons from Saint Lawrence for the Regent Park Redevelopment Process.* Toronto: Toronto Community Housing Corporation.

REICH, ROBERT B. 1991. *The Work of Nations: Preparing Ourselves for 21st Century Capitalism.* New York: Alfred A. Knopf.

RESTON. 2002. http://fairfaxtimes.com/ffxguide/ community.html#reston. Accessed January 24, 2003.

RIIS, JACOB. 1890, 1957. *How the Other Half Lives.* New York: Hill and Wang.

ROBERTS, BRYAN R. 2005. "Globalization and Latin American Cities," *International Journal of Urban and Regional Research* 29:110–23.

RODRIGUEZ, CLARA E. 1996. "The Puerto Rican Community in the South Bronx: View from Within and Without." In *Sociology,* 5th ed., edited by Beth B. Hess, Elizabeth W. Markson, and Peter J. Stein. Boston: Allyn and Bacon.

RODWIN, LLOYD, AND HUGH EVANS. 1982. "The New Communities Program and Why It Failed." Pp. 115–36 in *Cities and City Planning,* edited by Lloyd Rodwin. New York: Plenum.

ROESNNER, JANE. 2000. *A Decent Place to Live: From Columbia Point to Harbor Point.* Boston: Northeastern University Press.

ROSENTHAL, J. 1974. "The Rapid Growth of Suburban Employment." Pp. 95–100 in *Suburbia in Transition,* edited by L. Masotti and J. Hadden. New York: New York Times Books.

ROSENZWEIG, ROY. 1998. *The Park and the People: A History of Central Park* reprint ed. Ithaca, NY: Cornell University Press.

ROSTOW, WALT W. 1978. *The World Economy: History and Prospect.* Austin: University of Texas Press.

ROUSSEAU, FRANCOIS, AND LIONEL STANDING. 1995. "Zero Effect of Crowding on Arousal and Performance: On 'Proving' the Null Hypothesis." *Perceptual and Motor Skills* 81 (August): 72–74.

RUBIN, LILLIAN. 1994. *Families on the Fault Line.* New York: HarperCollins.

RUSK, DAVID. 1995. *Cities Without Suburbs.* Washington, DC: Woodrow Wilson Center Press.

RUSTEMLI, AHMET. 1992. "Crowding Effects of Density and Interpersonal Distance." *The Journal of Social Psychology* 132 (February): 51–58.

RYAN, MARY. 1979. *Womanhood in America: From Colonial Times to the Present.* 2nd ed. New York: Franklin Watts.

SAGAN, CARL. 1977. *The Dragons of Eden.* New York: Ballantine.

ST. CLAIRE, CLYDE, AND ROBERT CLYMER. 2000. "Racial Residential Segregation by Socioeconomic Status." *Social Science Quarterly* 81:701–15.

SALT LAKE CITY. 2005. Accessed at www.ci.slc.ut.us on August 6, 2005.

SALZAR, CARLA. 1997. "Rescued Film Crew Tells Tale of Lost City." *Boston Globe,* November 9, p. A4.

SANDBURG, CARL. 1944. *Chicago Poems.* New York: Harcourt Brace Jovanovich.

SASSEN, SASKIA. 2000. *Cities in a World Economy.* 2nd ed. Thousand Oaks, CA: Pine Forge Press.

———. 2001. *The Global City: New York, Tokyo, and London.* 2nd ed. Princeton: Princeton University Press.

———. 2002. *Global Networks: Linked Cities.* London: Brunner-Routledge.

SCHEIN, VIRGINIA E. 1995. *Working from the Margins: Voices of Mothers in Poverty.* Ithaca, NY: Cornell University Press.

SCHMITT, ERIC. 2001. "Most Cities in U.S. Expanded Rapidly Over Last Decade." *New York Times,* May 7, pp. A1, A12.

SCHWIRIAN, KENT P., F. MARTIN HANKINS, AND CAROL A. VENTRESCA. 1990. "The Residential Decentralization of Social Status Groups in American Metropolitan Communities, 1950–1980." *Social Forces* 68(4):1143–63.

SCOTT, ALLEN J. 1980. *The Urban Land Nexus and the State.* London: Pion.

———. 1988. *Metropolis.* Berkeley: University of California Press.

SENNETT, RICHARD. 1969. *Classic Essays on the Culture of Cities.* Englewood Cliffs, NJ: Prentice Hall.

SEWELL, JOHN. 1993. *The Shape of the City: Toronto Struggles with Modern Planning.* Toronto: University of Toronto Press.

SHEVKY, ESHREF, AND WENDELL BELL. 1955. *Social Area Analysis.* Stanford, CA: Stanford University Press.

SHEVKY, ESHREF, AND MARILYN WILLIAMS. 1949. *The Social Areas of Los Angeles.* Berkeley: University of California Press.

SIERRA CLUB. 1999. "What Is Sprawl?" At www.sierraclub.org/sprawl/report, accessed on February 17, 2006.

SIGELMAN, LEE, AND JEFFREY R. HENIG. 2001. "Crossing the Great Divide: Race and Preferences for Living in the City Versus the Suburb," *Urban Affairs Review* 37: 3–18.

SIMMEL, GEORG. 1964. "The Metropolis and Mental Life." Pp. 409–24 in *The Sociology of Georg Simmel,* edited by K. Wolff. New York: Free Press; originally published 1905.

SIMON, JULIAN L. 1999. *Hoodwinking the Nation.* New Brunswick, NJ: Transaction Publishers.

SINCLAIR, UPTON. 1947. *The Jungle.* New York: Viking.

SJOBERG, GIDEON. 1965. *The Preindustrial City.* New York: Free Press.

———. 1973. "The Origin and Evolution of Cities." Pp. 19–27 in *Cities: Their Origin, Growth, and Human Impact.* San Francisco: W. H. Freeman.

SKIDMORE, THOMAS E., AND PETER H. SMITH. 2004. Modern Latin America. 6th ed. New York: Oxford University Press.

SMITH, JANE I. 2005. *Patterns of Muslim Immigration.* Accessed at http://usinfo.state.gov/products/pubs/muslimlife/immigrat.htm on August 1, 2005.

SOLUTIONS NOT SPRAWL. 2005. "Here We Go Again." Accessed at www.solutionsnotsprawl.org/issue.htm on June 21, 2005.

SORKIN, MICHAEL, ed. 1992. *Variations on a Theme Park: The New American City and the End of Public Space.* New York: The Noonday Press, Farrar, Strauss, and Giroux.

SOUTHERN CALIFORNIA ASSOCIATION OF GOVERNMENTS. 2003. *Year 2000 Post-Census Regional Travel Survey.* Austin, TX: NuStats.

SOWELL, THOMAS. 1977. "New Light on Black I.Q." *New York Times Magazine,* March 27, p. 57.

SOJA, EDWARD W. 2000. *Postmetropolis.* New York: Bladewell.

SPAIN, DAPHNE. 1992. *Gendered Spaces.* Chapel Hill: University of North Carolina Press.

SPECTORSKY, A. C. 1957. *The Exurbanites.* New York: Berkley.

SPENGLER, OSWALD. 1928. *The Decline of the West.* New York: Knopf. Excerpted in *Classic Essays on the Culture of Cities,* edited by Richard Sennett. Englewood Cliffs, NJ: Prentice Hall, 1969.

SROLE, LEO. 1972. "Urbanization and Mental Health: Some Reformulations." *American Scientist* 60:576–83.

STACK, CAROL. 1997. *All Our Kin.* New York: Basic Books.

STARK, ANDREW. 2002. *Conflict of Interest in American Public Life.* Cambridge, MA: Harvard University Press.

STARR, ROGER. 1985. "Crime." *New York Times Magazine,* January 17, pp. 19–25, 58–60.

STATISTICS CANADA. 2004. Accessed at www.statcan.ca on July 17, 2005.

STAVRIANOS, LEFTEN. 1998. *Global History: From Prehistory to the 21st Century.* 7th ed. Englewood Cliffs, NJ: Prentice Hall.

STEELE, JEFFREY. 1998. "Profile: Gage Park," *Chicago Tribune,* July 24, p. 16.

STEFFENS, LINCOLN. 2004. *The Shame of the Cities.* Mineda NY: Dover Publications. Org. Published 1904.

STEIN, CLARENCE. 1957. *Toward New Towns for America.* Cambridge, MA: MIT Press.

STEINBECK, JOHN. 1962. *Travels with Charley: In Search of America.* New York: Franklin Watts.

STENGEL, RICHARD. 1986. "Down and Out and Dispossessed." *Time,* November 24, 27–28.

STEPHENSON, R. BRUCE. 1997. "A Vision of Green: Lewis Mumford's Legacy in Portland, Oregon." *Journal of the American Planning Association* 65 (Summer): 259–69.

STEPHENSON, SUSIE. 1999. "DINKS Dine Out." *Restaurants & Institutions,* April 1, pp. 78–81.

STILL, BAYRD. 1974. *Urban America.* Boston: Little, Brown.

———. 1994. *Mirror for Gotham: New York as Seen by Contemporaries from Dutch Days to the Present.* New York: Fordham University Press.

STONEBACK, DIANE. 2005. "Ironbound Ambiance: Historic District in Newark, N.J., Is Packed with the Tasty, the Spicy and All Good Things Portuguese," *Allentown Morning Call,* June 26, p. F1.

STRAIN, CHRISTOPHER. 2004. "Soul City, North Carolina: Black Power, Utopia, and the African American Dream," *Journal of African American History* 89:57–74.

STREET, D., AND ASSOCIATES. 1978. *Handbook of Contemporary Urban Life.* San Francisco: Jossey-Bass.

STRONG, JOSIAH. 1885. *Our Country: Its Possible Future and Its Present Crisis.* New York: Baker and Taylor.

SUISMAN, DOUGLAS R. 1990. *Los Angeles Boulevard: 8 X-Rays of the Body Politic.* Princeton, NJ: Princeton Architectural Press.

SUTTLES, GERALD. 1968. *The Social Order of the Slum.* Chicago: University of Chicago Press.

———. 1972. *The Social Construction of Communities.* Chicago: University of Chicago Press.

———. 1984. "The Cumulative Texture of Local Urban Culture." *American Journal of Sociology* 90:283–304.

SWEETSER, FRANK. 1965. "Factor Structure as Ecological Structure in Helsinki and Boston." *Acta Sociologica* 26:205–25.

TAEUBER, KARL, AND ALMA TAEUBER. 1965. *Negroes in Cities.* Chicago: Aldine.

TAYLOR, R. 1991. "Urban Communities and Crime." Pp. 106–34 in *Urban Life in Transition,* edited by M. Gottdiener and C. G. Pickvance. Newbury Park, CA: Sage.

TAYLOR, ROBERT L. 1985. *The Travels of Jaimie McPheeters.* New York: Arbor House.

TEAFORD, JON C. 1990. *The Rough Road to Renaissance.* Baltimore: Johns Hopkins University Press.

———. 1997. *Post-Suburbia: Government and Politics in the Edge Cities.* Baltimore: Johns Hopkins University Press.

THILL, JEAN-CLAUDE, AND DANIEL Z. SUI. 1993. "Mental Maps and Fuzziness in Space Preferences." *The Professional Geographer* 45 (August): 264–76.

THOMAS, JERRY, AND ANDREW MARTIN. "Notorious Block's Deadly Legacy." *Chicago Tribune,* Web posted November 23, 1996.

THOMAS, JIM. 1983. "Toward a Critical Ethnography." *Urban Life* 11:477–90.

THOMAS, JUNE, JOHN SCHWEITZER, AND JULIA DARNTON. 2004. *Mixed-Income Neighborhoods in Grand Rapids: A Summary of Findings.* East Lansing: Michigan State University.

TIMMER, DOUG A., D. STANLEY EITZEN, AND KATHRYN D. TALLEY. 1994. *Paths to Homelessness: Extreme Poverty and the Housing Crisis.* Boulder, CO: Westview Press.

TOBIN, G. 1976. "Suburbanization and the Development of Motor Transportation: Transportation Technology and the Suburbanization Process." Pp. 95–111 in *The Changing Face of the Suburbs,* edited by B. Schwartz. Chicago: University of Chicago Press.

TOCH, THOMAS. 1998. "The New Education Bazaar." *U.S. News & World Report,* April 27, pp. 34–46.

TOCQUEVILLE, ALEXIS DE. 1955. *The Old Regime and the French Revolution.* New York: Anchor Books; originally published 1856.

TODARO, MICHAEL P. AND STEPHEN C. SMITH. 2005. *Economic Development.* 9th ed. Boston: Addison-Wesley.

TONNIES, FERDINAND. 1963. *Community and Society.* New York: Harper & Row; *Gemeinschaft und Gesellschaft,* originally published 1887.

TORONTO. 2005. Accessed at www.city.toronto.on.ca/ on September 2, 2005.

TREESE, CLIFFORD J. 1999. *Community Associations Factbook.* Alexandria, VA: Community Associations Institute Research Foundation.

TRIMET. 2002. www.trimet.org/factsandphotos/index.htm.

TRIMET. 2005. *Facts About TriMet.* Accessed at http://www.trimet.org/news/pdf/factsheet.pdf. Accessed on February 17, 2006.

UCLA DEPARTMENT OF URBAN PLANNING. 1998. *The Byzantine-Latino Quarter.* Accessed at www.sppsr.ucla.edu/blq/home.html on July 11, 2005.

ULLMAN, EDWARD L. 1941. "A Theory of Location for Cities." *American Journal of Sociology* 46:853–64.

UN-HABITAT FEATURES. 2004. *State of the World's Cities 2004/05.* Accessed at www.unhabitat.org on February 17, 2006.

UNITED NATIONS DEVELOPMENT PROGRAMME. 1995. *Human Development Report 1995.* New York: Oxford University Press.

UNITED NATIONS DEVELOPMENT PROGRAMME. 1996. *Human Development Report 1996:*256. New York: Oxford University Press.

UNITED NATIONS POPULATION DIVISION. 2004. *World Population Prospects:* 2004 Revision. Accessed at http://esa.un.org/unpp/ on August 8, 2005.

———. 2003. *World Urbanization Prospects: 2003 Revision.* Accessed at http://esa.un.org/unup/ on August 9, 2005.

UNITED WAY OF GREATER ONTARIO. 2004. *Poverty by Postal Code.* Accessed at http://www.unitedwaytoronto.com/ on June 29, 2005.

U.S. Bureau of Justice Statistics. 2005. Accessed at www.ojp.usdoj.gov/bjs/ on August 4, 2005.

U.S. Census Bureau. 2002a *Profile of Selected Social Characteristics: 2000,* Summary File 3.

———. 2002b. Accessed at www.census.gov/hhes/www/ahs.html on January 24, 2003.

———. 2002c. *American Factfinder.* Accessed at http://factfinder.census.gov on July 8, 2005.

———. 2003. "Back Bay-Beacon Hill," *2000 Census of Population and Housing,* Summary File 3 Data.

———. 2004a. *American Housing Survey for the United States: 2003.* Washington, DC: U.S. Government Printing Office.

———. 2004b. *The Foreign-Born Population in the United States: 2003.* Washington, DC: U.S. Government Printing Office.

———. 2005. *Income, Poverty, and Health Insurance Coverage in the United States, 2004.* Washington, DC: U.S. Government Printing Office.

———. 2006. *Statistical Abstract of the United States: 2006.* Washington, DC: U.S. Government Printing Office.

U.S. Conference of Mayors. 2005. *A Status Report on Hunger and Homelessness Surveys.* Accessed at www.usmayors.org on February 17, 2006.

U.S. Department of Education. 2000. *The State of Charter Schools: Fourth-Year Report.* Washington, DC: U.S. Government Printing Office.

———. 2004. *Indicators of School Crime and Safety: 2004.* Washington, DC: U.S. Government Printing Office.

———. 2005. *Education for Homeless Children and Youth.* Accessed at www.ed.gov/programs/homeless/index.html on July 15, 2005.

U.S. Federal Deposit Insurance Corporation. 2002. *Statistics on Banking.* Washington, DC: U.S. Government Printing Office.

U.S. Office of Immigration Statistics. 2005. *2004 Statistical Yearbook.* Washington, DC: U.S. Government Printing Office.

Utt, Ronald D. 1996. *Time for a Bipartisan Reform of Public Housing.* Heritage Foundation. Accessed at www.heritage.org/library/categories/regulation/bg1081.html on September 14, 1999.

Valdez, Al. 2000. "18th Street: California's Most Violent Export," National Alliance of Gang Investigators Associations. Accessed at www.nagia.org/18th_street.htm on July 11, 2005.

Valentine, Betty Lou. 1980. *Hustling and Other Hard Work.* New York: Free Press.

Valentine, Charles A. 1968. *Culture and Poverty: Critique and Counterproposals.* Chicago: University of Chicago Press.

Verbrugge, Lois M., and Ralph B. Taylor. 1980. "Consequences of Population Density and Size." *Urban Affairs Quarterly* 16:135–60.

Vidich, Arthur, and Joseph Bensman. 1958. *Small Town in Mass Society.* Princeton: Princeton University Press.

Vidich, Charles. 1976. *The New York Cab Driver and His Fare.* Cambridge, MA: Schenkman.

Vigdor, Jacob L. 2002. "Does Gentrification Harm the Poor?" Brookings-Wharton Papers on Urban Affairs, pp. 133–82.

Vigil, James Diego. 1991. "Car Charros: Cruising and Low Riding in the Barrios of East Los Angeles." *Latino Studies Journal* 2 (May): 71–72.

Wacquant, Loïc J.D. 1997. "Three Pernicious Premises in the Study of the American Ghetto," *International Journal of Urban & Regional Research* 21:341–53.

Wadsworth, Tim, and Charis E. Kubrin. 2004. "Structural Factors and Black Interracial Homicide: A New Explanation of the Causal Process," *Criminology* 42:647–72.

Wahab, Mallika. 2003. "Bangladesh Slums Demand Access to Clean Water," *International Journal of Humanities and Peace* 19:46–47.

Waldinger, Roger. 1999. *Still the Promised City? African-Americans and New Immigrants in New York.* Reprint ed. Cambridge, MA: Harvard University Press.

Wallerstein, Immanuel. 1974; 1997. *Modern World-System I: Capitalist Agriculture and the Origins of the European World-Economy in the Sixteenth Century.* New York: Academic Press.

———. 1979. *The Capitalist World-Economy.* New York: Cambridge University Press.

———. 1983. "Crises: The World Economy, the Movements, and the Ideologies." Pp. 21–36 in *Crises in the World-System,* edited by Albert Bergesen. Beverly Hills, CA: Sage.

———. 1984. *The Politics of the World Economy: The States, the Movements, and the Civilization.* Cambridge: Cambridge University Press.

Walton, John. 1981. "The New Urban Sociology." *International Social Science Journal* 33.

———. 1993. "Urban Sociology: The Contributions and Limits of Political Economy." *Annual Review of Sociology* 19:301–20.

Ward, Steven V. 1998. *Selling Places: The Marketing and Promotion of Towns and Cities 1850–2000.* London: Spon Press, Taylor & Francis Group.

Warner, Sam Bass, Jr. 1978. *Streetcar Suburbs.* 2nd ed. Cambridge, MA: Harvard University Press/MIT Press.

Washington, DC. 2005. Accessed at www.washington.org on July 17, 2005.

Waterfield, Robin. 2004. *Athens: A History—From Ancient Ideal to Modern City.* New York: Basic Books.

Wayne, Gary. 2005. *The Universal CityWalk.* Accessed at www.seeing-stars.com/Shop/CityWalk.shtml on December 27, 2005.

Weber, Adna. 1899. *The Growth of Cities.* New York: Columbia University Press.

Weber, Max. 1966. *The City.* New York: Free Press.

Weibel-Orlando, Joan. 1999. *Indian Country, L.A.: Maintaining Ethnic Community in a Complex Society.* Rev. ed. Urbana: University of Illinois Press.

Weillisz, Christopher. 1983. "Bronx Neighborhood: 'One Big Family.'" *New York Times,* September 14, p. B1.

Weisner. Thomas S. 1981. "Cities, Stress, and Children." Pp. 783–803 in *Handbook of Cross-Cultural Human Development,* edited by Ruth H. Moore, Robert I. Monroe, and Beatrice B. Whiting. New York: Garland.

WENKE, ROBERT J. 2005. *Patterns in Prehistory: Humankind's First Three Million Years.* New York: Oxford University Press.

WEST, KIMBERLY C. 1994. "A Desegregation Tool That Backfired: Magnet Schools and Classroom Segregation." *Yale Law Journal* 103 (June): 2567–92.

WHITE, KERRY A. 1999. "Ahead of the Curve." *Education Week on the Web,* January 13.

WHITE, MORTON, AND LUCIA WHITE. 1977. *The Intellectual Versus the City.* New York: Oxford University Press.

WHITMAN, DAVID. 1995. "Welfare: The Myth of Reform." *U.S. News & World Report,* January 16, pp. 30–39.

WHITMAN, WALT. 1959. *Leaves of Grass.* New York: Viking Press. Originally published 1855.

WHITMEYER, JOSEPH M. 2002. "A Deductive Approach to Friendship Networks," *Journal of Mathematical Sociology* 26:147–65.

WHYTE, MARTIN K. AND WILLIAM L. PARISH. 1985. *Urban Life in Contemporary China,* reprint ed. Chicago: University of Chicago Press.

WHYTE, WILLIAM FOOTE. 1981 (orig. 1943). *Street Corner Society.* 3rd ed. Chicago: University of Chicago Press.

WHYTE, WILLIAM H. 1974. "The Best Street Life in the World." *New York,* July 14, pp. 26–33.

———. 1980. *The Social Life of Small Urban Spaces.* New York: Project for Public Spaces.

WIDHOLM, PAULA. 2005. "Chicago Is Back on the Upswing," *National Real Estate Investor* 47 (Fall): 34–38.

WIESE, ANDREW. 2004. "Robbins, IL," *The Encyclopedia of Chicago.* Chicago: Chicago Historical Society.

WIKIPEDIA ENCYCLOPEDIA. 2005. *New Orleans.* Accessed at http://en.wikipedia.org/wiki/New_Orleans,_Louisiana# Economy on September 9, 2005.

WILFORD, JOHN NOBLE. 1985. "A Legendary 'Lost City' in Andes Gives Hint of Mysterious Culture." *New York Times,* February 1, pp. A1, A11.

WILLIAMS, ROGER M. 1977. "The New Urban Pioneers: Homesteading in the Slums." *Saturday Review,* July 23, pp. 9–14.

———. 1978. "The Assault on Fortress Suburbia." *Saturday Review,* February 18, pp. 17–24.

WILLIE, CHARLES, AND HOWARD TAYLOR. 1995. "The Bell Curve Debate." Panel discussion at Eastern Sociological Society annual meeting, Philadelphia, March.

———. 1991. "Urbanism, Migration, and Tolerance: A Reassessment." *American Sociological Review* 56:117–23.

WILSON, WILLIAM J. 1990. *The Truly Disadvantaged.* Reprint ed. Chicago: University of Chicago Press.

WIMBERLEY, HOWARD. 1973. "Conjugal-Role Relationships and Social Networks in Japan and England." *Journal of Marriage and the Family* 35:125–30.

WIRTH, LOUIS. 1938. "Urbanism as a Way of Life." *American Journal of Sociology* 44:1–24.

———. 1964. *On Cities and Social Life.* Chicago: University of Chicago Press.

WOLFE, TOM. 1998. *A Man in Full.* New York: Farrar, Straus, Giroux.

WOLFINGER, NICHOLAS H. 1995. "Passing Moments: Some Social Dynamics of Pedestrian Interaction." *Journal of Contemporary Ethnography* 24:323–40.

WOLINSKY, JULIAN. 2004. "What Follows the Millennium?" *Railway Age* 205 (July): 27–29.

WORLD HEALTH ORGANIZATION. 2005. *World Health Report: 2005.*

WRIGHT, ARTHUR F. 1977. "The Cosmology of the Chinese City." Pp. 33–74 in *The City in Later Imperial China,* edited by G. William Skinner. Stanford, CA: Stanford University Press.

YALNYZIAN, ARMINE. 1998. *The Growing Gap.* Toronto: Centre for Social Justice.

YOSHIHASHI, PAULINE, AND SARAH LUBMAN. 1992. "Intra- and Inter-Ethnic Group Conflicts: The Case of Korean Small Business in the United States." *Wall Street Journal,* June 16, p. A1.

ZANGWILL, ISRAEL. 1919. *The Melting Pot.* New York: Macmillan.

ZHOU, MIN. 2003. "Urban Education: Challenges in Educating Culturally Diverse Children," *Teachers College Record* 105:208–25.

ZIA, HELEN. 2001. *Asian American Dreams: The Emergence of an American People.* New York: Farrar, Straus, and Giroux.

ZIELENBACH, SEAN. 2005. "Understanding Community Change: A Look at Low-Income Chicago Neighborhoods in the 1990s," *Neighborhood Change in America.* Washington, DC: The Urban Institute.

ZIPP, YVONNE, AND CHRISTOPHER D. COOK. 1999. "Genuine Urban Renewal, At Last in This Golden Economy, Even Bastions of Blight Start to Sparkle." *Christian Science Monitor,* August 19, p. 1.

ZUKIN, SHARON. 1993. *Landscapes of Power: From Detroit to Disney World.* Berkeley: University of California Press.

———. 1995. *The Cultures of Cities.* Malden, MA: Blackwell.

PHOTO CREDITS

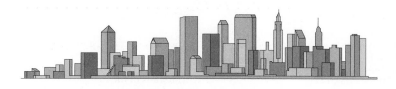

INDEX